Concurrency in
Programming
and
Database Systems

Concurrency in Programming *and* Database Systems

Arthur J. Bernstein
Department of Computer Science
State University of New York at Stony Brook

Philip M. Lewis
Department of Computer Science
State University of New York at Stony Brook

Jones and Bartlett Publishers
Boston   London

Editorial, Sales, and Customer Service Offices
Jones and Bartlett Publishers
One Exeter Plaza
Boston, MA 02116

Jones and Bartlett Publishers International
P.O. Box 1498
London W6 7RS
England

Library of Congress Cataloging-in-Publication Data

Bernstein, Arthur J.
    Concurrency in programming and database systems / Arthur J.
Bernstein and Philip M. Lewis.
        p.   cm.
    Includes bibliographical references.
    ISBN 0-86720-205-X
    1. Parallel programming (Computer science)   2. Database
management.   I. Lewis, Philip M., 1931–   .   II. Title.
QA76.642.B47   1993   92-2253
005.1′1--dc20   CIP

Printed in the United States of America
96 95 94 93 92   10 9 8 7 6 5 4 3 2 1

To our wives – Edie and Rhoda

Contents

Preface

The area of concurrent programming systems is exciting from both a practical and theoretical viewpoint. A concurrent system consists of a set of processes, each running independently but communicating with each other from time to time, and cooperating to perform a common task. An increasing number of the most challenging issues facing system designers involve concurrency. Concurrency has always been a major aspect of operating systems, database systems, and communication systems. More recently, concurrency has been playing an increasing role in the applications area. This trend has been accelerated by the introduction of hardware and software that support concurrency. Multiprocessor systems and computer networks, made possible by the explosive growth of hardware technology and the introduction of new communication techniques (such as local area networks), are now commonplace. Furthermore, languages supporting concurrency – such as Ada – are in wide use. Indeed, timely solutions to some of the most demanding problems in the applications area (for example, scientific modeling and weather forecasting) can be achieved only through the use of such concurrent software and hardware.

The design, implementation, and validation of concurrent programs is quite difficult – stretching the abilities and intuition of even the most knowledgeable system designer. The complexity of a concurrent program arises not from its size, but rather from the asynchronous nature of its execution: the individual operations of its component processes can be interleaved in an astronomical number of ways at execution time. In reasoning about such a program, it is difficult to even conceive of all the possible sequences of events that might occur. Program failures are often not reproducible, since the exact sequence of events that causes a failure cannot be identified.

Partly because of the unexpected difficulties uncovered in early concurrent systems, and partly because of their intriguing mathematical structure, researchers have developed a large body of mathematical theory addressed to the design of concurrent systems. The theory provides a basis on which a formal proof of the correctness of a concurrent system can be built. Producing such a proof, however, is itself a significant intellectual challenge for even a relatively simple system. Thus, it appears unlikely that, even with computer assistance, complete formal proofs will be made for even a small percentage of the concurrent systems that will be implemented in the foreseeable future. Nevertheless, we believe that a formal approach to concurrency has an important role to play in concurrent system design. It provides us with a tool for precisely describing the behavior of concurrent control constructs. Furthermore, an understanding of the considerations that underlie the formal reasoning process provides powerful support for the informal design process.

This book is addressed to both theoreticians, who want an introduction to the mathematical design theory, and practitioners, who want to use that design theory in the implementation of real-world concurrent systems.

A major organizing concept in any formal discussion of concurrency is that each component process is made up of *atomic* operations, which cannot be interrupted. These atomic operations are the unit of interleaving: the execution of a concurrent program involves the interleaving of the atomic operations of its component processes. At the lowest level, the atomic operations are the individual cycles of activity of the hardware. Although it is possible to use the techniques presented in the text to analyze a concurrent system at this level, the degree of detail is overwhelming. Instead, we choose as our starting point programs written in a high level language and assume that interleaving actually occurs at the statement level. We examine concurrent programs in this context and investigate various techniques for analyzing and controlling interleaving.

We introduce still higher levels of modularity as a means of dealing with complex systems. We examine procedures as the unit of interleaving and study their use in data abstraction and monitors. Since interleaving at execution time actually occurs at a much finer level, a major issue here is techniques for guaranteeing that the effect of an execution is the same as if the interleaving had been at the procedure level. The distinction between actual and effective interleaving appears again at the next higher level, as we move from procedures to transactions in a database system. Concurrency control is now a major issue and notions of data abstraction reappear in object oriented systems.

Several other issues cut across this hierarchy of interleaving. First we consider distributed systems as contrasted with shared memory systems. At the statement level, we consider message passing; at the procedure level, remote procedure calls; and at the transaction level, distributed transactions. A second issue is the relationship between failures and atomicity. How do we ensure that an inherently non-atomic unit, such as a procedure or transaction, executes atomically when failures can occur? We consider algorithms for dealing with processor, storage, and communication failures.

We have been very careful in selecting the level of formality of the discussion. We give the intuition underlying the mathematics and tools from which formal proofs can be built, but we do not employ the degree of formality necessary for mathematically complete and rigorous proofs. Our goal is not to teach formal techniques to theoreticians, but to give computer scientists and engineers the understanding that should form the basis of the design and construction of concurrent systems. We expect that in any significant system implementation, a detailed use of the design theory presented here might be possible for only some small, but key parts of the system, that other parts might be designed with a much less formal use of the theory, and still others with only intuition based on the theory. We want to give our readers the ability to perform in all of these modes.

This book is intended for a senior-level undergraduate or a graduate course in a computer science or engineering department. The prerequisites for the book are general in nature. A student should have the mathematical sophistication of a senior in computer science or engineering, be comfortable with the techniques for constructing ordinary sequential programs, and be familiar with practical issues relating to concurrency in the operating systems area. This foundation can be supplied by the standard, introductory-level, undergraduate mathematics and computer science courses, together with an undergraduate course in operating systems. We review much of this material in the first three chapters of the book. Chapter 1 covers those aspects of an undergraduate operating systems course that are relevant, while Chapters 2 and 3 contain an introduction to the mathematics of formal reasoning and develop the Hoare logic approach to reasoning about sequential programs. In Chapter 3 we present methods for reasoning about abstract data types. Later we use abstract data types as a structuring mechanism when we consider monitors, remote procedure calls, and databases. Also in Chapter 3 we discuss coroutines which, although sequential, involve some of the same reasoning techniques as concurrent constructs.

Chapters 4 and 5 cover shared memory systems, including critical sections, semaphores, and monitors. Chapters 6, 7, and 8 cover message passing systems, including synchronous and asynchronous message passing, virtual circuits and datagrams, and remote procedure calls and rendezvous. Chapter 9 discusses failures in centralized and distributed systems, including failure atomicity and stable storage. It also contains several distributed algorithms relevant to issues in the text, including distributed synchronization, the Byzantine Generals Problem, and clock synchronization.

Chapters 10, 11, and 12 discuss centralized and distributed transaction processing systems. Topics include typed and untyped databases, nested transactions, replication, and atomic commit protocols. We develop the design theory of database concurrency control and failure atomicity. We show how this theory can be used to obtain increased concurrency in object oriented databases, where the database items are instances of abstract data types. Distributed algorithms for leader election are also introduced because of their relationship to atomic commit protocols.

We complement the discussion of the underlying design theory with a discussion of practical issues and illustrate the theory with numerous examples. We use the bounded buffer problem as a common example throughout the book – showing how each of the techniques we develop can be used (and reasoned about) to obtain a bounded buffer design. We present several solutions to the Readers-Writers Problem, again in different contexts. We consider applications in data acquisition, banking, and communication. We discuss various implementation issues, such as the design of a concurrency kernel and the ISO reference model. The discussion on databases gives practical designs for centralized and distributed systems.

Rather than base the book on any particular computer language, we discuss each theoretical concept in terms of a "pure" language construct that embodies that concept and then show how to formally and informally reason about that construct. To make the discussion more realistic, however, in Chapters 3, 6, 7, 8, and 11 we discuss commercially available computer languages that employ a theoretical construct from that chapter as one of their central features. We discuss Modula-2 as an example of coroutines, Occam as an example of synchronous message passing, Ada as an example of rendezvous, Argus as an example of nested transactions, and Linda as an example of an interesting combination of paradigms. Other languages are also touched on. Our goal is not to make the reader an expert in a particular language, but to show the compromises, extensions, and trade-offs the language designer felt obliged to make in order to embody a concept into a practical language – and the effect of those compromises on our ability to reason about programs written in that language.

The text contains more material than can be covered in a one semester course. Hence, the instructor has the flexibility to organize the material in a variety of ways to adjust it to particular student groups and interests. For example, an undergraduate course could spend more time on the first three chapters than a graduate version, which might omit Chapter 1 entirely and cover Chapters 2 and 3 briefly, stressing only a few topics, such as procedures and data abstraction.

The unstarred sections constitute a path through the text that includes all the fundamental concepts but eliminates the details of the theory and those topics that are not required for an understanding of later chapters. These sections form a skeleton for a one semester course, which the instructor can flesh out with other sections as desired.

We have been particularly fortunate in obtaining reviews of much of the material from very highly qualified researchers in the concurrency area, many of whom have developed results covered in the text. We would especially like to thank Mohammed Gouda, Vassos Hadzilacos, Maurice Herlihy, Dave Musser, Fred Schneider, and Dale Skeen for their perceptive comments. We would also like to thank Ariel Frank who reviewed the section on Occam, Narain Gehani and Ike Nassi who reviewed the section on Ada, Rick Spanbauer who reviewed the section on Modula-2, and Anita Wasilewska who reviewed the introductory discussion on mathematical logic. Gurdip Singh and Narayanan Krishnakumar provided general comments and were of particular help in developing the exercises. Laura Dillon, Richard Schultz, Vasant Balasubramanian, and Joe Trubisz commmented on various versions of the text.

Finally, we would like to thank the Department of Computer Science at the State University of New York at Stony Brook and the Department of Computer Science at the University of California at Santa Barbara for the use of their facilities in preparing this text

1

Introduction and Brief Survey

A concurrent system consists of a set of processes, each running independently of the others, but all cooperating to perform a common task. Almost invariably this cooperation involves the exchange of information among the processes, usually through a shared memory or by message passing.

One example of a concurrent system is an airline reservation system, where hundreds of reservation request transactions are being processed concurrently, all sharing a common flight reservation database. Another example is an air traffic control system, where a different process is assigned to track each airplane being controlled by the system and these processes share information with other processes that prepare displays or perform other processing. Perhaps the most common, and certainly the most studied, example of concurrency occurs in operating systems, where different user and operating system processes operate concurrently and share system data structures.

We are particularly interested in concurrent systems in which the individual processes do not execute in lockstep. In an airline reservation system, for example, the processes may be executing on a distributed system consisting of thousands of computers and terminals at sites around the country. In an air traffic control system, the processes may be executing on a multiprocessor system, where a number of processors are all located at the same site and share a common memory but are not synchronized. Even in the operating system example, where all the processes may be executing on a single central processing unit (cpu), the processes are interacting with devices, such as terminals and disks, that are not synchronized with the cpu.

Since the individual processes in such systems are running independently, their actions can be arbitrarily interleaved. However, when they need to share information, they may have to temporarily synchronize their actions; for example, a process that wants to read some data may need to know that the process that was supposed to have written that data has already done so. This combination of temporary synchronization at certain times and arbitrary, unpredictable interleavings at others makes the design, implementation, validation, and debugging of concurrent systems considerably more difficult than that of ordinary (sequential) systems.

In this chapter we discuss concurrency in hardware and software and introduce some elementary concepts and definitions for dealing with the subject.

1.1   Synchronous and Asynchronous Hardware

A *processor* is a physical device (for example, a cpu) that executes operations. We use the word *operation* in a general sense. For example, an operation on a cpu might be an instruction. For a processor that directly executes some high level language, an operation might be an expression or a statement. A processor executes operations sequentially, atomically, and deterministically. By *sequential* we mean that no more than one operation is executing at any time. By *atomic* we mean that once selected for execution, the operation is executed completely; its execution is not interrupted at some intermediate stage to allow the processor to execute another operation. By *deterministic* we mean two things:

Each operation in its repertoire performs a well defined action that always produces the same result when operating on the same input data;

Upon completion of the execution of an operation, the next operation to be executed is determined (except in the case of an operation that halts the processor, in which case no successor is determined).

A control unit for a processor controls the steps necessary to sequence operations. We can think of each operation in a program as being referred to by a *control point*. A control point is *enabled* if the operation it refers to is eligible for execution. When the operation is executed we say that its control point is being *serviced*. After an operation is executed, its control point is disabled and a new control point, which refers to the next statement to be executed, is enabled. The control unit is usually driven by a *clock*, which provides a sequence of pulses that are directed by the unit to the various gates that need to be activated for each operation. Hence, all actions of the device are synchronized to its clock. A control unit contains a register that identifies an enabled control point. For example, the cpu has an *instruction counter* (IC), which stores the address of the next instruction to be executed.

Primitive computers are frequently constructed from a single processor and are controlled by a single control unit. The entire computer – including both the arithmetic/logic unit and I/O devices – can perform only one operation at a time. An I/O transfer is accomplished by executing an instruction. The computer waits until the transfer is complete before beginning the execution of the next instruction. Hence, at any time, either computation or I/O, but not both, is in progress.

A computer is *sequential* if no more than one control point can be serviced at a time.

Thus, the primitive computer with a single control unit is sequential.

While sequential operation is simple (an advantage not to be underestimated), it is also inefficient. An I/O transfer might involve mechanical motion, which is slow compared to electronic speeds, and hence, during the time it takes to execute an I/O transfer, considerable computation could be performed.

A common way to increase the efficiency of such a computer is to provide multiple processors, each with its own control unit. The control unit for the cpu controls the execution of instructions in the arithmetic/logic unit. The control unit for the I/O device controls I/O transfers. By providing separate control units, we create a computer that can have several enabled control points at the same time and hence can carry on several activities simultaneously.

A computer is *concurrent* if multiple control points can be serviced at the same time.

Thus, the new organization is concurrent; the cpu can request that the I/O controller perform I/O, and once the I/O controller has been initiated, the cpu can continue executing instructions and thus proceed concurrently with the I/O device.

In this type of computer organization, the I/O controller is frequently referred to as the *channel*. Although the cpu and channel can operate concurrently, the cpu must have some mechanism to direct the actions of the channel because programs running on the cpu must control the time at which an I/O transfer is to take place, the locations in main memory and on the mass storage device to or from which the data is to be moved, and the number of bytes to be transferred. In simple systems, the cpu program constructs a channel command at a particular location in memory known to the channel and then executes a *start I/O (SIO)* instruction. The *SIO* instruction wakes up the channel, which then fetches the contents of the designated location and executes the requested channel command – for example, move the disk head to a specified track or transfer n words from the magnetic tape starting from the current position of the head to a buffer in main memory.

In a more sophisticated computer, the designated location in memory contains the first command (or a pointer to it) of a channel program consisting of a number of commands. In this case the channel contains a register, called the *command counter* (CC), which stores the address of the next command to be executed, and operates in a manner quite analogous to the way the cpu executes its program. Both devices access the common memory to fetch instructions and fetch or store data. The channel also contains a status register – readable by the cpu – that the channel loads with completion status when the execution of the channel program has been completed. The status might indicate successful execution of the channel program or some error situation

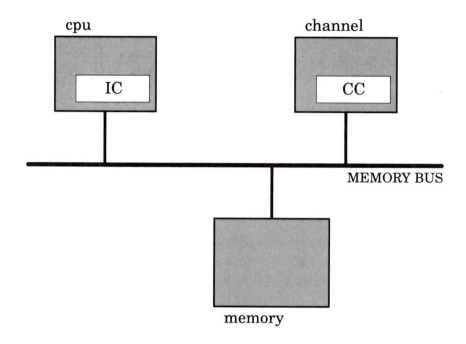

Figure 1.1: The channel and cpu are co-equal processors.

if the channel program could not be completed properly. The channel should
be viewed as a complete processor co-equal to the cpu, as shown in Figure 1.1.
The enabled control points referred to by each processor are the contents of
the instruction and command counters for the programs executing on that
processor.

   If the channel and I/O devices were driven by the same clock as the cpu,
the two processors could be made to progress in the execution of their programs at fixed rates with respect to one another. Since the number of clock
pulses necessary to execute a cpu instruction or channel command would be
known in advance, we could predict where the two processors would be in their
respective programs at any time.

   Usually, we cannot make such a prediction. Each processor in the system
runs at its own speed. The speed with which the channel program executes
is determined by the speed of the device, which may vary from day to day.
For example, if the I/O device is a disk, the time to perform an I/O transfer
might depend on the viscosity of the oil in the bearings (which affects the
rotational speed) and its angular position when the *SIO* is executed (which
affects the latency). Such factors do not affect the cpu, which executes at a

speed determined by its own internal clock. Thus, one cannot predict how far
one processor has proceeded in the execution of its program at the time the
other has reached some particular point in its program. As a result, in two
runs of the same program, the number of instructions executed by the cpu
while the channel is executing its program will generally be different.

Two processors are *synchronous* if their operations are driven by a common clock. Otherwise they are *asynchronous*.

Thus, the channel and the cpu are asynchronous processors.

Asynchronous processors can explicitly synchronize their execution from
time to time. When such synchronization occurs, we can infer something about
the enabled control point of one processor from the enabled control point of
another. The channel and cpu are synchronized for an instant at the time
the *SIO* is executed, since at that time it is known which control points are
enabled in each processor (the first channel command in the channel program
and the instruction following the *SIO* in the cpu). A point of synchronization
must also be established when the channel program completes, so that the cpu
knows when its request has been fulfilled. Points of synchronization involve an
explicit exchange of signals between the processors. One of two mechanisms
is commonly used to synchronize the cpu to the channel when the channel
program completes: polling or interrupts.

1.1.1   Polling

Polling involves the use of a register, the channel indicator, that is set by the
channel while it is executing a channel program and reset when it completes.
The cpu implements an instruction that reads the indicator. Thus, after executing *SIO*, the cpu can periodically check, or *poll,* the indicator and determine
when it has been reset. At this point the program executing on the cpu can
infer that the control point referring to the completion operation has been enabled. This test must be explicitly coded into the program executing on the
cpu.

The more frequently this test is made, the more quickly the cpu program
will become aware of the termination of channel activity, and thus the more
effectively it can keep the channel busy if other channel programs are waiting
to be executed. Unfortunately, the more frequently the indicator is tested by
the cpu program, the less efficiently that program will run, since the tests are
concerned with synchronization, not productive computation.

Figure 1.2 illustrates the polling technique in a situation in which there is
no operating system and the user program is controlling the channel (executing
SIO and testing the channel indicator) directly. We describe the program using
a Pascal-like language augmented in two ways. First, we assume a library
routine called *read*, which initiates channel activity. Once the channel has
been initiated, the cpu continues asynchronously. The channel indicator is

the boolean variable *busy*, which the channel sets to true when it initiates its execution and false when it completes.

Second, we have augmented the language by adding the coroutine statement. In the example, there are two coroutines, *Cp* and *Iop*, which together comprise the cpu program. Control is passed back and forth between them, but at any given time, only one control point is enabled. When an active coroutine, such as *Cp*, executes resume *Iop*, control is passed to *Iop* at the statement just after the last resume that *Iop* executed (or at its first statement, if it has not yet executed). Note that control is passed between the coroutines at points selected in advance by the program designer (using resume).

The program processes information from (an infinite) file, *file*, in sequence using a bounded buffer. The main routine, *Cp*, is an infinite loop that calls *getbuf, compute,* and *releasebuf*. The routine *getbuf* performs a synchronization function by idling if there is no buffer filled with unprocessed information. *compute* performs an unspecified computation on the next full buffer. *releasebuf* releases the buffer when computation has been completed. The channel indicator, *busy*, is polled by both *getbuf* and *releasebuf*, which transfer control to *Iop* only when the channel is idle.

Initially all buffers are empty and control resides in *Cp*. Since the channel is not busy when the main loop calls *getbuf* for the first time, *getbuf* executes resume, causing control to pass to *Iop* at its first statement. *Iop* calls *read*, which initiates the channel program (by executing *SIO*), causing *busy* to become true. *Iop* then executes resume, returning control to *Cp*, which continues processing at the point that it last executed (after the resume statement in the repeat loop in *getbuf*). Control remains in the repeat loop until *busy* becomes false (indicating I/O completion), at which point control returns to *Iop*. *Iop* updates variables, initiates another read, and then returns control to *getbuf*, still inside its repeat loop. Now, however, *count* is greater than 0, so the loop ends and *getbuf* returns. The routine *compute* is then called to process the data in *buf*[0], which is now known to have been filled by the channel. When *releasebuf* is called, it updates the necessary variables and polls *busy* so that *getbuf* and *Iop* act to synchronize cpu and channel activity. When the processing of buffers is proceeding more quickly than the filling of buffers and the cpu is ready to process a buffer but no buffer is full, *getbuf* delays the processing until there is a full buffer. Similarly, when the filling of buffers is proceeding more quickly than the processing of buffers and the channel is ready to fill a buffer but no buffer is empty, *Iop* returns to *Cp* without initiating channel activity. We return to this example in Section 3.3.

One way to view the activities of the two coroutines is to think of *Iop* (together with the channel) as producing information to be stored in the buffer and *Cp* as consuming that information. The two coroutines occupy what is commonly known as a *Producer-Consumer* relationship, examples of which will be seen throughout the book. These two synchronization conditions, which are concerned with situations in which one process proceeds more quickly than the other, must always be dealt with when such a relationship exists and

```
var
    count : integer 0..N := 0;        -- number of full buffers
    last : integer 0..N - 1 := 0;     -- next buffer to be filled
    first : integer 0..N - 1 := 0;    -- next buffer to be processed
    busy : boolean := false;          -- true when channel is busy
    buf : array[0..N - 1] of buffer_element;

coroutine
Cp ::
    begin
        procedure getbuf ();
            begin
                repeat if not busy then resume Iop;
                until count > 0;
            end getbuf;
        procedure releasebuf ();
            begin
                count := count - 1;
                first := (first + 1) mod N;
                if not busy then resume Iop;
            end releasebuf;
        begin
            repeat                          -- main routine
                getbuf (); compute(buf [first]); releasebuf ();
            until false;
        end;
    end Cp;
#
Iop ::
    begin
        repeat
            read(buf [last], file);
            resume Cp;
            last := (last + 1) mod N;
            count := count + 1;
            if count = N do resume Cp;
        until false;
    end Iop;
coend;
```

Figure 1.2: A program for processing a stream of information using a bounded buffer and polling.

resources (*e.g.,* the number of buffers) are limited.

1.1.2 Interrupts

One deficiency of the polling technique is that, unless the cpu constantly interrogates the channel indicator, it is not made aware of channel completion the instant it happens, and thus the opportunity to maximize the overlap between cpu and channel activity is reduced. More sophisticated computer systems use an *interrupt* technique that makes the cpu instantly aware of channel completion.

Once again the channel has an associated register, which we refer to as the channel flag, to differentiate it from the channel indicator described above. The flag is set on when the channel completes its program and is turned off when the cpu recognizes the completion. The cpu program no longer polls the flag; polling is now done automatically by the cpu hardware at the completion of the execution of each instruction. Thus, channel completion can be detected immediately by the cpu without the need to execute nonproductive polling instructions.

After the cpu hardware has detected channel completion, some mechanism must be provided whereby this information is conveyed to the cpu program so that code can be executed to process the channel status, synchronize the operation of various parts of the program, or initiate execution of a new channel program. Typically, when the hardware detects channel completion, it causes the cpu to interrupt the current sequence of instructions being executed and to transfer control to a routine for handling the situation. When the interrupt occurs, the channel flag is reset.

The occurrence of the interrupt causes the instruction counter to be reloaded from some fixed location in memory, thus forcing a transfer of control. Since the contents of that location can be set by the cpu program prior to initiating channel operation, the cpu program can specify that control be transferred to a routine located at an arbitrary address in memory as soon as the channel completes. We refer to that routine as an *interrupt handler* and its code as *interrupt-driven code*. The interrupt is said to *occur* when this transfer of control takes place. Once again a relationship has been established between enabled control points: the control point at the entry of the interrupt handler is enabled after the control point referring to the channel completion operation has been enabled.

After the interrupt handler has been executed, the cpu is expected to resume the sequence of instructions that was interrupted. Since the channel and cpu are asynchronous processors, the point in the cpu program at which the interrupt occurs cannot be predicted in advance (indeed, as pointed out previously, if the identical program is executed twice, the interrupt will most probably not occur when the same control point is enabled in the cpu program). Thus, the contents of the instruction counter and certain other cpu registers must be saved by the hardware prior to reloading these registers when the interrupt occurs. The contents of these registers are referred to as the *cpu state*. Since entry to and exit from the interrupt handler is managed like an ordinary subroutine call and return, we assume that the same mechanism is used for both. Hence, we assume the existence of a stack, S, for saving the return linkages for subroutines and interrupt-driven routines. The cpu state is automatically pushed onto S by the hardware when the interrupt occurs. The interrupt handler can therefore resume the interrupted code by simply popping the top entry of S back into the cpu registers.

More precisely, an interrupt involves two steps. In the first step the channel flag is set and a new control point is enabled (in addition to the control point that is enabled at the interrupted instruction). In the second step the interrupt occurs, causing a transfer of control, and hence the new control point is serviced. As we shall see, there can be an arbitrary delay between the first and second steps.

Figure 1.3 is a program that has similar functionality to that of Figure 1.2, except that now an interrupt mechanism is assumed in the hardware. The routine *Iop* is the interrupt handler. Since *Iop* is executed as soon as the interrupt occurs, it is synchronized with channel operation; it is the epilogue to the channel program even though it happens to be executed on the cpu. We cannot predict between which pair of successive instructions in *Cp* the execution of *Iop* will take place. Stated in a different way, when the control point at the entry to *Iop* is enabled, we cannot determine which control point in *Cp* is enabled. We say that the execution of these two routines is *interleaved*. *Iop* is executed, in its entirety, between the execution of two successive instructions of *Cp*. The example does not exhibit the full potential of interleaving; a more general form of interleaving occurs when the sequence of instructions executed is an arbitrary merge of the execution sequences of two routines. Note that instructions – or more generally operations – are the unit of interleaving. Since operations are atomic, the execution of operations of one routine must occur between successive operations of another, not in the midst of a single operation.

Note that, since our concern is with the order of instruction execution and not the processor on which the instructions are executed, we could execute the routines on separate processors of a multiprocessor system and get the same effect as we would by interleaving their execution on a single processor. An interesting question is whether the equivalence works in the opposite direction: can the execution of routines in parallel on a multiprocessor system always be duplicated by interleaving their execution on a single processor? If a difference exists, it must occur in a situation in which instructions are executed simultaneously on two processors of the multiprocessor. If the instructions do not access a common data element, their interleaved execution in either order will have the same effect as simultaneous execution. If they do access a common data element, almost invariably the hardware will serialize their references to the location in memory containing the element, and hence the instructions will not actually be executed simultaneously on the multiprocessor system.

```
var
    count : integer 0..N := 0;           -- number of full buffers
    last : integer 0..N − 1 := 0;        -- next buffer to be filled
    first : integer 0..N − 1 := 0;       -- next buffer to be processed
    busy : boolean := false;             -- true when channel is busy
    buf : array[0..N − 1] of buffer_element;

Cp ::
  begin
    procedure getbuf ();
      while count = 0 do;
    procedure releasebuf ();
      begin
        < count := count − 1;
        if count = N − 1 then read(buf [last], file);
        first := first + 1 mod N; >
      end releasebuf ;
    begin                                -- initialize
        read(buf [last], file);
      repeat                             -- main routine
        getbuf (); compute(buf [first]); releasebuf ();
      until false;
    end;
  end Cp;

Iop ::
  begin                                  -- enter on interrupt
    < last := (last + 1) mod N;
    count := count + 1;
    if count < N then read(buf [last], file);>
  end Iop;
```

Figure 1.3: An interrupt driven program for processing a stream of information using a bounded buffer.

We mention two situations in which inherent simultaneous execution is called for:

Architectures have been proposed in which the effect of simultaneous writes to the same location in memory is that the disjunction of the values being written is stored in the target location. Such an effect cannot be simulated by the interleaved execution of the individual writes.

In Chapter 6 we define communication statements that must be executed simultaneously and, hence, cannot be directly simulated by interleaved execution on a single processor.

Returning to our discussion of Figure 1.3, when the main routine is entered for the first time, it initiates a read and then calls *getbuf,* which idles in its wait loop until *count* is greater than 0. This situation, in which execution cycles in a loop until some condition is satisfied, is frequently referred to as a *busy wait*. The cpu is busy, but is not executing instructions productively.

Since *count* was initialized to 0 and can have been changed only within *Iop*, when *Cp* finally leaves the wait loop in *getbuf,* an interrupt must have occurred, indicating that the first read has completed. Hence, synchronization has been established between *Cp* and *Iop*. *Cp* returns from *getbuf,* since a full buffer is available for processing. Similarly, the wait loop synchronizes *Cp* and *Iop* at times other than start-up, whenever *getbuf* is called and all buffers are empty.

We refer to this type of synchronization, in which one routine notifies another about some specific item of mutual interest (in this case the state of the buffers), as *signaling*. The details of how signaling is accomplished and what information is to be signaled are usually highly application dependent.

If empty buffers exist when the interrupt occurs, *Iop* can immediately initiate the next transfer, hence achieving maximum overlap between cpu and I/O activity. Unfortunately, because the channel and cpu are asynchronous processors, it is not possible to guarantee that empty buffers will always be available when an interrupt occurs and *Iop* is entered. Hence, it is necessary to violate the division of responsibility adhered to in Figure 1.2 by allowing an I/O transfer to be initiated within *Cp*. *Cp* calls *read* in two places: at start-up time and from within *releasebuf* when it is discovered that the buffer that has just been released is the only free buffer. In the latter case, the last execution of *Iop* could not have restarted the channel and the channel must therefore be idle. Note that *getbuf* and *Iop* perform the same synchronization functions in Figure 1.2 as in Figure 1.3.

1.2   Programs, Processes, and Atomicity

By a *program* we mean a finite description of a task in some programming language. By an *address space* we mean the collection of all the variables that the program references. By a *program state* we mean the values of all the variables in the address space.

In the program shown in Figure 1.3, when the channel flag is set, a new control point is enabled at the entry to the interrupt handler, in addition to the enabled control point that refers to the interrupted instruction. Hence, the program can contain multiple enabled control points.

A program is *concurrent* if during its execution multiple control points can be enabled at the same time.

A program is *sequential* if during its execution no more than one control point can be enabled at a time.

A *process* is an agent that (1) executes instructions on a processor in an address space and (2) has a unique associated control point that designates the next instruction it will execute. The process is *ready* to execute if the control point is enabled. If the control point is not enabled, we say that the process is *waiting*. By a *process state* we mean the identity of the control point and an indication of whether or not the control point is enabled. The execution of a concurrent program involves more than one process; the execution of a sequential program only one. A process executing a concurrent program can frequently be identified with a particular routine within that program that it executes. In that case we refer to the process by the name assigned to the routine.

We view *Cp* and *Iop* as processes within the concurrent program of Figure 1.3. With only one cpu, only one of these processes can be serviced at a time. We generally choose to give priority to the interrupt handler – and refer to it as an interrupt-driven process – but this policy masks the real issues. As we shall see, there are occasions when the handler is not given priority and, in cases where there are multiple cpus, both enabled control points might be serviced at the same time.

We can extend our notions of synchronous and asynchronous behavior to software:

A concurrent program is *asynchronous* if, given the identity of one enabled control point, we cannot infer the identities of other enabled control points.

Thus the program of Figure 1.3 is an asynchronous program, and we say that *Cp* and *Iop* are *asynchronous processes* within it. As with asynchronous processors, asynchronous processes establish points of synchronization through the explicit execution of instructions that cause communication. The various forms that this communication might take are a major topic of this text.

A concurrent program is *synchronous* if, given the identity of one enabled control point, we can always infer the identities of the remaining enabled control points.

The program of Figure 1.2 is not concurrent, since an enabled control point can exist in only one coroutine at a time (*Cp* and *Iop* are not asynchronous processes). While I/O is in progress, however, an enabled control point does exist in the channel program as well as in one of the two coroutines. Hence, if the channel program is included, the program as a whole is an asynchronous, concurrent program: the identity of the enabled control point in the channel program does not allow us to infer the identity of the enabled control point in the cpu program and vice versa.

The asynchronism between Cp and Iop in Figure 1.3 gives rise to a new situation. Consider the variable *count* in Figure 1.3. It is updated in both Cp and Iop. Although these updates are accomplished in a single assignment statement, their actual implementation in the corresponding machine language program involves several instructions. Thus, the translation of the statement

$$count := count - 1$$

in *releasebuf* into assembly language might be:

$$LOAD\ reg, COUNT$$
$$SUB\ reg = 1$$
$$STORE\ reg, COUNT$$

where $COUNT$ is the location of variable *count*, *reg* is an arithmetic register in the cpu, and = denotes literals (*e.g.,* that the 1 refers to the number one).

Suppose an interrupt occurs after the $LOAD$ has been executed but before the $STORE$. The value of *count* will already have been copied into *reg* and the contents of *reg* pushed onto the stack when Iop is entered. Iop will increment the value of *count* stored at location $COUNT$. When Cp resumes, the state of the cpu at the time the interrupt occurred will have been restored and Cp will store the old value of *count* minus 1 back in $COUNT$. Thus, the final value stored in $COUNT$ is one less than the original value and the effect of the increment in Iop has been lost.

This malfunction is characteristic of situations in which asynchronous processes access shared data. One way to avoid such problems is to insist that once an update has been initiated by one process, all the instructions that implement the update must be completed before another process can initiate an access. That is, all other accesses must occur either before or after the update. Of course, if both processes are simply reading (and not changing) the shared data, their execution can be arbitrarily interleaved. But if interleaving is allowed while one process is in the midst of performing an update, the other process might view the data while it is in an inconsistent state (in the example Iop operates on an outdated value of *count*). Note that this situation does not arise in the polling example, since in that case Cp and Iop are coroutines that switch control at predictable points in the program where the designer has placed resume statements (not in the midst of updates).

One common method for dealing with such situations is to synchronize the processes. In each process we define regions of code, called *critical regions* or *critical sections*, and enforce the requirement that when one process is executing in a critical section, no other process is allowed to enter a critical section. This type of synchronization is referred to as *mutual exclusion* of critical sections. It represents a second form of synchronization that is frequently required of concurrently executing programs. Whereas signaling is application dependent, mutual exclusion is application independent. Critical sections must exclude one another independent of the semantics of the shared variables.

Note that critical sections come in sets. Thus we might define one set of critical sections (perhaps all of which access some common data) and require mutual exclusion in that set. We might also define a different set of critical sections (perhaps accessing different common data) and require mutual exclusion in that second set. But we could allow one process to be executing in a critical section from the first set while another process is executing in a critical section from the second set (since they would not be accessing common data).

One way (although not a very elegant one) to guarantee mutual exclusion between *Cp* and *Iop* in Figure 1.3 is to prevent the occurrence of interrupts during the execution of critical sections. Thus, once a process enters its critical section, it will not be interrupted and hence no other process will be allowed to execute (whether that other process enters a critical section or not). To implement this approach, some mechanism must exist so that the cpu program can prevent the interrupt from occurring. We refer to the invocation of such a mechanism as the *disabling of interrupts*. We can view the disabling of interrupts as a mechanism by which we cause the enabled control point at the entry to the interrupt handler to have lower priority for service from the cpu than the enabled control point in the critical section. Hence, disabling of interrupts can be viewed as a scheduling mechanism.

While interrupts are disabled, the interrupt does not occur even if the channel has, in fact, completed. Since the flag is not reset until the interrupt occurs, the flag will remain set until interrupts are later enabled. Thus, the fact that the channel has completed while interrupts are disabled will not be lost. In the example in Figure 1.3, we disable interrupts during the execution of *releasebuf*.

The control of interleaving is a central topic of this text.

A sequence of instructions (statements) is *atomic* if interleaving never occurs during its execution.

Once the first instruction in an atomic sequence is executed, the sequence is executed to completion before any other instructions are executed. We use angle brackets, $<$ and $>$, to indicate atomic sequences. One way to implement atomicity is to disable interrupts. Note that atomicity is a stronger property than is actually required to achieve the mutual exclusion of critical sections, since atomicity prohibits any interleaving while mutual exclusion only requires that critical sections accessing common data not be interleaved. We sometimes describe this weaker property by saying that a computation is *atomic with respect to* some other computation (or event).

The critical section issue is not quite as simple as we have indicated. For example, it is not sufficient to simply disable interrupts in *releasebuf* while *count* is being decremented, since an interrupt occurring after *count* is decremented but before the subsequent test on *count* has been completed can also cause difficulties. If *count* is decremented to $N - 2$ and an interrupt occurs,

Iop will increment *count* and restart the channel. When *Iop* returns, *count* will have value $N - 1$ and *releasebuf* will attempt to start a channel that has already been started. Therefore, in this case, the critical section must at least include the assignment and the following conditional.

It is also convenient to disable interrupts during the execution of the interrupt handler. While it is not possible for an interrupt to occur during the execution of the first few statements of *Iop*, once the channel has been restarted an interrupt could conceivably occur. Since no purpose is served by allowing a channel to interrupt its own interrupt handler, such interrupts are generally disabled.

While we have dealt in some detail with the particular issues of the bounded buffer example, it is worth noting that our techniques are not very general. For one thing, in a multiprocessor system, disabling interrupts on one cpu does not prevent them from occurring on another. Secondly (although it is not a problem in our example), we must in general consider the possibility that the cpu program and the channel program may be accessing common data and interfering with each other.

When the system involves multiple channels, each capable of causing its own interrupt, interrupts from one channel might occur during the execution of an interrupt handler for another channel. A simple system of this type might disable all interrupts during the execution of any interrupt handler. A more sophisticated system might implement a priority interrupt structure in which channels are ordered in accordance with the speed with which we want to respond to their channel completion events. During the execution of a handler at priority level i, all interrupts from channels at priorities less than or equal to i are disabled. In this way the disabling mechanism is employed as a low level scheduler. We will see later how scheduling can be done in a more uniform way.

The bounded buffer example illustrates the roots of the issues addressed in this book. Asynchronous concurrent programs are significantly more difficult to deal with than are sequential programs. This difficulty is not a function of the size of the program but relates to the arbitrary interleaving of statement execution at run time. The number of ways in which the statements of even moderate size routines can be interleaved during execution is astronomical, yet the program must work in all cases. Testing is out of the question because of the number of alternatives. Error situations cannot be reproduced, since they depend on a particular interleaving whose timing requirements cannot, in general, be reproduced.

It is not unusual for large asynchronous concurrent programs that have been functioning correctly for long periods of time to suddenly crash because a particular interleaving occurs. Usually, in this situation, the system is simply restarted, since there is not enough information available to trace the problem and there is no way to force the problem to repeat so that it can be studied. Software designers refer to such situations as transient hardware malfunctions, while the hardware maintenance staff speak of bugs in the software.

1.3 Multiprogramming and Multiprocessing

We have been assuming that the computer is a *uniprocessor* system, meaning that it contains only one cpu. The term uniprocessor, however, is somewhat misleading, since such a system might contain a number of channels and, as we have pointed out, each channel is essentially an independent processor. In addition, we have been assuming that the execution of only one user program – we refer to this as a *job* – is in progress on the computer at a time. In such a *uniprogrammed* system, if the single job is *compute bound* (*i.e.,* does mostly cpu processing with relatively little I/O) the channel will be idle most of the time. Even when the job is *I/O bound* (*i.e.,* requires I/O frequently, with relatively little computation), if the user is not clever enough to design the program so that it can effectively use the cpu while I/O is in progress (for example, incorporate a properly designed multiple buffering scheme), the cpu will not be busy while the channel is operating.

To increase the efficiency of the overall system, many modern operating systems are *multiprogrammed*. Several jobs reside in main memory at the same time. The operating system interleaves their execution so as to maximize the utilization of the cpu and the channel processors. If one job requests I/O, the operating system initiates the channel operation and then passes control to another job that needs the cpu, thereby keeping both devices busy. If some job is compute bound, the operating system may interleave it with other jobs that make more frequent use of the I/O channels. Jobs are generally allocated some fixed unit of time, referred to as a time quantum, by the operating system so that it can reassess the situation periodically. The time quantum is thus a major factor in determining the granularity of interleaving. A variety of scheduling disciplines have been developed to maximize utilization of resources. Since all the jobs make progress, the operating system creates the abstraction that each job is executing on its own dedicated processor. This abstraction is called a *virtual processor*.

The interleaved execution of processes described in previous sections was not symmetric. The interrupt-driven process could interrupt the non-interrupt-driven process, but not vice versa. By contrast, in multiprogrammed systems, the jobs are peer-related and the interleaving among them is symmetric. If we view the set of user programs as a single program, it is concurrent, since multiple control points can be enabled, and it is asynchronous, since the identities of these control points are determined by such factors as the time quantum and scheduling algorithm in the operating system and therefore their relationship cannot be predicted.

It might be argued that, if a fixed time quantum and round robin scheduler were used (and if the asynchronism associated with channel operation had no impact on the interleaving of jobs), the enabled control point in one job could be inferred from the enabled control point of another, and hence the program would be synchronous. The problem with this reasoning is that at the user level the time quantum and scheduling algorithm are not known (in fact might change with each new version of the operating system) and so the jobs cannot be designed with these factors in mind. They must execute correctly for any choice of quantum and scheduler; that is, they must execute as if no inferences of this type were possible.

When a single cpu system is multiprogrammed, the different jobs are multiplexed, or time shared, on the cpu. Although a multiprogrammed system operates more efficiently than a uniprogrammed system, any one job is not running any faster than it would if the system were uniprogrammed; in fact, it is probably running more slowly because of the interleaving. To increase the speed of execution of an individual job or to create a more powerful multiprogrammed system, many computers are built with multiple cpus. We refer to them as *multiprocessor* systems. The operating system can either assign each cpu to a different job or assign several cpus to the same job. In the second case the job is a concurrent program which supports a number of processes that can execute concurrently and can therefore be assigned to different cpus. Hence the overall program execution time may be reduced.

Multiprocessor systems are concurrent, since more than one enabled control point can be serviced. For our purpose an important distinction between multiprocessors is whether their cpus are synchronized or not. Since the same clock pulses drive all cpus in the synchronous case, their progress is completely predictable with respect to one another and we can organize them so that certain designated computations are performed simultaneously on different cpus. On the SIMD (single instruction/multiple data) variety of this organization, each processor has some private memory and all processors execute the same program, in lockstep, using corresponding data elements in their private memories. Although a program executing on a SIMD machine is concurrent, it is not asynchronous, since given the identity of one enabled control point, we can always infer the identities of the others. In the pipelined variety, data is streamed through a sequence of processors, each of which performs a different transformation on the stream. Transformations are synchronized so that the stream flows through each processor at a uniform rate and hence, once again, the program is not asynchronous.

In asynchronous multiprocessor systems, the individual cpus do not share a common clock (each processor has its own local clock) but do share access to a common memory. In a *distributed computer system*, complete computers – each with its own private memory – are interconnected through communication devices. Processes communicate using messages, which carry data and provide synchronization.

Certain kinds of computations are particularly appropriate for each organization. For example:

A SIMD machine consisting of a two dimensional array of processors would be appropriate for the solution of partial differential equations relating quantities in a two dimensional geometry. Each processor would store information about a different point in the (x, y)-plane. A copy of a program to compute derivatives might be simultaneously executed on each processor to compute the derivative at its (x, y) point.

A pipelined organization would be appropriate for matrix multiplication. The addends for a particular element of the product matrix might be accumulated in a linear array of adders, each of which takes the output of its predecessor as one of its inputs. Successive elements of the product would be in various stages of completion at the same instant.

An asynchronous multiprocessor would be useful in supporting concurrent access to a database. The database would be stored in the shared memory and the individual processors might be executing different transactions against that database.

A distributed computer system would be useful when the concurrent computations were distinct and involved small amounts of shared information that could be transferred over the communication lines. One application might be performing a distributed search through a game tree.

Since asynchronism is the main topic of this book, our interest lies in systems that support asynchronous execution. Asynchronism between a channel and a cpu exists in all systems that perform I/O. Asynchronism among cpus exists in asynchronous multiprocessors and distributed computer systems.

In multiprocessor systems, as well as systems having a single cpu and a channel, asynchronism causes interleaving at the memory reference level. In multiprogrammed systems, interleaving occurs at the time quantum level. In both cases, mutual exclusion is a major issue, since processors can be accessing shared data structures.

In distributed computer systems, processors can no longer access information through a shared memory. Mutual exclusion might still be an issue, however. Client processes, executing on distinct computers, might send messages to a server process, which monitors some data. The messages request access to the data, and these accesses are performed by the server on behalf of the client. In many cases, such accesses must be grouped into critical sections.

1.4   Nondeterminism

A program is constructed from simple statements. A simple statement is a statement that does not contain other statements. Examples of simple statements are the Pascal assignment and goto statements. Statements are combined into nonsimple statements using the constructors of the language. Examples of nonsimple statements are the Pascal conditional and compound statements, both of which contain other statements. The semantics of each constructor specifies how control points are to be enabled. For example, the compound statement

begin S_1; S_2;...; S_n; **end**

specifies that after each component statement is executed, the control point referring to the following statement is enabled. Since only one enabled control point exists at a time, the constructor is sequential. Similarly, the Pascal if statement

if B **then** S_1 **else** S_2

is a sequential program fragment, since a control point is enabled at either S_1 or S_2 depending on whether B is true or false.

The concept of determinism, previously defined for processors, applies to statements as well. A simple statement is *deterministic* if it always maps a particular program state in the same way (*i.e.*, a particular argument always yields the same results and the same final control point). A constructor is deterministic if, when the constructor is entered and also after each statement within the constructor is executed, the next enabled control point to be serviced is completely determined given the program state. With both the begin/end and if constructors, the newly enabled control point is completely specified given the program state; hence, they are deterministic (sequential) constructors. In fact, all of the constructors within Pascal are deterministic and sequential; hence, Pascal is a deterministic, sequential language. Deterministic, sequential languages are the software counterparts of processors.

Some languages have constructors which specify that only one statement out of a designated group of statements is to be executed, but the choice of which statement is to be executed is not completely determined by the program state. A constructor is *nondeterministic* if, when the constructor is entered or after some statement within the constructor is executed, the next statement to be executed is not completely determined given the program state. For example, in the next chapter we define a nondeterministic version of the if statement using the [] separator

$$\textbf{if } B_1 \rightarrow S_1; \text{ [] } B_2 \rightarrow S_2; \text{ []} \ldots \text{[] } B_n \rightarrow S_n; \textbf{ fi}$$

where the B_i are boolean expressions. The semantics of the if statement specifies that if more than one of the boolean expressions is true, one of the true expressions, B_i, is nondeterministically selected and the control point immediately preceding S_i is enabled. This constructor is sequential, since only one control point at a time is enabled. If all the other constructors in the language are also sequential, the language is nondeterministic and sequential.

This particular type of nondeterminism, in which one of a set of statements is nondeterministically chosen for execution, is called *choice* nondeterminism. (Note that the choice is arbitrary; probability and randomness are not involved.) It might appear that choice nondeterminism is not implementable if the underlying processor or support software is deterministic and always makes choices in the same way. From the point of view of the user of the language, however, the algorithm for making the choice is unknown. Furthermore, because of the semantics of the language, the program must work correctly if the underlying hardware and support software is changed so that a new choice algorithm is used. Hence the user must view the choice as being made nondeterministically.

Some languages have constructors which specify that all statements in a designated group of statements are to be executed, and that multiple control points are enabled within the group so that execution is concurrent. In this case we say that the constructor is concurrent and the language is a concurrent language. For example, in Chapter 4 we define the cobegin/coend constructor with the // separator

$$\textbf{cobegin } S_1; \text{ // } S_2; \text{ // } \ldots \text{ // } S_n; \textbf{ coend}$$

The semantics of this statement specifies that upon entry, control points are enabled at each of the component statements $S_1, S_2, \ldots, S_n$, thus simultaneously making all eligible for execution. After all statements have completed, a single control point is enabled at the statement following the coend. While control resides within the cobegin statement, several enabled control points coexist and therefore several statements are eligible for execution. The semantics of the cobegin constructor does not specify which statement is to execute next or whether any are to be executed simultaneously. We view the cobegin as creating a process to execute each of the component statements.

Since the next statement(s) to be executed is not determined by the program state, the cobegin constructor exhibits nondeterminism. To differentiate this type of nondeterminism from choice nondeterminism, we define the nondeterminism associated with the arbitrary interleaving permitted by this concurrent constructor to be *order* nondeterminism. The program fragment formed by an order nondeterministic constructor is asynchronous and concurrent.

The order in which enabled control points are serviced within the cobegin statement determines a particular interleaving of statement execution. Different implementations of cobegin may interleave execution in different ways. For example, each component could execute in parallel on a different processor in an asynchronous multiprocessor system, or all could execute in some arbitrarily interleaved fashion on a single processor in a multiprogrammed system. As with our discussions of multiprogrammed systems and of choice nondeterminism, although the underlying mechanisms in any particular system might be deterministic, the user must view the constructor as nondeterministic.

Other concurrent constructors can be defined in which the concurrency is constrained to be performed in a synchronous fashion. For example, the semantics of the constructor might specify that corresponding statements in each component of the construct are executed simultaneously. Such constructors are deterministic and are appropriate for implementation on a synchronous multiprocessor (*e.g.,* a SIMD machine). Since we are not concerned with such languages in this book, our use of the term concurrency will henceforth imply order nondeterminism and asynchronism.

Ada[1] is an example of a concurrent language that exhibits both choice and order nondeterminism. Ada tasking, which is analogous to the cobegin statement, allows multiple tasks to proceed concurrently and exhibits order nondeterminism. Tasks can communicate using entry calls, which essentially correspond to sending messages. A situation might occur in which a task is ready to receive messages from several other tasks, and more than one of these other tasks is ready to send a message. This situation is specified using a constructor that exhibits choice nondeterminism, allowing the receiver to accept a message from any one of the senders, but not specifying which.

The cobegin statement is a structured way to describe concurrent execution within a programming language. Another way to describe concurrent execution is to specify a number of sequential programs and state (outside of the framework of any programming language) that they are to execute concurrently. For example, the interrupt handling program shown in Figure 1.3 is concurrent, although no concurrent constructor is shown. The routines *Cp* and *Iop* execute concurrently; the interleaving is controlled by the timing of the interrupts.

1.4.1 Determinate and Indeterminate Programs

Programs written in a sequential, deterministic language have the property that their execution causes a deterministic transformation of the program state: a particular state is always transformed in the same way. Programs having this property, and processes executing them, are said to be *determinate*. As we shall see, programs written in a nondeterministic sequential language or a concurrent language may be either determinate or indeterminate.

Figure 1.4 shows the main loop of a determinate program that reads information sequentially from a file, modifies it, and appends the result to another file. We assume that I/O is performed synchronously – that the program waits after requesting I/O until the service has been completed – and indicate that through the use of the procedure identifiers *readblock* and *writeblock*. Because I/O is synchronous, each run that starts with *file1* in a particular state will produce the same values in *file2*; hence the program is determinate.

Suppose, instead, that the task is to be performed on an asynchronous multiprocessor and, since the files are quite large, it is desired to take advantage of the additional cpu power to speed its execution. We can explicitly designate the parts of the program that can be executed concurrently using the cobegin constructor.

Figure 1.5 shows the main loop of a concurrent version of the program that performs this function using three buffers. The cobegin statement indicates that the statements for reading, processing, and writing are to be executed concurrently. When all three statements have been completed, the information in *buf 3* is no longer needed, since it has been written to *file2*. The contents

---

[1]Ada is a trademark of the U.S. Department of Defense.

```
            . . .
        repeat
          begin
            readblock(buf, file1);
            compute(buf );
            writeblock(buf, file2);
          end;
        until false;
            . . .
```

Figure 1.4: A sequential program for processing a file.

```
            . . .
        repeat
          begin
            cobegin
              readblock(buf 1, file1);
            //
              compute(buf 2);
            //
              writeblock(buf 3, file2);
            coend;
            buf 3  :=  buf 2;
            buf 2  :=  buf 1;
          end;
        until false;
            . . .
```

Figure 1.5: A concurrent program for processing a file.

of the buffers can then be shifted as shown and the loop repeated. Since each of these statements is performed using a distinct buffer, no synchronization among them is required and the program will execute determinately. In general, concurrent programs perform determinately if their asynchronous parts operate on disjoint sets of variables (but they may be determinate even if this is not so.). Hence, concurrency need not imply indeterminate behavior.

Note, however, what happens if the program is written incorrectly and the argument of the call to *compute* is *buf 3*. In this case the information written to *file2* might be only partially updated. The extent of the update will depend on the relative speeds of *compute* and *writeblock*. Furthermore, the program will behave indeterminately. Since the speeds will be different on different runs, the state of *file2* on termination might be different even though the state of *file1* is the same – greatly complicating debugging. Indeterminacy occurs in this case because the two asynchronous components now share common variables. The debugging of such a program is substantially complicated by the fact that errors are no longer reproducible.

Like concurrent programs, sequential nondeterministic programs do not necessarily perform indeterminately. For example, to find the maximum of two numbers, x and y, a nondeterministic conditional statement can be used with the conditions $x \leq y$ and $x \geq y$. In the case when $x = y$, either of the corresponding statements can be executed and the program will give the same (correct) answer. In fact, a nondeterministic version of the conditional statement might be preferable, since it reflects the symmetry of the situation being dealt with.

In summary, we can draw two conclusions from the above discussion:

Determinate programs are considerably simpler to deal with than indeterminate ones;

The use of concurrent and nondeterministic constructors does not necessarily lead to indeterminacy.

Unfortunately, the system designer does not always have the luxury of dealing only with programs that exhibit determinate behavior. Programs that function in an environment in which events occur asynchronously must reflect that asynchronism and as a result might behave indeterminately. Such behavior is not necessarily erroneous, since frequently in these situations more than one result is acceptable. For example, in an airline reservation system in which clients at two separate locations request the same seat at approximately the same time, unpredictable communication delays might make the result indeterminate (*i.e.,* in one run one client might get the seat, and in another run, even though the requests are made at the same times, the other client may get it). Both results are equally acceptable (although perhaps not to the clients involved). The problem is not necessarily to eliminate indeterminacy, but to control it.

1.5 Modularization

Modularization is a technique for dealing with the analysis and design of many types of complex systems. The system is constructed as a collection of modules, each of which performs a relatively simple function. One module may draw upon the services of another. Each module can be analyzed and/or designed in isolation. The only information required about other modules when a particular module is designed is the specifications of the modules from which it draws its services. The functioning of the overall system can then be understood as the interaction of the individual modules without concern for the details of their internal structure. Our goal in this section is to begin to define an appropriate modularization for a concurrent program.

The modules we choose are the sequential programs, S_i, that are composed by concurrent constructors to form a concurrent program. Methods exist for reasoning about sequential programs, and these methods can be used as part of a two step procedure for analyzing and designing concurrent programs. In the first step, each of the S_i is analyzed or designed in isolation using the existing methods. In the second step, the interactions between the S_i are studied. It is the second step that is of primary concern in this text.

There are a number of possible degrees of interaction. At one extreme the sequential programs do not interact at all. That is, they neither share variables nor send messages to each other. In this case, the results produced by the overall system are simply the union of the results produced by each component. The fact that component execution is interleaved has no effect, since there is no communication. From a practical standpoint, if each of the sequential programs functions correctly in isolation, the entire set will function correctly together. Thus, in this case, step two is vacuous.

At the other extreme, considerable communication may occur between the sequential programs. In this case, the correct functioning of the individual programs does not imply the correct functioning of the overall system. Substantial mismatches may exist between the assumptions made by one program about the nature of the interaction with another and the actual interaction that occurs during execution. In this case, step two will be complex and may involve detailed analysis of the component programs.

Most decompositions of real concurrent programs fall between these two extremes. Their component sequential programs have limited interaction with one another, and these interactions tend to follow simple patterns. Step two of the analysis procedure can be dealt with effectively by developing techniques for dealing with these patterns. Hence we can break the analysis of the concurrent program into two manageable steps.

Figures 1.5 and 1.3 are examples of concurrent programs that are constructed from sequential programs. In Figure 1.5 no interaction occurs between the three sequential components of the cobegin statement, and thus, if each functions correctly, the entire cobegin statement will also function correctly.

In Figure 1.3 the concurrent program is made up of the sequential programs *Cp* and *Iop*. These programs interact through *buf* and *count*, and thus, even though each sequential part functions correctly, the overall program may not. However, in this example, we have argued that a solution to the mutual exclusion problem and appropriate signaling synchronization is all that is needed to make the program as a whole function correctly.

In all of these examples, the sequential programs interact through shared variables. By contrast, in many other systems, particularly distributed systems, programs do not share memory and a message passing mode of interaction is used. In either case, a mechanism is needed to support the concurrent sequential processes that execute the programs and handle issues such as mutual exclusion and message passing. This mechanism, frequently referred to as a *kernel*, is actually a mini-operating system. The kernel supplies the run-time support structure for a concurrent program by implementing the abstraction of virtual processors as well as appropriate synchronization and communication features.

The cobegin/coend constructor allows the designer to declare a fixed number of components in the program. Since this number is specified when the program is designed, decisions concerning resource allocation can be made at compile time. A more flexible approach is to allow a process to dynamically create an arbitrary number of other processes at run time. Ada is an example of a language that permits dynamic process creation. Dynamic process creation requires that the kernel make resource allocation decisions at run time, thus adding substantially to its complexity.

1.6   Semaphores and Mutual Exclusion

As we have seen, one way to control the interaction that occurs when concurrent processes access shared variables is by mutual exclusion of critical sections. We view a process as alternately executing code in critical and noncritical sections. The code in a noncritical section accesses variables that are local to the process, while the code in a critical section accesses variables that are shared with other processes. To maintain the integrity of the shared data, it is necessary to guarantee that no two processes concurrently execute critical sections that access the same shared data area.

The mutual exclusion problem involves finding a protocol that can be used by individual processes when they want to enter or leave a critical section. A satisfactory protocol must, of course, guarantee mutual exclusion and is usually also required to satisfy the following properties to assure that the overall system operates in a reasonable fashion:

All processes should be treated equally: they should execute the same algorithm and the protocol must not statically assign a higher priority to one process than to another.

A process trying to enter its critical section when all other processes are executing in their noncritical sections must not be delayed. Thus, the termination of a process outside its critical section will not affect the progress of other processes. (Note that the termination of a process while it is executing in its critical section will necessarily prevent others from entering their critical sections.)

If several processes are trying to enter their critical sections simultaneously, the decision as to which one succeeds must not be put off indefinitely.

A process trying to enter its critical section must eventually succeed. It must not be forever bypassed by other processes entering their critical sections. This property is an example of a *fairness* property.

Designing a mutual exclusion protocol using ordinary variables is more difficult than it might first appear. The exercises at the end of the chapter discuss some examples of proposed protocols that do and do not work correctly. To overcome the complexity of these solutions and to avoid the need for busy waiting, Dijkstra proposed a new data type called a *semaphore*. Variables of type semaphore can take on only nonnegative integer values. As a special case, we define *binary semaphores*, which take only the values 0 and 1. Semaphores that are not binary are referred to as *general*.

Only two operations are defined on semaphores. Corresponding to semaphore s, $P(s)$ is a decrement operation and $V(s)$ is an increment operation. Both operations are guaranteed to be performed atomically. When a control point is enabled at an operation $P(s)$, a test is made on the value of s; if the value is 0, the control point is disabled and remains disabled until some future time when the value of s is positive. Hence, a process enters the wait state if it attempts to decrement a semaphore with value 0. When a semaphore with value 0 is incremented as the result of the execution of a V operation, the control point of one waiting process (if such a process exists) is enabled.

By definition, the wait associated with a P operation is not a busy wait. Waiting processes do not utilize the cpu. Semaphores are generally part of the abstraction supported in the kernel, which maintains a queue of currently waiting processes that are not considered for execution.

Since several processes might be waiting for a particular semaphore to be incremented, at the time the increment occurs a choice must be made of which process's control point to enable. The algorithm for making the choice is not specified, except that a fairness requirement is imposed, that no process can be passed over indefinitely.

A mutual exclusion protocol can be implemented by associating a binary semaphore having initial value 1 with each shared data object, as shown in Figure 1.6. A process wishing to enter a critical section that accesses a particular shared data object performs a P operation on the associated semaphore. The process performs a V operation on exiting. Mutual exclusion is achieved, since (1) when a process is in its critical section, the semaphore has value 0 and hence no other process can execute a P operation and enter its critical section and (2) if two processes attempt to enter simultaneously, only one will succeed because semaphore operations are atomic. Furthermore, fairness follows from the fairness requirement of the definition of semaphores.

Although only two processes are shown in Figure 1.6, the same protocol works when n processes are competing for the data object. If we modify the specification of the problem so that as many as m of the n processes are allowed to access the object concurrently, the same protocol applies using a general semaphore initialized to m.

$\mathcal{P}_1$::
  $\cdots$ $--$ noncritical section
  $P(s)$;
  $\cdots$ $--$ critical section
  $V(s)$;
  $\cdots$ $--$ noncritical section
  $\cdots$

$\mathcal{P}_2$::
  $\cdots$ $--$ noncritical section
  $P(s)$;
  $\cdots$ $--$ critical section
  $V(s)$;
  $\cdots$ $--$ noncritical section
  $\cdots$

Figure 1.6: Two processes using semaphore s to achieve mutual exclusion. The initial value of s is 1.

At first it may seem strange that the solution to the problem of achieving mutually exclusive access to a shared data object involves the introduction of another shared data object, the associated semaphore. The reason this approach works is that the only accesses permitted to the new shared data object are the P and V operations, and they mutually exclude one another, since they are atomic.

1.6.1   Readers-Writers Problem

Mutual exclusion may be too stringent a requirement in many applications. When information is known about the semantics of the operations performed by the processes, it is frequently possible to identify shared accesses to common data that can be executed concurrently by different processes. For example, consider a class of problems known as the *Readers-Writers Problem*. We assume there is a data object that is shared among a number of processes, some of which (the readers) want only to read the value of the object, and some of which (the writers) want to change its value. Since the value of the object is not changed by a reader, multiple readers can be allowed to execute their read accesses concurrently. But, since writers change the value of the object, a writer must exclude other writers as well as all readers.

We want to design a protocol that will allow any number of readers or exactly one writer to be accessing the object at any given time. Several versions of the problem have been proposed, depending on whether readers or writers get priority in certain situations. (For example, suppose some readers are using the data object, a writer is waiting, and a new reader makes a request. Does that reader join the group of readers, or does it wait until after the writer accesses the object?) In Figure 1.7 we give a solution to the simplest version, called the reader priority solution, in which a continuing sequence of new reader requests can indefinitely delay any writers. In later chapters, we give other solutions, in which the priorities are decided differently.

The protocol given in Figure 1.7 uses two semaphores, *mutex* and *wrt*, both

P *(mutex)*;
   readcount := *readcount* + 1;
   if *readcount* = 1 **then** P *(wrt)*;
V*(mutex)*;
   ··· **- -** reading
P *(mutex)*;
   readcount := *readcount* − 1;
   if *readcount* = 0 **then** V*(wrt)*;
V*(mutex)*;

       (a)

P *(wrt)*;
   ··· **- -** writing
V*(wrt)*;

       (b)

Figure 1.7: Reader priority solution to the Readers-Writers problem using semaphores: (a) typical reader and (b) typical writer.

initialized to 1. *mutex* guarantees mutual exclusion among the readers in their accesses to *readcount* (which keeps track of the number of readers).

The key to the protocol is the use of the semaphore *wrt*. If the shared object is free, *wrt* can be successfully decremented by either a reader or a writer. If a writer is successful, then, until that writer completes, all subsequent readers and writers will wait. If a reader is successful, then, as long as *readcount* is greater than 1, subsequent readers do not attempt to further decrement *wrt* and hence can perform their reads. Writers, however, do attempt to decrement *wrt* and hence will wait. When *readcount* is set back to 0 by the last reader, that reader increments *wrt*, thus releasing mutual exclusion.

1.7 Semaphores and Signaling

Semaphores are a powerful synchronization tool and can be used in the solution of problems other than mutual exclusion. Their use in signaling is illustrated in Figure 1.8, where a solution is given to the bounded buffer problem first discussed in Figure 1.2.

Here, two general semaphores, *free* and *full*, are used to count the number of free and full buffers, respectively. They replace the variable *count*. The semaphore *full* is initialized to 0, denoting that initially no buffers are full. (Note that, for convenience, we use assignment in the declaration to indicate the initial value of a semaphore. The only allowed operations in the body of the program are P and V, however.) Thus, when the process Cp first calls *getbuf*, *full* cannot be decremented. This situation remains true until the process *Iop* has performed at least one read and incremented *full*. *full* can be decremented only when at least one buffer is full. Similarly, the semaphore *free* is initialized

```
var
   last : integer 0..N − 1 := 0;            − − next buffer to be filled
   first : integer 0..N − 1 := 0;           − − next buffer to be processed
   buf : array[0..N − 1] of buffer_element;
   free : general semaphore := N;           − − counts number of free buffers
   full : general semaphore := 0;           − − counts number of full buffers

cobegin
Cp ::
   begin
     procedure getbuf ();
        P (full);
     procedure releasebuf ();
        begin
          V(free);
          first := (first + 1) mod N;
        end releasebuf ;
     begin
       repeat                               − − main routine
          getbuf (); compute(buf [first]); releasebuf ();
       until false;
     end;
   end;
//
   Iop ::
   begin
     repeat
       P (free);
       readblock(buf [last], file);
       last := (last + 1) mod N;
       V(full);
     until false;
   end;
coend;
```

Figure 1.8: Solution to the bounded buffer problem using semaphores.

to N, denoting that initially N buffers are available. *free* can be decremented only when at least one buffer is empty.

Mutual exclusion is achieved indirectly, since the synchronization provided by the semaphores guarantees that the processes will never attempt to access the same buffer concurrently.

1.8 Conclusion

Most of this chapter has been a review of those aspects of an undergraduate operating systems course that are relevant to the subject area of this text. We have emphasized the asynchronous aspects of systems and discussed several classic problems.

You should feel rather uneasy about your understanding of the examples we have discussed. Although we have talked through their operation, we certainly have not addressed all the issues, nor have we reasoned about all the possible interleavings of the processes involved. In fact, it should be evident that informal discussions, such as we have given, are inadequate to analyze or design concurrent programs. In the remaining chapters we develop a more formal approach that can be used to analyze the behavior of concurrent programs and, for example, to reason about "all possible interleavings".

1.9 Bibliographic Notes

Peterson and Silberschatz [110] and Tanenbaum [128] are two good texts for introductory operating systems courses, which cover most of the material discussed in this chapter in more depth. A more complete discussion of parallel architectures can be found in Hwang and Briggs [73].

The early work on treating concurrent programs as collections of sequential programs, the mutual exclusion problem, and semaphores was done by Dijkstra [35], [36], [37], [38]. A simple solution of the mutual exclusion problem using ordinary variables was given recently in Peterson [109]. The layered approach to operating system design, with processor multiplexing at the lowest level, was described in Dijkstra [37]. More recent discussion of this approach can be found in Haberman, Flon, and Cooprider [60] and in Bernstein and Siegel [19]. The Readers-Writers problem was originally stated and solved in Courtois, Heymans, and Parnas [33].

1.10 Exercises

1. A banking application involves two types of transactions. A transfer transaction, in which money is transferred from one account to another, is constructed from the two assignments

$$account1 := account1 - num;$$
$$account2 := account2 + num;$$

A printing transaction prints out bank statements using the assignment

$$print(account1 + account2);$$

For each possible interleaving of the two transactions under concurrent execution, state what the printing transaction prints. You may assume that assignment and print statements are atomic. How could you make the program work correctly?

2. Suppose, in Figure 1.7, one writer is accessing the shared data object, and m readers and n writers are waiting. State at which semaphore each of the readers and writers is waiting.

3. Give a scenario demonstrating that the mutual exclusion protocol in the following concurrent program does not satisfy the desired properties given in Section 1.6. You may assume that $turn$ is initialized to either 1 or 2.

$\mathcal{P}_1$::	$\mathcal{P}_2$::
$\cdots$ – – noncritical section	$\cdots$ – – noncritical section
while $turn = 2$ **do**;	**while** $turn = 1$ **do**;
$\cdots$ – – critical section	$\cdots$ – – critical section
$turn := 2;$	$turn := 1;$
$\cdots$ – – noncritical section	$\cdots$ – – noncritical section

4. Give a scenario demonstrating that the mutual exclusion protocol in the following concurrent program does not satisfy the desired properties given in Section 1.6. Assume $q1$ and $q2$ are initialized to false.

$\mathcal{P}_1$::	$\mathcal{P}_2$::
$\cdots$ – – noncritical section	$\cdots$ – – noncritical section
$q1 := true;$	$q2 := true;$
while $q2$ **do**;	**while** $q1$ **do**;
$\cdots$ – – critical section	$\cdots$ – – critical section
$q1 := false;$	$q2 := false;$
$\cdots$ – – noncritical section	$\cdots$ – – noncritical section

5. Give a scenario demonstrating that the mutual exclusion protocol in the following concurrent program does not satisfy the desired properties given in Section 1.6. Assume $q1$ and $q2$ are initialized to false.

$\mathcal{P}_1::$
$\cdots$ $--$ noncritical section
while $q2$ **do**;
$q1 := true$;
$\cdots$ $--$ critical section
$q1 := false$;
$\cdots$ $--$ noncritical section

$\mathcal{P}_2::$
$\cdots$ $--$ noncritical section
while $q1$ **do**;
$q2 := true$;
$\cdots$ $--$ critical section
$q2 := false$;
$\cdots$ $--$ noncritical section

6. Informally demonstrate that the following program, due to G. Peterson [109], is a satisfactory mutual exclusion protocol as described in Section 1.6. Assume $q1$ and $q2$ are initialized to *false* and *turn* is initialized to either 1 or 2.

$\mathcal{P}_1::$
$\cdots$ $--$ noncritical section
$q1 := true$;
$turn := 1$;
while $q2$ **and** $turn = 1$ **do**;
$\cdots$ $--$ critical section
$q1 := false$;
$\cdots$ $--$ noncritical section

$\mathcal{P}_2::$
$\cdots$ $--$ noncritical section
$q2 := true$;
$turn := 2$;
while $q1$ **and** $turn = 2$ **do**;
$\cdots$ $--$ critical section
$q2 := false$;
$\cdots$ $--$ noncritical section

7. The following algorithm, due to L. Lamport [81], sometimes referred to as the Bakery Algorithm, solves the mutual exclusion problem for N processes without the use of semaphores. An N dimensional vector of integer variables, n, is shared among all processes. The ith process can modify its own entry in the vector, $n[i]$, and read all other entries. $n[i]$ is initially 0 and is set to a larger value when process i wishes to enter its critical section. The basic idea is that each process sets its entry to be larger than the values in the entries of every other process and then waits until its entry is the smallest of all waiting process (similar to taking numbers in a bakery). A lexicographic comparison between pairs of integers is used in the busy wait statement so that if $n[i] = n[j]$, the comparison is between i and j (note that this implies a static priority in the case of a tie and hence violates one of the desired properties given in Section 1.6). Give an argument for the correctness of the algorithm. Show that the protocol does not work correctly if the ith process does not initially set $n[i]$ to 1.

$n[i] := 1;$
$n[i] := max(n[1], n[2], \cdots, n[N]) + 1;$
for $j := 1$ **to** N **do**
    while $(n[j] \neq 0)$ **and** $((n[i], i) > (n[j], j))$ **do**;
   $\cdots$ $--$ critical section
$n[i] := 0;$
   $\cdots$ $--$ noncritical section

8. Two asynchronous processes, $\mathcal{P}_1$ and $\mathcal{P}_2$, are to be synchronized so that they both execute at designated points in their respective programs at the same time. Thus if $\mathcal{P}_1$ reaches statement $L1$ before $\mathcal{P}_2$ reaches $L2$, then $\mathcal{P}_1$ waits until $\mathcal{P}_2$ reaches $L2$ and vice versa. Using semaphores, design synchronizing statements that can be used at $L1$ and $L2$ to achieve this effect. Specify the initial value of each semaphore.

9. Revise the solution to the bounded buffer problem given in Figure 1.8 so that each time *Iop* completes the filling of N buffers (*i.e.*, after it fills $buf[N-1]$), it waits until Cp has emptied all N before refilling the buffers.

10. Revise the solution to the Readers-Writers Problem shown in Figure 1.7 so that, although it still gives priority to readers, at most N readers can be reading at the same time.

11. Revise the solution to the Readers-Writers Problem shown in Figure 1.7 so that it gives priority to writers.

12. Use semaphores to solve the Dining Philosophers Problem:

> Five philosophers sit around a circular table and alternate between thinking and eating spaghetti. A philosopher needs two forks to eat. A fork is placed between each pair of philosophers and a philosopher can only use the forks on his immediate left and right. Design a solution that avoids the deadlock situation in which all philosophers decide to eat simultaneously, each picks up one fork and then all wait for the other adjacent fork to be made available.

(Hint: Model each fork as a semaphore.)

13. A system contains a set of user processes and a single process, C, which is awakened by a hardware clock each time the clock ticks. From time to time a user may want to synchronize with the clock – that is, it might want to wait until the next clock tick. Design two procedures, *wakeme* and *tick*, for this purpose, using semaphores for synchronization. Users call *wakeme* when they want to synchronize and C calls *tick* each time it is awakened by the clock. Make sure that all users that have called *wakeme* prior to the call to *tick* get awakened.

14. Two infinitely looping processes must access a shared database in a mutually exclusive fashion. An additional constraint is imposed: neither process is to be allowed to make three accesses in a row without the other having made at least one. Give a solution to the problem using semaphores.

15. Design a protocol using binary semaphores to solve the "Restroom Problem," described as follows:

> There exist two types of users (*M* and *F*). Instances of each type compete for use of a single shared resource (the restroom). Multiple users of one type may use the resource simultaneously but it is forbidden for users of different types to be accessing the resource at the same time.
>
> We say that we are in a Type 1 (2) phase if the resource is being used by one or more Type 1 (2) users. A fairness constraint is imposed to prevent users of a single type from monopolizing the resource. If there is a waiting user of Type 1 and the number of Type 2 users who have used the resource during the current Type 2 phase is N or more, then all subsequently arriving Type 2 users will be made to wait until the next Type 1 phase completes. A symmetric constraint with 1 and 2 interchanged also applies. Thus, for example, a Type 1 user waits if (1) a Type 2 phase is in progress or (2) a Type 1 phase is in progress in which N or more Type 1 users have been admitted to the restroom and there is a waiting Type 2 user.

16. The reader priority solution to the Readers-Writers problem given in Figure 1.7 has the property that, if a writer is writing and both readers and writers are waiting, priority will not necessarily be given to a waiting reader. Give an alternative solution to the problem that always gives priority to waiting readers in this situation.

2

Sequential Programs

Our plan is to consider a concurrent system as a set of sequential processes, each running independently of the others and sharing information. We want to reason about the behavior of such a system by first reasoning about the behavior of its component sequential processes and then taking into account the effect of the information sharing. We begin that plan in this chapter by learning how to reason about sequential programs. Rather than use any specific language as the basis of our study, we consider particular constructs that are common to virtually all languages. In this chapter we discuss individual statements; in the next chapter we consider subprograms.

2.1 Sequential Constructs

In the previous chapter we used the word semantics in a rather informal way. In this chapter we are somewhat more precise and distinguish between two kinds of semantics: formal and informal. By informal semantics we mean a description, in English, of the effect of executing some program fragment. We refer to this type of description as *operational semantics*, since it describes how each statement operates. By its nature such a description tends to be imprecise. By *formal semantics* we mean a description, in a formal system, of the effect of executing a program fragment on the state of the program. By formalizing the semantics we make it precise. In this section we present the syntax and operational semantics of the language we use in the text. Later, we present its formal semantics.

In addition to giving the operational and formal semantics of the language, we specify which language constructs are atomic. (Recall that atomic operations are the unit of interleaving.) We assume the existence of a control point before and after each atomic construct. When the control point at the end of a program fragment is enabled, the fragment is said to terminate normally – more frequently, we simply say it terminates.

2.1.1 Skip Statement

The simplest construct of all is the skip statement:

skip

The operational semantics of the skip statement is as follows:

> The only effect of its execution is to enable a control point at the next
> operation. The skip statement is atomic.

The skip statement is equivalent to the Pascal empty statement and the Ada
null statement.

2.1.2 Halt Statement

Another simple construct is the halt statement:

halt

The operational semantics of the halt statement is as follows:

> Its execution has no effect and no new control point is enabled. The halt
> statement is atomic.

Since no new control point is enabled, the program does not continue executing.
Typically, the halt statement is executed only in situations where some fatal
error or exception has occurred. Hence we say that the program has failed or
terminated abnormally.

2.1.3 Multiple Assignment Statement

We generalize the ordinary assignment statement to one in which a vector of
expressions is first evaluated and then assignments are made to corresponding
elements of a vector of variables. The general form of the multiple assignment
statement is

$$\bar{v} := \bar{e}$$

where

> $\bar{v}$ is a vector of variables;
> $\bar{e}$ is a vector of expressions.

The operational semantics of the multiple assignment statement is as follows:

> First the address of each left-hand-side variable is computed (for indexed
> variables, this address computation might involve the evaluation of some
> expression); then each of the right-hand-side expressions is evaluated;

then each right-hand-side expression value is assigned to the corresponding variable (*i.e.,* the value of the first expression is assigned to the first variable, that of the second expression to the second variable, etc.). The multiple assignment statement is atomic.

Note that the order of evaluation is such that if any variable appears on both the left and right side of the assignment operator, its original value is used in the expression evaluation and in the computation of left-hand-side variable addresses.

Our assumption that the assignment statement is executed atomically is convenient for our later development of a formal system, but it is not realistic, since the statement can be quite complex. (For example, the assumption would be particularly unrealistic if the evaluation of an expression involved the invocation of a function. We do not include functions in our language.) However, the techniques we discuss can be used to develop a formal system without making this assumption.

We assume that each variable in $\bar{v}$ is distinct (since otherwise the order in which assignments were made would have to be specified). Furthermore, we assume here, as well as in the constructs that follow, that expression evaluation has no side effects (*i.e.,* that evaluating an expression does not change the value of any variables). Specifically, we assume no side effects in the evaluation of the right-hand-side expressions or any of the expressions encountered during address calculation. Side effects have a number of unfortunate consequences, some of which will be pointed out as we proceed. In assignment statements, for example, the order of expression evaluation might affect the outcome of the assignment.

Two examples of multiple assignment statements are

$$x,\ y,\ z\ :=\ 3,\ 4,\ 5$$

$$c1,\ c2\ :=\ c2,\ c1$$

Not only is the multiple assignment statement more compact than a sequence of conventional assignments but, as shown in the second example, it also permits a reduction in the number of temporary variables, which would otherwise clutter the program.

To obtain the usual assignment statement, the multiple assignment statement can be specialized to

$$v\ :=\ e$$

2.1.4   Compound Statement

Composition is used to group statements together into a compound statement:

begin S_1; S_2; ...; S_n; **end**

The operational semantics of the compound statement is as follows:

Each of the S_i is executed in sequence.

2.1.5 Conditional Statement

We use a nondeterministic generalization of the conventional conditional statement. It has the form

$$\textbf{if } G_1 \rightarrow S_1;\ [] \ G_2 \rightarrow S_2;\ [] \ldots [] \ G_n \rightarrow S_n;\ \textbf{fi}$$

where

G_i is a boolean expression (each G_i is called a guard);
S_i is a statement.

The operational semantics of the conditional, or alternative, statement is as follows:

First each of the guards is evaluated; if all the guards are false, the statement fails (*i.e.*, its execution has no effect and no new control point is enabled; we say that its execution has terminated abnormally); otherwise, one of the true guards is nondeterministically selected and the corresponding statement is executed; when its execution terminates, the conditional statement terminates. The evaluation of each guard is atomic.

We assume that guard evaluation has no side effects. Since guard evaluation is atomic, a control point exists at each guard and on entry to the corresponding statement. The nondeterminism involved in this statement is an example of the choice nondeterminism discussed in Chapter 1.

When a guard is true, both the guard and its corresponding statement are said to be *open*; otherwise they are *closed*. Thus, the operational semantics states that one of the open component statements is nondeterministically selected for execution.

A simple example of a conditional statement is

$$\textbf{if } x \leq 0 \rightarrow x := -x;\ [] \ x \geq 0 \rightarrow \textbf{skip};\ \textbf{fi}$$

The example illustrates an advantage of nondeterminism: the programmer is not forced to choose an alternative when either is acceptable (in the example, when $x = 0$).

To obtain the usual if-then-else construct, the statement can be specialized to

$$\textbf{if } B \rightarrow S_1;\ [] \ \neg B \rightarrow S_2;\ \textbf{fi}$$

2.1.6 Loop Statement

For the looping statement we use a nondeterministic generalization of the conventional looping statement. Its form is

$$\textbf{do } G_1 \rightarrow S_1;\ [] \ G_2 \rightarrow S_2;\ [] \ldots [] \ G_n \rightarrow S_n;\ \textbf{od}$$

where

> G_i is a boolean expression (each G_i is called a guard);
> S_i is a statement.

The operational semantics of the loop statement is as follows:

First each of the guards is evaluated; if all are closed, the statement terminates; otherwise one of the open guards is nondeterministically selected and the corresponding statement is executed; then the entire loop statement is reexecuted. The evaluation of each guard is atomic.

We make the same assumptions concerning side effects, atomicity, and control points as were made in connection with the if statement. The nondeterminism involved in this statement is once again an example of the choice nondeterminism discussed in Chapter 1.

A simple example of a loop statement is

> **do** *BufferNotFull* $\rightarrow$
> $\quad\cdots\qquad\quad$ – – accept input from producer
> [] *BufferNotEmpty* $\rightarrow$
> $\quad\cdots\qquad\quad$ – – give output to consumer
> **od**

This statement maintains a buffer that is written by a producer and read by a consumer. The statement is nondeterministic in that if the buffer is both not full and not empty, either statement can be executed.

To obtain the usual while construct, the loop statement can be specialized to

$$\textbf{do } B \rightarrow S;\ \textbf{od}$$

2.2   Introduction to Reasoning about Programs

Our approach to reasoning about programs is to use assertions to make statements about the values of program variables. An assertion might be true or false depending on the values of those variables. Thus

$$(x = 4) \wedge (y \geq z)$$

is an example of an assertion that might be true or false depending on the values of x, y, and z.

We *annotate* a program by placing assertions (enclosed in curly brackets) at control points in the program text. When we place an assertion at a particular point in the text of a program, we mean that whenever the corresponding control point is enabled, the value of the variables is such that the corresponding assertion is true. In some cases the truth of a particular assertion is obvious; in most cases a proof is necessary.

We might annotate an assignment statement with the assertions

$$\{x = 2\}$$
$$x := x + 1;$$
$$\{x = 3\}$$

These assertions state that before the execution of the assignment statement the value of x is 2 and (assuming the assignment terminates) afterward the value of x is 3. If we can somehow prove that one of these assertions is true when its control point is enabled, the truth of the other when its control point is enabled follows immediately from the operational semantics of the assignment statement.

In a slightly more complicated program, the assertions might be

$$\{x = 5\}$$
$$x := 1;$$
$$\{x = 1\}$$
$$y := x + 1;$$
$$\{(x = 1) \wedge (y = 2)\}$$

These assertions state that before the first statement is executed the value of x is 5, after the first statement is executed the value of x is 1, and after the second statement is executed the value of x is 1 and the value of y is 2. (Note that we made no statement about the value of y after the first assignment is executed.)

Reasoning about such assertions is trivial for assignment statements but becomes more complex for the other sequential constructs and still more complex for the concurrent constructs discussed in subsequent chapters. For this reason, we make a short digression in the next section to introduce the concepts of formal logic and formal reasoning techniques. Our purpose is to build a formal system within which the effect of a program can be precisely understood.

2.3   Logic and Formal Reasoning

Formal reasoning is done using a formal, or logical, system. Such a system provides a means for deriving sequences of symbols (from some alphabet) from other sequences (logicians would say "inferring sequences from other sequences"). Formal systems are analogous in many ways to context free grammars, which also provide a means for deriving sequences from other sequences. In the next section we develop a formal system called *Program Logic* for reasoning about programs.

A formal logical system consists of a set of symbols, a set of well formed formulas, a set of axioms, and a set of inference rules.

A Set of Symbols

The set of symbols contains the symbols that can appear in sequences derived within the system. It may contain constants, variables, logical connectives, and function and predicate symbols, as well as symbols that are specific to a particular application area (*e.g.,* Program Logic). This set is analogous to the lexical symbols in a context free grammar. A sequence of symbols is referred to as a *formula*.

A Set of Well Formed Formulas

The set of well formed formulas (logicians call them wffs) is the subset of formulas that are constructed in accordance with certain rules of formation. The well formed formulas are analogous to the sequences that can be generated by a context free grammar. Given a formula, there is a simple mechanical procedure (analogous to a parser) to test whether or not it is well formed. Within Program Logic, the well formed formulas are composed of assertions and program statements. Since our discussion deals only with well formed formulas, we frequently refer to them simply as formulas.

A Set of Axioms

The axioms are a distinguished subset of the well formed formulas. Axioms are analogous to start symbols in a context free grammar in that they are used to start derivations (or inference chains) within the system. The set of axioms can generally be divided into two parts: the *logical* axioms and the *specific* axioms. An appropriate set of logical axioms can be used to form the basis of a wide variety of formal systems and can be thought of as formalizing the basic reasoning process. The specific axioms describe a particular application to which the reasoning is to be applied. For example, Program Logic contains specific axioms that describe the effect of each assignment statement.

The set of axioms need not be finite. One way to express an infinite set of axioms is by using an *axiom schema*. An axiom schema is a sequence of symbols that can include some new symbols not in the formal system. (Hence an axiom schema is not itself a well formed formula.) These new symbols are meant to represent well formed formulas. An axiom can be derived from an axiom schema by systematically substituting appropriate well formed formulas for these new symbols. The next section contains a number of examples of axiom schemas.

A Set of Inference Rules

An *inference rule* is a rule for deriving (or inferring) a new well formed formula given a set of other well formed formulas. Inference rules are given in the form

$$\frac{H_1, \; H_2, \ldots, \; H_n}{C}$$

where the H_i are formulas called the *hypotheses* and C is a formula called the *conclusion*. We say that the inference rule can be used to infer the conclusion from the hypotheses.

Once again we can separate the inference rules into those that are application independent and those that are specific to a particular application. An example of an application dependent inference rule within Program Logic is a rule in which the hypotheses describe the effect of two different statements and the conclusion describes the effect of the composition of those statements.

Inference rules can be used to form a *proof*. A proof is a sequence of well formed formulas, where each formula either is an axiom or can be derived from previous formulas using inference rules. Any formula in a proof is called a *theorem*.

We have yet to introduce a concept of *truth* in a formal system. The set of axioms is just a distinguished subset of the set of well formed formulas, and theorems are just well formed formulas that can be syntactically derived from these axioms using inference rules; it is not necessary to ascribe a meaning to either axioms or theorems. The process of deriving new theorems is purely mechanical, requiring no creativity. (However, the process of producing a proof for a particular theorem may, and often does, require considerable ingenuity.) The fact that proofs are syntactic derivations and have no semantics is one of the strengths of this approach to formal reasoning; it ensures that the reasoning is valid and is not tainted by any appeal to intuition based on a particular application.

However, to make a formal system useful, we have to relate it to some *domain of discourse* – a particular application. Our goal is to reason about programs; hence our domain of discourse involves formulas that are annotated program fragments, and we are interested in determining if the assertions are meaningful in the context of the fragments.

To relate a formal system to a domain of discourse, we introduce meaning, or *semantics*. The semantics is provided through a mapping of each well formed formula to T or F, where T and F are meant to denote truth and falsity in the domain of discourse. Obviously, our intention is to choose a mapping that maps a formula to T if and only if it makes a true statement about the domain of discourse.

The details of how a particular mapping from formulas to T or F is performed depend on the application and the system of formal logic being used. Mappings usually involve several concepts:

A *state*, which is an assignment of a value to each variable in the formula. (As we shall see, we have to extend the notion of a state when we discuss Program Logic.)

An *interpretation*, which assigns a meaning to each function and predicate symbol that appears in the formula.

The utilization of the standard meaning for certain special symbols (*e.g.*, $\wedge, \neg, \forall$).

For example, consider the formula

$$p \wedge \neg q$$

where p and q are boolean variables. Using the standard meanings for $\wedge$ and $\neg$, in the state in which both p and q are assigned the value T, the formula is mapped to F. Next consider the formula

$$sin(x/2) = 1 \qquad (2.1)$$

In the state in which x is assigned the value π, the formula maps to T if the function symbol sin is interpreted as the sine function, the function symbol $/$ is interpreted as division, and the predicate symbol $=$ is interpreted as equality. In general, mapping involves substituting the values from the state for the variables of the formula, using the interpretation to evaluate the functions and predicates, and evaluating expressions using the standard meaning for the special symbols. If this process yields the value T, we say that a formula is *mapped to T in that state*. We sometimes say that the state *satisfies* the formula or that the formula is true[1] in that state as a shorthand for "maps to T in that state." Sometimes we leave out the phrase "in that state" when the state is obvious from the context.

We say that a particular formula is *valid* in some interpretation if it maps to T in all states.

Thus, the formula (2.1) is not valid, since, for example, it does not map to T in the state in which x is equal to 0. However, the formula

$$sin^2(x) + cos^2(x) = 1$$

is valid under an interpretation in which sin^2 is the square of the sine function, cos^2 is the square of the cosine function, and $+$ is the addition function (since by a theorem in trigonometry, it maps to T for all values of x).

---

[1] We distinguish this unitalicized use of the word "true" from the italicized version, *true*, introduced later, which is a constant in a formal system.

The purpose of a formal system is to help us reason in a precise way so that, starting with well formed formulas known to be valid (axioms), we can deduce the validity of other well formed formulas. We perform the deductions using inference rules. We say that an inference rule is *sound* under a particular interpretation if, whenever its hypotheses are valid, its conclusion is valid.

If a formal system has the property that, for some particular interpretation, each of its axioms is valid and each of its inference rules is sound, then any theorem provable within that system is valid and we say that the formal system is *sound* with respect to that interpretation.

When a formal system is sound under some interpretation I, I is referred to as a sound interpretation, or a *model*, for that system. We are interested in systems that have sound interpretations in some domain of discourse, since then we can mechanically derive valid statements about that domain; that is, we can automate the reasoning about that domain.

A formal system is sound with respect to some interpretation if every theorem that can be derived in that system is valid. If, conversely, every formula that is valid under some particular interpretation is a theorem, the system is said to be *complete* with respect to that interpretation. In other words, a formal system is complete with respect to some interpretation if every valid formula can be proven. Thus, in a formal system that is both sound and complete with respect to some interpretation, a well formed formula is valid if and only if it is a theorem.

We would like Program Logic to be both sound and complete with respect to the interpretation that describes the behavior of programs. Unfortunately, this perfectly sensible wish cannot be realized. Since programs deal with numbers, Program Logic must encompass all of arithmetic, and Gödel has shown that no sound formal system that encompasses arithmetic can be complete. Thus Program Logic will be sound, but not complete (that is, there will be valid statements about programs that our logic will not be able to prove).

Before developing Program Logic, we briefly study two formal systems on which Program Logic is based: Propositional Logic and Predicate Calculus.

2.3.1 Propositional Logic

Propositional Logic is a formalization of the system we commonly call boolean algebra. More precisely, it is a system for formally reasoning about propositions. A *proposition* is a declarative statement that makes an assertion about a domain of discourse. Each proposition makes a true or false statement about a particular domain of discourse. Thus, the proposition "The sky is blue" makes an assertion about the domain of discourse, which in this case is today's weather, that might be true or false, depending on what the weather happens to be.

The well formed formulas of Propositional Logic are strings that consist of propositional variables and logical connectives and use the usual syntax for boolean algebra. The propositional variables can be thought of as standing

p	q	$p \Rightarrow q$
F	F	T
F	T	T
T	F	F
T	T	T

Figure 2.1: Truth table for the *implies* connective.

for particular propositions. Thus, if the propositional variable p represents the proposition "The sky is blue" and q represents the proposition "It is not raining," the formula

"The sky is blue" implies "It is not raining"

can be written in Propositional Logic as

$$p \Rightarrow q$$

By substituting variables for propositions, we can concentrate on the reasoning process independent of a meaning in a particular domain. Corresponding to the fact that a proposition can be true or false in a domain, we allow a propositional variable to take on two possible values: T and F.

The assignment of meaning to well formed formulas in Propositional Logic is somewhat simpler than previously described because no special symbols are involved (*e.g.,* predicate and function symbols) and hence no interpretation is needed. A state is an assignment of T or F to each variable. For each state, a well formed formula can be mapped to T or F as follows. A propositional variable takes the value assigned to it in the state. A well formed formula is mapped by mapping all propositional variables in the formula and then simplifying using the standard truth tables that define the connectives. The truth tables are not chosen arbitrarily. They formulate our understanding of the logical connectives so that, if a well formed formula is mapped to T by this procedure, it will also be a true statement about the domain of discourse. For example, Figure 2.1 shows the truth table for the *implies* connective.

A formula that is mapped to T in all possible states – a valid formula – is known as a *tautology*. For example, the formula

$$x \vee y \vee (\neg x \wedge \neg y)$$

is a tautology, as can readily be verified by just evaluating the formula in its four possible states.

The method of truth tables is an effective procedure for determining whether or not a particular well formed formula is a tautology. All that is necessary is to evaluate the formula in all possible states. Since the number of states is finite, the decision procedure is finite.

Tautologies play an important role in Propositional Logic, since it can be shown that a formula is a theorem in the formal system for Propositional Logic (described below) if and only if it is a tautology. Thus there is a simple decision procedure to determine whether or not a given formula is a theorem: just verify that it evaluates to T in all possible states using the truth tables. Reasoning in the context of a formal system is not required. Unfortunately, more complex logics, such as Predicate Calculus and Program Logic, cannot be analyzed in such a simple way. An alternative approach based on a formal system is needed.

Although in Propositional Logic we can demonstrate that a formula is a theorem without reasoning in the context of a formal system, we present a formal system here as an example. We give a formulation of the system using only the $\neg$ (not) and $\Rightarrow$ (implies) connectives. The more familiar boolean connectives $\vee$ (or) and $\wedge$ (and) can be defined in terms of $\neg$ and $\Rightarrow$. Our formulation does not even require propositional constants. Thus, the constant *true*, which is assigned the value T, can be represented by any tautology, such as $(p \Rightarrow p)$, since a tautology maps to T in all states. Similarly, the constant *false* can be represented by any contradiction, such as $\neg(p \Rightarrow p)$, since a contradiction maps to F in all states. For convenience, in subsequent sections we freely use these additional symbols. We use upper case symbols P, Q, ... to represent well formed formulas (but note that these are not symbols of the formal system itself).

The Set of Symbols

The set of symbols is

Propositional Variables	$p, q,$ ...
Propositional Connectives	$\neg$ (not), $\Rightarrow$ (implies)
Punctuation marks	$(,)$

The Set of Well Formed Formulas

The set of well formed formulas is defined by two rules:

A propositional variable is a well formed formula;
If P and Q are well formed formulas, then so are $(\neg P)$ and $(P \Rightarrow Q)$.

Thus, the set of well formed formulas includes all the usual formulas in boolean algebra; for example

$$q$$

$$(p \Rightarrow q)$$

$$(p \Rightarrow (q \Rightarrow r))$$

The Set of Axioms

The set of axioms is defined by three axiom schemas:

$$(P \Rightarrow (Q \Rightarrow P))$$

$$((P \Rightarrow (Q \Rightarrow R)) \Rightarrow ((P \Rightarrow Q) \Rightarrow (P \Rightarrow R)))$$

$$(((\neg Q) \Rightarrow (\neg P)) \Rightarrow (((\neg Q) \Rightarrow P) \Rightarrow Q))$$

The Set of Inference Rules

Only one inference rule, known as *modus ponens*, is needed:

$$\frac{P,\ (P \Rightarrow Q)}{Q}$$

This rule states that if P and $(P \Rightarrow Q)$ are theorems, then Q can be inferred.

2.3.2 Predicate Calculus

Predicate Calculus is a generalization of Propositional Logic that allows us to reason about members of a set that may be very large or even infinite. To understand the limitations of Propositional Logic, consider the problem of stating that all students in a particular graduate course have B.A. degrees. If the course enrollment consisted of the three students John, Mary, and Bill, the following statement would cover the situation:

(John has a B.A.) $\wedge$ *(Mary has a B.A.)* $\wedge$ *(Bill has a B.A.)*

We can easily transform this into a well formed formula in Propositional Logic by substituting propositional variables for each of the conjuncts. Unfortunately, as the number of students in the class gets large, the formula gets unwieldy and if the number becomes infinite, the statement cannot be formulated in a finite way using only propositional operators.

As another example, consider the following assertions:

All prime numbers greater than 2 are odd numbers.

The number x is a prime number greater than 2.

From the meaning of the word "all," we would like to use *modus ponens* to infer that:

The number x is an odd number.

We cannot make this inference using Propositional Logic.

To overcome these limitations, Predicate Calculus introduces several new concepts:

Variables that can take on other than propositional values (*e.g.,* student names or integers) and a *domain, D,* from which these variables draw their values (*e.g.,* the set of all students in the course or the set of all integers);

Quantification operators, such as "all," that allow us to reason about membership in a set;

Functions and predicates.

The formulas in Predicate Calculus are built from the two quantification operators ∀ (for all) and ∃ (there exists), as well as the logical connectives (∃ can be expressed in terms of ¬ and ∀). For example, a formula involving a quantification operator might take one of the following forms:

$$((\forall x)P)$$

$$((\exists x)P)$$

Just as a standard meaning is assumed for the logical connectives (*e.g.,* ⇒), the quantifiers also have a standard meaning. The first expression states that for all values of x in D the predicate P is mapped to T. The second states that there exists a value of x in D for which the predicate P is mapped to T. Thus, quantified expressions express properties of sets of values.

As an example, the statement "All prime numbers greater than 2 are odd numbers" expresses a property of the set of prime numbers greater than 2 and can be written

$$((\forall x)(x \text{ is a prime number greater than 2}) \Rightarrow (x \text{ is an odd number}))$$

To transform this into a statement in Predicate Calculus, we need a way to express such properties as greater than, prime, and odd. We denote these using the predicates >, *prime,* and *odd* and rewrite the statement as

$$((\forall x)(prime(x) \wedge (x > 2)) \Rightarrow odd(x))$$

Quantified expressions can be combined and nested in the obvious way. For example, to say that there is a smallest prime number, we might write

$$((\exists x) \, prime(x) \wedge ((\forall y) \, prime(y) \Rightarrow (x \leq y)))$$

Quantified variables are referred to as *bound* variables. Occurrences of variables that are not bound are said to be *free.* The scope of the binding is specified by the parentheses around the quantified subexpression. Thus, in the expression

$$((\forall i)(0 \leq i \leq n) \Rightarrow (i^2 \leq 5i)) \vee (i > n)$$

the variable i within the parentheses around the quantified subexpression is a bound variable. The variable i outside the parentheses is a different variable and is free. The variable n is free throughout the entire expression. Bound and free variables in a formula are analogous to local and global variables of a program fragment, since bound variables, like local variables, are only defined within the scope of the binding. A well formed formula with no free variables is *closed*, otherwise it is *open*.

We argued that a formal theory is not necessary for Propositional Logic because the validity of well formed formulas can be easily tested using truth tables. In the case of Predicate Calculus, however, the domains of interest may be arbitrarily large or infinite, so it is no longer possible to use such an approach. Hence, a proof within a formal system is needed to determine whether a formula is valid.

We do not give a complete description of a formal system for Predicate Calculus but only mention some relevant issues. The set of symbols includes

The constants, connectives, and punctuation marks of Propositional Logic;

The symbol $\forall$ (for all);

A denumerable set of variables, constants, function symbols, and predicate symbols.

The function and predicate symbols are just symbols and have no meaning as functions or predicates. It is only when an interpretation is given to the formal system that specific functions and predicates are supplied for each symbol. Function and predicate symbols are assumed to have an associated *arity*, which indicates the number of arguments that they take.

Constants and variables are referred to as *terms*. Function symbols are used to combine terms to form other terms. Thus, if t_1 and t_2 are terms and f is a binary function symbol, then $f(t_1, t_2)$ is a term. Similarly, predicate symbols are used to combine terms into *atomic formulas*. Thus, if A is a binary predicate symbol, then $A(t_1, t_2)$ is an atomic formula. The propositional constants *true* and *false* are also atomic formulas. The well formed formulas are defined by two rules:

Every atomic formula is a well formed formula;

If P and Q are well formed formulas, then so are $(\neg P)$, $(P \Rightarrow Q)$, and $((\forall x)P)$, where x is a variable (as well as formulas properly constructed using other connectives, such as $\wedge$ and $\vee$).

(For simplicity, we drop the rules governing the use of parentheses.)

The logical axioms include those of Propositional Logic, together with other axiom schemas that deal with quantification. One of these, under certain restrictions concerning the scope of bound variables, is

$$((\forall x)A(x)) \Rightarrow A(t)$$

where t is a term. Informally, if A is true for all x, then it is true for any particular term t.

The rules of inference are *modus ponens* and generalization:

$$\frac{Q}{((\forall x)Q)}$$

Informally, this rule states that if a formula Q, which might involve a free variable x, is valid, then it is true for any value that x can assume.

An interpretation consists of a specification of

The domain, D, from which the variables and constants draw their values;

An assignment to each constant symbol of a value from D;

The mapping from D^n into D performed by each n-ary function symbol;

An n-ary relation (a subset of D^n) corresponding to each predicate symbol, indicating the n-tuples for which the predicate is mapped to T.

The mapping of a well formed formula to T or F involves the following actions. Assume a particular state (mapping of variables to elements of D). Free variables are replaced by their values in the state. A function symbol and its arguments are replaced by the value specified in the interpretation (hence terms assume a value in D). A predicate symbol is then mapped to T if its argument tuple is in the relation associated with the predicate symbol by the interpretation, and F otherwise (hence atomic formulas are mapped to T or F). The logical connectives and quantifiers are used in the standard way to assign T or F to the formula. For example, $((\forall x)((\forall y)P))$ is mapped to T if the binary relation associated with the predicate symbol P contains all pairs in $D \times D$. Open formulas are mapped to T or F depending on the values assigned to the free variables in the state. For example, the formula

$$((\forall i)(0 \le i \le n) \Rightarrow (i^2 \le 5i)) \lor (i > n)$$

maps to T for the state in which $n = 3$ and $i = 273$ (since the quantified subexpression within the parentheses maps to T for any $n \le 5$). The interpretation reinforces the analogy between bound and free variables in a formula and local and global variables in a program fragment, since the values assumed by local variables are determined entirely within the fragment while global variables have a value when the fragment is entered.

A well formed formula is valid in an interpretation if it is mapped to T in all states. It can be shown that the inference rules produce valid conclusions from valid hypotheses. Hence, an interpretation is a model if all axioms are valid in the interpretation. It can be shown that under any interpretation that is a model, Predicate Calculus is both sound and complete.

Predicate Calculus includes only logical axioms and inference rules. To reason about programs, specific axioms and inference rules must be added.

2.4   Program Logic

Program Logic is a formal logical system used to reason about programs written in the language described in Section 2.1 (and extended in subsequent chapters). Program Logic is an extension of Predicate Calculus in that any well formed formula in Predicate Calculus is also a well formed formula in Program Logic. In addition to the axioms and inference rules of Predicate Calculus, Program Logic includes the axioms and inference rules describing the data types of the language (*e.g.*, integers) (which we do not discuss) and new symbols (*e.g.*, **if**), well formed formulas, axioms, and inference rules related to the program constructs of the language.

The new well formed formulas are called *triples* and have the form:

$$\{P\}\,S\,\{Q\}$$

where P and Q are well formed formulas of Predicate Calculus, which we refer to as *assertions*, and S is a syntactically correct statement or sequence of statements. The free variables of the assertions are of two types: program variables and logical variables. We discuss logical variables shortly.

Recall that by a program state we mean a mapping from program variables to values. We assume, as in Predicate Calculus, that an interpretation gives meaning to all function and predicate symbols. An assertion defines a set of states, namely all states in which the assertion is mapped to T when the state values are assigned to the corresponding program variables in the assertion.

The interpretation must do more than provide a mechanism for mapping assertions; it must map triples as well. This mapping is provided by an *operational model*.

Operational Model

The triple $\{P\}\,S\,\{Q\}$ is valid in the operational model if and only if, whenever S starts execution in some state for which P is mapped to T, either S terminates, leaving the program in some state for which Q is mapped to T, or S does not terminate.

Recall that in Predicate Calculus a well formed formula is mapped to T or F in a particular state and is valid if it is mapped to T in all states. In Program Logic we must consider pairs of states, where the first element of a pair is an arbitrary initial state (corresponding to the program state before S executes) and the second element is the final state that results after execution of S terminates. A triple describing S is valid if and only if, for all such pairs, whenever the assertion preceding S in the triple is mapped to T in the initial state, the assertion following S is mapped to T in the final state. If the assertion preceding S is mapped to F in the initial state, the triple is mapped to T for any final assertion. For example, assuming the state consists only of the value of x, the set of pairs defined by the assignment $x := 1$ contains (0,1), (1,1),

(2,1), ... The triple

$$\{x = 0\}\ x\ :=\ 1\ \{x = 1\}$$

meets the required condition for all such pairs. (Note that for the first pair, (0,1), both assertions are mapped to T – and hence the triple is mapped to T – and for the remaining pairs, the first assertion is mapped to F but the triple is still mapped to T.)

The assertion P is called the *precondition* and the assertion Q is called the *postcondition*. If, for some reason, S does not terminate when started in a state satisfying P, then by definition any triple of the form $\{P\}\ S\ \{Q\}$ is mapped to T.

In addition to program variables, an assertion can involve logical variables. A *logical variable* is a variable that does not appear in the program text. We designate logical variables by upper case letters. For example, in the triple

$$\{x = X\}\ x\ :=\ x + 1\ \{x = X + 1\} \tag{2.2}$$

X is a logical variable. Logical variables are useful in recording some part of the program state. In the above example, we can view the role of X as that of taking on the value of x prior to the execution of the assignment. In general, logical variables are used to describe the effect of executing some program fragment, such as a procedure, in which the values of variables in the final state are some function of their initial values.

More formally, our operational model must be extended to triples whose assertions involve logical variables. We refer to an assignment of values to the logical variables as a *logical state* to differentiate it from a program state.

Operational Model with Logical Variables

The triple $\{P\}\ S\ \{Q\}$ is valid if and only if, whenever S starts execution in a program and logical state for which P is true, either S terminates and Q is true in the new program state and the original logical state or S does not terminate.

Thus a triple containing a logical variable must be true for any consistent assignment of a value to that logical variable in both the pre- and postcondition of the triple (in the example, for all values of X). For example, the set of state pairs (values of x) defined by the assignment in (2.2) includes (0,1),(1,2),(2,3),..., whereas logical states (values of X) include 0,1,2,.... If we choose the program state pair (1,2) and the logical state 0, the precondition of (2.2) is mapped to F and hence the triple is mapped to T. If we choose the logical state 1, both the pre- and postconditions are mapped to T and again the triple is mapped to T.

As with Predicate Calculus, the condition for a triple to be valid involves determining that it is true in a large, possibly infinite, number of situations – all possible initial states. A formal logical system enables us to make this determination: first we prove that the triple is a theorem in Program Logic; then we use the soundness of Program Logic with respect to the operational model to demonstrate that any theorem of the form $\{P\}$ S $\{Q\}$ that can be proven in Program Logic is valid. Since a theorem of this form does not prove termination, we say that it demonstrates *partial correctness*. Proof techniques that also prove termination are said to demonstrate *total correctness*.

Our approach to extending Predicate Calculus to Program Logic is to define axioms of the form $\{P\}$ S $\{Q\}$ for each of the constructs described in Section 2.1. These axioms provides a formal description of the effect of executing the construct. We refer to the axioms for each construct in the language as the *formal semantics* of that construct. We refer to the set of such axioms for all constructs in the language as the *formal semantics* of the language. The axioms corresponding to each construct are valid by definition – they define the semantics of the construct.

In contrast to operational semantics, formal semantics can be embedded in a formal logical system for proving properties of programs. Clearly, the formal and operational semantics of a language must closely correspond to each another.

We obtain the axioms for each construct by defining an axiom schema or rule of inference that describes that construct. These are the specific axioms and rules that extend Predicate Calculus to Program Logic. Since the constructors given in Section 2.1 include all the allowable ways of combining individual statements to get programs (for example, the compound and conditional statements both combine statements), we have the tools to reason about entire programs, as well as individual statements. In later chapters, we introduce additional constructors that deal with concurrency and define their formal and operational semantics.

Because our main purpose in this text is to study concurrency (rather than, for example, numerical computations), we restrict our formal presentation of Program Logic to programs involving only simple variables. We (informally) use structured variables in some of the examples, but be aware that certain subtleties must be dealt with (see [58] for a more complete treatment).

2.4.1   Skip Statement

The axiom schema describing the skip statement is

Skip Axiom

$$\{P\}\ \textbf{skip}\ \{P\} \qquad\qquad (2.3)$$

where P is an arbitrary assertion. Since the execution of the skip statement has no effect on the program state, any assertion that is true in the state before the statement executes will remain true afterwards.

2.4.2   Halt Statement

The axiom schema describing the halt statement is

Halt Axiom

$$\{P\}\ \mathbf{halt}\ \{Q\} \tag{2.4}$$

where P and Q are arbitrary assertions. Since execution of the halt statement does not enable a new control point, from a formal point of view the halt statement does not terminate. Hence any assertion can be asserted as a postcondition.

2.4.3   Multiple Assignment Statement

The axiom schema describing the multiple assignment statement $\bar{v} := \bar{e}$ is

Assignment Axiom

$$\{P_{\bar{e}}^{\bar{v}}\}\ \bar{v}\ :=\ \bar{e}\ \{P\} \tag{2.5}$$

where P is an arbitrary assertion and $P_{\bar{e}}^{\bar{v}}$ denotes P with all free occurrences of the variables $\bar{v}$ replaced by the corresponding expressions $\bar{e}$.

A few simple examples will clarify the use of this axiom.

1. For the assignment statement $x := x + 1$, let the postcondition, P, be $x = 3$. Then the precondition, P_{x+1}^{x}, is $(x + 1) = 3$. Thus,

$$\{x + 1 = 3\}\ x\ :=\ x + 1\ \{x = 3\}$$

   is an axiom that clearly conforms to the operational semantics of the language.

2. For the assignment statement $x := 3$, let the postcondition, P, be $x = 3$. Then the precondition, P_3^x, is $3 = 3$. Thus,

$$\{3 = 3\}\ x\ :=\ 3\ \{x = 3\}$$

   is an axiom. Since the assertion $3 = 3$ is a tautology (it is mapped to T in all program states), it can be replaced by *true*. Hence, this triple indicates that the postcondition will be mapped to T in all final states regardless of the initial state.

3. For the assignment statement $x := 2$, let the postcondition, P, be $x = 3$. Then the precondition, P_2^x, is $2 = 3$. Thus,

$$\{2 = 3\}\ x\ :=\ 2\ \{x = 3\}$$

   is an axiom. Since the assertion $2 = 3$ is a contradiction (it is mapped to F in all program states), it can be replaced by *false*. Hence, this triple indicates that there is no starting state that yields $x = 3$ as a postcondition.

4. For the assignment statement $x := y + 1$, let the postcondition, P, be $x = 3$. Then the precondition, P_{y+1}^x, is $y + 1 = 3$. Thus,

$$\{y + 1 = 3\}\ x := y + 1\ \{x = 3\}$$

is an axiom.

5. For the assignment statement $x, y := y, x$, let the postcondition, P, be $(x = 1) \wedge (y = 2)$. Then the precondition, $P_{y, x}^{x, y}$, is $(y = 1) \wedge (x = 2)$. Thus,

$$\{(y = 1) \wedge (x = 2)\}\ x, y := y, x\ \{(x = 1) \wedge (y = 2)\}$$

is an axiom.

For the Assignment Axiom to be valid, we must make the assumption of no side effects during expression evaluation. For example, a side effect could change the value of a variable not occurring in $\bar{v}$ but mentioned in P. The assertion $P_{\bar{e}}^{\bar{v}}$ would not reflect that change and thus would not be a complete description of the effect of the assignment. Hence, we must assume these side effects do not occur. The fact that it is difficult to account for side effects is an indication that side effects are poor programming practice.

2.4.4 Composition

Composition is described by an inference rule that uses as its hypotheses triples describing the two statements being composed and as its conclusion a triple describing the composed statements.

Rule of Composition

$$\frac{\{P\}\ S_1\ \{Q\},\ \{Q\}\ S_2\ \{R\}}{\{P\}\ S_1;\ S_2;\ \{R\}} \tag{2.6}$$

Thus, if statement S_1 can be described by triple $\{P\}\ S_1\ \{Q\}$ and statement S_2 by triple $\{Q\}\ S_2\ \{R\}$, where the postcondition for S_1 is the same as the precondition for S_2, then the composition of these two statements, $S_1;\ S_2;$, can be described by triple $\{P\}\ S_1;\ S_2;\ \{R\}$. For example, given the triples

$$\{true\}\ x := 1\ \{x = 1\}$$

and

$$\{x = 1\}\ x := x + 1\ \{x = 2\}$$

we can infer

$$\{true\}\ x := 1;\ x := x + 1;\ \{x = 2\}$$

We do not provide a separate rule for the compound statement. The pre- and postconditions of a compound statement are identical to the pre- and postconditions of the sequence of statements contained within.

2.4.5   Consequence

Before giving the schemas for the other control constructs, we present an inference rule that shows how the implication operator can be used to strengthen or weaken assertions. If the formula $P \Rightarrow Q$ is true, then for all states for which P is true, Q must also be true, and for those states for which P is false, Q can be either true or false. Thus Q is larger than P in the sense that it is true for at least all the states for which P is true, and possibly more. For example, for any P, $P \Rightarrow true$ and $false \Rightarrow P$. When P implies Q, we say that P is *stronger* than Q and Q is *weaker* than P. Thus *false* is the strongest assertion and *true* the weakest.

Using the implication operator, we obtain the Rule of Consequence:

Rule of Consequence

$$\frac{P' \Rightarrow P, \ \{P\} \, S \, \{Q\}, \ Q \Rightarrow Q'}{\{P'\} \, S \, \{Q'\}} \tag{2.7}$$

Thus, given a triple $\{P\} \, S \, \{Q\}$, we can replace P by a stronger assertion and Q by a weaker one. To see that this rule is sound, note that (1) for all states for which the new precondition, P', is true, the original precondition, P is also true and hence S can be expected to yield Q; (2) after S executes, the program is in some state for which the original postcondition, Q, is true and hence the new postcondition, Q', is also true.

As a simple example of the use of this rule, suppose we have the program fragment

$$x := 1;$$
$$x := 2;$$

Using the Assignment Axiom and substituting *true* where appropriate, we get the following triples:

$$\{true\} \, x := 1 \, \{x = 1\}$$

$$\{true\} \, x := 2 \, \{x = 2\}$$

We cannot use the Rule of Composition directly to compose these triples, since the postcondition of the first is not the same as the precondition of the second. However, the Rule of Consequence can be invoked as follows:

$$\frac{\{true\} \, x := 1 \, \{x = 1\}, \ (x = 1) \Rightarrow true}{\{true\} \, x := 1 \, \{true\}}$$

to yield a triple that can be used in the Rule of Composition to get the desired result:

$$\frac{\{true\} \, x := 1 \, \{true\}, \ \{true\} \, x := 2 \, \{x = 2\}}{\{true\} \, x := 1; \, x := 2; \, \{x = 2\}}$$

2.4.6 Weakest Preconditions

In reasoning about a complete program, *prog*, we generally begin with a notion
of the nature of the calculation the program is to perform and then translate
that notion into a postcondition for the program as a whole, Q. Starting with
this assertion, which is also the postcondition for the final program statement,
we can then reason backwards, using an axiom or rule of inference to obtain
a precondition for the final statement. This precondition can be used as a
postcondition for the prior statement, and then the entire process can be iter-
ated until a precondition, P, for the entire program is obtained. We then have
proven the triple

$$\{P\}\ prog\ \{Q\}$$

P asserts assumptions about the starting program state. Only if the program is initiated in a state satisfying these assumptions can we utilize the
triple to assert that Q will be mapped to T in the final state. If these assumptions are not satisfied by all possible starting program states implied
by the program requirements, the triple does not demonstrate that Q will always be true on completion of all possible runs. This failure does not mean
that P must be met in order for the program to work correctly, only that this
particular proof requires P. Other proofs might allow weaker preconditions.
Clearly it is desirable to produce a proof that utilizes the weakest possible
precondition at each step, leading to the weakest possible precondition for the
triple describing the program, since such a condition states the actual minimum requirements for the correct execution of the program. Note that the
Rule of Consequence is of no help in this process, since it can be used only to
strengthen, not weaken, preconditions.

For any program fragment S and any postcondition Q for that fragment,
we define the *weakest precondition, $wp(S, Q)$*, to be the weakest precondition
that guarantees termination of S and produces Q on termination. Hence, the
triple

$$\{wp(S, Q)\}\ S\ \{Q\}$$

not only is valid, but is an example of a strongest triple describing S, in the
sense that its precondition cannot be weakened without including either a
state for which S does not terminate or one for which S terminates in a state
that does not satisfy Q. Note that, although the preconditions and postconditions specified by the triples in Program Logic do not ordinarily guarantee
termination, the weakest precondition is defined so that it does.

The axiom schema for the skip statement clearly specifies a weakest precondition. The axiom schema for the assignment statement also specifies a
weakest precondition – with one caveat. While the specified precondition is
the weakest that will guarantee the postcondition on termination, termination will not occur if an exception occurs while the statement is being executed
(*e.g.*, due to overflow or division by zero). For simplicity here, and elsewhere in
the book, we ignore the possibility of exceptions that can prevent termination.

Similarly, if the preconditions of the hypotheses of the Rule of Composition are the weakest preconditions, the precondition of the conclusion is also the weakest precondition. Thus we have

$$wp(skip,\ Q)\ =\ Q$$

$$wp(\overline{v}\ :=\ \overline{e},\ Q)\ =\ Q_{\overline{e}}^{\overline{v}}$$

$$wp(S_1;S_2;,\ Q)\ =\ wp(S_1,\ wp(S_2, Q))$$

2.4.7   Conditional Statement

The formal semantics of the conditional statement

$$\textbf{if } G_1 \rightarrow S_1;\ []\ G_2 \rightarrow S_2;\ []\ldots[]\ G_n \rightarrow S_n;\ \textbf{fi}$$

is specified by an inference rule. The hypotheses are triples describing the component statements, S_i, and the conclusion is a triple for the conditional statement:

If Rule

$$\frac{\{P \wedge G_1\}\, S_1\, \{Q\},\ \{P \wedge G_2\}\, S_2\, \{Q\}, \ldots,\ \{P \wedge G_n\}\, S_n\, \{Q\}}{\{P\}\ \textbf{if } G_1 \rightarrow S_1;\ []\ G_2 \rightarrow S_2;\ []\ldots[]\ G_n \rightarrow S_n;\ \textbf{fi } \{Q\}} \tag{2.8}$$

One way to understand this rule intuitively is to assume that Q is to be the postcondition of the entire statement and P its precondition. Then, since any of the S_i might be executed, Q should be the postcondition of each. Furthermore, since S_i is executed only when G_i is true, G_i and P should both be conjuncts of the precondition of S_i.

In trying to reason backwards about a program, we might know the postcondition, Q, for a given conditional statement and want to find an appropriate precondition, P. If, working backward through each component statement, S_i, we can prove the triple $\{P_i\}\ S_i\ \{Q\}$, one choice for P is

$$(G_1 \Rightarrow P_1) \wedge (G_2 \Rightarrow P_2) \wedge \cdots \wedge (G_n \Rightarrow P_n)$$

This condition asserts that in any program state in which a guard is true, the precondition of the corresponding guarded statement is also true. Using this choice for P we obtain $P \wedge G_i \Rightarrow P_i$. We can then use the Rule of Consequence to derive, for each i, the triple $\{P \wedge G_i\}\ S_i\ \{Q\}$, which yields the hypotheses of the If Rule and justifies our use of P as a precondition of the if statement.

To express the condition that the if statement terminates, we define the assertion GG, which is true exactly when at least one of the guards is true.

$$GG = G_1 \vee G_2 \vee \cdots \vee G_n$$

```
if x ≥ y → m := x;
[] y ≥ x → m := y;
fi;
```

Figure 2.2: A statement that finds the maximum of two numbers.

If we know the weakest precondition of each of the component statements, we can express the weakest precondition of the entire if statement, S, as

$$wp(S, Q) = GG \wedge (G_1 \Rightarrow wp(S_1, Q)) \wedge (G_2 \Rightarrow wp(S_2, Q)) \wedge \ldots \wedge (G_n \Rightarrow wp(S_n, Q))$$

As a simple example, consider the statement in Figure 2.2 that sets m equal to the maximum of x and y. We would like the postcondition, Q, of the entire statement to be

$$\{(m \geq x) \wedge (m \geq y)\}$$

Q must be the postcondition of each of the component statements. Using the Assignment Axiom, we obtain for the first component statement the triple

$$\{(x \geq x) \wedge (x \geq y)\} \; m := x \; \{(m \geq x) \wedge (m \geq y)\}$$

Since *true* implies $x \geq x$, we can use the Rule of Consequence to derive

$$\{true \wedge (x \geq y)\} \; m := x \; \{(m \geq x) \wedge (m \geq y)\}$$

Similarly, for the second component statement we get the triple

$$\{(y \geq x) \wedge true\} \; m := y \; \{(m \geq x) \wedge (m \geq y)\}$$

Note that the precondition of each S_i is of the form

$$true \wedge G_i$$

Thus, the If Rule can be used to combine the triples for the component statements to obtain

$$\{true\} \; \mathbf{if} \; \cdots \; \mathbf{fi} \; \{(m \geq x) \wedge (m \geq y)\}$$

Since we have derived *true* as the precondition of the if statement and, since GG is *true*, we have shown that the if statement terminates and gives the desired result (m is set to the larger of x and y) for all possible initial states. In Figure 2.3 we show an annotated program fragment that illustrates the reasoning informally. Assertions have been inserted in the program text at control points where triples indicate they will be true at execution time. We use annotated programs throughout the text as a convenient way of presenting detailed properties of a program.

$$\{true\}$$
$$\textbf{if } x \geq y \rightarrow$$
$$\{ \ true \wedge (x \geq y)\}$$
$$m \ := \ x;$$
$$\{(m \geq x) \wedge (m \geq y)\}$$
$$[] \ y \geq x \rightarrow$$
$$\{(y \geq x) \wedge true\}$$
$$m \ := \ y;$$
$$\{ \ (m \geq x) \wedge (m \geq y)\}$$
$$\textbf{fi};$$
$$\{ \ (m \geq x) \wedge (m \geq y)\}$$

Figure 2.3: An annotated statement that finds the maximum of two numbers.

2.4.8   Invariance

As we shall see, the notion of invariance plays an important role in reasoning about programs. In this section we discuss several forms of invariance and how they can be demonstrated.

We say that an assertion, I, is *invariant to the execution* of some program fragment, S, if, assuming that I is true before S executes, it is true after S terminates – *i.e.* if

$$\{I\} \ S \ \{I\}$$

is a theorem. We say that S *maintains the truth* of I. Note that I need not be true during the intermediate steps of the execution of S.

Invariants are particularly useful in reasoning about loop statements. We say that an assertion I is a *loop invariant* for a particular loop if I is true prior to entry to the loop and after each iteration. Hence, in order for I to be a loop invariant for the statement

$$\textbf{do } G_1 \rightarrow S_1; \ [] \ G_2 \rightarrow S_2; \ [] \ldots [] \ G_n \ \rightarrow S_n; \ \textbf{od}$$

it is necessary that for each i,

$$\{I \wedge G_i\} \ S_i \ \{I\}$$

Note that I need not be "invariant to the execution" of each component statement, since the component statement is required to maintain the truth of I only when its guard is true.

A related concept is that of a program invariant. An assertion, I, is a *program invariant* of a program if, assuming that I is true in the initial program state, it is true in every state reached during program execution. To demonstrate that an assertion is a program invariant, we exhibit a proof of the program in which I is the program's precondition and the assertion at each control point implies I. Also, an assertion that is invariant to the execution of every atomic construct in the program is clearly a program invariant.

2.4.9   Loop Statement

The formal semantics of the loop statement

$$\textbf{do } G_1 \rightarrow S_1; \text{ } [] \text{ } G_2 \rightarrow S_2; \text{ } [] \ldots [] \text{ } G_n \rightarrow S_n; \text{ } \textbf{od}$$

is specified in terms of an inference rule in which the hypotheses are triples describing the component statements, S_i, and the conclusion is a triple describing the loop statement as a whole. These triples are expressed in terms of a loop invariant.

Do Rule

$$\frac{\{I \wedge G_1\} S_1 \{I\}, \ldots, \{I \wedge G_n\} S_n \{I\}}{\{I\} \textbf{ do } G_1 \rightarrow S_1; \text{ } [] \ldots [] \text{ } G_n \rightarrow S_n; \text{ } \textbf{od } \{I \wedge \neg G_1 \wedge \ldots \wedge \neg G_n\}} \tag{2.9}$$

Consider the program of Figure 2.4, which performs division of x_0 by y_0 using the method of repeated subtraction. (We use lower case subscripted letters to represent constants that appear in the program text. Constants should not be confused with logical or program variables.) The assertion

$$I: \text{ } (x_0 = r + y \times q) \wedge (y = y_0) \tag{2.10}$$

is a loop invariant. To demonstrate that I is a precondition of the first iteration of the loop, we use an instance of the Assignment Axiom to get the triple

$$\{(y_0 = y_0) \wedge (x_0 = x_0) \wedge (0 = 0)\} \text{ } y, \text{ } r, \text{ } q \text{ } := \text{ } y_0, \text{ } x_0, \text{ } 0 \text{ } \{(y = y_0) \wedge (r = x_0) \wedge (q = 0)\}$$

Since the precondition of this triple is implied by *true*, and

$$((y = y_0) \wedge (r = x_0) \wedge (q = 0)) \Rightarrow I$$

is an assertion that can be proven in a formalization of arithmetic (and hence in Program Logic, which includes arithmetic), it follows from the Rule of Consequence that

$$\{true\} \text{ } y, \text{ } r, \text{ } q \text{ } := \text{ } y_0, \text{ } x_0, \text{ } 0 \text{ } \{I\}$$

Hence, I is a precondition of the first iteration. To prove that it is a loop invariant, we use the strategy of working backwards through the loop to determine a precondition of the first statement of the loop body that ensures that I will be a postcondition of the last statement of the body. The following two triples are instances of the Assignment Axiom:

$$\{(x_0 = r + y \times (q + 1)) \wedge (y = y_0)\} \text{ } q \text{ } := \text{ } q + 1 \text{ } \{I\}$$

```
var
    y, r, q : integer;
begin
    y, r, q := y₀, x₀, 0;
    do y ≤ r →
        begin
            r := r − y;
            q := q + 1;
        end;
    od;
end;
```

Figure 2.4: A program for performing division by repeated subtraction.

$$\{(x_0 = (r - y) + y \times (q + 1)) \wedge (y = y_0)\}\ r\ :=\ r - y\ \{(x_0 = r + y \times (q + 1)) \wedge (y = y_0)\}$$

Using the Rule of Composition and simplifying, we get

$$\{I\}\ r\ :=\ r - y;\ q\ :=\ q + 1;\ \{I\}$$

Since I is true initially and is invariant to the execution of the loop body, we have demonstrated that it is indeed true before and after each iteration of the loop. The Do Rule yields

$$\{I\}\ \mathbf{do} \cdots \mathbf{od}\ \{I \wedge (y > r)\}$$

Figure 2.5 is a formal presentation of the proof of the program in Figure 2.4 (the proof is taken from [66]). It follows exactly the form of a proof of a theorem in Predicate Calculus. The proof consists of a sequence of numbered lines, where each line contains either a triple or a well formed formula of Predicate Calculus. Each line either is an axiom or is derived from previous lines using a rule of inference. The validity of each line of the proof can be checked mechanically using the justification. Hence, rigor is guaranteed. Unfortunately, the construction of such a proof is tedious. In the text we rely on annotated programs as an informal way of presenting some aspects of the proof. Still, the proof technique provides the foundation of all the reasoning and should be kept clearly in mind. We say that an annotation is *valid* if its assertions are derived from a formal proof.

The postcondition demonstrated by the proof only seems to state the desired result. In actuality it does not imply division. Suppose x_0 is a negative number and y_0 is a positive number. The postcondition will be satisfied but in a way that perhaps was not anticipated, since the loop will not be executed. Hence, the program executes correctly only if it starts in a state satisfying $x_0 \geq 0$. Since the value of x_0 is not changed in the program, the assertion $x_0 \geq 0$ is invariant

Line	Well Formed Formula	Justification
1	$\{(y_0 = y_0) \land (x_0 = x_0) \land (0 = 0)\}\ y, r, q := y_0, x_0, 0$ $\{(y = y_0) \land (r = x_0) \land (q = 0)\}$	Assignment
2	$true \Rightarrow (y_0 = y_0) \land (x_0 = x_0) \land (0 = 0)$	arithmetic
3	$((y = y_0) \land (r = x_0) \land (q = 0)) \Rightarrow I$	arithmetic
4	$\{true\}\ y, r, q := y_0, x_0, 0\ \{I\}$	Consequence; Lines 1, 2, 3
5	$\{(x_0 = (r - y) + y \times (q + 1)) \land (y = y_0)\}\ r := r - y$ $\{(x_0 = r + y \times (q + 1)) \land (y = y_0)\}$	Assignment
6	$I \Rightarrow (x_0 = (r - y) + y \times (q + 1)) \land (y = y_0)$	arithmetic
7	$\{I\}\ r := r - y\ \{(x_0 = r + y \times (q + 1)) \land (y = y_0)\}$	Consequence; Lines 5, 6
8	$\{(x_0 = r + y \times (q + 1)) \land (y = y_0)\}\ q := q + 1\ \{I\}$	Assignment
9	$\{I\}\ r := r - y;\ q := q + 1;\ \{I\}$	Composition; Lines 7, 8
10	$\{I\}\ \textbf{do} \cdots \textbf{od}\ \{I \land (y > r)\}$	Do; Line 9
11	$\{true\}\ program\ \{I \land (y > r)\}$	Composition; Lines 4, 10

Figure 2.5: A formal proof of the division program.

to the execution of every statement within the program and is a program invariant. Hence, if we assume that it is a conjunct of the precondition of the program (*i.e.*, it is true initially), it can be conjoined to every assertion in the proof and the justifications will remain unchanged. In addition, the conjunct $y_0 > 0$ is required to guarantee loop termination (recall that the postcondition of a triple must be true if the statement terminates, but the triple says nothing about whether termination will occur). Once again, assuming $y_0 > 0$ is true initially, it is a program invariant and can be conjoined with every assertion to yield a new proof. Thus the program's precondition is transformed from *true* to $(x_0 \geq 0) \land (y_0 > 0)$, indicating the minimum conditions necessary for the program to work properly. Finally note that the postcondition of the loop does not rule out the possibility that the loop has been executed too many times, causing r to become negative – in which case q and r would not be the quotient and remainder. To eliminate this possibility, we can prove a stronger

$$\{(y_0 > 0) \wedge (x_0 \geq 0)\}$$

var

$y, r, q : integer;$

begin

$y, r, q := y_0, x_0, 0;$

$$\{I' \wedge (y_0 > 0) \wedge (x_0 \geq 0)\}$$

do $y \leq r \rightarrow$

$$\{I' \wedge (y \leq r) \wedge (y_0 > 0) \wedge (x_0 \geq 0)\}$$

begin

$r := r - y;$

$$\{(x_0 = r + y \times (q + 1)) \wedge (y = y_0) \wedge (y_0 > 0) \wedge (x_0 \geq 0)\}$$

$q := q + 1;$

$$\{(I' \wedge (y_0 > 0) \wedge (x_0 \geq 0)\}$$

end;

od;

end;

$$\{I' \wedge (y > r) \wedge (y_0 > 0) \wedge (x_0 \geq 0)\}$$

Figure 2.6: An annotated version of the division program.

loop invariant, I'

$$I' : I \wedge (r \geq 0)$$

To prove that I' is a loop invariant, we note that the conjunct $r \geq 0$ is true prior to entry to the loop (since $x_0 \geq 0$) and the triple

$$\{I' \wedge (y \leq r)\} r := r - y; q := q + 1; \{I'\}$$

is a theorem.

Figure 2.6 is an annotated version of the program with the new conditions added. The annotation is not a complete proof. (For example, the use of the Rule of Consequence is not indicated; hence, where the postcondition of a statement is stronger than the precondition of the next statement, only the precondition is shown.) However, using the above discussion, it is easy to construct a complete proof similar to that of Figure 2.5.

The Do Rule is sound for any loop invariant, I. Any given loop has a great many invariants, and the Do Rule yields a different triple corresponding to each. However, most of these invariants are not useful in reasoning about the loop. For example, in the program of Figure 2.4, the expression $y = y_0$ is true before and after each iteration, but using it as the invariant of the Do Rule is not helpful when we are trying to prove that the program performs division correctly. A common technique for finding an appropriate invariant (and the one used in the example of Figure 2.4) is to attempt to capture in the invariant the intent of each iteration of the loop.

In working backwards from a program's postcondition to generate a proof, the choices of invariants for each loop are the only points at which the weakest precondition analysis cannot be used. If the precondition of the program generated in this fashion is not true in all desired initial states, we can attempt to find a different proof that uses weaker loop invariants. (Weakening a loop invariant weakens the derived precondition of the loop and hence can serve to weaken the precondition of the program.) Failing this, the program is either incorrect or not sufficiently robust to deal with all the possible initial states it may be presented.

2.4.10 Loop Termination

Turing's result on the undecidability of the halting problem for Turing machines implies that there is no general algorithm for determining whether or not a given loop statement terminates. Hence, given a loop statement, there is no general algorithm for finding the weakest precondition (which guarantees termination) for an arbitrary postcondition. This does not imply that we cannot prove termination for a specific loop statement. It implies that any proof method we use will not work for all possible loop statements. (In other words, we may have to use creativity to find a proof.)

One way to prove termination is to find a numeric function, E, of the program variables such that when the loop is entered, the initial value of E is positive; E decreases by at least some positive constant value on each iteration; and if the value of E becomes negative, no guards are true. Thus, the initial value of E divided by the constant is an upper bound on the number of iterations of the loop.

In the division example we can let E be a function of r and define $E(r) = r$. From the precondition of the loop body in Figure 2.6 it follows that $E(r) \geq 0$. Furthermore, the theorem

$$\{(r = A) \wedge (y = y_0) \wedge (y_0 > 0)\}\ r\ :=\ r - y;\ q\ :=\ q + 1;$$
$$\{(r = A - y) \wedge (y = y_0) \wedge (y_0 > 0)\}$$

(where A is a logical variable) is easily proven, demonstrating that, if the loop body terminates, $E(r)$ is decremented by a positive constant on each iteration. Termination of the loop body is guaranteed, however, since it consists only of assignment statements (the precondition is thus the weakest precondition for the given postcondition). Finally, $E(r) < 0$ implies that the guard ($y \leq r$) is false. Hence, loop termination is guaranteed.

A more general way to prove termination is through the concept of a *well founded set*. A well founded set is a partially ordered set of elements such that every decreasing sequence of elements from the set reaches a smallest element in a finite number of steps. (The set of positive integers is well founded, while the set of positive rational numbers is not.) To prove termination, find a function, F, of program variables and a proof whose assertions guarantee that

The range of F is a well founded set;

$f_1 \succ f_2$, where f_1 and f_2 are the values of F before and after an iteration of the loop, and $\succ$ is the partial order.

Since every such decreasing sequence of values is finite, the loop is guaranteed to terminate. Such a proof is referred to as a *termination proof*. Analysis based on well founded sets is frequently used in symbolic programming where loops involve nonnumeric quantities.

2.5 Safety and Liveness Properties

Our goals in developing Program Logic are to allow us to reason about the behavior of programs. In particular, we are able to demonstrate that when a particular control point in a program is enabled, the assertion attached to that control point is true of the program state that exists at that time. The truth of the assertion is independent of the sequence of statements that have been executed up to that time. There may be many (perhaps infinitely many) such sequences, but we have succeeded in deducing some fact about all of them through an examination of the (finite) program text.

For some purposes, an alternative view of a program is more appropriate. In this view a program is treated as a (possibly infinite) set of execution sequences, where an *execution sequence* is a sequence of program states. A particular execution sequence is in the set that characterizes a program if it is a sequence of states that can be produced by executing the program and each state (other than the first) is the result of executing an operation in the prior state. As we shall see in this and the following section, the execution sequence viewpoint allows us to discuss the behavior of a subset of the execution sequences of a program, whereas our previous approach allows us to discuss only the behavior of all execution sequences.

The purpose of reasoning about programs is to prove some property of their behavior. Two types of properties are of interest: safety and liveness.

2.5.1 Safety Properties

A safety property stipulates that some "bad" condition never occurs during the execution of a program. Examples of safety properties are

the value of the variable x never exceeds 1000;

the square root routine is never called with a negative argument;

the buffer never overflows;

requests for resources are never granted in an order different from that in which they were made;

process A and Process B are never in their critical sections at the same time.

Note that while the first three properties might reasonably be applied to a sequential program, the last two are appropriate for a concurrent program.

The bad condition can be represented by an assertion, P_{bad}, which is mapped to T in exactly those states in which the condition is true. Therefore, if the safety property is true of a program, no execution sequence in the set characterizing the program contains such a state. Conversely, if the safety property is not true of a program, there is an execution sequence in the set that contains such a state. Hence, the bad condition happens at some particular point in the execution.

For a safety property to be true of a program, $\neg P_{bad}$ must be a program invariant. One way to demonstrate a safety property is to find a program invariant, I, such that

$$I \Rightarrow \neg P_{bad}$$

The important point to note is that we can use Program Logic to demonstrate safety properties.

Most of the reasoning we have done so far using Program Logic deals with partial correctness. Partial correctness can be stated as a safety property: the program never terminates with the wrong answer. (We are more used to dealing with the contrapositive of that property: if the program terminates, it gives the correct answer – its postcondition is mapped to T in the final state.) Partial correctness allows us to prove properties of a program, assuming that the program terminates. Safety properties are more general in that they allow us to prove properties of intermediate states of programs and hence are useful in dealing with nonterminating programs. In general, Program Logic provides a method for reasoning about safety properties, since it allows us to demonstrate that an assertion is a program invariant.

2.5.2   Liveness Properties

A liveness property stipulates that some "good" condition eventually occurs during the execution of a program. Examples of liveness properties are

the program will eventually terminate;

the value of the variable x will eventually exceed 1000;

every statement in the program will eventually be executed at least once;

procedure p will eventually be called an infinite number of times;

every process that requests a resource will eventually receive it;

every message sent by Process A to Process B will eventually be received by Process B.

Once again, the first four properties might reasonably be applied to a sequential program, while the last two are appropriate for a concurrent program.

Consider a program with an infinite loop containing an if statement. The good thing might be that a particular component of the if statement gets selected an infinite number of times. This is an example of a case in which the good thing is a property of the entire execution sequence; no discrete point can be identified at which the good thing happens. Hence, it is not possible to attach an assertion to a control point indicating the good thing, and thus Program Logic is not appropriate for demonstrating the property. Furthermore, the example illustrates an interesting difference between safety and liveness: the bad thing in a safety property must be a discrete event that occurs at some point in the execution, while the good thing in a liveness property need not be discrete or occur at some particular point.

Safety and liveness properties are complementary in another way. For safety properties, once the bad thing happens in some partial execution, its effect is irremediable; no subsequent portion of the execution sequence can cause the safety property to hold. By contrast, for liveness properties, no partial execution is irremediable; the good thing might conceivably still occur during the subsequent execution.

Thus, some method other than Program Logic is generally necessary to prove liveness. Recall that we used such a method to prove termination of loops. Frequently other liveness properties can be proved using similar methods based on well founded sets. A formal method for dealing with liveness, Temporal Logic, is briefly introduced in Chapter 4.

2.6   Fairness in Nondeterministic Constructs

We have defined choice nondeterminism to be such that when a choice of actions is to be made, any one of the open actions can be selected for execution. Suppose, however, that a nondeterministic construct is executed in an infinite loop, and each time there is a choice of the same two open actions and each time the first choice is taken. We would say, intuitively, that the choice was not made in a "fair" manner and might anticipate that the program would exhibit somewhat unexpected behavior.

As an example, consider the program fragment shown in Figure 2.7. When the do statement is initially entered, both guards are true and hence both component statements are open. Suppose the first is selected. After its execution, the do statement is re-executed with both statements still open and another selection is made. The first might be selected again. If the second component statement is ever selected, the do statement will terminate, but if the first is always selected, the do statement will never terminate. Thus, to prove termination, we must postulate some fairness condition which guarantees that the second alternative is eventually selected.

Nondeterminism is a feature associated with a language construct. It states that, at a particular execution of the construct, the scheduler (which makes the choice) can choose any of the alternatives. When we reason in terms

```
var
  x : integer := 0;
  b : boolean := true;
begin
  do b → x := x + 1;
  [] b → b := false;
  od;
end;
```

Figure 2.7: A program that requires a fairness assumption for termination.

of nondeterminism, we prove properties of all possible executions, including some that might be unfair, since any choice made when a nondeterministic construct is executed is acceptable.

Fairness, on the other hand, is a feature associated with the scheduler. It is therefore a property of the implementation. Fairness places restrictions on the scheduler which require that in computations in which the same nondeterministic choice is made an infinite number of times, certain choices will eventually be made – it is a liveness property. Hence, fairness restricts the set of execution sequences associated with a program. Since Program Logic does not distinguish between fair and unfair schedulers, it is not a suitable mechanism for proving those properties that apply only to fair implementations.

We define two fairness properties that an implementation might have:

An implementation is *weakly fair* if, in every infinite execution sequence in which a particular nondeterministic construct is entered an infinite number of times and a particular one of its alternatives is continuously open, that alternative is selected infinitely often (thus if we start looking from any point in any infinite execution sequence, that alternative will eventually be selected).

An implementation is *strongly fair* if, in every infinite execution sequence in which a particular nondeterministic construct is entered an infinite number of times and a particular one of its alternatives is open infinitely often (but not necessarily continuously), that alternative is selected infinitely often.

(Even stronger fairness properties can be defined.)

Any infinite execution sequence of the program shown in Figure 2.7 must be unfair, since both alternatives of the do statement are continuously open and yet the first is always selected. If the implementation is weakly fair, the second alternative must eventually be selected and hence the program will terminate. We say that this program terminates under the assumption of weak fairness. (Clearly, the program would terminate under the assumption

```
var
  b, c : boolean := true, true;
begin
  do b → c := ¬c;
  [] (b ∧ c) → b := false;
  od;
end;
```

Figure 2.8: A program that requires a strong fairness assumption for termination.

of strong fairness as well.)

By contrast, in the program shown in Figure 2.8, the second alternative is not continuously open. Whenever the first alternative is selected, the value of c is negated. Therefore, we cannot use the weak fairness assumption to prove that the second alternative will eventually be selected and the program will terminate. However, in any infinite sequence of selections of the first alternative, the second alternative is open infinitely often. Hence if the implementation is strongly fair, the second alternative will eventually be selected and the program will terminate. We say that this program terminates under the assumption of strong fairness.

Fairness assumptions are needed to prove other liveness properties of non-deterministic programs in addition to termination. For example, suppose n processes in a concurrent system are all continuously trying to send messages to a single process, which can nondeterministically select any one of the processes from which to receive. To prove the property "any message that is sent is eventually received," we have to make some assumptions about the fairness of the implementation.

2.7   Bibliographic Notes

An early discussion of the use of nondeterminism and guarded commands in a sequential language appears in Dijkstra [39]. An excellent introduction to the Propositional Logic and Predicate Calculus from a mathematical point of view can be found in Mendelson [99]; Gallier [51] provides a more intuitive approach to the subject. Hoare [66] has made a major contribution to the development of Program Logic and we have taken the division example from that source. Two excellent texts that present a rigorous approach to the development of sequential programs and emphasize weakest preconditions have been written by Dijkstra [40] and Gries [58]. These texts also consider the issue of termination. An exhaustive discussion of fairness can be found in Francez [49]. Fairness is also treated in Apt, Francez, and Katz [13]. A nice discussion of the relationship between safety and liveness can be found in Alpern and Schneider [10].

2.8   Exercises

In the following exercises, the word "prove" means that formal reasoning is to be used to produce an annotated program, while the word "demonstrate" means that a convincing argument is sufficient.

1. A concurrent program is made up of a set of N sequential programs, P_i, where $1 \le i \le N$. Each program has a critical section. The property that a process executing P_i is in its critical section is expressed by the assertion CR_i. Give an assertion which expresses the property that when one process is in its critical section, no other process can be in its critical section.

2. Give an example showing that $E_{u, v}^{x, y}$ is in general different from $(E_u^x)_v^y$, where u and v are arbitrary expressions.

3. State the conditions under which $x, y := u, v$ is semantically equivalent to $x := u; y := v$; where u and v are arbitrary expressions. Prove your statement using Program Logic.

4. Give the weakest precondition, P, for each of the following statements:

$$\{P\} \text{ if } y > 0 \to x := x + 1; \; [] \; y \le 0 \to x := x + 2; \; \textbf{fi} \; \{x = 10\}$$

$$\{P\} \text{ if } y \ge 0 \to x := x + 1; \; [] \; y \le 0 \to x := x + 2; \; \textbf{fi} \; \{x = 10\}$$

5. Consider a deterministic version of the if statement

$$\textbf{if } G_1 \Rightarrow S_1; \; \% \; G_2 \Rightarrow S_2; \; \% \ldots \% \; G_n \Rightarrow S_n; \; \textbf{fi}$$

with the following operational semantics:

If G_1 is true execute S_1 and exit, else if G_2 is true execute S_2 and exit, ..., else if G_n is true execute S_n and exit, else halt.

Give an inference rule that describes the formal semantics of the statement in terms of the formal semantics of $S_1, S_2, \ldots, S_n$.

6. Consider the modified if statement

$$\textbf{if } G_1 \to S_1; \; [] \ldots [] \; G_n \to S_n; \; \textbf{else } S; \; \textbf{fi}$$

whose operational semantics are the same as the semantics of the standard if statement except that S is executed if and only if all G_i are false. Give the strongest rule of inference you can to describe the formal semantics of this statement.

7. Assume the operational semantics of the if statement is changed so that if all guards are false, the statement terminates normally. Give an inference rule that describes the formal semantics of the statement.

8. Demonstrate that the expression given for the weakest precondition of the if statement is correct.

9. Under what restrictions on the assertion P is the following triple valid?

$$\{P\}\, x \; := \; y \, \{P_x^y\}$$

10. The Pascal repeat statement has the syntax

repeat S until B

The operational semantics of the repeat statement is as follows:

First the statement S is executed; then the boolean expression B is evaluated; if B is true, the execution of the repeat statement is terminated; otherwise, the entire repeat statement is reexecuted.

Assuming S has a single exit (*i.e.*, the language does not have a goto type statement), give an inference rule that specifies a triple for the repeat statement in terms of an assertion I that is invariant to the execution of S.

11. The repeat forever statement has the syntax

repeat S forever

The operational semantics of the repeat forever statement is as follows:

The statement S is executed repeatedly forever.

Assuming S has a single exit (*i.e.*, the language does not have a goto type statement), give an inference rule that specifies a triple for the repeat statement in terms of an assertion I that is invariant to the execution of S.

12. The Pascal for statement (with integer loop index) has the syntax

for i := e_1 to e_2 do S;

The operational semantics of the for statement is as follows:

First the expression e_1 is evaluated and assigned to i; then the expression e_2 is evaluated; then i is compared with the value of e_2; if i is greater than this value, the for statement is terminated; otherwise, the statement S is executed (S cannot change the value of i); then the value of i is incremented by 1 and the for statement is re-executed from the point where the value of i is compared with the (previously computed) value of e_2.

Assuming S has a single exit (*i.e.,* the language does not have a goto type statement), give an inference rule that specifies a triple for the for statement in terms of an assertion I that is invariant to the execution of S. Demonstrate that the for statement always terminates.

13. Assume statement labels and a goto statement are added to the sequential language described in this chapter. Give an axiom schema for the statement **goto** X, where X is a statement label. What new considerations have to be taken into account in the proof of a program to deal with labeled statements? Discuss the issue of termination when goto statements can transfer control to earlier points in the program.

14. The exit statement is used to unconditionally exit from the most immediately surrounding do statement. Explain how the inclusion of an exit statement in the language modifies the formal semantics of the do statement.

15. Using the result that the halting problem for a Turing machine is undecidable, sketch a proof of the undecidability of termination of the loop statement. (Hint: Construct a loop containing a statement that performs a simulation of one step of the operation of a Turing machine.)

16. The following program sets m equal to the maximum of three integers, x, y, and z:

```
var
    x, y, z : integer := x₀, y₀, z₀;
begin
    if x ≥ y → m := x; [] y ≥ x → m := y; fi;
    if m ≤ z → m := z; [] z ≤ m → skip; fi;
end;
```

Assuming *true* as a precondition, prove that

$$(m \geq x) \wedge (m \geq y) \wedge (m \geq z)$$

can be asserted as a postcondition of the program.

17. Find an appropriate loop invariant and prove that the following program terminates and satisfies the given triple.

$$\{n_0 > 0\}$$

var
    $j, \ x, \ n : $ **integer** $:= \ 0, \ 1, \ n_0;$
$$\{n > 0\}$$
begin
   do $j < n \to$
      $j, \ x \ := \ j + 1, \ 2 * x;$
   od;
$$\{x = 2^n\}$$
end;

18. After the execution of the program fragment shown below, the variable *count* is supposed to contain the number of elements in the array A that have the value *true*. Prove that the fragment terminates and that the variable *count* does have the correct value.

var
   $i, \ count : integer;$
   $A : $ **array** $[1..N]$ **of** *boolean*;
begin
   $\cdots$ $-\!-$ initialize A
   $i, \ count \ := \ 1, \ 0;$
   do $i \le N \to$
     if $A[i] \to$
       $i, \ count \ := \ i + 1, \ count + 1;$
     $[] \ \neg A[i] \to$
       $i \ := \ i + 1;$
    fi;
   od;
end;

19. The Fibonacci Numbers $(F_0, F_1, \ldots)$ are defined by the equations

$$F_0 \ = \ F_1 \ = \ 1$$
$$F_n \ = \ F_{n-1} + F_{n-2} \ \text{ for } n \ge 2$$

Construct a (nonrecursive) program to compute F_m and prove that your program works correctly.

20. The following program, *prog*, finds the maximum element stored in the array A.

```
var
    A : array [1..N] of integer;
    i, max : integer;
begin
    ...    -- initialize A
    max, i := A[1], 2;
    do i ≤ N →
        if A[i] > max → i, max := i + 1, A[i];
        [] A[i] ≤ max → i := i + 1;
        fi;
    od;
end;
```

Prove the following theorem:

$$\{N \geq 1\} \; prog \; \{(i > N) \land ((\forall k)(0 < k < i)(max \geq A[k]))\}$$

Prove that the program terminates.

21. The following program is alleged to compute the product of integer a and nonnegative integer b. Prove it. Your proof should involve a proof of termination.

```
var
    prod : integer := 0;
    a : integer := a₀;
    b : integer := b₀;
    c : integer;
begin
    c := b;
    do c > 0 →
        prod, c := prod + a, c - 1;
    od;
end;
```

Hint: Take the loop invariant to be

$$(prod = (b - c) * a) \land (c \geq 0)$$

Prove that the program terminates.

22. The following program is alleged to compute the factorial of a positive integer, n.

```
var
    m1 : integer := 0;
    m2 : integer := 1;
    n : integer := n0;
begin
    do m1 < n →
        begin
            m1 := m1 + 1;
            m2 := m1 * m2;
        end;
    od;
end;
```

Show that the assertion $(m2 = m1!) \land (m1 \leq n)$ is a loop invariant and that when the program terminates, $m2 = n!$.

23. Since a safety property guarantees that something never happens and a liveness property guarantees that something eventually happens, why is every liveness property not just the complement of some safety property? Give examples to support your argument.

24. Demonstrate that the following program fragment cannot be proved to terminate under strong fairness. Define an even stronger fairness assumption, equifairness, under which termination can be proved.

```
x := 1;
do x ≥ 0 → x := x + 1;
[]  x ≥ 0 → x := x - 2;
od;
```

3

Structuring Sequential Programs

In this chapter we continue our discussion of sequential programs by considering three structuring mechanisms: procedures, abstract data types, and coroutines. As we shall see in subsequent chapters, procedures play an important role in concurrent systems. Both monitors, which are a structured approach to shared memory systems, and remote procedure calls, which are a structured approach to message passing systems, are based on procedure calls. As we shall also see, both monitors and remote procedure calls are commonly used to provide access to abstract data types, which themselves are a structured way to deal with complex data structures. Furthermore, as we shall see in the chapters on transaction processing, abstract data types provide a structuring mechanism for complex databases.

We also discuss another structured use of subprograms: coroutines. Although coroutines are sequential constructs, reasoning about them is somewhat similar to reasoning about concurrent programs, and hence they provide a good introduction to the material in later chapters. To gain some insight into a number of the practical issues underlying the use of coroutines, we include a brief discussion of the Modula-2 language, which uses coroutines as a basic structuring mechanism.

3.1 Procedures

We use a conventional form of procedure declaration and invocation. Procedures can have in, out, and in out parameters analogous to Ada procedures.

For simplicity, we do not consider the declaration of local variables in the axiomatization of procedures. We discuss the relationship between variable declarations and concurrency in Section 4.8.

The general form of procedure declaration and invocation is as follows:

Procedure Declaration

> **procedure** $p(\overline{a} :$ **in** *atype*; $\overline{b} :$ **out** *btype*; $\overline{c} :$ **in out** *ctype*);
> **begin**
> S;
> **end** p;

where

> $\overline{a}, \overline{b},$ and $\overline{c}$ are vectors of parameters;
> S is a sequence of statements.

Procedure Invocation

$$p(\overline{x}, \overline{y}, \overline{z})$$

where

> $\overline{x}$ is a vector of arbitrary expressions
> $\overline{y}$ and $\overline{z}$ are vectors of variables

Assuming a value/result parameter passing mechanism, the operational semantics of procedure invocation is as follows:

First the in and in out arguments are evaluated and assigned to the corresponding parameters; then the statement S is executed; then the values of the out and in out parameters are assigned to the corresponding variables. Argument passing is atomic, and result passing is atomic.

A simple example of a procedure declaration is

> **procedure** *swap*$(c1, c2 :$ **in out** *integer*);
> **begin**
> $c1, c2 := c2, c1$;
> **end** *swap*;

Procedures are somewhat different from the other constructs we have considered in that both declaration and invocation must be dealt with. We view these activities as occurring in the following manner. The procedure designer publishes the formal semantics of the procedure as an inference rule specifying the relationship between the precondition and the postcondition of a call. The procedure designer has made a contract with the users of the procedure to implement the procedure body so as to guarantee that it satisfies the published conditions. The user can then use that inference rule to reason about invocations of the procedure. The rule can be quite complex in a completely general situation, so we consider a special case that is adequate for the discussion in this text.

The special case we consider is one in which the only effect of procedure invocation is to (deterministically) assign new values to the out and in out arguments (no side effects), and these new values can be expressed as functions of the values of the in and in out arguments. Thus, procedure invocation has the effect of a multiple assignment statement, and its formal semantics can be described in a manner similar to that of the Assignment Axiom. Procedures that have this property are said to satisfy *assignment semantics*. As we shall see shortly, assignment semantics is particularly useful in the implementation of abstract data types.

Consider a code fragment, S, whose only global accesses are to the variables $\overline{a}$, $\overline{b}$, and $\overline{c}$. We say that S has assignment semantics (we generalize this definition shortly) if it can be described by the triple

$$\{(\overline{a} = \overline{A_0}) \land (\overline{c} = \overline{C_0})\} \, S \, \{(\overline{a} = \overline{A_0}) \land ((\overline{b}, \overline{c}) = f(\overline{A_0}, \overline{C_0}))\} \qquad (3.1)$$

where f is a function mapping a vector whose number and type match $(\overline{a}, \overline{c})$ to a vector whose number and type match $(\overline{b}, \overline{c})$, and $\overline{A_0}$ and $\overline{C_0}$ are logical variables. When S has assignment semantics, its only effect is to update the variables $\overline{b}$ and $\overline{c}$ with values that can be expressed as a function of the initial values of $\overline{a}$ and $\overline{c}$. The variables $\overline{a}$ are not modified by S, and S does not reference the initial values of the variables $\overline{b}$. The effect of S is that of the multiple assignment statement

$$\overline{b}, \, \overline{c} \, := \, f(\overline{a}, \overline{c})$$

Hence, we obtain the following rule, which describes the effect of executing S in terms of any postcondition, Q

$$\frac{\{(\overline{a} = \overline{A_0}) \land (\overline{c} = \overline{C_0})\} \, S \, \{(\overline{a} = \overline{A_0}) \land ((\overline{b}, \overline{c}) = f(\overline{A_0}, \overline{C_0}))\}}{\{Q^{\overline{b}, \, \overline{c}}_{f(\overline{a}, \overline{c})}\} \, S \, \{Q\}} \qquad (3.2)$$

In some situations, assignment semantics applies only when some assertion, Y, is true of $\overline{a}$ and $\overline{c}$. S might make some assumptions about the values of these variables and only work correctly when those assumptions are true. For example, S might implement an algorithm for calculating the sine of an angle, but might produce the correct value only when a value between 0 and 2π is input – if fact, it might not even terminate for values outside of this range. We say that S has assignment semantics and that $assign(S, f, Y)$ is true if

$$((\overline{a} = \overline{A_0}) \land (\overline{c} = \overline{C_0}) \land Y) \Rightarrow wp(S, (\overline{a} = \overline{A_0}) \land ((\overline{b}, \overline{c}) = f(\overline{A_0}, \overline{C_0})))$$

Thus, whenever Y is true, S terminates and f describes the effect of its execution. Again, the only effect of S is to update the the values of $\overline{b}$ and $\overline{c}$. Code fragments that have assignment semantics can be characterized by the following rule:

Assignment Semantics Rule

$$\frac{assign(S, f, Y),\ P \Rightarrow (Q_{f(\bar{a},\bar{c})}^{\bar{b},\ \bar{c}} \wedge Y)}{\{P\}\ S\ \{Q\}} \qquad (3.3)$$

Our immediate goal is to apply assignment semantics to procedures. In this case, S is the procedure body and $\bar{a}$, $\bar{b}$, and $\bar{c}$ are the in, out, and in out parameters, respectively. We assume that there is a value/result parameter-passing mechanism and that S does not modify $\bar{a}$. Our earlier assumption that the only global references within S are to $\bar{a}$, $\bar{b}$, and $\bar{c}$ implies that the procedure does not reference global variables. We make one further assumption:

No Aliasing. We assume that all out and in out arguments are distinct and none appear in the list of expressions that constitutes the in arguments.

We can motivate the requirement that all out and in out arguments be distinct as we did with the restriction that all variables on the left-hand side of the multiple assignment statement must be distinct (otherwise the order of assignment affects the final values). A more subtle problem underlies the restriction that these arguments not appear in any expression passed to an in parameter. Consider the procedure *double* with the heading

procedure *double*(a : **in** *integer*, b : **out** *integer*)

that returns twice the value of a in b. One would like to assert $y = 2x$ as a postcondition of the invocation *double*(x, y). Unfortunately, however, if aliasing is allowed, the invocation *double*(x, x) would lead to the assertion $x = 2x$. The difficulty is that assertions used in proving a triple describing the procedure body (such as $b = 2a$ for the body of *double*) are formulated in terms of the parameters but are actually intended to assert something about the arguments that are associated with the parameters by a particular invocation. Those assertions might not be applicable if aliasing is allowed.

Under these assumptions, procedure invocation can be viewed as the execution of the code fragment consisting of three assignment statements shown in Figure 3.1. We can see that the annotation is valid by working backwards from the postcondition. It follows from the Assignment Axiom that if U is to be the postcondition of the call, $U_{\bar{b},\ \bar{c}}^{\bar{y},\ \bar{z}}$ must be a postcondition of S. Assuming $assign(S, f, Y)$, we can use the conclusion of the Assignment Semantics Rule to demonstrate that a precondition of S is $(U_{\bar{b},\ \bar{c}}^{\bar{y},\ \bar{z}})_{f(\bar{a},\bar{c})}^{\bar{b},\ \bar{c}} \wedge Y$, which reduces to the assertion shown in the figure, since U is not a function of $\bar{b}$ or $\bar{c}$. Finally, using the Assignment Axiom again, the precondition of the call must be $(U_{f(\bar{a},\bar{c})}^{\bar{y},\ \bar{z}} \wedge Y)_{\bar{x},\ \bar{z}}^{\bar{a},\ \bar{c}}$, which reduces to the assertion shown in the figure, since U is not a function of $\bar{a}$ or $\bar{c}$. Hence, the following inference rule specifies the formal semantics of the invocation of procedures that have assignment semantics:

$$\{U^{\bar{y},\,\bar{z}}_{f(\bar{x},\bar{z})} \wedge Y^{\bar{a},\,\bar{c}}_{\bar{x},\,\bar{z}}\}$$
$$\bar{a},\ \bar{c} := \bar{x},\ \bar{z};$$
$$\{U^{\bar{y},\,\bar{z}}_{f(\bar{a},\bar{c})} \wedge Y\}$$
$$S;$$
$$\{U^{\bar{y},\,\bar{z}}_{\bar{b},\,\bar{c}}\}$$
$$\bar{y},\ \bar{z} := \bar{b},\ \bar{c};$$
$$\{U\}$$

Figure 3.1:   Assertions relating to the invocation of a procedure with a value/result parameter-passing mechanism.

Assignment Procedure Rule

$$\frac{assign(S, f, Y),\ T \Rightarrow (U^{\bar{y},\,\bar{z}}_{f(\bar{x},\bar{z})} \wedge Y^{\bar{a},\,\bar{c}}_{\bar{x},\,\bar{z}})}{\{T\}\, p(\bar{x}, \bar{y}, \bar{z})\, \{U\}} \tag{3.4}$$

With the Assignment Procedure Rule, the user can view a procedure with assignment semantics as a new language construct that performs a multiple assignment and use it without any knowledge of (or the need to prove anything about) its body. More precisely, if the procedure designer specifies to the user that $assign(S, f, Y)$ is true of the body of a procedure, the user can reason about an invocation of that procedure using an axiom schema

$$\{T\}\, p(\bar{x}, \bar{y}, \bar{z})\, \{U\}$$

for any T and U such that

$$T \Rightarrow (U^{\bar{y},\,\bar{z}}_{f(\bar{x},\bar{z})} \wedge Y^{\bar{a},\,\bar{c}}_{\bar{x},\,\bar{z}})$$

Note that a proof that a procedure has assignment semantics can be performed once by the designer of the procedure body and need not be performed separately for each invocation.

As an example, the body of the *swap* procedure

> **procedure** *swap*$(c1, c2 :$ **in out** *integer*$)$;
> $c1,\ c2 := c2,\ c1$;
> **end** *swap*;

can be described by the triple

$$\{(c1 = C_{01}) \wedge (c2 = C_{02})\}\ c1,\ c2 := c2,\ c1\ \{(c1 = C_{02}) \wedge (c2 = C_{01})\}$$

which satisfies assignment semantics with $f(c1, c2) = (c2, c1)$ and Y equal to *true*. Hence, invocations of *swap*(x, y) can be described by any triple of the form:

$$\{U^{z1,\ z2}_{z2,\ z1}\}\ swap(z1, z2)\ \{U\}$$

3.1.1   Variable Scoping*

In most languages, each variable has an associated scope within which it exists. For some variables, declared globally, that scope is the entire program. Many languages are block structured and allow the declaration of local variables whose scope is a block. Procedures are blocks, since they can contain local variables (including parameters) that do not exist outside of the procedure.

An assertion attached to a control point describes the state of variables when that control point is enabled. Hence, if P is an assertion at a control point and P refers to a variable x, then x must exist when that control point is enabled. To capture this idea in a more formal way, we introduce, for each variable declared in the program, a predicate called an *existence predicate*. *exist_x* has the following semantics with respect to entry to and exit from the block in which x is declared:

$$\{P^{exist\_x}_{true}\}\ block\ entry\ \{P\}$$

$$\{P^{exist\_x}_{false}\}\ block\ exit\ \{P\}$$

Thus entrance to the block sets *exist_x* to true, and exit from the block sets it to false. We require that *exist_x* be a conjunct of any assertion involving x. One result of this requirement (which we make use of later) is that an assertion in a program that calls a procedure cannot refer to variables local to that procedure.

Since it is intuitively clear what variables exist at any particular control point in most programs (and in all sequential programs), we do not reason about *exist_x* in most proofs in this and subsequent chapters. However, as we shall see, issues arise in concurrent programs that require us to be aware of this predicate.

3.2   Abstract Data Types

So far we have discussed how to reason about various constructs operating on simple data types such as integers. We have assumed that the operations on those data types work correctly. This assumption is based on a contract with the hardware designer. For example, the hardware designer has told us that there is a built-in data type called integer, which is constrained to take on values in some specified range. The designer has published a set of operations on that data type, described by a set of axioms. We use these operations, and reason using the axioms, without further thought.

The hardware designer has to satisfy the contract by implementing a suitable data structure for integers and instructions to carry out the promised operations. As users we do not particularly care what data structure is used (twos-complement binary, ones-complement binary, binary-coded decimal, etc.) as long as it and the associated machine instructions satisfy the axioms.

3.2.1   Abstract Specification

We would like to use this same approach in dealing with user-defined data types, such as queues, stacks, buffers, etc. Informally, the simple data types are those supplied with a language, and the user-defined, or abstract, types are those built explicitly by the user. One of the advantages of modern languages is that users can build their own data types and then use them in programs much like simple data types. The advantage of these user-defined data types is that they allow the user to work at a higher level of abstraction (thinking about queues instead of integers) and to reason about a program in terms of these higher level types, without having to be concerned with the details of their implementation.

By a *data type* we mean a set of possible values (which variables of that type might take on) and a collection of operations that can be performed on an instance of the type. This description applies to simple as well as abstract types. Our goal is to specify abstract data types using the formalism of Program Logic and then to demonstrate how a particular implementation can be shown to support that specification. In later chapters we show how Program Logic can be used to reason about abstract data types shared among multiple concurrent processes.

We specify the set of possible values of an abstract data type with an assertion that constrains the values that variables of that type can take on. For example, the assertion for the data type integer on a 32-bit machine might be

$$-(2^{31}) \leq i \leq (2^{31} - 1) \tag{3.5}$$

This assertion is true at each control point in the program that uses the type. Hence, it is a program invariant and is called the *abstract invariant* of the data type.

We assume that the operations of the abstract data type are carried out by procedures. We use the syntax

$$t.p(\bar{x}, \bar{y})$$

to designate an invocation of abstract operation p on an instance, t, of the type, where $\bar{x}$ and $\bar{y}$ are in and out arguments, respectively. For simplicity we assume that p has no in out parameters, but the treatment we give extends to such parameters easily.

Assume t is an instance of an abstract data type, I_a is the abstract invariant, and p_j is a procedure that performs an abstract operation. Then I_a must be invariant to the execution of p_j:

$$\{I_a\}\; t.p_j(\overline{x}, \overline{y})\; \{I_a\} \tag{3.6}$$

The subscript a is used to indicate that the subscripted item is relevant to the abstract domain. Note that I_a is a program invariant at the abstract level only. It makes no sense to talk about I_a when the enabled control point is at a statement within p_j, since p_j may be modifying t and its value is therefore undefined.

We specify the effect of each procedure as a triple. This is analogous to the way we describe operations on simple data types. Thus, we describe the effect of an increment operation on a variable of the (simple) type integer with the triple

$$\{P_{x+1}^x\}\; x \;:=\; x+1\; \{P\} \tag{3.7}$$

where P is an arbitrary assertion that describes the state of the program that invokes the operation.

We must also describe the conditions under which the procedure terminates. An abstract operation might not be defined in all circumstances. For example, an attempt to push a new element onto a full stack cannot be completed without violating the stack's abstract invariant, which places a limit on the size of the stack. The issue here is the same as that encountered in dealing with simple data types. Thus, the description (3.7) does not tell us that an exception occurs if we attempt to increment an integer variable having the maximum allowable value: $2^{31} - 1$. Under these circumstances, we assume that the assignment statement does not terminate. To guarantee termination, we must ensure as a precondition of the assignment that overflow will not occur: $x < 2^{31} - 1$. Such an assertion ensures termination in a state in which the invariant (3.5) is true. Note that, in contrast to P, which describes the (arbitrary) state of the invoking program, this assertion is simply a restriction on the state of the integer variable.

In a similar fashion we must specify the weakest precondition that ensures that p_j terminates. In the general case, the weakest precondition defines the combinations of values of $\overline{x}$ and t for which termination should occur. In the remainder of the text, however, we consider only the case in which the weakest precondition depends on t alone; it defines the subset of all possible values of t that, when input to p_j, must result in termination. Termination must occur for all initial values of t in the subset. When termination occurs, the state satisfies I_a since I_a is a program invariant at the abstract level. (The triple describing p_j ensures in addition that, *if* termination occurs, t will have the correct value.) Hence we must choose the assertion $wp(t.p_j(\overline{x}, \overline{y}), I_a)$ to be true for exactly those initial values of t for which p_j should terminate. For simplicity we denote this assertion by $WP_a^j(t)$. In the case of a stack, the weakest precondition for the *push* operation must constrain the initial value of the stack to one whose length is less than the maximum allowed. Since $WP_a^j(t)$ is a restriction on the values that t might assume, it follows that

$$WP_a^j(t) \Rightarrow I_a$$

If the inputs do not satisfy $WP_a^j(t)$, the procedure does not terminate. Thus, execution of the body, S_j, of p_j can be described by

$$\textbf{if } \neg WP_a^j(t) \rightarrow \textbf{ halt}; \; [] \; WP_a^j(t) \rightarrow S_j; \; \textbf{fi}$$

Note that the triple (3.6) is true even if $WP_a^j(t)$ is not a precondition, since when the procedure does not terminate, any postcondition can be asserted.

We consider only abstract data types in which the operations on the data type are performed by procedures characterized by the Assignment Procedure Rule. Hence, operations are characterized at the abstract level by triples of the form:

$$\{P_{f_a^j(\bar{x},t)}^{\bar{y},\,t}\} \; t.p_j(\bar{x},\bar{y}) \; \{P\} \tag{3.8}$$

where $f_a^j(\bar{x}, t)$ is a vector that can be decomposed into two parts:

$$f_a^j(\bar{x}, t) \; = \; (f_{a1}^j(\bar{x}, t), f_{a2}^j(\bar{x}, t))$$

such that $f_{a1}^j(\bar{x}, t)$ is the vector of out parameters produced by p_j and $f_{a2}^j(\bar{x}, t)$ is the new value of t. Hence, if $WP_a^j(t_0)$ is true, not only will termination occur when p_j is invoked with an argument having value t_0, but, using (3.8), we are also guaranteed that the effect of p_j is characterized by f_a^j.

The four components of the specification of an abstract data type are as follows.

Abstract Specification

(1) an abstract invariant, I_a, that constrains the values of the abstract variable, t;

(2) an initial value, t_{init}, for each variable of the type;

(3) for each procedure, p_j, an abstract weakest precondition, $WP_a^j(t)$, such that[1]:

$$WP_a^j(t) \; \equiv \; wp(t.p_j(\bar{x},\bar{y}), I_a)$$

where $U \equiv V$ means $U \Rightarrow V$ and $V \Rightarrow U$;

(4) for each procedure, p_j, the procedure heading and a triple that describes its intended operation:

$$\{P_{f_a^j(\bar{x},t)}^{\bar{y},\,t}\} \; t.p_j(\bar{x},\bar{y}) \; \{P\} \tag{3.9}$$

---

[1]Since the values returned by p_j (as specified by its heading) must be contained in the set of values that define the type, as we pointed out earlier it follows that if p_j terminates, I_a is true. Hence $wp(t.p_j(\bar{x},\bar{y}), true) \equiv wp(t.p_j(\bar{x},\bar{y}), I_a)$

Again, there is a contract involved. The designer of an abstract data type publishes the abstract specifications. The user can then assume that the operations are new constructs in the language and reason about them using the given specifications. To satisfy the contract, the designer has to build an implementation of the data type and prove that the implementation satisfies the specification.

As an example of an abstract data type we use a bounded queue, which we also refer to as a bounded buffer. Informally a queue is a sequence of elements of a particular type such that an element can be appended at one end (the back) and removed from the other end (the front). The following operations are provided for manipulating an instance of a queue:

procedure *Enqueue*(a : **in** *element*)

which appends a new element with value a to the back of the queue and

procedure *Dequeue*(b : **out** *element*)

which deletes the first element from the front of the queue and returns its value in b. An initialization routine assigns an empty queue to initial versions of the instance. We assume that a queue is of bounded (non-negative) length and can hold at most N elements. Thus, the abstract invariant states that the length of an instance must be between 0 and N.

The assertions used in the abstract specification are formulated in terms of related mathematical objects. Thus, the data type integer is described in terms of the mathematical object integer, which obeys the axioms for integers. Similarly, in specifying more complex abstract data types, we frequently use mathematical objects such as sequences and sets, which obey the appropriate mathematical axioms. These mathematical objects are not themselves abstract data types; they are used only in reasoning about the program, not in its implementation.

In the example of the queue, we specify the triples and invariant using a notation for sequences. A sequence consisting of the elements a, b, and c, in that order, is described by the notation

$$< a, b, c >$$

where a is at the front of the sequence and c is at the back. We use $\circ$ as the sequence concatenation operator. Thus

$$< a, b, c > \circ < d, e > = < a, b, c, d, e >$$

We use λ to denote the empty sequence, and α to denote a generic sequence. We denote the number of elements in the sequence α as *Length*(α). Thus

$$Length(< a, b, c >) = 3$$

$$Length(\lambda) = 0$$

(1) The invariant, I_a, is
$$0 \leq Length(q) \leq N$$

(2) The initial value is
$$q_{init} = \lambda$$

(3) The weakest preconditions for termination of each procedure are
$$WP_a^{Enqueue}(q) \equiv (0 \leq Length(q) \leq (N-1))$$
$$WP_a^{Dequeue}(q) \equiv (1 \leq Length(q) \leq N)$$

(4) Procedure headings are
    procedure $Enqueue(a :$ **in** $element)$
    procedure $Dequeue(b :$ **out** $element)$
and axiom schemas specifying the semantics of procedure invocation are
$$\{P_{q \,\circ\, <x>}^{q}\}\ q.Enqueue(x)\ \{P\}$$

$$\{P_{First(q),\ Tail(q)}^{y,\ q}\}\ q.Dequeue(y)\ \{P\}$$

Figure 3.2: An abstract specification for the queue.

For a nonempty sequence α, we denote its first element by $First(\alpha)$ and the sequence consisting of all the elements except the first by $Tail(\alpha)$. Thus;

$$First(<a, b, c>) = a$$

$$Tail(<a, b, c>) = <b, c>$$

By definition

$$First(<a>) = a$$

$$Tail(<a>) = \lambda$$

$First(\lambda)$ and $Tail(\lambda)$ are both undefined.

    Using this notation, the specification for an abstract queue, q, is given in Figure 3.2. For example, assignment semantics for the procedure $Dequeue$ involves the function

$$f_a^{Dequeue}(q) = (First(q),\ Tail(q)) \tag{3.10}$$

    The users of the abstract type queue can access variables of type queue in a program in much the same way as variables of type integer. They can invoke the supplied procedures to perform operations on queues and reason

```
i := 0;
do i < N →
    begin
        i := i + 1;
        q.Enqueue(A[i]);
    end;
od;
```

Figure 3.3: A program using the queue data type.

about the results of those procedures. For example, in the program fragment of Figure 3.3, assuming that the initial value of q is λ, a loop invariant is

$$(q = < A[1], A[2], \ldots, A[i] >) \land (i \leq N)$$

and an appropriate postcondition for the entire fragment is

$$q = < A[1], A[2], \ldots, A[N] >$$

3.2.2 Concrete Implementation

The second task in the construction of an abstract type is to build an implementation. The implementation consists of a concrete data structure to represent the values of the abstract type and a procedure body to implement each of the specified procedures. We refer to the implementation as the *concrete* domain and subscript relevant quantities with c.

Consider the two choices we have for implementing an abstract object, t, in terms of a concrete data structure, denoted by $\bar{c}$. We can view $\bar{c}$ as an in out argument of p, in which case its value is passed to p, perhaps changed, and then passed back out. In the dot notation for the invocation statement, $t.p(\bar{x}, \bar{y})$, t represents this argument. In this case we must assume that, since $\bar{c}$ is an instance of an abstract object, it cannot be directly accessed at the calling site (*i.e.*, by any means other than through one of its procedures) as an ordinary in out argument might be. Alternatively, we might encapsulate $\bar{c}$ in a module together with the procedures of the type. In this case t names the module, and the dot notation, $t.p(\bar{x}, \bar{y})$, invokes procedure p to operate on that instance. The variables $\bar{c}$ are *permanent* variables: they retain their values between invocations of the module's procedures and are accessible only to those procedures. Thus, there is no need to pass the instance through in out parameters. When an abstract operation is invoked, the named procedure within the module is called, and it updates $\bar{c}$.

In actuality, the two views are not very different. The essential points are that, in both, the concrete variables retain their values between calls and are accessible only to the procedure bodies. The only difference is in the way a procedure body refers to the variables: in the first view the reference is to in out parameters, while in the second it is to variables global to the body. We take the second view because it extends to the shared abstract types we study later. However, in our formal treatment, we treat permanent variables as if they were in out arguments. This enables us to use the formalization of procedures developed earlier. Be aware that a more formal treatment of this subject would deal directly with permanent variables.

Our plan, then, is to encapsulate the concrete variables as permanent variables within the module implementing the abstract object, but to treat them formally as in out arguments to the procedures implementing the abstract operations. We simplify the following discussion by assuming that these are the only in out arguments. This matches the notation used previously for in out parameters.

The task of building the concrete implementation can be divided into the following four steps:

(1) Design a concrete data structure, $\bar{c}$, that can encode all values of the abstract type, and specify a concrete invariant, I_c, that constrains the values of $\bar{c}$.

(2) Specify an initial value, $\bar{c}_{init}$, for the concrete variables, and implement the initialization routine, S_{init}, such that

$$true \equiv wp(S_{init}, ((\bar{c} = \bar{c}_{init}) \wedge I_c)) \qquad (3.11)$$

(3) For each procedure, p_j, specify an assertion, $WP_c^j(\bar{c})$, that is true for all values of $\bar{c}$ that encode values of t for which p_j is defined. Implement S_j satisfying

$$WP_c^j(\bar{c}) \equiv (wp(S_j, I_c) \wedge I_c) \qquad (3.12)$$

(4) For each procedure, p_j, prove

$$assign(S_j, f_c^j, WP_c^j(\bar{c})) \qquad (3.13)$$

Since I_c is true of $\bar{c}_{init}$ (step 2) and, since each procedure transforms states satisfying I_c to states satisfying I_c, S_j need not check that $\bar{c}$ satisfies I_c prior to computing the new state – it is guaranteed that this is true. Hence in a particular implementation, $wp(S_j, I_c)$ might include values of $\bar{c}$ that do not satisfy I_c (but are guaranteed never to be supplied as inputs). For example, if the implementation of *Enqueue* in Figure 3.6 were given a queue of length -1, it would terminate in a state in which I_c is true (the length would be 0). In step 3 we exclude such "don't care" states from our analysis by requiring that

$$WP_c^j(\bar{c}) \equiv (wp(S_j, I_c) \wedge I_c)$$

[*i.e.*, $WP_c^j(\overline{c})$ specifies the weakest condition on the input states such that S_j terminates in a state satisfying I_c, and the input state itself satisfies I_c.] The procedure need work correctly only for states in $WP_c^j(\overline{c})$.

In step 4 we specify that each procedure body, S_j, has assignment semantics. The condition, Y, restricting the parameters is required to be $WP_c^j(\overline{c})$, which defines the set of concrete states – corresponding to the set of abstract values – for which S_j must terminate. Hence, we are requiring that for all such values, S_j implements assignment semantics with f_c^j. By designing f_c^j in such a way that it performs at the concrete level a transformation corresponding to what f_a^j does at the abstract level, and by choosing $WP_c^j(\overline{c})$ to define exactly the set of concrete states that correspond to the range of values defined by $WP_a^j(t)$, we guarantee that S_j will implement the appropriate transformation on the appropriate input states.

f_c^j describes the new values of the out parameters and the concrete variables produced by S_j as a function of the initial values of the in parameters and the concrete variables. We find it convenient to break f_c^j up into two parts so that

$$f_c^j(\overline{a}, \overline{c}) \;=\; (f_{c1}^j(\overline{a}, \overline{c}),\; f_{c2}^j(\overline{a}, \overline{c}))$$

where $f_{c1}^j(\overline{a}, \overline{c})$ is a vector of out parameters and $f_{c2}^j(\overline{a}, \overline{c})$ is a new concrete state.

We now present a concrete implementation of the queue and later prove that it supports the abstract specification given in Figure 3.2. The implementation is in a language based on the control constructs introduced in Section 2.1, informally augmented with a mechanism that allows the declaration of simple variables, arrays, and records.

For the data structure representing the queue, we use a record, *Qrecord*, shown in Figure 3.4, having three fields: an array, *Qarray*, with bounds 0 to $N - 1$, and two integers, *last* and *count*. Assuming g is a variable of type *Qrecord*, *g.last* is the index of the location in the array where the last element of the queue is stored (where the last call to *Enqueue* stored its element) and *g.count* records the number of elements stored in the queue. We assume that the queue can "wrap around" the end of the array, so that the first element of the queue (where the next call to *Dequeue* will obtain its element) is at array location

$$(g.last - g.count + 1) \;\; \mathrm{mod} \;\; N$$

The concrete specifications are shown in Figure 3.5, where g is the permanent (concrete) variable corresponding to the queue and h is the parameter corresponding to the element being added or deleted. We use $A|_x^i$ to denote the array A with the contents of the ith element replaced by x. Note that, in the fourth part of the concrete specification, the new values of the concrete variables and out parameters are represented as functions of the initial values of the concrete variables and the in parameters, hence enabling us to utilize assignment semantics.

type
  Qrecord = **record**
    Qarray : **array**$[0..(N-1)]$ **of** *element*;
    last : $0..(N-1)$:= 0;
    count : $0..N$:= 0;
  end;

Figure 3.4: The declaration for the concrete data type queue.

(1) The invariant, I_c, is
 $0 \le g.count \le N$

(2) The initial value is
 $g.last = 0$
 $g.count = 0$

(3) The weakest precondition for each procedure is
 $WP_c^{Enqueue}(g) \equiv (0 \le g.count \le (N-1))$
 $WP_c^{Dequeue}(g) \equiv (1 \le g.count \le N)$

(4) Axiom schemas specifying the semantics of each procedure body
 $\{WP_c^{Enqueue}(g) \wedge (g = G) \wedge (h = H)\}\ S_{Enqueue}\ \{(g.count = G.count + 1)$
  $\wedge(g.last = (G.last + 1)\ \text{mod}\ N)$
   $\wedge(g.Qarray = G.Qarray|_H^{(G.last+1)\ \text{mod}\ N})\}$

 $\{WP_c^{Dequeue}(g) \wedge (g = G)\}\ S_{Dequeue}\ \{(g.count = G.count - 1)$
  $\wedge(g.last = G.last) \wedge (g.Qarray = G.Qarray)$
   $\wedge(h = G.Qarray[(G.last - G.count + 1)\ \text{mod}\ N])\}$

Figure 3.5: A concrete specification of the queue.

Concrete implementations of the procedures are shown in Figure 3.6. It is easy to verify that these procedures satisfy the specifications shown in Figure 3.5 and hence satisfy the appropriate assignment semantics. In this simple example, S_{init} is the assignment statements in the type declaration (Figure 3.4).

procedure *Enqueue*(*h* : **in** *element*);
begin
  if (*g.count* = *N*) → **halt**;
  [] (*g.count* < *N*) →
    g.Qarray[(*g.last* + 1) **mod** *N*], *g.last, g.count*
      := *h*, (*g.last* + 1) **mod** *N*, *g.count* + 1;
  fi;
end *Enqueue*;

procedure *Dequeue*(*h* : **out** *element*);
begin
  if (*g.count* = 0) → **halt**;
  [] (*g.count* > 0) →
    g.count, h := *g.count* − 1, *g.Qarray*[(*g.last* − *g.count* + 1) **mod** *N*];
  fi;
end *Dequeue*;

Figure 3.6: A concrete implementation for the queue. The queue is a permanent variable in this module.

3.2.3   Relating Abstract and Concrete Domains*

After the concrete implementation has been specified, the next task is to prove that it is a correct implementation of the abstract specification. The proof is done using a mapping from concrete states that satisfy I_c to abstract states. This mapping is called the *representation mapping* and is denoted by R. Note that there may be more than one concrete state that maps to a particular abstract state under R. For example, in the representation of the queue, if $g.count < N$, the value stored in array element $(g.last + 1)$ mod N (a value not actually in the abstract queue) can be changed, but the new concrete state maps to the same abstract state as the original concrete state. When two concrete states, c and c', map to the same abstract state, we require that each procedure return the same result and transform both c and c' into other concrete states that map into the same abstract state

$$(R(c) = R(c')) \Rightarrow ((f_{c1}^j(\overline{a}, \overline{c}) = f_{c1}^j(\overline{a}, \overline{c'})) \land (R(f_{c2}^j(\overline{a}, \overline{c})) = R(f_{c2}^j(\overline{a}, \overline{c'}))))$$

In the example, when the value of *g.Qarray* is Q, the value of *g.last* is L, and the value of *g.count* is C, we say the concrete state is $\ll Q, L, C \gg$. The representation mapping describes how the value of the concrete state corresponds to the contents of the abstract queue. Informally, the content of the abstract queue is the concatenation of all the elements stored in Q between $(L - C + 1)$ mod N and L.

$$Seq(\ll Q, L, 0 \gg) = \lambda$$
$$Length(Seq(\ll Q, L, C \gg)) = C$$
$$First(Seq(\ll Q, L, C \gg)) = Q[(L - C + 1) \mod N]$$
$$Tail(Seq(\ll Q, L, C \gg)) = Seq(\ll Q, L, C - 1 \gg)$$
$$Seq(\ll Q, L, C \gg) \circ <x>$$
$$= Seq(\ll Q|_x^{(L+1) \mod N}, (L + 1) \mod N, C + 1 \gg)$$

Figure 3.7: Some examples of the representation map, *Seq*, for queues.

Formally, the mapping is best described with a recursive definition. In the case of a queue, R is the function *Seq*

$$q = R(\ll Q, \ L, \ C \gg) = Seq(\ll Q, \ L, \ C \gg)$$

where

$$Seq(\ll Q, \ L, \ C \gg) \equiv if \ C = 0 \ then \ \lambda \ else$$
$$Seq(\ll Q, (L - 1) \mod N, C - 1 \gg) \circ <Q[L]>$$

This mapping states that if C is zero, the queue is empty; otherwise, the queue is the element pointed to by L, concatenated with the rest of the queue.

Some properties of the sequence specified by *Seq* are shown in Figure 3.7. For example, concatenation with a single element involves incrementing the number of elements, C, and the pointer to the last element, L, and then storing the new element in the location pointed to by the incremented value of L.

The key part of the proof showing that the concrete implementation correctly supports the abstract specification is to demonstrate that after its inputs and outputs are suitably mapped by R, each concrete procedure performs the same operation as does the corresponding abstract procedure. The situation is shown pictorially in Figure 3.8. Intuitively, we want to show that, starting with any concrete state, we can obtain the same abstract state by either

Mapping the concrete state to its corresponding abstract state and then applying an abstract operation; or

Applying the corresponding concrete operation to that concrete state and then mapping the concrete result to its corresponding abstract value.

The formal statement of the proof requirements indicated in Figure 3.8 for procedures that have assignment semantics is

$$f_{a1}^j(\overline{a}, R(\overline{c})) = f_{c1}^j(\overline{a}, \overline{c}) \tag{3.14}$$

$$f_{a2}^j(\overline{a}, R(\overline{c})) = R(f_{c2}^j(\overline{a}, \overline{c})) \tag{3.15}$$

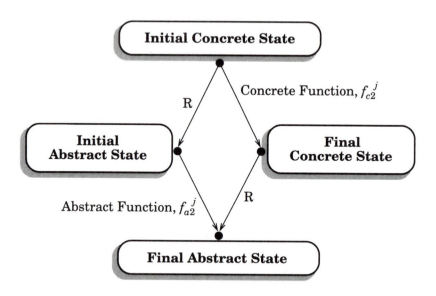

Figure 3.8: Illustration of the proof requirements showing that the concrete implementation supports the abstract specification.

Note that (3.15) implies that every abstract state is represented by some concrete state (*i.e.*, that each possible value of the abstract state is reachable from t_{init} by some sequence of operations).

The proofs of conditions (3.14) and (3.15) and the condition

$$WP_c^j(\bar{c}) \equiv WP_a^j(R(\bar{c})) \tag{3.16}$$

(for all j and all $\bar{c}$ satisfying I_c) are part of the proof obligation that a particular concrete implementation supports a given abstract specification. Before we state the complete proof obligation, we prove the following:

Assuming conditions (3.14), (3.15), and (3.16) are satisfied, each concrete procedure correctly implements the corresponding abstract operation.

At the concrete level we have already demonstrated $assign(S_j, f_c^j, WP_c^j(\bar{c}))$ (step 4 in the design of the concrete implementation). Thus, we have shown

$$(\bar{a} = \overline{A_0}) \wedge (\bar{c} = \overline{C_0}) \wedge WP_c^j(\bar{c})\} \ S_j$$
$$\{(\bar{a} = \overline{A_0}) \wedge (\bar{b} = f_{c1}^j(\overline{A_0}, \overline{C_0})) \wedge (\bar{c} = f_{c2}^j(\overline{A_0}, \overline{C_0})) \wedge I_c\}$$

Note that we have added I_c as a conjunct on the right hand side, as justified by (3.12). Since $WP_c^j(\bar{c})$ (which implies I_c) is a conjunct of the precondition and

I_c is a conjunct of the postcondition, we can use (3.16) and apply the mapping, R, to concrete states, $\overline{c}$, in these assertions to restate them in terms of the abstract object, t:

$$\{(\overline{a} = \overline{A_0}) \wedge (t = t_0) \wedge WP_a^j(t)\}\, S_j\, \{(\overline{a} = \overline{A_0}) \wedge (\overline{b} = f_{c1}^j(\overline{A_0}, \overline{C_0})) \wedge (t = R(f_{c2}^j(\overline{A_0}, \overline{C_0})))\}$$
$$(3.17)$$

where $t_0 = R(\overline{C_0})$.

Assuming that we can demonstrate (3.14) and (3.15), we can apply them to (3.17) and obtain

$$\{(\overline{a} = \overline{A_0}) \wedge (t = t_0) \wedge WP_a^j(t)\}\, S_j\, \{(\overline{a} = \overline{A_0}) \wedge (\overline{b} = f_{a1}^j(\overline{A_0}, t_0)) \wedge (t = f_{a2}^j(\overline{A_0}, t_0))\}$$
$$(3.18)$$

(3.18) is just $assign(S_j, f_a, WP_a^j(t))$. We can therefore use the Assignment Procedure Rule (3.4) as follows:

$$\frac{assign(S_j, f_a^j, WP_a^j(t)),\ (U_{f_a^j(\overline{x},t)}^{\overline{y},\, t} \Rightarrow WP_a^j(t))}{\{U_{f_a^j(\overline{x},t)}^{\overline{y},\, t}\}\, t.p_j(\overline{x}, \overline{y})\, \{U\}}$$
$$(3.19)$$

to justify the triple describing an invocation in the abstract specification. Thus we have shown that the concrete implementation supports the abstract specification; this completes the proof.

We can now say that the following four steps are sufficient to prove that the concrete implementation supports the abstract specification. Each step corresponds to one of the four parts of the formulation of the abstract specification given earlier, and the proof consists of demonstrating that the mapping of the concrete implementation satisfies each of these parts.

Proving the Concrete Implementation Supports the Abstract Specification

(1) Prove that if the concrete invariant is true for some state, $\overline{c}$, the abstract invariant is true in the corresponding state:

$$I_c(\overline{c}) \Rightarrow I_a(R(\overline{c}))$$

and that every abstract state can be encoded as a concrete state:

$$((\forall t)(I_a(t) \Rightarrow ((\exists \overline{c})((t = R(\overline{c})) \wedge I_c(\overline{c})))))$$

(2) Prove that the initial value of an abstract variable is t_{init}:

$$true = wp(S_{init}, (\overline{c} = \overline{c}_{init} \wedge I_c))$$

$$R(\overline{c}_{init}) = t_{init}$$

(3) For each j, prove that the abstract conditions for termination are equivalent to the concrete conditions for termination:

$$WP_c^j(\overline{c}) \equiv WP_a^j(R(\overline{c}))$$

(4) For each j, prove that the abstract semantics are supported by the corresponding concrete procedure body:

$$f_{a1}^j(\overline{x}, R(\overline{c})) = f_{c1}^j(\overline{x}, \overline{c})$$

$$f_{a2}^j(\overline{x}, R(\overline{c})) = R(f_{c2}^j(\overline{x}, \overline{c}))$$

We complete our example of the queue by proving that the concrete implementation is correct.

(1) Invariants:

$$(0 \leq C \leq N) \Rightarrow (0 \leq Length(R(\ll Q, L, C \gg)) \leq N)$$

This condition follows directly from the definition of *Length* given in Figure 3.7.

(2) Initial value:

$$R(\ll Q, 0, 0 \gg) = Seq(\ll Q, 0, 0 \gg) = \lambda$$

(3) Termination:

Enqueue: Follows from

$$(0 \leq C \leq N - 1) \equiv (0 \leq Length(R(\ll Q, L, C \gg)) \leq N - 1)$$

Dequeue: Follows from

$$(1 \leq C \leq N) \equiv (1 \leq Length(R(\ll Q, L, C \gg)) \leq N)$$

(4) Operation Semantics:

Enqueue: Follows from

$$f_{a1}^{Enqueue}(x, R(\ll Q, L, C \gg)) = Seq(\ll Q, L, C \gg) \circ <x>$$

$$
\begin{aligned}
R(f_{c1}^{Enqueue}&(x, \ll Q, L, C \gg)) \\
&= R(\ll Q|_x^{(L+1) \bmod N}, (L+1) \bmod N, C+1 \gg) \\
&= Seq(\ll Q, L, C \gg) \circ <x>
\end{aligned}
$$

Dequeue: Equivalence for the changes to the queue follows from

$$f_{a1}^{Dequeue}(x, R(\ll Q, L, C \gg)) = Seq(\ll Q, L, C - 1 \gg)$$

$$R(f_{c1}^{Dequeue}(x, \ll Q, L, C \gg)) = R(\ll Q, L, C - 1 \gg)$$
$$= Seq(\ll Q, L, C - 1 \gg)$$

Equivalence for the element returned follows from

$$f_{a2}^{Dequeue}(x, R(\ll Q, L, C \gg)) = First(R(\ll Q, L, C \gg))$$
$$= Q[(L - C + 1) \mod N]$$

$$f_{c2}^{Dequeue}(x, \ll Q, L, C \gg) = Q[(L - C + 1) \mod N]$$

3.3 Coroutines*

Coroutines are a structuring tool for decomposing a complex sequential program into simpler subprograms. We have already discussed one such tool, the subroutine (which we call a procedure). A key difference between coroutines and subroutines is that, while a program has an asymmetrical relationship with a subroutine it invokes, coroutines have a more symmetrical relationship. For example, the state of a process containing coroutines must include the identity of the control point in each coroutine at which execution will resume when that coroutine becomes active. By contrast, no such information is retained about an inactive procedure. Thus, in this sense, each coroutine *appears* to be executed by a distinct process. Note, however, that the coroutine construct is sequential since only one coroutine is active at a time and hence only one control point is enabled at a time.

One example of the use of coroutines is in a compiler. A lexical coroutine reads ASCII characters from the input stream until it has constructed a token and then calls the syntax coroutine to process that token. The syntax coroutine appends that token to the list of tokens it has previously been passed. If this list can be used to recognize a production, the syntax coroutine recognizes the production and calls the code generator coroutine to process the recognized production. If the token list cannot be used to recognize a production, the syntax coroutine calls the lexical coroutine, which continues reading from the input stream until it has constructed a new token, and then again calls the syntax coroutine to process that token. Note that between calls the lexical coroutine remembers its place in the input stream and the syntax coroutine remembers its place in the token list.

Coroutine Statement

We use the coroutine statement

$$\textbf{coroutine } \mathcal{P}_1 :: S_1; \ \# \ \mathcal{P}_2 :: S_2; \ \# \cdots \# \ \mathcal{P}_n :: S_n; \ \textbf{coend}$$

to introduce coroutines into our language. Each S_i is referred to as a coroutine and can have a name, $\mathcal{P}_i$. The operational semantics of the coroutine statement is as follows:

> When control reaches the coroutine statement, a control point is enabled at the statement S_1; when execution of S_1 has completed, the construct is exited through the coend. If one of the S_i, $i \neq 1$, terminates, the coroutine statement fails.

Other operational semantics are possible (particularly as they define termination) but, since our primary purpose in discussing coroutines is as a pedagogical tool for introducing concurrency, we choose this one due to its simplicity.

Resume Statement

The resume statement

$$\textbf{resume } \mathcal{P}_i$$

is used for transferring control to the named coroutine, $\mathcal{P}_i$. The operational semantics of the resume statement is as follows:

> If $\mathcal{P}_i$ has not yet executed, a control point is enabled at the first statement in S_i. Otherwise, a control point is enabled after the last executed resume statement in $\mathcal{P}_i$. The resume statement is atomic.

For simplicity we consider only the case in which n, the number of coroutines, is 2.

The coroutine statement is sequential, since at any given time there is only one enabled control point. Note, however, that the state of the process executing the coroutine statement must include the control points of both the active and the inactive coroutines, since it must contain the information needed to continue executing the inactive coroutine should a resume be executed by the active coroutine.

Our goal is to develop a two stage process for reasoning about a coroutine statement. In the first stage we analyze each coroutine separately to obtain a triple that describes its behavior. In the second stage we use the triples for the individual coroutines to infer a triple describing the coroutine statement as a whole. In this way we can break a complex analysis task into several simpler tasks. We have already presented the tools necessary for analyzing a single coroutine (*i.e.*, the axioms and inference rules describing our sequential language) with one exception: we have no way to reason about the resume statements that might appear within a coroutine. Hence, we need an axiom schema that relates the pre- and postconditions of a resume.

Unfortunately, our goal of reasoning in the first stage about each coroutine in isolation makes it difficult to reason about individual resume statements. A resume, $\rho_{1,i}$, in $\mathcal{P}_1$ transfers control to $\mathcal{P}_2$. An arbitrary sequence of statements is then executed in $\mathcal{P}_2$ before the control point following $\rho_{1,i}$ is enabled, resulting in an arbitrary change in the state of program variables. Since we do not wish (at this stage) to use information about $\mathcal{P}_2$ in reasoning about $\mathcal{P}_1$, we have no way of relating the postcondition of $\rho_{1,i}$ to its precondition.

We resolve this difficulty by noting that, if we view a coroutine as an isolated program, a resume does not terminate and can therefore be described by an arbitrary triple (as with a halt statement). It is only when the individual coroutines are assembled into a coroutine statement that it is possible for the control point following a resume to be enabled. Hence, in the first stage of our reasoning process, we derive a proof of each coroutine in isolation using the following axiom schema:

Resume Axiom

$$\{P\} \ \textbf{resume} \ \mathcal{P}_i \ \{Q\}$$

where P and Q are arbitrary assertions.

The Resume Axiom allows us to choose an arbitrary postcondition for each resume during the first stage. Using the Resume Axiom (and the other axioms and inference rules describing our sequential language), we can derive a triple describing each coroutine. In the second stage we are obliged to justify those choices. We do this by satisfying a proof obligation called a satisfaction condition.

Suppose the ith resume statement in $\mathcal{P}_1$, $\rho_{1,i}$, is described by the triple

$$\{P_{1,i}\} \ \textbf{resume} \ \mathcal{P}_2 \ \{Q_{1,i}\}$$

When $\rho_{1,i}$ is executed, a control point is enabled either after some resume statement – assume it is the jth resume statement, $\rho_{2,j}$ – in $\mathcal{P}_2$ or at the first statement in $\mathcal{P}_2$ if $\mathcal{P}_2$ has not yet executed. For simplicity we assume that the first statement in $\mathcal{P}_2$ is a dummy resume statement and that execution of $\mathcal{P}_2$ is initiated at the control point following that resume. Since the only effect of $\rho_{1,i}$ is to enable a new control point, the postcondition of $\rho_{2,j}$ will be $P_{1,i}$. Hence, if $\rho_{2,j}$ is described by the triple

$$\{P_{2,j}\} \ \textbf{resume} \ \mathcal{P}_1 \ \{Q_{2,j}\}$$

we must prove the satisfaction condition

$$P_{1,i} \Rightarrow Q_{2,j} \tag{3.20}$$

In general, if we assume that the execution of each resume in $\mathcal{P}_1$ can result in the enabling of the control point after any resume in $\mathcal{P}_2$ and vice versa (we return to this assumption shortly), satisfaction requires that we demonstrate (3.20) and

$$P_{2,j} \Rightarrow Q_{1,i} \tag{3.21}$$

for i and j ranging over all resume statements in $\mathcal{P}_1$ and $\mathcal{P}_2$, respectively. (3.20) and (3.21), together, are called the *satisfaction conditions*, since they demonstrate that the assumed postcondition of a resume statement in one coroutine is satisfied in any program state that can exist prior to the execution of a resume statement in the other coroutine.

As with the other control constructs, we define the formal semantics of the coroutine statement in terms of the formal semantics of its component coroutines. Each coroutine is described by a triple and the triples are related by satisfaction. We have the following rule of inference:

Coroutine Rule

$$\frac{\{R\}\ S_1\ \{T\},\ \{U\}\ S_2\ \{X\},\ satisfaction}{\{R\}\ \textbf{coroutine}\ \mathcal{P}_1\ ::\ S_1;\ \#\ \mathcal{P}_2\ ::\ S_2;\ \textbf{coend}\ \{T\}} \tag{3.22}$$

To understand the rule, we first note that, since control starts and ends in S_1, its pre- and postcondition must be identical to the pre- and postcondition of the coroutine statement as a whole. Second, the postcondition of S_2 is of no interest, since under normal circumstances, S_2 does not terminate (if S_2 terminates, the coroutine statement fails). Hence, we allow the proof of S_2 to yield an arbitrary postcondition. Finally, the satisfaction condition relates the pre- and postconditions of all resume statements in S_1 and S_2 [including the initial (dummy) resume statement in S_2].

Although coroutines are not concurrent, they do exhibit one characteristic of asynchronous programs: the execution of one coroutine (between a pair of resumes) might affect assertions made in the other. For example, suppose the assertion $x = 1$ is a precondition of a resume statement, $\rho_{1,i}$, in $\mathcal{P}_1$, and suppose x is incremented in $\mathcal{P}_2$ after $\rho_{1,i}$ is executed but before control is returned to $\mathcal{P}_1$. Then, when the control point following $\rho_{1,i}$ is enabled, the assertion $x = 1$ will be false. Hence, the assertion $x = 1$ is not invariant to the execution of $\rho_{1,i}$. The Resume Axiom accommodates this possibility by allowing the choice of an arbitrary postcondition for $\rho_{1,i}$ (in this case the postcondition might contain the assertion $x = 2$). A similar situation occurs with asynchronous programs, but there the reasoning becomes more complex, since we do not know in advance how process execution will be interleaved. With coroutines, interleaving is specified by the placement of resume statements.

We are often interested in identifying assertions that can be conjuncts of both the pre- and postconditions of some particular resume – that is, assertions that are invariant to the execution of that resume. As a simple example, even though $\mathcal{P}_1$ and $\mathcal{P}_2$ share a common global environment, they might be performing different subtasks and hence each might have a set of local variables associated with it to which the other does not refer. We can therefore expect that, if the precondition of $\rho_{1,i}$ implies an assertion, $C_{1,i}$, involving only $\mathcal{P}_1$'s local variables, $C_{1,i}$ will also be a postcondition of $\rho_{1,i}$ (since $\mathcal{P}_2$ does not even reference variables in the set). The restriction that the variables involved in $C_{1,i}$ are not accessed in $\mathcal{P}_2$ is too strong. $C_{1,i}$ might involve variables that $\mathcal{P}_2$ references but does not modify, and still be invariant to the execution of $\rho_{1,i}$. We can even go one step further. Suppose $C_{1,i}$ involves variables that $\mathcal{P}_2$ modifies. Suppose further that s_2 denotes a sequence of statements in $\mathcal{P}_2$ that can be executed between a pair of successively executed resume statements in $\mathcal{P}_2$, and let $Q_{2,j}$ be the precondition of s_2 (i.e., the postcondition of the immediately preceding resume statement). If the precondition of $\rho_{1,i}$, $P_{1,i}$, satisfies $P_{1,i} \Rightarrow C_{1,i}$ and

$$\{C_{1,i} \wedge Q_{2,j}\} \; s_2 \; \{C_{1,i}\} \tag{3.23}$$

is true for all s_2 in $\mathcal{P}_2$, then even though the execution of s_2 may update variables in $C_{1,i}$, its execution leaves $C_{1,i}$ invariant. (3.23) uses the fact that $Q_{2,j}$ is true on entry to s_2 and asserts that $C_{1,i}$ is invariant to the execution of s_2 under that precondition. Conditions such as (3.23) are referred to as *non-interference* conditions, because they assert that the execution of statements in one coroutine (or, as we shall see in the next chapter, in one process) do not interfere with assertions used in the proof of another. If (3.23) is true for all s_2 in $\mathcal{P}_2$, we say that $C_{1,i}$ is not interfered with. For example, if $C_{1,i}$ asserts $x > 0$ and the only update to x in any s_2 is an increment, then (3.23) is true.

We can now state the satisfaction conditions in a more general form. Although the satisfaction conditions (3.20) and (3.21) can be used within the Coroutine Rule, if we can find a set of assertions ($C_{1,i}$ and $C_{2,j}$) that are not interfered with, we can use those assertions to state a weaker form of the satisfaction proof requirement.

Satisfaction Condition for Resume Statements

In the proof of $\mathcal{P}_1$, let $\rho_{1,i}$ be annotated

$$\{P_{1,i}\} \; \textbf{resume} \; \mathcal{P}_2 \; \{Q_{1,i}\}$$

and in the proof of $\mathcal{P}_2$, let $\rho_{2,j}$ be annotated

$$\{P_{2,j}\} \; \textbf{resume} \; \mathcal{P}_1 \; \{Q_{2,j}\}$$

Furthermore, let $C_{1,i}$ and $C_{2,j}$ satisfy $P_{1,i} \Rightarrow C_{1,i}$, and $P_{2,j} \Rightarrow C_{2,j}$, where $C_{1,i}$ and $C_{2,j}$ are not interfered with. Then for i and j ranging over all resume statements in $\mathcal{P}_1$ and $\mathcal{P}_2$, respectively, prove

$$(P_{1,i} \wedge C_{2,j}) \Rightarrow Q_{2,j} \tag{3.24}$$

$$(P_{2,j} \wedge C_{1,i}) \Rightarrow Q_{1,i}$$

(3.24) states that when control is transferred from $\rho_{1,i}$ to $\rho_{2,j}$, not only is $P_{1,i}$ true, but any assertion, $C_{2,j}$, that is invariant to the execution of $\rho_{2,j}$ is true as well. The conjunction of these two assertions must imply $Q_{2,j}$. $C_{2,j}$ might assert something about the state of $\mathcal{P}_2$'s computation that is independent of the computation being carried out by $\mathcal{P}_1$ and hence does not form a part of the annotation of $\mathcal{P}_1$. To demonstrate that $C_{2,j}$ is still true when $\mathcal{P}_2$ resumes (as part of the continuity of reasoning about $\mathcal{P}_2$), we must show that $C_{2,j}$ is not interfered with.

Suppose we can find assertions $P_{1,i}$ and $C_{2,j}$ satisfying

$$(P_{1,i} \wedge C_{2,j}) \Rightarrow false \tag{3.25}$$

(3.25) implies that (3.24) is trivially true but, more interestingly, it implies that it is not possible to have the control point following $\rho_{2,j}$ be the next to be enabled in $\mathcal{P}_2$ when the control point preceding $\rho_{1,i}$ is enabled in $\mathcal{P}_1$. In other words it implies that the coroutine statement is so structured that it is impossible for $\rho_{1,i}$ to transfer control to $\rho_{2,j}$. Thus assertions such as (3.25) can be used to reason about the flow of control between the components of the coroutine statement. We return to this point in the next chapter when we introduce the technique of auxiliary variables, which can be used to develop assertions of the form of (3.25).

Example

As a simple example, consider the two coroutines shown in Figure 3.9. The variable x is shared, while y is local to $\mathcal{P}_2$. The given annotation meets the general satisfaction conditions. For example, the satisfaction condition corresponding to the transfer of control between the resume in $\mathcal{P}_1$, $\rho_{1,1}$, and the dummy resume at the beginning of $\mathcal{P}_2$ is

$$((x = 1) \wedge (y = 0)) \Rightarrow ((x = 1) \wedge (y = 0))$$

To show that $\rho_{1,1}$ cannot transfer control to the (actual) resume in $\mathcal{P}_2$, $\rho_{2,1}$, we note that (1) the precondition, $P_{1,1}$, of $\rho_{1,1}$ contains the conjunct $y = 0$ and (2) the assertion $C_{2,1} : y = 1$, which is a precondition to $\rho_{2,1}$, is not interfered with. Thus we have

$$(P_{1,1} \wedge C_{2,1}) \Rightarrow false$$

which implies that $\rho_{1,1}$ cannot transfer control to $\rho_{2,1}$.

Example

The program of Figure 1.2 has two coroutines, *Cp* and *Iop*, each of which has two resume statements. Since *Iop* does not check *busy* prior to initiating a read, we must demonstrate that $\neg busy$ is true whenever control is passed to *Iop*. But this follows easily, since $\neg busy$ is a precondition of each resume in *Cp*.

var
    x : *integer*;
    y : *integer* := 0;
coroutine
$\mathcal{P}_1$::
    begin
        $\{y = 0\}$
        $x := 1;$
        $\{(x = 1) \wedge (y = 0)\}$
        resume $\mathcal{P}_2$;
        $\{(x = 0) \wedge (y = 1)\}$
    end;
$\#$
$\mathcal{P}_2$::
    begin
        $\{(x = 1) \wedge (y = 0)\}$
        $x, y := 0, 1;$
        $\{(x = 0) \wedge (y = 1)\}$
        resume $\mathcal{P}_1$;
        $\{y = 1\}$
    end;
coend;
        $\{(x = 0) \wedge (y = 1)\}$

Figure 3.9: An example of satisfaction between two coroutines.

We must also demonstrate that $count < N$ is true whenever control is passed to *Iop*, since otherwise either the invariant $count \leq N$ will be violated or *read* will be called with a full buffer. We must prove that $count < N$ is a precondition of each resume in *Cp*. The proof is obvious for the resume in *releasebuf*, since *count* is decremented in *releasebuf* prior to execution of that resume. The formal proof for the resume in *getbuf* requires the use of auxiliary variables and is not included here. Intuitively we note that *getbuf* is called either at the beginning of the program, at which point $count = 0$, or right after a return from *releasebuf*. A call to *releasebuf* indicates that a particular buffer, $buf[i]$, has been emptied and therefore *releasebuf* decrements *count* (hence ensuring that it is less than N). If the channel is idle, *releasebuf* resumes *Iop* before returning. Although *Iop* might initiate I/O into $buf[i]$ at this time, it will not make an increment to *count* corresponding to the filling of $buf[i]$ until it is resumed at a later time and finds that $buf[i]$ is full. Hence, $count < N$ is true when *Iop* executes resume (and control returns to *releasebuf*), when *releasebuf* itself returns, and hence on the subsequent call to *getbuf*. Thus we have shown that *count* < *N* is a precondition to every invocation of *getbuf*. The resume in *getbuf* might be executed 0 or more times during a particular invocation. It follows from the previous reasoning that *count* < *N* must be true prior to the first execution. Furthermore, *count* = 0 is true prior to any subsequent execution. Hence, *count* < *N* is a precondition of the resume in *getbuf*.

Note that the variable *first* is local to *Cp*, and hence any assertion involving *first* that is a precondition to a resume statement in *Cp* is not interfered with by *Iop*. Similarly, an assertion involving *last* that is a precondition to a resume statement in *Iop* is not interfered with by *Cp*.

3.4   Coroutines in Modula-2*

The language Modula-2[2] is an outgrowth of Modula and Pascal. All were designed by Niklaus Wirth, whose intention was to produce languages that would encourage the development of well structured programs. While Pascal is a general purpose language, both Modula and Modula-2 were conceived as languages for implementing systems programs. Modula-2 has gradually replaced Modula for this purpose, so we discuss only Modula-2.

The major distinction between Modula-2 and Pascal is the introduction of the module concept, which is a departure from the normal nested scope rules for controlling variable visibility. A *module* is a construct within which variables can be declared and selectively exported for external use. A module can be decomposed into two parts: a definition module and an implementation module. A definition module, *M*, contains the list of exported objects. It makes available to other modules the information they need (*e.g.,* identifiers, procedure headings) to make use of the exported items. An implementation module contains a full elaboration of all objects in the module, whether or not they are exported. Since the exporting of variables and procedure names is under program control, the module facilitates the construction of abstract objects. The definition module contains information about the abstract specification, and the implementation module implements that specification. For example, concrete variables and concrete procedure bodies can be hidden within the implementation module.

Our interest in Modula-2 stems not from the module concept, but from features relevant to systems development – in particular, coroutines. While the facility for creating coroutines in a Modula-2 program is different from the coroutine statement described in the previous section, the facility for transferring control between coroutines is quite similar to the resume statement.

Since Modula-2 gives the programmer control over the structure of the overall program, the creation of a new coroutine involves a specification of its workspace as well as the code to be executed. A workspace is an area in which

---

[2]Our discussion of Modula-2 in this section follows the description of the language contained in [138].

the coroutine's local variables and state-related information are stored. Hence, the manipulation of coroutines involves storage management and utilizes features not normally included in a high level language. To keep the language relatively device independent, such low level features are not included in the language itself, but instead are made available as abstractions exported from modules generally included in a library.

Coroutines can be created at any point in the program using the procedure *NEWPROCESS*, exported from the module *SYSTEM*. The arguments provided in the call specify the coroutine's code and define its workspace, but the procedure does not transfer control to the newly created coroutine. The procedure *NEWPROCESS* is declared as follows:

$$PROCEDURE\ NEWPROCESS(p : PROC;\ a : ADDRESS;$$
$$n : CARDINAL;\ VAR\ co : PROCESS)$$

The coroutine's code is specified as the procedure *p*. The procedure type mechanism in Modula-2 is used to pass this procedure as an argument to *NEWPROCESS*. In general, the declaration of a procedure type specifies the number and type of all parameters and the type of the value returned, if any. Thus, the declaration

$$TYPE\ utility\ =\ PROCEDURE\ (REAL) : REAL$$

declares *utility* as a procedure type. Values of that type must be procedures that have a single parameter of type real and return a value of type real. If we subsequently declare a variable *specific* as

$$VAR\ specific : utility$$

then the assignment

$$specific := sin$$

assigns *sin* to *specific*, where *sin* is a procedure declared in the program with a specification matching that of the type. The invocation

$$x := specific(y)$$

actually invokes *sin*. Similarly, a value of type *utility* can be passed as an argument to a procedure that has a parameter of type *utility*.

A coroutine's code must be an instance of a parameterless procedure that does not return a value. The type *PROC*, which is predefined in the language, satisfies these requirements. *p* must be of type *PROC* and, in addition, must be declared at level 0 in the program, thus ensuring that the global environment of *p* is not deallocated until the entire program terminates.

The second and third parameters of *NEWPROCESS* describe the workspace of the coroutine: *a* is its starting address, and *n* is its size. Values of type *ADDRESS* are pointers to locations in memory. The object pointed at can be of any type. *ADDRESS* is considered a low level facility and is exported from the module *SYSTEM*. If *wsp* is the argument passed to the parameter *a*, *wsp* ↑ denotes the workspace itself. The routine that invokes *NEWPROCESS* must explicitly allocate storage for the workspace (by calling an appropriate library module) before making the call. Modula-2 does no automatic deallocation of space.

NEWPROCESS assigns a value to the variable *co*, which is a reference to the newly created coroutine. *co* is of type *PROCESS*, which is exported from the module *SYSTEM*. (*PROCESS* is an unfortunate choice of words: *COROUTINE* would have been better.) A coroutine reference is used when control is passed between coroutines to store information about the routine whose execution is being suspended and to obtain information about the routine being resumed.

NEWPROCESS simply creates the new coroutine; it does not transfer control to it. The analog of the resume statement in Modula-2 is the procedure *TRANSFER*, which is also exported from *SYSTEM* and is declared as

$$PROCEDURE \ \ TRANSFER(VAR \ old, \ new \ : \ PROCESS)$$

TRANSFER obtains the reference to the coroutine to be resumed from the variable *new*, puts the reference to the coroutine to be suspended in *old*, and resumes the coroutine referred to by *new*.

Hence, if P_1 executes *TRANSFER(source, destination)* with the value of *destination* being a reference to coroutine P_2, *TRANSFER* will transfer control to P_2 at the statement following its last call to *TRANSFER* (or at the first statement of the procedure body from which P_2 was formed if it has not yet executed), and the new value of *source* will be a reference to P_1. If, at a later time, P_2 decides to resume P_1, it executes *TRANSFER(x, source)*, and P_1 will be resumed at the statement following its last call to *TRANSFER*. *x* can be any variable of type *PROCESS* – the reference to P_2 need not always be stored in *destination*.

Using these facilities, a Modula-2 program can dynamically create an arbitrary number of coroutines (subject to the limitation of storage for workspaces). By contrast, in the coroutine statement described in the previous section, the number of coroutines created on entry to the statement is fixed at design time. The formal semantics of transferring control between coroutines is similar, however: the postcondition of an invocation of *TRANSFER* must be implied by the precondition of the invocation of *TRANSFER* that passed control to it [perhaps conjoined with an invariant assertion as in (3.24)].

The semantics chosen for the coroutine statement specifies that the normal exit through coend occurs when P_1 terminates; hence the postcondition of the coroutine statement is the postcondition of P_1. The statement fails if any other coroutine terminates. Modula-2 has no analog to coend and hence the entire program is similar to a single coroutine statement. A Modula-2 program terminates when any one of its coroutines terminates. Hence, the postcondition of the program is the postcondition of the coroutine that terminates, a slightly more general situation than we considered in the previous section.

3.4.1   Interrupt Handling*

To complete our discussion, we show how the coroutine mechanism in Modula-2 can be enhanced to implement interrupt handling. A language that provides for interrupt handling can be used to program a bare machine. Interrupt handling features would not generally be provided in a language used to implement applications that interface to an existing operating system.

In the Modula-2 implementation for the PDP-11, interrupt handlers can be built as coroutines, and the language provides a special version of *TRANSFER*, called *IOTRANSFER*, that can be used by interrupt handling coroutines. *IOTRANSFER* is declared as

PROCEDURE IOTRANSFER(VAR h, u : PROCESS; int : CARDINAL)

where *int* is the address associated with the interrupt handled by the calling coroutine. The operational semantics of the invocation

IOTRANSFER(handler, user, intadr)

is as follows:

The coroutine whose reference is stored in *user* is resumed using the same semantics as

TRANSFER(handler, user)

If subsequently an interrupt corresponding to the address *intadr* occurs, the effect is as if the statement

TRANSFER(user, handler)

were executed in the interrupted coroutine at the time of interrupt.

Normally, control is passed by a coroutine requesting I/O service, $\mathcal{P}_{user}$, to the interrupt handling coroutine, $\mathcal{P}_{handler}$, with the call

TRANSFER(user, handler)

where *handler* is a reference to $\mathcal{P}_{handler}$. After $\mathcal{P}_{handler}$ has initiated the requested service, it executes

IOTRANSFER(handler, user, intadr)

to relinquish control until the interrupt occurs. As a result, a reference to $\mathcal{P}_{handler}$ is stored in *handler*, and $\mathcal{P}_{user}$ is resumed through *user*. When an interrupt at location *intadr* subsequently occurs (indicating the completion of the requested service), $\mathcal{P}_{handler}$ is resumed, and a reference to the interrupted coroutine is stored in *user*. Note that the interrupted coroutine need not be $\mathcal{P}_{user}$; some other coroutine, $\mathcal{P}'$, may have taken control. This simulated call to *TRANSFER* could not actually be programmed into $\mathcal{P}'$, since the interrupt occurs asynchronously. When $\mathcal{P}_{handler}$ has completed processing the interrupt, it can return control to $\mathcal{P}'$ either with the call

$$IOTRANSFER(handler,\ user,\ intadr)$$

if it has initiated a new request for service and hence is expecting another interrupt or with the call

$$TRANSFER(handler,\ user)$$

if not.

The introduction of *IOTRANSFER* complicates the formal semantics of the language. Assume for simplicity that the program contains only the two coroutines $\mathcal{P}_{user}$ and $\mathcal{P}_{handler}$. Since invocation of either *TRANSFER* or *IOTRANSFER* by $\mathcal{P}_{handler}$ causes the resumption of $\mathcal{P}_{user}$, the satisfaction condition must relate the preconditions of both to the postcondition of any call to *TRANSFER* in $\mathcal{P}_{user}$. In this respect the semantics of *TRANSFER* and *IOTRANSFER* are the same. However, the resumption of $\mathcal{P}_{handler}$, after it has relinquished control by invoking *IOTRANSFER* and an interrupt has subsequently occurred, is not the result of an actual call to *TRANSFER* by $\mathcal{P}_{user}$. Hence, the postcondition of *IOTRANSFER* in $\mathcal{P}_{handler}$ will not be the same as it would be if $\mathcal{P}_{handler}$ had relinquished control by invoking *TRANSFER*. In fact, since the interrupt occurs asynchronously with respect to $\mathcal{P}_{user}$, we cannot identify a unique point in the execution of $\mathcal{P}_{user}$ at which the transfer will occur and hence a unique precondition that will be carried over as the postcondition of *IOTRANSFER*. To make matters even more complicated, the operational semantics associated with interrupts does not correspond to the Rule of Composition. If an interrupt occurs between two statements, $s_{user,j}$ and $s_{user,j+1}$, in $\mathcal{P}_{user}$, we cannot guarantee that the postcondition of the first statement, which is true when the interrupt occurs, will still be true when we are about to execute the second statement, since the execution of statements in $\mathcal{P}_{handler}$ has been interleaved between the two and the state may have been changed as a result. These complications are a direct result of the asynchronous nature of the interrupt. By managing asynchronous hardware using *IOTRANSFER* in a coroutine, we cause the coroutine statement to become concurrent, since two enabled control points can exist: one in $\mathcal{P}_{user}$ at $s_{user,j+1}$ and one following the call to *IOTRANSFER* in $\mathcal{P}_{handler}$. Priority is given to the latter. The program is asynchronous, since given the identity of the enabled control point in $\mathcal{P}_{handler}$, we cannot infer the identity of the enabled control point in $\mathcal{P}_{user}$. We return to exactly this situation when we discuss concurrency in the next chapter.

In Chapter 1 we discussed the relationship between such issues as shared variables, mutual exclusion, and interrupts. Restated in the current context, if $\mathcal{P}_{handler}$ is allowed to share variables with $\mathcal{P}_{user}$, mutual exclusion of critical sections cannot be guaranteed. An interrupt occurring while $\mathcal{P}_{user}$ is in a critical section will cause a transfer to $\mathcal{P}_{handler}$, which might then enter its critical section – thus violating mutual exclusion. One approach to guaranteeing mutual exclusion in this situation is to provide a mechanism in the language for disabling interrupts while a coroutine is in a critical section. Since shared variables and the corresponding critical sections can be encapsulated within modules, it is convenient to associate the disabling mechanism with the module. Thus an interrupt priority level, i, can be associated with a module, and all code within the module is then executed with interrupts at level i and lower disabled.

3.5   Bibliographic Notes

The treatment of procedures follows the development in Hoare [67]. A more comprehensive treatment of the subject is contained in Gries and Levin [59]. Our discussion of proof techniques for abstract data types is based on the work of Hoare [68]. Other relevant material on the subject can be found in Wulf, London, and Shaw [139] and Wulf, Shaw, Hilfinger, and Flon [140]. A discussion of proof techniques for coroutines is contained in Clarke [32]. Wirth's book on Modula-2 [138] served as the basis of our description of the language.

3.6   Exercises

In the following exercises, the word "prove" means that formal reasoning is to be used to produce an annotated program, while the word "demonstrate" means that a convincing argument is sufficient.

1. Consider the procedure *swap* with declaration

> **procedure** $swap(c1, c2 :$ **in out** $ctype)$;
> **begin**
> $c1, c2 := c2, c1$;
> **end** $swap$;

Use the assignment semantics given for *swap* in Section 3.1 to prove that $(x = 2) \land (y = 1) \land (z = 3)$ is a postcondition of the following program:

> $x, y, z := 1, 2, 3$;
> $swap(x, y)$;

2. Demonstrate that the following statement terminates. Prove that after termination $x1$, $x2$, $x3$, and $x4$ will be in sorted order. Use the assignment semantics given for *swap* in Section 3.1.

$$\textbf{do}\ x1 > x2 \rightarrow swap(x1, x2);$$
$$[]\ x2 > x3 \rightarrow swap(x2, x3);$$
$$[]\ x3 > x4 \rightarrow swap(x3, x4);$$
$$\textbf{od};$$

3. Prove that the following procedure has assignment semantics. Give an axiom schema that describes its invocation.

$$\textbf{procedure}\ max(a1, a2 : \textbf{in}\ atype;\ b : \textbf{out}\ btype);$$
$$\textbf{begin}$$
$$\quad \textbf{if}\ a1 \geq a2 \rightarrow b := a1;$$
$$\quad []\ a2 \geq a1 \rightarrow b := a2;$$
$$\quad \textbf{fi};$$
$$\textbf{end}\ max;$$

4. Demonstrate that the following procedure does not have assignment semantics:

$$\textbf{procedure}\ p(a : \textbf{in}\ atype;\ b : \textbf{out}\ btype);$$
$$\textbf{begin}$$
$$\quad \textbf{if}\ a \geq 0 \rightarrow b := 1;$$
$$\quad []\ a \leq 0 \rightarrow b := 0;$$
$$\quad \textbf{fi};$$
$$\textbf{end}\ max;$$

5. Give examples of three different ways in which a procedure body might not have assignment semantics.

6. Suppose the parameter passing mechanism for a procedure call is call by reference instead of value/result. How does that affect the discussion on assignment semantics?

7. Suppose that code fragment S can be characterized by the following triple:

$$\{x = A\}\ S\ \{x = f(A)\}$$

where A is a logical variable, f is a function, and S modifies only x. S is to be used as the body of a macro, which can be substituted in line at various places in a program. x is not a parameter of the macro but is a variable that is visible at the point where the macro is substituted. State an inference rule that can be used to reason about such macros.

8. Using the operations of the queue abstract data type, construct a program that takes as input two sorted queues of integers, Q_1 and Q_2, and an empty queue, Q_3, and transfers the elements of Q_1 and Q_2 to Q_3 in such a way that Q_3 contains all the elements that were in Q_1 and Q_2 in sorted order and Q_1 and Q_2 are empty. (Q_3 is a merge of Q_1 and Q_2.) Prove that the elements of Q_3 are in sorted order.

9. Define an abstract data type for a bounded natural number (a non-negative integer) less than or equal to N with initial value 0. The data type has two operations: $Add1$, which adds 1 to the natural number and $Subt2$, which subtracts 2 from the natural number. Provide implementations for both operations and prove that they support the abstract specification.

10. Modify the requirements of the previous exercise so that the data type supports two operations: $Add(n)$, which adds n to the natural number, and $Subt(m)$, which subtracts m from the natural number (both n and m are natural numbers). Provide implementations for both operations and prove that they support the abstract specification.

11. The queue abstract data type given in the text is to be augmented with the procedures

> **procedure** $Full(b :$ **out** $boolean)$

and

> **procedure** $Empty(b :$ **out** $boolean)$

On return, b is true if and only if the queue is full or empty, respectively. Give abstract triples for each procedure (using the specification of Figure 3.2). Expand the concrete implementation of queues given in the text to include an implementation of each procedure, and prove the realization is correct.

12. Prove that the concrete implementation of the data type queue given in Figure 3.6 satisfies the specification given in Figure 3.5.

13. Define an abstract data type for a bounded stack of nonnegative integers. Assume procedures $Push$ and Pop that perform the usual stack operations. If the stack is empty, Pop returns -1, but does not decrement the stack pointer. If the stack is full, $Push$ halts. The specification should indicate that initial versions of a stack are empty. Define an abstract invariant for the data type and abstract triples for the procedures. Design a concrete implementation for the stack, and prove that the implementation is correct. Specify the representation mapping used in your proof.

14. A deque is a data structure that is similar to a queue except that elements can be added or removed from either end. Design an abstract data type for a bounded deque of integers that contains four procedures: *InsertFront*, *InsertBack*, *RemoveFront*, and *RemoveBack*. The specification should indicate that initial versions of a deque are empty. Design a concrete implementation for the bounded deque and prove it is correct. Specify the representation mapping used in your proof.

15. In the following program, coroutine $\mathcal{P}_1$ produces tokens from an input stream by calling the function *get_next_token*, and coroutine $\mathcal{P}_2$ analyzes the token stream using the routine *process_token*. Assuming that P asserts "the value of T is an unprocessed token," annotate each control point in the following coroutine statement using P, and indicate the satisfaction conditions that must be demonstrated.

```
var
    T : token;
coroutine
P₁ ::
    do true →
        begin
            T := get_next_token();
            resume P₂;
        end;
    od;
#
P₂ ::
    do true →
        begin
            process_token(T);
            resume P₁;
        end;
    od;
coend;
```

16. Define an abstract data type for a set of nonnegative integers. The set has two operations

procedure *insert*(x : **in** *integer*)

and

procedure *delete*(x : **out** *integer*)

The procedure *insert* adds the element x to the set; if the set already contains x, then *insert* has no effect. The procedure *delete* deletes an arbitrary element in the set and returns its value, or returns -1 if the set is empty. The specification should indicate that initial versions of a set are empty. Design a concrete implementation for the data type (including implementations for both operations), and prove that it supports the abstract specification. Specify the representation mapping used in your proof.

17. In the Operational Model with Logical Variables a valid triple involving a logical variable maps to T for all values of the logical variable. Use this fact to specify an inference rule that specializes a triple involving a logical variable, X, to one in which the logical variable is replaced by a specific value, x_0. Now consider a code fragment, S, which is described by the triple

$$\{x = X\}\ S\ \{x = 2X\}$$

where X is a logical variable. S is embedded in the program fragment

$$x := 1;$$
$$S;$$
$$x := x + 1;$$

Use your rule to prove that $x = 3$ is a postcondition of this fragment.

18. The following coroutine statement scans an array, a, containing N elements and replaces each element, $a[i]$, for which $p(a[i])$ is true with $f(a[i])$, where p is a predicate and f is a function. Assume the computation s in $\mathcal{P}_2$ is described by the triple

$$\{p(x)\}\ s\ \{y = f(x)\}$$

Thus coroutine $\mathcal{P}_1$ checks whether the predicate p is true for each array element, and coroutine $\mathcal{P}_2$ performs the function f on those elements for which it is true. Note that s is not guaranteed to work correctly when p is false. Show that the coroutine statement satisfies the triple

$$\{((\forall i)(1 \le i \le N) \Rightarrow (a[i] = A[i]))\}\ \textbf{coroutine} \cdots \textbf{coend}$$
$$\{((\forall i)(1 \le i \le N) \Rightarrow$$
$$((p(A[i]) \Rightarrow (a[i] = f(A[i])) \land (\neg p(A[i]) \Rightarrow (a[i] = A[i]))))\}$$

where A is an array of logical variables. Show that the program terminates.

```
coroutine
𝒫₁ ::   ⋯
  begin
    i := 1;
    do i ≤ N →
      begin
        if p(a[i]) →
          begin
            x := a[i];
            resume 𝒫₂;
            a[i] := y;
          end;
          [] ¬p(a[i]) → skip;
        fi;
        i := i + 1;
      end;
    od;
  end;
#
𝒫₂ ::
  do true →
    begin
      s;
      resume 𝒫₁;
    end;
  od;
coend;
```

4

Shared Memory Concurrent Programs

In this chapter we begin our discussion of concurrent programming systems. We develop axiomatic techniques for reasoning about concurrent programs that use shared memory. Once again, our interest in formal methods is not specifically with producing detailed proofs of programs. Rather, we use the axiomatic approach to obtain a precise specification of the constructs used in building concurrent systems and a rigorous exposition of the issues involved in designing them.

The intermittent synchronization of the asynchronous components of a concurrent system is the central issue. We show how the axiomatic approach provides the basis for determining when components should be synchronized. A typical form of synchronization is one in which asynchronous computations are made to run atomically with respect to one another. In Chapters 2 and 3 we discussed atomicity in the context of the execution of individual statements in a programming language. In this chapter we extend the notion of atomicity to arbitrary computations.

4.1 Axiomatization of Concurrency

As described in Chapter 1, we use as our concurrency construct the cobegin statement.

$$\textbf{cobegin } \mathcal{P}_1 :: \ S_1; \ /\!/ \ \mathcal{P}_2 :: \ S_2; \ /\!/ \ldots /\!/ \ \mathcal{P}_n :: \ S_n; \ \textbf{coend}$$

Each S_i is a statement and can have a label, $\mathcal{P}_i$. We frequently use the label to name the process that executes the statement. The operational semantics of the cobegin statement is as follows:

When control reaches the cobegin statement, control points are enabled at each of the component statements, $S_1, S_2, \ldots, S_n$ (hence, the component statements execute concurrently); after all have completed, the construct is exited and a single control point is enabled at the statement following the coend. The cobegin statement fails if any of its component statements fail.

Note that we make no assumptions concerning the hardware on which the cobegin statement is executing. The processes could be executing on a uniprocessor system,, a multiprocessor system, or a distributed computer system.

As with the other control constructs, we define the formal semantics of the cobegin statement in terms of the formal semantics of its component statements. First we analyze each component statement, S_i, in isolation and summarize its semantics with a triple $\{P_i\}\, S_i\, \{Q_i\}$. Then we combine these triples to make assertions about the concurrent statement as a whole. Using this approach, we describe the semantics of the cobegin statement with an inference rule of the form

$$\frac{\{P_1\}\, S_1\, \{Q_1\}, \ldots, \{P_n\}\, S_n\, \{Q_n\},\ \textit{additional requirements}}{\{P_1 \wedge \cdots \wedge P_n\}\ \textbf{cobegin}\ S_1;\ /\!/\ldots/\!/\ S_n;\ \textbf{coend}\ \{Q_1 \wedge \cdots \wedge Q_n\}} \qquad (4.1)$$

When the cobegin statement is initiated, an enabled control point is created at each of the component statements. Hence, it is reasonable for the precondition of the cobegin statement to be the conjunction of the preconditions of all the component statements. Similarly when the cobegin statement terminates, all the component statements have terminated; hence it is reasonable for the postcondition of the cobegin statement to be the conjunction of the postconditions of all the component statements. However, these pre- and postconditions do not completely describe the semantics of the construct. As we saw informally in Chapter 1, when concurrent statements share memory, interactions can occur that affect the operation of the overall program. Such interactions are dealt with in (4.1) under the heading of *additional requirements*. A large part of this and later chapters is devoted to characterizing these requirements and their effect on the semantics of the construct.

The component statements might be sequential programs or might themselves contain nested cobegin statements, in which case the rule of inference can be applied recursively. Consider the simple case in which each S_i is a sequential program: $s_{i,1}; s_{i,2}; \ldots; s_{i,m_i}$. By treating each S_i as an isolated program, we can derive the triple $\{P_i\}\, S_i\, \{Q_i\}$ from the triples $\{p_{i,j}\}\, s_{i,j}\, \{q_{i,j}\}$, using the techniques described in Chapters 2 and 3, where $q_{i,j} \Rightarrow p_{i,j+1}$ for all $1 \le j < m_i$, $P_i = p_{i,1}$, and $Q_i = q_{i,m_i}$.

The triples $\{p_{i,j}\}\, s_{i,j}\, \{q_{i,j}\}$ are valid if, whenever $s_{i,j}$ is executed starting in some state satisfying $p_{i,j}$, it either does not terminate or terminates in some state satisfying $q_{i,j}$. The fact that the theorem $\{P_i\}\, S_i\, \{Q_i\}$ actually describes the effect of executing S_i is based on the assumption that in the operational model the state of the system is modified only by the execution of the $s_{i,j}$. While this assumption is reasonable during the first stage of the analysis when we are examining each S_i in isolation, it is not true when we analyze the concurrent program formed by the cobegin statement as a whole.

Entry to the cobegin statement enables control points at all of the S_i and allows them to be executed in an arbitrarily interleaved fashion. Hence, although the execution of $s_{i,j}$ in isolation establishes the precondition of $s_{i,j+1}$, when concurrency is present, the execution of $s_{i,j}$ and $s_{i,j+1}$ might be separated by the execution of statements $s_{k,l}$, $k \neq i$, in other components of the cobegin. Therefore, the state produced by $s_{i,j}$ might have been modified before $s_{i,j+1}$ is initiated and $p_{i,j+1}$ might no longer be true. As a result, the operational model introduced in Chapter 2 and used to map triples in Program Logic might no longer reflect the effect of execution in the presence of concurrency, since without some restrictions, its inference rules are no longer sound.

For example, the Rule of Composition does not necessarily reflect program execution, since we cannot assume that the postcondition of the first statement is still true when the second is initiated. More precisely, at the instant the control point preceding the second statement is enabled, the assertion corresponding to the postcondition of the first statement is true; but before that control point is serviced, some other statement in a concurrent component of the cobegin statement might execute and cause that assertion to become false. A similar situation exists for the If Rule. Let $G \rightarrow S$ be a component of an if statement in S_i. Although $P \wedge G$ might be true at the instant the control point preceding S is enabled, before that control point is serviced and hence before the execution of S, the state might be changed by a concurrent component of the cobegin to one in which G is false. Note that in both of these cases the trouble arises when S_i and the concurrent component statements share variables – in particular, when a concurrent component statement modifies a variable that appears in an assertion in the proof of S_i. We are faced, in a formal way, with the shared variable problem first discussed in Chapter 1.

Our plan for reasoning about a cobegin statement is to first reason about each component statement as a sequential program. Then, to ensure that the operational model for sequential programs accurately describes concurrent execution within a cobegin, we impose the *additional requirements* alluded to in (4.1). The purpose of these requirements is to ensure that the assertions in the proof of any one component statement cannot be invalidated by the execution of statements in another. Suppose $p_{i,j}$ is an assertion in the proof of S_i. We want to prove that the execution of some other component statement, $s_{k,l}$, $k \neq i$, does not invalidate $p_{i,j}$. Since $s_{k,l}$ is executed in a state in which its precondition is true, we must demonstrate that

$$\{p_{i,j} \wedge p_{k,l}\} \, s_{k,l} \, \{p_{i,j}\} \tag{4.2}$$

Thus, if $p_{i,j}$ is true before the execution of $s_{k,l}$, it will also be true afterwards. From the point of view of program execution, $p_{i,j}$ remains true even if $s_{k,l}$ is interleaved between the execution of $s_{i,j-1}$ and $s_{i,j}$.

It should be clear[1] that the interleaving of $s_{k,l}$ between the execution of $s_{i,j-1}$ and $s_{i,j}$ is analogous to the interleaved execution of one coroutine at the point where another executes a resume statement. The difference between these two situations is that with the cobegin the interleaving is implicit and nondeterministic, whereas with coroutines the interleaving is explicitly specified in the program and hence deterministic. The issue of interference is, however, quite similar. The notion of non-interference, as expressed by (3.23), is analogous to (4.2). An assertion in one coroutine (process) is invariant to the interleaved execution of statements in another coroutine (process). Since interleaving of coroutines only occurs at resume statements, these are the only assertions that can possibly suffer interference.

If (4.2) is not a theorem, we say that $s_{k,l}$ *interferes* with the proof of S_i. Note that $s_{k,l}$ may access, and even change, variables named in $p_{i,j}$, but interference does not occur if (4.2) is a theorem.

The precondition of the triple in (4.2) is the conjunction of the assertion that might be interfered with and the precondition of the potentially interfering statement. In some situations, it might be impossible for the execution of $s_{k,l}$ to be interleaved between the execution of $s_{i,j-1}$ and $s_{i,j}$. The proof of non-interference in such cases consists of showing that the preconditions satisfy

$$(p_{i,j} \wedge p_{k,l}) = false \qquad (4.3)$$

Hence, (4.2) is valid, since its precondition is mapped to F in all states. (4.3) implies that control points at $s_{i,j}$ and $s_{k,l}$ cannot be simultaneously enabled[2].

Since interference might exist between any assertion and any concurrently executable statement, we must in general prove the following theorems.

Proof Obligations for Interference Freedom

$$\{p_{i,j} \wedge p_{k,l}\}\, s_{k,l}\, \{p_{i,j}\}, \quad 1 \le i, k \le n, \; i \ne k, \; 1 \le j \le m_i, \; 1 \le l \le m_k \qquad (4.4)$$

$$\{Q_i \wedge p_{k,l}\}\, s_{k,l}\, \{Q_i\}, \quad 1 \le i, k \le n, \; i \ne k, \; 1 \le l \le m_k \qquad (4.5)$$

Clearly, to cause interference, the statement $s_{k,l}$ must change the state of free variables in $p_{i,j}$. Hence, when testing to see whether or not interference occurs, we need consider only assignment statements. (Later we discuss the occurrence of assignments within procedures and await statements.) If each of the triples in (4.4) and (4.5) is a theorem, the proofs of each of the components of the cobegin are said to be *interference free* and the operational model is an accurate reflection of concurrent execution.

Using the idea of interference freedom, we can describe the formal semantics of the cobegin statement with the inference rule:

---

[1]This paragraph refers back to the discussion on coroutines in Section 3.3 and can be omitted if that section was skipped.

[2]Again this situation is analogous to a similar situation that can occur with coroutines.

Cobegin Rule

$$\frac{\{P_1\}\, S_1\, \{Q_1\}, \ldots, \{P_n\}\, S_n\, \{Q_n\},\ \textit{interference free}}{\{P_1 \wedge \cdots \wedge P_n\}\ \textbf{cobegin}\ S_1;\ /\!/ \ldots /\!/\ S_n;\ \textbf{coend}\ \{Q_1 \wedge \cdots \wedge Q_n\}} \tag{4.6}$$

Interference freedom is also involved in proofs of program invariance. The concept of a program invariant of a concurrent program carries over directly from the concept of a program invariant of a sequential program. I is a program invariant of a concurrent program if, assuming that I is true in the initial program state, it is true in every state reached (in all possible interleavings) during the execution of the program. To demonstrate that an assertion I is a program invariant of a concurrent program, we first show that it is a program invariant of each component program. We then show that the proofs of invariance for the component programs are not interfered with.

We have not precluded the possibility that an assertion, A, in one process, $\mathcal{P}_1$, can refer to some variable, x, that is declared in another process, $\mathcal{P}_2$, and is therefore not visible in $\mathcal{P}_1$. We shall see examples of this later. A must include the (perhaps implicit) conjunct $exist\_x$. Then, in demonstrating that A is not interfered with, we must show that the implicit assignments to $exist\_x$ on block entry and exit in $\mathcal{P}_2$ do not interfere with the conjunct $exist\_x$ of A.

Note that the details of our discussion of interference depend on our choice of which constructs are atomic. Since we can place assertions only before and after such constructs, these are the only places where interference can occur. It might seem more natural, for example, to say that interleaving occurs at the individual memory reference level (instead of at the level of complete expression or statement executions). Although the techniques discussed in this chapter are general enough to apply to such a fine granularity of interleaving, it would be necessary to express algorithms in a language in which each individual program action corresponded to a single memory reference. For simplicity we use the larger granularity defined in Chapter 2.

Example

Consider a banking database system that allows concurrent access by transactions. (We use the word "transaction" here in its informal sense. In Chapter 10 we give a formal definition of transactions.) Let transaction T_dep be a deposit transaction and T_cred be a transaction that checks the credit rating of a customer. T_cred returns the value $true$ if there is more than $1000 in the customer's account. T_dep and T_cred may be complex transactions, but we restrict our attention to the central statement in each. These statements, together with a partial annotation, are shown in Figure 4.1. The variable bal is the balance in the account and dep is the amount to be deposited. Note that in the annotation we have introduced a logical variable, B. As before, we assume that the annotation must be valid for all values of the logical variable.

T_dep ::

 . . .

$\{(bal = B) \wedge (dep > 0)\}$
$bal \; := \; bal + dep;$

$\{(bal = B + dep) \wedge (dep > 0)\}$
 . . .

(a)

T_cred ::

 . . .

$\{true\}$
if $(bal > 1000) \rightarrow$
 $credit \; := \; true;$
$[] \; \neg(bal > 1000) \rightarrow$
 $credit \; := \; false;$
fi;
 $\{credit \Rightarrow (bal > 1000)\}$
 . . .

(b)

Figure 4.1: Concurrent banking transactions: (a) T_dep, a deposit transaction, and (b) T_cred, a credit check transaction.

We first demonstrate that the annotation is valid when the transactions are considered in isolation. Reasoning backward from the postcondition, we find that the precondition of the assignment statement in T_dep follows from the Assignment Axiom. The justification for the precondition of the if statement begins with two instances of the Assignment Axiom

$$\{true \Rightarrow (bal > 1000)\} \; credit \; := \; true \; \{credit \Rightarrow (bal > 1000)\}$$

$$\{false \Rightarrow (bal > 1000)\} \; credit \; := \; false \; \{credit \Rightarrow (bal > 1000)\}$$

Simplifying, we get

$$\{bal > 1000\} \; credit \; := \; true \; \{credit \Rightarrow (bal > 1000)\}$$

$$\{true\} \; credit \; := \; false \; \{credit \Rightarrow (bal > 1000)\}$$

Since the first precondition is equivalent to $true \wedge (bal > 1000)$ and $true \wedge \neg(bal > 1000)$ implies the second, we can use the If Rule to demonstrate that $true$ is a precondition of the if statement. A completely annotated version of the program is shown in Figure 4.2.

We have demonstrated that the annotation of Figure 4.2 is valid when the transactions are considered in isolation. To use the Cobegin Rule to combine proofs, we must ensure that statements in one transaction do not interfere with assertions in the other. The only possibility for interference is through the shared variable bal, which is modified in T_dep and appears in assertions of T_cred. Thus we must show that the statement

$$bal \; := \; bal + dep$$

does not interfere with the assertions in T_cred that involve bal. Intuitively we can see that interference does not take place because the assignment can only increase the value of bal.

T_dep ::
    . . .
      $\{(bal = B) \wedge (dep > 0)\}$
      $bal := bal + dep;$

T_cred ::
    . . .
      $\{true\}$
    if $(bal > 1000) \rightarrow$
        $\{(bal > 1000)\}$
        $credit := true;$
        $\{credit \Rightarrow (bal > 1000)\}$
    $[] \neg(bal > 1000) \rightarrow$
        $\{true\}$
        $credit := false;$
        $\{credit \Rightarrow (bal > 1000)\}$
    fi;

$\{(bal = B + dep) \wedge (dep > 0)\}$
    . . .

      $\{credit \Rightarrow (bal > 1000)\}$
    . . .

(a)   (b)

Figure 4.2: Completely annotated versions of (a) T_dep, the deposit transaction, and (b) T_cred, the credit check transaction.

To formally prove that interference does not take place, consider, for example, the postcondition of T_cred. We must demonstrate that

$$\{(credit \Rightarrow (bal > 1000)) \wedge ((bal = B) \wedge (dep > 0))\}$$
$$bal := bal + dep \; \{credit \Rightarrow (bal > 1000)\}$$

From the Assignment Axiom we have

$$\{credit \Rightarrow ((bal + dep) > 1000)\} \; bal := bal + dep \; \{credit \Rightarrow (bal > 1000)\}$$

Since

$$((credit \Rightarrow (bal > 1000)) \wedge ((bal = B) \wedge (dep > 0))) \Rightarrow$$
$$(credit \Rightarrow ((bal + dep) > 1000)) \tag{4.7}$$

no interference occurs.

Note that if T_dep had been a withdrawal transaction, the assignment statement would have been

$$bal := bal - wdr$$

where $wdr > 0$, and it would not have been possible to prove an assertion of the form (4.7). Hence, the proofs of the two transactions would no longer be interference-free. (Intuitively, the credit check transaction might return true, even though the withdrawal transaction had reduced the balance below $1000.)

Note further that the specifications for the credit check transaction were designed by the bank, not the customer. The postcondition states that when the credit check transaction completes, if credit has been granted, the balance is greater than 1000; it does not say that if credit has not been granted, the balance is not greater than 1000. A program that never grants credit, no matter what the balance, satisfies the given specification. The given program for *T_cred* also satisfies the specifications and is a bit fairer to the customer. However, consider the scenario in which, when the guard is evaluated, the balance is less than 1000. The second alternative is selected, but before the statement *credit := false* is executed, a deposit transaction is performed and 1001 is deposited. Under this scenario, when *T_cred* completes, credit has not been granted despite the fact that the balance is greater than 1000. This scenario does not cause a violation of the postcondition of *T_cred*, and no interference has taken place (although the customer may not be too happy). If we try to make the credit check transaction fairer to the customer by making its postcondition

$$(credit \Rightarrow (bal > 1000)) \wedge (\neg credit \Rightarrow \neg(bal > 1000))$$

we find that interference exists and, correspondingly, the above scenario causes the postcondition to be violated.

4.2 Eliminating Interference

4.2.1 Weakening Assertions

Frequently a given program is correct, but we have difficulty making a formal proof because the initially chosen assertions are interfered with. In such cases, a common technique is to use a weaker set of assertions that still implies correct execution but does not cause interference. As a somewhat contrived example, consider two concurrent deposit transactions, in which the first deposits *dep*1 dollars and the second *dep*2 dollars, where *dep*1 ≠ *dep*2. Furthermore, for convenience, assume that *bal* is initially 0. Then the two deposit transaction are described by the triples

$$\{bal = 0\}\ bal := bal + dep1\ \{bal = dep1\}$$

$$\{bal = 0\}\ bal := bal + dep2\ \{bal = dep2\}$$

We have ignored the conjuncts *dep*1 > 0 and *dep*2 > 0, which do not affect the argument.

It is intuitively clear that concurrent execution of the two transactions works correctly, since we have assumed that assignments are carried out atomically and hence the two deposits will be correctly added to *bal*. However, it is also clear that interference occurs with the chosen assertions because execution of the first transaction interferes with the assertion $bal = 0$ in the triple of the second and vice versa.

To make a formal proof, we weaken the assertions. Suppose that the following weaker triple is used to describe the first deposit transaction:

$$\{(bal = 0) \lor (bal = dep2)\} \; bal := bal + dep1$$
$$\{(bal = dep1) \lor (bal = dep1 + dep2)\}$$

and a similar triple is used to describe the second transaction. Interference no longer occurs. For example, the following theorem, easily demonstrated using the Assignment Axiom, proves that the postcondition of the second deposit transaction is not interfered with by the execution of the first deposit transaction.

$$\{[(bal = 0) \lor (bal = dep2)] \land [(bal = dep2) \lor (bal = dep1 + dep2)]\}$$
$$bal := bal + dep1 \; \{(bal = dep2) \lor (bal = dep1 + dep2)\}$$

Furthermore, the conjunction of the new postconditions of the two deposit transactions implies $bal = dep1+dep2$ (since we have assumed that $dep1 \neq dep2$) and thus we have shown that bal is updated correctly. Although the example is artificial, it demonstrates the point that interference might be a problem of the proof and not the program, and that by using assertions that are only strong enough to yield the desired result, we may be able to eliminate interference.

4.2.2   Auxiliary Variables

To remove the artificiality of the previous section, we drop the assumption that the amounts deposited by each transaction are distinct. Suppose now that deposits can be made into a given account concurrently from several Automatic Teller Machines (ATMs). We refer to a deposit transaction run at the ith ATM as T_depi. Only one deposit transaction can be run at a time at a particular ATM, but several may be running concurrently at different ATMs. Again we can see that concurrent deposits perform correctly because the assignment statements execute atomically, but the assertion weakening approach we used in the previous section is no longer adequate to yield a proof. References to the value of bal in assertions of one transaction (for example, $bal = B+dep$) will be interfered with by assignments to bal in another. Hence, we once again appeal to a new proof technique – this time we use auxiliary variables.

By an *auxiliary variable* we mean a variable introduced into a program in a restricted way for the sole purpose of facilitating the proof process. Such variables are used in the proof, but are eliminated when the program is actually implemented. To ensure that auxiliary variables do not affect the flow of control or the values of actual program variables in any way, we impose the following restriction on their use:

Restriction on Auxiliary Variables

An auxiliary variable, a, can appear in the program only in assignment statements $a := e$, where e is an expression that can contain auxiliary variables and program variables.

Our plan is to augment a program with auxiliary variables and prove that the augmented program satisfies some particular property. Then we would like to conclude that the same program with the auxiliary variables removed exhibits the same behavior with respect to program variables. Since the auxiliary variables do not affect the flow of control or the values of program variables, any property we can prove about the program variables in the augmented program is also true in the original program – with one caveat: we must also prove that all the statements involving auxiliary variables, which we have added to the program, terminate. If one of these added statements does not terminate, we can assert anything as its postcondition. Hence we can prove any postcondition for the augmented program, but that postcondition might not be true for the original program. The only statements involving auxiliary variables that we are allowed to add to programs are assignment statements, and the only way an assignment statement can fail to terminate is if some exception occurs. For example, the assignment

$$\{x = 0\} \; aux \; := \; 1/x \; \{any \; assertion\}$$

does not terminate. Hence, we must demonstrate that the preconditions of assignments to auxiliary variables are strong enough to guarantee termination.

In the example, we use an array of auxiliary variables, $totaldep[i]$, to indicate the total amount of money that has ever been deposited (in the given account) by the ith ATM. $totaldep[i]$ therefore records the deposit history of the ith ATM. When auxiliary variables are used in this way (to record history), they are referred to as *history variables*. Note the distinction between auxiliary variables and logical variables. Logical variables are generally used to preserve initial values for reference in assertions and hence are not introduced into the program text.

Figure 4.3 shows a new annotation of the deposit transaction augmented with a history variable, $totaldep[i]$, and a logical variable, D_i. $depi$ is the amount to be deposited by the deposit transaction running at the ith ATM. Note that the value of $totaldep[i]$ does not affect the flow of control or the value of actual program variables, so the program will update program variables in the same way when auxiliary variables are removed. The key point is that the assertions in this annotation are not interfered with, since $totaldep[i]$ is not accessed in T_depj and does not appear in assertions of that transaction.

Unfortunately, however, although the final postcondition in Figure 4.3 tells us that $totaldep[i]$ has been correctly updated, it says nothing about *bal*. To

T_depi ::
　　$\cdots$

　　$\{(totaldep[i] = D_i) \wedge (depi > 0)\}$
　　$totaldep[i], \ bal \ := \ totaldep[i] + depi, \ bal + depi;$
　　$\{(totaldep[i] = D_i + depi) \wedge (depi > 0)\}$
　　$\cdots$

Program Invariant:
　$I : \ bal = \sum_i totaldep[i]$

Figure 4.3: The deposit transaction T_depi at the ith ATM.

demonstrate that bal has been correctly updated, we use the assertion, I:

$$I : \ bal = \sum_i totaldep[i]$$

I is true initially (since bal and $totaldep[i]$ are initially 0) and, since it is preserved by the assignment statement in T_depi, it is a program invariant of the deposit transaction. Since it is invariant to the execution of the multiple assignment statement, it is also a program invariant of the concurrent program consisting of several deposit transactions and can therefore be conjoined with each assertion in that program. I conjoined with the postcondition implies that bal is updated correctly. Once again we have reasoned about the program in two different ways, one of which was interference-free and the other not. Remember, proofs can be interfered with, not programs.

4.2.3   Strengthening Assertions by Synchronization

The failure of a non-interference proof might indicate a problem with the program and not that improper assertions have been chosen. In such cases the precondition of a statement, $s_{i,j}$, can be invalidated by the execution of a concurrent statement, $s_{k,l}$, and there is no weaker precondition of $s_{i,j}$ that implies correct execution and is not interfered with.

　　One way to eliminate interference in such situations is to make it impossible for control points at $s_{i,j}$ and $s_{k,l}$ to be simultaneously enabled. Then $s_{k,l}$ cannot possibly interfere with the precondition of $s_{i,j}$, and, as discussed in relation to (4.3), the required non-interference proof obligation becomes trivial. In this section we consider the approach of synchronizing the two processes to ensure that the offending statements cannot be simultaneously enabled. Synchronization allows us to strengthen the preconditions of the two offending statements so that their conjunction is false.

　　To illustrate the need for such synchronization and a method for providing it, we expand the banking example to consider start-up procedures at the

```
         . . .
ATMs := off;
cobegin
T_book::
  begin
       . . .    -- do bookkeeping activities
     ATMs := on;
  end;
//
T_tot::
  begin
    total, j := 0, 1;
    do j ≤ n →
      total, j := total + bal_array[j], j + 1;
    od;
  end;
coend;
```

Figure 4.4: Start-of-day banking transactions.

beginning of the day. Suppose that two concurrent activities take place in the morning. The first performs some standard bookkeeping on all account records and then turns on the ATMs (which we represent with the assignment statement *ATMs := on*) to allow transactions to be input. The second accumulates the sum of the balances of all accounts in the variable *total* before the day starts. The two transactions are shown in Figure 4.4. *bal_array* is an array whose jth element is the balance in the jth account (including deposits from all ATMs), and *total* is the sum of all the balances.

We wish to show that *ATMs = off* is a conjunct of the postcondition of the loop in *T_tot*, since it ensures that, for all j, the correct value of *bal_array[j]* was accumulated in *total*. Unfortunately, the code that turns on the ATMs in *T_book* interferes with this assertion. Thus there is no assurance that the second transaction reads *bal_array[j]* at the proper time.

In Figure 4.5 we have inserted code to synchronize the execution of the two transactions. Synchronization is accomplished through the shared variable *fin*, which is set by *T_tot* when it has completed accumulating the total. *T_book* waits in its loop until *fin* has been set before turning on the ATMs.

To prove that the program works correctly, we show that the annotation in Figure 4.5 is valid and hence that the assertion, I, defined as

$$I : \neg fin \Rightarrow (ATMs = off)$$

is a program invariant of the cobegin statement (note that the annotation

$\cdots$

$$\textit{fin, ATMs} := \textit{false, off};$$
$$\{I \land \neg\textit{fin}\}$$
cobegin
T_book::
  begin
$$\{I\}$$
$\cdots$ -- do bookkeeping activities
$$\{I\}$$
  do $\neg\textit{fin} \rightarrow$ **skip**; **od**;
$$\{I \land \textit{fin}\}$$
  $\textit{ATMs} := \textit{on};$
$$\{I \land \textit{fin}\}$$
  end;
//
T_tot::
  begin
$$\{I \land \neg\textit{fin}\}$$
  $\textit{total, j} := 0, 1;$
  do $j \leq n \rightarrow$
    $\textit{total, j} := \textit{total} + \textit{bal}[j], \ j + 1;$
  od;
$$\{I \land \neg\textit{fin}\}$$
  $\textit{fin} := \textit{true};$
$$\{I \land \textit{fin}\}$$
  end;
coend;

Program Invariant:
$$I : \ \neg\textit{fin} \Rightarrow (\textit{ATMs} = \textit{off})$$

Figure 4.5: Start-of-day banking transactions with synchronization.

implies that I is true at each control point). It is clear that I is a program invariant of each transaction in isolation. For example, $I \land \neg\textit{fin}$ is true after the initial assignment statement (before the cobegin) because of the Assignment Axiom and the Rule of Consequence. Hence I is true on entry to *T_book*, and on entry to the loop in *T_book* (since bookkeeping does not change the value of any of I's variables). Then $I \land \textit{fin}$ is a postcondition of the loop (by the Do Rule) and a postcondition of the following assignment statement (by the Assignment Axiom and the Rule of Consequence). Similar reasoning applies to the annotation in *T_tot*.

Furthermore, the proofs of the two transactions are interference-free. Since *I* is a program invariant of both transactions individually, it is not interfered with. Hence, only the assignment to *fin* in *T_tot* can possibly cause interference. This assignment, however, does not interfere with any assertions in *T_book* (since all such assertions involve only the conjunct *fin*, and *fin* is set to *true* in *T_tot*). Thus, the annotation demonstrates that the transactions correctly synchronize, since the postcondition of the loop in *T_tot* implies *ATMs = off*.

The process just described involved two steps. First, our inability to satisfy the non-interference obligations suggested that we add synchronization code. Then, the synchronization code allowed us to strengthen the assertions so as to eliminate the interference.

4.3   Atomicity and Mutual Exclusion

As we discussed informally in Chapter 1, concurrent systems that communicate through shared variables frequently require synchronization to eliminate troublesome interleavings. In the previous section this synchronization was implemented through the use of a delay. In Chapter 1 two mechanisms were introduced for controlling interleaving through delays: interrupt disabling in uniprocessor systems and a more general technique using semaphores. Our goal in this section is to place mechanisms such as these in the context of our more formal approach to concurrency.

The purpose of these mechanisms is to eliminate certain interleaved executions and hence control interference. Consider two concurrent programs, S_1 and S_2; let $s_{1,i}$ be a statement in S_1, and let $s_{2,j}$ and $s_{2,j+1}$ be consecutive statements in S_2. During concurrent execution, control points at $s_{1,i}$ and $s_{2,j+1}$ might be simultaneously enabled; $s_{1,i}$ might execute first and modify the values of shared variables, thus causing interference with the precondition of $s_{2,j+1}$, which was previously established by $s_{2,j}$.

One way to eliminate this interference is to use a mechanism which ensures that the execution of $s_{2,j}$ and the execution of $s_{2,j+1}$ are not separated by the execution of any other statement: the statements are executed *atomically*. In Chapter 1 we introduced angle brackets, $< \cdots >$, to denote such a mechanism. Thus, if we describe S_2 by

$$\cdots < s_{2,j};\ s_{2,j+1};\ > \cdots$$

we mean that $s_{2,j}$ and $s_{2,j+1}$ are executed atomically. It should be clear that while one component is executing some program fragment atomically, the other components are delayed; delay is an essential ingredient of any synchronization technique. By introducing atomicity we reduce the number of possible interleavings and eliminate certain situations in which interference can occur. Hence, to reason formally about concurrent programs in which statements are grouped in angle brackets, we use the Cobegin Rule, but we are not required to demonstrate that assertions within angle brackets are not interfered with.

An alternative to using angle brackets is to specify atomicity using the following construct which is more appropriate to a high level language:

Await Statement

$$\textbf{await } B \rightarrow S$$

The operational semantics of the await statement is as follows:

> When a control point is enabled at the await, the boolean expression B is evaluated and, if B is true, S is executed atomically. If B is false, the control point is disabled until a later time when B is true, at which point S is executed atomically. No interleaving occurs between the final evaluation of B and the execution of S, and the execution of S is not interleaved with the execution of statements in concurrent components.

Note that it would be both unwise and unnecessary to nest another await within S.

The await statement is extremely powerful, since it not only specifies atomicity but also causes execution of S to be delayed until some application-related condition, B, is true. In Chapter 1 we referred to such a mechanism as signaling. The formal semantics of the await statement is described by the following rule:

Await Rule

$$\frac{\{P \wedge B\}\, S\, \{Q\}}{\{P\}\, \textbf{await } B \rightarrow S\, \{Q\}} \tag{4.8}$$

The rule states that if S transforms $P \wedge B$ to Q, an await in which B guards S transforms P to Q. The rule is identical to that for the if statement (with a single guarded statement) and thus the formal semantics of the await and if statements are the same; however their operational semantics are different in that: (1) if the guard is false, the if statement fails while the await statement waits until the guard becomes true and (2) the await statement is atomic, while the if statement has a control point between the guard and the guarded statement.

Since S might contain assignment statements or procedure invocations, the await statement might interfere with assertions in other components. Therefore, in testing for interference, each await statement that contains assignment statements or procedure invocations (as well as each assignment statement and procedure invocation not within an await) must be examined for its effect on assertions in other components of the cobegin. Assignment statements and procedure invocations within awaits need not be considered separately, since their effect is considered as part of the await. Since the await statement is executed atomically, only its pre- and postconditions need be tested for interference; assertions within await statements cannot be interfered with, by definition.

Although the await statement can be used to produce atomic execution of an arbitrarily large program fragment, S, such atomic execution is generally undesirable, since it unnecessarily restricts concurrency. While S is executing atomically, no other concurrent component can be executing at all. The notion of atomicity is more powerful than generally required, since it excludes any interleaving. It excludes not only the interleaved execution of statements that might interfere with assertions within S, but also the interleaved execution of statements that do not interfere with those assertions. Typically, S is a program fragment that manipulates some variables shared with concurrent components, and the assertions in S that are in jeopardy deal with those variables. Statements in other components that do not access the shared variables will not cause interference, and therefore interleaving their execution with S can be allowed. Hence, atomicity has too gross an effect and unnecessarily limits concurrency.

In Chapter 1 we discussed a more efficient approach to synchronization through the use of critical sections and mutual exclusion. Using that approach, we identify regions in each component that interfere with one another as critical sections, and we ensure that the execution of statements in a critical section in one component is not interleaved with the execution of statements in a critical section of another component. However, we do not require that execution within a critical section be atomic; while one process is executing in a critical section, any other process can be executing in a noncritical section.

Mutual exclusion is generally implemented with semaphores. In their most primitive form, semaphores can be implemented with a special machine instruction such as *test-and-set*. This instruction has the property that it does two things as a single atomic unit: it returns the initial value of a variable and subsequently sets the variable to some particular value. The atomicity here is not harmful, since it involves only a few memory cycles, but it is powerful enough to implement a semaphore. Semaphores built in this way delay processes through busy waiting.

Semaphores can also be implemented through a disciplined use of the await statement, which does not unduly restrict concurrency. An integer variable, *sem*, is used to store the value of the semaphore, and the only atomicity required is in the testing and setting of *sem*. The P operation is realized as

$$\textbf{await } sem > 0 \rightarrow sem \ := \ sem - 1$$

and the V as

$$sem \ := \ sem + 1$$

(Recall that the assignment statement is executed atomically.)

Example

We once again concentrate on a single bank account and consider a transaction, T_wdri, that attempts to withdraw $wdri$ dollars from the account using the ith ATM. The transaction might contain the statement

$$\textbf{if } (bal \geq wdri) \rightarrow$$
$$bal, amtwdri := bal - wdri, wdri;$$
$$[] \, (bal < wdri) \rightarrow$$
$$amtwdri := 0;$$
$$\textbf{fi};$$

where $amtwdri$ is the amount of money issued to the customer. As described previously, if we state the pre- and postconditions of this statement in terms of the variable bal, those assertions might be interfered with by concurrent transactions that change its value. Thus, our plan is to introduce auxiliary variables that will not be interfered with and to state our pre- and postconditions in terms of these variables. We define an array of auxiliary variables, $totwdrn[i]$, to indicate the total amount of money that has ever been withdrawn (from the given account) by the ith ATM since the account was first opened.

Figure 4.6 shows an annotated version of a withdrawal transaction at the ith ATM, augmented with the history variable $totwdrn[i]$ and a logical variable, W_i. Q_i is the assertion

$$Q_i : \; (totwdrn[i] = W_i + amtwdri) \wedge ((amtwdri \neq 0) \Rightarrow (amtwdri = wdri))$$

Consider T_wdri as an isolated sequential program. To see that the annotation in Figure 4.6 is valid, it is only necessary to use instances of the Assignment Axiom (with Q_i as a postcondition) for each of the component statements and show that the preconditions of the components in Figure 4.6 imply the preconditions indicated by the axioms.

Again, the final postcondition, Q_i, says nothing about whether bal has been updated properly, so we introduce an assertion, I:

$$I : \; (bal = \sum_i totaldep[i] - \sum_i totwdrn[i]) \wedge (bal \geq 0)$$

where $totaldep[i]$ is the history variable used in the deposit transaction. I is a program invariant for the withdrawal transaction in isolation. To demonstrate that I is an invariant, it is only necessary to note that if I is true initially, the precondition of the multiple assignment statement is $I \wedge (bal \geq wdri)$ and the following is a theorem, establishing I as its postcondition.

$$\{I \wedge (bal \geq wdri)\}$$
$$bal, amtwdri, totwdrn[i] := bal - wdri, wdri, totwdrn[i] + wdri \; (4.9)$$

T_wdri ::

   ...

        $\{totwdrn[i] = W_i\}$

if $(bal \geq wdri) \rightarrow$

        $\{(totwdrn[i] = W_i) \wedge (bal \geq wdri)\}$

        $bal,\ amtwdri,\ totwdrn[i] := bal - wdri,\ wdri,\ totwdrn[i] + wdri;$

        $\{Q_i\}$

[] $(bal < wdri) \rightarrow$

        $\{totwdrn[i] = W_i\}$

      $amtwdri := 0;$

        $\{Q_i\}$

fi;

       $\{Q_i\}$

Program Invariant

   $I:\ (bal = \sum_i totaldep[i] - \sum_i totwdrn[i]) \wedge (bal \geq 0)$

Figure 4.6: A withdrawal transaction, *T_wdri*, for the *i*th ATM.

Since *I* is a program invariant, it can be conjoined with any assertion in the annotation. The postcondition, $I \wedge Q_i$, implies that *bal* is updated correctly.

Consider now the concurrent execution of two withdrawal transactions, *T_wdr*1 and *T_wdr*2. Having developed a proof for a withdrawal transaction in isolation, we must now test for interference before the Cobegin Rule can be invoked. The only shared variable is *bal*, and hence we need examine only assertions that involve *bal*. It is intuitively clear that concurrent withdrawal transactions will not work correctly, since the value of *bal* can be decreased between the time a guard is evaluated and the time the corresponding assignment is executed.

Formally, interference takes place between the precondition of the multiple assignment statement in *T_wdr*1 [including the precondition of (4.9)] and the execution of that same statement in *T_wdr*2. Specifically, we cannot prove the following triple, which represents the test to determine if the multiple assignment in *T_wdr*2 interferes with the conjunct $bal \geq wdr1$ of the precondition of the multiple assignment in *T_wdr*1.

$\{[(totwdrn[1] = W_1) \wedge I \wedge (bal \geq wdr1)]$

    $\wedge\ [(totwdrn[2] = W_2) \wedge I \wedge (bal \geq wdr2)]\}$

$bal,\ amtwdr2,\ totwdrn[2] := bal - wdr2,\ wdr2,\ totwdrn[2] + wdr2$

   $\{bal \geq wdr1\}$ (4.10)

Since this triple is not a theorem, interference occurs and the Cobegin Rule cannot be used. One way to eliminate this interference is to make the entire if statement atomic by bracketing it with an await statement:

$$\textbf{await } true \rightarrow \textbf{if } \dots \textbf{ fi}$$

Since assertions within await statements cannot be interfered with, we no longer require that (4.10) be a theorem. Furthermore, since the postcondition of the await in T_wdr1 ($I \wedge Q_1$) is invariant to the execution of the await in T_wdr2, no interference takes place and the Cobegin Rule can be used.

A more efficient way to eliminate interference is to make the if statement a critical section. A semaphore, sem, can be used to implement mutual exclusion by bracketing the if statement as follows:

$$P(sem); \textbf{ if } \dots \textbf{ fi}; V(sem)$$

Now interference cannot take place between the various incarnations of the withdrawal transaction.

Consider next the deposit transaction. Since its effect is to increase bal, it does not interfere with any assertions in the withdrawal transaction. (Note that we rely here on the atomicity of assignment statements.) Hence, the deposit transaction need not be made a critical section – its execution can be arbitrarily interleaved with that of a withdrawal. This is an example of the flexibility achieved through the use of critical sections, rather than atomicity, to eliminate interference. The concurrent execution of withdrawal and deposit transactions illustrates a situation in which a variable in an assertion of one component of a cobegin is modified by a statement in another component without invalidating the assertion.

4.4   Proving Mutual Exclusion

We have argued that atomicity is too strong a tool for eliminating interference and that a better way is to selectively prevent the interfering statements from being enabled at the same time as the statements whose preconditions are interfered with. We identify the interfering and interfered with sections of code as critical sections and guarantee that they are executed in a mutually exclusive fashion.

We have stated that a common approach to achieving mutual exclusion of critical sections is to use semaphores; the critical sections are bracketed with P and V operations on a particular semaphore. However, we are obliged to show that such a scheme actually achieves mutual exclusion before we can claim that interference has been eliminated.

Because we implement semaphores using the await construct, we can use the Await Rule to reason about them. Figure 4.7 shows an annotated program which demonstrates that mutual exclusion is achieved. The two auxiliary variables, $in1$ and $in2$, illustrate a new way in which such variables can be used: to reason about the location of enabled control points. $in1$ is equal to 1 when the first process is in its critical section and equal to 0 otherwise. Similarly, $in2$ denotes when the second process is in its critical section. The assertions concerning the values of these variables at various points in the program follow from the Assignment and Await Axioms.

To demonstrate that the assertion I, denoted by

$$I : (sem = (1 - in1 - in2)) \wedge (0 \le sem \le 1) \wedge (0 \le in1, in2 \le 1)$$

is a program invariant, we note that it is true initially and it is preserved by the execution of each statement in the program. For example, consider the await statement that implements P in the first component. From the Assignment Axiom and the Rule of Composition we have

$$\{(sem = (1 - in2)) \wedge (0 \le (sem - 1) \le 1) \wedge (0 \le in2 \le 1)\}$$
$$sem := sem - 1; \ in1 := 1 \ \{I\}$$

Since the precondition of this triple is implied by $I \wedge (in1 = 0) \wedge (sem > 0)$ (where $sem > 0$ is the wait condition of the await statement), we can use the Await Rule to conclude

$$\{I \wedge (in1 = 0)\} \ \textbf{await} \ sem = 1 \rightarrow \textbf{begin} \ sem := sem - 1; \ in1 := 1; \ \textbf{end} \ \{I\}$$

We wish to prove that this protocol achieves mutual exclusion – *i.e.*, that the two components are never in their critical sections simultaneously. Mutual exclusion is an example of a safety property in which P_{bad} is the assertion $(in1 = 1) \wedge (in2 = 1)$. Since $I \Rightarrow \neg P_{bad}$, the safety property is true and we have demonstrated mutual exclusion.

We also wish to show that this protocol does not exhibit deadlock, *i.e.* that the two components are never simultaneously waiting to enter their critical sections. In this case we define P_{bad} to be the assertion that both components are in their noncritical sections, $(in1 = 0) \wedge (in2 = 0)$, and the semaphore can cause delay, $\neg(sem > 0)$. The absence of deadlock is implied by the fact that, once again, $I \Rightarrow \neg P_{bad}$.

4.5   Invariants and Shared Variables

In previous sections we have used the concept of a program invariant in various ways to aid in the proof process. In this section we take a somewhat more systematic view of the role played by program invariants and provide some motivation for their use in later chapters.

If each assertion, $p_{i,j}$, in the proof of the ith component of a concurrent program can be decomposed into a conjunction $I \wedge p'_{i,j}$, where I is a program invariant of each component (considered individually) that includes all the

var
  sem : *integer* := 1;
  *in*1, *in*2 : *integer* := 0, 0; -- auxiliary variables
cobegin
   do *true* →
     begin
         {*I* ∧ (*in*1 = 0)}
         . . .   -- noncritical section
         {*I* ∧ (*in*1 = 0)}
       await *sem* > 0 → **begin** *sem* := *sem* − 1; *in*1 := 1; **end**;
         {*I* ∧ (*in*1 = 1)}
         . . .   -- critical section
         {*I* ∧ (*in*1 = 1)}
       await *true* → **begin** *sem* := *sem* + 1; *in*1 := 0; **end**;
         {*I* ∧ (*in*1 = 0)}
     end;
   od;
//
   do *true* →
     begin
         {*I* ∧ (*in*2 = 0)}
         . . .   -- noncritical section
         {*I* ∧ (*in*2 = 0)}
       await *sem* > 0 → **begin** *sem* := *sem* − 1; *in*2 := 1; **end**;
         {*I* ∧ (*in*2 = 1)}
         . . .   -- critical section
         {*I* ∧ (*in*2 = 1)}
       await *true* → **begin** *sem* := *sem* + 1; *in*2 := 0; **end**;
         {*I* ∧ (*in*2 = 0)}
     end;
   od;
coend;

Program Invariant:
  I : $(sem = (1 - in1 - in2)) \wedge (0 \leq sem \leq 1) \wedge (0 \leq in1, in2 \leq 1)$

Figure 4.7: Proof of mutual exclusion.

references to shared variables and $p'_{i,j}$ is an assertion involving only variables local to the ith component, then the proofs are guaranteed to be interference-free: since $p'_{i,j}$ involves only variables local to the ith component, it cannot be invalidated by statements in the jth component, $i \neq j$, and since I is a program invariant of the jth component, it also cannot be invalidated. When such a decomposition is made, we can assemble the proofs of the individual programs into a proof of the concurrent program as a whole, with no interference proof obligations to be satisfied – thus achieving true modularity of the proof process.

The modularity of the proof corresponds to the modular decomposition of a concurrent program into a set of sequential programs, discussed in Section 1.5. We pointed out that in most decompositions the sequential components have limited interaction with one another and that these interactions tend to follow simple patterns – for example, producers and consumers interacting through shared queues. In such cases the assertions describing the behavior of a component can often be partitioned into two parts: one that describes the state of the local variables and another that describes the state of the shared variables. If this second part can be stated as a program invariant, the proof is modularized as described above.

We saw in Chapter 3 that abstract objects, such as queues, which can be used to support interaction between processes, are characterized by abstract invariants. Unfortunately, such invariants are not program invariants, since they are not required to be true of intermediate states reached during the execution of abstract operations. In Chapter 5 we consider the approach of designing concurrent programs hierarchically, with an abstract level (which involves operations on abstract objects) and a concrete level (which implements the abstract objects). At the abstract level, abstract operations can be viewed as atomic; thus the abstract invariant is invariant to the execution of every statement at the abstract level. (Note that we are arguing informally here.) To complete the design, we must then separately prove the correctness of the concrete level, as we did in Chapter 3. Since the abstract objects are shared, concurrent execution of concrete operations can cause interference and may require appropriate use of mutual exclusion. A second issue is that the abstract invariant is generally a weak assertion, which simply states that the value of the abstract item satisfies the constraints of its data type. If a stronger assertion is needed for some proof, that assertion might not be a program invariant of the concurrent program and, hence, might be interfered with. We return to this discussion in Chapter 5.

4.6   Termination of Concurrent Programs

For some applications we may have to reason about the termination of a cobegin construct. In this section we informally discuss some of the issues involved.

In the simplest situation, the component processes that make up the concurrent program can each be proven to terminate when run independently (for example, by the proof methods given in Section 2.4.10). To prove that the concurrent program terminates, we must in addition show that the assertions in the individual termination proofs are not interfered with. For example, suppose that in demonstrating the termination of a loop in a particular component, S_i, we have found a function, F, from program variables to the elements of a well founded set. We must show that the execution of statement $s_{k,l}$ in a concurrent component, S_k, satisfies

$$\{(F(\cdots) = F_0) \wedge p_{k,l}\}\ s_{k,l}\ \{F(\cdots) \prec F_0\}$$

If one or more of the component processes do not terminate when run independently, a number of issues may be involved. For instance, in the program shown in Figure 4.5, the first component will not terminate when run by itself. Assume, in the concurrent case, that the do statement in the first component and the assignment statement that sets *fin* to true in the second component are both enabled. The implementation can nondeterministically select either for execution. If the do statement is selected, the situation repeats itself. If the do statement is selected every time, *fin* will never be set to *true* and the first component will never terminate. Thus, to prove termination, we must make some fairness assumption about the implementation of the cobegin construct.

We can make the same kind of fairness assumptions for order nondeterminism in concurrent systems that we made for choice nondeterminism in Chapter 2. Specifically, we can define weak fairness and strong fairness, depending on whether components are enabled continuously or infinitely often. The program of Figure 4.5 terminates under the assumption of weak fairness, since both control points are continuously enabled. In most cases an assumption of weak fairness is sufficient to ensure that each component of a cobegin makes progress in its computation. Strong fairness might be required to ensure a component's progress if it contains an await statement whose boolean expression can be turned on and off by another component.

More generally, when a component contains an await (do) statement we have to reason about whether the guard will ever become true (false). Even when fairness assumptions are made, such reasoning may be difficult. In the general case, determining whether a specific variable will ever have a specific value is undecidable; hence any proof may require considerable creativity.

As a special case it may be possible to prove that a particular component terminates with a postcondition that implies the ultimate termination of another component. In Figure 4.5, for example, the second component can easily be proven to terminate (assuming a fair implementation) with a postcondition which implies that *fin* is true; hence we can reason that the first component will escape from its do statement and terminate as well.

Another issue that may arise is that of deadlock: all components are simultaneously waiting. For example, deadlock might occur in the statement **cobegin** $S_1;//S_2;$ **coend** if S_1 has terminated and S_2 is waiting at an await statement, $s_{2,l}$, for the guard, B, to become true. Note that deadlock may or may not occur, depending on the precondition of the cobegin. Thus, there may be certain starting states that lead to deadlock and others that do not. If those states that lead to deadlock are not included in the precondition, deadlock will not occur. In the example, if we have demonstrated that, under some precondition of the cobegin, S_1 terminates with postcondition Q_1, and $p_{2,l}$ is the precondition of the await, then deadlock does not occur if

$$(\neg B \wedge p_{2,l} \wedge Q_1) = \textit{false}$$

As previously mentioned, the absence of deadlock is a safety property, which can be proven using a suitable invariant.

4.7   Coenter Statement

Some languages use a construct related to the cobegin statement, called the coenter statement:

$$\textbf{coenter } \mathcal{P}_1 :: S_1; \ \# \ \mathcal{P}_2 :: S_2; \ \#\ldots\# \ \mathcal{P}_n :: S_n; \ \textbf{coend}$$

where each S_i is a statement. The operational semantics of this statement is as follows:

> When control reaches the coenter statement, one of the component statements is selected nondeterministically, a control point is enabled at that statement, and the statement is executed to completion; then another component is selected nondeterministically, a control point is enabled at that statement, and the statement is executed to completion; and so on, until all components have been executed. The construct is then exited and a control point is enabled at the statement following the coend. The coenter fails if any of its component statements fail.

Since the component statements are executed sequentially in some nondeterministically selected order, the construct is sequential and nondeterministic. (We can take the view that each component statement is a single critical section and that all critical sections are run in a mutually exclusive fashion.)

We can describe the formal semantics of this construct with the same inference rule as for the cobegin except that the interference condition is different.

Coenter Rule

$$\frac{\{P_1\}\, S_1\, \{Q_1\},\ \ldots,\ \{P_n\}\, S_n\, \{Q_n\},\ \textit{interference free}}{\{P_1 \wedge \cdots \wedge P_n\}\ \textbf{coenter}\ S_1;\ \#\ldots\#\ S_n;\ \textbf{coend}\ \{Q_1 \wedge \cdots \wedge Q_n\}} \qquad (4.11)$$

Since the components run sequentially, assertions internal to a component statement cannot be interfered with. However, the pre- and postconditions of an entire component statement can be interfered with by another component. We leave the exact statement of the interference condition for the exercises. Even though interference can occur, its form is restricted; consequently, systems based on the coenter construct are relatively easy to design and reason about.

In one common application of the coenter statement, the pre- and postconditions for all the components are an invariant, I. In this case, no interference can take place and the Coenter Rule becomes

Coenter Rule for Components That Maintain an Invariant

$$\frac{\{I\}\ S_1\ \{I\},\ \ldots,\ \{I\}\ S_n\ \{I\}}{\{I\}\ \textbf{coenter}\ S_1;\ \#\ldots\#\ S_n;\ \textbf{coend}\ \{I\}} \qquad (4.12)$$

One example of the use of a construct similar to the coenter is in a transaction processing system that controls access to a database. Each transaction can be thought of as a component of a coenter statement that maintains an invariant: the consistency constraint of the database. The system actually executes the component statements concurrently, but their execution has the same effect as if they ran sequentially according to the semantics of the coenter statement. We show how this type of execution can be implemented in Chapters 10 and 11.

4.8 Procedure Calls in Concurrent Processes*

A call to a procedure that has assignment semantics looks to the caller as if it were an assignment statement. That viewpoint is adequate for sequential programs, but not for concurrent programs where atomicity must be considered.

The call of a procedure, p, with assignment semantics occurs in three steps:

The assignment of in and in out arguments, $\bar{x}$ and $\bar{z}$, to in and in out parameters, $\bar{a}$ and $\bar{c}$;

The execution of the procedure body, S, which assigns some function, f, of the in and in out parameters to out and in out parameters;

The assignment of out and in out parameters, $\bar{b}$ and $\bar{c}$, to out and in out arguments, $\bar{y}$ and $\bar{z}$.

We take the first and third steps to be atomic (because of the assumed atomicity of the multiple assignment statement). Since we have assumed that S does not access global (and hence shared) variables, each incarnation of S accesses only parameters and locally declared variables – we refer to these as p's local variables – and hence has exclusive access to the variables on which it operates. Therefore, the result produced by S is independent of the way its execution is interleaved with concurrent processes. Since one such sequencing is the

$$\{U_{f(\bar{x},\bar{z})}^{\bar{y},\,\bar{z}} \wedge Y_{\bar{x},\,\bar{z}}^{\bar{a},\,\bar{c}}\}$$
$$\bar{a},\ \bar{c}\ :=\ \bar{x},\ \bar{z};$$
$$\{U_{f(\bar{a},\bar{c})}^{\bar{y},\,\bar{z}} \wedge Y\}$$
$$\bar{b},\ \bar{c}\ :=\ f(\bar{a},\bar{c});$$
$$\{U_{\bar{b},\,\bar{c}}^{\bar{y},\,\bar{z}}\}$$
$$\bar{y},\ \bar{z}\ :=\ \bar{b},\ \bar{c};$$
$$\{U\}$$

Figure 4.8: An annotated program fragment describing procedure invocation.

atomic execution of S, the second step can be viewed as occurring atomically. Hence, under the assumption that S does not access global variables, the call is equivalent to a sequence of three (atomic) assignment statements:

$$\bar{a},\ \bar{c}\ :=\ \bar{x},\ \bar{z};$$
$$\bar{b},\ \bar{c}\ :=\ f(\bar{a},\bar{c});$$
$$\bar{y},\ \bar{z}\ :=\ \bar{b},\ \bar{c};$$

If a call of p is described by the triple

$$\{U_{f(\bar{x},\bar{z})}^{\bar{y},\,\bar{z}} \wedge Y_{\bar{x},\,\bar{z}}^{\bar{a},\,\bar{c}}\}\, p(\bar{x},\bar{y},\bar{z})\,\{U\}$$

then the annotation shown in Figure 4.8 (which is essentially the same as that of Figure 3.1) describes the intermediate states.

Assume p is called by process $\mathcal{P}_1$, and $\mathcal{P}_2$ is a concurrent process. Note that $\mathcal{P}_1$ and $\mathcal{P}_2$ might synchronize at some time before p is called or after values have been returned, but not in between, since in order for synchronization to take place between call and return, $\mathcal{P}_1$ and $\mathcal{P}_2$ must have access to common variables. (For example, the condition in an await statement in one process might refer to a variable modified in the other.) But S makes no global references and, since parameters are passed by value/result, they cannot be used to synchronize the two processes. Suppose an assertion, A, attached to a control point in $\mathcal{P}_2$ were to refer to one of p's local variables, d. Then *exist_d* must be a conjunct of A. But, because of the absence of synchronization, it is not possible to demonstrate that d exists whenever that control point is enabled. Hence, $\mathcal{P}_2$ can make no assertions about a local variable of p and thus argument passing and the execution of S cannot interfere with assertions in $\mathcal{P}_2$. However, the final assignment is to the arguments, which are not local to p, and that assignment can cause interference with assertions in $\mathcal{P}_2$. In addition, statements in $\mathcal{P}_2$ can interfere with the assertions of Figure 4.8.

As an example, consider the procedure *increment* with the following declaration:

```
procedure increment(c : in out integer);
begin
    c := c + 1;
end increment;
```

Assume *increment* is called in the program shown in Figure 4.9(a) which, by our previous argument, is equivalent to the program in Figure 4.9(b). Although we might expect the final value of z (in both programs) to be 3, if the execution of the statement $z := z + 2$ is interleaved between, for example, the passing of arguments and the execution of the procedure body, the final value of z will be 1. Hence, it is impossible to prove the assertion $z = 3$ as a postcondition. To illustrate the problem, a program annotation based on the reasoning used in Section 4.2 is shown in Figure 4.9(c). Unfortunately, the assignment corresponding to the return of values interferes with the postcondition of the first process, since the proof requirement

$$\{(((z = 2) \lor (z = 3)) \land ((c = 1) \lor (c = 3)))\}\ z := c\ \{((z = 2) \lor (z = 3))\}$$

cannot be demonstrated. If the procedure call had been atomic, this interference would not have taken place.

4.9 Control Predicates*

The assertions in Program Logic are mapped to T or F depending on the state of the program. All the axioms and inference rules we have discussed so far involve only assertions defined over program variables; they do not involve the location of the control point(s). In this section we show how to include information about control points in assertions.

We expand our model of a program by allowing names to be optionally given to (arbitrarily complex) program fragments. We denote a program fragment, S, that has name α as $\alpha : [S]$. (Note that α is the name of the program fragment, not the label of a single statement.) For example, the program in Figure 4.10 is the same as the program we used to prove mutual exclusion in Figure 4.7 except that we have removed the auxiliary variables and introduced names. The program uses the await statement to build a semaphore, which, in turn, is used to implement mutual exclusion. Each of the statements and each of the critical and noncritical sections has been given a name.

We define a new type of predicate called a *control predicate*. Using α as a generic fragment name, we define three control predicates, $at(\alpha)$, $in(\alpha)$, and $after(\alpha)$, with interpretations:

$at(\alpha)$ is mapped to T in any state in which a control point is enabled at the beginning of the program fragment named α;

$in(\alpha)$ is mapped to T in any state in which a control point is enabled at the beginning of or within the program fragment named α;

```
z := 0;
cobegin
  z := z + 2;  // increment(z);
coend;
```

(a) A program fragment

```
z := 0;
cobegin
  z := z + 2;
//
  begin
    c := z;
    c := c + 1;
    z := c;
  end;
coend;
```

(b) An equivalent program fragment

```
z := 0;
        {z = 0}
cobegin
        {(z = 0) ∨ (z = 1)}
  z := z + 2;
        {(z = 2) ∨ (z = 3)}
//
  begin
        {(z = 0) ∨ (z = 2)}
    c := z;
        {(c = 0) ∨ (c = 2)}
    c := c + 1;
        {(c = 1) ∨ (c = 3)}
    z := c;
        {(z = 1) ∨ (z = 3)}
  end;
coend;
```

(c) An annotation that exhibits interference.

Figure 4.9: Interference due to nonatomicity of a procedure execution.

```
        var sem : semaphore := 1;
        start : [cobegin
          loop₁ :: [do true →
              begin
                noncrit₁: [⋯]              -- noncritical section
                C₁ : [await sem > 0 → sem := sem − 1;]
                crit₁ : [⋯]               -- critical section
                D₁ : [sem := sem + 1;]
              end;
              od;]
     //
          loop₂ :: [do true →
              begin
                noncrit₂ : [⋯]            -- noncritical section
                C₂ : [await sem > 0 → sem := sem − 1;]
                crit₂ : [⋯]              -- critical section
                D₂ : [sem := sem + 1;]
              end;
              od;]
        coend;]
```

Figure 4.10: A labeled version of a program involving critical sections.

$after(\alpha)$ is mapped to T in any state in which a control point is enabled at the beginning of the program fragment following the fragment named α.

The condition that the two processes in Figure 4.10 not be simultaneously in their critical sections can now be expressed using control predicates as

$$\neg(in(crit_1) \wedge in(crit_2))$$

and the condition that the processes not deadlock can be expressed as

$$\neg(at(C_1) \wedge at(C_2) \wedge (sem = 0))$$

(*i.e.*, both processes are not simultaneously waiting to perform the P operation on the semaphore, and the semaphore has value 0).

We can also use control predicates to express the information contained in an annotated program. Thus, the fact that the annotated version of a program contains the assertion P_i as a precondition of the program fragment α_i can be expressed as

$$at(\alpha_i) \Rightarrow P_i$$

which states that when the first atomic operation in α_i is enabled, P_i is true.

This idea can be expanded to allow us to formulate a single assertion that includes all the assertions in an annotated program. Suppose each assertion P_i, $1 \leq i \leq N$, is a precondition of a program fragment named α_i. Then the single assertion

$$(at(\alpha_1) \Rightarrow P_1) \wedge (at(\alpha_2) \Rightarrow P_2) \wedge \cdots \wedge (at(\alpha_N) \Rightarrow P_N)$$

contains the same information as the annotated program. It has the interesting property that it is a program invariant if and only if the annotation is valid. Some approaches to reasoning about programs are based on this idea of a single program invariant.

We have given some examples of how to include control predicates in assertions. To reason formally using such predicates, we must expand Program Logic to include axioms and inference rules describing their semantics. We do not give such a formalization, but include two of the more intuitive axioms:

Sequential Control Axiom

For a program fragment S

$$\{at(\alpha)\} \; \alpha : [S] \; \{after(\alpha)\}$$

This axiom describes the effect of executing the fragment S on the enabled control point.

Concurrent Control Axiom

For $<S>$, a program fragment that is executed atomically in one process, and β, the name of a program fragment in a different process

$$\{at(\beta)\} \; <S> \; \{at(\beta)\}$$

This axiom states that the atomic execution of a program fragment in one process does not change the location of the enabled control point in a concurrent process.

Although we have not shown how to reason formally using control predicates, we can easily see that the following assertion is an invariant of the program of Figure 4.10 (by noting that it is true initially and invariant to the execution of all statements):

$$[(sem = 0) \wedge ((in(crit_1) \wedge \neg in(crit_2)) \vee (\neg in(crit_1) \wedge in(crit_2)))]$$
$$\vee ((sem = 1) \wedge \neg in(crit_1) \wedge \neg in(crit_2))$$

and that this invariant implies mutual exclusion:

$$\neg (in(crit_1) \wedge in(crit_2))$$

4.10   Temporal Logic*

One way to talk about safety and liveness properties is to use concepts related to time such as "never" and "eventually." However, ordinary Program Logic does not offer a convenient way to reason about time. We briefly discuss another formal system, called Temporal Logic, which allows us to do this.

In Program Logic, an assertion, which we now refer to as an *immediate assertion*, is true or false when evaluated in a particular state (including the enabled control point). In Temporal Logic, an assertion, called a *temporal assertion*, is true or false when evaluated on a particular execution sequence (*i.e.*, a sequence of program states). Since temporal assertions include all immediate assertions, we must first explain what it means for an immediate assertion to be evaluated on an execution sequence. The interpretation maps an immediate assertion to T or F when evaluated on an execution sequence depending on whether the assertion is mapped to either T or F in Program Logic when evaluated in the first state of that sequence.

Since we are interested in making assertions about a program and not just a single execution sequence, we extend the previous definition and say that a temporal assertion is true of a program if it is mapped to T when evaluated on all of the program's execution sequences. While an immediate assertion describes the present (the first state in an execution sequence), Temporal Logic introduces two new operators on assertions, $\square$ (always) and $\diamond$ (eventually), which refer to the future and have the following interpretation:

$\square P$ is true of a program if, in all of the program's execution sequences, P is true in the first state of the sequence and will be true in all future states (*i.e.*, after the execution of each subsequent atomic operation).

$\diamond P$ is true of a program if, in all of the program's execution sequences, P either is true in the first state of the sequence or will become true in some future state (*i.e.*, after the execution of some subsequent atomic operation).

The two temporal operators are related by the axiom

$$\neg \square P \equiv \diamond \neg P$$

which says that P is not always true if and only if it is eventually false.

To make assertions of this type, we have to assume that an executing program makes progress: if there exists at least one enabled control point in the program, some atomic operation eventually is executed. (Note that this assumption is not necessary in Program Logic, since the interpretation of triples is always conditional: *if* the statement terminates, the postcondition is true in the final state.)

Frequently, the properties we would like to prove about a program are only true under some assumption of fairness. For example, the program shown in

Figure 4.5 terminates only if scheduling is fair. Hence, to prove that this program eventually terminates, we must restrict the set of execution sequences of the program to those that are produced by a fair scheduler.

We can use temporal operators to express a number of properties of programs. For example, we can say that x will always be less than or equal to 1000:

$$\Box\,(x \leq 1000)$$

or that x will eventually equal 1000:

$$\Diamond\,(x = 1000)$$

Program invariance is conveniently expressed in temporal terms. An assertion, I, is a program invariant if

$$I \Rightarrow \Box I$$

A condition, P_{bad}, that is guaranteed never to occur is expressed as a safety property:

$$\Box\,\neg P_{bad})$$

A condition, Q_{good}, that is guaranteed to eventually happen is expressed as a liveness property:

$$\Diamond\,Q_{good}$$

Some properties require a combination of the two temporal operators. For example, consider a concurrent program consisting of two components, one whose termination is dependent on an await with condition B and the other that changes the value of B. A condition for termination of this program can be expressed as

$$\Box\,\Diamond\,B$$

which states that it is always the case that B will eventually be true. Thus, no matter when the first component reaches the await, at some later time B will become true.

Another useful temporal operator that can be derived from $\Diamond$ and $\Box$ is $\leadsto$ (leads to), defined by

$$(P \leadsto Q) \equiv (\Box\,(P \Rightarrow \Diamond\,Q))$$

Intuitively, $P \leadsto Q$ is true of a program if and only if, in any execution sequence of the program, if P becomes true then Q eventually becomes true.

The $\leadsto$ operator is particularly useful for expressing liveness properties. For example, to state that a loop eventually terminates, we can say that entrance to the loop statement "leads to" the statement following the loop. We can express this property for the loop

$$\alpha : [\textbf{do}\ldots\textbf{od}]$$

as

$$at(\alpha) \leadsto after(\alpha)$$

Similarly, we can express the termination property for the program

$$\alpha : [Prog]$$

as

$$at(\alpha) \leadsto after(\alpha)$$

These examples use the temporal operators to precisely state certain properties of program fragments. Such statements are frequently quite useful in informal reasoning about program behavior. To perform formal reasoning using these operators, we would have to develop a formal system that includes these operators and expand the axioms and inference rules of Program Logic. We do not present such a formalization but do include some of its more intuitive axioms:

Single Exit Rule

For any program fragment $\alpha : [S]$,

$$in(\alpha) \Rightarrow (\Box\, in(\alpha) \vee \Diamond\, after(\alpha))$$

which states that the only way control can leave S is by enabling the control point following α. (This axiom is true only in languages that do not contain goto type statements.)

Liveness of the Cobegin Statement

The liveness axiom for the statement

$$\alpha : [\textbf{cobegin}\ \alpha_1 : [S_1;\,]\, /\!/\ \cdots\ /\!/\ \alpha_n : [S_2;\,]\ \textbf{coend}]$$

is

$$\bigwedge_{i=1}^{n} at(\alpha) \leadsto at(\alpha_i)$$

which states that after a control point is enabled at the beginning of a cobegin statement, a control point will eventually be enabled at each of the component statements.

4.11   Bibliographic Notes

Much of the material in this chapter is based on the original work in Owicki and Gries [105]. A more recent treatment of the material and one upon which we have also drawn substantially is Schneider and Andrews [118]. Their treatment is somewhat different in that the formal system is based on well formed formulas that are annotated programs. The more traditional approach based on triples is used in Hoare [66] for sequential programs and in Owicki and Gries [105] for concurrent programs. Another approach to the verification of concurrent programs can be found in Ashcroft [14], where an invariant constructed of control predicates and the assertions in a program annotation is used. A discussion of the relationship between the proofs of programs before and after auxiliary variables have been removed appears in McCurley [97]. A more complete description of the use of control predicates can be found in Owicki and Lamport [106] and Manna and Pneuli [96]. The relative merits of control predicates and auxiliary variables are discussed in Lamport [82]. An introduction to temporal logic operators can be found in Alford, Lamport, and Mullery [9], and the use of temporal logic to prove liveness properties of concurrent programs is covered in Owicki and Lamport [106]. A discussion of the relationship between safety and liveness is contained in Alpern and Schneider [10].

4.12 Exercises

In the following exercises, the word "prove" means that formal reasoning is to be used to produce an annotated program, while the word "demonstrate" means that a convincing argument is sufficient.

1. Demonstrate how coroutines can be implemented using the cobegin and await constructs.

2. Describe why it is unwise to nest an await statement within an await statement.

3. Assume that the operational semantics of the if statement is revised so that if all guards are closed the executing process waits. In a purely sequential program the process will wait forever, but in a concurrent program a concurrent process might change the value of a variable in a guard and cause it to become open. In that case the waiting process can resume. The same formal semantics describes either operational semantics. Demonstrate that the formal semantics of the busy wait implemented by the statement

$$\textbf{do } \neg B \rightarrow \textbf{skip; od}$$

is the same as the formal semantics of

$$\textbf{if } B \rightarrow \textbf{skip; fi}$$

4. Using auxiliary variables, formalize the argument given in Section 3.3 for the correctness of the program in Figure 1.2. Prove that the second resume statement in *Iop* cannot cause a transfer of control to the resume statement in *releasebuf*.

5. Suppose the execution of some statement, $s_{i,j}$, in the ith component of a cobegin statement interferes with an assertion, $p_{k,l}$, used in the proof of the kth component, $k \neq i$. We would like to embed $s_{i,j}$ in an if statement with operational semantics as described in the previous problem, and thereby delay its execution to avoid the interference. Thus, the if statement has the form

$$\textbf{if } B \to s_{i,j};\ \textbf{fi}$$

Express, in terms of $p_{k,l}$ and $wp(s_{i,j}, p_{k,l})$, the weakest B that achieves this result.

6. Prove that the await construct is no more powerful than a semaphore.

7. The State Banking Commission has just issued a regulation that the balance of any bank account cannot exceed \$100,000. The deposit transaction of Figure 4.3 must be redesigned to accommodate the new regulation (if a deposit would make the balance exceed \$100,000, the amount deposited is reduced to the amount required to make the balance exactly equal \$100,000). Intuitively, it appears that two of the new deposit transactions might interfere with each other, but that a deposit and a withdrawal transaction do not interfere. Thus we can define two sets of critical sections, one for deposit transactions and one for withdrawal transactions (using different semaphores). Design the new deposit transaction using this intuition, and prove that it works correctly.

8. Implement the Producer-Consumer program of Figure 1.2 as a concurrent program in which $Prod$ and $Cons$ are components of a cobegin statement. Use the await construct for synchronization. Add auxiliary variables num_{in} and num_{out}, where num_{in} counts the number of items added to buf and num_{out} counts the number of items removed. Prove that the assertion $num_{in} = num_{out} + count$ is a loop invariant of each process.

9. Consider the cobegin statement

$$\textbf{cobegin } S_1;\ /\!/\ S_2;\ \textbf{coend}$$

where S_1 contains the statement

$$\textbf{if } x > 20 \to x := x - 1;\ [\,]\ x \leq 20 \to x := x + 1;\ \textbf{fi}$$

Can interference occur between S_1 and the assertion $x > 10$ that appears in the proof of S_2? What would your answer be if we assumed that the if statement is executed atomically?

10. Prove that, in the following program fragment, when the second process assigns 1 to x, the boolean variable $b1$ is true.

```
var
  x : integer := 0;
  b1, b2 : boolean := false, false;
cobegin
  begin
    b1 := true;
    await b2 → skip;
    b1 := false;
  end;
//
  begin
    await b1 → skip;
    x := 1;
    b2 := true;
  end;
coend;
```

11. Prove that, upon termination of the following program fragment, *num* = $N - 2M$, assuming that N and M are nonnegative integers.

```
var
  num, i, j : integer := 0, 0, 0;
cobegin
  do i < N →
    i, num := i + 1, num + 1;
  od;
//
  do j < M →
    j, num := j + 1, num - 2;
  od;
coend;
```

12. State the conditions for non-interference in the coenter statement as described by the Coenter Rule (4.11).

13. Reimplement the solution of the Readers-Writers Problem given in Figure 1.7 using the await construct to implement semaphores. Add appropriate auxiliary variables and prove that the solution is correct: when one writer is writing, no other writer is writing and no reader is reading.

14. Prove that, upon termination of the following program fragment, $y = 1$.

```
var
  b : boolean := false;
  x, y, z : integer := 0, 0, 0;
cobegin
  begin
    x := x + 1;
    b := true;
    z := x + 3;
  end;
//
  await b → y := x ;
coend;
```

15. Prove that, upon termination of the following program fragment, $x = 2$ and $y = 1$.

```
var
  b : boolean := false;
  x, y : integer := 0, 0;
cobegin
  begin
    x := 1;
    b := true;
    await ¬b → skip;
    x := 2;
  end;
//
  begin
    await b → skip;
    y := x;
    b := false;
  end;
coend;
```

16. The goal of the following program fragment [105] is to find the index of the first positive element in the array $x[1..M]$. The two components of the cobegin statement search the odd and even array elements separately. Prove that if the program terminates, the variable k is equal to the index of the first positive element (or $M+1$ if all elements are nonpositive). Prove that the program terminates by first proving that each component of the cobegin terminates when run by itself and then proving that the execution of the other component does not interfere with your termination proof.

```
var
  x : array [1..M] of integer;
  i, j, oddtop, eventop : integer := 1, 2, M + 1, M + 1;
begin
  cobegin
    do (i < min(oddtop, eventop)) ∧ (x[i] ≥ 0) →
        oddtop := i;
    [] (i < min(oddtop, eventop)) ∧ (x[i] < 0) →
        i := i + 2;
    od;
  //
    do (j < min(oddtop, eventop)) ∧ (x[j] ≥ 0) →
        eventop := j;
    [] (j < min(oddtop, eventop)) ∧ (x[j] < 0) →
        j := j + 2;
    od;
  coend;
  k := min(oddtop, eventop);
end;
```

17. Give an example of a concurrent program that terminates under conditions of strong fairness, but not under weak fairness.

18. Describe the difference in meaning between the two assertions

$$\{at(\alpha)\}\ \alpha : [S]\ \{after(\alpha)\}$$

and

$$at(\alpha) \rightsquigarrow after(\alpha)$$

19. Using temporal logic and control predicate operators, express the liveness property that in the program $S_1; S_2; \ldots; S_n;$, each statement, S_i, is executed at least once.

20. The goal of the following program fragment is to copy the contents of the array A into the array B using a one element buffer buf. Prove that if the program terminates $B[k] = A[k]$ for $1 \le k \le M$. Prove that the program terminates.

```
var
  A, B : array [1..M] of elemtype;
  buf : elemtype;
  full : boolean := false;
  i, j : integer := 1, 1;
cobegin
  do i ≤ M →     -- producer
    begin
      await ¬full → skip;
      buf, full, i := A[i], true, i + 1;
    end;
  od;
//
  do j ≤ M →     -- consumer
    begin
      await full → skip;
      B[j], full, j := buf, false, j + 1;
    end;
  od;
coend;
```

5

Monitors

In this chapter we continue our discussion of concurrent programs operating in a shared memory environment. As we saw in Chapter 4, demonstrating interference freedom significantly complicates the proofs of such programs. The purpose of this chapter is to introduce techniques for imposing a discipline on the use of shared variables that greatly reduces this complication.

Once again, modularization is at the core of these techniques. The strategy is to view the shared memory as a collection of shared data objects, similar to those discussed in Chapter 3, and to encapsulate each object inside a module called a *monitor*. Any process wishing to access a shared object performs its access through the monitor associated with that object. The required synchronization mechanisms are contained within the monitor.

As might be expected, proof obligations are greatly simplified when such an approach is used. Mutual exclusion is provided automatically in monitors. Signaling is also provided but, as we shall see, different monitor implementations provide signaling mechanisms that differ in the extent to which object code efficiency is traded off for language support of correct synchronization.

Thus, monitors preserve the advantages of data abstraction from both an implementation and a proof point of view.

5.1 Structured Synchronization

In Chapter 1 we described algorithms involving only simple variables that concurrent processes can use to synchronize their actions. Such algorithms range from simple polling to more elaborate techniques for achieving mutual exclusion. From a conceptual viewpoint, these algorithms exhibit a surprising amount of subtlety and complexity, particularly as the number of processes to be synchronized grows. From a practical viewpoint, efficiency is a problem, since busy waiting is involved.

The semaphore was proposed as a means of overcoming these shortcomings. Conceptually, a semaphore is a simple data structure that provides an effective synchronization tool. From a practical viewpoint, semaphores integrate nicely into the kernel of an operating system and eliminate the need for busy waiting.

Although semaphores are conceptually simple and easy to implement, they are not consistent with a high level approach to synchronization. While for simple applications they can be used in a syntactically structured way (for example, mutual exclusion can be achieved by bracketing critical sections with P and V operations), more complex synchronization problems can easily involve the use of multiple semaphores with no syntactic structure to aid in the design or comprehension of the solution. P and V operations need not balance each other. Instead, they may be spread throughout the program in a seemingly random way so that their role in solving the synchronization problem is not apparent. Hence, although powerful, semaphores provide the programmer with insufficient structure to deal with complex synchronization problems.

Perhaps the simplest way to structure mutual exclusion is to provide a lock construct within which to embed critical sections:

$$\textbf{lock } l \rightarrow S$$

where S is a statement. Typically, S is a critical section, which performs a complete update on some shared data, bringing it from one consistent state to another. l is an instance of a data type – called a *mutex* in the language Modula-3 (a successor to Modula-2) – that can assume two values: locked and unlocked. l is initially unlocked and is set to the locked state while control resides in S. A process attempting to execute a lock construct involving l is blocked if l is found to be in the locked state. In a formal sense, if $\mathcal{P}_1$ executes

$$\textbf{lock } l \rightarrow S1$$

and $\mathcal{P}_2$ executes

$$\textbf{lock } l \rightarrow S2$$

assertions within $S1$ (excluding its pre- and postconditions) cannot be interfered with by statements in $S2$ (and vice versa). Typically, l is associated in a program with some set of shared variables, and all statements that access those variables do so in the context of a lock construct that tests l. (Different sets of shared variables would use different instances of the mutex type.) Although the lock construct structures mutual exclusion, it is the programmer's responsibility to ensure that accesses to shared variables are performed within a lock construct.

Instead of viewing the individual processes as executing in a common addressing environment containing the shared data, we can add yet more structure by encapsulating each process and shared data object in a distinct module. Each module has procedure and data components. The data in a module can be accessed only by executing the associated procedures; hence module address spaces are disjoint, a feature that can be enforced by the compiler. The operations on a shared data object, which previously had been critical sections within the processes, are now implemented as calls to procedures in the module implementing the object. That module is referred to as a *monitor*. Within a given monitor, only one procedure is allowed to execute at a time. Thus, a monitor guarantees mutual exclusion of operations on the shared data. Concurrent Pascal, Modula, and Mesa are examples of concurrent programming languages that incorporate monitors.

A monitor can be viewed as an implementation of a shared abstract data type. The monitor procedures implement the abstract operations, and the shared data is the concrete implementation of some data abstraction. The data abstraction is characterized by an abstract invariant, and each monitor procedure is required to preserve this invariant, thus bringing the data from one consistent state to another.

Process modules are the initial sites of activity of the processes of the concurrent program. A one-to-one correspondence exists between the process modules and the processes of the program. Each process module contains data local to the corresponding process. Processes execute asynchronously. When access to shared data is required, a process calls a monitor procedure. The call results in a change of addressing environment for the process: the shared data is now accessible, and the local data in the process module is temporarily inaccessible. Nested calls, from a procedure in one monitor to a procedure in another, are possible (although, as we shall see later, may cause difficulties). When the access to the shared data has been completed, the process returns to its process module. Hence, a process migrates from one addressing environment to another. Each process module in a concurrent program can become the site of a concurrent thread of activity and hence corresponds roughly to a component in a cobegin statement. Note that a monitor is not a separate process, since it does not have its own individual thread of control.

In Figure 5.1, m processes are initiated in the m process modules. We denote both the ith process and its corresponding process module by $\mathcal{P}_i$. The context differentiates the usages. Processes $\mathcal{P}_1$ and $\mathcal{P}_2$ both call monitor $\mathcal{M}_2$ and hence can communicate through the shared data accessible there.

The implementation of a monitor must guarantee mutual exclusion among the monitor procedures. One simple way of implementing mutual exclusion is to associate with each monitor, $\mathcal{M}_i$, a semaphore, s_i, initialized to 1. $P(s_i)$ is compiled into each call of a procedure in $\mathcal{M}_i$, and $V(s_i)$ is compiled into each return. Hence, the monitor structure makes critical sections visible to the compiler and eliminates the need to explicitly program mutual exclusion.

The glue that links the various modules of the concurrent program together is a kernel, similar to those we discussed in Chapter 1. The kernel can be viewed as a library procedure that is linked together with the compiled versions of the modules of the concurrent program. It multiplexes the processes and provides synchronization – perhaps by implementing semaphores. We have seen one use for a semaphore in providing mutual exclusion for each monitor; we shall see other uses shortly. The kernel is bounded by a dotted line in Figure 5.1 to emphasize the fact that it is not a visible part of the program.

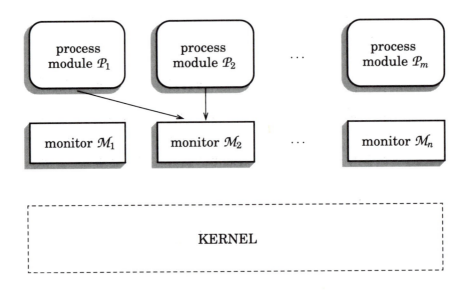

Figure 5.1: A concurrent program built of monitors and process modules.

Figure 5.2 illustrates a concurrent program corresponding to the diagram in Figure 5.1. The syntax used is not meant to correspond to any particular language. The program contains the declaration of process modules and monitors, followed by a body. The body can serve to initialize various components of the system and initiate new processes. Many concurrent languages use a construct similar to a *fork* to initiate a new process. A statement consisting of the name of a process module creates a new process in that module. The invoking process then continues execution. Thus, in the figure, new processes are created in each of the modules P_1, P_2, ..., P_m in turn.

The structure of a monitor is shown in Figure 5.3. The variable *sdb* represents the shared database that is accessed by the processes of the system through calls to the monitor's procedures. *sdb* is a permanent variable of the module, accessible to monitor procedures and retaining its value between monitor calls, but inaccessible outside the monitor. Each procedure contains the code that was formerly a critical section. Such a procedure is referred to as an *entry procedure* to distinguish it from a procedure that is strictly internal and cannot be invoked from outside the monitor. The monitor body is executed when the monitor declaration is elaborated (when control enters the module containing the monitor declaration) and can be used to initialize *sdb*. Since the monitor body is executed at elaboration time, *sdb* will be initialized before the first call to a monitor procedure is executed.

An example of a concurrent program that processes a job stream is shown

```
system
    process 𝒫₁ ··· end 𝒫₁;
    process 𝒫₂ ··· end 𝒫₂;
        ···
    process 𝒫ₘ ··· end 𝒫ₘ;
    monitor ℳ₁ ··· end ℳ₁;
    monitor ℳ₂ ··· end ℳ₂;
        ···
    monitor ℳₙ ··· end ℳₙ;
begin
    𝒫₁; 𝒫₂; ...; 𝒫ₘ;
end;
```

Figure 5.2: The concurrent program corresponding to the diagram in Figure 5.1.

```
monitor ℳᵢ;
    var sdb;              -- the shared database
    procedure cs1(···);
        var locals1;
            ···          -- critical section 1 code
    end cs1;
    procedure cs2(···);
        var locals2;
            ···          -- critical section 2 code
    end cs2;
        ···
    procedure csk(···);
        var localsk;
            ···          -- critical section k code
    end csk;
begin
        ···              -- body: initialize sdb
end ℳᵢ;
```

Figure 5.3: An example of monitor syntax.

in Figure 5.4. The program includes three process modules:

input reads information from an input device, assembles it into jobs, and enqueues the jobs on an input queue, *in_q*.

execute dequeues jobs from *in_q*, executes them, and places their output on an output queue, *out_q*.

output dequeues output from *out_q* and prints it.

Each queue, or bounded buffer, is implemented by a monitor, and each monitor exports procedures *Enqueue* and *Dequeue*. Standard dot notation is used to reference a particular monitor procedure.

5.2 Signaling

We have previously noted that in addition to mutual exclusion, application-related synchronization, or signaling, is generally required in constructing a concurrent program. While mutual exclusion can be supplied automatically by the compiler, signaling must be programmed explicitly, since the requirements of each application are different. Hence, some mechanism for signaling is needed in a concurrent programming language. The mechanism must allow a process to wait when continued execution is not appropriate and to be awakened (have its state returned to ready) at a later time. We discuss one approach to signaling in this section and several others in later sections.

The usual approach to signaling within monitors uses a new data type, called *signal*. Two operations, *sig.wait* and *sig.send*, are permitted on a variable, *sig*, of type signal. The operational semantics of these operations is as follows:

A process executing *sig.wait* waits. At any given time, *sig* has associated with it a set of waiting processes that have previously executed *sig.wait* and have not yet been awakened.

The execution of *sig.send* causes one of the waiting process in the set associated with *sig* to be awakened (its state is set to ready) and removed from the set. If there are no processes in the set at the time *sig.send* is executed, the operation has no effect.

From an implementation point of view, *sig* is the name of a set. When a process executes *sig.wait*, it waits and its name is placed in the set named *sig*. When a process executes *sig.send*, some waiting process from the set *sig* (if there is one) is removed from the set and awakened.

Note that the operational semantics of the send operation does not specify which process is to be awakened if more than one waiting process is in the set associated with the signal at the time send is executed. This type of nondeterminism is exactly analogous to that associated with the *V* operation

```
system
  process input();
  begin
    do true →
      begin
          ···          -- read input and assemble into job
        in_q.Enqueue(job);
      end;
    od;
  end input;
  process execute();
  begin
    do true →
      begin
        in_q.Dequeue(job);
          ···          -- execute job
        out_q.Enqueue(res);
      end;
    od;
  end execute;
  process output();
  begin
    do true →
      begin
        out_q.Dequeue(res);
          ···          -- print output
      end;
    od;
  end output;
  monitor in_q;
    var concrete_vars;
    procedure Enqueue(h :  in job_info) ··· end Enqueue;
    procedure Dequeue(h :  out job_info) ··· end Dequeue;
    begin ··· end in_q;
  monitor out_q;
    var concrete_vars;
    procedure Enqueue(r :  in results) ··· end Enqueue;
    procedure Dequeue(r :  out results) ··· end Dequeue;
    begin ··· end out_q;
begin
  input; execute; output;
end;
```

Figure 5.4: A concurrent program for processing a job stream.

```
monitor in_q;
  var
    Qarray : array[0..(N – 1)] of job_info;
    last : 0..(N – 1);              – – pointer to last position filled
    count : 0..N;                   – – count of filled positions
    nonempty, nonfull : signal;
  procedure Enqueue(h : in job_info);
    begin
      if count = N → nonfull.wait; [] count < N → skip; fi;
      Qarray[(last + 1) mod N], last, count
         := h, (last + 1) mod N, count + 1;
      nonempty.send;
    end Enqueue;
  procedure Dequeue(h : out job_info);
    begin
      if count = 0 → nonempty.wait; [] count > 0 → skip; fi;
      count, h := count – 1, Qarray[(last – count + 1) mod N];
      nonfull.send;
    end Dequeue;
  begin
    count := 0;
    last := 0;
  end in_q;
```

Figure 5.5: A monitor implementing a bounded buffer.

on semaphores, and once again we impose a fairness requirement, that no waiting process be passed over indefinitely.

An example of the use of signals is shown in Figure 5.5, which is an implementation of the monitor *in_q* of Figure 5.4. The data structure is stored (as a permanent variable) within the monitor, together with the two procedures for accessing the queue and an initialization routine.

In designing *in_q*, we must consider two application-related synchronization issues: the process *input* must wait if the queue is full when it makes a call to *Enqueue*, and the process *execute* must wait if the queue is empty when it makes a call to *Dequeue*. To provide this synchronization, we define two signals: *nonfull* and *nonempty*. We associate with each signal a boolean expression describing the synchronization condition it represents. Since *nonfull* represents the condition that the buffer is not full, we associate with it the boolean expression $count < N$. Our intention is that if a process attempts to execute *Enqueue* when that condition is not true, it will be made to wait at the signal *nonfull*, and that later, when it is awakened, the condition is guaranteed to be true. Thus, the first statement in *Enqueue* checks this condition and, if it is false, executes *nonfull.wait*. When the execution of *Dequeue* has completed, the queue cannot be full (an element has just been removed); hence the last statement in *Dequeue* is *nonfull.send*. It is possible, of course, that no process is waiting when the send is executed, but then the send has no effect so no harm is done.

Similarly, the signal *nonempty* represents the condition that the queue is not empty: *count* > 0. Thus, the first statement of *Dequeue* evaluates the condition *count* = 0 and executes *nonempty.wait* if it is true. The last statement of *Enqueue*, which can be executed only when the queue is not empty, is *nonempty.send*.

Whereas signaling is explicitly handled in the monitor using wait and send, mutual exclusion is implicit. The *Enqueue* and *Dequeue* procedures correspond to critical sections so that if, in Figure 5.4 for example, *execute* invokes *in_q.Dequeue* at a time when *input* is executing *in_q.Enqueue*, *execute* will be made to wait on the hidden semaphore associated with *in_q*. Hence, one process executes in a monitor at a time.

The notion of "one process executing in a monitor at a time" is a little more subtle than the notion of "one process executing in a critical section at a time." First of all, we cannot count a waiting process as executing, since if we did, there would be no way of awakening it. Since a signal is visible only within the monitor, a second process executing a monitor procedure is needed to awaken the waiter. Hence, provision must be made to allow other processes to execute in the monitor when a process waits.

More troubling, however, is the situation that arises when a process is awakened by a send. At that time two processes, neither of which is waiting, exist within the monitor: the process that executed the send and the awakened process. Some restrictions must be applied in this situation, since we wish to prevent the arbitrarily interleaved execution of the two processes within the monitor. The restriction usually adopted is that one of the two processes *pauses* until the other relinquishes control of the monitor. A process that has paused is not eligible to execute. Hence, although neither process is waiting, one is given higher priority than the other until it relinquishes control of the monitor. By *relinquish control* we mean that the process either exits the monitor or executes a wait. Note that more than one process might be in this paused state; for example, the process chosen for execution could send a signal awakening a third process, so two of the three processes must pause.

The monitor *in_q* is an example of a special case of the use of send: each send is the last statement of a monitor procedure. In this commonly occurring situation, the sender can simply exit the monitor, leaving only one active process and avoiding the need to place a process in the paused state. The scheduling algorithm within the kernel might well take advantage of this special case. The concurrent programming language Concurrent Pascal requires that a send occur only as the last statement of a monitor procedure.

A monitor implementing shared access to an abstract data object, *t*, generally has the form shown in Figure 5.5. The first statement of each monitor procedure conditionally waits. The condition tests whether the corresponding operation can be performed in t's current state. In the treatment of data abstraction in Chapter 3, we referred to that condition as $WP_c^j(\overline{c})$. Once again, since the procedure can assume that the concrete invariant, I_c, is true on entry, it need only test for any additional restrictions beyond I_c that are required for $WP_c^j(\overline{c})$ to be true (for example, in Figure 5.5, *Enqueue* need only check that the queue is not full).

Since only sequential execution was involved in Chapter 3, if $WP_c^j(\overline{c})$ was false on entry to p_j, an exception occurred, which caused the program to halt. In a concurrent environment, the falsity of $WP_c^j(\overline{c})$ indicates that the corresponding operation cannot be performed until the state of t is changed by the execution of some concurrent process. Hence, the caller does not halt; it waits until that state change has occurred (in which case the process that caused the change will execute a send). The last statement of each monitor procedure unconditionally sends on an appropriate signal if that procedure can have the effect of making some condition, $WP_c^j(\overline{c})$, true.

While a monitor providing access to a shared data abstraction is common, the use of wait and send need not be restricted to the first and last statements of monitor procedures; they may appear at arbitrary points. Later we shall see examples of such monitors, which are used as schedulers to provide ordered access to a resource. When send is not the last statement in a monitor procedure, we must decide which process is made to pause when the send executes: the newly awakened process or the process that executed the send. Although it might seem that the decision could be based purely on considerations of efficiency (in which case the newly awakened process would pause and the sender continue, thus avoiding a context switch), we shall see in the next section that another factor is involved.

5.3   Axiomatization of Monitors

Our approach to proving the correctness of a monitor that provides access to a shared abstract object follows the treatment of data abstraction in Chapter 3. At the abstract level, we assume some abstract data object, t, described by an abstract invariant, I_a, which constrains the values that t can assume, and an initial value, t_{init}. We no longer specify the weakest precondition for termination of each operation, since halting has been replaced by waiting. Termination now depends on the invocation of operations on t by concurrent processes. Lastly, we specify the pre- and postconditions for each operation invocation.

On the concrete level, we express the constraints on the possible values of concrete variables by a concrete invariant, I_c, and specify their initial values, $\overline{c}_{init}$. In Chapter 3 we pointed out that to ensure that I_c is true on entry to each procedure body, S_j, we must demonstrate that it is true as a postcondition of S_{init} and of each procedure body. In the case of a monitor we have additional proof obligations, since mutual exclusion may be released, and hence a procedure body can be entered, when a wait is executed. Thus, to ensure that I_c is a precondition to S_j, I_c must be true just prior to relinquishing control as a result of the wait. Since I_c must be a precondition of the wait and, since the wait should appear to the executing process as a pure delay, it must be a postcondition as well. Hence, we have argued that the triple

$$\{I_c\} \; sig.wait \; \{I_c\}$$

must be true of each wait, where sig is any signal.

Next we must decide, when a send is executed, whether the sender or the awakened process is to pause. Note that the awakened process originally waited because the state of $\bar{c}$ was inappropriate for its continued execution. That is, some condition, B, on $\bar{c}$ was false. In the case of an abstract data structure, that condition is $WP_c^j(t)$. The reason for performing the send at some later time is that a concurrent process has made B true. For example, in the monitor in_q, the condition B that allows the producer to enqueue an element is $count < N$. The producer waits if, on entry to $Enqueue$, $count = N$; and the consumer sends on exit from $Dequeue$, since it knows that B must be true and the producer might be waiting.

Suppose that whenever a send is executed, the sender pauses and a context switch is performed to the awakened process. If B is true as a precondition of send, it will necessarily be true as a postcondition of wait. If, instead, when a send was executed, the awakened process were to pause, there would be no guarantee that B would still be true when it ultimately resumed; the sender might have performed subsequent actions that made B false. Hence, the connection between the precondition of the send and the postcondition of the wait is supported by the kernel when a "switch on send" rule is implemented. As we have already pointed out, however, this support of the axiomatic structure comes at the price of efficiency – the cost of two extra context switches. (If we require that each send be in the last statement of a monitor procedure, this cost can be avoided.)

Assume we choose to switch on send (as we shall see later, other choices are possible). Since I_c is a postcondition of each wait, we must require that it be a precondition of the send. Thus, the following pair of axiom schemas describes the desired formal semantics of the wait and send.

Axioms for Wait and Send under "Switch on Send" Semantics

$$\{I_c\} \; sig.wait \; \{I_c \wedge B\} \tag{5.1}$$

$$\{I_c \wedge B\} \; sig.send \; \{I_c\} \tag{5.2}$$

I_c is a postcondition of the send, since the sender resumes when a process relinquishes control of the monitor (either through exiting or waiting) and at that time I_c is always true. Note that B is not a postcondition of the send, since the awakened process may invalidate it before the sender resumes.

We have assumed that B is an assertion over the concrete variables, $\bar{c}$, and does not involve variables local to a monitor procedure. Without such a restriction, the sender has no way of determining whether the synchronization condition for which the waiting process is waiting has become true (since that condition might be dependent on variables local to the waiting process). Furthermore, note that the values of local variables do not change when a process executes a send or wait. Hence, any assertion involving only local variables that is true before the send or wait will be true afterwards. Therefore, such an assertion can be conjoined to the pre- and postconditions of the send or wait. (It is invariant to the execution of the send or wait in a manner that is analogous to an assertion that is invariant to the execution of a resume statement as discussed in Section 3.3.)

In contrast to the formal semantics of other language constructs, the axioms for wait and send must be understood as a pair – they support each other. Recall that B is not part of the definition of the signal *sig*, but has been associated with *sig* as part of the design. The axioms state that if I_c is a precondition of each operation *sig.wait* and if $I_c \wedge B$ is a precondition of each operation *sig.send*, then it can be concluded that $I_c \wedge B$ will be a postcondition of each operation *sig.wait* and I_c will be a postcondition of each operation *sig.send*.

We can now apply to monitors the approach described in Chapter 3 for building sequentially accessed abstract data objects. At the concrete level, we demonstrate that the implementation supports the concrete specification. A monitor procedure is simply a sequential program. With the addition of axioms for wait and send, we have a complete description of each statement that can appear in such a program and hence we can carry out a proof of each procedure in isolation. The proof of a monitor procedure cannot be interfered with, for the following reasons:

Processes executing concurrently in other modules operate in disjoint address spaces and hence cannot interfere with assertions describing the state of concrete variables declared in the monitor.

Interleaving within the monitor is controlled by mutual exclusion, with process switching occurring only during the execution of wait and send statements. The effect of such switches is described by the wait and send axioms, which ensure that interleaved execution establishes the proper postconditions when the control point following the wait or send is serviced.

Having demonstrated correctness at the concrete level, we can demonstrate that the concrete implementation supports the abstract specification in exactly the same way as for sequentially accessed objects. Then we can use the abstract specification in proving the correctness of the invoking program.

5.4   Example – The Bounded Buffer Monitor*

While we have shown that interference does not occur in monitor implementations at the concrete level, interference may still be an issue at the abstract level, since concurrent processes manipulate a shared (abstract) data object. To illustrate the issues, we once again consider a queue. The various assertions used in Chapter 3 to characterize a queue at the abstract level were formulated with a sequential environment in mind. In a concurrent environment, the queue is shared, and its value may change as the result of actions taken in any of the processes. Hence, an assertion about the value of the abstract queue in one process may be interfered with by the invocation of an abstract operation in another. For example, it would be unwise, after enqueueing an item e on a queue, to assert that e is the last element, since a concurrent call to *Enqueue* would interfere with the assertion. Hence, we restrict ourselves to assertions that are not subject to interference. It should be kept in mind that our concern about interference goes beyond a desire to construct proofs; the circumstances that result in interference are exactly those that the program designer must keep in mind, even if a formal proof is not to be constructed.

To avoid interference in reasoning about the queue, we introduce two history (auxiliary) variables, *in* and *out*, of type sequence. *in* is the sequence of all the elements that have ever been enqueued on the abstract queue, in_q, and *out* is the sequence of all the elements that have ever been dequeued. Then the following assertion is a program invariant of any program that uses in_q.

$$in = out \circ in\_q \tag{5.3}$$

The invariant states that every element that has ever been enqueued either has been dequeued or is still in the queue.

Our motivation for introducing *in* and *out* is that, since elements are never deleted from these sequences, they possess certain properties that are not subject to interference. Hence, assertions at the abstract level about in_q can be stated in terms of *in* and *out* and then related to in_q using (5.3). To describe these assertions, we define *prefix(s)*, where s is a sequence, to be the set of all prefixes of s. Thus, if

$$s = <a, \ b, \ c, \ d>$$

then

$$prefix(s) = \{\lambda, \ <a>, \ <a, b>, \ <a, b, c>, \ <a, b, c, d>\}$$

The prefix operator is useful because an assertion of the form

$$u \in prefix(in)$$

cannot be interfered with. Since the value of *in* can be changed only by appending new elements at the end, initial portions of *in* cannot be altered. The same statement applies to *out*.

(1) The invariant, I_a, is
$$(0 \le Length(in\_q) \le N) \wedge (in = out \circ in\_q)$$

(2) The initial values are
$$in = out = in\_q = \lambda$$

(3) Procedure headings are
procedure *Enqueue*(*a* : **in** *element*)
procedure *Dequeue*(*b* : **out** *element*)

and axiom schemas specifying the semantics of procedure invocation are
$$\{P^{in,\ in\_q}_{in\ \circ\ <x>,\ in\_q\ \circ\ <x>}\}\ in\_q.Enqueue(x)\ \{P\}$$

$$\{P^{out,\ y,\ in\_q}_{out\ \circ\ <First(in-out)>,\ First(in-out),\ Tail(in\_q)}\}\ in\_q.Dequeue(y)\ \{P\}$$

Figure 5.6: An abstract specification for a shared queue.

With such considerations in mind, we show the abstract specification of a concurrently accessed queue in Figure 5.6. It should be compared with the abstract specification of the sequentially accessed queue given in Figure 3.2. The pre- and postconditions of the procedures indicate the effect of invocation on *in* and *out* as well as *in_q*. Assertions at the abstract level, however, should be formulated in terms of the auxiliary variables to avoid interference. Conclusions about *in_q* can be derived from (5.3), which has been added as a conjunct to I_a. The proof that (5.3) is an invariant follows easily from the abstract specifications. Note that the precondition of *Dequeue* involves the expression $in - out$, which is the sequence *in* with the prefix *out* removed.

in and *out* are permanent variables of the monitor. Although they can appear in assertions in the calling processes, they are not otherwise accessible to those processes and hence, as discussed in Chapter 3, we can deal formally with them in the same way as we deal with in out parameters.

As an illustration of how this specification can be used, suppose a process enqueues an element, *a*, on the queue *in_q*. We do not wish to use, as a postcondition of *Enqueue*, that *a* is the last element of *in*, since that assertion can be interfered with by a concurrent execution of *Enqueue*. Instead, we use as the postcondition that there is some prefix of *in* for which *a* is the last element

$$((\exists r)\ (r \in prefix(in)) \wedge (a = Last(r)))$$

where $Last(r)$ denotes the last element of sequence *r*. Substituting this postcondition into the axiom schema for *Enqueue* given in Figure 5.6 we obtain for the precondition

$$((\exists r) \; (r \in prefix(in \; \circ < a >)) \wedge (a = Last(r)))$$

which is equivalent to *true*, since $(in \; \circ < a >) \in prefix(in \; \circ < a >)$. Thus, we have

$$\{true\} \; in\_q.Enqueue(a) \; \{((\exists r) \; (r \in prefix(in)) \wedge (a = Last(r)))\}$$

In contrast, the triple

$$\{true\} \; in\_q.Enqueue(a) \; \{a = Last(in\_q)\}$$

can also be proven, but is subject to interference.

Now suppose that a second call on *Enqueue* from the same process enqueues an element, b, on in_q. We would like to assert, as a postcondition of the second call, that if a and b are dequeued, a will be dequeued before b, despite any concurrent activity. Stating such a property in terms of in_q is difficult, since a may have already been deleted from in_q when the second call on *Enqueue* is made, and hence we cannot claim that a precedes b in in_q. Instead, it is sufficient to assert that a precedes b in *in*, since *out* is a prefix of *in*. Thus, we use as a postcondition of the second call to *Enqueue*

$$((\exists r, s) \; (r, s \in prefix(in)) \wedge (r \in prefix(s)) \wedge (a = Last(r)) \wedge (b = Last(s)))$$

Substituting this postcondition into the axiom schema for *Enqueue* given in Figure 5.6 we obtain for the precondition

$$((\exists r, s) \; (r, s \in prefix(in \; \circ < b >)) \wedge (r \in prefix(s)) \wedge (a = Last(r)) \wedge (b = Last(s)))$$

Note that proof of the existence of an s that satisfies this assertion is trivial: s is $in \; \circ < b >$, which is an element of $prefix(in \; \circ < b >)$. Thus, the postcondition of the first call to *Enqueue* implies the precondition of the second; hence, their triples can be composed as

$$\{true\}$$
$$in\_q.Enqueue(a);$$
$$in\_q.Enqueue(b);$$
$$\{((\exists r, s)(r, s \in prefix(in)) \wedge (r \in prefix(s))$$
$$\wedge(a = Last(r)) \wedge (b = Last(s)))\}$$

The postcondition of the second triple states the desired property. The point to keep in mind with respect to these assertions is that, since they are formulated in terms of the prefix operator, they are not subject to interference by concurrent invocations of *Enqueue* and *Dequeue*.

Having decided upon an abstract specification for the concurrently accessed queue, we must now consider the concrete level. The monitor procedure bodies and the queue data structure shown in Figure 5.5 are essentially the same as those shown in Figure 3.6. Hence, the concrete specifications and the proof that the concrete implementation supports the abstract specification follow the same lines as for the sequential case. Several additional points need to be addressed, however.

First, consider the concrete specification. The introduction of *in* and *out* changes the specification shown in Figure 3.5 in a straightforward way. The concrete invariant, I_c, is now

$$I_c : (0 \leq count \leq N) \wedge (in = out \circ R(\ll Qarray, last, count \gg))$$

in and *out* must be initialized to λ, and they must be updated properly in *Enqueue* and *Dequeue*. Termination conditions need no longer be specified. To support this specification, procedure *Enqueue* in Figure 5.5 must be augmented with the assignment statement

$$in := in \circ <h>$$

and procedure *Dequeue* must be augmented with the assignment statement

$$out := out \circ <h>$$

The modified implementation is shown in Figure 5.7. *in* and *out* are initialized to λ and are accessed only from within monitor *in_q*. Thus, the updates to *in* and *out* specified in both the abstract and the concrete specification for the two procedures (and the initialization) are clearly valid. Also, based on the abstract specification given in Figure 3.2, *in_q* is updated correctly. Hence, the augmented forms of I_c and I_a are maintained.

in and *out* are concrete (auxiliary) variables in the program of Figure 5.7, since they appear in assignment statements within the procedures. We can also take the view that there are abstract (auxiliary) variables called *in* and *out* for use at the abstract level. We have used the same names for the abstract and concrete versions of *in* and *out* because the representation mapping between the two versions is the identity function.

Second, the procedure bodies used in the sequential case have been modified with wait and send statements, and we must take this into account before we can claim that the implementation supports the concrete specification. Consider the first conjunct of I_c. We must prove (among other things) that if I_c is a precondition of the body of *Enqueue*, this conjunct will be a postcondition. Since the second conjunct of I_c plays no role in the proof, it will be omitted in what follows. Although *Enqueue* involves only a wait on the signal *nonfull* and a send on the signal *nonempty*, the two axiom schemas for each signal must be considered as a pair. Thus, we instantiate the two schemas for *nonempty* as

$$\{0 \leq count \leq N\} \; nonempty.wait \; \{(0 \leq count \leq N) \wedge (count > 0)\} \qquad (5.4)$$

```
monitor in_q;
  var
    Qarray : array[0..(N – 1)] of job_info;
    last : 0..(N – 1);           – – pointer to last position filled
    count : 0..N;                – – count of filled positions
    nonempty, nonfull : signal;
    in, out : sequence;          – – auxiliary variables
  procedure Enqueue(h : in job_info);
    begin
      if count = N → nonfull.wait; [] count < N → skip; fi;
      Qarray[(last + 1) mod N], last, count
         := h, (last + 1) mod N, count + 1;
      in := in ∘ < h >;
      nonempty.send;
    end Enqueue;
  procedure Dequeue(h : out job_info);
    begin
      if count = 0 → nonempty.wait; [] count > 0 → skip; fi;
      count, h := count – 1, Qarray[(last – count + 1) mod N];
      out := out ∘ < h >;
      nonfull.send;
    end Dequeue;
  begin
    count := 0;
    last := 0;
    in, out := λ, λ;
  end in_q;
```

Figure 5.7: A bounded buffer monitor augmented with auxiliary variables.

$$\{(0 \leq count \leq N) \wedge (count > 0)\} \ nonempty.send \ \{0 \leq count \leq N\} \qquad (5.5)$$

While we do not need (5.4) to reason about *Enqueue*, the demonstration of invariance requires that we consider *Dequeue* as well, and (5.4) must be used to describe the semantics of the statement *nonempty.wait*.

Starting with the last statement in *Enqueue* and working backwards using (5.5), we find that the postcondition of the if statement is

$$0 \leq count < N$$

(since *count* is incremented in the assignment statement). We can obtain a precondition of the if statement sufficient to ensure this postcondition using the If Rule, with a hypothesis obtained from the following axiom describing skip:

$$\{0 \leq count < N\} \; \mathbf{skip} \; \{0 \leq count < N\}$$

and an axiom describing wait. Once again, the schemas for wait and send must be instantiated as a pair, this time for *nonfull*. We use

$$\{0 \leq count \leq N\} \; nonfull.wait \; \{(0 \leq count \leq N) \wedge (count < N)\} \qquad (5.6)$$

$$\{(0 \leq count \leq N) \wedge (count < N)\} \; nonfull.send \; \{0 \leq count \leq N\} \qquad (5.7)$$

and obtain as a precondition of the if statement

$$0 \leq count \leq N$$

which is the first conjunct of I_c, thus demonstrating that this conjunct is invariant to the execution of *Enqueue*. As before, (5.7) must be used in carrying through the proof of *Dequeue*.

Having demonstrated that the implementation supports the concrete specification, we must show that the concrete specification supports the abstract specification. This is done as in the sequential case.

5.5 Monitor Implementation

We have seen that the mutual exclusion associated with monitors can be implemented by associating with each monitor a unique semaphore (which we assume is implemented within the kernel). In this section we show that a signal can also be implemented using a semaphore. Thus, we will have shown that a monitor can be built on a kernel that implements the abstraction of a semaphore and hence that semaphores are at least as powerful as monitors. The reverse is also true: a monitor can be designed that presents the abstraction of a semaphore. Hence, monitors and semaphores are equally powerful.

Our implementation of signals involves associating with each signal a record whose type is shown in Figure 5.8. The record has two fields: a semaphore and an integer to count the number of processes waiting on that semaphore. We assume that the semaphore associated with the monitor for the purpose of mutual exclusion is called *mutex* and that the signal *sig* has been declared within the monitor using the declaration

$$sig : signal$$

One possible implementation of wait and send is shown in Figure 5.9. A switch on send semantics is implied. Assume that when a sending process, $\mathcal{P}_1$, executes *sig.send*, the resulting execution of V(*sig.sem*) awakens a single waiting process, $\mathcal{P}_2$, leaving two active processes in the monitor. If the kernel elects to continue executing $\mathcal{P}_1$, $\mathcal{P}_1$'s next action will cause it to wait on *mutex* (since *mutex* must have value 0 at this point), which achieves the desired

type
   signal = **record**
      sem : *semaphore* := 0;
      count : *integer* := 0;
   end;

Figure 5.8: The data type used to implement a signal.

sig.count := *sig.count* + 1;   **if** *sig.count* > 0 →
V(*mutex*);   **begin**
P(*sig.sem*);   *V*(*sig.sem*);
sig.count := *sig.count* − 1;   *P*(*mutex*);
                                                               end;
                                                            [] *sig.count* = 0 →
                                                               skip;
                                                            fi;

            (a)   (b)

Figure 5.9: Implementation of (a) wait and (b) send operations on signal *sig*.

result, since P_2 is then the only active process in the monitor. If, instead, the kernel elects to run P_2, the desired result (of executing P_2) is obtained immediately. If the kernel elects to run some third process, that process will not be able to enter the monitor because the value of *mutex* is zero and hence the decision as to whether to run P_1 or P_2 first will simply be postponed.

Note that a process relinquishes control by performing *V*(*mutex*) when either exiting or waiting, and that the sender pauses by performing *P*(*mutex*). This use of *mutex* for both waiting and pausing results in some (perhaps) unexpected behavior for the send. Since pausing involves waiting on *mutex*, the paused process cannot be distinguished from other processes that are waiting to enter the monitor. Hence, the sender might not be the next process selected to run in the monitor after control of the monitor is next relinquished [since, other than fairness, nothing can be assumed about which process resumes when *V*(*mutex*) is executed]. The crucial question that must be answered is "Does this situation violate the assumed formal semantics?" The sender resumes at some future time when a process executing in the monitor relinquishes control (*i.e.*, waits or exits). Since I_c is a precondition of both wait and exit, it will necessarily be true as a postcondition of the send, and that is all that is required by (5.2). Hence, such a sequencing of processes does not violate the assumed formal semantics, and the implementation is therefore acceptable. The concurrent language Modula (Modula is an ancestor of both Modula-2 and Modula-3) treats paused processes in this way (although the original Modula compiler did not implement signals using semaphores).

We can also design a more intuitively satisfying implementation of waiting that gives priority to senders that have paused over processes trying to enter the monitor. In this case an additional semaphore is associated with the monitor to implement pause. If a sender is waiting on this semaphore when control is relinquished, it is awakened and mutual exclusion is not released. Since the additional semaphore enables us to distinguish paused processes from those trying to enter the monitor, the unexpected behavior is eliminated.

5.6   A Kernel Implementation in Modula-2*

In the previous section we demonstrated that a monitor could be constructed on top of a kernel that supports the abstraction of a semaphore. Such a kernel could be used in a multiprocessor or time sliced system. In such a system, a process might attempt to enter a monitor at a time when another process was active within that monitor. By explicitly using semaphores, we ensure that the process attempting to enter will be made to wait. The kernel implementation must also deal with another issue: in a multiprocessor system the kernel data structures themselves are subject to concurrent access and hence must be protected. Typically this protection is provided with busy waits, using special instructions implemented in hardware (*e.g.,* test-and-set).

In this section we describe a kernel appropriate for a uniprocessor system that does not implement time slicing. The kernel uses coroutines to support the abstraction of concurrent processes. If we view the kernel together with the hardware on which it executes as a single system, and calls to the kernel as abstract operations, each coroutine appears to be a process. Thus we henceforth refer to these coroutines as processes. The kernel supports the abstraction of process synchronization. Processes (coroutines) synchronize from time to time through calls to procedures *WAIT* and *SEND* (implemented in the kernel) and otherwise appear to run asynchronously.

The kernel implements switch on send semantics. Hence, process switching occurs only on calls to *WAIT* and *SEND*. Under these circumstances, when a process attempts to enter a monitor, any process within the monitor must have its control point at a call to *SEND* or *WAIT*. Therefore, mutual exclusion is automatically ensured – semaphores are not needed. If interrupt-handling processes are supported by the kernel, process switching also occurs on interrupts. To avoid violations of mutual exclusion, (1) all routines accessing data structures pertinent to the handling of a particular interrupt are encapsulated in a *device module* and interrupts are disabled whenever control resides in that module and (2) calls to interruptible modules are not permitted from within device modules. Using these techniques, we can avoid the need for

DEFINITION MODULE kernel;

EXPORT QUALIFIED SIGNAL, StartProcess,
  SEND, WAIT, Queue, Init;

TYPE SIGNAL;

PROCEDURE StartProcess(P : PROC; n : CARDINAL);
  (*start a program P as a concurrent process with workspace size n*)

PROCEDURE SEND(VAR s : SIGNAL);
  (*resume one process waiting for the signal s*)

PROCEDURE WAIT(VAR s : SIGNAL);
  (*wait for some other process to send the signal s*)

PROCEDURE Queue(s : SIGNAL) : BOOLEAN;
  (*true if the queue for signal s is nonempty*)

PROCEDURE Init(VAR s : SIGNAL);
  (*initializes the queue for signal s to empty*)
END kernel.

Figure 5.10: A Modula-2 definition module for a kernel.

semaphores in this case as well.

Figures 5.10, 5.11, and 5.12 illustrate an implementation of a kernel in Modula-2 (taken from [138]). Figure 5.10 shows the definition module, which contains the list of exported items. Figures 5.11 and 5.12 show the implementation module. Two import lists follow the heading in the implementation module. The function *TSIZE* takes a type as its argument and returns the number of storage units occupied by a variable of that type. The procedure *ALLOCATE* returns in its first argument the address of a storage area whose size is specified in its second argument. We have assumed a single processor system; hence mutually exclusive access to kernel variables cannot be violated as a result of concurrent calls to the kernel by two processes executing on different processors. However, if we allow the kernel itself to be interrupted, mutual exclusion could be violated if interrupt-driven code made a kernel call. To avoid this situation, we disable interrupts in the kernel. In the example, we have assumed two priority levels, 0 and 1, and have indicated that the kernel is to be executed at the higher level by placing the (bracketed) 1 in the module heading.

```
IMPLEMENTATION MODULE kernel [1];
FROM SYSTEM IMPORT ADDRESS, TSIZE, PROCESS,
   NEWPROCESS, TRANSFER;
FROM Storage IMPORT ALLOCATE;

TYPE SIGNAL = POINTER TO ProcessDescriptor;

ProcessDescriptor = RECORD
   ringptr : SIGNAL;
   sigptr : SIGNAL;
   pro : PROCESS;
   ready : BOOLEAN
END;

VAR cp : SIGNAL;                          (*current process*)

PROCEDURE StartProcess(P : PROC; n : CARDINAL);
   VAR s0 : SIGNAL; wsp : ADDRESS;
BEGIN s0 := cp; ALLOCATE(wsp, n);
   ALLOCATE(cp, TSIZE(ProcessDescriptor));
   WITH cp ↑ DO
      ringptr := s0 ↑ .ringptr; s0 ↑ .ringptr := cp;
      ready := TRUE; sigptr := NIL
   END;
   NEWPROCESS(P, wsp, n, cp ↑ .pro); TRANSFER(s0 ↑ .pro, cp ↑ .pro)
END StartProcess;

PROCEDURE SEND(VAR s : SIGNAL);
   VAR s0 : SIGNAL;
BEGIN
   IF s ≠ NIL THEN
      s0 := cp; cp := s;
      WITH cp ↑ DO
         s := sigptr; ready := TRUE; sigptr := NIL
      END;
      TRANSFER(s0 ↑ .pro, cp ↑ .pro)
   END
END SEND;
```

Figure 5.11: A Modula-2 implementation of a kernel: first part.

```
PROCEDURE  WAIT(VAR s : SIGNAL);
  VAR s0, s1 : SIGNAL;
BEGIN
  IF s = NIL  THEN s := cp
  ELSE  s0 := s; s1 := s0 ↑.sigptr;
     WHILE  s1 ≠ NIL  DO
        s0 := s1; s1 := s0 ↑.sigptr
     END;
     s0 ↑.sigptr := cp
  END;
  s0 := cp;                            (*search ring*)
  REPEAT cp := cp ↑.ringptr UNTIL  cp ↑.ready;
  IF cp = s0 THEN  HALT  END;     (* deadlock*)
  s0 ↑.ready := FALSE; TRANSFER(s0 ↑.pro, cp ↑.pro)
END  WAIT;

PROCEDURE Queue(s : SIGNAL) : BOOLEAN;
BEGIN  RETURN s ≠ NIL
END  Queue;

PROCEDURE  Init(VAR s : SIGNAL);
BEGIN s := NIL
END Init;

BEGIN                                (*kernel initialization*)
ALLOCATE(cp, TSIZE(ProcessDescriptor));
  WITH cp ↑ DO
     ringptr := cp; ready := TRUE; sigptr := NIL
  END
END kernel.
```

Figure 5.12: A Modula-2 implementation of a kernel: second part.

A process is described in the kernel by a record of type *ProcessDescriptor*
(hidden within the implementation module), which contains a flag (to indicate
whether the process is ready or waiting on a signal), the process reference,
and two list pointers. All process descriptors are permanently linked into a
circular list, called the ring, which is traversed in sequence each time the next
ready process is to be identified. Each signal is implemented as a list of process
descriptors of processes waiting for a send on that signal. The descriptor of a
waiting process is therefore linked to two lists, while the descriptor of a ready
process is linked only to one.

A user of the kernel can create a new signal by declaring a variable of type *SIGNAL* (the type is exported from *kernel*) and calling *Init* to initialize it.

The procedure *QUEUE* tests whether the list associated with the signal passed as an argument is empty.

The procedure *WAIT* links the descriptor of the executing process to the end of the list associated with the signal passed as an argument. Then *WAIT* searches the ring for the next ready process; if none is found, the system deadlocks.

The procedure *SEND* deletes the process descriptor at the head of the list associated with the signal passed as an argument and passes control to the corresponding process. Thus, the processes waiting on a signal are treated in a first-in-first-out fashion, and the discipline for awakening processes is fair.

A new process is created by a call to *StartProcess*, with a procedure (the new process's code) and a workspace size passed as arguments. Space is first allocated for the process's workspace and descriptor using the procedure *ALLOCATE*. The process reference returned in the call to *NEWPROCESS* is stored in the descriptor, and control is transferred to the newly created process.

The initial process, *main*, is treated somewhat differently. *main*, which is the thread of control that executes the main program module, can create any number of coroutines by calling *StartProcess*. It is a peer of these coroutines but, since it is not created by a call to *StartProcess*, it is created without a descriptor. Hence, a descriptor must be created separately for it. We create this descriptor within the body (*i.e.*, the initialization portion) of *kernel*. The body is executed only once after the *kernel* has been imported into some module. The initialization code places in the ring a single descriptor to be used to store information about *main*. Thus, when *main* makes its first call to *StartProcess* and control is transferred to the new process, a process reference to *main* will be stored in this descriptor so that *main* can be resumed at a later time.

5.7 Resource Scheduling

The bounded buffer example illustrates how monitors can be used to control access to an abstract data object that can be thought of as a shared resource. By implementing mutual exclusion, the monitor guarantees that only one process accesses the object at a time, and by providing signals, it enables the designer to guarantee that the object state is appropriate for each access. While both of these synchronization methods involve delaying one process in favor of another, they are scheduling decisions in only a very primitive sense. In both cases the next process to access the abstract object is chosen arbitrarily using the selection mechanism built into the semaphore implementation. In situations in which a particular discipline is to be imposed on the order in which processes are to access a resource, the semaphore selection mechanism is inadequate.

In general we need to consider situations in which an arbitrary algorithm must be implemented in the monitor for controlling the order in which processes access a shared resource. For example, consider an alarmclock monitor that causes a calling process to wait for an interval of time that the caller specifies. The abstract interface presented to the user involves a single procedure:

procedure *wakeme*(*n* : **in** *integer*)

whose effect is to delay the caller by *n* units of time. Note that the abstract invariant in this case is simply *true*, since there is no abstract data structure involved.

The alarmclock monitor can be implemented in several ways. One possibility is to declare an array of records whose dimension is equal to the number of potential callers, where each record contains a signal and an integer. A caller, executing in *wakeme*, calculates its wake-up time, stores the value in the integer field of its record, and waits on the corresponding signal. A clock process (which is a device handler for a physical clock) maintains the current time and periodically enters the monitor to wake processes whose wake-up time has arrived. In this implementation, at most one process at a time waits on any one signal, and therefore the clock process has complete control over which process it awakens. Concurrent Pascal imposes such a limitation on the use of signals (*i.e.,* only one process at a time can wait on a given signal).

In addition to complexity, this implementation suffers from the need to allocate a number of signals proportional to the maximum number of caller processes, a potentially significant waste of space if, on the average, only a small number of processes are waiting at a given time. To develop simpler implementations for situations such as this, we generalize wait to permit the caller to specify a priority. The operational semantics of *sig.wait*(*p*) is as follows:

Execution of *sig.wait*(*p*) causes the caller to wait on the signal *sig* with priority *p*. Execution of *sig.send* wakes the process with the smallest priority waiting on *sig*.

With this modification, we can construct the simpler alarmclock monitor shown in Figure 5.13 (taken from [69]). In this implementation, a caller to *wakeme* uses the time at which it wishes to be awakened as the priority in its wait on the signal *wakeup*. Each send on *wakeup* awakens the waiting process with the smallest wake-up time. Procedure *tick* is called by a clock process when a unit of time has elapsed. *tick* unconditionally wakes the process with the smallest priority, since it has no way of knowing whether the wake-up time for that process has occurred (if the wake-up time has not occurred for the process with the smallest priority, it certainly has not occurred for any other process). From an axiomatic point of view, since *alarmsetting* is not a monitor permanent variable, the clock process cannot evaluate the expression *now* ≥ *alarmsetting*; therefore the precondition, *B*, of the send is simply *true*. Thus, the awakened process cannot assume that *now* ≥ *alarmsetting* is a

```
monitor alarmclock;
  var
    now : integer;
    wakeup : signal;
  procedure wakeme(n : in integer);
    var
      alarmsetting : integer;
    begin
      alarmsetting := now + n;
      do now < alarmsetting → wakeup.wait(alarmsetting); od;
      wakeup.send;
    end wakeme;
  procedure tick();
    begin
      now := now + 1;
      wakeup.send;
    end tick;
  begin
    now := 0;
  end alarmclock;
```

Figure 5.13: A monitor implementing an alarmclock.

postcondition of the wait and so it must explicitly check this condition (and perhaps resume waiting) each time it is awakened. From a formal point of view, we see that the construction is correct, since the Do Rule guarantees that $now \geq alarmsetting$ is a postcondition of the loop. The send that is in procedure *wakeme* takes care of the case in which two processes must be awakened at the same time. Note that this example illustrates a situation in which wait is not invoked as part of the first statement of a monitor procedure.

When reasoning about the prioritized wait, we can use the fact that no scheduling discipline is specified for an unprioritized wait, and hence, any discipline for implementing it will do, including the one used for a prioritized wait. Thus, the axiom schemas (5.1) and (5.2) are still valid. The prioritized wait, however, is not fair.

While the alarmclock monitor illustrates the usefulness of a prioritized wait in performing scheduling, it does not actually illustrate scheduled access to an arbitrary shared resource. Consider now a shared resource, R, whose operating characteristics are such that it is reasonable to expect a queue of users to build up waiting to access it. For reasons of efficiency we would like to order this queue in an application-dependent way. A typical example of such a situation is a latency reduction algorithm for scheduling access to a disk. Our assumptions imply that each access to R takes a nonnegligible amount of time, and hence it would be self-defeating to place the scheduler for R in the same monitor as R itself. If we were to do so, a process requesting access to R at a time when R was being used by another process (which is therefore active within the monitor) would be forced to wait for entry to the monitor as a result of mutual exclusion. A queue of requestors would build up in this way but, since none could enter the monitor while R was in use, the scheduling algorithm implemented within the monitor could place no order on them. Instead, when R was released, an arbitrary waiting process would be chosen (by the semaphore selection algorithm applied to *mutex*) and that process would enter and immediately be granted access to R. Since no queue of waiting processes would ever build up inside the monitor, the application-related scheduling algorithm within the monitor would serve no purpose.

Thus, the routines for scheduling access to R and the routines for accessing R should be encapsulated in separate modules. Clearly the scheduling module must be a monitor, since it will be subject to concurrent access. If the process awakened within that monitor for the purpose of being granted next access to R simply made a nested call to the accessing module, as shown in Figure 5.14(a), the situation described in the previous paragraph would remain unchanged, since mutual exclusion is not released when a nested call from a monitor procedure to another module is made.

Figure 5.14(b) illustrates an implementation that overcomes these difficulties and allows scheduling decisions to be made within a scheduling monitor. A user calls the scheduling monitor to request access to the resource. Control is returned to the user when access has been granted. The user then accesses the resource directly. Thus, one user can enter the scheduling monitor at the same time that another is accessing the resource. After completing an access to the resource, the user is required to make an additional call to the scheduler to indicate that the resource is free. The resource itself need not be a monitor, since it is never subject to concurrent access.

Note two disadvantages of this protocol. First, an improperly coded user process that does not observe the protocol (*e.g.*, accesses R without first making a request to the scheduler, or fails to release R after using it) can obstruct the use of R by other processes. Thus, the correctness of the monitor in ordering the accesses to R cannot be proven without taking into account the sequence in which its procedures are invoked by routines at a higher level. Hence, not only has additional complexity been introduced into the proof process, but the correctness of a level of code that implements an abstraction depends upon the correctness of a level that uses the abstraction – an unfortunate situation. Second, the user interface is complicated, since scheduling and access are separately revealed to the user level. From the user's viewpoint, the fact that the use of the resource must be scheduled indicates that the resource is shared with other processes, a detail that can be hidden.

These objections can be overcome by interposing an *envelope* level between the user modules and the scheduler/resource level, as shown in Figure 5.15.

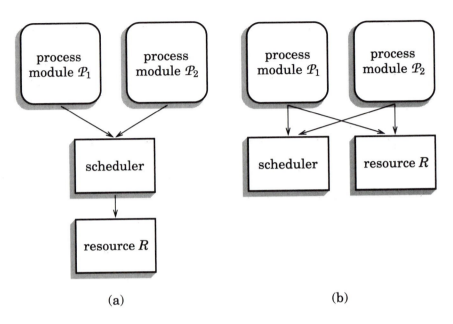

Figure 5.14: Scheduling a resource: (a) nested call, (b) request/release proto-col.

The envelope presents the abstraction of a scheduled resource to the user. The user appears to have exclusive access to a scheduled resource, when in fact the resource is being shared with other processes. Thus, the interface presented to the user by the envelope is essentially the interface presented by R itself. The envelope is responsible for observing the request/release protocol. Each user is provided with its own envelope module through which it must access the resource.

We introduce one further modification of the signal mechanism to enhance the ease with which scheduling algorithms can be implemented. The new construct is called *sig.queue*; its operational semantics is as follows:

The boolean function *sig.queue* returns the value *true* if a process is wait-ing on the signal *sig* and *false* otherwise.

sig.queue introduces a new element into the program state: an indication of whether or not processes are waiting on *sig*. Wait and send affect the value of this element; hence the axioms for wait and send must be revised if we are to reason about this aspect of the state. (We shall see an example of such a revision shortly.)

As an example of a resource scheduled using the organization shown in Figure 5.14(b) and of the use of *sig.queue*, consider the solution to the Readers-

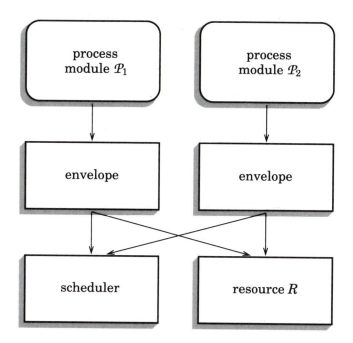

Figure 5.15: An envelope layer implements the request/release protocol.

Writers Problem shown in Figure 5.16 (taken from [69]). A process that wants to perform a read calls *startread* and, when that call returns, it can perform the read. When the reader is finished reading, it calls *endread*. A process wanting to write follows a similar protocol with *startwrite* and *endwrite*. Hence the solution has the structure shown in Figure 5.14(b).

In contrast to the solution given in Chapter 1, this implementation does not give readers unconditional priority over writers. Instead, if a writer arrives while reading is in progress, subsequently arriving readers must wait. As a result, *readcount* will eventually fall to zero and a waiting writer will be allowed to resume. When a writer completes, all waiting readers will be allowed to resume even if additional writers are waiting. The solution is therefore referred to as a fair solution.

Note that this solution does not implement a first-come-first-served protocol, since readers arriving during a write phase when a writer, W, is waiting will precede W to the resource when the write phase terminates. Note also that the condition for waiting is not always the negation of the condition for waking. Although an arriving reader must wait if there are waiting writers, it may also be awakened when there are waiting writers. Hence, the postcondition of *read_q.wait* is simply $\neg writerbusy$ and not $\neg writerbusy \land \neg write\_q.queue$.

It is interesting to place shared abstract data objects in the context of

```
monitor fair_rdr_wrtr;
  var
    readcount : integer := 0;
    writerbusy : boolean := false;
    read_q, write_q : signal;
  procedure startread();
    begin
      if writerbusy ∨ write_q.queue  →  read_q.wait;
      [] ¬writerbusy ∧ ¬write_q.queue  →  skip;
      fi;
      readcount := readcount + 1;
      read_q.send;
    end startread;
  procedure endread();
    begin
      readcount := readcount − 1;
      if readcount = 0  →  write_q.send;
      [] readcount > 0  →  skip;
      fi;
    end endread;
  procedure startwrite();
    begin
      if (readcount > 0) ∨ writerbusy  →  write_q.wait;
      [] (readcount = 0) ∧ ¬writerbusy  →  skip;
      fi;
      writerbusy := true;
    end startwrite;
  procedure endwrite();
    begin
      writerbusy := false;
      if read_q.queue  →  read_q.send;
      [] ¬read_q.queue  →  write_q.send;
      fi;
    end endwrite;
end fair_rdr_wrtr;
```

Figure 5.16: A fair solution to the Readers-Writers Problem.

generalized resource scheduling. The data object can be regarded as a resource in which the only scheduling to be performed is the delay of accesses that are inconsistent with the object's state. Hence, a separate scheduling module is not required, since we do not need to control the order in which processes are awakened.

5.8   Monitor Critique I: Semantic Support for Signaling

The introduction of monitors was motivated by a desire to provide high level support for synchronization in concurrent programs. While monitors are a significant step forward over semaphores, a number of criticisms have been made concerning the definition and implementation of the monitor concept.

One criticism is that a monitor does not provide sufficient semantic support for signaling. When we declare a signal, *sig*, we implicitly associate with it some boolean expression, B, and we must demonstrate that B is a precondition of *sig.send* in order to ensure that B is a postcondition of *sig.wait*. The fact that the monitor itself does not guarantee that B is a postcondition of the wait is a shortcoming.

One suggested alternative to the signal is to make the association with B explicit using the construct *wait(B)*, where B is an arbitrary boolean expression that can include monitor permanent variables as well as parameters or variables declared local to the monitor procedure. *wait(B)* has the following operational semantics:

> If B is not true, the process executing *wait(B)* waits. It is awakened at some future time when control of the monitor is relinquished and B is true.

wait(B) has two important advantages. First, a send is no longer needed. Since the expression being awaited is explicitly stated as part of the wait operation, the kernel can evaluate the expression at appropriate times and awaken the waiting process when it is found to be true. Thus, the designer is relieved of the need to explicitly code the send. Second, from an axiomatic viewpoint, the truth of B can be assumed as a postcondition of the wait (whereas formerly it had to be proven that B was a precondition of the send); hence a proof obligation is removed. Thus, the formal semantics is given by

$$\{I_c\}\; wait(B)\; \{I_c \wedge B\}$$

Clearly the construct provides significant additional support for synchronization compared with that provided by signals.

Unfortunately, a substantial price in efficiency must be paid for these advantages. Since the kernel is not in a good position to determine exactly when B becomes true, it might re-evaluate B unnecessarily. The use of an explicit send reduces this overhead. The sending process need only check B when it performs some action that might make B true. In some cases no evaluation of B at all is required. For example, in the monitor in_q (Figure 5.5), execution of the body of *Dequeue* guarantees that the condition associated (implicitly) with the signal *nonfull* must be true.

An even more serious source of inefficiency is that, since B is allowed to be a function of variables local to the waiting process, its evaluation may require a context switch, thus introducing additional overhead. For example, in the monitor *alarmclock* (Figure 5.13), the variable *alarmsetting* is not a monitor permanent variable. Hence, evaluation of the condition $now < alarmsetting$ requires that the kernel perform a context switch into the addressing environment of the waiting process.

Another approach to signaling involves a new data type called *condition*. A condition, *cond*, is a monitor permanent variable that is explicitly associated with a boolean expression, B, in a declaration of the form

$$cond : condition\ B$$

Since B is part of the declaration in the monitor heading, it can be a function only of monitor permanent variables; hence conditions are not as flexible as $wait(B)$. For example, a condition appropriate for use in the monitor in_q is

$$nonempty : condition\ count > 0$$

Note that *count* is a monitor permanent variable. A condition can be used in an enhanced version of the wait construct, *cond.wait*, which has the same operational semantics as $wait(B)$, the only difference being that B is now the expression in the declaration of *cond*.

The advantage of the condition is that, since B contains only monitor permanent variables, its evaluation need not occur in the context of any particular process. Thus, B can be evaluated by the kernel without a context switch, eliminating one source of inefficiency. The formal semantics of a wait on the condition, *cond*, is given by the axiom schema

$$\{I_c\}\ cond.wait\ \{I_c \wedge B\}$$

Once again, send has been eliminated. Also, as with $wait(B)$, a proof obligation is removed since the truth of B can be assumed as a postcondition of the wait.

The implementation of conditions requires that when control of the monitor is relinquished by some process, the kernel must evaluate the boolean expressions associated with conditions on which processes are waiting. If one or more of these expressions is true, one of the waiting processes is awakened. As with $wait(B)$, this evaluation entails additional kernel overhead, which is not required when signals are used.

The use of a condition is illustrated in Figure 5.17, which shows a writer priority solution to the Readers-Writers Problem (taken from [75]). The simplicity of this solution is partly due to the absence of both a send and the

```
monitor wrtrprior_rdr_wrtr;
  var
    readcount, writecount : integer := 0;
    writerbusy : boolean := false;
    read_allowed : condition (writecount = 0);
    write_allowed : condition (readcount = 0) ∧ ¬writerbusy;
  procedure startread();
    begin
      read_allowed.wait;
      readcount := readcount + 1;
    end startread;
  procedure endread();
    begin
      readcount := readcount - 1;
    end endread;
  procedure startwrite();
    begin
      writecount := writecount + 1;
      write_allowed.wait;
      writerbusy := true;
    end startwrite;
  procedure endwrite();
    begin
      writerbusy := false;
      writecount := writecount - 1;
    end endwrite;
end wrtrprior_rdr_wrtr;
```

Figure 5.17: A writer priority solution to the Readers-Writers Problem using conditions.

expression evaluation associated with waking a process. *readcount* counts the number of active readers while *writecount* counts the number of active and waiting writers. Consider the situation immediately after a writer exits from the procedure *endwrite*. If there are both waiting readers and waiting writers, the boolean associated with the condition *read_allowed* will be false but the boolean associated with *write_allowed* will be true. Hence, only a writer can be awakened, as specified in a writer priority solution. Note also that, since the boolean expression is specified explicitly in the condition declaration, the condition for waiting must be the negation of the condition for waking. Thus, another element of flexibility is lost. A fair solution to the Readers-Writers Problem using conditions would not be as simple as this example.

5.9 Monitor Critique II: Efficiency

Concurrent languages are often used to implement systems in which code efficiency is a crucial consideration. Issues such as the cost of monitor entry and exit (which involve semaphore operations) are important. Similarly, a system implementor who demands tight control over the runtime code might object to the send operation, since a context switch is always required and, under certain circumstances, such a switch can be disadvantageous.

For example, Modula provides two types of signals. In addition to the signal whose semantics are described by (5.1) and (5.2), Modula also allows a signal in which a context switch does not occur as part of the send. The justification is that the sending process, P_1, might have higher priority than the waiting process, P_2, and so should not be required to give up control. This situation might occur if P_1 is controlling a device in real time. P_2 might have issued a request for device service. The interrupt indicating service completion is handled by P_1, which must awaken P_2, quickly start device service for the next request (to ensure efficient utilization of the device), and arrange to wait for the next interrupt. A send operation that can be used to awaken P_2 without switching contexts is useful in this case.

Weaker semantics are implied for this type of send. The postcondition of the wait is no longer the same as the precondition of the send, since execution of the waiting process no longer follows immediately after the send. The axiom schema for the wait in this case is simply

$$\{I_c\} \; sig.wait \; \{I_c\} \tag{5.8}$$

Hence, an appropriate way to wait is

$$\textbf{do } \neg B \rightarrow sig.wait; \textbf{ od} \tag{5.9}$$

where sig is a signal and the executing process is waiting for the boolean expression B to become true. Thus, if the process is awakened and B is not true, it immediately initiates a new wait. An advantage of this mode of waiting is that B can be a function of variables local to the waiting process.

The send is described by the schema

$$\{P\} \; sig.send \; \{P\} \tag{5.10}$$

where P is an arbitrary assertion. We use an arbitrary assertion here instead of I_c, since send does not involve context switching and hence the invariant need not be true before and after its execution. (Note that we have implicitly assumed that P does not involve $sig.queue$. If it did, P would not be invariant to the execution of send.) The use of wait is similar to its use in the alarm clock monitor. The difference is that in that case send caused context switching.

The concurrent programming language Mesa takes a similar approach to signaling. The send operation (called *notify* in Mesa) awakens a single waiting process but does not cause a context switch. The fact that the awakened process cannot assume the truth of B makes it possible to use signals somewhat more flexibly. Thus, Mesa allows a timeout interval, T, to be associated with each signal. A process waiting for T units of time will be awakened regardless of whether a send has been executed. Such a feature makes sense only in the context of the weaker semantics of (5.8), since B cannot be assumed as a postcondition of the wait.

Similarly, Modula-3 does not implement a switch on send rule, and therefore condition checking on wake up might be necessary (in addition, Modula-3 does not guarantee that only a single process will be awakened when a send is executed).

Finally, both Mesa and Modula-3 allow a broadcast operation in which all waiting processes on a particular signal are awakened (as before, however, only one process is active in the monitor at a time). Such broadcast awakenings are useful in situations in which B is a function of a variable local to a process and hence the sender is not in a position to know which of the waiting processes should be awakened. For example, a monitor that implements dynamic storage allocation might provide a procedure, *allocate*, in which the number of units of storage desired is specified as a parameter. A requesting process waits if insufficient storage is available. The monitor might also provide a procedure *deallocate*, which releases storage and awakens processes that are waiting for their storage requests to be filled. Unfortunately, unless the amount requested by each waiting process is recorded in monitor permanent variables, *deallocate* has no way of determining which waiting process(es) to awaken. Hence, a broadcast is appropriate: each process rechecks B on resumption and returns to the wait state if insufficient storage is available.

A second source of inefficiency in monitors relates to the rigid enforcement of mutual exclusion. For example, requiring that all shared variables be stored in monitors and accessed through monitor procedures may be unnecessarily restrictive. Thus, in the monitor *alarmclock* (Figure 5.13), the variable *now* contains the current time. To make this variable available to processes that simply wanted to know the time, we would have to implement a new procedure to return the value of *now*. Reading the current time would incur the cost of procedure invocation and semaphore operations on entry and exit. Such a cost could be eliminated if variables could selectively be made available for direct external access. Thus, *now* could be exported in addition to the entry procedure identifiers *wakeme* and *tick*.

While selective exportation is available in many languages, it must be done carefully when concurrency is involved. Processes executing externally to the monitor are not synchronized with processes executing within the monitor, which may be updating the monitor's data structures. Hence, any data structure that cannot be updated atomically may be viewed by external processes in a state in which its invariant is false. Such data structures should therefore not be exported. Thus, if the increment operation used to update *now* is atomic, *now* can be exported. (It should be kept in mind, however, that such exportation is outside of the monitor model and can lead to problems. For example, *alarmclock* might be moved to a new machine in which the increment operation is not atomic. Alternatively, the implementation of *alarmclock* might be changed so that *now* is updated in a non-atomic fashion.) A further restriction, which would normally be imposed, is that variables be exported solely for read only purposes.

A similar criticism relates to situations in which not all computations done within monitor procedures require mutual exclusion. For example, the storage allocation monitor described above might have an additional procedure for expanding a process's current allocation. *expand* might (1) obtain a new (larger) block of storage, (2) copy the contents of the old block into the new block, and (3) release the old block. While *expand* should logically reside within the storage management module, the potentially time-consuming process of copying information from one block to another need not be executed in a critical section. Mesa deals with this situation by allowing a monitor procedure to be declared *public*. Public procedures are not subject to mutual exclusion. If *expand* is made a public procedure, it can still perform functions (1) and (3) under mutual exclusion by calling entry procedures *allocate* and *deallocate*, but it has the flexibility to perform (2) without mutual exclusion, thus allowing a more efficient use of the monitor.

Modula-3 provides a different kind of flexibility by including both the lock construct and signals. In this way, mutual exclusion need not be tied to monitor entry and exit, a potentially awkward requirement. To accommodate this flexibility, wait specifies a mutex in addition to a signal. A process waiting within a lock construct specifies the associated mutex. The mutex is unlocked when the process waits and is relocked when the process is resumed.

5.10   Monitor Critique III: Deadlock

Monitors have been criticized from a number of other points of view. Many of these criticisms are of a very practical nature (*e.g.*, crash recovery) and will not be discussed here. As a final issue, we consider the problem of deadlocks. Deadlock can occur in any system involving resource acquisition and waiting. Hence, the introduction of monitors cannot be expected to eliminate deadlocks. In the monitor context, two processes might be waiting, each expecting the other to execute a send. Mutually recursive monitor calling is another obvious source of difficulty.

A deadlock situation that is more closely related to the monitor structure itself is shown in Figure 5.18. Suppose P_1 executing in M_1 makes a nested call to a procedure in M_2 and then waits before returning. If the process that is to awaken P_1 must traverse M_1 before entering M_2, a deadlock results. Although mutual exclusion is released on wait, and hence entry to M_2 is possible, mutual exclusion is not released when a nested call is made from a monitor to an external procedure, and hence entry to M_1 is not possible. We refer to this

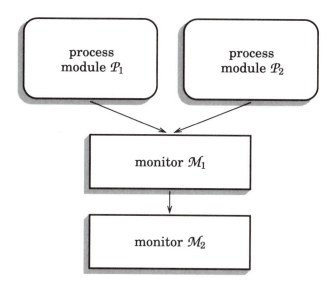

Figure 5.18: Nested monitor calls and hierarchical deadlock.

situation as *hierarchical deadlock*.

One approach to eliminating hierarchical deadlocks is to release mutual exclusion when a nested call is made. However, this approach is not attractive, since it requires that I_c be restored prior to the call and that additional semaphore operations be invoked in the calling monitor, even though the calling process might not wait in the called procedure. Furthermore, this approach is unsatisfactory from the viewpoint of data abstraction, since if the called procedure implements an abstract operation, the requirements on the precondition of the call should be no different from those imposed on access to any data structure maintained within the calling monitor itself. Thus, I_c would have to be a precondition of access to any data structure, whether implemented within the monitor or outside.

Deadlock is an extreme case of a more general problem, referred to as *remote delay*. As we have seen, monitors are used for scheduling access to shared resources. It is frequently important in designing a scheduling algorithm to be able to estimate the time necessary to perform various functions. Consider a nested call from one monitor to a procedure in another. The elapsed time between call and return will depend on the amount of waiting in the called monitor, a quantity that not only is out of the control of the caller, but might not even be predictable. This unpredictable delay not only might have a negative impact on the ability of the calling monitor to make good scheduling decisions, but, by leaving the calling monitor in a locked state, might inhibit its ability to service other requests.

5.11 Real Time Programming

Up to this point we have studied two categories of programs: sequential programs and concurrent programs. From an operational point of view, concurrent programs involve the asynchronous execution of a collection of sequential programs. Although asynchronism has the potential for introducing extraordinary complexity into program execution, we have shown in this chapter that the task of verifying a concurrent program can be effectively dealt with if a discipline is imposed on the way the concurrent program is structured. Thus, if shared variables are confined to monitors (which guarantee mutual exclusion) and if the asynchronous sequential processes exchange signals to synchronize their actions, the technique for verifying a concurrent program is a relatively small extension of the technique for verifying a sequential program. A key reason for this simplicity is that, even though the relative execution speeds of the component processes affect the actual execution interleaving, time itself plays no role in the proof process. The arbitrary interleaving of processes accessing local data does not result in interference. Mutually exclusive access to shared data, together with the exchange of synchronization signals, makes it possible to ensure that certain timing relationships between concurrent processes are maintained and hence, as with sequential programs, correctness depends solely on the program text.

By a *real time program* we mean a program whose validity does depend upon the relative execution speeds of its component processes. Hence, correctness can no longer be deduced solely from the program text, and new reasoning techniques are needed. Unfortunately, time greatly complicates verification, and good techniques for dealing with arbitrary real time programs do not yet exist. In this section we discuss some problems that arise when time is introduced and some approaches to dealing with these problems.

Real time programs generally interact with physical devices. Such interactions occur when a program sends control signals to a device or when the device interrupts or stores values in registers accessible to the program. In many respects these interactions are analogous to the interaction between the processes of a concurrent program. Device registers accessible to the program or memory locations accessed by a channel act like shared variables. Interrupt handling processes wait for interrupts from the device. Hence, interrupts act like send events. Similarly, the device waits for a start signal (*e.g., SIO*) from the controlling program, which is similar to a send event.

We intend to think of a device as a process, called a *device process*, that interacts with normal processes as in a concurrent program. There is one important difference, however. Device processes are not programmable, and hence have fixed, and sometimes undesirable, behavior. The behavior that is particularly problematic from our point of view is that many device processes cannot be made to wait in order to synchronize their actions with the other processes of the program.

For example, a data acquisition device, *dev*, may sample a voltage sensor every T_d seconds and convert the value read into a digital signal, which it stores in a register accessible to the program. Hence, it acts like a producer. The program is the consumer. If it does not read the register within T_d seconds of the time the signal is stored, the value will be overwritten by the next sample. The register is like a bounded buffer with length one. As we have seen, two synchronization requirements must be met by such a buffer: the consumer must wait for a full buffer and the producer must wait for an empty buffer. Since the consumer waits for an interrupt, one of the synchronization requirements is met. Unfortunately, *dev* cannot be made to wait. Thus, the correctness of the program depends upon our ability to guarantee that the consumer empties the buffer within T_d seconds. In other words, correctness depends on time.

With the analogy between devices and processes in mind, we outline a method for designing a real time program in the following steps:

1. Design the entire system as a concurrent program, treating devices as co-operating processes that exchange all necessary synchronization signals;

2. Analyze (perhaps validate) the concurrent program using axiomatic techniques;

3. For each synchronization event that is not actually implemented by the device, derive the time bound which ensures that the program will correctly synchronize with the device;

4. Check whether the bound is actually met by the program.

A goal of step (1) is to develop a structure in which device-dependent code is confined to a small number of modules. This is the code that must satisfy the time constraints that are the subject of steps (3) and (4). By concentrating the code in a few modules, we reduce the complexity of the additional proof obligations.

A standard method for interfacing to a device is to design an interrupt handling process, *handler*, that executes in an infinite loop. Each iteration of the loop services a single interaction with the device. Consider the data acquisition device, *dev*, mentioned above. Assuming that *dev* interrupts each time it stores a new value in the register, the loop in *handler* might have the form shown in Figure 5.19.

handler's responsibility is to transfer values from the device register to the buffer, *buf*, which it shares with some application-related process (whose responsibility is to actually process the information). We assume that *buf* is sufficiently large that it never overflows. *handler* is acting like a consumer with respect to the device register and like a producer with respect to *buf*. It is the consumer interaction that is of concern here. Since *dev* does not wait for the register to be emptied (this is the unimplemented synchronization event), *handler* must be able to execute one iteration of the loop in a time less than the

```
do true →
  begin
    ⋯ – – wait for next interrupt
    ⋯ – – fetch value from device register
    ⋯ – – store in buf
  end;
od;
```

Figure 5.19: The loop of a simple interrupt handling process, *handler*.

minimum time separating two successive interrupts, in this case T_d seconds. This is the time bound referred to in step (3).

If *handler* executes on a dedicated processor with its own private memory, step (4) is fairly easy to check. The execution time of straight line code on a dedicated machine is obtained by summing the execution times of each instruction in the object code. Even in more complex situations, where *handler* contains a nested loop, an upper bound can be placed on execution time since the maximum number of iterations of any loop within an interrupt handler is generally easy to determine. If T_h represents the time to execute one pass through *handler*, then for step (4) we need only verify that

$$T_h \leq T_d \tag{5.11}$$

A more serious problem arises in situations in which *handler* shares the processor with other processes in the system. Execution of *handler* may now be delayed because of contention for the processor. For example, an arbitrary amount of time may be spent between the execution of two successive instructions in *handler* because of the execution of instructions in another process. Hence, summing instruction times would not be an appropriate way to measure the time to execute one pass through *handler*.

Frequently, the device-related code is regarded as having higher priority than application-related code, and hence *handler* cannot be delayed by the execution of application code when an interrupt occurs. If the system only controls a single device, inequality (5.11) is once again the bound to be satisfied.

Consider, however, the more likely case that arises when several devices, dev_i, $1 \leq i \leq N$, must be serviced, and assume that only two priority levels are available in the machine. Then all interrupt handlers are executed at the higher priority level, and all application-related processes are executed at the lower level. Since interrupts are disabled when the processor is at the higher level, once a particular handler, $handler_i$, takes control, the time to execute its code is T_{h_i}. If dev_i attempts to interrupt at a time when some other handler is in control, its interrupt will be disabled until the priority returns to the lower level, thus causing an additional delay in servicing dev_i. If several devices attempt to interrupt in this fashion, their interrupts will typically be enabled in some order fixed by the hardware. If the order is first-come-first-served, for example, the worst case delay for responding to the interrupt from dev_i occurs when all devices interrupt at the same time and dev_i's interrupt is at the end of the queue. In this case, execution of $handler_i$ is delayed by $\sum_{j, j \neq i} T_{h_j}$ and step (4) is satisfied if

$$\sum_{i=1}^{N} T_{h_i} \leq min_j(T_{d_j})$$

The situation becomes much more involved if multiple priority levels are permitted, since then not only can *handler* be interrupted by higher priority interrupts but a particular device might interrupt the same invocation of *handler* several times, depending on the frequency of interrupts from that device. Good solutions to problems involving priority interrupts and conflicting scheduling requirements are not currently available.

One approach that is common when real time constraints are unusually severe is to use a very simple operating system that does not allow interrupts. The kernel schedules all processes (including device handlers) in a round robin manner, allowing each process to execute for a fixed period of time. Each process is designed so that it is guaranteed to accomplish its task within its given time slice, and the time slices are selected so that all real time constraints are guaranteed to be satisfied.

5.12 Bibliographic Notes

The monitor concept was suggested by the work of Dijkstra [38]. The early work on monitors was done primarily by Brinch Hansen and Hoare. The language Concurrent Pascal [24], [25], which was designed and implemented by Brinch Hansen, incorporated the monitor construct for controlling concurrency. Hoare's early paper [69] described a somewhat more general monitor construct. Much of the description in this chapter and the examples are based on that paper. The concurrent language Modula [136] was subsequently developed by Wirth with a goal of producing highly efficient code. Monitors appeared there under the name "interface modules." Application-dependent synchronization is performed in both of these languages using the signal construct as described in this chapter. Modula-2 [138] was designed by Wirth as a successor to Modula to allow the programmer to custom design a kernel. A description of the language Modula-3 can be found in [103]. The condition construct was discussed by Hoare [69] and a concrete proposal was described by Kessels [75]. A more recent implementation of monitors was done in the Mesa language developed by Lampson and Redell [86]. A comprehensive critique of the monitor construct, with an emphasis on practical issues, can be found in Keedy [74]. Techniques for proving the correctness of monitors are discussed in Howard [72] and Owicki [104]. The discussion of real time programs is based on the work of Wirth [137].

5.13 Exercises

In the following exercises, "design" means provide abstract and concrete specifications and a concrete implementation. Unless otherwise stated, use signals for synchronization in your solutions.

1. Design a monitor *sem* that implements the abstraction of a general semaphore, S, with initial value 0. The monitor is to have two (entry) procedures, P and V. As with the bounded buffer, we use two auxiliary variables in the abstract specification of the monitor. num_p counts the total number of P operations that have ever been performed and num_v counts the total number of V operations. Just as with in and out, we can avoid interference with assertions formulated using num_p and num_v. The abstract invariant is $(0 \le S) \wedge (num\_v \ge num\_p)$. The triples describing the semantics of the two abstract operations are

$$\{Q^{num\_p,\ S}_{num\_p+1,\ S-1}\}\, P()\, \{Q\}$$

$$\{Q^{num\_v}_{num\_v+1,\ S+1},\ S\}\, V()\, \{Q\}$$

Prove that your implementation satisfies the abstract specifications.

2. Give a concrete specification for the queue implemented in the monitor of Figure 5.5. Prove that the monitor supports this specification.

3. Design a monitor that implements an abstract data type for a bounded natural number (a nonnegative integer less than or equal to N) with initial value 0. The data type has operations $Add1$, which adds 1 to, and $Subt2$, which subtracts two from the natural number. Implement both operations and prove that they support the abstract specification.

4. Modify the requirements of the previous exercise so that the monitor supports two operations: $Add(n)$, which adds n to the natural number, and $Subt(m)$, which subtracts m from the natural number (both n and m are natural numbers). Design a monitor for this data type, and prove that the implementation supports the abstract specification.

5. Give an abstract specification for a shared set, t, which is accessed using two procedures, **procedure** *insert*(x : **in** *elem*) and **procedure** *delete*(x : **out** *elem*). The procedure *delete* deletes an arbitrary element in the set and returns its value or returns *null* if the set is empty. The specification should indicate that t is initially empty and should include an abstract invariant and triples for each of the two procedures. Use auxiliary variables so the triples will be useful in a program where interference is an issue.

6. Use the abstract specification of the previous exercise. Assume that as the result of a previous call to *insert*, a particular component of a cobegin

statement has inserted the element with value a in t. Given the following subsequent program fragment in that component:

$$delete(x);$$
$$\textbf{if } x = null \rightarrow S; \; [] \; \cdots \; \textbf{fi};$$

we should be able to assert as a postcondition of S that the value a has been deleted. Show how your specification enables you to do that.

7. Give an alternative implementation of monitor entry, exit, wait, and send which guarantees that paused processes resume execution before additional processes are allowed to enter the monitor.

8. Give an alternative implementation for the alarmclock monitor that uses only a single signal but avoids the need to awaken the process with smallest priority at each clock tick.

9. The Readers-Writers Problem comes in three varieties:

   (a) Reader priority: A stream of readers can indefinitely exclude waiting writers.

   (b) Writer priority: A stream of writers can indefinitely exclude waiting readers.

   (c) Fair: A waiting writer prevents additional readers from entering; after a writer completes, all waiting readers can enter.

   We have given a fair solution using signals and a writer priority solution using conditions. Find solutions to the other combinations.

10. Give the abstract specification for a monitor that implements a shared, unbounded stack. The stack is to be characterized by an auxiliary variable, in_out, which is a sequence of elements that have been stored in the stack. An element is appended to in_out when it is pushed on the stack and again when it is popped off the stack. We say that a sequence, S, has the property $paren$ if it satisfies the following recursive rules of formation:

    (a) If S is the empty sequence, then $paren(S)$.

    (b) If $paren(S)$, and S' is obtained by inserting the sequence $< e, e >$ anywhere in S, then $paren(S')$.

    Show that the assertion $paren(in\_out \circ s)$, where s is the contents of the stack (ordered so that the top element of s follows the last element of in_out), is an abstract invariant.

11. State why there is a $read\_q.send$ operation in the $startread$ procedure in Figure 5.16 and not one in the equivalent procedure in Figure 5.17.

12. Implement an envelope that can be used to present the abstraction of a scheduled resource to a user of a resource scheduling monitor similar to that of Figure 5.14(b).

13. Design a monitor solution to the Dining Philosophers Problem. The monitor should have procedures for starting and ending eating and must not deadlock.

14. Implement a monitor for performing latency reduction scheduling for a disk. The monitor is to implement an elevator algorithm in which the disk head is to sweep alternately up the disk (move to higher numbered cylinders) and then down the disk (move to lower numbered cylinders). While the disk head is sweeping up, all requests for accesses at cylinders higher than the current position of the head are to be handled in cylinder order; the reverse is true on the downsweep. Newly arriving requests for the cylinder at which the disk head currently resides should be serviced during the following sweep to ensure fair scheduling. The monitor is to have two entry procedures:

$$\textbf{procedure } request(dest : \textbf{ in } cylinder)$$

$$\textbf{procedure } release()$$

15. Implement a monitor for performing latency reduction scheduling for a disk. The monitor is to implement a shortest seek time first algorithm and to have the same entry procedures in the previous problem. Note that fairness is no longer ensured.

16. Are the following proof rules an adequate description of wait and send (assuming switch on send semantics)? Explain.

$$\{I_c\} \; sig.wait \; \{B\}$$

$$\{(B \wedge sig.queue) \vee (I_c \wedge \neg sig.queue)\} \; sig.send \; \{I_c\}$$

17. In Section 5.6 we described a monitor implementation for a uniprocessor system that does not require semaphores. We imposed two rules concerning device modules to ensure that interrupts did not result in violations of mutual exclusion. Explain why these rules are sufficient.

18. Extend the formal model to include *sig.queue*. Treat *sig.queue* as a boolean variable that has value *true* (*false*) if at least one process is waiting on *sig* (no processes are waiting on *sig*). *sig.wait* and *sig.send* (potentially) change the value of *sig.queue* (i.e., they act like assignment statements). Keep in mind that I_c and B might be functions of *sig.queue*. Your solution should include new axioms for wait and send. (Hint: Replace *sig.queue* with two auxiliary variables of type integer, *num_wait* and *num_sucsend*. *num_wait* counts the number of times a process has waited on *sig* and *num_sucsend* counts the number of times a process waiting on *sig* has been awakened.)

6

Synchronous Communication

Many concurrent systems are designed so that the individual processes exchange information by sending each other messages rather than through a shared memory. The processes may be executing on different processors that do not share a common memory, or they may be on the same processor but executing in different address spaces so that it is inconvenient to access a common memory location. Alternatively, the designer may want the freedom to have the processes execute either on different processors or on the same processor with no coding changes required. Or, the designer may simply believe that message passing is a conceptually cleaner approach to communication among concurrent processes.

In this and the next two chapters we develop methods for reasoning about message passing systems. We introduce new constructs for specifying message passing and then axiomatize their behavior. Before proceeding with this formal presentation, however, we give an informal description of some issues related to the design and use of message passing systems.

6.1 Overview of Communication

A number of alternatives arise in connection with the design and use of message passing systems. These alternatives are in many respects orthogonal, so that appropriate choices can lead to significantly different system configurations. We discuss these alternatives briefly in the following subsections.

6.1.1 Communication Paradigms

Figures 6.1 and 6.2 illustrate two common patterns used when processes communicate with messages. In the *client-server* paradigm, shown in Figure 6.1,

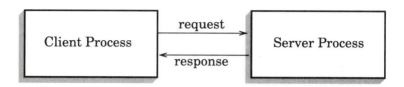

Figure 6.1: The client-server paradigm.

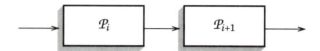

Figure 6.2: The pipeline paradigm.

the client process sends a message to the server process, requesting it to perform some activity; the server performs that activity and then sends a message back to the client informing it that the activity has been completed. For example, the server may be a disk controller, and the client may request that a particular record be stored on the disk.

A monitor is an example of a server which provides service to client processes that want to access the resource it is managing. As discussed in Chapter 5, however, a monitor is not a separate process; it is a routine with which clients interface through procedure calls. We shall see later how to build a monitor-like server process with which clients communicate using rendezvous or remote procedure call mechanisms. These mechanisms can be implemented with simple message passing primitives, but appear to the client processes as if they were procedure calls.

The *pipeline* paradigm, shown in Figure 6.2, is appropriate for a task that can be divided into stages, each of which is performed by a separate process. The process responsible for the ith stage, P_i, receives a message containing a block of data from the process responsible for the $(i-1)$st stage, performs some operation on that data, and then sends a message containing the transformed data to the process responsible for the $(i+1)$st stage. Meanwhile, P_i is available to perform an operation on the next block of data. For example, the pipeline may be processing graphical information for a display system and one stage may be performing a change of coordinates while another is doing a clipping operation.

Other paradigms are possible, but these two capture the ideas of one-way and two-way communication between processes.

6.1.2   Naming

When a process wishes to communicate, it must provide information concerning the location to which a message is to be sent and/or the location from which it is to be received. The simplest alternative is *direct naming*, in which each communication primitive names the process with which communication is to take place. A request from P_1 to send a message containing a vector of values, $\bar{e}$, to P_2 might be expressed as

$$\textbf{send } \bar{e} \textbf{ to } P_2$$

The corresponding receive primitive in P_2 is

$$\textbf{receive } \bar{v} \textbf{ from } P_1$$

where $\bar{v}$ is a corresponding list of variables. The number and types of the values and variables must match. The result of executing this pair of primitives is to store the values in the corresponding variables.

Direct naming is simple in concept and easy to implement. However, it has severe limitations in certain situations, particularly for client-server relationships. With direct naming, the server process must know in advance the names of all the processes that can ever be its clients. For a general system utility, the possible clients can include any active process in the system. It is clearly impractical to name them all in receive primitives. A similar situation occurs for any server process included in a system library.

One approach to overcoming this limitation is to use *one-way direct naming*, in which the sending process names the receiving process, but the receiver is willing to accept a message from any sender. Thus, a send request within P_1 might be

$$\textbf{send } \bar{e} \textbf{ to } P_2$$

with the corresponding receive in P_2

$$\textbf{receive } \bar{v}$$

The ability to receive from any process has the advantage of not requiring the receiver to know in advance which process will be the source of the next message, a requirement that generally cannot be met in a client-server relationship.

One disadvantage of both direct naming and one-way direct naming is that the receiver knows nothing about the content of the message before actually receiving it. A server may be in a state in which it can provide service for some classes of requests but not for others. For example, a server managing a bounded queue may be in a state where the queue is full and so it can fulfill a request to delete from the queue but not one to add to the queue. Monitors deal with this situation by using different procedure names to distinguish different classes of service requests. A similar demultiplexing can be achieved in a message passing environment through the use of ports (sometimes referred to as mailboxes). A *port* is a data object that serves as a common location at which the sender and receiver can store and retrieve messages. The receive primitive might be of the form

receive $\bar{v}$ from port1

Processes can send to the port using a primitive of the form

send $\bar{e}$ to port1

In a client-server relationship, different types of requests can be directed to different ports. The server can selectively accept requests by receiving only from those ports associated with services it is willing to perform at a particular time.

Ports can be created in a variety of ways. In the simplest case, a port is statically declared within the receiving process. The port name is exported, with send only access, to potential senders, so that only the declaring processes can receive messages at that port. In a client-server relationship, the server declares a port for each type of request, and the client addresses a port using the naming structure *processname.portname*.

This approach to port declaration is inadequate in a situation in which several server processes are willing to perform a given service. In this case the port can be declared global to the clients and the servers. (This is the approach taken in Linda.). All servers can now receive requests addressed to a given port. Both clients and servers now refer to the port with its global name, *portname*. Once again, it is desirable to limit receive access to servers.

A port can also be defined dynamically at run time by some process. In this situation, there must be a way to convey the identity of the newly created port to the communicating partner. If the communicants are in a parent/child relationship, the port can be created by the parent and then passed to the child when the child is created (the approach taken in UNIX). Alternatively, the port name can be a first class value in the sense that it can be assigned to a variable and passed in a message to another process. In the case where processes are already able to communicate, a process creates a new port and passes a reference to it in a message to one or more other processes. If the processes are not already in direct communication, the reference is passed through some utility process to which all processes can communicate through known, statically created ports. Clearly, static naming is easier to implement, but dynamic naming is more general. In particular, dynamic naming is often required in environments where an unbounded number of new processes can be created at run time.

Note that with one-way direct naming or statically declared local ports, the identity of the sender might not be known to the receiver, and with globally declared or dynamically created ports, the identity of the sender and the receiver might not be known to each other. Hence, in a client-server relationship, the server might not know the identity of the process that requested the service and therefore might not know to whom to reply when the service is complete. Of course, the client can include its name in the request message, and the server can use that in its reply. However, the server cannot be sure that the name supplied by the client is correct. If it is not, the reply will be returned to the wrong process, causing anomalous behavior. By contrast, with a remote procedure call the system is responsible for returning the reply message to the sender, and thus this problem is avoided.

6.1.3   Dynamic Process Creation

We have been assuming that a server is a single process and that request messages are placed in a queue and dealt with one at a time: when the server is ready to receive a message, it executes a receive primitive. Another possibility is to statically create a fixed pool of server processes within a server module. The processes share access to the module's addressing environment, and all receive messages from the queue. Alternatively, a new server process could be created dynamically each time a message arrives (this is the approach taken in the Argus language.) The process receives the message, services the request, and then is deallocated. The newly created process executes a passive object, a procedure or *handler*, which is declared in the module. The module, sometimes referred to as a *guardian*, contains the permanent data that is shared by all created processes and may include some permanent processes as well.

When all requests are handled by a single process, mutual exclusion is guaranteed. When processes are dynamically created or a pool of processes exists, multiple requests are handled concurrently in a common addressing environment. Hence, some method for achieving mutual exclusion may be needed to eliminate interference within the server.

6.1.4   Synchronization

The extent to which the execution of message passing primitives results in the synchronization of the communicating processes is another design alternative. Message passing systems can be characterized as being synchronous or asynchronous.

In an *asynchronous* message passing system, the only synchronization that occurs is the minimum required of any communication system – a message cannot be received until after it is sent. If a send is executed before the corresponding receive, the system buffers the message and the sending process proceeds without delay. Later, when the receive is executed, the message is delivered. If the receive precedes the corresponding send, the receiver waits until the send is executed.

In a *synchronous* message passing system, the send and receive operations must be executed simultaneously. Hence, the sender and receiver are temporarily synchronized when information is exchanged. If the send is executed before the corresponding receive, the sending process waits until the receiving process executes the receive, and vice versa. When information is exchanged, we say that a *rendezvous* has occurred, after which the processes continue their asynchronous execution.

Higher level synchronous communication exhibits a still more constrained synchronization structure. From the sender's viewpoint, communication is accomplished through ordinary procedure invocation. Thus, the sender executes

$$x.y(\overline{arg})$$

where x is the name of the remote server (*i.e.,* the server resides in a distinct module), y is the name of the procedure the sender wishes to call, and $\overline{arg}$ is the list of arguments passed to that procedure. Information describing the invocation is sent in a message to the receiver.

The receiver can be structured in two ways. *Remote procedure call* (or *rpc*) utilizes dynamic process creation. x is the name of a module, and y is the name of a procedure declared within x. When the invocation message arrives at x, a new process is immediately initiated to execute procedure y. Type matching in accordance with the parameter list in the declaration of y is required.

Alternatively, x is the name of the receiver process, and the sender waits until x executes a corresponding accept statement, which might take the form

accept $y(\overline{par})$ **do** S; **end** y

The statement S is referred to as the body of the accept statement and is executed when a rendezvous takes place between the execution of the invocation statement by the sender and the execution of the accept statement by the receiver. In many respects the accept statement resembles a procedure declaration; for example, $\overline{par}$ is generally a list of parameters, indicating their types and whether they are to be treated as in, out, or in out parameters. The important difference is that while a procedure declaration is passive, the accept is an executable statement within the server process. When a receiver is organized in this way, we speak of *rendezvous* rather than rpc. Hence, the word rendezvous is used in two senses: the generic sense of the coming together of two processes for the exchange of information and the specific sense of a particular form of high level synchronous communication. We rely on the context of the discussion to distinguish between the two.

As an example of the use of an accept statement, consider a process that controls the printing of information that is read from a device. One accept statement within that process might accept an invocation from the device driver, which transfers a single item of information. The process might execute a sequence of such accept statements until it had filled its print buffer and then invoke a remote procedure in the printer driver to print the buffer.

With both rendezvous and rpc, the sender awaits a response from the receiver containing the values of out and in out parameters. While the receiver might not know the identity of the sender, the run time system retains information about the source of the message and automatically returns the results. Hence, in addition to waiting for the invocation message to be received, the sender waits until the body of the procedure or accept statement has been executed and a response has been returned. The applicability of remote procedure call and rendezvous to the client-server paradigm is obvious.

Send and receive primitives that can be made to wait are said to be *blocking*, and those that never wait are said to be *nonblocking*. We have defined synchronous message passing to use a blocking send and a blocking receive, and asynchronous message passing to use a nonblocking send and a blocking receive. It is possible to define a nonblocking receive primitive such that, if it is executed before the corresponding send primitive, no communication takes place and the receiver proceeds without delay. This type of nonblocking receive is useful in the implementation of polling and is related to timeout.

Most implementations of message passing use system buffers to temporarily store messages between the time they are sent and the time they are received. If infinite buffer space is available, an unbounded number of messages can be stored for as long as necessary. The sender need never wait, and a complete implementation of asynchronous message passing is possible. Real systems have only finite size buffers, and a sender may find that the buffer is full, in which case it must be delayed until buffer space is freed or the system must return a "buffer full" exception. Hence a complete implementation of asynchronous message passing is not achieved. With synchronous message passing, no system buffers are used; the message can be transferred directly from sender to receiver when the rendezvous takes place.

Another way to compare message passing systems is by looking at the knowledge the sending process has about the state of the receiving process after a send terminates. In an asynchronous system, the sender does not know if the receiver has received the message, while in a synchronous system, the sender knows that the message has been received but does not know if it has been processed. With rpc or rendezvous, the sender waits until the message has been both received and processed. In this case, the sender may be able to make rather strong assertions about the state of the receiving process.

6.1.5   Timeout

In many situations there may be a limit, T, on the time a sender or receiver process is willing to wait for a rendezvous to take place. This limit may be due to a performance requirement or the need to deal with error situations in which, for example, one partner to the communication has failed. As a special case, a process may wish to engage in communication only if a rendezvous is immediately possible and to continue its computation otherwise. In this case, $T = 0$ and the communication primitive is nonblocking. When a process periodically checks to see if a rendezvous can take place, we say that the process is polling.

If we assume that the correctness of the communicating processes does not depend on real time considerations, the assertions describing their behavior are not a function of T. Thus, we can ignore the actual value of T in our formal reasoning, but we must still distinguish between situations in which communication occurs and situations in which timeout occurs, since different postconditions may apply in the two cases.

6.1.6 Multicast Communication

The type of communication we have been discussing, in which each message is sent to a single destination process, is called *unicast* communication. *Multicast* communication occurs when a message is addressed to a group of processes. *Broadcast* is a special case of multicast in which the group includes all processes, and unicast is a special case in which the group has only one member. A system implementing multicast communication provides mechanisms for naming a group and, perhaps, for allowing processes to dynamically be added to or deleted from the group.

A number of interesting questions arise in connection with multicast. Since group membership may change concurrently with a multicast communication to the group, how can we specify which processes actually receive the message? If the memberships of two multicast groups overlap and concurrent multicasts are addressed to each group, will messages arrive in the same order to all processes that are in both groups? In situations in which messages can be lost, should multicast be atomic (either all group members get the message or none do)? We deal with some of these questions in Chapter 9.

6.2 Axiomatization of Synchronous Communication

For our formal discussion of synchronous message passing systems, we use direct naming constructs. We adopt a widely used notation to represent synchronous message passing. The synchronous send is denoted by

$$\mathcal{P} \,!\, \bar{e}$$

where $\mathcal{P}$ is the name of the process to which the message is to be sent and $\bar{e}$ is a vector of expressions that is to be evaluated and sent to $\mathcal{P}$. The synchronous receive is denoted by

$$Q \,?\, \bar{v}$$

where Q is the name of the process from which a message is to be received and $\bar{v}$ is a vector of variables into which the received message is to be placed.

Neither of these commands terminates when executed in isolation, since each must wait until a matching command is executed. A send and a receive are said to *match* when

1. The process executing the receive is named in the send;

2. The process executing the send is named in the receive;

3. The sizes of the vectors $\bar{e}$ and $\bar{v}$ are the same and corresponding elements are of compatible types.

The operational semantics of synchronous communication is as follows:

> When matching commands are executed, communication occurs. The vector of expressions, $\bar{e}$, in the sending process is evaluated, and its value is sent to the receiving process, where it is assigned to the vector of variables, $\bar{v}$. A communication command fails if the process it names has terminated. Once the match is detected, the evaluation and send in the sending process is atomic and the receive and assignment in the receiving process is atomic.

The combined behavior of matching synchronous send and receive commands is often referred to as a *distributed assignment statement*, since the overall effect is the assignment of the values of the expressions $\bar{e}$ in the sending process to the variables $\bar{v}$ in the receiving process. For example, the effect of the message exchange in

$$\textbf{cobegin } \mathcal{P}_1 :: \textbf{begin } x := 4; \mathcal{P}_2 \mathbin{!} x; \textbf{ end}; \; /\!/ \; \mathcal{P}_2 :: \mathcal{P}_1 \mathbin{?} y; \textbf{ coend} \qquad (6.1)$$

is to assign the value 4 to the variable y.

Message passing commands can be contained within other constructs. For example, the process

$$\textit{Buff} :: \textbf{do } \textit{true} \rightarrow \textbf{begin } \mathcal{P}_1 \mathbin{?} x; \; \mathcal{P}_2 \mathbin{!} x; \textbf{ end}; \textbf{ od}$$

is an infinite loop that maintains a buffer, x. Each iteration of the loop accepts a message from $\mathcal{P}_1$, filling the buffer, and then sends the message to $\mathcal{P}_2$, emptying it.

To reason about a program, we must start with a precise description of each construct in the language. Since we have introduced message passing into the language, we must now provide an axiom schema that describes the effect of all possible instances of the communication statements. We can then construct proofs for each process in the program by combining the axioms for each construct using rules of inference. Finally, we can study how the proofs interact. The inference rule describing the cobegin statement has the form

$$\frac{\{P_1\}\, S_1\, \{Q_1\}, \ldots, \{P_n\}\, S_n\, \{Q_n\}, \; \textit{additional requirements}}{\{P_1 \wedge \ldots \wedge P_n\}\, \textbf{cobegin } S_1; \; /\!/ \ldots /\!/ \; S_n; \; \textbf{coend }\{Q_1 \wedge \ldots \wedge Q_n\}} \qquad (6.2)$$

As in the shared memory case, the *additional requirements* deal with the interactions between the individual proofs.

Recall that neither of the synchronous communication commands terminates when executed in isolation, and that triples specify meaningful postconditions only for terminating constructs. Since any triple is valid for a nonterminating construct, the following axiom schemas describe synchronous communication when each process is considered in isolation:

Axiom Schemas for Synchronous Message Passing

$$\{T\}\ \mathcal{P}\,!\,\bar{e}\ \{U\} \tag{6.3}$$

and

$$\{V\}\ Q\,?\,\bar{v}\ \{W\} \tag{6.4}$$

where T, U, V, and W are arbitrary assertions.

Since there is no relationship between T and U or between V and W, each schema can be instantiated to produce an axiom with arbitrary pre- and post-conditions. At first thought it might seem that we could select any assertions, and hence we might be able to derive arbitrary, or even contradictory, conclusions about the results produced by the program. As we shall see, however, when a message passing command does terminate, only meaningful conclusions can be derived.

The message passing commands terminate when executed in matching pairs with the effect of a distributed assignment statement. Since more than one process is now involved, we reason about the effect of matching execution under the *additional requirements* hypotheses of the inference rule for the cobegin statement. For each matching pair of communication commands we must prove a particular theorem called a satisfaction formula (analogous to the satisfaction requirement for coroutines).

Consider the execution of a specific matching pair of message passing commands described in their respective processes by the triples

$$\{T\}\ \mathcal{P}\,!\,\bar{e}\ \{U\}$$

$$\{V\}\ Q\,?\,\bar{v}\ \{W\}$$

Since the effect of communication is the distributed assignment

$$\bar{v}\ :=\ \bar{e}$$

and, since the overall state of the two processes is described before the assignment by $T \wedge V$ and after the assignment by $U \wedge W$, we have from the Assignment Axiom that the following condition is necessary and sufficient to guarantee the stated postconditions:

$$(T \wedge V) \Rightarrow (U \wedge W)^{\bar{v}}_{\bar{e}}$$

We refer to such a condition as a *satisfaction condition*. Satisfaction restricts the choice of postconditions permitted in (6.3) and (6.4) to assertions that can be supported by the communication that has occurred.

For example, in the program (6.1), the message passing commands can be described by the triples

$$\{x = 4\}\; \mathcal{P}_2 \,!\, x \;\{x = 4\}$$

$$\{true\}\; \mathcal{P}_1 \,?\, y \;\{y = 4\}$$

for which the satisfaction condition

$$((x = 4) \wedge true) \Rightarrow ((x = 4) \wedge (y = 4))_x^y$$

is obviously true. Note that the postconditions of these triples were chosen with the expected behavior of the processes in mind.

Since satisfaction must be demonstrated between every matching pair of message passing commands, we must in general prove the following theorems.

Proof Obligations for Satisfaction

For each matching pair of message passing commands described in the proofs of individual processes by the triples

$$\{T\}\; \mathcal{P} \,!\, \bar{e} \;\{U\}$$

$$\{V\}\; \mathcal{Q} \,?\, \bar{v} \;\{W\}$$

prove the satisfaction condition

$$(T \wedge V) \Rightarrow (U \wedge W)_{\bar{e}}^{\bar{v}}$$

Since processes in message passing systems do not usually share variables, one might think that the condition for interference freedom could be omitted from the inference rule for the cobegin statement. However, we have not precluded the possibility of shared variables, and, as we shall soon see, when we try to formulate proofs we frequently have to introduce shared auxiliary variables. Operations on these variables in one process might interfere with assertions involving them in another. Also, even though two processes have no shared variables, an assertion, A, in one process, $\mathcal{P}_1$, can refer to some variable, x, declared in another process, $\mathcal{P}_2$. In this second situation, we must demonstrate not only that A is not interfered with, but also that the implicit assignments to $exist\_x$ on block entry and exit in $\mathcal{P}_2$ do not interfere with the implicit conjunct, $exist\_x$, of A in $\mathcal{P}_1$.

Demonstrating interference freedom for message passing systems is the same as demonstrating it for shared memory systems, except that now we must take into account that the distributed assignment that occurs with message passing can also cause interference. Hence, in addition to the interference condition discussed in Chapter 4, we must show that the transfer of a message between two processes does not interfere with an assertion in a third process. (Note that no assertion in either of the communicating processes can be interfered with by the distributed assignment, since only one control point can be enabled in a sequential process at a time and, in order for the assignment to take place, control points must be enabled at each of the communication statements in the two processes.)

Additional Proof Obligations for Interference Freedom

For each pair of matching communication commands described in the proofs of individual processes by the triples

$$\{T\}\ \mathcal{P}\,!\,\bar{e}\ \{U\}$$

$$\{V\}\ Q?\,\bar{v}\ \{W\}$$

and each assertion, A, in a process different from the two communicating processes, show that

$$(A \wedge T \wedge V) \Rightarrow A^{\bar{v}}_{\bar{e}}$$

Clearly we need only check assertions A that involve variables in $\bar{v}$.

The formal semantics of the cobegin statement can now be described by the inference rule:

Extended Cobegin Rule

$$\frac{\{P_1\}\ S_1\ \{Q_1\},\ \ldots,\ \{P_n\}\ S_n\ \{Q_n\},\ interference\ free,\ satisfaction}{\{P_1 \wedge \ldots \wedge P_n\}\ \textbf{cobegin}\ S_1;\ /\!/\ldots/\!/\ S_n;\ \textbf{coend}\ \{Q_1 \wedge \ldots \wedge Q_n\}} \tag{6.5}$$

An annotated version of the program (6.1) is shown in Figure 6.3. The annotation describes a valid proof of each process. The proofs are constructed using axioms (6.3) and (6.4) and satisfy the satisfaction and noninterference conditions.

6.3 Satisfaction Proofs and Deadlock

Many programs have multiple matching sends and receives. Satisfaction must be demonstrated for each matching pair. For example, in Figure 6.4, $\mathcal{P}_1$ has two sends and $\mathcal{P}_2$ has two receives. Assuming $B1$ and $B2$ have been assigned values that are independent of one another, either send in $\mathcal{P}_1$ can rendezvous with either receive in $\mathcal{P}_2$. Thus, four satisfaction theorems must be demonstrated. After communication takes place, the value of x and y can be either 1 or 2. One example of a set of axioms for the communication commands for which satisfaction can be demonstrated is

$$\{true\}\ \mathcal{P}_2\,!\,1\ \{true\}$$

$$\{true\}\ \mathcal{P}_2\,!\,2\ \{true\}$$

$$\{true\}$$
cobegin
$\mathcal{P}_1::$
  begin
    $\{true\}$
    $x := 4;$
      $\{x = 4\}$
    $\mathcal{P}_2 \, ! \, x;$
      $\{x = 4\}$
  end;
    $\{x = 4\}$
//
$\mathcal{P}_2::$
    $\{true\}$
    $\mathcal{P}_1 \, ? \, y;$
      $\{y = 4\}$
coend;
    $\{(x = 4) \land (y = 4)\}$

Figure 6.3: An annotated version of a simple message passing program.

cobegin
$\mathcal{P}_1::$
  if $B1 \rightarrow \mathcal{P}_2 \, ! \, 1;$
  $[]\neg B1 \rightarrow \mathcal{P}_2 \, ! \, 2;$
  fi;
//
$\mathcal{P}_2::$
  if $B2 \rightarrow \mathcal{P}_1 \, ? \, x;$
  $[]\neg B2 \rightarrow \mathcal{P}_1 \, ? \, y;$
  fi;
coend;

Figure 6.4: A program with several possible rendezvous.

$$\textbf{cobegin}$$
$$\mathcal{P}_1::$$
$$\textbf{begin}$$
$$\mathcal{P}_2 \; ! \; 1;$$
$$\mathcal{P}_2 \; ! \; 2;$$
$$\textbf{end};$$
$$//$$
$$\mathcal{P}_2::$$
$$\textbf{begin}$$
$$\mathcal{P}_1 \; ? \; x;$$
$$\mathcal{P}_1 \; ? \; y;$$
$$\textbf{end};$$
$$\textbf{coend};$$

Figure 6.5: A program with a unique rendezvous pattern.

$$\{true\} \; \mathcal{P}_1 \; ? \; x \; \{(x = 1) \vee (x = 2)\}$$

$$\{true\} \; \mathcal{P}_1 \; ? \; y \; \{(y = 1) \vee (y = 2)\}$$

It is possible that a matching send and receive cannot rendezvous. For example, in Figure 6.5, the first send in $\mathcal{P}_1$ can rendezvous with the first receive in $\mathcal{P}_2$, but not the second. Similarly, the second send in $\mathcal{P}_1$ cannot rendezvous with the first receive in $\mathcal{P}_2$. We can demonstrate that a particular rendezvous cannot take place by displaying an annotated version of the program in which the conjunction of the preconditions of the send and receive is *false*, thus showing that the control points at those two statements cannot simultaneously be enabled. Since *false* implies any assertion, the satisfaction condition is trivially true in that case.

As pointed out in Chapter 4, it is often necessary to strengthen assertions using auxiliary variables to produce a conjunction of preconditions having value *false*. A common technique is to introduce a shared auxiliary variable that counts the message transmissions in the program. For the program of Figure 6.5, we introduce a shared auxiliary variable, *step*, which is incremented whenever communication takes place. Figure 6.6 shows the modified program.

Assuming *step* is not changed elsewhere in the program, one set of axioms that describes the communication and for which satisfaction can be demonstrated is

$$\{step = 0\} \; \mathcal{P}_2 \; ! \; (1, step + 1) \; \{step = 1\}$$

$$\{step = 1\} \; \mathcal{P}_2 \; ! \; (2, step + 1) \; \{step = 2\}$$

$$\{step = 0\} \; \mathcal{P}_1 \; ? \; (x, step) \; \{(x = 1) \wedge (step = 1)\}$$

$$step := 0;$$
cobegin
$\mathcal{P}_1::$
   begin
      $\mathcal{P}_2 ! (1, step + 1);$
      $\mathcal{P}_2 ! (2, step + 1);$
   end;
  //
$\mathcal{P}_2::$
   begin
      $\mathcal{P}_1 ? (x, step);$
      $\mathcal{P}_1 ? (y, step);$
   end;
  coend;

Figure 6.6: The previous program with the auxiliary variable *step* added.

$$\{step = 1\} \; \mathcal{P}_1 ? (y, step) \; \{(y = 2) \wedge (step = 2)\}$$

Satisfaction is demonstrated for the first send and receive in each process by the theorem

$$(step = 0) \Rightarrow ((x = 1) \wedge (step = 1))^{x, \; step}_{1, \; step+1}$$

while the conjunction of the preconditions of the first send and the second receive is *false*. Note that interference is not an issue, since *step* is only modified in the distributed assignments and there is no third process whose assertions can be interfered with by these assignments.

The programs in Figures 6.7 and 6.8 are the same as that of Figure 6.5 except that in each case one send has been changed to a receive and one receive changed to a send. Note that the program in Figure 6.7 deadlocks, since $\mathcal{P}_1$ and $\mathcal{P}_2$ will both wait forever at their send primitive. Since deadlock is undesirable, we would like to have proof techniques for demonstrating its absence. The program shown in Figure 6.8 would deadlock if it ever reached a state in which $\mathcal{P}_1$ and $\mathcal{P}_2$ were both waiting to send. We can prove that this state is not reachable, using the same technique that was applied to the program of Figure 6.6. As shown in Figure 6.9, we use the variable *step*, which is incremented whenever a rendezvous takes place.

Again, assuming *step* is not changed elsewhere in the program of Figure 6.9, one set of axioms that describes communication and for which satisfaction can be demonstrated is

$$\{step = 0\} \; \mathcal{P}_2 ! (1, step + 1) \; \{step = 1\}$$

$$\{step = 1\} \; \mathcal{P}_2 ? (y, step) \; \{(step = 2) \wedge (y = 2)\}$$

```
cobegin
P₁::
    begin
        P₂ ! 1;
        P₂ ? x;
    end;
//
P₂::
    begin
        P₁ ! 2;
        P₁ ? y;
    end;
coend;
```

Figure 6.7: A program that deadlocks.

```
cobegin
P₁::
begin
        P₂ ! 1;
        P₂ ? y;
    end;
//
P₂::
    begin
        P₁ ? x;
        P₁ ! 2;
    end;
coend;
```

Figure 6.8: A program that does not deadlock.

$$\{step = 0\}\ P_1\ ?\ (x, step)\ \{(x = 1) \wedge (step = 1)\}$$

$$\{step = 1\}\ P_1\ !\ (2, step + 1)\ \{step = 2\}$$

These triples demonstrate that both processes cannot simultaneously be waiting to send, since the conjunction of their preconditions is *false*.

It might be thought that this program could exhibit a related kind of undesirable behavior. If P_1 is waiting at one of its communication commands for P_2 to reach a matching command but P_2 has completed, the command in P_1 will fail. The same reasoning as before shows that this situation also cannot

```
step := 0;
cobegin
P₁::
  begin
    P₂ ! (1, step + 1);
    P₂ ? (y, step);
  end
//
P₂::
  begin
    P₁ ? (x, step);
    P₁ ! (2, step + 1);
  end;
coend;
```

Figure 6.9: The previous program with the auxiliary variable *step* added.

occur. When P_2 has completed, the assertion ($step = 2$) is true, while when P_1 is waiting at one of its communication commands, one of the assertions ($step = 0$) or ($step = 1$) is true.

More generally, to prove that processes cannot deadlock in a state in which they are waiting at particular control points, we can find a program annotation in which the conjunction of all the assertions at those control points is *false*.

6.4   Example – The Bounded Buffer*

Figure 6.10 shows a process, BB, that is maintaining a bounded buffer similar to that defined in Section 5.4. We use essentially the same concrete implementation (and the same variable names) as in that section. The buffer is implemented using an array, *Qarray*, with pointers *last* and *count* (initialized to 0). The entire process is a single loop. The guards guarantee that BB will accept a message from process P_1 to add an element to the buffer only if the buffer is not full, and will send a message to process P_2 containing an element from the buffer only if the buffer is not empty. If the buffer is both not full and not empty, BB can nondeterministically choose either one of the two actions. As in Section 5.4, we define two auxiliary variables, *in* and *out*, where *in* is the sequence of all the messages that have ever been received by BB and *out* is the sequence of all the messages that have ever been sent by BB. To ensure that *in* and *out* maintain this interpretation, we update them only within the communication constructs.

We prove two properties of this implementation: (1) the sequence of mes-

var
  in, out : *sequence* := λ, λ;

cobegin
$\mathcal{P}_1$ ::
  $\cdots$ $\mathcal{BB}$! (*e*, *in* $\circ$ < *e* >); $\cdots$
//
$\mathcal{BB}$ ::
  var
    Qarray : **array**[0..(N − 1)] **of** *job_info*;
    last : 0..(N − 1) := 0;
    count : 0..N := 0;
  begin
    do *count* < N →
      begin
        $\mathcal{P}_1$? (*Qarray*[(*last* + 1) **mod** N], *in*);
        last, count := (*last* + 1) **mod** N, *count* + 1;
      end;
    [] *count* > 0 →
      begin
        $\mathcal{P}_2$! (*Qarray*[(*last* − *count* + 1) **mod** N],
          out $\circ$ < *Qarray*[(*last* − *count* + 1) **mod** N] >);
        count := *count* − 1;
      end;
    od;
  end;
//
$\mathcal{P}_2$ ::
  $\cdots$ $\mathcal{BB}$? (*v*, *out*); $\cdots$
coend;

Loop Invariant:
  I : (0 ≤ *count* ≤ N) ∧ (*in* = *out* $\circ$ *Seq*(*Qarray, last, count*))

Figure 6.10: Communication through the bounded buffer.

sages sent by $\mathcal{BB}$ to $\mathcal{P}_2$ is the same as the sequence received by $\mathcal{BB}$ from $\mathcal{P}_1$, and (2) the sequence received by $\mathcal{BB}$ is the same as the sequence sent by $\mathcal{P}_1$. [The proof that the sequence sent by $\mathcal{BB}$ is the same as the sequence received by $\mathcal{P}_2$ is similar to that for (2).]

For the first proof, we want to prove that when $\mathcal{BB}$ has both received and sent a sequence of M messages, the sequence sent and the sequence received are the same. Our plan is to demonstrate that the assertion I, shown in Figure 6.10, is an invariant of the loop in $\mathcal{BB}$ [where $Seq()$ is defined as in Section 3.2.3]. The invariance of I implies that the buffer works correctly, since when $\mathcal{BB}$ has both sent and received M messages, the lengths of in and out are both M. From I it follows that the lengths of in and out can only be equal when the sequences in and out are themselves equal. Hence, $\mathcal{BB}$ has sent exactly the sequence of messages it received.

To demonstrate the invariance of I, consider the first component of the do statement and assume I is its postcondition. Working backwards, using the Assignment Axiom, we obtain

$$\{(0 \le count + 1 \le N)$$
$$\wedge(in = out \circ Seq(Qarray,\ (last + 1) \bmod N,\ count + 1))\}$$
$$last,\ count := (last + 1)\ \textbf{mod}\ N,\ count + 1$$
$$\{(0 \le count \le N) \wedge (in = out \circ Seq(Qarray,\ last,\ count))\}$$

We now instantiate (6.4) to obtain a triple that describes the receive. Since any triple is an acceptable instantiation, we can choose as the postcondition of the receive the precondition of the assignment statement. The precondition of the receive must have two properties: it must be implied by the precondition of the first component of the do statement, so that it can be used in a sequential proof, and it must support the satisfaction condition. We choose the following axiom to describe the receive and denote its precondition as Q_1:

$$\{(0 \le count + 1 \le N)$$
$$\wedge\ ((in \circ < Qarray[(last + 1)\ \text{mod}\ N] >)$$
$$= (out \circ Seq(Qarray,\ (last + 1)\ \text{mod}\ N,\ count + 1)))\}$$
$$\mathcal{P}_1\ ?\ (Qarray[(last + 1)\ \textbf{mod}\ N],\ in)$$
$$\{(0 \le count + 1 \le N)$$
$$\wedge(in = out \circ Seq(Qarray,\ (last + 1)\ \text{mod}\ N,\ count + 1))\}$$

Using the same approach for the second component of the do statement, we obtain as the precondition of the send the assertion Q_2:

$$(0 \le count - 1 \le N)$$
$$\wedge(in = out \circ < Qarray[(last - count + 1)\ \text{mod}\ N] >$$
$$\circ Seq(Qarray,\ last,\ count - 1))$$

Now we must show that this choice of axioms for the two communication primitives supports a proof that the loop in $\mathcal{BB}$ has I as a loop invariant. Clearly, I is initially true. For the first component of the do statement we must show that

$$(I \wedge (count < N)) \Rightarrow Q_1 \tag{6.6}$$

Note that $Seq()$ can be expanded to make its last element visible:

$$Seq(Qarray, (last + 1) \bmod N, count + 1)$$
$$= Seq(Qarray, last, count) \circ < Qarray[(last + 1) \bmod N] >$$

Thus, (6.6) can be written as

$$((0 \leq count < N) \wedge (in = out \circ Seq(Qarray, last, count))) \Rightarrow$$
$$[(0 \leq count + 1 \leq N) \wedge ((in \circ < Qarray[(last + 1) \bmod N] >)$$
$$= (out \circ Seq(Qarray, last, count) \circ < Qarray[(last + 1) \bmod N] >))]$$

which is obviously true. Similarly, for the second component it can be shown that

$$(I \wedge (count > 0)) \Rightarrow Q_2$$

Thus, I is a loop invariant.

To demonstrate satisfaction for the postcondition of the receive, we show that

$$Q_1 \Rightarrow [(0 \leq count + 1 \leq N)$$
$$\wedge (in = (out \circ Seq(Qarray, (last + 1) \bmod N, count + 1)))]_{in \circ <e>, e}^{in, Qarray[(last+1) \bmod N]}$$

which can be demonstrated by expanding $Seq()$ to make its last element visible. Satisfaction must also be demonstrated for the corresponding send in $\mathcal{P}_1$ (when that postcondition is chosen). Similar reasoning can be applied to the second component of the do statement. Also, assuming that in and out are modified only in $\mathcal{BB}$, the assertions in $\mathcal{BB}$ are not interfered with. Hence, we have completed the first proof.

For the second proof, assume that $\mathcal{P}_1$ wishes to send the sequence of messages stored in array m to $\mathcal{BB}$ (these elements replace the variable e in Figure 6.10). We assume that the array has dimension M and hence the sequence to be sent can be denoted by $Seq(m, M, M)$. We add two additional auxiliary integer variables, $step$ and j, as shown in Figure 6.11. $step$ is a global variable, initialized to 0. It is incremented at every communication between $\mathcal{BB}$ and $\mathcal{P}_1$ and allows us to describe an aspect of how the loops in the two processes are synchronized. j counts the number of messages received by $\mathcal{BB}$.

The theorem we want to prove is that when communication is complete,

$$in = Seq(m, M, M)$$

which is implied by the loop invariant $I_{\mathcal{BB}}$ shown in Figure 6.11 when $j = M$. We first show that $I_{\mathcal{P}_1}$ is a loop invariant of $\mathcal{P}_1$. It is true initially and its

```
var
  in, out : sequence := λ, λ;
  step : integer := 0;

cobegin
P₁ ::
  var
    i : integer := 0;
    m : array [1..M] of job_info;
  begin
    do i < M →
      begin
        BB ! (m[i + 1], in ∘ < m[i + 1] >, step + 1);
        i := i + 1;
      end;
    od;
  end;
//
BB ::
  var
    Qarray : array[0..(N − 1)] of job_info;
    last : 0..(N − 1) := 0;
    count : 0..N := 0;
    j : integer := 0;
  begin
    do count < N →
      begin
        P₁ ? (Qarray[(last + 1) mod N], in, step);
        last, count := (last + 1) mod N, count + 1;
        j = j + 1;
      end;
    [] count > 0 →
      . . .
    od;
  end;
coend;
```

Loop Invariants:
I_{BB} : $(step = j) \land (in = Seq(m, j, j))$
I_{P_1} : $(step = i)$

Figure 6.11: Analysis of the messages received by the bounded buffer.

invariance is demonstrated if we choose the axiom

$$\{I_{\mathcal{P}_1}\} \; \mathcal{BB} \, ! \, (m[i+1], \; in \circ < m[i+1] >, \; step+1) \; \{step = i+1\}$$

to describe the send in $\mathcal{P}_1$.

We next show that $I_{\mathcal{BB}}$ is an invariant of the loop in $\mathcal{BB}$. It is true initially. We assume that the second component of $\mathcal{BB}$, which communicates with $\mathcal{P}_2$, does not access any variables in $I_{\mathcal{BB}}$ and therefore $I_{\mathcal{BB}}$ is invariant to its execution. If the axiom:

$$\{I_{\mathcal{BB}}\} \; \mathcal{P}_1 \, ? \, (Qarray[(last+1) \; \textbf{mod} \; N], \; in, \; step)$$
$$\{(step = j+1) \wedge (in = Seq(m, \, j+1, \, j+1))\}$$

is chosen to describe the receive in the first component, it follows that $I_{\mathcal{BB}}$ is invariant to the execution of that component and hence of the loop in $\mathcal{BB}$ as well.

The key part of the proof involves demonstrating satisfaction. The conjunction of the postconditions of the send and receive in $\mathcal{P}_1$ and $\mathcal{BB}$, respectively, is

$$Q_3 : \; [(step = i+1) \wedge (step = j+1) \wedge (in = Seq(m, \, j+1, \, j+1))]$$

We must prove the satisfaction formula:

$$(I_{\mathcal{P}_1} \wedge I_{\mathcal{BB}} \wedge (count < N)) \Rightarrow (Q_3)^{Qarray[(last+1) \; mod \; N], \; in, \; step}_{m[i+1], \; in \, \circ \, < m[i+1] >, \; step+1}$$

Making the indicated substitutions and expanding $Seq(m, j+1, j+1)$ to make its $(j+1)$st element visible, we obtain for the right-hand side of the implication

$$((step + 1) = (i+1)) \wedge ((step+1) = (j+1))$$
$$\wedge \, ((in \, \circ < m[i+1] >) = (Seq(m, \, j, \, j) \circ < m[j+1] >))$$

from which the truth of the satisfaction formula is evident. Note that the use of the auxiliary variable *step* was crucial, since it allowed us to conclude $i = j$ in the satisfaction proof (*i.e.*, it showed that the loops in $\mathcal{P}_1$ and $\mathcal{BB}$ were synchronized so that the *i*th element sent by $\mathcal{P}_1$ was the *j*th element received by $\mathcal{BB}$). Finally, we must demonstrate that the proofs of $\mathcal{P}_1$ and $\mathcal{BB}$ do not interfere with one another. The only variable that plays a role in both proofs is *step*, and it is modified only by the communication statements. Execution of these statements cannot interfere with an assertion, A, since the control point to which A is attached cannot be enabled when the communication takes place.

6.5   Guarded and Nondeterministic Communication

The implementation of the bounded buffer in Figure 6.10 satisfies its specifications but suffers from a serious problem. Assume the buffer is both not full and not empty and the implementation nondeterministically selects the first alternative. If P_1 is not ready to send, the system will wait despite the fact that P_2 may be ready to receive. Hence, communication with the second process is unnecessarily delayed for an indefinite period of time.

This difficulty can be overcome by allowing a message passing command to (optionally) appear in a guard. Thus, in addition to allowing guards to have the form G, where G is a boolean expression, we also allow guards of the form

$$G; P \# x$$

where $P \# x$ stands for either a synchronous send to or a synchronous receive from process P (*i.e.*, $\#$ can be either ! or ?). G can be omitted when its value is *true* and a communication command is present. Letting C_i denote either a communication command or a null statement, the form of a do statement is

$$\textbf{do } G_1; C_1 \rightarrow S_1; \text{ } [] \dots [] \text{ } G_n; C_n \rightarrow S_n; \textbf{ od} \tag{6.7}$$

As in the sequential case, a guard in which G_i is false is said to be *closed*; otherwise the guard is *open*. An open guard is said to be *executable* if it has no communication command or if it has a communication command, $P \# x$, that is matched by a command in P that P is waiting to execute. The operational semantics of this statement is as follows:

First, the boolean in each guard is evaluated. If all guards are closed, the statement terminates. If one or more executable guards exist, one is nondeterministically selected, its communication operation (if any) is executed, and the corresponding component statement is executed. If none of the open guards is executable, the process waits until at least one open guard becomes executable and then performs the above sequence of steps. Then the entire loop statement is re-executed. The evaluation of the boolean in each guard is atomic. Each boolean is evaluated only once so that, while a process is waiting for an open guard to become executable, no open guard can become closed and no closed guard can become open.

As an example, Figure 6.12 shows an implementation of the bounded buffer process with communication commands in the guards.

Note that the only difference between statement (6.7) and the statement

$$\textbf{do } G_1 \rightarrow C_1; \text{ } S_1; \text{ } [] \dots [] \text{ } G_n \rightarrow C_n; \text{ } S_n; \textbf{ od} \tag{6.8}$$

occurs when there exists an i such that C_i is not null. In (6.7) we can choose the ith component only if its guard is executable and hence the communication specified by C_i is immediately possible. In (6.8) we can choose the ith component even when the communication specified by C_i is not immediately possible and then wait an indefinite amount of time until C_i can be executed. In both cases communication occurs before S_i is executed. The formal semantics specified for (6.8), as given by the Do Rule (Section 2.4), allows for

$\mathcal{BB}$ ::
do *count* $< N$; $\mathcal{P}_1$? *Qarray*[(*last* + 1) **mod** *N*] $\rightarrow$
    last, count := (*last* + 1) **mod** *N, count* + 1;
[] *count* > 0; $\mathcal{P}_2$! *Qarray*[(*last* − *count* + 1) **mod** *N*] $\rightarrow$
    count := *count* − 1;
od;

Figure 6.12: A bounded buffer process implemented with communication guards.

an arbitrary choice to be made among open guards, including the choice algorithm described for (6.7). Statement (6.8) is more subject to delay and perhaps to deadlock than is (6.7), but the assertions in Program Logic do not deal with time. Hence, we expect that both versions of the do statement have the same formal semantics. Thus, the proof given for the bounded buffer process of Figure 6.10 should also apply to the bounded buffer process of Figure 6.12. Before drawing such a conclusion, however, we must address one additional issue, which is discussed in the next section.

Communication guards can also be used to generalize the if statement. Again, we expect the new form of the statement to have the same semantics as the original but be less subject to delays and deadlocks.

6.5.1   Termination and Failure

A program that does not execute an infinite computation either terminates normally (we simply say that it terminates) or fails (terminates abnormally). A concurrent program fails when one of its component processes fails; a process fails when one of its component statements fails. A statement can fail as a result of some purely sequential run-time event, such as an attempt to divide by zero or to execute an if statement in which all guards are closed.

Communication introduces new failure modes. Thus, the operational semantics of synchronous send and receive commands call for a process to fail if it attempts to communicate with another process that has already terminated. These are reasonable semantics, since if we did not consider this a failure situation, the process would wait forever for a match to occur.

The question of failure and termination becomes more involved when we allow communication statements to appear in guards. To be consistent with the above notion of communication failure, an if statement in which all open guards have communication commands naming terminated processes should be considered as having failed, since the executing process will wait forever. The introduction of this additional failure mode to the operational semantics does not have an impact on the formal semantics (*i.e.*, the If Rule still applies), since the if statement does not terminate under either the original or the augmented operational semantics when all communicants have terminated, and the postcondition only describes the state when the program terminates normally.

When we try to apply this notion to the do statement, we find that the equivalent assumption does affect the formal semantics. With the original operational semantics, a do statement waits if it has open guards, even if all those guards have communication statements naming terminated processes. Since a do statement terminates when all its guards are closed (rather than failing as does an if statement), one approach to defining the augmented operational semantics for the do statement is to require that the do statement terminate (rather than wait) if all its open guards have communication commands naming terminated processes. Do statements that have this operational semantics are said to satisfy the *distributed termination convention* (DTC). DTC does have an impact on formal semantics, as we shall see shortly, since it introduces a new condition under which the do statement can terminate normally.

Figure 6.13 illustrates a client-server system in which DTC is used to notify the server that the client has terminated. The client might invoke *Server* several times before terminating, at which point the guard in the server's loop fails, resulting in (normal) loop termination. *Server* then terminates, and the entire parallel command terminates.

While DTC is convenient, it suffers from several drawbacks. From a theoretical viewpoint, it complicates the formal semantics of the do statement. With DTC, a guard $G_i; C_i$ fails if G_i is true and C_i refers to a terminated process, $\mathcal{P}_i$. Hence, $\neg G_i$ is no longer necessarily a postcondition of the loop. We can only assert the weaker postcondition:

$$I \wedge \bigwedge_{i=1}^{n} (\neg G_i \vee term(\mathcal{P}_i))$$

where I is the loop invariant and $term(\mathcal{P}_i)$ is a function that returns true if $\mathcal{P}_i$ has terminated. From a practical standpoint, the implementation of DTC implies that a process executing a do statement be aware of the state of another process, thus requiring an implicit exchange of messages on each iteration of the loop. Furthermore, since loop termination is not explicitly dealt with in the program, the modification of a previously terminating process, $\mathcal{P}_1$, so that it terminates in a different way might affect the termination of a loop in a process, $\mathcal{P}_2$, with which it was communicating, requiring a major restructuring of $\mathcal{P}_2$.

For these reasons, many languages do not use DTC. Thus a do loop does not terminate when all its open guards name terminated processes. In such languages, loop termination can be accomplished using explicit communication. A component is added to the do statement corresponding to each communicant, $\mathcal{P}_i$, that might terminate. Each such component is prepared to receive a termination message, which $\mathcal{P}_i$ sends prior to its termination. The body of the

```
        cobegin
        Server ::
           begin
              . . .
              do Client ? mess  →
                 begin
                    . . .        -- perform requested service
                    Client ! reply;
                 end;
              od;
           end;
        //
        Client ::
           begin
              . . .              -- requests for service
           end;
        coend;
```

Figure 6.13: Client-server example using the distributed termination convention.

component closes any guard that communicates with $\mathcal{P}_i$.

Figure 6.14 illustrates this explicit coding for the client-server example. After the client has finished sending requests to the server, it sends the constant *false*. The receipt of this message causes all guards in the server to become closed and hence results in loop exit. (Note that we have assumed that *mess* is not of type boolean so that requests for service match only the receive command in the first guard while a request for termination matches only the receive command in the second.)

Henceforth we assume that the operational semantics of the do statement does not involve DTC and thus guard failure must be explicitly coded. Under this assumption the Do Rule can be used for statements involving communication guards as follows:

$$\frac{\{I \wedge G_1\}\, C_1;\, S_1\, \{I\},\ \ldots,\ \{I \wedge G_n\}\, C_n;\, S_n\, \{I\}}{\{I\}\ \textbf{do}\ G_1; C_1 \to S_1;\ []\cdots[]\ G_n; C_n \to S_n;\ \textbf{od}\ \{I \wedge \neg G_1 \wedge \cdots \wedge \neg G_n\}}$$

While explicit coding is a reasonable alternative to DTC, the problem of detecting when loop termination should take place can be subtle. The client-server example is asymmetric and, hence, easy. The client informs the server when its services are no longer required and the server can then exit its loop and terminate. A symmetric situation is more difficult to handle. For example, consider a cobegin statement involving n processes, $\mathcal{P}_1,\ \mathcal{P}_2, \ldots,\ \mathcal{P}_n$, in which each process has the form shown in Figure 6.15. The overall computation

```
cobegin
Server ::
  var
    continue : boolean;
  begin
    . . .
    continue := true;
    do continue; Client ? mess →
      begin
        . . .            — — perform requested service
        Client ! reply;
      end;
    []
    continue; Client ? continue → skip;
    od;
  end;
//
Client ::
  begin
    . . .              — — requests for service
    Server ! false;
  end;
coend;
```

Figure 6.14: Client-server example explicitly providing for termination.

to be performed is divided among the n processes, each of which has two responsibilities. Not only must a process perform its part of the computation (which might cause it, as a client, to request service from another process), it also must be available to satisfy requests for service from other processes. Figure 6.15 indicates that, acting as a server, $\mathcal{P}_i$ is willing to accept m different types of service requests from other processes. A service request might cause $\mathcal{P}_i$ to revert to its role as a client (i.e., it might request service from within S_i or it might exit the loop and reenter the loop at a later time. Hence, each process is both a client and a server. This dual role complicates the problem, since a process cannot decide locally when it can terminate. Even after it has completed its part of the computation, it cannot terminate unless it is sure that no subsequent requests for service will arrive from other processes. The goal here is to avoid a situation in which all processes complete their computations, but none exit their loop. Each process is waiting in its loop for a possible request, which will never arrive. While this problem can be solved using the explicit exchange of termination signals, the algorithm is not simple.

$$\mathcal{P}_i ::$$
$$\cdots$$

do $G1; C1 \rightarrow S1;$
[] $G2; C2 \rightarrow S2;$
$$\cdots$$
[] $Gm; Cm \rightarrow Sm;$
od;
$$\cdots$$

Figure 6.15: Process structure illustrating termination detection.

Ada provides a special mechanism to deal with a related situation. We discuss this construct in Chapter 8.

6.5.2 Else Construct

The if statement we have defined is not powerful enough to implement polling. Suppose a receiver process wants to operate in a polling mode in which it checks whether the matching sender process is ready to send and, if not, performs some other operation (and then checks later to see if the sender is ready). We might try to implement this using

$$\textbf{if } \mathcal{P}_2 \, ? \, e \rightarrow S_1; \, [] \, true \rightarrow S_2; \, \textbf{fi}$$

Unfortunately this construct does not implement polling correctly. The receiver will certainly execute S_2 whenever the sender is not prepared to communicate, but when the sender is ready to communicate, both guards are executable and therefore the second alternative might be selected even though communication is possible. Fairness ensures that the first alternative will eventually be selected, but we cannot place a bound on the number of times it may be passed over, and hence the intent of polling is not achieved.

To allow polling and similar modes of operation, many languages define an extension of the if and do statements that allows a new alternative, denoted by *else*, which is selected if and only if all the other alternatives cannot be selected. For the polling example, the new form of the if statement is

$$\textbf{if } \mathcal{P}_2 \, ? \, e \rightarrow S_1; \, \textbf{else } S_2; \, \textbf{fi}$$

The operational semantics of this statement is that the first alternative is selected if its guard is executable and the second alternative is selected otherwise. Thus, the new construct allows a polling mode of operation.

The general form of the if statement involving an else alternative is

$$\textbf{if } G_1; C1 \rightarrow S_1; \, [] \ldots [] \, G_{n-1}; C_{n-1} \rightarrow S_{n-1}; \, \textbf{else } S_n; \, \textbf{fi}$$

Only one else alternative is allowed and it must be the last. The formal semantics of this statement is

$$\frac{\{P \wedge G_1\}\, C_1;\, S_1\, \{Q\},\ \dots,\ \{P \wedge G_{n-1}\}\, C_{n-1};\, S_{n-1}\, \{Q\},\ \{P\}\, S_n\, \{Q\}}{\{P\}\ \textbf{if}\ G_1; C_1 \rightarrow S_1;\ []\cdots[]\ G_{n-1}; C_{n-1} \rightarrow S_{n-1};\ \textbf{else}\ S_n;\ \textbf{fi}\ \{Q\}}$$

Only P is assumed as a precondition of S_n in the hypothesis, since the else alternative may have been chosen because no guard is executable, not because no guard is open.[1] (Thus, from the viewpoint of Program Logic, the semantics of this statement is the same as if the word else were replaced by the word *true*.) Note that this form of the if statement can never fail, since the final alternative can always be selected.

A similar extension can be made to the do statement, allowing a final else alternative. Such a statement never terminates because the else alternative can always be selected. Nonterminating processes form an integral part of many systems, such as operating systems, that are designed to run continuously.

6.6   Transferring Assertions Between Processes*

In addition to the data explicitly transferred between processes in a message passing system, there may be an implicit exchange of information. For example, the receiver may be able to make assertions about the state of the sender, not only at the time the message was sent, but at times between message transmissions.

The two processes in Figure 6.16 interact with the same physical device. P_1 turns the device switch on and then later turns it off. P_2 samples output from the device that is only meaningful when it is on. P_1 sends messages to P_2 after turning the switch on and before turning it off. P_2 waits before initiating data acquisition until it receives the first message and then periodically polls P_1 to determine whether it is ready to turn the device off. P_1 does not actually turn the switch off until P_2 has received the second message. We represent the switch as a global variable, *switch*, which is accessed only by P_1.

To prove that the system works correctly, we must demonstrate that the device is on while P_2 is sampling. We can easily show that it is on at the instant the first message is sent, but P_1 could conceivably turn the switch off immediately afterwards, and so we must prove that the assertion (*switch = on*) is true while P_2 is sampling. Thus, we must reason in P_2 about a variable accessed only by P_1.

The proof centers on demonstrating that the assertion

$$I:\ ok \Rightarrow (switch = on) \tag{6.9}$$

---

[1]Note that we could have chosen a stronger precondition for S_n using the same reasoning we used when discussing DTC in Section 6.5.1.

```
cobegin
𝒫₁::
  begin
      · · ·
      switch := on;          – – turn on device
      𝒫₂ ! true;
      · · ·
      𝒫₂ ! false;
      switch := off;         – – turn off device
  end;
//
𝒫₂::
  var
      ok : boolean := false;
  begin
      𝒫₁ ? ok;
      do ok →
        if 𝒫₁ ? ok → skip;
        else · · ·               – – sample device output
        fi;
      od;
  end;
coend;
```

Figure 6.16: A program that communicates the assertion "switch=on".

is a program invariant of $\mathcal{P}_2$. Since *ok* is true while $\mathcal{P}_2$ is sampling the device, the result follows.

Figure 6.17 is an annotated version of the program. We first show that the annotation forms the basis of individual proofs of each process. In the proof of $\mathcal{P}_1$, the assignment and send axiom schemas have been used (the send axiom enables us to choose arbitrary pre- and postconditions) and we have assumed that the computation between the two sends does not affect the values of *switch* and *ok*. In the proof of $\mathcal{P}_2$, we have instantiated the axiom schema for the if statement as

$$\frac{\{ok \ \wedge I\} \ \mathcal{P}_1 \ ? \ ok; \ \textbf{skip} \ \{I\}, \ \{ok \ \wedge I\} \ \text{sample device output} \ \{I\}}{\{ok \ \wedge I\} \ \textbf{if} \ \cdots \textbf{fi} \ \{I\}}$$

Note that the boolean part of the guard of the first component is simply *true*, and in the hypothesis the receive statement is treated as part of the component itself. Note also that we have weakened the postcondition of the sampling statement in the annotation using the Rule of Consequence in order to apply the If Rule. As with P_1, we have assumed that sampling does not affect *switch* and *ok*.

Although the proofs are constructed independently, assertions in P_2 refer to the variable *switch* used in P_1. The validity of the theorems from which these assertions are derived follows from the synchronization enforced by the communication commands and is demonstrated in the satisfaction proofs. Note, however, that information about *switch* is not explicitly passed in messages between P_1 and P_2. Synchronization has enabled us to pass assertions between the processes.

Satisfaction between the first send and the first receive follows from

$$((switch = on) \wedge \neg ok \; \wedge I) \Rightarrow ((switch = on) \wedge ok \; \wedge I)^{ok}_{true} \qquad (6.10)$$

Satisfaction between the first send and the second receive cannot be demonstrated using the assertions shown in Figure 6.17. The communication structure of this program, however, is identical to that of the program shown in Figure 6.5. In that case, to prove that the first send in P_1 could not rendezvous with the second receive in P_2, we introduced the auxiliary variable *step*. Satisfaction followed trivially, since the conjunction of the preconditions of the two statements was *false*. Exactly the same technique can be used for the program of Figure 6.17, and we do not repeat the argument. Similar reasoning applies to the second send.

Assertions in P_2 can refer to *switch*, since we can assert *exist_switch* in P_2 (since *switch* is a global variable and exists throughout the program). Consider the variable *ok*, which is local to P_2. We cannot assert *exist_ok* prior to the first send in P_1 (or after the second send), since we cannot demonstrate that block entry has actually occurred (or block exit has not occurred) in P_2. (It would, however, be possible to demonstrate *exist_ok* at control points between the two sends, but we have no need to do so.)

Having demonstrated satisfaction, we must next show non-interference. Since the distributed assignments cannot interfere with assertions in the two processes, the only statement in one process that can interfere with an assertion in the other is the assignment of *off* to *switch* in P_1 (since that assignment has the potential for making I false). In the subsequent discussion we refer to this assignment statement as s.

It follows easily that the assertion $\neg ok \wedge I$ is not interfered with, since the triple

$$\{(\neg ok \wedge I) \wedge (switch = on)\} \; switch := \; off \; \{\neg ok \wedge I\}$$

can be demonstrated using the Assignment Axiom and the Rule of Consequence.

To demonstrate non-interference for the assertions I and $ok \wedge I$, we must strengthen the precondition of s, since, for example, the triple

$$\{I \wedge (switch = on)\} \; switch := \; off \; \{I\}$$

is not a theorem. It is tempting to add $\neg ok$ as an additional precondition, but it would be interfered with by the termination of P_2 (*i.e.*, P_2 might terminate and

```
cobegin
𝒫₁ :: begin
        . . .
                {true}
        switch := on;          -- turn device on
                {switch = on}
        𝒫₂ ! true;
                {switch = on}
        . . .
                {switch = on}
        𝒫₂ ! false;
                {switch = on}
        switch := off;          -- turn device off
                {switch = off}
    end;
//
𝒫₂ :: var
        ok : boolean := false;
    begin
                {¬ok ∧ I}
        𝒫₁ ? ok;
                {ok ∧ I}
        do ok →
                {ok ∧ I}
          if 𝒫₁ ? ok →
                {¬ok ∧ I}
            skip;
                {I}
          else
                {ok ∧ I}
            . . .                -- sample device output
                {I}
          fi;
                {I}
        od;
                {¬ok ∧ I}
    end;
coend;
```

Program Invariant of $\mathcal{P}_2$:
$\quad I \ : \ ok \Rightarrow (switch = on)$

Figure 6.17: An annotated version of the previous program.

hence deallocate *ok* before *s* is executed). Instead we use as the precondition of *s* the assertion

$$(switch = on) \wedge (\neg ok \vee \neg exist\_ok)$$

which says that either *ok* is false or block exit has occurred in $\mathcal{P}_2$. This assertion can be justified, since anything can be asserted as the postcondition of the second send when $\mathcal{P}_1$ is considered in isolation, and satisfaction follows from

$$((switch = on) \wedge ok \wedge I) \Rightarrow ((switch = on) \wedge (\neg ok \vee \neg exist\_ok) \wedge \neg ok \wedge I)^{ok}_{false}$$

Since *exist_ok* is an implicit conjunct of *I*, non-interference now follows. For example, the assertion $ok \wedge I$ is not interfered with, since its conjunction with the precondition of *s* is *false*, indicating that the control point at *s* cannot be enabled when $ok \wedge I$ is true.

Having demonstrated satisfaction and non-interference, we can use the Cobegin Rule to combine the proofs.

6.7   Implementation of Guarded Communication

The implementation of synchronous message passing is straightforward when the send and receive commands do not appear in guards. Once a process attempts to execute a message passing command, it must wait until the specified match has been achieved. For example, with one-way direct naming the rendezvous can be detected at the receiver. Sending processes register requests for a rendezvous with the receiver (perhaps through the use of control messages exchanged by the kernels and a rendezvous table, which we discuss in Chapter 7). When the receiver executes a statement that matches one of the pending requests, the rendezvous occurs. (Note that the events could occur in the opposite order.) This implementation is simple because, once the sender has registered its request, it is committed to wait for that particular rendezvous: it cannot withdraw the request. Hence, the receiver can be confident that any registered requests are valid.

The same implementation approach can be used when if and do statements are permitted to have only receive commands in their guards. When such a statement is executed, the receiver can choose any send request that matches a receive statement in an open guard with confidence that that sender is still waiting for a rendezvous.

A major complication arises, however, when send commands are also allowed in guards. Under this circumstance, it is no longer possible to be sure that a sender that submits a request for rendezvous will wait for that rendezvous to occur. For example, suppose process $\mathcal{P}_2$ attempts to establish a rendezvous with either $\mathcal{P}_1$ or $\mathcal{P}_3$ as a result of executing the following if statement:

$$\textbf{if } \mathcal{P}_1 \, ? \, x \rightarrow S_1; \, [] \, \mathcal{P}_3 \, ! \, y \rightarrow S_2; \, \textbf{fi}$$

If we adopt the convention that the rendezvous is to be detected at the receiver, P_2 will send a request for rendezvous to P_3. Suppose P_3 is in a similar situation executing the statement

$$\textbf{if } P_2 ? x \rightarrow S_3; \; [] \; P_1 ! y \rightarrow S_4; \; \textbf{fi}$$

The request from P_2 may arrive at a time when P_3 has sent a request for rendezvous to P_1. P_3 cannot respond positively or negatively to P_2's request until it learns the outcome of its own request to P_1. If the rendezvous algorithm calls for P_3 to delay its response to P_2's request until it gets a response from P_1, a deadlock could result if P_1 was similarly engaged with P_2 and P_3. On the other hand, if we adopt a rendezvous algorithm in which P_3 refuses to accept P_2's rendezvous request and instead asks it to try again at a later time, under the same circumstances, a situation can result in which each process repeatedly requests a rendezvous and is refused, and no process ever makes any progress. This situation is generally referred to as a *livelock*.

The problem results from the symmetry of the situation and is independent of whether rendezvous is detected at the sender or at the receiver. Solutions can be constructed using a technique for breaking symmetry. For example, priorities can be assigned to processes so that a process, P, delays responding to a request from a lower priority process but refuses to accept a request from a higher priority one if P has a request outstanding.

Because of the added complication involved in implementing rendezvous when both send and receive commands are permitted in guards, many languages do not allow guards to contain send commands.

6.8 Synchronous Communication in Occam*

We have been considering synchronous communication in a rather abstract context. In this section we take a more practical view. We give a brief description of some aspects of the programming language Occam 2, which we refer to as Occam.[2] Occam is of interest to us because it is virtually a direct implementation of the synchronous message passing paradigm discussed in detail in this chapter. Our goals are to illustrate those language features that were added to the basic communication constructs to support real applications and to discuss how the addition of those features affects our ability to reason about programs written in the language. The description is not intended to be complete.

Occam is a "high level language designed to express concurrent algorithms and their implementations on a network of processing components" [71]. The development of Occam has been closely related to the development of the IN-MOS transputer, a microprocessor particularly suited for distributed systems. Occam is the native language of the transputer and can be used to program a single transputer or a network of transputers.

---

[2]Occam is a trademark of the INMOS group of companies.

6.8.1 Processes*

Following the Occam terminology, every executable statement is considered to be a process. In contrast to the cobegin statement in which each component can be named, Occam processes are not named. Examples of primitive processes follow.

Skip

> *SKIP*

The process *SKIP* starts, then immediately terminates. (Note that line indentation is part of the Occam syntax.)

Stop

> *STOP*

The process *STOP* starts, but does not terminate.

Multiple Assignment

> $x, y := z + 2, 13$

These primitive processes can be combined into larger processes using a number of constructs. The language has (deterministic) if, while, and case constructs similar to those in other languages and also the following constructs, which are important for our discussion.

Sequence

> *SEQ*
> $x := 4$
> $y := 3$

The seq is similar to a compound statement and corresponds to sequential execution of the component processes.

Procedure Declaration

A procedure declaration provides a name for the process that is the body of the procedure. A use of the name within a program has the semantics of a procedure call.

> *PROC decrement(INT x, VAL INT y)*
> $x := y + z - 1$
> :

VAL parameters cannot be modified in the body of the procedure.

Parallel

Concurrent execution of processes is initiated by the par construct, which is analogous to the cobegin statement:

> *PAR*
> $x := x - 1$
> $y := y + 1$

The operational semantics of the par is as follows:

When control enters the par, control points are enabled at each of the component processes and hence they execute concurrently; when all have terminated, the par is exited.

In the following example the component processes are procedures.

> *PAR*
> $p1(x)$
> $p2(y)$

Concurrent processes communicate over named channels, which we discuss shortly. Communication is performed using input and output processes

Input

> $c1 \, ? \, x$

The execution of the input process causes the value received on channel $c1$ to be stored in the variable x.

Output

> $c1 \, ! \, y$

The execution of the output process causes the value of y to be sent over channel $c1$.

Communication occurs when an input and an output in two concurrent processes rendezvous. An attempt to communicate over a channel with a terminated component of a par does not cause the communication statement to fail; it simply waits forever.

Component processes in a par can share variables, but in a restricted way. Variable visibility is based on the usual scoping rules, which in this language are apparent in the level of program indentation. Components within a par can read the same global variables, but if one component assigns to a variable (either in an assignment or in an input), that variable cannot appear in any other component in that par (this condition is checked by the compiler). An array can be used by more than one component in a par only if the compiler can evaluate the subscripts used and verify that the condition on multiple accesses is satisfied. The language has a construct called an *abbreviation*, which can be used to decompose an array into nonoverlapping parts, called *segments*, which can then be accessed by different components in the same par.

Replicators

The seq, if, par, and, as we shall see later, alt constructs can have *replicators*, which allow multiple copies of component processes to be specified. An example of a replicated seq is

> *SEQ i = 0 FOR size*
>   *c[i] ! a[i]*

where *c* is an array of channels and *a* is an array of variables. *i* is called the *index* and *size* is called the *count* of the replicator. The operational semantics of this construct is that a number of processes equal to the value of *size* and indexed from 0 to *size* $-$ 1 are executed in sequence. For example, if *size* is equal to 3, the construct is equivalent to

> *SEQ*
>   *c[0] ! a[0]*
>   *c[1] ! a[1]*
>   *c[2] ! a[2]*

An example of a replicated par is

> *PAR i = 0 FOR 4*
>   *c[i] ! msg*

which sends the same message on four channels and is equivalent to

> *PAR*
>   *c[0] ! msg*
>   *c[1] ! msg*
>   *c[2] ! msg*
>   *c[3] ! msg*

Unlike the seq, if, and alt replicators, the par replicator must have a constant for the initial value of both the index and the count. As a result, the process structure in Occam is completely static and the number of processes in a program can be determined at compile time. Within a replicator, the index can be used in expressions but cannot be assigned to in an assignment or input.

6.8.2 Channels*

Processes communicate through named *channels*. Each channel provides synchronous, unidirectional message passing between a unique sender and a unique receiver. The sender and receiver each name that channel in their input and output processes. A protocol is associated with each channel as part of the channel declaration. The protocol describes the messages transmitted; for example,

> *CHAN OF BYTE screen*1, *screen*2 :
> *CHAN OF* [72]*BYTE line* :

The first declaration declares two channels, each using a protocol in which a message is a single byte. The second declaration declares a channel named *line* that uses a protocol in which each message is a 72-byte array.

Arrays of channels can be declared. For example,

> [10]*CHAN OF BYTE screen*1, *screen*2 :

declares two arrays of channels, *screen*1 and *screen*2, where each array contains 10 channels, numbered from 0 to 9, and the protocol for each channel is a byte.

Protocols can be defined separately and given names. Named protocols can specify a sequence of simpler protocols. For example,

> *PROTOCOL COMPLEX IS REAL*64; *REAL*64 :

defines a protocol named *COMPLEX* in which each message is a sequence of two 64-bit real numbers. An example of a channel with this protocol is

> *CHAN OF COMPLEX c*1 :

A process sending over channel *c*1 might use

> *c*1 ! *realpart*; *imagpart*

When a single channel is to be used to communicate messages with different formats, a *variant* protocol can be defined, where a *tag* is used to differentiate the format. For example, in the protocol

> *PROTOCOL MSG*
>   *CASE*
>   *character*; *BYTE*
>   *number*; *INT*
>   *error*

character, *number*, and *error* are tags. The tag *character* is associated with the protocol *BYTE*; the tag *error* has no associated protocol. A channel with this variant protocol would be declared as

CHAN OF MSG mess :

To send a byte on this channel, we would use

mess ! *character*; *c*

where *c* is a variable of type byte. The tag, in this case *character*, and the value of *c* are sent as two separate communications. The tag is sent first, followed by the value of *c*. To receive on this channel, we could use

mess ? *CASE*
    character; *c*1
        ···   – – process the character
    number; *x*1
        ···   – – process the number
    error
        ···   – – respond to the error

A process need not be prepared to accept all possible variants that might be sent on a channel with a variant protocol. Hence, if the receiver is only prepared to deal with a character, it might execute the special form of input

mess ? *CASE character*; *c*1

Suppose now that the sender executes

mess ! *number*; *n*

The semantics of the variant construct is that the first communication, containing the tag, will succeed whether or not the receiver is prepared to accept that variant. Since the tag, *number*, does not match the only tag that the receiver is willing to accept, the second communication, consisting of the value of *n*, does not succeed, and neither the input nor the output terminates. (It is as if both processes executed *STOP* .)

Note an anomaly. Suppose the sender executes

mess ! *error*

Since communication of the tag succeeds and that is all the sender wants to communicate, the output terminates. However, since *error* does not match *character*, the input does not terminate. This operational semantics is different from that usually associated with synchronous communication.

Communication through Occam channels is similar to direct naming, discussed earlier in the chapter, in the following ways:

Each channel interconnects only one pair of component processes;

Each component process must name the channel it wants to communicate over in each communication statement.

Hence, channels have a disadvantage similar to that of direct naming: a server process must know the names of the channels used by all the clients. With direct naming we observed that the analogous restriction – that the server must know the names of all of its clients – is particularly awkward when the server is a library module that must communicate with an arbitrary number of clients. Although channel and process naming are similar, the use of channels makes the design of a library server somewhat easier. A channel array of size n can be declared globally, with the value of n chosen to accommodate the needs of the clients that are concurrent with the server in a particular application. The value chosen is equal to the maximum number of clients that can be created within that program. Replicators can be used within the server to deal with inputs from the n channels (for example, a replicated alt with count equal n, as described in Section 6.8.4).. Note that the value of n need not be known at the design time of the server. The allocation of channels to clients is done externally to the server.

6.8.3   Timers*

A timer is declared as

> *TIMER clock*1 :

A value input from a timer is of type integer and is derived from a clock that advances at regular intervals. Since the clock periodically wraps around, the most positive value is followed by the most negative value. A timer can be accessed by two special forms of the input process.

> *clock*1 ? *t*

assigns the value of *clock*1 to the variable *t*.

> *clock*1 ? *AFTER t*

called a delayed input, suspends execution until the value of *clock*1 is greater than *t*, then resumes execution, leaving the value of *t* unchanged. The following construct can be used to obtain a delay of *d*:

> *SEQ*
>   *clock*1 ? *now*
>   *clock*1 ? *AFTER now PLUS d*

where *PLUS* means modulo arithmetic. A timer input can appear anywhere an input can appear. Since a timer can only be read, it can be used by any number of processes in a par.

6.8.4   Alternation*

The alt process corresponds to the nondeterministic if statement. An example of an alt is

```
ALT
  c1 ? x
    p1(x)
  y > 0 & c1 ? x
    p2(y, x)
  y > 0 & SKIP
    p3()
```

where *p*1, *p*2, and *p*3 are procedures. Guards must contain either an input, preceded by an optional boolean expression, or a *SKIP*, preceded by a boolean expression. Outputs are not permitted in guards. Open, closed, and executable guards are defined as before. If all guards are closed, the alt acts like a stop. If one or more guards are open but none is executable, the alt waits until one or more become executable. If one or more guards is executable, a process with an executable guard is nondeterministically selected for execution. If a guard contains a delayed input, the guard becomes executable when the delay period is over.

The alt can have a replicator; for example,

```
ALT i = 0 FOR n
  c[i] ? a[i]
       ...        -- processing for channel c[i]
```

where *c* is an array of channels and *a* is an array of variables.

6.8.5 Configuring an Occam Program*

Occam provides several features that can be used to map a program onto a physical system. The system can consist of a set of interconnected computers (transputers), which are referred to in the language as processors. If multiple computers are used, processes can be assigned to specific computers by using the placed par. For example,

```
PLACED PAR
  PROCESSOR 1
    p1(c1, c2)
  PROCESSOR 2
    p2(c2)
  PROCESSOR 3
    p3(c1)
```

(where *c*1 and *c*2 are channels) assigns process *p*1 to processor 1, and so on. A placed par can involve a replicator:

```
PLACED PAR i = 0 FOR 4
  PROCESSOR i
    c[i] ! msg
```

Priorities can be assigned to the component processes of a par executing on the same processor by using a prioritized par; for example,

> *PRI PAR i = 0 FOR* 4
>   *c[i] ! msg*

assigns higher priority to lower numbered process. When a replicator is not used, higher priority is given to processes occurring earlier in the textual order. A process is executed only when all higher level processes cannot execute.

Priorities can also be assigned to processes in an alt; for example,

> *PRI ALT*
>   *c1 ? x*
> $x := x + 1$
>   *c2 ? x*
> $x := x + 2$

Priorities are based on the ordering within the alt, with processes mentioned earlier having higher priorities. Whenever more than one alternative is executable, the one with the highest priority is selected. Although Occam does not have an else construct, an else construct can be simulated with a prioritized alt.

Communication can be performed with external devices by defining a *port*, which acts like a single ended channel whose other end is connected to the device. Ports can then be used in inputs and outputs wherever channels can appear. An example of a port declaration is

> *PORT OF INT*16 *state* :
> *PLACE state AT* 5

where the *PLACE* construct maps the port to memory location 5. Ports can appear anywhere a channel can; for example

> *state ? val*
> *state ! 0*

A specific port can be used in only one component of a par.

6.8.6   Reasoning About Occam Programs*

Occam is a simple language that was developed with a minimalist approach. Its communication constructs are quite similar to the message passing constructs described earlier in this chapter; hence, it might be assumed that the proof techniques described there apply to Occam. Small differences in the language, however, can have a major impact on the way we reason about Occam programs. In this section we describe how some of these differences affect the reasoning process.

Variant Protocols

To an extent, we can reason about variant channel protocols using the formal methods described earlier. A channel using a protocol with n variants is semantically equivalent to n channels using nonvariant protocols. The case construct in the input is replaced by a nondeterministic choice among the n channels using an alt. One situation that falls outside of our formal techniques arises when an output process communicates only a tag and that tag does not match any of the cases in the input process. The output terminates but the input does not; hence, an entirely different satisfaction condition must be developed.

Priority

A prioritized par or alt is not fair. In the case of a par, if a high priority process never waits, a lower priority process will never progress. In the case of an alt, a guard, g, might be executable infinitely often, but if a higher priority guard is executable whenever g is, the component guarded by g will never be selected.

Replicators

A par replicator can be reasoned about using our usual methods, since its index and count values are constants and hence, at design time, it can be expanded into a fixed number of processes. A complication arises with the seq, if, and alt replicators because their index and count values may be dynamic and determined at execution time. Hence, there may be no bound, known at design time, on the number of processes that will be generated. To make an assertion about such a replicator, we might have to reason inductively.
For example, in

```
x := 0
SEQ i = 1 FOR n
    x := x + i
```

a triple for the jth replicated process can be shown inductively to be:

$$\{x = j(j-1)/2\} \; x \; := x + j \; \{x = j(j+1)/2\}$$

Hence, a postcondition for the entire seq construct is $x = n(n+1)/2$.

6.9   Bibliographic Notes

The features described in the overview appear in a variety of languages and language proposals. For example, synchronous communication is found in

Hoare [70], asynchronous communication in Andrews [11], remote procedure call in Andrews [11] and in the Ada language [1], port naming in Carriero and Gelernter [29], and dynamic process creation in Liskov and Scheifler [93]. Much of the material in the chapter is based on Hoare's language proposal Communicating Sequential Processes (CSP) [70] and the proof technique developed for it in Levin and Gries [88]. The distributed termination convention was introduced in Hoare [70] and criticized in Kieburtz and Silberschatz [76]. A technique for transforming a CSP program that utilizes DTC to one that uses an explicit exchange of signals is given in Apt and Francez [12]. A solution to the problem of detecting the termination of a set of processes was first discussed in Dijkstra [41] and then dealt with in a specifically CSP context in Francez [48] and Misra and Chandy [100]. An early discussion of the role of output commands in guards was presented in Bernstein [17]. Buckley and Silberschatz [26] focus on the implementation of such a feature. A description of Occam can be found in the Occam manual [71] and in the book by Burns [27].

6.10 Exercises

1. Give an example in which a server process, using different ports to perform demultiplexing of request messages, cannot simulate a monitor using *wait* and *send*. Consider situations in which the solution depends on the values sent in the message.

2. Describe the conditions on T, U, V, and W such that the satisfaction condition for a matching pair of message passing commands

$$\{T\} \; \mathcal{P} \, ! \, \bar{e} \; \{U\}$$

$$\{V\} \; Q \, ? \, \bar{v} \; \{W\}$$

simplifies to

$$V \Rightarrow W_{\bar{e}}^{\bar{v}}$$

and

$$T \Rightarrow U$$

3. Consider a synchronous message passing paradigm in which a process can send the same message simultaneously to two other processes. All three processes synchronize when the communication takes place. The syntax of the communication is as follows:

In process $\mathcal{P}$

$$(Q_1, Q_2) \, ! \, \bar{e}$$

In Q_1 and Q_2

$$\mathcal{P} \, ? \, \bar{v}$$

State the satisfaction condition for this communication. Intuitively describe a situation in which, after the communication takes place, process Q_1 can make some inference about the state of Q_2, even though Q_1 and Q_2 have not communicated. Produce a modified version of the "switch on" example of Section 6.6 in which Q_2 turns a switch on and Q_1 reasons that it is on. Sampling is delayed, however, until $\mathcal{P}$ sends the message $\bar{e}$ to both Q_1 and Q_2

4. (Hoare [70]) Design a pipeline system that reads a sequence of 80-character punch cards and prints them on a 125-character line printer. In printing, a space should be inserted between the last character of one card and the first character of the next, and the last line should be completed with spaces if necessary. Your system should consist of three processes: *rdr*, which reads the cards, using a procedure *getchar* to return the next character (or $\perp$ if there are no more characters); *print*, which formats the lines; and *ptr*, which prints a line using the procedure *writeln*. (Assume that *getchar* and *writeln* are given.) *print* accepts characters one at a time from *rdr*. When a line is complete (or the execution of *rdr* is complete), *print* sends the line as a 125-character array to *ptr*. The processes communicate with synchronous send and receive primitives. Do not assume DTC. A process that wishes to indicate to some other process that it has completed sends a boolean process to that other process.

5. (Hoare [70]) Adapt the previous problem so that whenever there is a pair of consecutive asterisks on a card the printer replaces those asterisks with an upward arrow.

6. A printer driver, *Driver*, accepts fixed size messages from a client process, *Client*, that wants those messages printed on the printer. The printer itself is represented by an asynchronous process, *Printer*, shown below. Unfortunately, if *Driver* sends a message while *Printer* is printing a previous message, a failure occurs. Hence, when *Printer* has completed printing a message, it sends a completion message back to *Driver*. Design *Driver* using synchronous send and receive primitives. Assume that *Driver* has embedded in it a bounded buffer abstract data object whose specification is given in Figure 3.2, with the modification that *count* is exported for read only purposes. Prove that *Driver* does not send a message when *busy* is true.

```
Printer::
    var
        busy : boolean := false;
        msg : message;
    begin
        do Driver ? msg →
            begin
                busy := true;
                ...        -- print message
                busy := false;
                Driver ! true;
            end;
        od;
    end;
```

7. Prove that when the following program terminates, the contents of array A have been copied into array B. Both arrays have dimension N. Note that the variable i is global to the two processes and is a shared variable. Describe in words how the shared variable is being used.

```
var
    i : integer := 0;
cobegin
P₁ :: ...
    do i < N → P₂ ! (A[i], i + 1); od;
//
P₂ :: ...
    do i < N → P₁ ? (B[i], i); od;
coend;
```

8. In the following program the process Sem acts like a semaphore to ensure that the critical sections in processes P₁ and P₂ are executed in a mutually exclusive fashion. Prove that the program correctly implements mutual exclusion. Note that all the P variables are of one type and all the V variables are of a different type, so that they imply different matchings in the synchronous communication. (Hint: To construct the proof, introduce auxiliary variables in the manner shown in Section 4.4.)

```
              cobegin
              𝒫₁ ::
                var
                   P1 : type1;
                   V1 : type2;
                do true →
                   begin
                     Sem ! P1;
                        ···  -- critical section
                     Sem ! V1;
                        ···  -- noncritical section
                   end;
                od;
              //
              𝒫₂ ::
                var
                   P2 : type1;
                   V2 : type2;
                do true →
                   begin
                     Sem ! P2;
                        ···  -- critical section
                     Sem ! V2;
                        ···  -- noncritical section
                   end;
                od;
              //
              Sem ::
                var
                   P3 : type1;
                   V3 : type2;
                do 𝒫₁ ? P3 → 𝒫₁ ? V3;
                [] 𝒫₂ ? P3 → 𝒫₂ ? V3;
                od;
              coend;
```

9. In a manner analogous to the previous problem, design a server process
   that implements a reader priority solution to the Readers-Writers Problem
   (Section 1.6.1) using synchronous message passing. Use auxiliary variables
   to record the number of active readers and the number of active writers at
   any time. Prove a safety property which asserts that the number of active
   readers and the number of active writers is never greater than zero simultaneously. Prove also that the number of active writers is never greater

than one.

10. In the following program, the function *input(b)* inputs a value and assigns
    it to the boolean variable, *b*. Describe in words what the program does.
    Prove that the program does not deadlock. Prove that a postcondition of
    the program is $b \Rightarrow (x = 1)$.

cobegin

$\mathcal{P}_1$::

  var

    b : *boolean*;

    y : *integer* := 0;

  begin

    input(b);

    $\mathcal{P}_2$! $\neg b$;

    if $b \rightarrow \mathcal{P}_2$! 1;

    []$\neg b \rightarrow \mathcal{P}_2$? *y*;

    fi;

  end;

//

$\mathcal{P}_2$::

  var

    x : *integer* := 0;

    b1 : *boolean*;

  begin

    $\mathcal{P}_1$? *b1*;

    if $b1 \rightarrow \mathcal{P}_1$! 2;

    []$\neg b1 \rightarrow \mathcal{P}_1$? *x*;

    fi;

  end;

coend;

11. Some languages generalize the else construct to allow timeout. The word
    "else" is replaced with the words **"when timeout(T)"**. The operational se-
    mantics of the new construct is that the final alternative is selected exactly
    when the else alternative would have been selected, except that if there
    are no processes waiting to rendezvous, the system waits for *T* seconds to
    see if any process become ready before selecting that alternative. If the
    words **"when timeout(T)"** were replaced by **"else"**, would the construct
    have the same formal semantics? If the words **"when timeout(T)"** were
    replaced by *"true* →*"*, would the construct have the same formal semantics?
    Explain.

12. Describe in words what the following program does. Prove that when the program terminates, the value of y is $M - 2N$, assuming M and N are nonnegative integers.

```
cobegin
P₁::
  var
    i : integer := 0;
  do i < M →
    begin
      P₃ ! 1;
      i := i + 1;
    end;
  od;
//
P₂::
  var
    j : integer := 0;
  do j < N →
    begin
      P₃ ! - 2;
      j := j + 1;
    end;
  od;
//
P₃::
  var
    k, y, x : integer := 0, 0, 0;
  do k < M + N →
    begin
      if true → P₁ ? x;
      [] true → P₂ ? x;
      fi;
      y, k := y + x, k + 1;
    end;
  od;
coend;
```

13. Some languages do not allow output commands in guards. We would like to design a bounded buffer implementation that used only input commands in its guards but nevertheless gives us the benefits of putting communication commands in guards. Assume the consumer process using the bounded

buffer repeatedly executes

$$\cdots \; \mathcal{BB}\,!\,more;\; \mathcal{BB}\,?\,x;\; \cdots$$

Using a method analogous to that in the text, prove that the following implementation words correctly. State in words the benefits of putting the communication commands in the guards.

$\mathcal{BB}$ ::
 $\cdots$

> **do** $count < N;\; \mathcal{P}_1\,?\,Qarray[(last+1)\,\mathbf{mod}\,N] \to$
> $last, count := (last+1)\,\mathbf{mod}\,N, count+1;$
> [] $count > 0;\; \mathcal{P}_2\,?\,more \to$
> > **begin**
> > $\mathcal{P}_2\,!\,Qarray[last-count+1\,\mathbf{mod}\,N];$
> > $count := count-1;$
> > **end**;
>
> **od**;

14. The following process uses message passing with one-way direct naming to implement a general semaphore with initial value 0. Prove that this process is a concrete implementation of the abstract semaphore data type defined in Exercise 5.1.

> **var**
> > $sem : integer := 0;$
> > $P : type1;$
> > $V : type2;$
>
> **begin**
> > **do** $?\,V \to$
> > > $sem := sem+1;$
> >
> > [] $sem > 0;\; ?\,P \to$
> > > $sem := sem-1;$
> >
> > **od**;
>
> **end**;

15. (Schlichting and Schneider [115]) A process, $\mathcal{M}erge$, receives inputs from two processes, In_1 and In_2. The input values received from In_1 and from In_2 are both strictly increasing. $\mathcal{M}erge$ sends to process Out a merged version of these values in strictly increasing order. A value that appears in both In_1 and In_2 should not be duplicated in the output. The input streams from both In_1 and In_2 are terminated with a special symbol, ∞, which is larger than any input and is not to be output. State in words how

the following version of *Merge* works. To prove that it works correctly, prove that all inputs sent to *Merge* are received by *Merge*; that all values received by *Merge*, except ∞, are sent to *Out*; and that the values sent to *Out* are strictly increasing.

Merge::
    $\cdots$
begin
    $In_1 ? v1;$
    $In_2 ? v2;$
    do $v1 < v2 \rightarrow$
        begin
            $Out ! v1;$
            $In_1 ? v1;$
        end;
    [] $v1 > v2 \rightarrow$
        begin
            $Out ! v2;$
            $In_2 ? v2;$
        end;
    [] $(v1 = v2) \wedge (v1 \neq \infty) \rightarrow$
        begin
            $Out ! v1;$
            $In_1 ? v1;$
            $In_2 ? v2;$
        end;
    od;
end

16. Consider the three processes, $\mathcal{P}_1$, $\mathcal{P}_2$, and $\mathcal{P}_3$, each of which executes an infinitely looping statement, whose body we refer to as a compute phase. We require that before $\mathcal{P}_i$ can enter its jth compute phase, all other processes must have completed their $(j - 1)$st compute phase. Processes exchange messages synchronously to guarantee that this requirement is satisfied. Design a protocol for this purpose, and prove that it satisfies the required condition.

17. Design an algorithm for implementing guarded communication when both send and receive commands are allowed in guards. Use a priority method to break symmetry.

18. Assume that two language constructs have the same formal semantics. Discuss three ways in which their operational semantics might differ.

19. To prove that the following variation of the program of Figure 6.16 works correctly, prove that the assertion $(ok \Rightarrow (switch = on))$ is a program invariant of $\mathcal{P}_2$.

```
cobegin
P₁::
   ...
   begin
       switch := on;        -- turn device on
       P₂ ! true;
       ...
       P₂ ! false;
       switch := off;       -- turn device off
   end;
//
P₂::
   var
       ok : boolean := false
   begin
       P₁ ? ok;
       do ok →
           ...              -- sample device output
           if P₁ ? ok → skip;
           else skip;
           fi;
       od;
   end;
coend;
```

20. To solve the symmetric termination problem illustrated by Figure 6.15, design an algorithm involving the explicit exchange of termination messages. The solution should involve the exchange of "I am passive" messages. A process can send such a message after it has completed its part of the computation and is ready to terminate. Explain why an algorithm in which a process sends one such message to each of its peers will not solve the problem.

7

Asynchronous Communication

In an asynchronous message passing system, communicating processes do not synchronize at the instant the message is transferred. The sending process sends the message and then continues executing; thus it does not know how much later in its execution the receiving process actually receives the message. When the receiving process does receive the message, it does not know how much earlier in its execution the sending process actually sent the message or how much further the sending process has proceeded since sending the message. Thus, as we shall see, there is often added complexity in reasoning in one process about the state of another.

The asynchronous mode of message passing allows a greater degree of asynchronous behavior than the synchronous mode, since the sender is not synchronized with the receipt of the message. In many situations, however, the logic of an application requires synchronization not provided in asynchronous mode. In such cases additional synchronization must be provided – perhaps through the use of additional messages. Thus, in many ways, synchronization is an attribute of the application, not the implementation.

We consider two types of asynchronous message passing systems: *virtual circuit* systems and *datagram* systems. In a virtual circuit system, the messages are received in the same order they were sent while in a datagram system the messages might be received in a different order. For both types of systems, we assume that all messages that are sent are eventually received; unreliable systems are discussed in Chapter 9.

7.1 Network Communication and the OSI Reference Model

Message passing systems require the use of communication protocols to ensure that messages are sent and received correctly. Much of the work on protocols

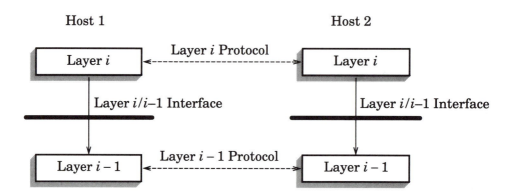

Figure 7.1: Adjacent layers in a hierarchical protocol.

in recent years has been done in the context of the model formulated by the International Standards Organization (ISO) for Open Systems Interconnection (OSI). The structure proposed involves a hierarchical model in which each layer of the hierarchy implements some abstraction for use by the next higher layer. Starting with the lowest, or *physical*, layer, which deals directly with the hardware, successive layers create increasingly more sophisticated abstractions, which are tailored to make communication convenient for a wide variety of end users.

The hierarchical organization is shown in Figure 7.1. Each layer of the structure at a particular site is composed of *entities* (*e.g.,* processes), which communicate with *peer related* entities in the same layer at other sites. Communication at layer i is performed using the *layer i protocol*. A *protocol* is a specification of the rules governing the conduct of a conversation between the entities. For example, the protocol might specify such things as the format of the messages exchanged between the entities, the meaning of the various fields in each message, which entity is allowed to speak next, and how conversations are started and terminated.

A conversation between two entities in layer i is conducted over a virtual link, which is an abstraction created by layer $i - 1$. A layer i entity uses this abstraction through the layer $i/i-1$ *interface*. This interface specifies primitive operations available for managing the abstraction. In the OSI model, the interface can be crossed in two directions. A layer i entity can invoke an operation supported by a layer $i - 1$ entity, or a layer $i - 1$ entity can inform a layer i entity of an event that has occurred, using, for example, an interrupt. Thus, a layer i entity at site A might invoke a primitive operation, implemented by layer $i - 1$, to send data to its layer i peer at site B over the virtual link. The layer $i - 1$ entity at site A sends the data to its (layer $i - 1$) peer at site B (using the layer $i-1$ protocol, over the virtual link created by layer $i-2$), which interrupts the layer i entity to inform it of the arrival of the data. Although the abstraction creates the illusion of direct communication between peer entities in layer i, in actuality a message must travel down the hierarchy at the sending site and back up the hierarchy at the receiver.

The interface presented by the physical layer involves such things as the mechanical dimensions of connectors, voltage levels, and the significance of sequences of voltage pulses on different interfacing wires. Whereas in other layers, the link between peer related entities is virtual, in this layer it is real, using, for example, a wire or the atmosphere as a transmission medium. A message in this layer is a bit, and the protocol specifies the format of the message. For example, with Manchester encoding, each bit involves either a positive pulse followed by a negative pulse or vice versa. The abstraction created by the physical layer is that of a pipe between directly connected sites in the net for the transmission of bits.

In general, when a layer i entity invokes a primitive to communicate with its layer i peer, it must provide both the message and parameters describing the requested transmission through the network. For example, a parameter might specify the address of the destination layer i entity to which the message is to be sent. The layer $i-1$ entity in turn constructs a message for its layer $i-1$ peer out of the information it has received through the interface. This message consists of the message received from layer i (which layer $i-1$ treats as an uninterpreted bit string) concatenated with a layer $i-1$ *header* containing control information in accordance with the layer $i-1$ protocol. In the example, the header contains the destination address. The combination is dispatched to the layer $i-1$ peer through the virtual link between entities in layer $i-1$, using the layer $i-1/i-2$ interface. Figure 7.2 illustrates the process. The layer $i-1$ header is interpreted by the layer $i-1$ (destination) peer and contains information about how the original layer i message is to be dealt with. In the example, the header is used to decide which layer i entity is to receive the message.

The sites of a network can be interconnected in a variety of ways. In the simplest case, network connectivity can be described by a completely connected graph. Such a situation arises most frequently in a *local area network*, or LAN, where sites are in close proximity to one another. In such cases, sites are frequently connected through a shared medium – for example, a common bus such as an ethernet. Not only does such a physical organization enable each site to communicate directly with every other site, but it also allows broadcast communication, in which each message sent can be received by every other site. In a *wide area network*, or WAN, where sites may be separated by large distances, a completely connected topology is generally not cost effective. Hence, each site is no longer directly connected to every other site and a store and forward technique must be used.

The protocol layer in the OSI model immediately above the physical layer is the *datalink* layer. It presents the abstraction of a virtual link between

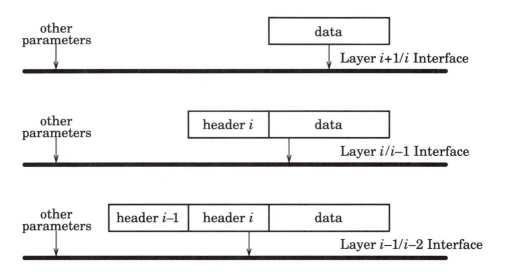

Figure 7.2: The layering of header information as a message passes through the hierarchy.

directly connected sites in the net for the transmission of sequences of bits (generally called *frames* in this layer). The next layer up in the hierarchy is the *network* layer. It presents the abstraction of a virtual link between arbitrary (not necessarily directly connected) sites in the net for the transmission of sequences of bits (generally called *packets* in this layer). An important role played by the protocol in this layer is that of routing messages through intermediate sites from source to destination.

While the network layer offers end-to-end service to its users, the service might not be reliable, might not hide network failures, and might transmit units of information whose size is tailored to the needs of the network, not the user. The next layer in the hierarchy is the *transport* layer. It translates the network layer abstraction into one that is more convenient for the user by creating the abstraction of a reliable end-to-end service that hides network failures and accommodates larger units of transfer. Higher layers in the protocol hierarchy (the session, presentation, and application layers) deal with such issues as the encoding of information, imposing rules on the way the application layer conversations are conducted, and providing mechanisms for synchronizing users.

The end-to-end service offered by the network layer makes it an appropriate boundary between the higher layers of protocol, which are primarily concerned with tailoring the communication abstraction to the needs of the application, and the lower layers, which are primarily concerned with simply moving blocks of information having some maximum length from the source to the destination. Public networks – networks that sell their services to a variety of customers – frequently provide a level of abstraction roughly equal to that prescribed by the OSI network layer, leaving the higher layers of the protocol to be implemented on the customer's host machines. For this reason, the network layer plays a particularly crucial role in the protocol hierarchy.

In this chapter we concentrate on the two major variations of the network layer abstraction that are most commonly offered: *connection-oriented* and *connectionless*. When service is connection-oriented, a communicating pair of customers first establish a connection, then transmit information over the connection, and finally destroy the connection. In the establishment phase, the customers may negotiate the terms under which communication is to take place (*e.g.*, are there to be messages of different priorities, who is to pay for the connection, will acknowledgments be sent). Full network addresses must be supplied by the customers to set up the connection, but once the connection has been established, the network layer returns a connection name, which is used by the customers in addressing all data transmitted over the connection in the next phase. The connection is viewed as a data pipe, meaning that the data packets are received in the order sent. Connection-oriented service generally offers a high probability that all packets will be delivered and none will be duplicated.

With connectionless service, each message is treated as an independent entity. No connection is set up. Instead, a customer must fully address each message it delivers to the network layer. There is no guarantee that messages will arrive in order, and, indeed, connectionless service generally does not offer the same high probability that messages will not be lost or duplicated.

Whereas connection-oriented service is appropriate when long streams of data are to be exchanged and the cost of connection establishment and destruction can be prorated over the amount of information to be communicated, connectionless service is appropriate for short messages. There are two schools of thought concerning the appropriate level of reliability that should be offered by the network layer. One school asserts that the lower level offered by connectionless service is appropriate, since applications that do not require high reliability should not be forced to pay (financially or in terms of transfer time) for unneeded features. Additional reliability can be provided by the transport layer for those applications that require it. The other school asserts that, since a certain level of reliability must be provided by the lowest layers of the system, rather than duplicate these algorithms at higher layers to obtain more reliable service, it is more efficient to deal with the issue in one place.

Two distinct techniques are generally used to implement connection-oriented and connectionless service: *virtual circuits* and *datagrams*. With a virtual circuit, a path through the network is constructed when the connection is established. The path involves entries in tables at nodes along the chosen route that contain information describing the state of the connection and enable packets in a message to be relayed along the path without re-executing routing algorithms. Resources can also be reserved at these nodes (*e.g.,* buffers, bandwidth). The reservation of resources reduces waiting time. The fact that all packets follow the same route makes it easier to guarantee that packets will arrive in order, but makes it more difficult to respond to node or link failures. Successive messages are numbered to enforce ordered delivery and detect lost messages. These *sequence numbers* are included in messages and also stored as state information at the source and destination sites.

By contrast, a datagram is a fully addressed message that is independent of all other messages and traverses the network without the aid of a previously constructed path. Successive datagrams from a particular source to a particular destination might travel different routes and hence arrive at the destination in an order different from the order in which they were sent. The network layer header of a datagram contains the final destination of the datagram and is interpreted by the network layer at intermediate sites in order to make dynamic routing decisions. Whereas in virtual circuit communication fixed data structures must be maintained at each node along the path from source to destination and a failure at any such node causes a major disruption, in datagram communication no data structures are maintained and messages can be easily rerouted when intermediate node failures occur. Sequence numbers are not used in a datagram; they would imply the maintenance of state information at the source and destination sites.

The most straightforward implementation of connection-oriented service is through virtual circuits. In fact, the terms are often used interchangeably, and we conform to that usage. Similarly, the most straightforward implementation of connectionless service is through datagrams, and again the terms are often used interchangeably. However, it is possible to build a connection-oriented service with a hybrid implementation that uses datagrams and stored state information at the source and destination sites. During the establishment phase, the network layer at the source and destination use datagrams to negotiate the terms under which the communication is to take place and agree on a connection name. Each establishes a correspondence between that name and the source and destination addresses. A user of the network layer addresses messages to the connection name, but the network layer at the source site translates the name into a destination address and dispatches the message as a datagram. Since data is sent in datagrams, ordered delivery at the destination is not guaranteed. However, sequence numbers are used, so the network layer at the destination site can detect lost datagrams and order the datagrams before returning them to the destination user. Thus, although the user sees the abstraction of a connection, no resources are reserved at intermediate sites and data does not flow along a unique path.

7.1.1   The Rendezvous Table

In any communication system, whether synchronous or asynchronous, datagram or virtual circuit, message transmission between a source and a destination cannot be completed until the system detects that a pair of events has occurred: each process has indicated a desire to communicate. In a connection-oriented system, this indication might involve requests to set up a connection; in a connectionless system, it might involve requests to send and receive a message. In other words, a rendezvous must be detected. A commonly used data structure for detecting a rendezvous is the *rendezvous table*. For example, the table might contain entries describing unmatched send and receive requests. Thus, when a receive is executed, the rendezvous table is searched for an entry created as the result of a matching send. The criterion for matching depends on the type of message passing being implemented. For example, with datagrams, full network addresses must match, whereas with virtual circuits, the receiver searches for an entry describing a send on the same virtual circuit. When message passing is handled through a high level language, matching involves the number and types of the individual data items sent or expected in a message. If a match is found in the rendezvous table by a receiver, the send entry is deleted from the table and the corresponding message is delivered to the receiver. If no matching entry is found, an entry for the receive is created in the table. A symmetric algorithm is executed for the send.

In the context of the OSI model, a rendezvous table can be implemented within any layer that has available to it end-to-end service. For example, if the table is implemented within the transport layer, the end-to-end facilities of the network layer are used for transmitting the control messages necessary for detecting the rendezvous.

In a distributed system, the rendezvous table may be stored at some known site in the net, or it may be distributed across the net. In the latter case, the sender and receiver must agree on where the rendezvous is to take place. Two commonly used alternatives exist: rendezvous at sender and rendezvous at receiver. If rendezvous at receiver is implemented, the sender and receiver use that portion of the distributed rendezvous table located at the receiver site to effect the rendezvous. The sender sends a request to the receiver, causing the system to search the receiver's rendezvous table for a matching entry and, if none is found, to create an entry for the send.

One problem with rendezvous at receiver concerns the management of buffers. If the rendezvous request sent to the receiver site contains the actual message, the receiver site must be prepared to buffer the message. However, since the sender site cannot be sure that the receiver site has enough space available to buffer the message, an exchange of control messages might be required before the message can be brought to the receiver site, thus resulting in additional message traffic. With rendezvous at sender, the buffer management problem can be handled locally, avoiding the message exchange. If buffer space exists (at the sender site), the message can be copied from the sender process to a buffer and the sender can continue executing. If not, the sender must be delayed until buffer space becomes available (since if the sender is allowed to continue, it might overwrite the message), or an exception can be returned to the sender rejecting the send request. When the rendezvous request from the receiver arrives at the sender site, either an entry can be made in the sender's portion of the rendezvous table (if the matching send request has not been executed) or the message can be immediately transferred to the receiver site (if it has). Furthermore, if the message exchange is aborted (*e.g.,* if the receiver terminates before accepting the message), no communication bandwidth has been wasted in transferring the message. Rendezvous at sender would not be appropriate in situations involving one-way direct naming.

7.2   Virtual Circuit Communication

We assume that each virtual circuit has a name and provides unidirectional communication between a unique sender and a unique receiver. To send and receive on virtual circuit V, we use the primitives

$$\mathbf{send_c}\ \bar{e}\ \mathbf{to}\ V$$

$$\mathbf{receive_c}\ \bar{v}\ \mathbf{from}\ V$$

where the subscript **c** denotes asynchronous virtual circuit communication, $\bar{e}$ is a vector of expressions, and $\bar{v}$ is a vector of variables. We assume that the number and type of the elements in a message transmitted through V is fixed and that $\bar{e}$ and $\bar{v}$ conform to that specification.

An ideal virtual circuit, V, can be viewed as a queue of unbounded length. The operational semantics of the send is as follows:

> The expressions $\bar{e}$ are evaluated and their values are appended to the queue corresponding to V; then the send terminates. The send operation is atomic.

The operational semantics of the receive is as follows:

> If the queue corresponding to V is empty, the receiver waits until the queue is nonempty; if the queue is nonempty, the vector of values at the head of the queue is removed and assigned to $\bar{v}$; then the receive terminates. The removal and assignment are done atomically.

For example, the effect of message passing in the program of Figure 7.3 is to assign the value 1 to the variable x and 2 to the variable y.

7.3   Axiomatization of Virtual Circuit Communication

As with synchronous message passing, we first state axiom schemas describing the virtual circuit send and receive primitives and then introduce satisfaction and non-interference conditions so that the proofs of processes using these primitives within a cobegin statement can be combined.

```
              cobegin
              𝒫₁::
                begin
                   send_c 1 to V;
                   send_c 2 to V;
                end;
              //
              𝒫₂::
                begin
                   receive_c x from V;
                   receive_c y from V;
                end;
              coend;
```

Figure 7.3: A simple program using a virtual circuit.

Before presenting the schemas, we define a formal model for the virtual circuit. Whereas in a synchronous message passing system messages are never buffered, in an asynchronous system there may exist at any time a sequence of messages that have been sent but not yet received. The contents of this set is a part of the system state, which we represent using auxiliary variables. A virtual circuit, V, is modeled by two auxiliary variables, σ_V and ρ_V, both of which are sequences initialized to λ. σ_V represents the sequence of all messages that have ever been sent on V, and ρ_V represents the sequence of all messages that have ever been received on V. Since the virtual circuit has been defined so that messages are received in the order sent, the following axiom describes virtual circuit behavior.

Virtual Circuit Axiom

$$\rho_V \in prefix(\sigma_V)$$

Given two sequences, α and β, where $\beta \in prefix(\alpha)$, we use the notation $\alpha - \beta$ to denote the suffix of α that is not contained in β.

It follows from the Virtual Circuit Axiom that there exists a sequence α_V such that

$$\sigma_V = \rho_V \circ \alpha_V$$

(in other words: $\alpha_V = \sigma_V - \rho_V$). α_V represents the messages that have been sent and not yet received. If $\alpha_V \neq \lambda$, there is at least one message that has been sent and not yet received.

The only effect of a send on virtual circuit V is to append the message sent to the end of σ_V. Thus it has the effect of an assignment statement, and the following axiom schema describes its semantics:

Virtual Circuit Send Axiom

$$\{U^{\sigma_V}_{\sigma_V \circ <\bar{e}>}\} \textbf{ send}_\textbf{c} \; \bar{e} \textbf{ to } V \, \{U\}$$

where U is an arbitrary assertion.

We can no longer state (as we could with synchronous message passing) that a receive does not terminate when the receiver process is executed in isolation. A process can send a message to itself, and if the receive follows the send, that receive will terminate. Nevertheless, we describe the receive primitive with an axiom schema that allows arbitrary pre- and postconditions and rely on satisfaction to relate these assertions to those of the corresponding send and to the message being sent.

Virtual Circuit Receive Axiom

$$\{P\} \textbf{ receive}_\textbf{c} \; \bar{v} \textbf{ from } V \, \{W\}$$

where P and W are arbitrary assertions.

The receive terminates only when the queue is nonempty. We describe the semantics of its execution with a satisfaction condition. The effect of the execution is to assign the value of the first message stored in the queue to $\bar{v}$ and append that value to ρ_V. In order for an execution to take place that has the effect of assigning some message, X, to $\bar{v}$, the system must be in a state in which the precondition, P, of the receive is satisfied, $(\sigma_V - \rho_V)$ is not empty, and $First(\sigma_V - \rho_V)$ is X. Thus, the satisfaction condition is

Proof Obligation for Satisfaction of Virtual Circuit Receive

For each virtual circuit receive,

$$\{P\} \textbf{ receive}_\textbf{c} \; \bar{v} \textbf{ from } V \, \{W\}$$

show that

$$[P \wedge ((\sigma_V - \rho_V) \neq \lambda) \wedge (First(\sigma_V - \rho_V) = X)] \Rightarrow W^{\bar{v}, \; \rho_V}_{X, \; \rho_V \circ <X>} \tag{7.1}$$

where X is a logical variable.

Whereas in the synchronous case satisfaction uses the precondition of the send to strengthen the left-hand side of the implication, in the asynchronous case the identity of the enabled control point of the sender at the time the receive is executed is not known. Hence, only the states of the receiver and the virtual circuit at the time the receive is executed can be used to validate the postcondition of the receive.

We must also prove non-interference for all virtual circuit sends and receives. Proving non-interference for a virtual circuit send is the same as proving it for any other assignment statement. To prove non-interference for the virtual circuit receive, we must demonstrate that the assignments to $\bar{v}$ and ρ_V do not interfere with any assertion in a parallel process.

Proof Obligations for Interference Freedom of Virtual Circuit Receive

For each virtual circuit receive statement,

$$\{P\}\ \textbf{receive}_C\ \bar{v}\ \textbf{from}\ V\ \{W\}$$

and each assertion, A, in a process different from that containing the receive, show that

$$[A \wedge P \wedge ((\sigma_V - \rho_V) \neq \lambda) \wedge (First(\sigma_V - \rho_V) = X)] \Rightarrow A_{X,\ \rho_V \circ <X>}^{\bar{v},\ \rho_V} \qquad (7.2)$$

Once again X is a logical variable, so the proof obligation reduces to demonstrating (7.2) for the value of X satisfying $X = First(\sigma_V - \rho_V)$.

Example

An annotated version of the program in Figure 7.3 is shown in Figure 7.4. The annotation abbreviates sequential proofs of processes $\mathcal{P}_1$ and $\mathcal{P}_2$, since the assertions in $\mathcal{P}_1$ satisfy the virtual circuit send axiom and the assertions in $\mathcal{P}_2$ trivially satisfy the virtual circuit receive axiom (any assertions would do). Furthermore neither $\mathcal{P}_1$ nor $\mathcal{P}_2$ interferes with the proof of the other.

To demonstrate satisfaction, consider the first receive in $\mathcal{P}_2$. Substituting the values of P and W from the annotation into the satisfaction condition (7.1), we obtain

$$[(\rho_V = \lambda) \wedge ((\sigma_V - \rho_V) \neq \lambda) \wedge (First(\sigma_V - \rho_V) = X)] \Rightarrow$$
$$[(x = 1) \wedge (\rho_V = <1>)]_{X,\ \rho_V \circ <X>}^{x,\ \rho_V} \qquad (7.3)$$

Unfortunately we cannot prove the truth of this implication without more information about σ_V. This additional information can be expressed by the assertion

$$(\sigma_V = \lambda) \vee (First(\sigma_V) = 1) \qquad (7.4)$$

which is a program invariant of $\mathcal{P}_1$. It is true initially, and, by the Virtual Circuit Send Axiom, its truth is preserved by each of the send statements (as can be demonstrated using the assertions in the proof of $\mathcal{P}_1$ in Figure 7.4). Similarly, it is a program invariant of $\mathcal{P}_2$, since $\mathcal{P}_2$ does not modify σ_V. To show that it is a program invariant of the entire program, we need to show

$$\{true\}$$
cobegin
$\mathcal{P}_1::$
  begin
    $\{\sigma_V = \lambda\}$
    send$_c$ 1 to V;
    $\{\sigma_V = <1>\}$
    send$_c$ 2 to V;
    $\{\sigma_V = <1, 2>\}$
  end;
    $\{\sigma_V = <1, 2>\}$
$//$
$\mathcal{P}_2::$
  begin
    $\{\rho_V = \lambda\}$
  receive$_c$ x **from** V;
    $\{(x = 1) \wedge (\rho_V = <1>)\}$
  receive$_c$ y **from** V;
    $\{(x = 1) \wedge (y = 2) \wedge (\rho_V = <1, 2>)\}$
  end;
    $\{(x = 1) \wedge (y = 2) \wedge (\rho_V = <1, 2>)\}$
coend;
  $\{(x = 1) \wedge (y = 2) \wedge (\rho_V = <1, 2>) \wedge (\sigma_V = <1, 2>)\}$

Program Invariant:
$\quad I \; : \; (\sigma_V = \lambda) \vee (First(\sigma_V) = 1)$

Figure 7.4: An annotated version of a simple virtual circuit program.

non-interference and satisfaction as well. Non-interference follows from the fact that it is a program invariant of each component and the assertions in the original annotation are not interfered with. Satisfaction for both receives follows from

$$[(\sigma_V = \lambda) \vee (First(\sigma_V) = 1)] \wedge ((\sigma_V - \rho_V) \neq \lambda) \wedge (First(\sigma_V - \rho_V) = X) \Rightarrow$$
$$[(\sigma_V = \lambda) \vee (First(\sigma_V) = 1)]_{X, \; \rho_V \circ <X>}^{x, \; \rho_V}$$

Hence (7.4) is a program invariant of the entire program and can be conjoined with all assertions in the annotation. In particular, if we add it as a precondition to the first receive, the satisfaction condition (7.3) becomes

$$(\rho_V = \lambda) \wedge (First(\sigma_V) = 1) \wedge (First(\sigma_V) = X) \Rightarrow$$
$$[(x = 1) \wedge (\rho_V = < 1 >)]_{X, \ \rho_V \ \circ \ <X>}^{x, \ \rho_V}$$

which is trivially true. Note that we need not include the invariant on the right side of the implication, since its invariance has already been demonstrated.

To demonstrate satisfaction for the second receive, we choose a new program invariant that describes the second value sent. An appropriate choice is

$$(\sigma_V = \lambda) \vee (\sigma_V = < 1 >) \vee (First(Tail(\sigma_V)) = 2)$$

Again, the satisfaction proof follows easily.

Since statements in $\mathcal{P}_1$ do not modify variables in assertions of $\mathcal{P}_2$ and vice versa, no interference is possible, and hence the annotation is valid.

7.4   Example – The Bounded Buffer with Virtual Circuits*

Figure 7.5 shows a process, $\mathcal{BB}$, that is maintaining a bounded buffer similar to that defined in Section 6.4. We use virtually the same implementation as in that section, except that instead of using synchronous message passing, $\mathcal{P}_1$ sends to $\mathcal{BB}$ on virtual circuit V1 and $\mathcal{BB}$ sends to $\mathcal{P}_2$ on virtual circuit V2.

To perform the proofs in Section 6.4, we introduced two auxiliary variables, *in* and *out*, where *in* was the sequence of all the messages that had ever been received by $\mathcal{BB}$ and *out* was the sequence of all the messages that had ever been sent by $\mathcal{BB}$. In the present implementation, auxiliary variables with this interpretation already exist: ρ_{V1} is the sequence of all the messages that have ever been received by $\mathcal{BB}$, and σ_{V2} is the sequence of all the messages that have ever been sent by $\mathcal{BB}$. Thus most of the proofs for the implementation in Section 6.4 can just be reformulated using the new variables.

In Figure 6.10 we used as the loop invariant that describes the behavior of that bounded buffer

$$(0 \le count \le N) \wedge (in = out \circ Seq(Qarray, last, count))$$

In a similar proof of $\mathcal{BB}$ in Figure 7.5, we can use as the loop invariant

$$(0 \le count \le N) \wedge (\rho_{V1} = \sigma_{V2} \circ Seq(Qarray, last, count)) \tag{7.5}$$

The proof that (7.5) is a loop invariant is similar to that given in Section 6.4. Now, however, the assignments to ρ_{V1} and σ_{V2} are done as part of the receive and send statements instead of in separate assignments. For example, to demonstrate the loop invariance of (7.5) for the first component of the do statement in Figure 7.5 we choose as an instance of the Virtual Circuit Receive Axiom the triple

```
cobegin
𝒫₁ ::
    ··· sendc e to V1; ···
//
ℬℬ ::
    var
        Qarray : array[0..(N – 1)] of job_info;
        last : 0..(N – 1) := 0;
        count : 0..N := 0;
    begin
        do count < N →
            begin
                receivec Qarray[(last + 1) mod N] from V1;
                last, count := (last + 1) mod N, count + 1;
            end;
        [] count > 0 →
            begin
                sendc Qarray[(last – count + 1) mod N] to V2;
                count := count – 1;
            end;
        od;
    end;
//
𝒫₂ ::
    ··· receivec v from V2; ···
coend;
```

Figure 7.5: A bounded buffer implementation using virtual circuits.

$\{(0 \le count < N) \land (\rho_{V1} = \sigma_{V2} \circ Seq(Qarray, last, count))\}$
receive$_c$ $Qarray[(last + 1) \bmod N]$ **from** $V1$;
$\quad \{(0 \le count + 1 \le N) \land (\rho_{V1} = \sigma_{V2} \circ Seq(Qarray, (last + 1) \bmod N, count + 1))\}$

Loop invariance is now trivially true, since the following triple is a consequence of the assignment axiom:

$\quad \{(0 \le count + 1 \le N) \land (\rho_{V1} = \sigma_{V2} \circ Seq(Qarray, (last + 1) \bmod N, count + 1))\}$
$last,\ count := (last + 1) \bmod N,\ count + 1$;
$\quad \{(0 \le count \le N) \land (\rho_{V1} = \sigma_{V2} \circ Seq(Qarray, last, count))\}$

We are left with the satisfaction proof obligation:

$$[(0 \le count < N) \wedge (\rho_{V1} = \sigma_{V2} \circ Seq(Qarray, last, count))$$
$$\wedge((\sigma_{V1} - \rho_{V1}) \ne \lambda) \wedge (First(\sigma_{V1} - \rho_{V1}) = X)] \Rightarrow$$
$$[(0 \le count + 1 \le N) \wedge (\rho_{V1} = \sigma_{V2}$$
$$\circ\, Seq(Qarray, (last + 1)\ mod\ N, count + 1))]_{X,\ \rho_{V1}\ \circ\ <X>}^{Qarray[(last+1)\ mod\ N],\ \rho_{V1}}$$

which follows easily.

This loop invariant, together with the invariants corresponding to the virtual circuit axioms,

$$\rho_{V1} \in prefix(\sigma_{V1}) \tag{7.6}$$

$$\rho_{V2} \in prefix(\sigma_{V2}) \tag{7.7}$$

can be used to formulate other proofs. For example, we can show that after $\mathcal{P}_1$ has sent a sequence of M messages and $\mathcal{P}_2$ has received a sequence of M messages, the sequence of messages received by $\mathcal{P}_2$ is the same as that sent by $\mathcal{P}_1$. To see this, observe that if the lengths of σ_{V1} and ρ_{V2} are both M, it follows from the invariants (7.5), (7.6), and (7.7) that

$$\sigma_{V1} = \rho_{V1} = \sigma_{V2} = \rho_{V2}$$

since, if sequences α and β are the same length and one is a prefix of the other, they are the same sequence.

Note that, since the receive statement is not in the guard in Figure 7.5, this formulation of $\mathcal{BB}$ is subject to added delay and possible deadlock. However, arguing as we did in Section 6.5, we can demonstrate that the proofs apply as well to a bounded buffer in which the receive statement is included in the guard. Since send is non-blocking, nothing is gained by allowing send statements in guards.

7.5 Transferring Assertions Between Processes*

As with synchronous message passing systems, there may be an implicit exchange of information between processes communicating through virtual circuits. The receiver process may be able to conclude something about the state of the sender process, not only at the time the message was sent, but at times between message transmissions.

We use the same example as in the previous chapter: we want to reason that a device turned on by one process is still on while another process is sampling output from the device. Because of the additional complexity of asynchronous message passing, we consider separately how to reason about the switch being turned on and being turned off. We do this by analyzing two separate programs: one that only turns the switch on and the other that only turns it off. The programs can be combined to obtain a complete solution to the problem.

```
                    cobegin
                    𝒫₁::
                      begin
                          . . .
                          switch  :=  on;
                          sendᴄ on to V;
                          . . .
                      end;
                    //
                    𝒫₂::
                      begin
                          receiveᴄ x from V;
                          . . .    - -  sample device output
                      end;
                    coend;
```

Figure 7.6: A program that communicates the assertion "switch on."

Figure 7.6 is an example of the first program. $\mathcal{P}_1$ turns the device switch on. $\mathcal{P}_2$ samples output from the device that is only meaningful when it is on. Thus, $\mathcal{P}_1$ sends a message to $\mathcal{P}_2$ after turning the switch on. $\mathcal{P}_2$ waits before initiating data acquisition until it receives the message from $\mathcal{P}_1$.

To prove that the system works correctly, we must demonstrate that the switch is on while $\mathcal{P}_2$ is sampling. We can easily show that the switch is on at the instant the message is sent, but $\mathcal{P}_1$ could conceivably turn the switch off right after it sends the message, and so we must prove that the assertion $switch = on$ is true while $\mathcal{P}_2$ is sampling.

We perform the proof by demonstrating that the assertion

$$I : ((on \sqsubseteq \sigma_V) \Rightarrow (switch = on)) \wedge ((\sigma_V = \lambda) \vee (\sigma_V = <on>))$$

is a program invariant, where $x \sqsubseteq S$ means that x is in the sequence S. In other words, for all time after on is sent, the switch is on. Then, after $\mathcal{P}_2$ receives on, it can conclude that $on \sqsubseteq \sigma_V$ (using the Virtual Circuit Axiom) and, therefore, that the switch is on. Hence, we have transferred the assertion $switch = on$ from the proof of $\mathcal{P}_1$ to the proof of $\mathcal{P}_2$.

Figure 7.7 shows an annotated version of the program. The annotation abbreviates individual proofs of each process, which exhibit no interference. I is a program invariant of the concurrent program, since it is true initially, $switch$ and σ_V are only changed in $\mathcal{P}_1$ (hence it is a program invariant of $\mathcal{P}_2$), and each of the assertions in $\mathcal{P}_1$ implies I (hence it is a program invariant of $\mathcal{P}_1$). Furthermore, using I, satisfaction can be shown.

Now we want to allow $\mathcal{P}_1$ to turn the switch off. Figure 7.8 is a first try at

```
cobegin
        {σ_V = λ}
P_1::
  begin
      . . .
        {σ_V = λ}
      switch := on;
        {(σ_V = λ) ∧ (switch = on)}
      send_c on to V;
        {(σ_V = < on >) ∧ (switch = on)}
      . . .
  end;
        {(σ_V = < on >) ∧ (switch = on)}
//
        {ρ_V = λ}
P_2::
  begin
        {ρ_V = λ}
      receive_c x from V;
        {ρ_V = < on >}
      . . .          -- sample device output
        {ρ_V = < on >}
  end;
        {ρ_V = < on >}
coend;
```

Program Invariant:
  I : $((on \sqsubseteq \sigma_V) \Rightarrow (switch = on)) \wedge ((\sigma_V = \lambda) \vee (\sigma_V = < on >))$

Figure 7.7: An annotated version of the previous program.

such a program, where for simplicity we assume that the switch is on initially.
Note that we now allow a virtual circuit receive statement (as contrasted with
a synchronous receive statement) to appear as the last component of a guard.
Such a guard is executable if its boolean component is true and if $(\sigma_V - \rho_V) \neq \lambda$. If
the guard is not executable, the else clause is chosen and hence the if statement
implements polling. Unfortunately this program does not exhibit the desired
behavior. Since P_1 does not have to wait until P_2 receives its message, P_1 may
send the *off* message and then turn the switch off while P_2 is sampling, thus
violating the requirements of the problem. (If we tried to make a formal proof
of this program, we would find that any pair of individual proofs that satisfied

```
cobegin
P₁::
  begin
    ...
      {switch = on}
    send_c off to V;
    switch := off;
  end;
//
P₂::
  var
    ok : boolean := false;
  begin
    ...
      {switch = on}
    ok := true;
    do ok →
      begin
        ...          -- sample device output
        if receive_c x from V → ok := false;
        else skip;
        fi;
      end;
    od;
  end;
coend;
```

Figure 7.8: An incorrect technique for turning the switch off.

the specifications was subject to interference.)

Figure 7.9 shows a second try at sampling the device properly. This time P_2 samples the device but does not immediately accept the output as valid; instead it saves the results in temporary storage. It then uses the if statement to check for the *off* message. If the message is present, it assumes that the device has been turned off and exits without saving the previous sample in permanent storage. If not, it assumes that the message has not been sent and, hence, that the device is still on and the sample previously acquired is valid. It therefore moves the data from temporary to permanent storage and repeats the loop.

Unfortunately, this program still does not exhibit the desired behavior. The implementation of asynchronous message passing might allow P_2 to check and find that there is no message for it to receive, even though P_1 has already

```
cobegin
  P₁::
    begin
      . . .
          {switch = on}
      send_c off to V;
      switch := off;
    end;
  //
  P₂::
    var
      ok : boolean := false;
    begin
      . . .
          {switch = on}
      ok := true;
      do ok →
        begin
          . . .        - -  sample output; save in temporary storage
          if receive_c x from V → ok := false;
          else . . . - -  move data from temporary to permanent storage
          fi;
        end;
      od;
    end;
coend;
```

Figure 7.9: A second version of the data acquisition program, which still works incorrectly.

sent a message (which is perhaps wending its way slowly to P_2 through the network). Thus, in the example, even though P_2 executes the else portion of the if statement, P_1 may previously have sent the message containing *off* and then turned off the switch, thus invalidating the previous sample. (Again, any attempt at a formal proof would be subject to interference.)

In general, problems of this type require additional synchronization. One way to provide this synchronization is to simulate a synchronous message passing system by having P_1 send an (asynchronous) message to P_2 and then wait for a reply from P_2 before actually turning the switch off. P_2 stops sampling after sending the reply. An alternative way of achieving the necessary synchronization is described in Section 7.7. Before describing that method, we digress to discuss some related implementation issues.

7.6   Semi-Synchronous Communication

Different types of message passing systems make different assumptions about how the sender and receiver are synchronized by accesses to the rendezvous table. In synchronous message passing systems, a process (either the sender or receiver) waits if no match is found in the rendezvous table and continues at a later time when the matching request is executed. The send and receive behave symmetrically, and both are blocking primitives.

In an asynchronous message passing system, the receive is generally blocking. If a receive is executed and no match is found, an entry is made in the table for the receiver and the receiver waits. The receiver resumes at some later time when its entry is deleted. The deletion might be the result of the execution of a matching send request or the expiration of a timeout interval associated with the receive. Alternatively, if the receiver is operating in a polling mode and the search does not yield a match, the receiver might simply continue without creating an entry. Figures 7.8 and 7.9 contain examples of receive statements that operate in polling mode.

The send in an asynchronous message passing system is generally non-blocking: the sender continues executing whether or not a match is detected. Of course the sender must wait until the message has been copied into a system buffer, but this buffer might be unrelated to the rendezvous table. We can distinguish two approaches to implementing a non-blocking send. In the first, the sender does not resume until the message has been copied into the system buffer and the sender's access into the rendezvous table is complete. Since the sender's progress is synchronized to its rendezvous table access, we refer to this implementation as *semi-synchronous*. Note that the sender is not delayed until a matching receive is executed, and hence the sender's progress is independent of the receiver's progress. If the sender and receiver reside at the same site or if rendezvous occurs at the sender's site, the additional delay to the sender required to create an entry in the rendezvous table is minimal. In the second approach, the sender resumes immediately after the message has been copied into the system buffer (and possibly before the rendezvous table has been accessed). In this case we say that message passing is totally asynchronous.

A semi-synchronous implementation has the property that, if a receiver fails to find a match in the rendezvous table, it can infer that the sender has not progressed beyond its send (since the sender cannot proceed beyond its send until after it has accessed the rendezvous table and we assume mutually exclusive access to the table). Since this inference cannot be made when message passing is totally asynchronous, we expect that the formal semantics of the two implementations will differ. The difference is apparent in exactly the case in which the receiver does not find a match and resumes, either because of timeout or because it is operating in polling mode (*i.e.,* timeout of 0). Since the only difference between these two situations is a time delay, which is not visible in the formal semantics, we can restrict our discussion to polling (*i.e.,* the else clause). The following inference rule applies to the simple polling construct used in the example of the previous section. It can be generalized to describe if statements with multiple guarded components. The subscript **sc** denotes semi-synchronous virtual circuit communication.

Simple Semi-Synchronous Virtual Circuit Polling Rule

$$\frac{\{W\} \, S_1 \, \{Q\}, \; \{U\} \, S_2 \, \{Q\}}{\{P\} \; \textbf{if receive}_{\textbf{sc}} \; \bar{v} \; \textbf{from} \; V \; \rightarrow \; S_1; \; \textbf{else} \; S_2; \; \textbf{fi} \; \{Q\}} \qquad (7.8)$$

The corresponding satisfaction condition is

Proof Obligations for Satisfaction of Simple Semi-Synchronous Virtual Circuit Polling

For each semi-synchronous receive within a simple polling statement with assertions as in (7.8), show that

$$[P \wedge ((\sigma_V - \rho_V) \neq \lambda) \wedge (First(\sigma_V - \rho_V) = X)] \Rightarrow W^{\bar{v}, \; \rho_V}_{X, \; \rho_V \circ <X>} \qquad (7.9)$$

$$[P \wedge ((\sigma_V - \rho_V) = \lambda)] \Rightarrow U \qquad (7.10)$$

We assume that when a message is sent, it is appended to σ_V when the corresponding entry has been made in the rendezvous table. Proof obligation (7.9) is identical to satisfaction condition (7.1), since a rendezvous has occurred when S_1 is executed. Proof obligation (7.10) deals with the situation that arises when the receiver resumes after failing to find a match (and, hence, can infer that there are no messages that have been sent and not yet received).

We must still show non-interference. For example, we must show that U is not interfered with by a send that is executed immediately after the polling performed by the receiver has failed to find a matching send.

7.7 Example – Polling*

Consider again the example of Figure 7.9. The program exhibits the correct behavior when semi-synchronous communication primitives are used. Figure 7.10 is an annotated version of the program that abbreviates the proof. We consider the problem of turning the switch off as separate from that of turning the switch on, and hence assume that σ_V and ρ_V are initially λ and the switch is on. Two auxiliary boolean variables, both initialized to *true*, have been added: *aux*, which is shared between $\mathcal{P}_1$ and $\mathcal{P}_2$, and *tmp*, which is accessed only by $\mathcal{P}_2$. *aux* is only changed in $\mathcal{P}_1$, where it is set to *false* after the *off* message is sent but before the switch is actually turned off. Thus, the following assertion is a program invariant of the cobegin statement:

$$((\sigma_V = \lambda) \Rightarrow aux) \wedge (aux \Rightarrow (switch = on)) \wedge [(\sigma_V = \lambda) \vee (\sigma_V = < off >)] \qquad (7.11)$$

since (1) it is true initially, (2) it is implied by each of the assertions in $\mathcal{P}_1$ and those assertions are not interfered with by any of the statements in $\mathcal{P}_2$ (hence it is a program invariant of $\mathcal{P}_1$), and (3) the statements in $\mathcal{P}_2$ do not affect the variables appearing in (7.11) (hence it is a program invariant of $\mathcal{P}_2$).

We plan to show that data moved from temporary to permanent storage in $\mathcal{P}_2$ was sampled when *aux* was true and, hence (using the second conjunct of (7.11)) when the switch was on. After each sample of data is taken, the current value of *aux* is stored in *tmp*. Thus, to prove that *aux* was true when the data was sampled, we just have to show that *tmp* is true when the data is moved from temporary to permanent storage. (The reason we store *aux* in *tmp* and then reason about *tmp* is that the value of *aux* is changed by $\mathcal{P}_1$, and hence assertions involving *aux* are subject to interference.)

The annotation indicates that *tmp* is true when the results are moved from temporary to permanent storage, so we just have to show that the annotation corresponds to a proof. The assertions of $\mathcal{P}_1$ obviously constitute an individual proof. To see that the assertions of $\mathcal{P}_2$ constitute an individual proof, note that (1) we have chosen

$$ok \Rightarrow (\rho_V = \lambda)$$

to be a loop invariant, (2) the two assertions in sequence following the assignment $ok := false$ indicate an application of the Rule of Consequence (the second assertion is implied by the first), and (3) the preconditions of the two branches of the if statement are arbitrarily chosen and must be subsequently justified by the satisfaction conditions (7.9) and (7.10).

No variables in assertions in $\mathcal{P}_1$ are modified by statements in $\mathcal{P}_2$, and therefore $\mathcal{P}_2$ does not interfere with the proof of $\mathcal{P}_1$. Two assertions in $\mathcal{P}_2$ contain variables modified by statements in $\mathcal{P}_1$: $((\sigma_V = \lambda) \Rightarrow aux)$ and $((\sigma_V = \lambda) \Rightarrow tmp)$. Since the first is a conjunct of the program invariant, it is not interfered with. The only statement in $\mathcal{P}_1$ that can interfere with the second assertion is the send, which appends an element to σ_V but, since this send negates the premise of the implication, it cannot invalidate the assertion. Hence, the proofs of the two processes are interference free.

It only remains to be shown that the assertions meet the satisfaction conditions (7.9) and (7.10). The first condition is

$$[ok \wedge [ok \Rightarrow (\rho_V = \lambda)] \wedge [(\sigma_V = \lambda) \Rightarrow tmp] \wedge [(\sigma_V = \lambda) \vee (\sigma_V = <\textit{off}>)]$$
$$\wedge [(\sigma_V - \rho_V) \neq \lambda] \wedge [First(\sigma_V - \rho_V) = X]] \Rightarrow [ok \wedge (\rho_V = <\textit{off}>)]^{x, \, \rho_V}_{X, \, \rho_V \circ X}$$

which is true (we have included the final conjunct of the program invariant on the left-hand side of the implication).

The second condition is

$$[ok \wedge [ok \Rightarrow (\rho_V = \lambda)] \wedge [(\sigma_V = \lambda) \Rightarrow tmp] \wedge [(\sigma_V - \rho_V) = \lambda]] \Rightarrow$$
$$[ok \Rightarrow (\rho_V = \lambda)] \wedge tmp$$

which is also true. The key part of the proof is that $\rho_V = \lambda$ when the else is

cobegin
$\mathcal{P}_1$:: **begin** $\cdots$
      $\{(switch = on) \wedge aux \wedge (\sigma_V = \lambda)\}$
    send$_{\mathbf{SC}}$ *off* **to** V;
      $\{(switch = on) \wedge aux \wedge (\sigma_V = \;<off>)\}$
    $aux := false$;
      $\{(switch = on) \wedge \neg aux \wedge (\sigma_V = \;<off>)\}$
    $switch := off$;
      $\{(switch = off) \wedge \neg aux \wedge (\sigma_V = \;<off>)\}$
  end;
//
$\mathcal{P}_2$:: **var** ok : *boolean* := *false*;
  begin $\cdots$
        $\{(\rho_V = \lambda) \wedge [(\sigma_V = \lambda) \Rightarrow aux]\}$
    $ok := true$;
        $\{ok \wedge [ok \Rightarrow (\rho_V = \lambda)] \wedge [(\sigma_V = \lambda) \Rightarrow aux]\}$
    do $ok \rightarrow$
      begin
          $\{ok \wedge [ok \Rightarrow (\rho_V = \lambda)] \wedge [(\sigma_V = \lambda) \Rightarrow aux]\}$
        $\cdots$ **--** sample output; save in temporary storage
          $\{ok \wedge [ok \Rightarrow (\rho_V = \lambda)] \wedge [(\sigma_V = \lambda) \Rightarrow aux]\}$
     $tmp := aux$;
          $\{ok \wedge [ok \Rightarrow (\rho_V = \lambda)] \wedge [(\sigma_V = \lambda) \Rightarrow tmp]\}$
    if receive$_{\mathbf{SC}}$ x **from** $V \rightarrow$
          $\{ok \wedge (\rho_V = \;<off>)\}$
     $ok := false$;
          $\{\neg ok \wedge (\rho_V = \;<off>)\}$
          $\{ok \Rightarrow (\rho_V = \lambda)\}$
    else
          $\{[ok \Rightarrow (\rho_V = \lambda)] \wedge tmp\}$
        $\cdots$ **--** move from temporary to permanent storage
          $\{[ok \Rightarrow (\rho_V = \lambda)] \wedge tmp\}$
    fi;
          $\{ok \Rightarrow (\rho_V = \lambda)\}$
      end;
     od;
    end;
coend;

Program Invariant:
    $((\sigma_V = \lambda) \Rightarrow aux) \wedge (aux \Rightarrow (switch = on)) \wedge [(\sigma_V = \lambda) \vee (\sigma_V = \;<off>)]$
Loop Invariant in $\mathcal{P}_2$:
    $ok \Rightarrow (\rho_V = \lambda)$

Figure 7.10: The "switch off" program with semi-synchronous communication.

```
cobegin
𝒫₁::
  begin
    switch := on;
    sendₛᴄ on to V;
      ...
    sendₛᴄ off to V;
    switch := off;
  end;
//
𝒫₂::
  var
    ok : boolean := false;
  begin
    receiveₛᴄ x from V;
    ok := true;
    do ok →
      begin
        ...        −− sample output; save results in temporary
        if receiveₛᴄ x from V → ok := false;
        else ··· −− move from temporary to permanent storage
        fi;
      end;
    od;
  end;
coend;
```

Figure 7.11: A program that turns the switch both on and off.

executed, and since the implementation is semi-synchronous, it follows that $(\sigma_V - \rho_V) = \lambda$ as well. Thus, we can conclude that $\sigma_V = \lambda$ and, since $(\sigma_V = \lambda) \Rightarrow tmp$, we have that *tmp* is true, which is what we wanted to demonstrate.

We can now combine the programs for turning the switch on and turning it off into a single program, as shown in Figure 7.11. The proof that this program exhibits the desired behavior can be constructed by appropriately modifying the two separate proofs we have described.

7.8 Datagram Communication

For our formal discussion we consider datagram systems that use one-way direct naming. The datagram send and receive primitives are

```
                    cobegin
                    𝒫₁::
                       begin
                          send_d 1 to 𝒫₂;
                          send_d 2 to 𝒫₂;
                       end;
                    //
                    𝒫₂::
                       begin
                          receive_d x;
                          receive_d y;
                       end;
                    coend;
```

Figure 7.12: A simple program using datagram communication.

$$\textbf{send}_\textbf{d} \ \bar{e} \ \textbf{to} \ \mathcal{P}$$

$$\textbf{receive}_\textbf{d} \ \bar{v}$$

where $\mathcal{P}$ is the name of the process to which the datagram is being sent and the subscript **d** denotes asynchronous datagram communication.

An ideal datagram system can be modeled by associating with each process a buffer $M_\mathcal{P}$ that contains all the messages that have been sent to $\mathcal{P}$ but not yet received. The operational semantics of the send is as follows:

> The vector of expressions, $\bar{e}$, is evaluated and its value is added to $M_\mathcal{P}$; then the send terminates. The send operation is atomic.

The operational semantics of the receive is as follows:

> If $M_\mathcal{P}$ is empty, $\mathcal{P}$ waits; if $M_\mathcal{P}$ is not empty, one of the messages in $M_\mathcal{P}$ is nondeterministically selected, removed from $M_\mathcal{P}$, and its value assigned to the vector of variables, $\bar{v}$; then the receive terminates. The removal and assignment are done atomically.

For example, the effect of message passing in the program shown in Figure 7.12 is to assign either 1 or 2 to x and the other to y.

7.9 Axiomatization of Datagram Communication

The formal semantics of a datagram system is expressed in terms of multisets. A *multiset* is similar to a set, except that repetitions of elements are allowed (a multiset is sometimes called a *bag*). One example of a multiset is

$$\{1, 2, 2, 3, 3, 3\}$$

We briefly review some notation for multisets.

The empty multiset is denoted by Φ.

$x \in M$ is a predicate that is true when at least one element with value x is contained in multiset M.

$N \subseteq M$ is a predicate that is true when multiset N is contained in multiset M.

$M \oplus N$ denotes the multiset consisting of all the elements in multiset M and all the elements in multiset N.

$M \ominus N$ denotes the multiset consisting of all the elements in multiset M except that, for each element x of N, one element with value x is deleted from M if such an element exists in M.

Formally, we model $M_{\mathcal{P}}$ by two auxiliary variables, $\sigma_{\mathcal{P}}$ and $\rho_{\mathcal{P}}$, both of which are multisets initialized to Φ. $\sigma_{\mathcal{P}}$ represents the multiset of all messages that have ever been sent to $\mathcal{P}$ and hence have ever been added to $M_{\mathcal{P}}$. $\rho_{\mathcal{P}}$ represents the multiset of all messages that have ever been received by $\mathcal{P}$ and hence have ever been removed from $M_{\mathcal{P}}$. Thus, the contents of $M_{\mathcal{P}}$ is

$$\sigma_{\mathcal{P}} \ominus \rho_{\mathcal{P}}$$

Since datagrams can be received in an order different from that in which they were sent, the following is an axiom:

Datagram Axiom

$$\rho_{\mathcal{P}} \subseteq \sigma_{\mathcal{P}}$$

In other words, the multiset of messages that have been received is contained in the multiset of messages that have been sent.

The datagram send has the effect of adding the message sent to $\sigma_{\mathcal{P}}$ and then terminating. Thus, it has the effect of an assignment statement.

Datagram Send Axiom

$$\{U_{\sigma_{\mathcal{P}} \oplus \{\bar{e}\}}^{\sigma_{\mathcal{P}}}\} \ \mathbf{send_d} \ \bar{e} \ \mathbf{to} \ \mathcal{P} \ \{U\}$$

where U is an arbitrary assertion and $\bar{e}$ is a vector of expressions.

As with virtual circuits, we cannot state that a receive does not terminate when the receiver process is executed in isolation (because a process can send a datagram to itself). Also as with virtual circuits, the axiom schema describing receive allows arbitrary pre- and postconditions, and we rely on satisfaction to relate these assertions to those of the corresponding send and to the message being sent. Thus the formal semantics of the receive is as follows:

Datagram Receive Axiom

$$\{P\} \ \textbf{receive}_\textbf{d} \ \bar{v} \ \{W\}$$

where P and W are arbitrary assertions and $\bar{v}$ is a vector of expressions.

The receive terminates only when $M_{\mathcal{P}}$ is nonempty. We describe the semantics of its execution with a satisfaction condition. The effect of the execution is to assign the value of some element, X, stored in $M_{\mathcal{P}}$ to $\bar{v}$ and add that value to $\rho_{\mathcal{P}}$. Thus, in order for an execution to take place that has the effect of assigning X to $\bar{v}$, the system must be in a state in which the precondition, P, of the receive is satisfied, $(\sigma_{\mathcal{P}} \ominus \rho_{\mathcal{P}})$ is not empty, and X is contained in $(\sigma_{\mathcal{P}} \ominus \rho_{\mathcal{P}})$. Hence, the satisfaction condition is

Proof Obligations for Satisfaction of Datagram Receive

For each datagram receive in process $\mathcal{P}$,

$$\{P\} \ \textbf{receive}_\textbf{d} \ \bar{v} \ \{W\}$$

show

$$[P \wedge ((\sigma_{\mathcal{P}} \ominus \rho_{\mathcal{P}}) \neq \Phi) \wedge (X \in (\sigma_{\mathcal{P}} \ominus \rho_{\mathcal{P}}))] \Rightarrow W_{X, \ \rho_{\mathcal{P}} \oplus \{X\}}^{\bar{v}, \ \rho_{\mathcal{P}}} \qquad (7.12)$$

We must also prove non-interference for all sends and receives. Proving non-interference for a datagram send is the same as proving it for any other assignment statement. To prove non-interference for the datagram receive, we must demonstrate that the resulting assignments do not interfere with any assertion in a parallel process.

Proof Obligations for Interference Freedom of Datagram Receive

For each datagram receive in process $\mathcal{P}$,

$$\{P\} \ \textbf{receive}_\textbf{d} \ \bar{v} \ \{W\}$$

and each assertion, A, in a different process, show

$$[A \wedge P \wedge ((\sigma_{\mathcal{P}} \ominus \rho_{\mathcal{P}}) \neq \Phi) \wedge (X \in (\sigma_{\mathcal{P}} \ominus \rho_{\mathcal{P}}))] \Rightarrow A_{X, \ \rho_{\mathcal{P}} \oplus \{X\}}^{\bar{v}, \ \rho_{\mathcal{P}}}$$

Although these satisfaction and non-interference conditions look similar to those for virtual circuit primitives, it should be noted that the conditions for datagrams are expressed in terms of multisets while those for virtual circuits are expressed in terms of sequences. Thus, for example, after receiving a message in a virtual circuit system, one can conclude that all previous messages have already been received; such a conclusion is not possible for a datagram system.

It does not make sense to consider a semi-synchronous implementation of datagrams. Consider a process that sends two datagrams. If we require that an entry be made in the rendezvous table for the first send before the sender can resume and execute the second, the entries are inserted in the table in the same sequence as the datagrams were sent, and hence sequenced delivery is easily implemented. Such a message passing system is essentially a virtual circuit system.

Example

An annotated version of the program in Figure 7.12 is shown in Figure 7.13. The annotation abbreviates individual proofs of the two processes, since the assertions in P_1 satisfy the datagram send axiom and the assertions in P_2 trivially satisfy the datagram receive axiom (any assertions would do).

We demonstrate satisfaction for the first receive. Satisfaction for the second receive is demonstrated in a similar fashion. Since the assertion

$$(\sigma_{P_2} = \Phi) \vee (\sigma_{P_2} = \{1\}) \vee (\sigma_{P_2} = \{1, 2\})$$

is a program invariant, the satisfaction condition for the first receive reduces to

$$[(\rho_{P_2} = \Phi) \wedge ((\sigma_{P_2} = \{1\}) \vee (\sigma_{P_2} = \{1, 2\})) \wedge (X \in \sigma_{P_2})] \Rightarrow$$
$$[[(x = 1) \wedge (\rho_{P_2} = \{1\})] \vee [(x = 2) \wedge (\rho_{P_2} = \{2\})]]_{X, \ \rho_{P_2} \ \oplus \ \{X\}}^{x, \ \rho_{P_2}}$$

which is true. Since no interference can take place, the annotation is valid.

7.10   Example – The Bounded Buffer with Datagrams*

Figure 7.14 shows a bounded buffer implementation similar to that of Figure 7.5 except that virtual circuit communication has been replaced by datagram communication. Since datagram communication does not preserve the ordering of messages, we must content ourselves with proving that any message received by P_2 was sent by P_1, and so if P_1 has sent M messages and P_2 has received M messages, the sequence of messages received by P_2 is some permutation of the sequence of messages sent by P_1.

$$\{true\}$$
cobegin
$\mathcal{P}_1::$
  begin
    $\{\sigma_{\mathcal{P}_2} = \Phi\}$
    send$_d$ 1 **to** $\mathcal{P}_2$;
    $\{\sigma_{\mathcal{P}_2} = \{1\}\}$
    send$_d$ 2 **to** $\mathcal{P}_2$;
    $\{\sigma_{\mathcal{P}_2} = \{1, 2\}\}$
  end;
    $\{\sigma_{\mathcal{P}_2} = \{1, 2\}\}$
//
$\mathcal{P}_2::$
  begin
    $\{\rho_{\mathcal{P}_2} = \Phi\}$
  receive$_d$ x;
    $\{[[(x = 1) \wedge (\rho_{\mathcal{P}_2} = \{1\})] \vee [(x = 2) \wedge (\rho_{\mathcal{P}_2} = \{2\})]]\}$
  receive$_d$ y;
    $\{[[(x = 1) \wedge (y = 2)] \vee [(x = 2) \wedge (y = 1)]]$
    $\wedge (\rho_{\mathcal{P}_2} = \{1, 2\})\}$
  end;
    $\{[[(x = 1) \wedge (y = 2)] \vee [(x = 2) \wedge (y = 1)]]$
    $\wedge (\rho_{\mathcal{P}_2} = \{1, 2\})\}$
coend;
    $\{[[(x = 1) \wedge (y = 2)] \vee [(x = 2) \wedge (y = 1)]]$
    $\wedge (\rho_{\mathcal{P}_2} = \{1, 2\}) \wedge (\sigma_{\mathcal{P}_2} = \{1, 2\})\}$

Figure 7.13: An annotated version of a simple datagram program.

We define $Bag()$ as the multiset consisting of all elements stored in $Qarray$ that have been received from $\mathcal{P}_1$ but not sent to $\mathcal{P}_2$. Formally

$$Bag(Qarray, last, count) \equiv if \ count = 0 \ then \ \Phi \ else$$
$$Bag(Qarray, (last - 1) \ mod \ N, count - 1) \ \oplus \{Qarray[last]\}$$

Note the similarity between this definition and that of $Seq()$ given in Chapter 3.

We can now express the invariant of the loop in $\mathcal{BB}$ as

$$(0 \leq count \leq N) \wedge (\rho_{\mathcal{BB}} = \sigma_{\mathcal{P}_2} \oplus Bag(Qarray, last, count)) \tag{7.13}$$

The expression is virtually identical to (7.5), and the same proof techniques can be used to demonstrate its invariance and to perform other reasoning with

```
𝒫₁ ::
   ··· send_d e to ℬℬ; ···
//
ℬℬ ::
   var
      Qarray :  array[0..(N − 1)] of job_info;
      last :  0..(N − 1) := 0;
      count :  0..N := 0;
   begin
      do count < N →
         begin
            receive_d Qarray[(last + 1) mod N];
            last, count := (last + 1) mod N, count + 1;
         end;
      [] count > 0 →
         begin
            send_d Qarray[(last − count + 1) mod N] to 𝒫₂;
            count := count − 1;
         end;
      od;
   end ;
//
𝒫₂ ::
   ··· receive_d v; ···
```

Figure 7.14: A bounded buffer implementation using datagrams.

it. As with the virtual circuit implementation, the receive statement in ℬℬ can be moved to the guard without affecting the proof.

7.11   Proving the Absence of Deadlock

Datagram (and virtual circuit) systems can deadlock if all processes are waiting at receive statements. Hence, one might think that the program in Figure 7.15 could deadlock in this way.

For synchronous message passing systems, we demonstrated the absence of deadlock by showing that all processes could not simultaneously be at nonmatching communication statements. We did this by showing that the conjunction of the preconditions of these statements was *false*. In an asynchronous message passing system, however, even though all processes are at

$$\{true\}$$

cobegin

$\mathcal{P}_1$::

    begin

        send$_\mathbf{d}$ 1 to $\mathcal{P}_2$;

        send$_\mathbf{d}$ 2 to $\mathcal{P}_2$;

        received$_\mathbf{d}$ z;

    end;

  //

$\mathcal{P}_2$::

    begin

        received$_\mathbf{d}$ x;

        received$_\mathbf{d}$ y;

        send$_\mathbf{d}$ 3 to $\mathcal{P}_1$;

    end;

coend;

Figure 7.15: Concurrent processes that exchange messages.

receive statements, one of the processes might be able to proceed if it can receive some message that was sent earlier by one of the other processes (which is now waiting at a receive). In the program of Figure 7.15, for example, both processes can be at receive statements, but the program does not deadlock because when $\mathcal{P}_1$ is at its receive statement, the system is in a state in which

$$\sigma_{\mathcal{P}_2} = \{1, 2\}$$

(*i.e.*, $\mathcal{P}_1$ previously sent the messages 1 and 2) and in that state both of the receives in $\mathcal{P}_2$ can be executed.

A program may or may not deadlock, depending on its precondition. To demonstrate the absence of deadlock between two datagram receive statements in some program S with precondition P, we must produce a proof of $\{P\}\ S\ \{Q\}$ in which the conjunction of the preconditions of the receives implies that $(\sigma_{\mathcal{P}_i} \ominus \rho_{\mathcal{P}_i}) \neq \Phi$ for at least one of the communicating processes, $\mathcal{P}_i$. This condition implies that the receive statement in $\mathcal{P}_i$ terminates. A similar condition can be stated for virtual circuit systems.

Figure 7.16 is a partially annotated version of the program in Figure 7.15 demonstrating that it does not deadlock. We have omitted assertions involving the values of x, y, and z. To demonstrate that when $\mathcal{P}_1$ is at its receive and $\mathcal{P}_2$ is at its second receive, $\mathcal{P}_2$ can execute, we show that

```
cobegin
𝒫₁::
  begin
```
$\{(\sigma_{\mathcal{P}_2} = \Phi) \wedge (\rho_{\mathcal{P}_1} = \Phi)\}$

send$_d$ 1 **to** $\mathcal{P}_2$;

$\{(\sigma_{\mathcal{P}_2} = \{1\}) \wedge (\rho_{\mathcal{P}_1} = \Phi)\}$

send$_d$ 2 **to** $\mathcal{P}_2$;

$\{(\sigma_{\mathcal{P}_2} = \{1, 2\}) \wedge (\rho_{\mathcal{P}_1} = \Phi)\}$

receive$_d$ z;

$\{(\sigma_{\mathcal{P}_2} = \{1, 2\}) \wedge (\rho_{\mathcal{P}_1} = \{3\})\}$

```
  end;
//
𝒫₂::
  begin
```
$\{(\rho_{\mathcal{P}_2} = \Phi) \wedge (\sigma_{\mathcal{P}_1} = \Phi)\}$

receive$_d$ x;

$\{[(\rho_{\mathcal{P}_2} = \{1\}) \vee (\rho_{\mathcal{P}_2} = \{2\})] \wedge (\sigma_{\mathcal{P}_1} = \Phi)\}$

receive$_d$ y;

$\{(\rho_{\mathcal{P}_2} = \{1, 2\}) \wedge (\sigma_{\mathcal{P}_1} = \Phi)\}$

send$_d$ 3 **to** $\mathcal{P}_1$;

$\{(\rho_{\mathcal{P}_2} = \{1, 2\}) \wedge (\sigma_{\mathcal{P}_1} = \{3\})\}$

```
  end;
coend;
```

Figure 7.16: A partially annotated version that demonstrates absence of deadlock.

$$(((\rho_{\mathcal{P}_2} = \{1\}) \vee (\rho_{\mathcal{P}_2} = \{2\})) \wedge (\sigma_{\mathcal{P}_1} = \Phi)) \wedge ((\sigma_{\mathcal{P}_2} = \{1, 2\}) \wedge (\rho_{\mathcal{P}_1} = \Phi))] \Rightarrow$$
$$((\sigma_{\mathcal{P}_2} \ominus \rho_{\mathcal{P}_2}) \neq \Phi)$$

which is clearly true.

7.12 Communication in Linda*

Linda[1] provides a novel approach to communication that has features resembling both shared memory and asynchronous message passing. Linda is a small set of commands for process communication and creation that can be integrated into a base sequential language, such as C or Fortran, to create a high level concurrent language. We use the syntax of C-Linda.

---

[1]Linda is a trademark of Scientific Computing Associates.

Linda programs manipulate tuples. There are two kinds of tuples: data tuples and process tuples. A *data tuple* is a sequence of typed fields. For example, (*"Joe"*, 1, 7.5) is a data tuple with three elements: a string with value *Joe*, the integer value 1, and the real value 7.5. A *process tuple* is like a data tuple except that its fields are expressions (which can include functions). For example, (*"Joe"*, *p+q*, *f*(*x*, *y*)) is a process tuple. We discuss process tuples later.

Data tuples are stored in a shared memory, called *tuple space*, which lies at the heart of a Linda program and is accessible to all processes. [When Linda is implemented on a system with no physical shared memory, tuple space is still viewed as being stored in a (conceptual) shared memory.]

A process accesses tuple space using four basic commands: *out* and *eval* to create new tuples, and *in* and *rd* (which abbreviates read) to remove and/or read them. Tuples exist independently of the process that created them.

The command *out* takes a data tuple as its argument. *out*(*"Joe"*, 1, 7.5) causes its argument data tuple to be atomically inserted into tuple space. *out* can be thought of as a non-blocking (asynchronous) send, except that no target process is named.

The command *eval* takes a process tuple as its argument and initiates a concurrent process to compute the values of the expressions in its argument. The process tuple is said to be *active*. Thus, *eval*(*"Joe"*, *p+q*, *f*(*x*, *y*)) initiates a process that computes the values of *Joe* (a trivial computation), *p+q*, and *f*(*x*, *y*) (using the environment of the process that executed the *eval*) and inserts those values into its argument. The new process then terminates, and the process tuple turns into a data tuple (in tuple space), which can be read by *in* or *rd*. (Process tuples cannot be read.)

The *in* and *rd* commands specify templates that are used to direct associative searches in tuple space. A *template* is a sequence of typed fields, some of which may be values (specified as either constants or the values of named variables) and some of which may be formals, which indicate only the type of the corresponding field. Thus, *in*(*"Joe"*, ? *i*, *x*) has an argument template whose second element is a formal having the type of variable *i* and whose third element is the value of variable *x*. The command causes a search in tuple space for a *matching* three-element data tuple that has a string with value *Joe* as its first element, the value of *x* as its third element, and a value whose type is consistent with variable *i* as its second element. For example, assuming *x* is a real variable with value 7.5, the argument of the *out* command above is a matching tuple. If at least one such matching tuple exists, one is nondeterministically chosen and atomically deleted from tuple space, the value in its second element is assigned to *i*, and the *in* terminates. If no such tuple exists, the *in* blocks until some future time at which a matching tuple exists in tuple space (*i.e.*, has been inserted into tuple space by some process executing *out* or *eval*). Hence, *in* can be thought of as a blocking receive. *rd* is the same as *in* except that the matching tuple is not deleted.

There are also nonblocking variants of *in* and *rd*, called *inp* and *rdp*. *inp* and *rdp* are predicates that return 0 (which corresponds to *false* in the C language) if no matching tuple is available; otherwise they return 1 (which corresponds to *true* in C) and have the same effect as *in* and *rd*, respectively. These variants allow a program to poll tuple space.

More generally, a tuple need not be a sequence of only values, but may contain formals as well. Thus, the tuple (*"Joe"*, *integer*, 7.5), which has a formal element of type integer as its second element, may be inserted into tuple space. A formal tuple element matches a corresponding template element having a value that is type consistent with the formal. (Formals in tuples, however, do not match type-consistent formals in templates.) The value in the template is not communicated backward to the formal in the tuple. In fact, tuples cannot be modified in tuple space; however, they can be deleted and reinserted in a modified form.

A comparison of communication in Linda with conventional message passing reveals some interesting features of the language. The tuple space can be used as a collection of global ports. For example, a value stored in the first field of a tuple or template can serve as a port name. A client creates a tuple by storing the arguments of a request in the remaining fields and then placing the tuple in tuple space using *out*. A server retrieves a request using *in* with an argument template whose first field is a value specifying the port name and whose remaining fields are formals to receive the arguments of a request. Multiple servers can retrieve requests posted to the same port. Moreover, a server is not limited to selecting requests based only on the port name. It can use the information in additional fields to select those specific requests for which it is willing to provide service at some particular time.

The *rd* command provides a bulletin board implementation of multicast:, since *rd* does not delete the tuple, the tuple can be read by all processes in some group. This implementation only approximates multicast, since it leaves unresolved the question of how the tuple ultimately gets deleted and how a particular process can avoid reading the same tuple twice. It is most naturally useful in situations in which information is simply being made available to processes that might want to refer to it. Examples of such information are the current time and the best result that has been found so far by a set of processes doing a parallel search.

A formal model for communication in Linda can be constructed that corresponds closely to the model of datagram communication described earlier. Instead of having a buffer, $M_\mathcal{P}$, which is associated with each process, $\mathcal{P}$, we have a common buffer, tuple space, which is accessed by all processes.

Tuple space can also be used as a conventional shared memory. The usual issues related to interference arise. Assertions in one process concerning the state of tuple space can be interfered with by any process in the program, since tuple space is global to all processes. Such assertions will generally state the existence of a (perhaps unique) tuple or the absence of a tuple in tuple space having fields with particular values.

Mutually exclusive access to a data structure that is completely contained

```
lmain() {
  int i;

  for (i = 2; i < N; ++i) {
    eval ("primes", i, is_prime(i));
  }
}

is_prime(me) int me; {
  int i, limit, ok;
  double sqrt();

  limit = sqrt((double) me) + 1;

  for (i = 2; i < limit, ++i) {
    rd ("primes", i, ? ok);
    if (ok && (me % i == 0)) return 0;
  }
  return 1;
}
```

Figure 7.17: A C-Linda program for finding primes.

within a single tuple is easily achieved. A critical section accessing that structure deletes it (atomically) from tuple space (hence making it unavailable to concurrent processes) and reinserts it (atomically) when the access has been completed. More generally, mutually exclusive access to an arbitrary set of tuples can be achieved by introducing a new tuple to serve as a token associated with that set. A process wishing to access the set deletes the token and reinserts it when the access is complete.

Example – Prime Finder

Figure 7.17 is a C-Linda program (taken from [29]) that produces a vector of tuples of the form ("primes", i, is_prime(i)), where $2 \leq i \leq N$, and is_prime(i) is 1 if i is a prime and 0 if not. The main program uses eval to produce each tuple. The process created to service the call to eval corresponding to integer i calls the function is_prime(i) to determine whether i is divisible by any prime less than or equal to sqrt(i). Note that each invocation of is_prime remains blocked until the tuples it uses have been produced. (Note also the use of the cast operator (double) to convert the integer me into the correct type for the argument of sqrt.)

7.13 Bibliographic Notes

Good discussions of the structure of virtual circuit and datagram systems can be found in Tanenbaum [129] and Stallings [127]. A comprehensive treatment of issues related to the rendezvous table is contained in Walden [130]. Our discussion of the formal semantics of virtual circuits and datagrams is based on Schlichting and Schneider [115]. Our discussion of semi-synchronous message passing is based on Bernstein [18]. Descriptions of Linda can be found in Carriero and Gelernter [29] [30] and Gelernter [54].

7.14 Exercises

1. Prove that the program given in Figure 7.11 exhibits the desired behavior when the switch is turned on and off.

2. Implement the switch on/switch off problem by having P_1 send an *off* message when it wishes to turn off the device. When P_2 receives the message, it stops sampling and sends an acknowledgment to P_1. When P_1 receives the acknowledgment, it turns the device off. Prove that your design is correct.

3. Prove satisfaction for the second receive in Figure 7.13.

4. State a condition under which processes communicating through virtual circuits will not deadlock. Prove that the following program does not deadlock:

> **cobegin**
> P_1::
>   **begin**
>   send$_c$ 1 to $V1$;
>   send$_c$ 2 to $V1$;
>   receive$_c$ z from $V2$;
>   **end**;
> //
> P_2::
>   **begin**
>   receive$_c$ x from $V1$;
>   receive$_c$ y from $V1$;
>   send$_c$ 3 to $V2$;
>   **end**;
> **coend**;

5. Given a synchronous message passing system and the following annotation of a matching send and receive:

$$\mathcal{P}_1 :: \cdots \qquad\qquad\qquad \mathcal{P}_2 :: \cdots$$
$$\{A\} \qquad\qquad\qquad\qquad \{C\}$$
$$\mathcal{P}_2 \, ! \, x; \qquad\qquad\qquad \mathcal{P}_1 \, ? \, y;$$
$$\{B\} \qquad\qquad\qquad\qquad \{D\}$$

show that the following program fragment can be annotated as shown (where m is an integer variable that does not appear in A, B, C, or D).

$$\mathcal{P}_1 :: \cdots \qquad\qquad\qquad\qquad \mathcal{P}_2 :: \cdots$$

$\{A\}$
send$_\mathbf{C}$ x **to** $V_{1,2}$;
receive$_\mathbf{C}$ m **from** $V_{2,1}$;
$\{B\}$

$\{C\}$
receive$_\mathbf{C}$ y **from** $V_{1,2}$;
send$_\mathbf{C}$ 0 **to** $V_{2,1}$;
$\{D\}$

In other words, show that the program fragment simulates synchronous message passing. (Hint: Show that

$$(x \in (\sigma_{V_{1,2}} - \rho_{V_{1,2}})) \Rightarrow A$$

is a program invariant.)

6. Implement the switch on/switch off problem using datagrams. Prove that your design is correct.

7. Consider the three processes, $\mathcal{P}_1$, $\mathcal{P}_2$, and $\mathcal{P}_3$, each of which executes an infinitely looping statement whose body we refer to as a compute phase. We require that before $\mathcal{P}_i$ can enter its jth compute phase, all other processes must have completed their $(j-1)$st compute phase. Processes exchange messages asynchronously to guarantee that this is so. Design a datagram protocol for this purpose, and prove that it satisfies the required condition.

8. In the following cobegin statement, $\mathcal{P}_1$ sends a datagram containing the value i to $\mathcal{P}_2$ when it finishes the ith phase of its computation. $\mathcal{P}_2$ alternates between performing some background computation and checking if a datagram has arrived. If a datagram containing a value larger than any $\mathcal{P}_2$ has yet seen is received, $\mathcal{P}_2$ prints a message describing $\mathcal{P}_1$'s progress. Letting Φ_i be a predicate that is true when $\mathcal{P}_1$ has completed the ith phase, prove that Φ_j is a precondition of the print statement. (Hint: First show that

$$((\forall k)(k < i) \Rightarrow \Phi_k)$$

is a loop invariant of $\mathcal{P}_1$.)

```
cobegin
𝒫₁::
  begin
    i := 1;
    do true →
      begin
        ...          -- phase i
        send_d i to 𝒫₂;
        i := i + 1;
      end;
    od;
  end;
//
𝒫₂::
  begin
    do true →
      begin
        ...          -- background computation
        if receive_d j →
              if j > max →
                begin
                  max := j;
                  print("completed phase, j");
                end;
              else skip;
              fi;
        else skip;
        fi;
      end;
    od;
  end;
coend;
```

9. Informally discuss the issues involved in using the OSI model for very high speed communication.

10. What are the proof obligations for satisfaction corresponding to (7.9) and (7.10) when a totally asynchronous implementation of virtual circuit message passing is used?

11. Processes $𝒫_1$ and $𝒫_2$ engage in computations *comp*1 and *comp*2, respectively, and then communicate as shown (we have violated the syntax in order to use the same program to represent different kinds of communication):

$$\mathcal{P}_1 :: \cdots$$
$$comp1;$$
$$\mathbf{send_x}\ M;$$

$$\mathcal{P}_2 :: \cdots$$
$$comp2;$$
$$\mathbf{if\ receive_x}\ m \to S1;$$
$$\mathbf{else}\ S2;$$
$$\mathbf{fi};$$

What can $\mathcal{P}_2$ deduce about which process finished its computation first at the time a control point is enabled at either $S1$ or $S2$? $comp1$ is finished when a control point is enabled at the send, and we consider two possibilities for defining when $comp2$ finishes: a control point is enabled at the if statement or a control point is enabled at either $S1$ or $S2$. Provide an answer for all combinations of choices of x in {c, sc, d} and the two choices of completion time of $comp2$. In a case in which a deduction can be made, formalize the reasoning.

12. Informally discuss the issues involved in the design of a rendezvous table for a dynamically declared port used in synchronous communication.

13. An implementation of remote procedure call is to be made using two virtual circuits, as shown below. The procedure body, S, is characterized by $assign(S, f, Y)$, and the server, $\mathcal{P}_2$, simply loops, accepting one invocation on each iteration. Prove that if

$$P_{f(\bar{x},\bar{z})}^{\bar{y},\ \bar{z}} \wedge Y_{\bar{x},\ \bar{z}}^{\bar{a},\ \bar{c}}$$

is the precondition of the send in $\mathcal{P}_1$, P will be the postcondition of the receive in $\mathcal{P}_1$.

$$\mathcal{P}_1 :: \cdots$$
$$\mathbf{send_c}\ (\bar{x}, \bar{z})\ \mathbf{to}\ VC1;$$
$$\mathbf{receive_c}\ (\bar{y}, \bar{z})\ \mathbf{from}\ VC2;$$

$$\mathcal{P}_2 :: \cdots$$
$$\mathbf{do}\ true \to$$
$$\mathbf{receive_c}\ (\bar{a}, \bar{c})\ \mathbf{from}\ VC1;$$
$$S;$$
$$\mathbf{send_c}\ (\bar{b}, \bar{c})\ \mathbf{to}\ VC2;$$
$$\mathbf{od};$$

14. Provide a formal model (including axioms and proof obligations) for a virtual circuit message passing system in which the send is blocking and the receive is non-blocking (*i.e.*, if the sender is not waiting at a send statement, the receive statement acts like a skip statement). Assume a semi-synchronous implementation and use the syntax given in the conclusion of the inference rule (7.8) for the non-blocking receive. Does it make any difference if a semi-synchronous or totally asynchronous implementation is used? Explain.

15. Describe how a virtual circuit system can be simulated within Linda.

16. Describe how a synchronous communication system can be simulated within Linda.

17. Describe how a general semaphore can be implemented in Linda.

18. Provide a formal model (including axioms and proof obligations) for a subset of Linda that includes *in*, *out*, and *rd*. (Hint: Your model should be based on the model of datagram communication.)

8

Remote Procedure Call and Rendezvous

Remote procedure call and rendezvous are widely accepted communication mechanisms for implementing the client-server paradigm. From the viewpoint of the caller, the syntax and semantics are virtually identical to those of ordinary, local procedure calls, so the designer of the client process can (in most cases) reason about the client as if it were sequential. There is one major difference, however, from the viewpoint of the client. If the server is executing on a different processor than the client, there is the possibility that before, during, or after the execution of the remote procedure body, one of the processors, or the associated communication network, might fail. We discuss such failures in Chapter 9. In this chapter, we assume that no failures occur.

8.1 Motivation

The client-server paradigm is a common mode of communication among cooperating processes. File servers (which processes call upon to access their files), name servers (which processes call upon for setting up connections), time servers (which processes call upon to get the time of day), and process servers (which processes call upon for initiating remote processes) are some examples of commonly used servers that are generally supplied at the systems level in a network environment. At the applications level, a hierarchical organization of modules frequently implies a client-server relationship between modules.

Because of the pervasive nature of the client-server model, we are particularly interested in communication structures that support client-server interactions. We have previously introduced two similar mechanisms that support such interactions: remote procedure call (rpc) and rendezvous. rpc involves dynamic process creation: each invocation by the client causes a new process to be created in the server module to execute the called procedure.

Rendezvous involves the coming together of a client and a server process so that the server can execute the called procedure on behalf of the client. In both cases, the client waits until the procedure completes and results are returned. (The meaning of rendezvous in this chapter conforms to its usage in the context of the Ada[1] programming language.) The interface presented to the client is identical in both mechanisms and is frequently referred to as an rpc interface. An rpc interface is similar to that of a procedure call and hence is simple, well understood, and can be embedded in a high level language. It is often preferable to a commonly used alternative client-server interface in which operations are invoked by system calls and notification is provided by an interrupt facility.

Since a client and server can exist anywhere in a network, rpc and rendezvous must be supported by an end-to-end communication facility. One obvious approach is to support client-server interactions within one of the higher levels of the OSI model. However, this approach has several shortcomings. Most implementations of the higher OSI levels are connection-oriented. As we have pointed out, connection-oriented communication is usually appropriate only when large amounts of information are to be transferred (so that the overhead of establishing the connection can be amortized over this large amount of information). For rpc and rendezvous, the arguments are transferred in one direction and the results in the other. In many applications these transfers represent a relatively small amount of information, and therefore the overhead of establishing a connection leads to inefficiency. Efficiency is further impacted by the number of levels that must be traversed at the source and destination hosts to provide the service.

An alternative approach, which frequently leads to a more efficient implementation, is to build the rpc interface on top of a (low level) datagram facility. Thus, the number of levels that must be traversed to invoke a remote procedure is reduced, and the establishment and destruction of a connection is eliminated.

A key goal of an rpc interface is *transparency*: the user should not be able to distinguish between calling a remote procedure and calling a local procedure. Unfortunately, this goal cannot be fully achieved. For one thing, new failure modes exist when the caller and callee are on different sites. Since communication uses (potentially unreliable) datagrams, messages may be lost, and a site crash may destroy the caller or the callee, but not both. Hence, failures result in situations that do not occur when the called procedure is local and that are difficult to hide from the communicating processes. We deal with such situations in Chapter 9.

Failure is not the only issue that stands in the way of full transparency. Access to global variables is both inappropriate and difficult to implement with remote invocation. Note, however, that we did not permit globals in our formal treatment of procedures in Chapter 3. A call by reference parameter passing

---

[1]Ada is a trademark of the U.S. Department of Defense.

mechanism is also difficult to implement in the remote case, since a reference to an argument at the caller's site is of little use to the callee. Furthermore, call by reference cannot entirely be simulated with a value/result mechanism. For example, the procedure

procedure $p(a, b :$ **in out** $integer);$ **begin** $a := a + 1;$ $b := b + 1;$ **end** p

gives different results for the two parameter passing mechanisms when invoked with the call $p(z, z)$. This anomaly is due to aliasing, which we also excluded in our formal treatment in Chapter 3. Finally, arguments that are pointer variables are difficult to implement. For example, the system cannot know (in the general case) how much of a list structure will be accessed by a procedure that has as a parameter a pointer to an element in the list.

8.2   Rendezvous

Whereas in a monitor procedure call the caller and the procedure body reside in different modules but are executed by the same process, with both rpc and rendezvous the procedure body is executed by a process different from the caller. In this and the following sections we center our attention on rendezvous. We use the following syntax for rendezvous:

Rendezvous Invocation Statement

$$\mathcal{P}.p(\bar{x}, \bar{y}, \bar{z})$$

where

> $\mathcal{P}$ is the name of a process;
> p is the name of a remote procedure;
> $\bar{x}$ is a vector of arbitrary expressions;
> $\bar{y}$ and $\bar{z}$ are vectors of variables.

Rendezvous Accept Statement

> **accept** $p(\bar{a} :$ **in** $atype;$ $\bar{b} :$ **out** $btype;$ $\bar{c} :$ **in out** $ctype)$ **do**
> $s;$
> **end** p

where

> $\bar{a},$ $\bar{b},$ and $\bar{c}$ are vectors of parameters;
> s is a sequence of statements.

A dot notation is used in the invocation statement to indicate the name of the process containing the remote procedure and the name of the remote procedure. We use one-way direct naming so that the callee can provide service to a set of clients. The syntax of these statements is quite similar to that of the call and declaration of a procedure as given in Chapter 3. Note, however, that the accept statement is an executable statement in the called process, not a declaration, and can therefore appear anywhere a statement can appear in the callee. When the control point preceding the accept statement is enabled, the callee is prepared to execute the procedure on behalf of a remote caller. As with local procedure calls, we assume no aliasing and no recursion (an accept statement cannot call itself).

As with the synchronous send and receive constructs, the invocation and accept do not terminate when executed separately; each waits until a matching statement is executed. An invocation and an accept statement are said to *match* when

The process executing the accept is the destination process named in the invocation;

The procedure named in the invocation is the same as the procedure named in the accept;

The arguments of the invocation are compatible in number and type with the parameters of the accept.

When an invocation statement executed in $\mathcal{P}_1$ matches an accept statement executed in $\mathcal{P}_2$, the two statements are said to rendezvous. The operational semantics of rendezvous is as follows:

$\mathcal{P}_1$ waits.

The in and in out arguments of the invocation are evaluated and sent from $\mathcal{P}_1$ to $\mathcal{P}_2$ and are assigned to the corresponding parameters in $\mathcal{P}_2$. The evaluation and send in $\mathcal{P}_1$ is atomic; the receive and assignment in $\mathcal{P}_2$ is atomic.

The body of the remote procedure, s, is executed by $\mathcal{P}_2$.

The values of the out and in out parameters are sent from $\mathcal{P}_2$ to $\mathcal{P}_1$ and assigned to the corresponding arguments in $\mathcal{P}_1$. The send in $\mathcal{P}_2$ is atomic; the receive and assignment in $\mathcal{P}_1$ is atomic.

Then $\mathcal{P}_1$ and $\mathcal{P}_2$ proceed asynchronously.

As a simple example consider the procedure *swap* described in Chapter 3, here implemented in the context of rendezvous:

Rendezvous Invocation:

$\mathcal{P}.swap(x, y);$

Accept (in process $\mathcal{P}$):

> **accept** $swap(c1, c2 :$ **in out** $ctype)$ **do**
> $c1, c2 := c2, c1;$
> **end** $swap;$

8.3 Axiomatization of Rendezvous, I

In this section we give a formal treatment of rendezvous for remote procedures that implement an abstract data object with assignment semantics. Later we consider a more general situation.

First consider the simple case, shown in Figure 8.1, in which the callee has no permanent variables and, therefore, its state before and after the rendezvous is characterized by the assertion *true*. Hence, apart from reasoning about the procedure body itself, we do not reason about the callee. As with the invocation of a local procedure, the in and in out arguments must first be passed to the callee (using messages in this case) and assigned to the parameters. The body is then executed, and finally the values of the out and in out parameters are returned to the calling site (again using messages) and assigned to the corresponding out and in out arguments.

For this simple case we make the same assumptions as we did for local procedures, namely that the only global references within s are to its parameters, $\bar{a}$, $\bar{b}$ and $\bar{c}$, that s does not modify $\bar{a}$, and that there is no aliasing: all out and in out arguments are distinct and none appear in the in argument expressions. Despite the fact that messages are now involved, the semantics of parameter passing is exactly as described in Section 3.1 for local procedures when a value/result parameter passing mechanism is used. Hence, in this case we can use the Assignment Procedure Rule (3.4) as follows:

$$\frac{assign(s, f, Y), \ U_{f(\bar{x},\bar{z})}^{\bar{y}, \bar{z}} \Rightarrow Y_{\bar{x}, \bar{z}}^{\bar{a}, \bar{c}}}{\{U_{f(\bar{x},\bar{z})}^{\bar{y}, \bar{z}}\} \ \mathcal{P}.p(\bar{x}, \bar{y}, \bar{z}) \ \{U\}}$$

to describe the invocation.

Since we treat the passing of arguments as a (distributed) assignment, the second hypothesis ensures that the precondition of the invocation, $U_{f(\bar{x},\bar{z})}^{\bar{y},\bar{z}}$, implies that Y is a precondition of s. Thus the caller is responsible for ensuring that Y is true.

Now consider the more general case of rendezvous in which the callee is a server process maintaining concrete variables, $\bar{c}$, and a function exists that

$$\mathcal{P}_1 :: \cdots \qquad\qquad\qquad \mathcal{P}_2 :: \cdots$$

$$\{U_{f(\overline{x},\overline{z})}^{\overline{y},\,\overline{z}}\} \qquad\qquad\qquad\qquad \{true\}$$

$\mathcal{P}_2.p(\overline{x},\overline{y},\overline{z});$ **accept** $p(\overline{a} :$ **in** $atype;$ $\overline{b} :$ **out** $btype;$

$$\overline{c} : \textbf{in out } ctype) \textbf{ do}$$

$$\{Y\}$$

$$s;$$

$$\textbf{end } p;$$

$\{U\}$ $\{true\}$

(a)   (b)

Figure 8.1: An annotated (a) remote invocation (b) and accept, assuming assignment semantics and no permanent variables in the callee.

maps $\overline{c}$ to an abstract data object, t, with assignment semantics. As in Section 3.2.2, we assume that the concrete variables are declared as permanent variables in the callee, and we simplify the discussion by assuming that no in out arguments are passed. We assume that no global references are made from within s to variables other than $\overline{c}$. Assignment semantics for s is conditioned on $WP_c(\overline{c})$ (*i.e.*, Y is $WP_c(\overline{c})$), and by definition,

$$\{WP_c(\overline{c})\}\ s\ \{I_c\} \tag{8.1}$$

where, as described in Section 3.2.2,

$$WP_c(\overline{c}) \equiv (wp(s, I_c) \wedge I_c)$$

The situation is shown in Figure 8.2. Note that if $WP_c(\overline{c})$ is a precondition of the accept statement, it will also be a precondition of s, since it is not a function of the parameters and hence is not affected by the passing of arguments. Similarly, if I_c is a postcondition of s, it will also be a postcondition of the accept statement, since it is not a function of the arguments and hence is not affected by the return of values. In contrast to the situation shown in Figure 8.1, the precondition of the accept statement must be guaranteed by the callee, not the caller. Hence, the Assignment Procedure Rule (3.4) can no longer be used in justifying the specifications of the abstract type. We introduce the following formal semantics to describe rendezvous in this case.

Rendezvous Rule for Abstract Data Types

The Caller:

$$\frac{assign(s, f_a, WP_a(t))}{\{U_{f_a(\overline{x},t)}^{\overline{y},\,t}\}\ \mathcal{P}.p(\overline{x},\overline{y})\ \{U\}} \tag{8.2}$$

$$\mathcal{P}_1 :: \cdots \qquad\qquad \mathcal{P}_2 :: \cdots$$

$$\{U_{f_a(\bar{x},t)}^{\bar{y},\,t}\} \qquad\qquad\qquad \{WP_c(\bar{c})\}$$

$$\mathcal{P}_2.p(\bar{x},\bar{y}); \qquad\qquad \textbf{accept } p(\bar{a}: \textbf{ in } atype;\ \bar{b}: \textbf{ out } btype)\ \textbf{do}$$

$$\{WP_c(\bar{c})\}$$

$$s;$$

$$\{I_c\}$$

$$\textbf{end } p;$$

$$\{U\} \qquad\qquad\qquad \{I_c\}$$

(a)   (b)

Figure 8.2: An annotated (a) remote invocation (b) and accept, in the case of a server implementing an abstract data object with assignment semantics.

The Callee:

$$\{WP_c(\bar{c})\}\ \textbf{accept } p(\bar{a}: \textbf{ in } atype;\ \bar{b}: \textbf{ out } btype)\ \textbf{do } s;\ \textbf{end } p\ \{I_c\} \quad (8.3)$$

The design of the abstract data type is similar to that described in Section 3.2 for the sequential case. The designer must provide a concrete implementation, prove $assign(s, f_c, WP_c(\bar{c}))$, and then demonstrate that (3.14), (3.15), and (3.16) are true. These proofs justify the use of the hypothesis of (8.2). In addition, the designer must demonstrate that $WP_c(\bar{c})$ is a precondition of s. This requirement is imposed by treating (8.2) and (8.3) as a pair. The designer must utilize the axiom (8.3) in the proof of the callee, hence guaranteeing that $WP_c(\bar{c})$ is a precondition of the accept statement and therefore of s. (In the next section we show one way in which this guarantee can be given.) The design is then complete and its abstract specification can be published.

The caller of the abstract data type can then use the abstract specification and reason about the call as if it were a local invocation of an abstract operation with assignment semantics.

8.4 Rendezvous and Nondeterminism

The asynchronous nature of concurrent processes implies that the order in which various procedures will be invoked remotely cannot be predicted. We use nondeterminism as a simple and elegant way of modeling this situation. We introduce a nondeterministic construct that the callee can use to accept invocations of different types. The construct is nondeterministic because the callee does not know the order in which the invocations will be received and must be prepared to accept them in any order.

As a first try, we might attempt to embed an accept statement within the ordinary if statement:

> **if** $G1 \rightarrow$ **accept** $p1(\cdots)$ **do** $s1$; **end** $p1$;
> [] $G2 \rightarrow$ **accept** $p2(\cdots)$ **do** $s2$; **end** $p2$;
> $\cdots$
> [] $Gn \rightarrow$ **accept** $pn(\cdots)$ **do** sn; **end** pn;
> **fi**

As we discussed in Chapter 6 with respect to send and receive, this use of the if construct can suffer from needless delays and even deadlocks. An open component statement (*i.e.*, a component that has a guard with value *true*) is nondeterministically chosen whether or not it is executable (*i.e.*, a rendezvous is immediately possible). Hence, the if statement might wait even though another component is executable. To avoid this situation, we generalize the if statement to a new construct, called the select statement, with the following syntax:

> **select** $G1 \rightarrow$ **accept** $p1(\cdots)$ **do** $s1$; **end** $p1$;
> [] $G2 \rightarrow$ **accept** $p2(\cdots)$ **do** $s2$; **end** $p2$;
> $\cdots$
> [] $Gn \rightarrow$ **accept** $pn(\cdots)$ **do** sn; **end** pn;
> **end select**

where the Gi are boolean expressions. The operational semantics of the select statement is

> The guards are evaluated atomically; if all guards are closed, the statement does not terminate; if one or more of the guards are open but no component is executable, the callee waits until one or more components become executable; if one or more components are executable, a nondeterministic choice is made among the executable components and the corresponding accept statement is executed; then the statement terminates. Each guard is evaluated only once so that, while the callee is waiting for an open guard to become executable, no open guard can become closed and no closed guard can become open.

It should be evident that the select statement provides a convenient mechanism for implementing an abstract data object. A simple server consists of an initialization section followed by a loop containing a select statement in which each component is an accept statement whose body implements a particular abstract operation. The guard for the jth component conjoined with the concrete invariant, I_c, is $WP_c^j(\overline{c})$. I_c is also the loop invariant. In each iteration of the loop, one client's remote invocation of an abstract operation is accepted, the corresponding request is serviced, and the results are returned. Waits and sends within the bodies of the accept statements are not needed, since the guards prevent the server from accepting a particular invocation when the state of the abstract object does not satisfy the weakest precondition for that operation (*e.g.*, the server does not accept an *Enqueue* if the bounded buffer is full).

Since Program Logic does not deal with delays, the select statement has the same formal semantics as the if statement. Specifically, the formal semantics of the select statement is given by the inference rule

Select Rule

$$\frac{\{G1 \wedge R\} \textbf{ accept } p1(\cdots) \textbf{ do } s1; \textbf{ end } p1 \{W\}, \ldots,}{\{Gn \wedge R\} \textbf{ accept } pn(\cdots) \textbf{ do } sn; \textbf{ end } pn \{W\}}{\{R\} \textbf{ select } \ldots \textbf{ end select } \{W\}} \tag{8.4}$$

In the general case, the validity of each triple in the hypothesis must be demonstrated using the general proof obligations for remote invocation and accept, which we have not yet discussed. However, in the case of an abstract data object we can apply our earlier analysis. $(Gi \wedge R)$ is $WP_c^i(\overline{c})$, and R and W are I_c.

Note that the select statement is useful only in the context of rendezvous. With rpc, a process is unconditionally created in the server module for each invocation. Hence, we get unconditional concurrency instead of guarded, nondeterministic sequencing.

8.5   Example – The Bounded Buffer Server Process*

Figure 8.3 shows a bounded buffer server process, $\mathcal{BB}$, similar to that of Figure 6.10, but implemented using rendezvous. The remote procedures *Enqueue* and *Dequeue* are called by the clients, the producer process $\mathcal{P}_1$ and the consumer process $\mathcal{P}_2$, respectively.

We reason about $\mathcal{BB}$ using the Select Rule and the Rendezvous Rule for Abstract Data Types. As before, we introduce the auxiliary variables *in* and *out* to aid in the proof. *in* and *out* are sequences of messages, initialized to λ, which denote, respectively, the elements that $\mathcal{P}_1$ has appended to and that $\mathcal{P}_2$ has removed from the buffer.

To demonstrate that $\mathcal{BB}$ has the abstract semantics given in Figure 5.6 requires three proofs: (1) we must prove the required properties of the concrete procedures as described in Section 3.2.2, (2) we must prove that $WP_c^j(\overline{c})$ is the precondition of each accept, for j equal to *Enqueue* and *Dequeue*, and (3) we must prove that the concrete implementation supports the abstract specifications as described in Section 3.2.3. We consider each of these proof obligations separately.

$\mathcal{P}_1$ ::
    $\cdots$ *$\mathcal{BB}$.Enqueue(x)*; $\cdots$
//
$\mathcal{BB}$ ::
   var
     Qarray : **array**$[0..(N-1)]$ **of** *job_info*;
     last : $0..(N-1)$:= 0;
     count : $0..N$:= 0;
     in, out : *sequence* := λ, λ;
   begin
     do *true* $\rightarrow$
       select *count* $< N \rightarrow$
         accept *Enqueue(a* : **in** *element*) **do**
           Qarray$[(last+1)$ **mod** $N]$, *last, count* :=
             a, $(last+1)$ **mod** N, *count* + 1;
           in := *in* $\circ$ *a*;
         end *Enqueue*;
       [] *count* $> 0 \rightarrow$
         accept *Dequeue(b* : **out** *element*) **do**
           b, count := *Qarray*$[(last-count+1)$ **mod** $N]$, *count* $- 1$;
           out := *out* $\circ < b >$;
         end *Dequeue*;
       end select;
      od;
     end;
//
$\mathcal{P}_2$ ::
    $\cdots$ *$\mathcal{BB}$.Dequeue(y)*; $\cdots$

Loop Invariant I_c:
   $(0 \le count \le N) \wedge (in = out \circ Seq(Qarray, last, count))$

Figure 8.3: A bounded buffer process that uses rendezvous to present a procedural interface.

To prove that $WP_c^j(\bar{c})$ is a precondition of each accept, we analyze each component of the do statement in $\mathcal{BB}$ separately. Consider the second component, corresponding to *Dequeue*. Assuming I_c, as given in Figure 8.3, is a postcondition of that component and working backwards using the Assignment Axiom and the Rule of Composition, we obtain the following triple describing the body of the second component:

$$\{(0 \leq (count - 1) \leq N)$$
$$\wedge(in = out \circ < Qarray[(last - count + 1) \bmod N] >$$
$$\circ \, Seq(Qarray, last, count - 1))\}$$
$$count, \, b \; := \; count - 1, \; Qarray[(last - count + 1) \bmod N];$$
$$out \; := \; out \circ < b >;$$
$$\{I_c\}$$

It is easily shown that the precondition of this triple is implied by $I_c \wedge (count >$ 0), which is $WP_c^{Dequeue}(\overline{c})$. Hence, I_c is an invariant of the second component. In a similar manner we can show that it is an invariant of the first component as well. Thus, I_c is a loop invariant, and $WP_c^{Dequeue}(\overline{c})$ is a precondition of the accept for *Dequeue*.

As an example of a required property of the concrete procedures, we must prove (3.13)

$$assign(s_{Dequeue}, f_c^{Dequeue}, WP_c^{Dequeue}(\overline{c}))$$

Hence, we must show

$$\{(C_0 = count) \wedge (L_0 = last) \wedge ((Q_0 = Qarray) \wedge (O_0 = out) \wedge WP_c^{Dequeue}(\overline{c}))\}$$
$$s_{Dequeue} \; \{(b, count, last, out) \; = \; f_c^{Dequeue}(C_0, L_0, Q_0, O_0)\}$$

where, for example, the value assigned to b by $f_c^{Dequeue}$ is

$$Q_0[(L_0 - C_0 + 1) \bmod N]$$

Once again we can show the validity of this triple using the Assignment Axiom and the Rule of Composition. A similar result holds for $s_{Enqueue}$.

Neither the proof that $WP_c^j(\overline{c})$ is a precondition of the jth accept nor the proof of $assign(s_j, f_c^j, I_c)$ for the two components depended on the arguments passed to the accept statements. Hence, these proofs need be done only once by the designer of the server and can (implicitly) be used by all clients.

8.6   Axiomatization of Rendezvous, II

In this section we consider the general case of rendezvous, in which we do not assume assignment semantics and we allow the procedure body to make global references. We develop a formal model by considering a possible implementation of rendezvous using synchronous message passing. Hence, instead of introducing new axioms or inference rules to describe rendezvous, we replace the invocation and accept statements with message passing commands and prove the correctness of the transformed program using the techniques of Chapter 6. When the procedure is invoked, the calling site sends a message containing the initial values of the in and in out arguments to the site at which the rendezvous takes place and then waits to receive a reply message

$$\mathcal{P}_1 :: \cdots$$
$$\{T\}$$
$$\mathcal{P}_2 \ ! \ (\bar{x}, \bar{z});$$

$$\{T'\}$$

$$\mathcal{P}_2 \ ? \ (\bar{y}, \bar{z});$$
$$\{U\}$$

$$\mathcal{P}_2 :: \cdots$$
$$\{V\}$$
$$\mathcal{P}_1 \ ? \ (\bar{a}, \bar{c});$$
$$\{P\}$$
$$s;$$
$$\{Q\}$$
$$\mathcal{P}_1 \ ! \ (\bar{b}, \bar{c});$$
$$\{W\}$$

Figure 8.4: A model for the general case of rendezvous using synchronous message passing primitives.

containing the final values of the out and in out arguments. The accept is implemented as a receive of the values to be assigned to the in and in out parameters, followed by the execution of s, followed by a send of the values to be assigned to the out and in out arguments.

Assuming that the execution of s can be described by the triple $\{P\} \, s \, \{Q\}$, we can describe the rendezvous by the annotated program shown in Figure 8.4. The assertions T, T', U, V, and W can be selected arbitrarily as far as the individual proofs are concerned, but must meet satisfaction and interference conditions.

Our model of rendezvous has a somewhat disconcerting property: between the caller's send and receive is a control point – and an attached assertion T' – that does not appear in the original program. T' describes the state of the caller while s is executing. More precisely, T' is that portion of the precondition of the call, T, that is (1) true after the arguments have been passed and (2) not interfered with by s.

While T' can be chosen arbitrarily (within the requirements of satisfaction), it is reasonable to choose it in such a way that it can be derived from the precondition of the call. Hence, we impose the condition

$$T \Rightarrow (T')_{\bar{x}, \, \bar{z}}^{\bar{a}, \, \bar{c}} \tag{8.5}$$

This condition allows us to simplify the satisfaction proof obligations. Whereas the general formulation of satisfaction for argument passing requires

$$(T \wedge V) \Rightarrow (P \wedge T')_{\bar{x}, \, \bar{z}}^{\bar{a}, \, \bar{c}}$$

using (8.5) we get the following satisfaction proof obligations:

Satisfaction Conditions for Rendezvous

$$(T \wedge V) \Rightarrow P_{\bar{x}, \, \bar{z}}^{\bar{a}, \, \bar{c}}$$

$$(T' \wedge Q) \Rightarrow (U \wedge W)^{\bar{y}, \bar{z}}_{\bar{b}, \bar{c}}$$

In addition we must demonstrate the non-interference condition:

$$\{T' \wedge P\} \, s \, \{T'\}$$

Note that we can always choose *true* for T', since it trivially satisfies the implication (8.5) and is not interfered with by s. (Of course, we might need a stronger T' to prove a desired postcondition.)

Note also that, since we assume that s does not modify its in parameters, the assertion $\bar{x} = \bar{a}$ can always be conjoined to T': it is not interfered with by s and it trivially satisfies the implication (8.5).

Example

Consider a server process, S, that allocates tracks on a disk to user processes. We assume it has been separately proven that a user never has allocated to it more than one track at a time. S attempts to even out the usage of tracks by selecting at random an unused track to assign to a user when a request is made. The annotated program shown in Figure 8.5 describes the situation.

Each user, $\mathcal{U}$, has a distinct process identification that it references using its local variable *myproc*. A user requests a track by calling the procedure *request* in S. (Presumably, S also contains a procedure *release* for deallocating tracks, and the two procedures are nested in a select statement in a loop in a manner similar to the structure of $\mathcal{BB}$ shown in Figure 8.3.) S records the status of each track in a boolean array, *alloc* (initialized to *false*), and randomly selects an unused track to assign to the caller using the function *rand*. Since a random choice is made, there does not exist a function that relates the values of the out arguments to the values of the in arguments and variables local to S. Hence, *request* does not have assignment semantics.

We introduce a (shared) auxiliary variable, *using*, to assist in constructing a proof. $using[j] = i$ if the user with process identification j has been assigned track i and is null otherwise. Assertion I

$$I : ((\forall i) \neg alloc[i] \Rightarrow ((\forall j) \, using[j] \neq i))$$

(which would be a loop invariant of the main loop in S), states that a track that has not been allocated is not being used by any user.

The annotation shown in Figure 8.5 provides a basis for constructing a proof of the triple (corresponding to $\{P\} \, s \, \{Q\}$)

$$\{I \wedge (using[a] = null)\} \, s \, \{I \wedge ((\forall j)(j \neq a) \Rightarrow (using[j] \neq b)) \wedge (using[a] = b)\} \quad (8.6)$$

where s is the body of *request*. A few points need clarification. The last conjunct of the postcondition of the loop in s, $((\forall j) \, using[j] \neq b)$, is obtained using the Rule

var
   using : **array**[0..*max_proc_no*] **of** *procid*;
cobegin
$\mathcal{U}$::
   . . .

      {*using*[*myproc*] = *null*}
   S.request(*myproc*, *track*);
      {(*using*[*myproc*] = *track*) $\wedge$ (($\forall k$)(*k* $\neq$ *myproc*) $\Rightarrow$ (*using*[*k*] $\neq$ *track*))}
   . . .

//

S::

  var
    alloc : **array**[0..*max_track_no*] **of** *boolean*;
    . . .

    {*I*}
  accept *request*(*a* : **in** *procid*; *b* : **out** *trackno*) **do**
     {*I* $\wedge$ (*using*[*a*] = *null*)}
    b := *rand*();
    do *alloc*[*b*] $\rightarrow$ *b* := *rand*(); **od**;
     {*I* $\wedge$ (*using*[*a*] = *null*) $\wedge$ (($\forall j$) *using*[*j*] $\neq$ *b*)}
    alloc[*b*] := *true*;
     {*I* $\wedge$ (*using*[*a*] = *null*) $\wedge$ (($\forall j$) *using*[*j*] $\neq$ *b*) $\wedge$ (*alloc*[*b*] = *true*)}
    using[*a*] := *b*;
     {*I* $\wedge$ (($\forall j$)(*j* $\neq$ *a*) $\Rightarrow$ (*using*[*j*] $\neq$ *b*)) $\wedge$ (*using*[*a*] = *b*)}
  end *request*;
    {*I*}
  . . .

coend;

I : (($\forall i$)$\neg$*alloc*[*i*] $\Rightarrow$ (($\forall j$) *using*[*j*] $\neq$ *i*))

Figure 8.5: A disk server process that randomly assigns unused tracks.

of Consequence and the Do Rule. The Do Rule allows us to assert $\neg alloc[b]$ as
a postcondition of the loop, and

$$(I \wedge \neg alloc[b]) \Rightarrow ((\forall j) \, using[j] \neq b)$$

Since the assignment of *true* to *alloc*[*b*] weakens the constraint placed on *using*
by *I*, it follows that *I* is a postcondition of that assignment. Finally, *I* is a postcondition of *s*, since *alloc*[*b*] has been assigned *true* and hence *I* does not pro-
hibit an element of *using* from having the value *b*. Formally, these assertions
can be demonstrated using instances of the Assignment Axiom in which asser-

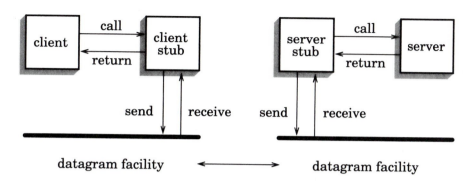

Figure 8.6: The implementation of a remote procedure call using stubs.

tions involving universal quantification are expanded so that each conjunct is visible.

We cannot choose T' to be identical to T, since s interferes with the assertion *using[myproc]* = *null*. Instead we take T' to be *true*. The satisfaction proof obligations are straightforward after we conjoin the assertion $a = myproc$ to T'.

8.7   Implementation of Remote Invocation

Remote invocation is frequently implemented using a mechanism known as a *stub*. Stubs are automatically generated at the client and server ends to act as intermediaries. The situation is shown in Figure 8.6. A client call invokes the client stub, whose role, called *marshaling*, is to pack the arguments into one or more packets and send them to the server site. The server stub receives the packets, unmarshals them, and invokes the server. Results are returned by the server to the server stub, which sends them back to the client stub. The client stub, in turn, returns them to the client. The stub mechanism is designed so that if the client and server are located on the same machine, the client invokes the server directly without stubs serving as intermediaries. Hence, the stub is transparent. The stub also plays a role in binding the client to the server.

8.8   Ada Tasking and Rendezvous*

Ada is a high level language originally sponsored by the U.S. Department of Defense for use in embedded systems, but now finding applications in nonembedded systems as well. (An embedded system is one in which the computer is part of a larger system, such as a missile, a process control system, or a washing machine.) Ada addresses such issues as data abstraction, encapsulation, generics, exception handling, and multitasking. It is the multitasking aspect of Ada that is of particular interest to us.

Ada provides for both multitasking and rendezvous. Because Ada is intended for mission-critical military applications where efficiency and robustness are crucial, it incorporates a number of additional features, which interact with multitasking and rendezvous in ways that sometimes complicate reasoning about the correctness of a program. For example, one such feature is exception handling, which allows a designer to conveniently provide appropriate actions when an unexpected event occurs. In this section, we discuss Ada multitasking and rendezvous in some detail and investigate how these additional features affect the reasoning methods we discussed earlier in the chapter.

8.8.1 Initiation and Termination of Tasks*

The construct that we have called a process is called a *task* in Ada. A task consists of two modules, a specification and a body, which are quite similar to the definition and implementation components of a Modula-2 module. The specification module lists the exported objects: in this case the procedures, or *entries*, as they are called in Ada, which can be invoked remotely. The task body contains the declaration of local objects and the implementation of the task. Tasks can be declared within a subprogram (Ada terminology for a procedure or function), block, task body, or package. A package is the declarative unit, comparable to a module in Modula-2, that implements information hiding. It also has a specification and a body. Tasks can be initiated either statically (in a manner analogous to a cobegin statement) or dynamically, in which case the number of tasks is determined at run time.

Figure 8.7 shows the static declaration of two tasks, $T1$ and $T2$, within a procedure, P. P is referred to as the *master* (note that the master need not be a task), and $T1$ and $T2$ as its *children*; $T1$ and $T2$ also are referred to as *siblings*. The specification of a task is separate from the task body. In Figure 8.7, tasks $T1$ and $T2$ present no interface to other tasks; hence they have null specifications. Interaction with a task requires knowledge only of its specification. The implementation of the task, as represented by the task body, is not accessible outside of the task.

Task execution occurs in two stages: *activation* and *execution* of the task body. Task activation involves the elaboration of the declarations local to the task body. *Elaboration* is Ada terminology for causing the effect of a declaration at run time: the declared item comes into existence and is assigned an initial value, if any is specified. Since elaboration includes the evaluation of initial value expressions, exceptions might be raised, indicating that some kind of failure has occurred. If a child task is declared, the elaboration of the master includes the elaboration of the entities in the child's specification and

```
procedure P is
    task T1;  - - specification of T1 (null)
    task T2;  - - specification of T2 (null)
    task body T1 is
    begin
        ...       - - body of task T1
    end T1;

    task body T2 is
    begin
        ...       - - body of task T2
    end T2;

begin          - - tasks become active here
    ...        - - body of procedure P
end P;
```

Figure 8.7: Statically declared tasks.

elaboration of the child's body (but not the elaboration of the declarations local to the child's body). The activation of a set of statically declared child tasks starts after the elaboration of the declaration of the master has completed (just after the master's first begin, but before its first executable statement). We do not speak of the activation of the master, since the master might not be a task. The activation of all the declared tasks must be completed before the execution of the body of the master is initiated (before the master can proceed beyond its begin). As soon as a child has completed its activation, it can begin execution of its body without regard to the activation of siblings. Hence, in Figure 8.7, when execution of the body of P commences, P, $T1$, and $T2$ are executing concurrently. P is exited when its body reaches its end statement and $T1$ and $T2$ have terminated. This sequence of events is defined precisely so that exceptions that occur while tasks are being activated can be handled properly. Note that in this example the master is a procedure (not a task), but the rules concerning child activation are the same whether the master is a task, block, or package.

Task types can be specified and used in the static declaration of multiple instances of the same task. Figure 8.8 shows the specification of a task type, $TTYPE$, and the declaration of two instances, $T1$ and $T2$, of that type. As with any other object, the declaration of the task instances need not occur in the same program unit as the specification of the type. With static task declaration, the unit in which the task instance is declared is assumed to be the master of the task. Once again, activation of the children starts after elab-

```
procedure P is
   task type TTYPE;

   task body TTYPE is
   begin
      ···     -- body of each task of type TTYPE
   end TTYPE;

   T1, T2 : TTYPE;

begin
   ···     -- body of procedure P
end P ;
```

Figure 8.8: Static task declaration using task types.

oration of the master's declaration completes and activation must complete before execution of the body of the master commences.

Figure 8.9 shows the dynamic declaration of a set of tasks. First we specify a task type *TTYPE* so that an arbitrary number of tasks of that type can be declared. Then we declare an access type (pointer type), *TPTR*, instances of which can point to instances of type *TTYPE*. Finally, we declare an array, *TARRAY*, of such pointers. We initiate instances of the task type *TTYPE* using the allocator new.

Each time the allocator (*i.e.*, new) is evaluated, activation is immediately started for a new instance of task type *TTYPE*. Control remains at the allocator until the activation of the new task is completed. The activation of the new task is immediate, even if the allocator is invoked within a declaration. Immediate activation ensures that the instance of the access type is properly initialized. Note that this semantics differs from that of a static declaration of a task, where activation of the child does not start until elaboration of the master's declaration completes.

In Figure 8.9 an array of N tasks is dynamically created, all of which execute concurrently with each other and with P. P can exit when its body reaches its end statement and all the tasks in the array have terminated.

We can use a pointer, together with an allocator, to create a task, T, and then later reassign that pointer to refer to another task, thus destroying the reference to T. Assuming that no other reference to T had been created, there would be no way to refer to T. Hence, T could continue to execute and call upon the entries of other tasks, but entries declared within T would no longer be callable and T could not be aborted by the abort statement (we discuss entries and the abort statement later).

```
procedure P is
   tasktype TTYPE;
   type TPTR is access TTYPE;
   TARRAY : array(1..N) of TPTR;

   task body TTYPE is
   begin
      ···    -- body of each task of type TTYPE
   end TTYPE;

begin
   for I in 1..N loop
      TARRAY(I) := new TTYPE;
   end loop;
end P;
```

Figure 8.9: Dynamic task declaration.

In general, each task is said to be *dependent* on its *master* (or *parent*). A task declared statically in a block, subprogram, task, or library package is said to be dependent on that program unit. (By a library package we mean a package that is not nested in some other module.) A task declared statically in a package, P, that is not a library package is dependent on the most immediately enclosing block, subprogram, task, or library package in which P is declared (we discuss a reason for this rule in the next paragraph). A task declared dynamically is dependent on the block, subprogram, task, or library package containing the declaration of the access type (not the program unit where the task was created or the program unit where the instance of the access type was declared). (It would not be appropriate to make the task dependent on the program unit in which the instance of the access type was declared since the task might be referred to by different instances declared in different program units over the task's lifetime.)

When a subprogram, block, or task has finished executing, we say that it has *completed*. Even though a master program unit has completed, its storage cannot be deallocated if it has dependent tasks, since they might subsequently access objects declared within the master. When a master program unit has completed and all its dependent tasks (if any) have terminated, all of the master's storage can be deallocated. If the master is a task, we say that it has *terminated*. Since the deallocation of the storage associated with a package, P, is related to the completion of the most immediately surrounding subprogram, block, or task, any task statically declared in P is dependent on that program unit (not on P).

A task can complete in four ways:

The final statement in its body has been executed.

An exception has been raised within the task for which there is no exception handler within the task (we discuss exceptions later).

An exception has been raised within the task for which the exception handler is at the outermost level of the task and the final statement of that handler has been executed.

The task has been aborted as the result of the execution of an abort statement. The abort statement can be executed by either the task itself or some other task.

A task can terminate in two ways:

It has completed, and all tasks that depend on it have terminated.

It has executed a terminate alternative while waiting for communication with another task (we discuss the terminate alternative later), and all tasks that depend on it have terminated.

Control does not leave a module until all the tasks that depend on it have terminated.

To understand the implications of some of these definitions, consider the structure of the program shown in Figure 8.10. Three tasks are created in the inner block. *TASK1* is statically declared in the inner block; hence the inner block is its master, and exit from the inner block will be delayed until *TASK1* has terminated. The task referred to by *TASK_PTR2* is dynamically created as part of the initialization of variables in the elaboration of the declaration of the inner block. Both the reference to it and the corresponding access type, *ACC_TYPE2*, are declared there. Because the access type is declared in the inner block, that block is the task's master, and hence exit from the inner block will be delayed until the task has terminated. Although the task referred to by *TASK_PTR1* is created in the inner block and the reference to it is declared there, its master is the outer block, since *ACC_TYPE1* is declared in the outer block. Hence, this task can continue to execute after execution has left the inner block. Since, at that time, *TASK_PTR1* will have been deallocated, there will be no way of referring to the task, although it will continue to execute.

8.8.2 Communication Between Tasks*

Ada tasks can communicate with each other in two ways: (1) through globally shared variables and (2) by remote invocation of an entry and rendezvous. The language provides virtually no support for accessing shared variables (for example, there is no semaphore data type) and guarantees correctness of its implementation of shared variables only in very restricted circumstances. Specifically, the language manual states that a program using shared variables

```
declare
   task type T;
   type ACC_TYPE1 is access T;
   task body T is . . .
begin
   . . .
   declare
      type ACC_TYPE2 is access T;
      TASK1 : T;
      TASK_PTR1 : ACC_TYPE1 := new T;
      TASK_PTR2 : ACC_TYPE2 := new T;
   begin
      . . .
   end;
end;
```

Figure 8.10: A task declaration structure.

will give unpredictable results if it violates either of the following rules. The rules are based on the concept of a synchronization point. A *synchronization point* occurs when a task is initiated or terminated and at the beginning and end of a rendezvous.

If a task reads a shared variable between the occurrence of two synchronization points, no other task is allowed to write that variable between those points.

If a task writes a shared variable between the occurrence of two synchronization points, no other task is allowed to read or write that variable between those points.

These rules allow an efficient implementation of shared variables. In particular, an implementation can choose to create a local copy of a shared variable for each task (on which that tasks can perform its updates) and update the global copy only at synchronization points. If the rules are followed, the effect is the same as if each task made its access directly to the global copy. If the rules are not followed, a local copy might not be up to date and a task might not see the current value of the variable. Hence, such a program, although syntactically correct, is erroneous, since its execution time environment does not support the program semantics. Although the rules result in a more efficient implementation, they place rather strict limitations on the use of shared variables. The language does allow the use of the construct

pragma *SHARED(V);*

(a pragma is an instruction to the compiler), which specifies that variable *V* is *SHARED*, in which case all accesses to *V* are made synchronization points (hence forcing access to the global copy), with some loss in efficiency.

Because of these issues, the intended mode of interprocess communication in Ada is through rendezvous invocations, which are referred to as *entry calls*. Hence, we limit the remainder of our discussion to entry calls and assume no shared variables. Figure 8.11 shows the tasks of Figure 8.7 augmented so that *T1* calls an entry in *T2*. Note that the entry name and parameters appear in the specification of *T2*. The syntax and – except for some peculiarities discussed later – the semantics of entry call and accept are the same as those given for rendezvous earlier in this chapter. Entries can be declared only in the specification of a task. Calls waiting for an entry are kept in a queue associated with that entry and are serviced in a first-in-first-out order. Figure 8.12 shows a server task implementing a one-element buffer. The task accepts first a call to fill the buffer, then one to empty it.

In the general case, a task body can contain more than one accept statement for the same entry, and the accept bodies in each case can be different. (See, for example, Figure 8.16.) The accept actually executed in a particular rendezvous depends on the location of the enabled control point of the called task when the call occurs. Hence, both the state of the variables in the called task and the control state of that task can affect the action taken in response to an invocation.

Figures 8.13 and 8.14 show two simple extensions of the concept of an entry. In Figure 8.13, an indexed family of *N* entries is defined. Each entry in the family can be called separately and maintains its own queue of waiting tasks. Figure 8.14 shows how Ada handles interrupts. An interrupt appears as an entry call performed by some (fictitious) external task. The for construct in the specification is called a *representation clause* and designates the hardware address associated with the interrupt. When the interrupt occurs, the body of the entry *INTRPT* is executed.

8.8.3 Select Statement*

The select statement is used to choose among alternatives in performing communication. There is a deterministic version of the select statement for the calling task and a nondeterministic version for the called task. For the calling task, the select statement has two forms. In the conditional entry call,

```
select
    entry_call;
    sequence_of_statements;
else
    sequence_of_statements;
end select;
```

```
procedure P is
    task T1;

    task T2 is
        entry Q(I : in INTEGER; J : out INTEGER; K : in out INTEGER);
    end T2;

    task body T1 is
        A, B, C : INTEGER;
    begin
        . . .
        T2.Q(A, B, C);
        . . .
    end T1;

    task body T2 is
    begin
        . . .
        accept Q(I : in INTEGER; J : out INTEGER; K : in out INTEGER) do
            . . .           -- body of Q;
        end Q;
        . . .
    end T2;

begin
    . . .                   -- body of P
end P;
```

Figure 8.11: Tasks communicating with a rendezvous.

the second sequence of statements is executed if a rendezvous cannot be established immediately with the called task. In the timed entry call,

```
            select
                entry_call;
                sequence_of_statements;
            or
                delay T;
                sequence_of_statements;
            end select;
```

the second sequence of statements is executed if a rendezvous cannot be es-

```
task ONE_ELEMENT_BUFFER is
  entry PUT(X : in ELEMENT);
  entry GET(Y : out ELEMENT);
end ONE_ELEMENT_BUFFER;

task body ONE_ELEMENT_BUFFER is
  B : ELEMENT;
begin
  loop
    accept PUT(X : in ELEMENT) do
      B := X;
    end PUT;
    accept GET(Y : out ELEMENT) do
      Y := B;
    end GET;
  end loop;
end ONE_ELEMENT_BUFFER;
```

Figure 8.12: A one element buffer.

```
task T is
  entry FAM(1..N) (I : in INTEGER);
end T;

task body T is
begin
  for K in 1..N loop
    accept FAM(K) (I : in INTEGER) do
      ...           -- accept body
    end FAM;
  end loop;
end T;
```

Figure 8.13: A family of entries.

```
task T is
    entry INTRPT;
    for INTRPT use at ADDR;
end T;

task body T is
begin
    loop
        · · ·
        accept INTRPT do
            · · ·          - - process the interrupt
        end INTRPT;
        · · ·
    end loop;
end T;
```

Figure 8.14: An entry corresponding to an interrupt.

```
loop
    select
        DEVICE.READ(X);
        · · ·          - - process the value of X;
        exit;
    else
        · · ·          - - do something else in the meanwhile;
    end select;
end loop;
```

Figure 8.15: A polling example

tablished within T time units. The alternative,

delay T;

suspends execution for at least T time units. In Figure 8.15, the first form is used to poll a task monitoring a device until it is ready to rendezvous. The exit statement allows the caller to leave the loop after processing input from the device.

For the called task, the select statement is nondeterministic and has several forms. An example of the simplest case is shown in Figure 8.16. After allowing a writer to initialize B, the select statement within the loop will subsequently nondeterministically rendezvous with either a reader or a writer.

```
task body T is
  B : ELEMENT;
begin
  accept WRITE(X : in ELEMENT) do
    B := X;
  end WRITE;
  loop
    select
      accept WRITE(X : in ELEMENT) do
          B := X;
      end WRITE;
      ...                    -- do additional computation
    or
      accept READ(Y : out ELEMENT) do
          Y := B;
      end READ;
    end select;
  end loop;
end T;
```

Figure 8.16: A task in which the variable *B* is available to concurrent tasks through entry calls.

Note that the example illustrates a situation in which two accept statements correspond to the same entry. It also illustrates that a component of a select (the first component in this case) can contain additional computation that the callee performs after the rendezvous with the caller has completed and hence concurrently with the caller. In this case the computation is appropriate only after *WRITE* has been called; hence it cannot be placed after the select statement.

Each accept alternative in a select statement can be guarded as follows:

when condition => accept_statement;

The guarded select statement (with slightly different syntax) was discussed in Section 8.4, and the semantics described there applies to Ada.

A select statement can also contain a terminate alternative. Figure 8.17 shows an implementation of a bounded buffer using a guarded select statement with a terminate alternative. The purpose of this alternative is to address the problem mentioned in Chapter 6 in which each process in a set of communicating processes functions as both a client and a server. When all processes have completed their (client) computations, they may all be waiting in select statements for service requests from other members of the set. Since all com-

```
task body BUFFER is
  N: constant := 100;
  QARRAY : array(0..N - 1) of ELEMENT;
  LAST : INTEGER range 0..N - 1 := 0;
  COUNT : INTEGER range 0..N := 0;
begin
  loop
    select
      when COUNT < N =>
        accept ENQUEUE(X : in ELEMENT) do
          QARRAY((LAST + 1) mod N) := X;
        end ENQUEUE;
        LAST := (LAST + 1) mod N;
        COUNT := COUNT + 1;
    or
      when COUNT > 0 =>
        accept DEQUEUE(Y : out ELEMENT) do
          Y := QARRAY((LAST - COUNT + 1) mod N);
        end DEQUEUE;
        COUNT := COUNT - 1;
    or
        terminate;
    end select;
  end loop;
end BUFFER;
```

Figure 8.17: A bounded buffer with a terminate alternative.

putations have completed, such requests will never occur and the processes will be deadlocked. The terminate alternative was designed to deal with this situation. A task waiting in a select statement having a terminate alternative can terminate if

Its master has completed;

All of its dependent tasks and all of its siblings (and all of their dependent tasks) either have completed or are themselves waiting at terminate alternatives.

Server tasks, such as the bounded buffer, are often designed with a terminate alternative so that when there are no possible clients, the server quietly terminates. A terminate alternative can be guarded.

The various forms of the select statement are described by the following formal syntax:

> **select**
>   select_alternative;
> {**or**
>   select_alternative;}
> [**else**
>   sequence_of_statements;]
> **end select**;

where the curly braces indicate that zero or more instances of the contained clause can be present in the select and the square brackets indicate that at most one else clause is permitted. A select alternative has the form

> [**when** condition =>] selective_wait_alternative;

and a selective_wait_alternative can have the following forms:

> accept_statement;
> sequence_of_statements;

or

> delay_statement;
> sequence_of_statements;

or

> **terminate;**

with the following restrictions:

A select statement that has an else part cannot have a delay or terminate alternative;

A select statement can have at most one terminate alternative;

A select statement that has a terminate alternative cannot also have a delay alternative.

The operational semantics of the select statement is as follows:

The guards are examined to determine whether any are open. If a delay alternative exists, the delay clock is started. (When an alternative has no guard, it is assumed to have an open guard.)

If there are no open guards and there is no else part, the exception *PRO-GRAM_ERROR* is raised.

If there are any open guards that are guarding accept statements for which a rendezvous can be immediately established – we refer to these as open alternatives – one of these accept statements is nondeterministically selected and its rendezvous performed; any statements that follow the selected accept statement are then executed, and the select statement is exited.

If no open alternative can be selected immediately and there is no else part, execution is suspended until an open alternative can be executed; then an open alternative is selected and its rendezvous performed; any statements that follow the selected accept statement are then executed, and the select statement is exited.

If there are no open guards or no open alternatives that can be selected immediately and there is an else alternative, the sequence of statements following the else clause is executed; then the select statement is exited.

If there is an open guard guarding a delay alternative for which the delay period has elapsed and no other alternative has been selected yet, the sequence of statements following the delay statement is executed; then the select statement is exited.

If there is an open guard guarding a terminate alternative and no other alternative can be selected immediately, and if the master of this task has completed and all dependent tasks and all sibling tasks (and their dependent tasks) have completed or are waiting at select statements with open terminate alternatives, then this task and all the dependents and siblings (and their dependents) are terminated.

An implementation may (but need not) support task priorities, which are assigned to tasks by including the pragma

pragma *PRIORITY(P)*;

in the task specification, where P is a static expression that can be evaluated at compile time. Priorities are static and cannot be changed at run time. When an implementation supports priorities, a higher priority task that is eligible to execute can never wait while a lower priority task executes. Hence, preemptive scheduling is implied. A rendezvous executes with the higher priority of the two tasks involved. However, priority does not affect the first-come-first-served queueing associated with entry calls nor does it affect the nondeterminism in choosing among executable alternatives (a task waiting on an accept queue is not eligible to execute).

Tasks and their entries have several attributes:

T'CALLABLE is a boolean attribute of a task that is false if the task is completed, terminated, or abnormal (is in the process of being aborted) and true otherwise.

T'TERMINATED is a boolean attribute of a task that is true if the task has terminated and false otherwise;

E'COUNT is an integer attribute of an entry that denotes the number of tasks waiting to rendezvous at that entry. This attribute is visible only within the task that contains the entry and is not visible in any subprogram, task, or package nested within that task.

For example, the *COUNT* attribute can be used in guards to prioritize the choice of open alternatives in a select statement such that a call on an entry is accepted only when no entry with a higher priority has any callers waiting on its queue. Thus, if E is a high priority entry, the guard of a lower priority entry might be $E'COUNT = 0$, thus closing the lower priority entry when a call is pending on E. However, care must be taken in using this approach. Since tasks can be aborted (see the next section), a caller with a pending call on E might be aborted between the time the guard is evaluated and the time a rendezvous is attempted. In this case, pending calls to the low priority entry will be made to wait unnecessarily.

8.8.4   Aborting Tasks*

A task can be explicitly terminated with the abort statement

$$\textbf{abort } T_1, T_2, \ldots, T_n;$$

where $T_1, T_2, \ldots, T_n$ are (references to) tasks. A task can abort itself or any other task that is visible to it.

   The operational semantics of the abort statement is as follows:

All of the tasks $T_1, T_2, \ldots, T_n$ that have not already terminated become *abnormal*.

When a task becomes abnormal, all of the tasks that depend on it also become abnormal.

An abnormal task suspended at an accept, select, or delay statement abandons its processing and enters the completed state.

An abnormal task suspended at an entry call for which the rendezvous has not yet occurred is removed from the queue and enters the completed state.

If a calling task becomes abnormal during a rendezvous, it is allowed to complete the rendezvous before entering the completed state (so that the data in the called task will be left in a consistent state and hence the called task will be able to serve other clients after the caller is terminated).

Otherwise, an abnormal task can proceed (the language reference is purposely not precise here), but it cannot be allowed to proceed beyond one of the following synchronization points before it abandons its processing and enters the completed state.

Its final end statement;
The activation of another task;
The start or end of an accept statement;
An entry call;
A select statement;
A delay statement;
An exception handler;
An abort statement.

If an abnormal task abandons its processing while it is updating a shared variable, the value of that variable is undefined.

As we shall see in the next section, if the called task becomes abnormal during a rendezvous, an exception is raised within the caller (since the service it requested was not performed).

8.8.5 Exceptions*

An exception is an unexpected event for which the program is supposed to perform some special actions. Examples of exceptions are numeric overflow and an attempt to communicate with a terminated task. Ada has extensive facilities for raising and dealing with exceptions, and these facilities interact in interesting ways with the tasking facilities.

Certain exceptions are predefined within the language and are raised automatically when the corresponding event occurs. For example, the predefined exception *PROGRAM_ERROR* is raised when all the guards in a select statement are closed and there is no else alternative. A program can provide its own, user defined exceptions with a declaration of the form

TEMP_OVER_LIMITS : **exception**;

A program can raise an exception, either user defined or predefined, using the raise statement:

raise *TEMP_OVER_LIMITS*;

When an exception is raised, the normal execution of the program is abandoned. If an *exception handler* has been provided, control is passed to the handler. An exception handler is a sequence of statements provided by the user at the end of a block, subprogram, package body, or task body. The general form of an exception handler is

when exception_name => sequence_of_statements;

(In the last of a sequence of exception handlers, exception_name can be replaced by the word **others**, denoting that that handler deals with all the exceptions for which a handler has not been explicitly specified.) An example of exception declaration, raising, and handling is shown in Figure 8.18.

The operational semantics of raising an exception is as follows:

```
declare
    PROBLEM : exception;                    – –  declare the exception
    ...
begin
    ...
    if ... then raise PROBLEM; endif;       – –  raise the exception
    ...
exception
    when PROBLEM => S;                       – –  handle the exception
end;
```

Figure 8.18: The declaration, raising, and handling of an exception.

1. If the program unit (block, subprogram, package, or task), U, that directly contains the location where the exception was raised has a handler for that exception, that handler is executed. After execution of the handler, U is considered to have completed and execution is resumed at the appropriate location outside of U (*i.e.*, at the location to which U would have transferred if it had completed normally).

2. If the program unit that directly contains the location where the exception is raised is a task and that task does not contain a handler for that exception, the task is considered to have completed.

3. If the program unit that directly contains the location where the exception is raised is the main program and the main program does not contain a handler for that exception, the program is terminated (*i.e.*, its execution and that of all its children are abandoned).

4. If the program unit, U, that directly contains the location where the exception is raised is a block, subprogram, or package and U does not contain a handler for that exception, U is considered to have completed and the exception is re-raised in the program unit from which U was entered, at the point at which U was entered. For example, if U is a subprogram, it is re-raised at the point of call, or if U is a block, it is re-raised at the point at which the block is embedded in the immediately enclosing module. This re-raising is called *propagating* the exception. Note that propagation is performed dynamically, based on the calling structure of the particular execution, rather than statically, based on the lexical structure of the program. If U has dependent tasks, propagation will occur after all dependents have completed.

5. An exception occurring during the elaboration of a declaration is not handled by a handler in the program unit, U, to which that declaration is local. U is

considered to have completed, and the exception is re-raised in the program unit from which U was entered, at the point at which U was entered.

6. If an exception is raised within an exception handler, the exception is propagated to the calling program unit as described in (4), unless the unit containing the handler is a task or the main program, in which case (2) or (3) applies.

The propagation semantics for exception handling gives the designer freedom to determine which program unit is the most appropriate for handling a particular exception. Since an exception raised within an exception handler is propagated to the calling unit, a handler can partially process an exception and then re-raise that exception so that the calling unit completes the handling. The raise statement has another form:

raise;

which can be used only in an exception handler labeled with **others** and re-raises in the calling program unit the exception (whose name is not known within the handler) that caused entry to the handler.

The language does not allow exceptions to be propagated out of a task to its master because the master is executing concurrently with the task and would have to be asynchronously interrupted to handle the exception.

We are particularly interested in those exceptions that can occur when a task is being initiated and while a rendezvous is taking place. As we shall see, not only can the predefined exception *TASKING_ERROR* occur, but other exceptions, both predefined and user defined, can also be raised. We must specify precisely where each exception is raised so that we know which handler will be called to process the exception.

If an exception occurs during the elaboration of the declaration of a master (for example, in the evaluation of an expression to initialize a variable), the children will not be activated (since children are not activated until activation of the master is complete). The master is considered to have completed, and the exception is re-raised in the program unit from which the master was entered at the point at which the master was entered.

If an exception occurs during the activation of a task (*i.e.*, during the elaboration of the declarations within the task body), the task is assumed to have completed (but its sibling tasks are allowed to continue) and the exception *TASKING_ERROR* is raised as follows:

For statically declared tasks, it is raised immediately after the initial begin (but before the first executable statement) in the master (only one *TASKING_ERROR* is raised even when exceptions occur in the activation of more than one task);

For dynamically declared tasks, it is raised at the evaluation of the allocator that caused the task to be activated;

Note that for statically declared tasks, these rules imply that a handler for *TASKING_ERROR* within the master will be invoked, while for dynamically declared tasks, such a handler might not be invoked, since the evaluation of the allocator might be contained within a different program unit.

If a calling task attempts a rendezvous and the called task is terminated, completed, or abnormal (or becomes completed or abnormal while the calling task is on one of its entry queues), the exception *TASKING_ERROR* is raised in the caller at the point of entry call.

If, during a rendezvous, the called task becomes abnormal, the exception *TASKING_ERROR* is raised in the caller at the point of entry call.

If, during a rendezvous, an exception is raised within the accept statement and that exception is not handled locally within the accept statement, the exception is raised in the caller at the point of entry call, and it is also propagated in the called task using the usual rules for exception propagation. (Note that the exception is raised in two places.)

If an entry call to a family of tasks uses an index outside of the defined range for the family, the *CONSTRAINT_ERROR* exception is raised in the caller.

Example

Figure 8.19 [53] illustrates some of the features of exception handling and propagation in the implementation of a server task performing storage allocation. We assume that the types *BLOCK* and *PTR_TO_BLOCK* as well as the procedure *GARBAGE_COLLECTOR* are declared in the global environment.

A client task calls the entry *ALLOCATE* when it wants a block of storage. The accept statement uses the allocator new to attempt to get a block of storage. If no storage is available, the predefined exception *STORAGE_ERROR* occurs. Since a handler for that exception is provided in the accept statement, that handler is executed. The handler first calls the procedure *GARBAGE_COLLECTOR* to attempt to reclaim storage and then again uses new to attempt to get a block. If the second attempt succeeds, the accept completes, the server enters another iteration of its loop, and the client resumes execution, ignorant of the fact that an exception has been raised. However, garbage collection might not reclaim sufficient storage, and the evaluation of new within the handler might again raise *STORAGE_ERROR*. Since this exception is raised inside the handler within the accept statement, it is now propagated outside of the accept statement to the calling task (the exception will be raised at the point of entry call and the caller will then know that no storage is available), and also within the called task. Since the accept statement is inside the block that is the loop body and, since a handler for that exception is provided in that block, that handler will be executed. Because that handler consists of only the null statement, no processing occurs. After the handler completes,

```
task body BLOCK_STORAGE is
begin
  loop
    begin
      accept ALLOCATE(P : out PTR_TO_BLOCK) do
        begin
          P := new BLOCK;
        exception
          when STORAGE_ERROR =>
            GARBAGE_COLLECTOR;
            P := new BLOCK;
        end;
      end ALLOCATE;
    exception
      when STORAGE_ERROR => null;
    end;
  end loop;
end BLOCK_STORAGE;
```

Figure 8.19: A storage allocator.

the containing block is exited, control passes to the beginning of the loop, and the server continues its execution. If the null handler had not been provided in the block, the exception would have caused the server to complete – not a desirable situation.

8.8.6   Reasoning About Ada Programs*

The communication facilities in Ada are based on rendezvous, and to some extent the formal methods developed earlier in this chapter can be used to reason about them. However, a number of features have been added to Ada to make it more useful in practical situations, and many of these features are not covered by the formal semantics we have presented. In some cases the formal semantics can be readily extended; in others the operational semantics cannot easily be described formally. Even when formal proofs cannot be constructed, the designer must be able to reason about the behavior of the program with sufficient precision so that a convincing argument for its correctness can be made. It is exactly those language features that make it difficult to construct a formal proof that also complicate the informal reasoning. In this section we consider a few features of Ada that relate to language structures we have analyzed earlier, and we discuss how they affect the reasoning.

Conditional and Timed Entry Call

The formal semantics of a conditional entry call is the same as that of an if statement in which all guards are *true*, since the choice of components does not depend on the state of variables in the task. Hence, we have

$$\frac{\{P\}\ T.E(\overline{X},\overline{Y},\overline{Z});\ S1\ \{Q\},\ \{P\}\ S2\ \{Q\}}{\{P\}\ \textbf{select}\ T.E(\overline{X},\overline{Y},\overline{Z});\ S1;\ \textbf{else}\ S2;\ \textbf{end select};\ \{Q\}}$$

Since we are not reasoning about time, the same semantics applies to the timed entry call.

Task and Entry Attributes

Attributes act like shared variables: they can be modified by actions of one task and inspected by another. Hence assertions based on these attributes are subject to interference. The *COUNT* attribute (which can only be accessed by the called task) might decrease (for example, if the caller times out) or increase asynchronously. Similarly, the *TERMINATED* attribute might change from false to true (but not true to false) and the *CALLABLE* attribute might change from true to false (but not false to true) asynchronously. For example, if a guard is dependent on the value of a *COUNT* attribute, interference may occur if the value of *COUNT* is used in a precondition of the corresponding selective_wait_alternative.

Aborts

Since the execution of an abort can result in the termination of a large number of tasks, its effect can be widespread, making it difficult to reason about the state of the program afterwards – particularly if globally shared variables are used. One possible way to circumvent this difficulty is to use an implementation that allows an abnormal task to proceed to a synchronization point before terminating. Then if the program design specifies an invariant characterizing the consistent states of the shared variables and requires that the invariant be true at all synchronization points, consistency of these variables would be guaranteed after an abort. Unfortunately, such an implementation leaves us with the problem of not being able to predict when the abort will take effect (which might be potentially dangerous if the abort were used to stop the program in certain emergency situations).

Fairness

The language manual specifies that calls to each entry must be handled in a first-come-first-served manner; hence, a strong notion of fairness is implied. However, fairness is specifically not required in choosing among executable components of a select statement. Since the implementation can use any arbitrary scheduling discipline, programs must be designed to work under all possible disciplines – even those that are completely deterministic or totally unfair.

Priorities

A program with prioritized tasks might not be fair. Although priorities will have no effect on safety properties, liveness properties (such as termination) might be affected. For example, a high priority calling task executing a loop containing a conditional entry call that invokes an entry in a lower priority task might run forever without achieving a rendezvous. The lower priority called task, although always ready to run, never gets a chance to execute and, hence, never reaches its accept statement.

Exceptions

An exception causes a disruption in the normal flow of control, not unlike that of a goto statement. Consider a program unit, U, consisting of a main body, U', and a handler, H, for an exception, E. We must demonstrate that if the precondition of H is P, the preconditions of all points in U' at which E can be raised must imply P. Among the approaches to the design of H are the following:

If H can always repair the situation indicated by E and then perform the computation contained in U' following any point at which E was raised, then H always returns normally to the caller of U. In that case, H can be described by a triple:

$$\{P\}\,H\,\{Q\}$$

where Q implies the postcondition of U'.

If H cannot always repair the situation indicated by E, it can re-raise E when the repair is not possible so that a normal return to the caller does not occur. In that case H can be described by an expanded triple that indicates two possible postconditions:

$$\{P\}\,H\,\{Q_n, Q_e\}$$

where Q_n is the postcondition when H returns normally (after completing the computation of U') and Q_e is the postcondition when H returns exceptionally by re-raising E. Then Q_n must imply the postcondition of U', and Q_e must imply the precondition of the handler in the caller that handles E. In general, a number of distinct exceptions might be raised in U and propagated out (they might be raised in U' or in some handler in U). In each case a different postcondition can be demonstrated and in each case propagation causes a different transfer of control. As a result, the proof obligations become more complex.

Shared Variables

Assuming the program satisfies the two rules concerning access to shared variables between synchronization points (so that the language implementation works correctly), shared variables can be reasoned about using the methods for global variables discussed in Chapter 4.

Distributed Termination

The terminate alternative provides an orderly way for server tasks to terminate when all clients have completed and, in particular, deals with the symmetric client-server problem discussed in Section 6.5.1. However, it significantly complicates the formal semantics of the language. Since it provides an alternative means for a task to terminate, it affects the postcondition of the task. The situation is not as straightforward as that described in connection with the distributed termination convention for do statements (Section 6.5.1), since in general the terminate statement can be executed only in cooperation with other related tasks that are also waiting at select statements with terminate alternatives. Using the distributed termination convention, a guard in a do statement can fail either because the boolean expression, G_i, is false or because the communicating partner, P_i, has terminated. The latter possibility required that we add a disjunct, $term(P_i)$ (a function returning true if P_i has terminated), in the postcondition of the do statement. Although the Ada terminate alternative can also be dealt with by adding an appropriate disjunct, D, in the postcondition of the task, the form of D is no longer simple. Consider a task, T, containing a select statement with precondition P. Let the select statement contain the component

$$\textbf{when } G \; \texttt{=>} \; \textbf{terminate};$$

Then the precondition of the terminate statement is $G \wedge P$. The terminate statement will execute when the program is in a state in which T's master has completed and all T's dependents and siblings (and their dependents) have completed or are at terminate alternatives. There are a number of ways that such a state can arise depending on whether a particular sibling or dependent has completed and, if not, at which of its select statements (having a terminate alternative) it is waiting. D can be expressed as a disjunction of terms with each disjunct describing one such situation. The jth situation is described by an assertion having the form $Q \wedge (G \wedge P) \wedge R_j$, where Q is the postcondition of the master and R_j contains a conjunct for each sibling or dependent describing that task's state (*i.e.*, its postcondition if it has completed; otherwise, the precondition of the terminate statement it will execute). Unfortunately, not every combination of possibilities within each sibling or dependent can actually occur (*i.e.* it may not be possible for task $T1$ to be waiting at select statement $S1$ when task $T2$ is at select statement $S2$), and hence assertions must be strong enough so that a disjunct corresponding to an impossible combination of task states has value *false*.

8.9   Critique of Rendezvous

The client-server paradigm is appropriate for many applications and can be implemented in a number of ways. An implementation using primitive message passing has the advantage that asynchronism is permitted between the two processes. The client can proceed with its own computation while its service request is being satisfied by the server. If communication is asynchronous, the client can proceed before the server even accepts the message. With synchronous message passing, the client is somewhat more constrained, since it must wait until the message has been received.

In this chapter we have considered clients that access servers through an rpc interface. Such an interface places a stronger synchronization constraint on the client, since the client must wait until the service request has been satisfied. Nevertheless, the rpc interface is an attractive alternative for a client-server system because, from the viewpoint of the client, it is simple (a single procedure call as contrasted with the exchange of two distinct messages), familiar, and has clean semantics.

On the other hand, the rendezvous mechanism, particularly as provided in Ada, has some shortcomings from the point of view of the server. One of these shortcomings is concerned with an important activity the server has to perform, namely scheduling its own operations (providing service to some clients while making others wait). Depending on the application, scheduling decisions are based on some or all of the following information:

1. The name of the requested operation – for example, a solution to the Readers-Writers problem might give priority to processes calling a *startread* procedure.

2. The state of the server – for example, a queue server might be in a state where it can fulfill requests to enqueue an element, but not to dequeue an element.

3. The arguments of the requested operation – for example, a storage server can only satisfy requests for blocks of storage smaller than the current amount of free storage.

4. The priority of the client – since priorities can be passed as arguments, this item is similar to (3).

5. The order in which the requests are made – for example, the server might be required to implement a first-in-first-out schedule.

Monitors use signals to implement scheduling algorithms. Items (1) through (4) are clearly available to the called monitor procedure, and hence a scheduling decision can be based on them. Item (5) is more difficult to obtain, since requests may be forced to wait for monitor entry. The monitor specification does not state the order in which these waiting processes are to be resumed. Note that when the initial processing of a request is performed, if the monitor procedure decides not to immediately provide the requested service, it can make the client process wait and service other processes instead.

A major shortcoming of a server module implemented using rendezvous (as in Ada) concerns its inability to perform scheduling using information contained in arguments. The decision by the server to accept a request can be based only on items (1) and (2), not on the value of the arguments passed. To understand this situation better, consider a server that has accepted a request and, after examining the arguments, finds that it cannot provide the requested service in its current state. Service must be delayed until some subsequent request is serviced and causes a change of server state. A monitor can deal with such a situation by making the requestor wait while it serves other processes. A server implemented with rendezvous can attempt to use a number of design alternatives to either deal with or avoid such situations:

Nested Accept Statements: If, while executing some accept statement, the server finds that it cannot provide the requested service, it executes a nested accept statement to provide some (perhaps different) service to a different client. The hope is that on returning, after providing this new service, the server will be in a state where it can provide the original service. Unfortunately, this approach is only a partial solution, since the server may find that the new request cannot be serviced, requiring a further nesting of accept statements. The nesting requires the server to use a last-in-first-out service discipline.

Family of Accept Statements: The server is constructed using a number of entries (and corresponding accept statements) for the same service, each corresponding to a different value (or range of values) of the arguments. A client decides which of the several entries for a given service to call, based on the arguments it is passing, and the server accepts only calls to entries that are invoked with argument values it can serve. For example, a disk server might declare a family of entries, with each entry corresponding to a different track. A client invokes the entry corresponding to the track it wants to access. By accepting a rendezvous only for a track it is willing to service, the server can impose a disk head scheduling algorithm. This approach is only a partial solution, since the range of argument values must be known at design time and any finite number of entries can only approximate a range of possible argument values. Furthermore, it complicates the client's interface, since the client must select the appropriate entry to call. Finally, it makes the correct functioning of the server dependent on the cooperation of the client.

Refusal: A service request that cannot be fulfilled is rejected. The client must resubmit the request at a later time. This approach can lead to a large number of resubmitted requests, causing an increase in communication traffic. Furthermore, it complicates the client's interface and offers the client no guidance as to when to resubmit.

Early Reply: The server accepts a request, records the arguments, and returns an immediate acknowledgment to the client, indicating only that the request has been queued for service. The server carries out the request at some later time, using a scheduling algorithm that can be based on the arguments passed and, hence, can be as general as an algorithm implemented in a monitor. Two techniques can be used to notify the client when the request has been satisfied: (1) In the out arguments of the original entry call, the server can return the name of a different entry within the server that the client should call and that the server will accept when the service is complete. (2) In the in arguments of the original call, the client can include the name of an entry within the client that the server should call when the service is complete. In both cases a second call is involved, thereby complicating the interface. The (high level) rendezvous mechanism is essentially being used to simulate (low level) synchronous message passing – not a desirable situation. Furthermore, both techniques put the server in jeopardy, since a faulty client might not engage in the second rendezvous (for example it might be aborted), leaving the server waiting indefinitely.

The last three protocols are best implemented through the use of an envelope, as described in Section 5.7. The envelope is provided by the server and acts as an interface between client and server. Rather than invoking the server directly, the client invokes the envelope, which then implements one of the protocols. Not only does this approach remove the added complication introduced into the client code (*e.g.,* the two communications used in the Early Reply approach are hidden within the envelope), but, since the envelope is provided by the server, potential security loopholes can be better controlled. The envelope can be implemented either as a separate process associated with the client or as a macro expansion of the client call.

The dynamic process creation aspect of rpc eliminates the problem of being unable to use the values of arguments in scheduling, since a process is unconditionally created for each request, making the arguments available within the server module. The competing concurrent processes must then schedule themselves using some synchronization mechanism (such as signaling) which must be provided for use within the server module. This approach has all the flexibility of monitors.

In Section 5.10 we discussed the problem of remote delay, in which some server, A, on behalf of one of its clients, requests service from another server, B. A must then wait an unpredictable amount of time until that service is supplied by B. Monitors do not provide adequate flexibility to deal with this situation, since, while monitor *A* waits, no service can be supplied to other clients. Servers implemented with rendezvous suffer from the same deficiency. Servers implemented using rpc can cope with this situation, since while one server process is waiting for a nested remote call to be serviced, other server processes can be providing service to other clients.

Finally, the rendezvous mechanism provided in Ada requires that entries be declared only in tasks. Hence, a call to a particular entry can be serviced only by the task that declares that entry, precluding a direct implementation of multiple server processes capable of providing the same service. A solution to this problem is to declare the multiple servers within a package that also contains a data structure designed to keep track of which servers are busy. The package exports a procedure that, when called by a client, locates an idle server, marks it as busy, and then invokes that server's entry. Accesses to the data structure must be synchronized. This synchronization can be enforced by requiring that accesses be done indirectly through a separate task declared within the package for this purpose.

8.10   Bibliographic Notes

A comprehensive description of all aspects of remote procedure calling can be found in Nelson [102] and a short critique in Liskov, Herlihy, and Gilbert [92]. A description of an implementation of the remote procedure call interface is contained in Birrell and Nelson [23]. The validation of remote procedures is dealt with in Schlichting and Schneider [115]. The Argus language [90], [91] uses rpc (as contrasted with rendezvous). The Reference Manual for the Ada Programming Language [1] provides the definitive description of the Ada language. A good general introduction to the language can be found in [16], while two excellent sources of information on the concurrent aspects of the language are Shumate [119] and Gehani [53]. A proof system for a subset of Ada is described in Gerth and de Roever [55]. The language SR [11] provides a flexible mechanism for scheduling rendezvous, since it allows parameters to be referenced in guards.

8.11   Exercises

1. Give an example of a monitor that cannot be simulated by a single server process using rendezvous. Discuss the difficulty of implementing the equivalent of an alarm clock monitor with rendezvous.

2. Show that, in the following program, the first call in P_1 cannot rendezvous with the second accept in P_2. You may add auxiliary variables, but you can use only rendezvous as a message passing mechanism. (Hint: Simulate rendezvous using synchronous message passing.)

```
cobegin
P₁::
  begin
     . . .
     P₂.p(a);
     . . .
     P₂.p(b);
     . . .
  end;
//
P₂::
  begin
     . . .
     accept p(x) do S₁; end p;
     . . .
     accept p(x) do S₂; end p;
     . . .
  end;
coend;
```

3. Design a process that uses rendezvous to implement an abstract data type for a bounded natural number (a nonnegative integer less than or equal to N) initialized to 0. The data type has two operations: $Add1$, which adds one to the natural number, and $Subt2$, which subtracts two from the natural number. Provide concrete implementations for both operations, and prove that the process correctly implements the abstract data type. Describe the difficulties that would be involved in implementing the operation $Add(n)$, which adds the natural number n to the natural number.

4. Give the syntax, operational semantics, and an inference rule that specifies the formal semantics of the do statement in which each component is a guarded accept statement.

5. Show how the $COUNT$ attribute in Ada can be used to prioritize the $SELECT$ statement.

6. Consider an invocation $P.insert(x)$ of the accept statement shown in the program below. Prove that if T is a precondition of the call, a postcondition is

$$T \wedge ((\exists j)(1 \le j \le m) \wedge (set[j] = x))$$

(Hint: Use the assertion $0 \le m \le N$ as loop invariant.)

$\mathcal{P}$ ::
  var
    m : *integer* := 0;
    set : **array** [1..N] **of** *element*;
    find : *boolean*;
    i : *integer*;
  begin
    do $m < N \rightarrow$
      accept *insert*(a : **in** *element*) **do**
        find, i := *false*, 1;
        do $(i \le m) \wedge \neg find \rightarrow$
          if *set*[i] = $a \rightarrow find$:= *true*;
          else i := $i + 1$;
          fi;
        od;
        if $\neg find \rightarrow set$[$m$], m := a, $m + 1$;
        else skip;
        fi;
      end *insert*;
    od;
      . . .
  end;

7. Treat the process $\mathcal{P}$ of the previous problem as a server implementing an abstract set, st, having the single operation *insert*, where I_a is $0 \le |st| \le N$, $st_{init} = \Phi$, $WP_a^{insert}(st)$ is $0 \le |st| < N$, and *insert* is described by

$$\{P_{st \cup <x>}^{st}\} \ \mathcal{P}.insert(x) \ \{P\}$$

To support this implementation, show at the concrete level that s, the body of *insert*, is described by

$$\{WP_c^{insert}(m, set) \wedge (a = A) \wedge (m = M) \wedge (set = SET)\} \ s$$
$$\{(a = A) \wedge (m = M + 1) \wedge (set = SET_{|A}^{M+1})\}$$

where I_c is $0 \le m \le N$ and $WP_c^{insert}(m, set)$ is $0 \le m < N$.

8. Suppose a module, U, contains a main body, U', and a handler, H, for an exception, E. Suppose further that H cannot always complete the computation that has been interrupted by the raising of E in U', but that H always returns normally (*i.e.*, it does not raise an exception). Relate the postconditions of U', H, and U. Design a simple convention whereby the caller of U can determine whether or not U has completed the requested computation.

(Hint: Introduce a boolean variable that U sets to true when it completes the computation and sets to false otherwise. Show how the variable fits into the postconditions.)

9. Prove the triple (8.6) and demonstrate the satisfaction conditions for the program of Figure 8.5.

10. Consider an implementation of rendezvous using datagrams. Translate an entry call and an accept statement into appropriate sequences of statements involving datagram communication. You can assume that process names can be passed in messages. Also assume, for simplicity, that the caller receives datagram messages only from the called task (*i.e.*, the receipt of a datagram by the caller indicates the completion of the rendezvous). In a manner analogous to the discussion in Section 8.6, give the proof obligations in this case.

11. Implement two reader priority solutions to the Readers-Writers Problem in Ada. (Recall that a reader priority solution was given in Figure 1.7.) In the first you may use the COUNT attribute. Do not use COUNT in the second. (Hint: Use nested select statements to avoid accepting a request from a writer once a read phase has started.)

12. Implement a disk head scheduling task in Ada, as described in Exercise 14 of Chapter 5. Use an early reply approach in which the procedure *request* has an additional out parameter of type integer that identifies an entry within a family of entries that the client should call to determine when access has been granted to the disk. The client accesses the task through a system-provided envelope, so the second call is guaranteed to be made. (Hint: The number of pending disk requests must be limited to the number of entries in the family.)

13. Give an inference rule for an Ada select statement that has an else clause as its last alternative.

14. Give an inference rule for an Ada select statement in which each component accept statement is followed by an arbitrary statement that is not part of the rendezvous (as in Figure 8.16).

15. Using the inference rules of the previous problem, prove that in the following variation of the polling example of Section 7.7, the switch is on when the samples are taken. Note that the entries *ON* and *OFF* have neither parameters nor bodies.

```
task body T1 is
begin
   ...
   switch := on;
   T2.ON;
   ...
   T2.OFF;
   switch := off;
end T1;

task body T2 is
begin
   ...
   accept ON;
   ok := true;
   while ok loop
       ...              - - sample device output
                        - - and save results in temporary storage
       select
          accept OFF;
          ok := false;
       else
          null;
       end select;
   end loop;
end T2;
```

16. In contrast to rendezvous, assume that a new process is dynamically created in the called module whenever a procedure is remotely invoked. The new process executes the procedure on behalf of the caller. Describe a set of proof obligations that would support proofs of the caller and callee. Take the case where each procedure has assignment semantics. You should first deal with the isolated case in which only one invocation of a procedure can be executed at a time (as discussed in Chapter 3) and then introduce non-interference (as discussed in Chapter 4). Since permanent variables within the callee can be accessed concurrently by concurrent invocations, some synchronization construct is needed. Assume the concurrent language provides mutex objects (as described in Chapter 5 in connection with Modula-3) and use invariants to characterize the state of permanent variables. For simplicity, assume that busy waits are used instead of signaling.

9

Distributed Systems and Failures

Previous chapters have been concerned with the mechanisms used by concurrent processes to communicate and with techniques to demonstrate that programs employing these mechanisms are correct. In this chapter our focus shifts away from the details of the individual mechanisms to questions about the program as a whole. Our focus also shifts more specifically to concurrent programs that are distributed across a network. We refer to such programs by the commonly used term *distributed systems*. In such systems, communication is achieved through message passing, and the time it takes to pass a message may be significant compared to the time to perform computation. We view each process as a sequence of events and study the relationship among events in a distributed system. An understanding of this relationship is fundamental to the analysis of distributed algorithms.

The second issue dealt with in this chapter is that of failure. Real systems are subject to a variety of failures, and our discussion would therefore not be complete if we did not introduce some techniques for dealing with failure. The failure modes of a distributed system are more complicated than those of a centralized system, since partial failure is more likely than total failure. We discuss failures in the three major components of the system: communication failures, storage failures, and processor failures. A major concern with respect to failure is once again atomicity. Whereas in earlier chapters we were concerned that computations accessing a common data object be performed atomically with respect to one another, here we are concerned that a computation be atomic with respect to a failure. We discuss failure recovery procedures whose goal is to ensure that either an interrupted computation is completed or it has no effect whatsoever. We return to this subject in Chapter 12, where we discuss failures in transaction processing systems.

9.1 Ordering the Events in a Distributed Algorithm

In Chapter 2 we developed a formal semantics for the constructs of a sequential language and saw that an assertion about the state produced by a particular computation – its postcondition – generally depends on an assertion describing the initial state seen by the computation – its precondition. The precondition is in turn the postcondition of the prior computation, and thus we get a chain of dependencies from which we can draw the (obvious) conclusion that the outcome of a computation (potentially) depends on all the prior computations that have been performed.

We view a process as executing a total order of computations. Depending on the level of granularity with which we view a process, a computation could be the execution of a single statement or of an entire routine. The meaning of the word "prior" in the context of a process is clear. The computations that are prior to a particular computation, e, are all the computations that precede e in the total order. It is easy to bring time into the discussion at this point, since our notion of prior has a simple temporal interpretation as well: computation e_1 is prior to computation e_2 if e_1 occurred at an earlier time.

The notion of prior is more complex in the context of a distributed system. When does a computation in one process influence the precondition of a computation in another process? Clearly time is no longer the only issue, since even if computation e_1 in one process occurs at an earlier time than computation e_2 in another process, e_1 cannot influence the precondition of e_2 if there is no communication between the processes. Hence, communication must play a central role in our understanding of how computations in different processes in a distributed system influence one another.

We view a distributed system as consisting of a set of sequential processes executing at distinct nodes, or sites, in a network. For simplicity we assume that processes communicate using datagrams. Recall that datagrams may be lost and, if not lost, may take an arbitrary amount of time to be delivered and may arrive at their destination in an order different from that in which they were sent. We define an *event* to be the execution of a datagram send or receive or a computation (not involving send or receive). Each node may have its own (local) real time clock, but these clocks are not necessarily synchronized and there is no global clock that all nodes can read.

While it might be a simple matter for a global observer of all the nodes in the system to determine the time ordering of all events, it is not at all simple for a local observer who can see only the events at a single node to do so. Even if such a local observer were to receive a datagram notifying it of each computation and the local time at which it occurred, the observer would have no way of determining the order in which those computations were performed, since the clock readings at different sites are not comparable. Thus, if an event e_1 at site A occurs at time 5 as read on A's clock and a local observer at A subsequently receives a message from site B announcing the occurrence of event e_2 at B at time 6 as read from B's clock, the observer has no way of determining which event occurred first. Since the clocks are not synchronized, B's clock might have read 6 before A's clock read 5.

Fortunately, it is not the temporal ordering of events that concerns us, but rather the flow of information and the identity of computations that can influence the outcome of a given computation. For this purpose we define the *happened-before* relation between events as follows:

Event e_1 *happened-before* event e_2 if and only if one of the following conditions holds:

1. e_1 and e_2 are events in the same process, and e_1 completed before e_2 started.
2. e_1 is a send event in one process, and e_2 is the receive event in a second process that receives the message sent by e_1.
3. There exists an event e such that e_1 *happened-before* e and e *happened-before* e_2.

Item 1 captures the information flow in a single process, item 2 captures the information flow between processes, and item 3 simply takes the transitive closure of related events. Figure 9.1 describes a distributed computation consisting of three processes, $\mathcal{P}_1$, $\mathcal{P}_2$, and $\mathcal{P}_3$. Vertical lines represent the passage of time within a single process, and events local to a process are totally ordered along each line. Diagonal lines represent messages passed between processes. For example $e_{1,2}$ and $e_{2,5}$ are the send and receive events for a particular message. Using (1) we have that $e_{1,1}$ *happened-before* $e_{1,2}$, using (2) we have that $e_{1,2}$ *happened-before* $e_{2,5}$, and using (3) we have that $e_{1,2}$ *happened-before* $e_{2,2}$. Note that $e_{1,4}$ and $e_{2,4}$ are not related by *happened-before*, and hence neither can influence the other's computation. We say that $e_{1,4}$ and $e_{2,4}$ are *concurrent*. Hence, *happened-before* is a partial ordering of the events in the system.

If C_A is the real time (local) clock at site A and e is an event at that site, we denote the time at which e occurs, as measured by C_A, as $C_A(e)$. We assume that the clock ticks fast enough so that any two successive events at a site are separated by at least one tick. Then it follows from (1) that if e_1 and e_2 are both events at A and e_1 *happened-before* e_2, $C_A(e_1) < C_A(e_2)$. Unfortunately, we cannot make a similar claim concerning events related by (2) [and hence events related by (3) as well]. For example, if e_1 is a send event at A and e_2 the corresponding receive event at B, it does not follow that $C_A(e_1) < C_B(e_2)$, since the clocks at the two sites are not necessarily synchronized. As we shall see, it is useful to have the clocks of a distributed system organized in such a way that the following condition holds for any pair of events in the system.

Clock Condition

For any events, e_1 and e_2, at (not necessarily distinct) sites A and B respectively, if e_1 *happened-before* e_2, $C_A(e_1) < C_B(e_2)$.

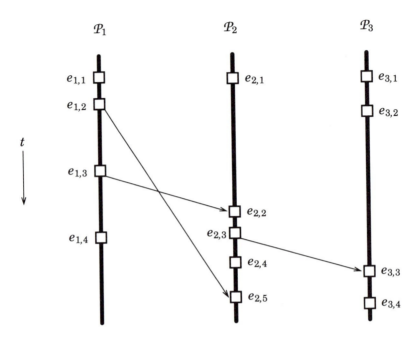

Figure 9.1: The events occurring in the three processes are related by *happened-before*. Time progresses in the downward direction.

Note that we cannot expect the converse of the clock condition to be true, since that would imply that concurrent events happen at the same time. For example, in Figure 9.1 that would lead us to require that $e_{3,1}$ and $e_{3,2}$ happen at the same time, since they are both concurrent with $e_{2,1}$.

To achieve the clock condition, we must have some control over the contents of the clocks. Since such control is not possible with real time clocks, we assume that each site is also equipped with a new kind of clock called a *logical clock*. A logical clock need not keep time in the same way as a real time clock. We can think of a logical clock as a register whose contents are monotonically increasing. Assuming e is an event that occurs at site A, and now letting $C_A(e)$ denote the time, as measured on A's logical clock, at which e occurs, we know that the clock condition will hold between any two events related by *happened-before* if the following two rules for updating a logical clock are observed:

1. In order for the clock condition to hold for two events in the same process, we require that the logical clock be advanced (tick) at least once between each pair of successive events in the same process.

2. In order for the clock condition to hold between corresponding send and receive events, e_1 at A and e_2 at B, we require that $C_A(e_1)$ be included in the message and, on receipt, C_B be set to a value that is greater than its current value and the value included in the message. Furthermore, we take $C_B(e_2)$ to be the value of C_B after this update has occurred.

The clock condition will automatically hold between any other pair of events related by *happened-before* as a result of these two rules.

It is a simple matter to use logical clocks to place a total (as contrasted with a partial) ordering on events that is consistent with *happened-before*. Ordering events in accordance with the value of their local logical clock at the time they occur is almost sufficient, but leaves open the possibility that (concurrent) events at different sites might be assigned the same value. To break such ties, we assume that each site has been statically assigned a unique site identifier, which we append (as the low order bits) to the value of the local logical clock to form a timestamp for the event. Timestamps are unique and the total order they impose on the events in the system is an extension of the *happened-before* partial order. We denote that total order by $\Rightarrow$. As we shall see in the next section, this total order can be useful in developing distributed algorithms.

9.2   Synchronization in a Distributed System

A central problem in distributed systems is that of synchronization: how do we ensure that the computations, or *actions*, at the various sites occur in an acceptable order? For example, to implement distributed mutual exclusion, we must guarantee that the actions within a critical section executed at one site are not interleaved with the actions within a critical section at another. As another example, consider a replicated database with processes at each site attempting to update their local copy of a data item. To ensure that all copies remain identical, it is necessary that each site learn of updates initiated at all other sites and that all sites apply these updates to their local copies in the same order.

A centralized system makes use of a shared memory. Concurrent processes communicate and synchronize using shared variables (perhaps semaphores). We can view the accesses to these shared variables as operations that perform some transformation on the variable's state. Each operation is atomic and, we assume, deterministic. Synchronization results from the fact that operations are totally ordered. Each operation sees the current state, and therefore its effect is a function of all prior operations invoked by all processes. For example, the shared memory might simply contain a semaphore with operations P and V and a state that reflects the difference between the total number of V operations and the total number of P operations that have been performed. Alternatively, the shared memory might contain (the unique copy of) an arbitrary database, and each operation might perform some update on the database.

We can take a more abstract view of this same situation, which eliminates issues related to the semantics of particular data items, by modeling the data item with a *state machine*. A state machine has a set of states (possibly infinite) to account for all possible values of an object, a set of input commands (corresponding to the operations), and a transition function that determines the new state based on the command to be executed and the current state (since the operations are deterministic, state transitions can be modeled by functions).

In a distributed environment, shared memory cannot be used to synchronize accesses to a data item. One approach to achieving synchronization is to replicate the state machine at all sites and broadcast each command invoked by a process at a particular site to all other sites. If all sites execute all commands (those that have been invoked locally as well as those invoked remotely) in the same sequence, then (since the commands are deterministic) each site mimics the behavior of the centralized system and synchronization can be achieved: when a command is executed at a site the state of the local state machine is the result of the execution of all prior commands at all other sites.

The task, then, is to ensure that the same sequence of commands is executed at all sites. We assume the availability of an atomic broadcast facility. A broadcast facility is *atomic* if it guarantees that either all sites receive a broadcast message or none do. If we assume that broadcast is atomic, all sites will come to know of each command that has been requested in the net. We further assume ordered delivery: the commands broadcast by a particular site arrive at every other site in the sequence in which they were broadcast. Hence, we have assumed (the equivalent of) virtual circuit communication between each broadcaster/receiver pair. A problem, however, remains. Commands broadcast from sites A and B might arrive at site C in an order different from the order in which they arrive at site D. Hence, if a site simply executes commands in the order in which they arrive, we cannot guarantee the same ordering at all sites.

To overcome this problem, we can require that sites timestamp all commands (using logical clocks as described in the last section) and then broadcast the timestamped commands to all other sites. We further require that each site invoke commands in timestamp order, rather than in the order in which they are received. Since timestamps are guaranteed to be unique, the sequence of executed commands will be the same at all sites. The only remaining issue is to determine how a site will know when to invoke a particular command with timestamp, TS, since it might well receive, at a later time, a command with a timestamp smaller than TS. However, if the site waits until it has received a message from every other site with a timestamp larger than TS, then, under the assumption of ordered delivery, it cannot receive a subsequent message containing a command with a timestamp smaller than TS. We say that a message (in this case a command) is *fully acknowledged* when a message with a larger timestamp has been received from every other site. Thus, distributed synchronization is achieved if we require that commands be executed in time-stamp order and only after they are fully acknowledged. Note, however, that for this technique to work, we must make the additional assumption that sites do not fail, since otherwise commands will never become fully acknowledged.

As a specific example, consider the problem of guaranteeing mutually exclusive access to some resource shared by the processes of a distributed system. In Chapter 1 we discussed the mutual exclusion problem and its role in organizing the activities of a set of concurrent processes. The standard solutions to the problem can be complex and involve the use of shared variables. We discussed the (shared) semaphore as a basic synchronizing mechanism and its use in providing mutual exclusion. Consider now the problem of a set of processes in a distributed system (with no shared memory) which, from time to time, wish to acquire mutually exclusive access to some resource. Centralized solutions no longer apply, and we want to avoid solutions that simulate their structure – solutions in which a central process in the net receives all request and release messages and controls access to the resource. Such solutions might perform poorly, since all requests must be funneled through a single site, and are subject to failure if the site crashes.

In addition to guaranteeing mutually exclusive access to the resource, we impose the requirement that requests be granted in some specified order. Unfortunately, with no global observer and only unsynchronized clocks, it is difficult to enforce an ordering that corresponds to real time. Hence, we settle for the ordering $\Rightarrow$, which means that concurrent requests might not be satisfied in the temporal order in which they are made, but if request r_1 *happened-before* request r_2, r_1 will be granted the resource first. It is important to recognize that this is not a simple requirement to satisfy, even if a centralized solution is implemented. We define a request to be the event in which a process sends a message requesting the resource to a central site. Suppose process $\mathcal{P}_1$ sends a message, M, to $\mathcal{P}_2$ after making request r_1, and that $\mathcal{P}_2$ makes request r_2 after receiving M. Then r_1 *happened-before* r_2, but since message delays in the net are unpredictable, r_2 might arrive at the central site before r_1.

We can use the model described above to develop a distributed (as contrasted with centralized) solution to the mutual exclusion problem that provides access to the resource in *happened-before* order. As in the shared memory case, we assume that a process alternates between critical and noncritical sections. Before entering a critical section, it requests the resource and waits until the resource is granted. On leaving a critical section, it releases the resource. The algorithm utilizes atomic broadcast as well as unicast messages: request and release events are now broadcast messages to all other processes; a process receiving a request unicasts an acknowledgment to the requestor. Each process maintains a queue that records requests in timestamp order. Note that concurrently executed requests do not necessarily arrive in timestamp order and hence may have to be inserted into the queue. When a request message is received, it is placed in the queue and acknowledged. When a release message is received, the corresponding request is deleted from the queue. For uniformity, we assume that the requestor enters its own request in its queue and removes it when it releases the resource. Suppose process P_i requests the resource by broadcasting a request message with timestamp TS_i. P_i can access the resource when (1) its request has reached the head of its queue and (2) that request is fully acknowledged.

The correctness of the algorithm follows from the fact that, given our assumption of ordered message arrival, once a process receives a message from process P_j with timestamp TS_j, it knows that it will not receive a message from P_j with a smaller timestamp. Hence, when P_i discovers that its request is fully acknowledged, it knows that no requests with smaller timestamps will subsequently arrive. If, in addition, its request is at the head of its queue, all previous accesses to the resource must have been completed. It can therefore access the resource, since its request is next in the $\Rightarrow$ order. Finally, note that a request is guaranteed to ultimately become fully acknowledged, since each process is obliged to acknowledge any request it receives.

9.3   Reliable Communication

Our treatment of communication has focused on individual exchanges of messages and the assertions that can be made if communication is successful. We assumed that messages were delivered reliably. Unfortunately, unreliable communication is a fact of life in distributed systems. In this section we briefly review a few mechanisms for providing reliable service and then show how the axiomatic techniques introduced in earlier chapters can be extended to describe them. A complete description of protocols for achieving reliable communication is more properly the subject of an entire book devoted to communication systems.

Error detecting and correcting codes are commonly used at the lowest levels of a communication system to deal with messages that have been corrupted during transmission. In both cases redundant bits are included in a message. Error correction requires significantly more redundancy than error detection, since for error correction the redundant bits must enable the receiver to reconstruct the message. Of the two, error detecting codes have proven most useful for two reasons. First, since errors occur infrequently, the cost of requesting retransmission when an error is detected is generally small compared with the cost of the redundancy necessary for error correction in each message sent. Second, transmission errors tend to occur in bursts. Hence, when a message is corrupted, it is likely to have many erroneous bits. The number of redundant bits necessary to correct multiple bit errors goes up rapidly with the number of bits to be corrected. Hence, error correction is generally uneconomical when retransmission is possible.

The general strategy, then, is to use an error detecting code – for example, a cyclic redundancy check – to detect corrupted messages and discard them. Such messages can be categorized as lost, since they are not even seen at any but the lowest levels of the system. Thus, we restrict our attention to channels that fail by losing messages.

In Chapter 7 we distinguished between communication using datagrams and communication using virtual circuits. The issues are somewhat different for lost messages in these two types of communication.

We modeled datagram communication using two auxiliary variables, σ_P and ρ_P, the multisets of datagrams sent to and received by process P. The model can easily be extended to encompass lost datagrams. A datagram in σ_P that is lost is never added to ρ_P. If, when P executes a receive, the only elements of $\sigma_P \ominus \rho_P$ are lost datagrams, P simply waits until a new datagram (which is not to be lost) is sent (inserted in σ_P). We must modify the operational semantics to allow a receiver to wait indefinitely if $\sigma_P \ominus \rho_P$ is not empty but, since the Datagram Receive Axiom says nothing about termination (*i.e.*, it does not require that the receive terminate when $\sigma_P \ominus \rho_P \neq \Phi$), the formal semantics of the datagram send and receive remains unchanged.

A virtual circuit provides for the delivery of messages in the order in which they are sent. While virtual circuits (in contrast to datagrams) are designed to be reliable, a physical transmission medium (*e.g.*, a wire or the atmosphere) can be regarded as a virtual circuit that occasionally loses messages. The state of a lossy virtual circuit, V, can again be represented by a pair of auxiliary variables, but the definitions have to be modified somewhat. σ_V is still the sequence of all messages sent over V. We redefine ρ_V to be the sequence of all messages received or lost on V. We assume that messages are either received or lost in the order in which they were sent. Thus, in the model, at the time message M is received, the sequence of messages, β, that precede M in σ_V (*i.e.*, were sent at an earlier time) and that have not yet been received or lost (*i.e.*, are not yet in ρ_V) is considered to have been lost. One effect of receiving M is to append the sequence $\beta \circ <M>$ to ρ_V. In other words, if, before M is received,

$$\sigma_V = \alpha \circ \beta \circ <M> \circ \gamma$$

and

$$\rho_V = \alpha$$

then afterwards σ_V is unchanged and

$$\rho_V = \alpha \circ \beta \circ <M>$$

The messages in β have been lost.

Using this model, we can apply to a lossy virtual circuit the Virtual Circuit Axiom, the Virtual Circuit Send Axiom, and the Virtual Circuit Receive Axiom given in Chapter 7 for an ideal virtual circuit, but the satisfaction condition becomes the following:

Proof Obligations for Satisfaction for Receive over Lossy Virtual Circuit

For each virtual circuit receive

$$\{P\} \ \mathbf{receive_{lc}} \ \bar{v} \ \mathbf{from} \ V \ \{W\}$$

show that

$$[P \wedge ((\sigma_V - \rho_V) \neq \lambda) \wedge ((\beta \circ < M >) \in \mathit{prefix}(\sigma_V - \rho_V))] \Rightarrow W_{M, \ \rho_V \ \circ \ \beta \ \circ \ <M>}^{\bar{v}, \ \rho_V} \quad (9.1)$$

We use the subscript lc to denote a lossy virtual circuit. The proof obligations for interference freedom must be modified in a similar fashion.

The problem of achieving reliable communication over a lossy virtual circuit can be stated as follows. We assume the existence of a pair of processes, *Sender* and *Receiver*, connected by a lossy virtual circuit. *Sender* has an infinite sequence, *Seq*, of values that it wants to transmit to *Receiver*. It encapsulates each value in a message that it sends over the circuit. *Receiver* may or may not deliver the value in the message that it receives to the application at the receiver site depending on *Receiver*'s state. We require that a solution to the problem satisfy two conditions: (1) at any time, the sequence of values delivered by *Receiver* must be a prefix of *Seq* (this is a safety property) and (2) every value sent is eventually delivered (this is a liveness property). *Sender* and *Receiver* execute a protocol that compensates for message loss by retransmitting messages. To prove (2), we must rule out a channel that loses all messages. For example, we might assume that if an infinite number of messages are sent, an infinite number must be (correctly) delivered.

An acknowledgment scheme can be used to cause retransmission. In a negative acknowledgment system, the receiver sends a negative acknowledgment message (*NAK*) to the sender, essentially requesting retransmission, if it detects that a message has been lost (*e.g.*, if it discards a corrupted message). In a positive acknowledgment system, the receiver sends a positive acknowledgment message (*ACK*) for each correct message received (and does not respond to corrupted messages). The sender uses a timeout mechanism to detect the absence of an *ACK* and then retransmits.

The introduction of acknowledgments, unfortunately, introduces a new problem: they can be lost as well. Consider a positive acknowledgment system. Since the loss of an *ACK* results in retransmission, a duplicate message will be sent. The receiver must have a mechanism for detecting duplicates so that they can be filtered out of the sequence delivered to the application at the receiver site (*i.e.*, the sequence of messages accepted). Detection is generally done with sequence numbers. The sender and receiver initialize themselves with a starting sequence number. The sender includes in each message a sequence number. A duplicate message contains the same sequence number as the original; otherwise the sequence number in a message is one greater than the sequence number assigned to the last original message sent. The

receiver records the sequence number of the next message it expects and re-
jects a message – even though it has been correctly received – if its sequence
number is not equal to that quantity. Since only a finite number of bits, N,
can be allocated to a sequence number, it is necessary to increment sequence
numbers modulo 2^N. Care must be taken in the choice of N to avoid confusion
due to the reuse of sequence numbers.

There are two distinct physical situations that must be considered in this
context. If the sender and receiver are directly connected, the receiver will
receive the messages in the order sent: one message cannot overtake another
during transmission. This is the situation described by the lossy virtual circuit
(9.1). In the following subsection we give a formal model that can be used to
analyze a protocol for communicating over a lossy circuit. Overtaking can
occur when the sender and receiver are not directly connected and messages
can travel different routes from sender to receiver. Overtaking introduces new
problems, which we discuss later.

9.3.1   Example – The Stop-and-Wait Protocol*

Figure 9.2 shows the main loop on the sender and receiver sides of a simple
protocol that uses positive acknowledgments and sequence numbers to achieve
reliable communication. This protocol is called a *stop-and-wait* protocol because the sender waits for an acknowledgment for one message before sending
the next. [It is also called the *alternating bit protocol* because the sequence
numbers for consecutive (original) messages alternate between 1 and 0.] The
sender-to-receiver virtual circuit is V, and the receiver-to-sender virtual circuit
is V'.

We assume that a message is of type *mess*, where *mess* is a record having
an *info* field, which contains the transmitted value, and a *seq* field, which contains a sequence number. The next value to be transmitted is returned by the
function *get_next_value*. Generally, a *type* field is also needed to distinguish
messages from acknowledgments, but is not used here, since, for simplicity,
we have assumed unidirectional (*simplex*) communication and hence only messages flow over V and only acknowledgments over V'.

We have used a delay alternative in the sender to implement timeout. The
sender waits T seconds after sending a message, M_1, to receive its acknowledgment, A_1. If timeout occurs, the sender assumes that either M_1 or A_1 has been
lost and performs another iteration of the loop, sending a duplicate of M_1. If A_1
was lost, the receiver will (assuming no transmission errors) receive M_1 twice.
It will recognize the copy, because it has the wrong sequence number, and can
simply discard it. The receiver sends a duplicate of A_1, since it knows that the
original might have been lost. Suppose neither (the original of) M_1 nor A_1 is
lost, but timeout occurs because A_1 arrives too late, as shown in Figure 9.3.
Then a copy of M_1 will be sent, and the receiver will respond with a copy of
A_1. If an acknowledgment does not identify the message it is acknowledging,
a new problem arises. The sender can send the next message, M_2, as soon as

Sender ::
  var
    s : *mess*; *s_ack* : *acknowledgment*;
    sndr_seq : *integer* := 0;
  begin
    s.seq, s.info := *sndr_seq, get_next_value*();
    send$_{lc}$ *s* **to** *V*;
    do *true* →
      if receive$_{lc}$ *s_ack* **from** *V'* →
        if *s_ack.seq* = *sndr_seq* →
          begin
            sndr_seq := (*sndr_seq* + 1) **mod** 2;
            s.seq, s.info := *sndr_seq, get_next_value*();
            send$_{lc}$ *s* **to** *V*;
          end;
        [] *s_ack.seq* ≠ *sndr_seq* → **send**$_{lc}$ *s* **to** *V*;
        fi;
      [] **delay** *T*;
        send$_{lc}$ *s* **to** *V*;
      fi;
    od;
  end;

Receiver ::
  var
    r : *mess*; *r_ack* : *acknowledgment*;
    rec_seq : *integer* := 0;
  begin
    do *true* →
      receive$_{lc}$ *r* **from** *V*;
      if *r.seq* = *rec_seq* →
        begin
          ···   −− pass *r.info* to application;
          r_ack.seq := *rec_seq*;
          rec_seq := (*rec_seq* + 1) **mod** 2;
          send$_{lc}$ *r_ack* **to** *V'*;
        end;
      [] *r.seq* ≠ *rec_seq* → **send**$_{lc}$ *r_ack* **to** *V'*;
      fi;
    od;
  end;

Figure 9.2: The stop-and-wait protocol for reliably transmitting data over a lossy virtual circuit.

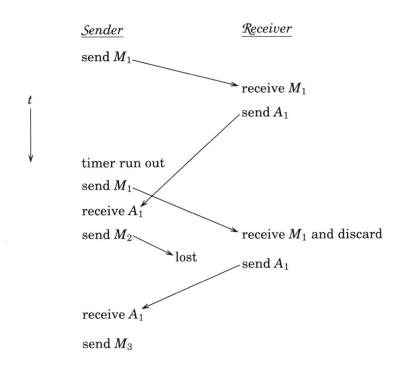

Figure 9.3: A situation that might arise if the timer runs out too quickly and an acknowledgment does not identify the message being acknowledged.

the original acknowledgment of M_1 arrives, since it knows that M_1 has been received. It has no way of knowing how to interpret the copy of A_1, however. If an acknowledgment does not identify the message it is acknowledging, the sender cannot be sure if the copy is an acknowledgment of the duplicate of M_1 (as it happens to be in the figure) or an acknowledgment of M_2 (if it happened to be the case that M_1, its copy, or one of the acknowledgments was lost). In the figure the sender makes the second choice and overwrites M_2 with the next message, M_3. If M_2 is lost in transmission, as shown in the figure, the protocol fails. This situation can be avoided if acknowledgments contain the sequence number of the message being acknowledged. Hence, in Figure 9.2 an acknowledgment is of type record and has a *seq* field containing a sequence number.

One way to develop a proof of the stop-and-wait protocol is to first consider a modified protocol in which sequence numbers have unbounded size (*i.e.,* eliminate modulo 2 arithmetic in Figure 9.2) and then later demonstrate that a one-bit sequence number is sufficient. We do not give such a proof here, but indicate invariants that can be used. (Some guidance in constructing such a proof can be found in the exercises at the end of the chapter.)

We describe the state of V with auxiliary variables σ and ρ, and V' with auxiliary variables σ' and ρ', and denote the ith message and its acknowledgment by M_i and A_i, respectively. Since we initially allow arbitrary size sequence numbers, i is also the sequence number of the message. Let α_i and μ_i denote the sequences $< A_0^+, A_1^+, \ldots, A_i^+ >$ and $< M_0^+, M_1^+, \ldots, M_i^+ >$, respectively, where A_j^+ and M_j^+ represent sequences consisting of one or more repetitions of the jth acknowledgment and message respectively and α_{-1} and μ_{-1} denote the empty sequence. We can demonstrate that the following assertion is a program invariant of the receiver:

$$I_r : ((\exists j)\, \sigma' = \alpha_j) \wedge ((\forall i)(A_i \in \sigma') \Rightarrow (M_i \in \rho)) \tag{9.2}$$

I_r states that σ' is a sequence having the form α_j for some value of j, and that an acknowledgment of M_i will not be sent by the receiver until after M_i has been received or lost. Furthermore, since the sender does not modify either σ' or ρ, I_r is a program invariant of the concurrent program consisting of both the sender and the receiver.

I_r has a form that allows it to be used to pass a predicate from the proof of the receiver to the proof of the sender. Thus, if in the sender we can demonstrate that $M_j \notin \sigma$, it follows from the Virtual Circuit Axiom that $M_j \notin \rho$, and using I_r we conclude that $A_j \notin \sigma'$.

In a symmetric fashion, we can show that the assertion

$$I_s : ((\exists j)\, \sigma = \mu_j) \wedge ((\forall i)(M_{i+1} \in \sigma) \Rightarrow (A_i \in \rho')) \tag{9.3}$$

which describes the state of variables that can be modified by the sender, is a program invariant of the concurrent program.

Since ρ does not differentiate between messages lost and received, it is convenient to introduce an auxiliary variable, δ, which records the sequence of messages delivered by the receiver to the application, and the notation $\bar{\rho}$ to denote the sequence ρ with all duplicate elements deleted. Then, using the above invariants, we can demonstrate that the assertion $\delta = \bar{\rho}$ is a loop invariant of the receiver. This assertion, together with the Virtual Circuit Axiom, yields the desired safety result. The desired liveness result rests on the assumption that if a message or acknowledgment is sent enough times, it will be received.

Since only a finite number of bits can be allocated to a sequence number, sequence numbers must be allowed to wrap around. In Figure 9.2, only the numbers 0 and 1 are used. To demonstrate that this is sufficient, it can be shown that a precondition of the statement in the sender's loop that sends a new message (*i.e.*, a message that has never been sent before) is $(\sigma - \rho) = M_{sndr\_seq-1}^*$ and a precondition to the statement in the receiver's loop that sends a new acknowledgment is $(\sigma' - \rho') = A_{rec\_seq-2}^*$, where M_j^* and A_j^* represent sequences containing zero or more repetitions of the jth message and acknowledgment, respectively, and A_{-1} is the null element. It follows that each channel never has more than two distinct (and successive) messages or acknowledgments pending and that these can be distinguished by a single bit.

The overhead of acknowledgment messages can be reduced when data is allowed to flow in both directions (*duplex* transmission). In that case, each data message is augmented with an acknowledgment field. The acknowledgment field of a data message in one direction contains the sequence number of the last received message in the other. The acknowledgment is said to be *piggybacked* on the data. Acknowledgment messages cannot be completely eliminated, however, since they are needed if there is insufficient reverse traffic.

The stop-and-wait protocol is simple but inefficient, since it allows only one message to be in transit at a time. Efficiency can be improved through the use of a *sliding window* protocol, in which a sequence of messages can be sent before the first is acknowledged. As with the stop-and-wait protocol, a message must be retained at the sender site until it is acknowledged, since it might have to be retransmitted. Hence, the sender maintains an array of buffers in which it stores each unacknowledged message.

To allow multiple unacknowledged messages, however, we must use additional sequence numbers, since other than assuming that errors are detectable, we make no assumptions about the number of messages that might be corrupted. For example, if, as in Figure 9.2, only two sequence numbers were used, the loss of two consecutive messages in the sequence of unacknowledged messages would not be detected. Since only a finite number, N, of bits can be allocated in a message, a sequence number is a number modulo 2^N. Acknowledgments need not be sent for each received message. Instead, an acknowledgment for a message with sequence number i implicitly serves to acknowledge all unacknowledged messages with smaller sequence numbers.

A lower bound on N is determined by the number of unacknowledged messages that are allowed. If the number of unacknowledged messages is greater than the number of distinct sequence numbers, a particular sequence number must be associated with more than one unacknowledged message and, as a result, the meaning of an acknowledgment containing that sequence number is ambiguous. Even if the number of unacknowledged messages is equal to the number of distinct sequence numbers, an ambiguous situation can still arise. An entire cycle of messages [i.e., messages numbered i through $(i-1)$ mod 2^N] can be dispatched before the first is acknowledged. The loss of the cycle could not be detected, since the same sequence number [$(i-1)$ mod 2^N] would be piggybacked onto reverse traffic whether the entire cycle was received or lost. In general, the number of distinct sequence numbers must be at least one greater than the number of unacknowledged messages. Thus, in the stop-and-wait protocol, two sequence numbers (0 and 1) are used.

If the sender and receiver are not directly connected, overtaking can occur and a message might appear at the receiver out of sequence. For example, a message, M, might be delayed in the network, and a duplicate might eventually be sent and acknowledged. At some future time, M might arrive at the receiver, and the problem is to distinguish it from a later message in the sequence (from the same sender) with the same sequence number. This can be done by limiting the length of time during which a message can be allowed to travel in the network. For example, the sender might store the (real) time at which a message is sent in the message. A (possibly intermediate) receiving site destroys the message if it is too old. The rate at which a sending site can produce new messages is similarly limited so that a message carrying a particular sequence number will be destroyed before that number is reused by the sender. Hence, two messages with the same sequence number from the same sender are never in transit at the same time. For a site to determine the age of a message it receives, however, it must compare the contents of its (local) clock with the time stored in the message. If the comparison is to be meaningful, synchronization between the sender's and the receiver's real time clock is required.

9.3.2 Broadcast

We have already noted the usefulness of broadcast in achieving distributed synchronization. A broadcast, or more generally a multicast, facility plays an important role when a group of processes cooperate in the performance of some task. It permits a process in the group to communicate a message to all other group members. For example, broadcast is an integral part of systems involving replication, where data or servers are replicated at different sites to enhance availability or performance. Similarly, complex tasks may be subdivided and parceled out to a set of workers who all must be aware of common status information.

A frequent requirement of broadcast communication is atomicity: either all group members receive a broadcast message or none do. For example, we have seen that such a requirement is needed in an algorithm for achieving distributed synchronization. (It might not, on the other hand, be required in a distributed search of a solution space, where a broadcast message simply reports on the current best solution to some problem.) As with unicast communication, the assurance that each member of a group has received the broadcast message generally involves the use of acknowledgments. The acknowledgment can be a direct response from each receiver, or, as we shall see when we discuss gossip messages, it can be indirect.

Another aspect of broadcast communication concerns the order in which broadcast messages are received. For example, if two broadcast messages are sent to a group, do all group members receive them in the same order? Note that this feature goes beyond the ordered delivery provided by a virtual circuit connection, since the broadcast messages may have different sources. The utility of a common ordering was illustrated in our discussion of distributed synchronization. There the goal is to act on broadcast messages in timestamp order. The technique of waiting until a message is fully acknowledged before acting on it is used to compensate for the fact that, although broadcast messages from a single site might arrive in the order sent, broadcast messages from different sites need not arrive at all sites in the same order. We make a distinction between the time at which a message arrives at a site and the (later) time at which the message is made available – the time it is delivered to or received by the application at that site. The broadcast layer of a hierarchically structured communication protocol might be made responsible for delivering broadcast messages that arrive at a site to the destination application at that site in a common order. In that case, the broadcast message is not delivered to the next higher level until it is fully acknowledged.

In general, a broadcast protocol providing a common delivery order need not be constrained as to what the order is to be as long as the order is the same at all sites. For example, if $M1$ and $M2$ are messages broadcast from two distinct sites, the broadcast layer is required to deliver $M1$ before $M2$ at all sites or vice versa. The requirement of a common delivery order is therefore less restrictive than the requirement of the distributed synchronization example, where a particular (timestamp) order was specified.

Instead of requiring a common order at all sites, one might require an ordering that is consistent with the *happened-before* order. Suppose e_1 and e_2 are events, other than communication events, that occurred at particular sites in a network and that information about them is of interest to all other sites. The information describing event e – the information to be broadcast – is contained in an *event record*, denoted $rec(e)$. If e_1 *happened-before* e_2, all sites should receive $rec(e_1)$ before receiving $rec(e_2)$. If, however, e_1 and e_2 are concurrent, no restriction is placed on the order of delivery at different sites. $rec(e_1)$ might be received first at one site and $rec(e_2)$ first at another. Such a requirement is referred to as a *causal* ordering. Thus, a broadcast protocol that ensures a common delivery order does not necessarily provide a causal ordering and one that provides a causal ordering does not necessarily provide a common ordering.

9.3.3 Gossip*

From the sender's viewpoint, broadcast can be synchronous or asynchronous: the sender might or might not be forced to wait until all group members have received the message. One drawback of synchronous broadcast is that it might incur substantial delays. Instead of having to wait for a single acknowledgment, the sender must wait for multiple acknowledgments.

Gossip messages have been proposed as a low level mechanism for implementing an asynchronous atomic broadcast facility with a causal order of delivery. Gossip messages are exchanged between neighboring sites in background at arbitrary times (unsynchronized with the events in the system about which information is to be broadcast[1]) for the purpose of disseminating broad-

---

[1]The sending or receipt of a gossip message is not an event about which information is to be

cast information. We assume that gossip messages might be lost, duplicated, or arrive in an order different from that in which they were sent. Nevertheless, we require that event records be delivered in causal order.

We assume that site s_i maintains a *record set*, R_i, and say that s_i *knows about* event e when $rec(e)$ is placed in R_i. If e occurs at s_i and information about e is to be broadcast, $rec(e)$ is placed in R_i immediately after e occurs. We assume that once s_i knows about e, it knows about e at all future times. Each gossip message contains a set of event records that the sender of that message knows about. When a gossip message from s_j arrives at s_i, the event records it contains are added (using set union) to R_i. Hence, s_i comes to know about events that are known to s_j.

A simple way of guaranteeing delivery in causal order, which we refer to as the *send all* protocol, is for s_i to include R_i in every gossip message it sends. To see that this method works, observe that if e_i occurred at s_i and e_1 *happened-before* e_2, then $rec(e_1)$ must have been in R_2 before the occurrence of e_2. [Assuming s_1 and s_2 are distinct sites, the only way that e_1 could have *happened-before* e_2 is if there was some chain of gossip messages starting at s_1 after the occurrence of e_1 and ending at s_2 before the occurrence of e_2. With the send all protocol, each message in the chain must contain $rec(e_1)$.] Hence, any gossip message sent by s_2 containing $rec(e_2)$ will also contain $rec(e_1)$. It follows that any gossip message sent by any sender containing $rec(e_2)$ will also contain $rec(e_1)$, and therefore, if a site has received $rec(e_2)$, it must also have received $rec(e_1)$. Thus, any gossip message that contains $rec(e)$ also contains an event record for all events that *happened-before e*.

The only remaining issue is how a receiving site delivers event records to an application at the site in causal order. We assume that each site has a logical clock that is incremented whenever an event occurs at the site and that events are timestamped as described in Section 9.1. The timestamp of event e is stored in $rec(e).ts$, with the high order, logical clock portion stored in $rec(e).ts.lc$ and the low order, site identification portion stored in $rec(e).ts.id$. To deliver records to an application in an order consistent with causal order, s_i maintains the following condition: when $rec(e)$ is delivered, all records, $rec(e')$, in R_i satisfying $rec(e).ts > rec(e').ts$ have already been delivered. This condition does not guarantee that all records are delivered in timestamp order. Undelivered records in R_i are delivered in timestamp order. Records arriving later are delivered later and might have smaller timestamps. If $rec(e)$ is delivered before $rec(e')$ and $rec(e).ts > rec(e').ts$, then e and e' are concurrent.

If the network is strongly connected and each site continually sends gossip messages to all its neighbors, atomic broadcast is guaranteed: all sites learn of all broadcast events (as before, we rule out channels that lose all messages).

The send all protocol is clearly impractical, since the size of gossip messages and record sets increases without bound. One way to decrease the required storage and message size is for each site to maintain information about the

---

broadcast.

knowledge state of other sites. If a site can place a lower bound on what a neighboring site knows about events that have happened, it can avoid including certain event records in the next gossip message it sends to that site. Furthermore, when s_i is certain that all other sites know about an event, it can delete the event record from its record set, since it need never send that record again (s_i, however, still knows about the event).

The information that s_i maintains about the knowledge state of other sites is contained in its *time table*, T_i, an N by N array, where N is the number of sites in the network. $T_i[i, i]$ is a logical clock (it is incremented each time an event occurs at s_i and its value may be increased when a gossip message arrives). When e occurs at s_i, $T_i[i, i]$ is assigned to $rec(e).ts.lc$. We will show that the algorithm maintains the following invariant.

Time Table Invariant

If $T_i[j, k] = t$, then s_i can place the following lower bound on what s_j knows: s_j knows about all events, e, satisfying $rec(e).ts.id = k$ (i.e., e happened at s_k) and $rec(e).ts.lc \leq t$ (i.e., e happened at a time less than or equal to t as measured on s_k's clock).

It would be imprecise to restate the Time Table Invariant as "If $T_i[j, k] = t$, then s_i knows that s_j knows about all events ... ", since our definition of "know" is limited to the contents of R_i. However, assuming that the reader understands the Time Table Invariant, we use "know" in this loose sense.

Note that gossip messages provide a generalized (indirect) acknowledgment mechanism. If event e happened at s_i at time t (as measured on s_i's clock), s_i can assume that s_j knows about e when $T_i[j, i] \geq t$.

Assuming the Time Table Invariant is true, it follows that

1. When s_i sends a gossip message to s_j it need not include any event record, $rec(e)$, satisfying $rec(e).ts.id = k$ and $rec(e).ts.lc \leq T_i[j, k]$ (if s_i knows that s_j knows about e, s_i need not include $rec(e)$ in any gossip message it subsequently sends to s_j).

2. Assuming $rec(e).ts.id = k$, s_i can delete $rec(e)$ from R_i if

$$((\forall j) \ (1 \leq j \leq N) \Rightarrow (rec(e).ts.lc \leq T_i[j, k]))$$

(if s_i knows that all sites know about e, s_i need not include $rec(e)$ in any gossip message it subsequently sends.)

We first give an algorithm that each site can use to keep its time table current and then show that the algorithm maintains the Time Table Invariant. Each site includes a current snapshot of its time table in each gossip message it sends. Let TT_j be the snapshot of s_j's time table, T_j, contained in a gossip message that s_i receives from s_j, and let RR_j be the set of event records in the message. The algorithm executed by s_i on receipt of the message is as follows:

Gossip Message Receive Algorithm

1. Assign $R_i \cup RR_j$ to R_i. (Note that timestamps are unique, so duplicate event records can be detected and deleted.)

2. Assign $max(T_i[i, i], TT_j[j, j])$ to $T_i[i, i]$.

3. For each q between 1 and N, assign $max(T_i[i, q], TT_j[j, q])$ to $T_i[i, q]$.

4. For each r between 1 and N such that $r \neq i$ and each q between 1 and N, assign $max(T_i[r, q], TT_j[r, q])$ to $T_i[r, q]$.

Assuming the Time Table Invariant is true, after step 1 s_i knows about all events that s_j knew about when it sent the message. Step 2 corresponds to the second rule for updating a logical clock. Step 3 reflects s_i's new knowledge by updating the ith row of T_i. Step 4 updates T_i with information derived from T_j concerning the knowledge status of other sites.

Assume that all entries in all time tables are initially 0. We use an induction argument to demonstrate the invariance of the following inequality:

$$T_k[k, k] \geq T_i[j, k], \quad 1 \leq i, j, k \leq N \tag{9.4}$$

It is true initially. Assume it is true at some time. The only actions that change values in a time table are the occurrence of an event and the receipt of a gossip message. If the next action is the occurrence of an event, (9.4) continues to hold, since the only effect is to increment $T_k[k, k]$ for some k. Assume that the next action is the receipt by s_i of a gossip message from s_j containing TT_j. Step 2 of the receive algorithm serves only to increase $T_i[i, i]$ and hence cannot cause a violation of (9.4). The new values of elements in the kth column of T_i assigned in steps 3 and 4 are values that existed in the kth column of T_i before the execution of the algorithm or values in the kth column of TT_j. By the inductive assumption,

$$T_k[k, k] \geq TT_j[r, k], \quad 1 \leq j, r, k \leq N$$

(since TT_j is a snapshot of T_j), and before the execution of the algorithm,

$$T_k[k, k] \geq T_i[j, k], \quad 1 \leq i, j, k \leq N$$

Hence, (9.4) continues to hold after the action.

We use an inductive argument to demonstrate that the Time Table Invariant is maintained. The invariant holds for T_i when the system is initialized. Assume it is true at some time. We must demonstrate that it remains true after the next action. Once again, the only actions that can affect its truth are the occurrence of an event and the receipt of a gossip message. If an event, e, happens at s_k, $k \neq i$, the invariant remains true of T_i, since $rec(e).ts.lc$ is assigned the incremented value of $T_k[k, k]$ and therefore, from (9.4), $rec(e).ts.lc > T_i[j, k]$ (the event occurred at s_k, and no other site knows about it). If e happens at s_i,

$T_i[i, i]$ is incremented and $rec(e)$ is stored in R_i; hence the invariant remains true of T_i (the event occurred at s_i, and s_i knows about it).

Suppose the next action is the receipt by s_i of a gossip message sent by s_j. Since, by the inductive assumption, the Time Table Invariant was true of T_j at the time the message was sent, no record of an event, e, known to s_j but not known to s_i at that time is omitted from RR_j. Hence, after step 1 of the Gossip Message Receive Algorithm, s_i knows of every event s_j knew about. Step 2 does not cause a violation of the invariant: since no new events have happened at s_i, increasing $T_i[i, i]$ does not imply a change to s_i's knowledge state. When the message was sent s_j knew of all events that happened at s_q up to time $TT_j[j, q]$ (as measured on s_q's clock). Since s_i now knows of all these events, step 3 maintains the invariant for the new value of row i of T_i. Similarly, by the inductive assumption, when the message was sent, s_r knew of all events that had occurred at s_q up to time $TT_j[r, q]$ (as measured on s_q's clock). Hence, the invariant holds for row r of T_i after the execution of step 4.

Note that the availability of a time table does more than simply improve the efficiency of the send all protocol. A site can use information about the knowledge state of other sites to synchronize its actions. Although the algorithm uses less message capacity than the send all protocol, it requires that a time table be sent in each gossip message. Since a time table has N^2 entries, significant communication resources may be required. Optimizations, however, are possible (see Bibliographic Notes).

9.4 Reliable Storage

A failure can cause the loss of the contents of some portion of memory. Storing information redundantly permits recovery from such a loss. The algorithm we now discuss for storing redundant information creates the abstraction of what has come to be called stable storage. A *stable storage* device is one whose contents are preserved despite failures. Stable storage is an abstraction that does not exist in the real world of fires and volcanos. However, we can implement stable storage approximately – usually using mass storage devices, such as disks and tapes – to protect information from the most common failures. We refer to these failures as *errors* and those failures from which our implementation provides no protection as *disasters*. Our goal is to specify a model of a computer system that distinguishes clearly between errors and disasters. The hope is that the probability of a disaster is much smaller than that of an error. We speak of failure-free behavior as *desired*.

Unfortunately, the price that must be paid for this added reliability is slow access (in addition to the price of the redundant memory capacity). Hence, a computer system built for reliability contains both stable storage and a fast main memory. Thus, in addition to the failures experienced by mass storage devices, we must consider failures of the processor and its associated main memory. Such failures are discussed in Section 9.5. In this section we assume that the processor and its main memory do not fail.

The stable storage model we describe is built in three hierarchical layers and is assumed to be implemented on random access mass storage devices, such as a set of disks. The lowest layer is the physical storage unit itself. The next layer is a software interface to physical storage that eliminates some of the errors to which physical storage is prone. We refer to the abstraction created by this layer as *careful storage*. The final layer is a software interface to careful storage that eliminates the remaining errors (but not the effect of disasters). This layer creates the abstraction of stable storage seen by the user.

9.4.1 Physical Storage*

We model a physical disk as a set of pages. Each page has an address of type *address* and can accommodate a block of data, having type *dblock*. The data in a page may be corrupted, and we assume that corrupted data can always be distinguished from correctly stored data (for example, parity bits might be stored in the page). We model this ability to distinguish good data from bad data by assuming that each page contains both a block of data and an associated status, which we represent as a type, *status_type*, with values *good* and *bad*. Hence, the contents of a page is a pair, *(status, data)*, where *status* is a variable of type *status_type* and *data* is a variable of type *dblock*. The data contained in a page with bad status can be ignored, and the content of such a page is represented *(bad,–)*.

Two operations are provided for accessing a physical disk:

> **procedure** *Put(at* : **in** *address*; *data* : **in** *dblock*)
> **procedure** *Get(at* : **in** *address*; *status* : **out** *apparent_status*;
>   *data* : **out** *dblock*)

Put writes a block of data to the page whose address is specified. It does not return status and hence no guarantee is made that the data has been written correctly. *Get* reads the block of data from the addressed page. The status returned indicates whether the read has been performed successfully, not whether the data is stored correctly in the page. Thus, a read of a page containing uncorrupted data might return status *looksbad* if the read does not transfer the data correctly. A subsequent read of the same page might transfer the data successfully and return a status of *good*. We define the type *apparent_status* to have an associated set of values *good* and *looksbad*.

We allow the following outcomes of *Get(a, st, db)*:

Correct read (desired) – The page at address *a* is *(good,d)* and *Get* returns *(good,d)*, or the page is *(bad,–)* and *Get* returns *(looksbad,–)*.

Soft read failure (error) – The page at address *a* is *(good,d)* and *Get* returns *(looksbad,–)*. However, the last of i repeated invocations of *Get*, where i is less than some bound, H, yields *(good,d)*.

Persistent read failure (disaster) – The page at address a is *(good,d)* and H successive invocations of *Get* return *(looksbad,–)*.

Undetected failure (disaster) – The page at address a is *bad* and *Get* returns *(good,d)*, or the page is *(good,d)* and *Get* returns *(good,d ')*.

The fact that we categorize a persistent read failure as a disaster is a technical matter. The model can deal with behavior of this type as an error by assuming that a page that cannot be successfully read in H attempts actually has decayed (a condition we describe below) and has bad status as a result.
We allow the following outcomes of a *Put(a, d)*:

Correct put (desired) – The page at address a becomes *(good,d)*.

Null write (error) – The page at address a is unchanged.

Bad write (error) – The page at address a becomes *(bad,–)*.

Finally, we allow one additional category of failures called decay events. A *decay event* occurs spontaneously and causes the contents of one or more pages to become *(bad,–)*. Clearly, if we are to construct a system in which information – even redundantly stored information – is to be preserved, we must place some restrictions on the way decay events occur. We impose two such restrictions. We limit the extent of damage a particular decay event can cause by subdividing the physical storage unit into *decay sets* in such a fashion that a particular decay event can affect only pages in a single decay set. For example, all the pages on a single cylinder or single surface of a disk might be grouped into a decay set (or, if the stable storage is being implemented using two disks, each disk might be a decay set). Furthermore, we define a time interval, T_D, that we use to limit the frequency of decay events. The following spontaneous events can occur in the system:

Infrequent decay (error) – A decay event occurs, preceded and followed by T_D units of time in which no other decay events occur. In addition, we require that any bad writes that occur during this interval affect only pages in the decay set contaminated by the decay.

Frequent decay (disaster) – Two decay events occur in different decay sets within an interval of T_D time units.

Mutation (disaster) – A page changes from *(good,d)* or *(bad,–)* to *(good,d ')*.

Since stable storage protects only against errors, these definitions imply that pages that become *bad* within an interval of T_D time units are confined to a single decay set. Since we categorize persistent read failures as disasters (and hence do not attempt to protect against them), the only unreadable pages are those with bad status. Thus, within the interval, at worst only the pages in a single decay set can become unreadable.

Other failures can be viewed as combinations of these events. For example, the event in which a block of data is written to the wrong address can be viewed as a null write to the intended address followed by a mutation at the wrong address. Since a mutation is a disaster, stable storage cannot protect against such a failure.

9.4.2 Careful Storage*

A careful storage device contains a set of careful pages that are accessed with two routines: *CarefulGet* and *CarefulPut*. A careful page is simply a physical page. The two routines are shown in Figure 9.4.

CarefulGet reads the specified page using *Get* until a good status is returned or until it has tried H times. This eliminates soft read failures. Since we have assumed that no disasters occur, if the status returned by each of H successive reads is *looksbad*, the status of the page on mass storage must be *bad*. *CarefulPut* writes the data to the specified page and then reads it back until a good status is returned and the data in the page matches the data written. This read-after-write eliminates null writes and bad writes. We have assumed that *CarefulPut* ultimately succeeds. To accommodate a situation in which the target page is permanently damaged, we could easily modify the algorithm so as to switch to a different target page after a sufficient number of tries.

9.4.3 Stable Storage*

Since careful pages can decay, we need a more elaborate mechanism to preserve information. In particular, we must store information redundantly. A stable page is built from an ordered pair of careful pages that are in distinct decay sets. Hence, in an interval of T_D time units, at most one of the pages can decay. We assume that the addresses of the two pages in the pair are related by a function, h, so that if at is the address of the first page in the pair, at' is the address of the second, where $at' = h(at)$. We take at to be the address of the stable page.

A stable page is accessed by operations *StableGet* and *StablePut*. It has no associated status, since assuming disasters do not occur, an access to a stable page is always successful. The content of a stable page is defined to be the content of the first careful page in the pair, if its status is good; otherwise it is the content of the second careful page. We show that the following assertion, I_{ss}, describing each stable page, is always true:

procedure *CarefulGet(at* : **in** *address*; *status* : **out** *status_type*;
        data : **out** *dblock*);
    var *fin* : *boolean* := *false*;
      i : *integer* := 0;
      st : *apparent_status*;
    begin
      do ¬*fin* ∧ (*i* < *H*) →
        begin
          Get(at, st, data);
          if *st* = *good* → *fin* := *true*;
          [] *st* = *looksbad* → *i* := *i* + 1;
          fi;
        end;
      od;
      if *st* = *looksbad* → *status* := *bad*;
      [] *st* = *good* → *status* := *good*;
      fi;
    end *CarefulGet*;

procedure *CarefulPut(at* : **in** *address*; *data* : **in** *dblock*);
    var *fin* : *boolean* := *false*;
      st : *apparent_status*;
      d : *dblock*;
    begin
      do ¬*fin* →
        begin
          Put(at, data);
          Get(at, st, d);
          if (*st* = *good*) ∧ (*d* = *data*) → *fin* := *true*;
          [] (*st* = *looksbad*) ∨ (*d* ≠ *data*) → **skip**;
          fi;
        end;
      od;
    end *CarefulPut*;

Figure 9.4: The operations for accessing a careful page are *CarefulGet* and *CarefulPut*.

```
procedure StableGet(at : in address; data : out dblock);
  var st : status_type;
  begin
    CarefulGet(at, st, data);
    if st = good → skip;
    [] st = bad → CarefulGet(h(at), st, data);
    fi;
  end StableGet;

procedure StablePut(at : in address; data : in dblock);
  begin
    CarefulPut(at, data);
    CarefulPut(h(at), data);
  end StablePut;
```

Figure 9.5: The operations for accessing a stable page are *StableGet* and *StablePut*.

I_{ss}: At most one of the careful pages has bad status. Pages with good status contain the data written by the most recent *StablePut*.

StableGet and *StablePut* are shown in Figure 9.5. Assuming I_{ss} is true, it is clear that *StableGet* returns the correct value of the data stored in a stable page. Furthermore, since it does no writing, it maintains I_{ss}. *StablePut* correctly writes to the stable page and maintains I_{ss}, even if a bad or null write occurs during execution. When *StablePut* completes, the stable page is left in the state

$$((good, d) \ (good, d)) \tag{9.5}$$

no matter what its state was on entry. (We have assumed that the time to perform *StablePut* is small compared with T_D.) Such a state is characterized by the assertion I_{good} given by

I_{good}: Both pages have good status, and both contain the data written by the most recent *StablePut*.

We must now deal with the problem of decays. Consider a T_D second interval and assume that I_{good} is true of each stable page at the beginning of the interval. Since the two careful pages making up a stable page are in distinct decay sets, a decay event can affect only one of them and, hence, produces either the pair $((good, d), \ (bad, -))$ or the pair $((bad, -), \ (good, d))$. If this is the only decay event that occurs during the interval, I_{ss} is true of each stable page at the end. Since decay and *StablePut* are the only events that modify the page, it follows that if a page is in state (9.5) (hence, satisfying I_{ss}) at

```
procedure Cleanup();
    var st1, st2 : status_type;
    d1, d2 : dblock;
    at : address;
begin
    do for all stable pages →
        begin
            CarefulGet(at, st1, d1); CarefulGet(h(at), st2, d2);
            if (st1 = st2) ∧ (d1 = d2) → skip;
            [] st1 = bad  → CarefulPut(at, d2);
            [] st2 = bad  → CarefulPut(h(at), d1);
            [] (st1 = st2) ∧ (d1 ≠ d2)  → CarefulPut(h(at), d1);
            fi;
        end;
    od;
end Cleanup;
```

Figure 9.6: Procedure $Cleanup$ is executed every T_D time units and after each crash.

the beginning of the interval, it will satisfy I_{ss} throughout the interval, and therefore $StableGet$ works correctly.

To avoid the cumulative effect of decay events, the procedure $Cleanup$, shown in Figure 9.6, is executed every T_D time units. The first component of the if statement applies to stable pages characterized by I_{good}. The second two components apply to a page that has suffered a decay event and restore it to a state satisfying I_{good}. We discuss the role of the final component when we introduce processor crashes. Clearly, for each stable page we can assert

$$\{I_{ss}\} \; Cleanup \; \{I_{good}\}$$

(We have assumed that the time it takes to execute $Cleanup$ is small compared with T_D.)

9.5   Reliable Processing

Processor failures in a distributed system can take a number of forms. In this section, we consider two extreme failure modes:

1. The processor simply stops, and the contents of main memory are lost. Since this is a common failure mode, main memory is generally referred to as volatile memory. The contents of stable storage are preserved and available

when the processor is restarted. This type of behavior is referred to as *fail-stop* or, more simply, as a *crash*. Fail-stop failures are said to be *benign*.

2. The processor becomes faulty but continues operating (and other processors might not be aware of the failure). We assume that the faulty processor can behave arbitrarily, performing spurious computations, sending spurious messages, and writing spurious information to its stable or volatile storage. In analyzing the effect of such a faulty processor, we must make the worst possible assumption – that the processor is performing some computation that is actively and maliciously attempting to sabotage whatever algorithm the distributed system is performing. This type of failure is called a *malicious failure*.

For benign failures, our goals are to continue the computation when the failed processor is restarted. For malicious failures, our goals are to complete the distributed algorithm in spite of the failure.

9.5.1 Programming a Fail-Stop Processor*

We assume that, when a crash occurs, we want the action, A, in progress at that time to be completed when the node is restarted. Completion is accomplished through the execution of a *recovery action, R*. Since the contents of volatile memory are lost, R must be stored in stable storage. Furthermore, R and A must be designed as a unit: R must be able to accomplish the same state transformation as A. Specifically, R must be able to perform A's entire computation, since the crash might occur the instant A starts. More generally, R must be able to resume A's computation at any intermediate stage at which A may fail. Finally, R must be able to recover for itself: if a crash occurs during the execution of R, restarting R completes the action.

It might appear that R and A are identical computations but that need not be so. For example, A might utilize data structures available in volatile memory at the time of its initiation, which, although not essential, speed execution (*e.g.*, A might utilize an index or cache prepared in volatile memory by an earlier computation for fast access to items of data on stable storage). Since these data structures are lost when the crash occurs, R might perform the same computation as A more laboriously by searching through all the data on stable storage. While R's algorithm might be very inefficient, it is executed only after a crash. Since crashes are likely to be infrequent, efficiency at recovery time is generally not as important as efficiency during normal operation.

By a *fault-tolerant action*, we mean an action together with its recovery action. We use the following syntax for the combination of the action and its recovery:

$$\textbf{action } A \textbf{ recovery } R \textbf{ end} \qquad (9.6)$$

where A and R are sequences of statements. If A and R are identical actions, the fault-tolerant action is called a *restartable* action and we use the syntax

action, recovery *A* **end**

A restartable action can be broken off and restarted any number of times. When it finally runs to completion, it achieves the same result as if it had run to completion the first time. A fault-tolerant action is a statement and can be combined with other statements in the standard way. A program might be a sequence of fault-tolerant actions (or of fault-tolerant and non-fault-tolerant statements), or one fault-tolerant action might be nested within another. Hence, a program might contain a number of recovery actions, and we speak of the *current recovery action* as the one in effect at a particular point in the program's execution.

The operational semantics of the fault-tolerant action *FTA* (9.6) is as follows:

First *R* is established as the current recovery action; then *A* is executed. If *FTA* is interrupted by a crash, on restart the recovery action in effect at the time of the crash is (1) re-established as the current recovery action and (2) initiated. Execution of *FTA* terminates when either *A* or *R* terminates. If *FTA* is followed by another fault-tolerant action, *FTA'* with recovery action *R'*, then on termination of *FTA*, *R'* is established as the current recovery action. Otherwise, the recovery action in effect when *FTA* was entered is re-established as the current recovery action. The switch from one recovery action to the next recovery action (in the case of the sequential composition of fault-tolerant actions) or to the recovery action in effect when *FTA* was entered is accomplished atomically.

We describe the formal semantics of a fault-tolerant action in terms of the formal semantics of its component actions. Assume that a proof of the theorem

$$\{P'\} A \{Q'\}$$

can be found with assertions $p'_1, p'_2, \ldots, p'_n$ at each control point, where $p'_1 = P'$ and $p'_n = Q'$. Similarly a proof of

$$\{P''\} R \{Q''\} \tag{9.7}$$

can be found with assertions $p''_1, p''_2, \ldots, p''_m$ at each control point, where $p''_1 = P''$ and $p''_m = Q''$. Furthermore, since the contents of volatile memory are lost when the crash occurs, assume that all variables mentioned in P'' are stored in stable storage. To conclude that despite a crash,

$$\{P\} \text{ action } A \text{ recovery } R \text{ end } \{Q\}$$

we must demonstrate the following hypotheses:

1. $P \Rightarrow P'$ and $Q' \Rightarrow Q$

2. $Q'' \Rightarrow Q$

3. If R is the current recovery action when the control point to which p_i' (p_j'') is attached is enabled,

$$p_i' \Rightarrow P'' \quad \text{and} \quad p_j'' \Rightarrow P''$$

4. p_i' and p_j'' must not mention variables stored in the volatile memory of a program executing at a different node.

Hypothesis 4 is needed, since a crash at a node other than the one at which the fault-tolerant action is executing might interfere with an assertion in the proof of the action. Hypothesis 3 guarantees that when R is initiated after a crash at an arbitrary point in the execution of A or R, P'' will be true of the state of stable storage, and hence Q'' will be true when R terminates. This condition is related to the notion of an idempotent routine. A routine S is *idempotent* with respect to some postcondition W if W is an invariant of S. Then, assuming $\{U\}\ S\ \{W\}$, n successive executions, for any $n > 0$, starting in U yields W as a postcondition. Thus a recovery action, R, described by (9.7) is idempotent with respect to Q'' if $Q'' \Rightarrow P''$. Note that R may be idempotent with respect to some postconditions but not with respect to others.

Example

We would like to make the annotated program fragment shown in Figure 9.7 resilient to crashes. Assume that x and y – which we refer to as program variables to distinguish them from variables introduced solely to cope with failures – are stored on stable storage. Suppose we wish to structure the program as a single fault-tolerant action by designing a recovery action and setting P, P', and P'' all equal to $(x = X) \wedge (y = Y)$ and setting Q, Q', and Q'' all equal to $(x = g(X)) \wedge (y = g(Y))$. (Note that, in general, P' and P'' will not be identical. For example, P' might assert something about the state of volatile memory.) Unfortunately, these assertions violate hypothesis 3, and hence a different approach is needed. Intuitively, we know that the difficulty arises from the fact that a recovery action cannot determine how far the program has progressed and, therefore, must redo the entire computation. Q cannot be guaranteed as a postcondition under these circumstances, since new values might have been assigned to x or y before the crash.

An alternative approach is to introduce additional variables in stable storage and structure the computation as two restartable actions, $\mathcal{FTA}1$ and $\mathcal{FTA}2$, as shown in Figure 9.8. Taking the pre- and postconditions of each restartable action (*i.e.*, P and Q) as the pre- and postconditions of the nested action itself (*i.e.*, P' and Q'), we see that hypotheses 1 and 2 are satisfied. Since the assertions within the actions of each restartable action are strengthened by the execution of each assignment statement, hypothesis 3 follows.

$$\cdots$$
$$\{(x = X) \wedge (y = Y)\}$$
$$x := g(x);$$
$$\{(x = g(X)) \wedge (y = Y)\}$$
$$y := g(y);$$
$$\{(x = g(X)) \wedge (y = g(Y))\}$$

Figure 9.7: A program fragment that updates two variables.

$\mathcal{F}TA1 ::$
  action, recovery
$$\{(x = X) \wedge (y = Y)\}$$
$$xtmp := g(x);$$
$$\{(x = X) \wedge (y = Y) \wedge (xtmp = g(X))\}$$
$$ytmp := g(y);$$
$$\{(x = X) \wedge (y = Y) \wedge (xtmp = g(X)) \wedge (ytmp = g(Y))\}$$
  end;

$\mathcal{F}TA2 ::$
  action, recovery
$$\{(xtmp = g(X)) \wedge (ytmp = g(Y))\}$$
$$x := xtmp;$$
$$\{(xtmp = g(X)) \wedge (ytmp = g(Y)) \wedge (x = xtmp)\}$$
$$y := ytmp;$$
$$\{(xtmp = g(X)) \wedge (ytmp = g(Y)) \wedge (x = xtmp) \wedge (y = ytmp)\}$$
  end;

Figure 9.8: The update program of the previous figure configured as two restartable actions.

The example illustrates a general technique that we use in later sections to cope with failures. Results are computed and stored in temporary records in stable storage, with no change made to the initial values of program variables. Hence the computation can be broken off at any point and restarted, and the same results will be computed. When all results have been computed, the temporary records are used to update the program variables. The updating process can also be broken off at any point and restarted. The set of temporary records is generally called an *intentions list*, or *do list*, since it contains the intended changes to be made by the program. Each record is referred to as a *do record*.

We now introduce crashes into the stable storage model of Section 9.4. We have assumed that crashes do not affect the contents of stable storage, and so it might at first appear that our previous treatment needs no modification. We must, however, consider the case of a crash during the execution of *StablePut*. Suppose we have made the call *StablePut*(a, d) and the crash occurs immediately after a bad write error. Since we have assumed that bad writes and decay events within an interval of T_D time units must occur in the same decay set, it follows that, after the crash, the page must be in either the state $((bad, -), (good, d'))$ or the state $((good, d), (bad, -))$, where d' is the data stored in the page before the call. In the first case we say that *StablePut* has not completed, while in the second case we assume that it has. In either case, I_{ss} is true.

Another possibility is that the crash occurs between the two invocations of *CarefulPut* in a *StablePut*, and hence the stable page is left in the state $((good, d), (good, d'))$. Although this state does not satisfy I_{ss}, we say that *StablePut* has completed. Hence, after the crash a stable page is characterized by the assertion I_{cr}.

I_{cr}: I_{ss} or both pages have good status and the first contains the data written by the most recent *StablePut*.

Consider the use of *Cleanup* as a recovery action. The last component of the if statement transforms a page characterized by I_{cr} to one satisfying I_{good}, and hence for each stable page we have

$$\{I_{cr}\} \ Cleanup \ \{I_{good}\}$$

Furthermore, at any intermediate point in the execution of *Cleanup*, a page is characterized by I_{cr}; hence hypothesis 3 is satisfied. It follows then that if *Cleanup* is executed every T_D time units and as a recovery action after a crash, I_{ss} will be true of each page during normal operation and as a postcondition of crash recovery. Note that we have not excluded the possibility that a crash occurs during the execution of *Cleanup*.

9.5.2   Failure Atomicity with Stable Storage

While fault tolerant actions guarantee that a computation is completed in spite of crashes, a more modest goal is often permissible. Consider an action that transforms the state of program variables on stable storage from S to S'. (In what follows we assume that the program variables we refer to are those on stable storage.) We say the action is *failure atomic* if, after recovery from a crash, the state of program variables is either S or S'. We no longer require that the action be carried through to completion. The goal is now only data consistency. Since a crash can occur at an arbitrary time during the execution of the action, program variables might be partially updated and left in an inconsistent state. Our concern is that recovery restore data to a consistent state, not that the action be carried through to completion. Thus if the action is not carried through to completion, we want recovery to restore the system state to the way it was before the action was initiated – which we assume was a consistent state.

To implement failure atomicity, we introduce two new operations, *commit* and *abort*, which direct the system to take certain actions during recovery after a crash. Consider an action, A, that is initiated in state S, and assume that A computes new values of program variables that cause the state to become S'. We assume that if a crash occurs while A is executing, but before it has executed either commit or abort, the recovery procedure restores the state to S. An action can execute either commit or abort, but not both. A commit operation executed by A has the following operational semantics:

Commit Operation

A executes commit after it has determined the values of program variables in state S'. The system makes the following commitment: if a crash occurs after A has committed, the new values computed by A will be assigned to the appropriate program variables by the recovery procedure (assuming these variables have not been subsequently modified by another committed action). The operation is executed atomically.

An abort operation allows an action to terminate prematurely. It has the following operational semantics:

Abort Operation

The system makes the following commitment: if a crash occurs after A has aborted, the values of program variables modified by A (and not subsequently modified by committed actions) will be restored to their values in S by the recovery procedure. The operation is executed atomically.

We consider two approaches to achieving failure atomicity: *deferred update* and *immediate update*. In deferred update, actions do not directly update program variables. Instead, new values are stored in an intentions list. After the action commits, the new values are transferred from the intentions list to the program variables.

Deferred Update Using an Intentions List

1. An intentions list is created on stable storage for the action. It consists of a commit flag (initially set to *non-committed*) and a list (initially set to null) of do records.

2. The action is executed, and as new values of program variables are computed, do records containing the new values are appended to the intentions list (program variables are not modified in this step).

3. The execution of commit by the action causes the commit flag in the intentions list to be set to *committed*. The action terminates and the do records in the intentions list are used to update program variables. Then the intentions list is discarded.

4. If the action executes abort, it terminates and the intentions list is discarded.

Since setting the commit flag is atomic, stable storage either records that the computation has committed or records that it has not. After a crash, the recovery action examines each intentions list. If an intentions list indicates that the corresponding action has committed, the do records are used to update program variables. In either case, the list is discarded. Thus, if a crash occurs before the action commits, the state of the program variables is the same as it was before the action began. If it occurs afterwards, the state of program variables reflects the complete execution of the action.

The algorithm implementing the intentions list approach involves two restartable actions separated by a commit point: the action described by step 2 and the action consisting of the installation of the intentions list. This structure is almost identical to the example of Section 9.5.1; the only difference is that we do not provide a mechanism for restarting the action if a crash occurs before the commit point. The application itself is responsible for any needed restarts. Since the installation of the intentions list is a restartable action, it can simply be restarted if a crash occurs during recovery from a prior crash.

Note that the do record need not be appended to the intentions list immediately after the new value of the program variable is computed. It is only necessary that all do records be in the intentions list before the commit is performed. This is an important observation, since it implies that the executing action need not wait until the stable put that appends the do record completes before continuing its computation. An operation that is requested by an action, but is carried out concurrently with subsequent computations within the action, is referred to as a *background operation*. The only requirement on the execution of a background update is that it complete before the action commits. Thus the append operation in step 2 can be a background operation.

An alternative implementation of deferred update is called *shadow paging*. Assume that the granularity of access to a mass storage device is an entire page and that the system maintains a *page table* containing the address of each page of an item on stable storage. An action makes a copy of the system's page table for each item that it updates and uses that page table during its execution. The original page table is retained and is called the *shadow page table*. Whenever the action wishes to update a page, a new version of that page is created and a pointer to it is placed in the new page table, leaving the shadow table and the original page unchanged. To commit an action, we simply substitute the new page table for the original and discard the original.

In the second approach to achieving failure atomicity, *immediate update*, the action makes its updates directly to program variables. Before updating a program variable, however, it saves the previous value of that variable in an *undo record*. Undo records are entries in a list on stable storage called the *write-ahead log* or *undo list*. If a crash occurs before the action commits, on recovery the write-ahead log is used to restore the state of each program variable to its value before the action began. It is important that the undo record be appended to the log before the program variable is updated, since if the operations were performed in the opposite order and a crash occurred after an update to a program variable but before the record was appended, there would be no way to restore the variable to its state before the action started. The name "write-ahead" is derived from this necessary ordering. Hence, an update to the write-ahead log must be a *forced operation* in the sense that the executing action is required to wait until the operation is complete.

Immediate Update Using a Write-Ahead Log

1. A write-ahead log is created on stable storage for the action. It consists of a commit flag (initially set to *non-committed*) and a list (initially set to null) of undo records.

2. The action is executed, and as new values for program variables are computed, undo records containing the old values are appended to the write-ahead log. Then the new values are written into the program variables.

3. The execution of commit by the action causes the commit flag in the write-ahead log to be set to *committed*. The action terminates and the write-ahead log is discarded.

4. If the action executes abort, it terminates and the undo records in the write-ahead log are used to restore program variables to their original state. Then the write-ahead log is discarded.

After a crash, the recovery action examines each write-ahead log. If a write-ahead log indicates that the corresponding action has not committed, the undo records are used to update program variables. Since the installation of the undo records is a restartable action, it can simply be restarted if a crash occurs during recovery from a prior crash.

9.5.3   Failure Atomicity with Recoverable Storage

Stable storage has the property that its contents are always immediately available. However, this property is obtained at the cost of doubling the required on-line storage capacity. In many applications, particularly those involving massive databases, providing duplicate on-line storage would be too expensive. For these applications, we can implement a less ambitious capability: recoverable storage. *Recoverable storage* protects against essentially the same failures as stable storage, but decays might cause the data to be temporarily unavailable. Once again, recoverable storage does not protect against disasters.

Recoverable storage is commonly implemented using a secondary, sequentially accessed mass storage device (such as a tape) to back up a primary, random access mass storage device (such as a disk). We assume that information written on the secondary device is not subject to decay (*i.e.,* decay of information on the secondary is considered a disaster). Like stable storage, recoverable storage is built from careful storage.

The basic approach is to store information redundantly on the primary and the secondary devices so that if a data item on the primary decays, the secondary can be used to restore it to its value before the decay. As with stable storage, implementing failure atomicity with recoverable storage requires that we carefully distinguish between those operations that must be forced and those that can be performed in the background. This distinction is particularly important for recoverable storage, since the access time for the secondary is generally quite large. Forcing all operations to the secondary would essentially limit the speed of the system to that of the secondary. Since failure atomicity is all that is required, however, we can take advantage of the fact that frequently only the order of operations is important; it is not essential that they complete at the time they are invoked: they can be background operations.

We now describe systems that implement actions that are failure atomic using recoverable storage. The systems are designed to protect against processor crashes and errors of the primary device. We assume that actions do not execute concurrently. In Chapter 12 we extend these systems to concurrent execution and demonstrate their application in transaction processing.

To recover from a crash, we use one of the methods discussed in the previous section, except that the intentions list or write-ahead log can be maintained on the primary device and need not be written to the secondary. Since the primary survives a crash, these lists are available to the recovery procedure.

To recover from a decay, we restore the primary from the secondary. Whereas with stable storage *Cleanup* is used periodically to restore decayed data, restoration is now done when the decay is detected – when a careful get operation returns a bad status. The plan is to periodically copy, or *dump*, the entire contents of the primary device to the secondary, effectively taking a snapshot. In addition, we keep a *journal* on the secondary of all changes made to the primary by actions that committed since the last dump was taken. If a decay is detected, we restore the primary by first reading in the latest dump and then using the information from the journal to incorporate updates made by actions that committed since that dump was taken.

To do this, we organize the secondary device into two files: a dump file and a journal file. We assume in this section that the dump file is made off line by shutting the system down at some convenient time. We do not discuss more sophisticated algorithms in which the dump is taken dynamically while the system is running.

Recoverable storage must be carefully managed to ensure that actions are failure atomic no matter when a crash or decay occurs, while also ensuring that the stored values can be accessed efficiently. We assume that there is a forced and a background careful put operation to the primary, *FPCarefulPut* and *BPCarefulPut*, respectively, and a forced and a background careful put operation to the secondary, *FSCarefulPut* and *BSCarefulPut*, respectively. As with *CarefulPut*, in all these operations the data is written and read back repeatedly until it has been ascertained that the data has been written successfully, and the transfer of data that results from the execution of each careful operation is assumed to be atomic with respect to crashes (*i.e.,* either all the data is transferred to the mass storage device or none is).

For the primary device, we assume that a (background or forced) careful get operation that addresses a particular region of storage returns the information written by the most recently requested prior (background or forced) careful put operation to that region. We do not assume anything about the order in which information written by *BPCarefulPut* operations to different regions is actually transferred to the primary device.[2] *FSCarefulPut* and *BSCarefulPut* append (rather than write) records to the secondary device. We assume that the appends are performed in the order in which the (background or forced) operations are invoked. (Hence, a background put to the secondary is forced to completion by a subsequent forced put.)

The following algorithm can be used to ensure both failure atomicity (with respect to crashes) and recoverability (with respect to decays).

Immediate-Update and Deferred-Update Systems Using Recoverable Storage

1. When an action begins, it uses *BSCarefulPut* to append a *begin action* record to the journal.

2. When an action computes a new value of a program variable, it records that value on recoverable storage differently in immediate-update and deferred-update systems:

   (a) *Deferred-update systems*: *BPCarefulPut* is used to append a do record to the intentions list, and *BSCarefulPut* is used to append a do record to the journal.

   (b) *Immediate-update systems*: *FPCarefulPut* is used to append an undo record to the write-ahead log. Then *BPCarefulPut* is used to overwrite the program variable with its new value, and *BSCarefulPut* is used to append a do record to the journal. (As before, we must make the entry in the write-ahead log before overwriting the program variable.)

---

[2]This assumption corresponds to the use of page buffers to retain recently accessed disk pages in main memory. When a get or a background put to a primary page is requested, a check is first made to see if the page resides in a buffer. If so, the access is done in main memory, avoiding a reference to the disk. The buffers are allocated to disk pages in such a way as to maximize the likelihood that a referenced page will be found in a page buffer (this is frequently referred to as a *hit*).

3. When an action commits, it uses *FSCarefulPut* to append a *commit* record to the journal. Since a forced operation is used, any do record that has been previously written using a background operation but has not yet been transferred to the journal will be forced out as well and will precede the commit record in the journal. Similarly, if an action aborts, it uses *FSCarefulPut* to append an *abort* record to the journal. The action is assumed to have committed when the commit record has been appended. The committed or aborted action is then terminated. The next activity depends on whether the system is deferred update or immediate update:

(a) *Deferred-update systems*: For committed actions, the commit flag in the intentions list is set, the do records in the list are used to update program variables, and the list is then discarded. For aborted actions, the list is discarded.

(b) *Immediate-update systems*: For committed actions, the commit flag in the write-ahead log is set, and then the log is discarded. For aborted actions, the undo records in the write-ahead log are used to roll back the changes made to program variables, and the write-ahead log is then discarded.

Since a crash does not affect the contents of the primary device, recovery is as described in Section 9.5.2, with one exception. The crash might have occurred after a commit record had been appended to the journal, but before the commit flag had been set in the corresponding intentions list (in a deferred-update system) or write-ahead log (in an immediate-update system). Hence, the recovery procedure must initially set the commit flag of any action active at the time of the crash for which a commit record exists in the journal. The recovery procedure must also append abort records to the journal for all actions that had neither committed nor aborted at the time of the crash (actions for which a begin action record exists in the journal, but no commit or abort records exist). The recovery procedure of Section 9.5.2 can then be executed.

Note that in an immediate-update system it is convenient (although not necessary) for the write-ahead log to contain do records (as well as undo records), since, when a crash occurs, all updates to program variables made by committed actions might not have been completed (since database updates are performed using background operations). If the write-ahead log contains do records, these background updates can be re-executed without referring to the secondary device.

To recover from the decay of a single item, the system searches backwards through the journal to locate the do record that updated the item and was written by the most recently committed action. This record contains the current value of the item. If no such actions exists, the current value of the item is contained in the most recent dump. To restore the entire primary device, the system first copies the dump file from the secondary to the primary; then it makes two sequential passes through the journal – a backward pass in which it makes a list of all the committed actions and a forward pass in which it uses the do records of committed actions in the journal to update program variables in commit order. The recovery procedure has the effect of aborting all uncommitted actions and discarding all intentions lists and write-ahead logs.

One further issue must be addressed: we must consider what action is to be taken if a decay corrupts the intentions list or write-ahead log, since they are not stored redundantly on the secondary. In a deferred-update system, if an action, A, commits and do records in A's intentions list are unreadable, copies of the do records in the journal (that have been forced by the put of A's commit record) can be used to update program variables. In an immediate-update system, if an action, A, aborts and undo records in A's write-ahead log are unreadable, the system can identify all program variables that have been modified by A, since their do records have been forced to the journal by the put of A's abort record. The system can then determine the original values of these variables by searching backwards through the journal until it finds the most recent committed action that has modified each such variable. Do records containing the original values have been written to the journal by these actions. If no action can be found in the journal for a particular program variable that has been modified by A, the original value of that variable can be found in the most recent dump.

Our purpose in this section has been to describe a framework for masking errors and to bring out the importance of properly ordering the steps that must be taken to ensure recovery. A practical system would involve considerable optimization.

9.5.4   Byzantine Generals Problem*

In this section we consider the problem of reaching agreement in a network in spite of malicious failures. Agreement is a fundamental issue in distributed systems. Distributed algorithms involve the cooperation of a set of nodes in achieving some goal. Generally, algorithms require that nodes agree on some aspects of the network state. For example, in Chapter 12 we consider a situation in which a set of nodes must agree on which node is to be the leader.

A simple form of the problem of reaching agreement is the *consensus problem* in which each node is initialized with a (potentially different) single bit of information and the goal is for nodes to ultimately agree on a (common) final value. To avoid trivial solutions, we require that the final value depend in some nontrivial way on all the initial values. The requirement generally imposed, referred to as *strong unanimity*, specifies that if all initial values are 0 (or all are 1), then all final values must be 0 (must be 1). Since we allow nodes to fail in an arbitrary way, we cannot require that all nodes agree on the final value. Instead, we must be satisfied if all correctly functioning, or *normal*, nodes agree when the algorithm terminates.

A related problem is that of *reliable broadcast*, in which a single, distinguished node – which we refer to as the *source* – sends a value to all others.

Once again, we require that normal nodes agree on a received value. The two problems are related in that it is easy to extend a solution of the consensus problem to a solution of the reliable broadcast problem. First the source sends the value to all other nodes. Then the nodes engage in a consensus algorithm using as initial values the values received from the source (the initial value used by the source is the value it sent). Although the consensus algorithm is formulated in terms of a single bit of information while the reliable broadcast algorithm is formulated in terms of an arbitrary value, we can execute the consensus algorithm (in parallel) for each bit of the value broadcast by the source.

We now permit malicious failures. Since a malicious failure allows a node to behave in a totally arbitrary way, it is not possible to develop strategies to defend against such failures at the failed node itself. Instead, we focus on a distributed algorithm executing in a network and devise strategies that can be used by normal nodes to reach agreement in spite of malicious failures at other nodes.

The reliable broadcast problem in the context of malicious failures has come to be referred to as the *Byzantine Generals Problem*, since the malicious form of failure is said to be reminiscent of the deviousness and intrigue that existed in the Byzantine Empire. The problem was originally described in terms of a general – the source – trying to broadcast an order – a value – to a set of lieutenants. It is this problem that we focus on in this section.

One complication of the Byzantine Generals Problem is that the source itself might have failed maliciously and not sent the same value to all other nodes. We require that, even when the source fails maliciously, normal nodes agree on some value. Hence, a solution to the Byzantine Generals Problem is an algorithm (*i.e.,* termination is implied) in which the following goals are satisfied:

G1: All normal nodes reach the same conclusion concerning the value broadcast by the source; and

G2: If the source is normal, the conclusion reached by all normal nodes is the value broadcast by the source.

Note that when the source is normal, G1 follows from G2.

Consider a network of n nodes in which each node is directly connected by bidirectional links to every other node. We assume that failures affect only the nodes and, hence, links are completely reliable. (This assumption is not really a restriction, since a link failure can be attributed to a failure of one of the nodes at either end.) Messages are delivered in the order in which they are sent. Since the network topology is fixed, the receiver of a message knows the identity of the sender.

An important issue is whether the network supports synchronous or asynchronous algorithms. A *synchronous algorithm* is generally structured as a sequence of *rounds*. In each round, a node first sends an arbitrary set of messages to other nodes, then it receives the messages that were sent to it in that round, and then it performs some computation ending the round. Implicit in this structure is the assumption that, if a faulty node fails to send a message expected by a normal node, the normal node can deduce that the sender has failed from the absence of the message (perhaps using a timeout) and take appropriate action. In an *asynchronous algorithm*, nodes progress at arbitrary (but nonzero) rates, and therefore the absence of a message can be due to the failure of the sender or to a situation in which the sending process and/or communication link connecting the sender and receiver is functioning slowly. Hence, the receiver cannot be certain that the sender is faulty.

It can be shown that agreement is not possible in the totally asynchronous case, even if only a single benign failure occurs [95]. This result has significant implications concerning the ultimate capabilities of distributed systems that are subject to failures. Hence, we assume that the network supports synchronous algorithms. Such support can be provided if we can assume that the maximum difference, or *skew*, between the readings of (nonfaulty) clocks, the maximum transmission time on a link, and the maximum computation time at a node are known. These quantities enable us to choose a timeout interval and the duration of time to be allocated to a round.

As might be expected, a solution to the reliable broadcast problem depends on placing some limit on the errors that can occur. In this case, the limit is on the number of failed nodes, t. It can be shown that if $t \geq n/3$, the goals cannot be satisfied. We do not prove that here, but illustrate the problem with a simple example. Consider the case $n = 3$, $t = 1$. In the situation shown in Figure 9.9(a), the source, S, has failed and the two receivers are normal (failed nodes are indicated by squares and normal nodes by circles). S has sent the value a to receiver R_1 and b to receiver R_2. To defend against a failure, the receivers exchange messages, each one telling the other the value it has received from S. Intuitively, we know that at this point each receiver has all the information available concerning what has transpired in the network and must decide on a final value (remember, this argument is not a proof).

Based on the information it has received, R_1 cannot distinguish this situation from the one shown in Figure 9.9(b), where S is normal and R_2 has failed. S has sent the same value, a, to both R_1 and R_2, but R_2 relays a value to R_1 different from the one it has actually received from S. Since R_1 cannot exclude the possibility that S is normal [*i.e.*, the situation is as shown in Figure 9.9(b)], it must choose a in order to satisfy G2. By the same argument, if R_2 receives b from S and a from R_1 [as it does in Figure 9.9(a)], it cannot exclude the possibility that S is normal and R_1 has failed and, hence, must choose b as the final value. We have derived a contradiction, since, when the situation is as shown in Figure 9.9(a), the two normal receivers choose different final values.

Next we present a family of algorithms, $A(t)$, for $t \geq 0$, that a source, S, can

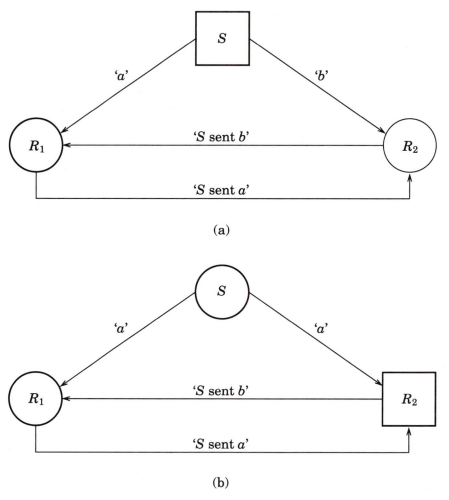

(a)

(b)

Figure 9.9: Two different failure situations: (a) a failed source sends different values to normal receivers, and (b) a normal source sends the same value to both receivers, but the failed receiver relays the wrong value to the normal receiver. Failed nodes are indicated by squares, normal nodes by circles.

use to reliably broadcast a value to $n - 1$ receivers.[3] $A(t)$ ensures that G1 and G2 will be satisfied if the number of failures is at most t, where $n = 3t + 1$. We assume that normal nodes execute the algorithms as specified; we make no assumption about the behavior of failed nodes.

   $A(t)$ utilizes a family of functions, maj, having i arguments, where i ranges up to $n - 1$. If the majority of its arguments have value v, maj returns v. Two functions satisfy this requirement:

1. maj returns the majority value among its arguments, if it exists; otherwise maj returns a default value, $\perp$ (we assume that $\perp$ is one of the values on which the receivers are allowed to agree);

2. maj returns the median of its arguments (assuming that the arguments come from an ordered set).

In this section we assume that maj is the majority function. In Section 9.7.2, we discuss a similar algorithm (for sites agreeing on the value of a clock) in which we use the median function for maj.

   To gain insight into what $A(t)$ should be, we first discuss a simpler – and, as it turns out, incorrect – two round protocol. In the first round, S sends its value to each receiver. In the second round, each receiver transmits the value it received to all the other receivers. Each receiver then applies maj to the values received from S and the other receivers and chooses its result as the final value. As an example, assume $n = 28$ (so that S is attempting to reliably broadcast its value to 27 receivers) and 9 nodes are faulty. Note that these numbers satisfy $n > 3t$, the condition for the correct operation of the (correct) algorithm we present later. Consider first the case when S is normal (and thus 9 of the receivers are faulty). In the first round, S sends the value a to each receiver. In the second round, all the normal receivers send a to each other. Thus, in the second round, each normal receiver receives at least 17 additional a's (a node does not send a message to itself). Hence, no matter what the faulty receivers do, when the normal receivers apply the maj function to the values they received, they all decide a. Thus, the simple protocol works for this case. Now consider the case when S is faulty. The simple protocol no longer works correctly. For example, suppose that during the first round S sends the value a to a group, G_1, of 9 normal receivers, the value b to another group, G_2, of 10 normal receivers, and $greetings$ to its friends, the 8 faulty receivers. During the second round, the 8 faulty receivers all send a to the members of G_1 and b to the members of G_2. Each member of G_1 receives 17 a's, and each member of G_2 receives 18 b's; hence members of different groups will choose different final values. The difficulty occurs because, in the second round, the faulty receivers were able to fool the normal receivers by sending inconsistent messages. Notice that the situation faced by the normal receivers in the second round is exactly the situation they faced at the beginning of the

---

[3]Strictly speaking, we should denote the algorithm as $A(t, n)$. We rely on the context, however, to make clear the number of nodes involved.

protocol – how to reach a consistent decision when the site sending a value is faulty. This observation suggests that during the second round the sites use the same protocol to transmit values to each other as they did in the first – in other words that the protocol be defined recursively.

Based on these ideas, we now present the algorithm $A(t)$ recursively in terms of the algorithm $A(t - 1)$. The assumption of synchronous operation is implicit in the fact that we assume that a node can detect when no message has been sent. In that case it chooses $\perp$ as a default received value. The base case of the recursion corresponds to $A(0)$.

Agreement Algorithm $A(0)$

1. S sends its value to every receiver R_i, $1 \le i \le n - 1$.

2. R_i chooses as the final value the value received from S, or $\perp$ if no value is received.

Agreement Algorithm $A(t)$, $t > 0$

1. S sends its value to every receiver R_i, $1 \le i \le n - 1$.

2. Let v_i be the value R_i receives from S in step 1 or $\perp$ if no value is received. R_i uses $A(t - 1)$ to send v_i to the $n - 2$ other receivers.

3. For each i and for each j not equal to i, let v_j be the value that R_i receives from R_j in step 2, or $\perp$ if no value is received. R_i chooses $maj(v_1, v_2, \ldots, v_{n-1})$ as the final value.

Clearly, $A(0)$ satisfies G2 if all nodes are normal, since if S is normal it sends the same value to all receivers and each receiver chooses that value as its final value. For $t > 0$, each receiver assembles a vector of $n - 1$ values, which it uses as an argument to maj to determine its final value. R_i stores the value sent by S in the ith position of its vector and, for $j \ne i$, the value sent by R_j to R_i in the jth position. The mechanism used by the receivers to exchange values happens to involve $A(t - 1)$, but in first attempting to understand the algorithm, we can ignore the recursion.

The recursion is implemented iteratively as a sequence of rounds. For $t > 0$, $A(t)$ operates in $t + 1$ rounds. In round 1, S sends a value to the $n - 1$ receivers. Consider a particular receiver, R_i. It then acts as a sender and uses $A(t - 1)$ to tell the other $n - 2$ receivers the value it has received from S. Hence, in round 2 of $A(t)$, R_i sends the value it received from S in round 1 to the other $n - 2$ receivers. Consider a particular one of these receivers, $R_j, j \ne i$. It then acts as a sender and uses $A(t - 2)$ to tell the other $n - 3$ receivers (*i.e.,* all nodes other than S, R_i, and R_j) the value received from R_i in round 2. Hence, in round 3 of $A(t)$, R_j sends the value it received from R_i in round 2 to $n - 3$ other receivers. Note that R_j has actually received $n - 2$ values in round 2 from other receivers and, therefore, invokes $A(t-2)$ a total of $n-2$ times. In each invocation it is telling a distinct set of $n-3$ other receivers one of the values it has received in round 2.

The procedure is complex, and it is difficult to gain insight into what is happening by looking at it in this way. Consider the case $n = 4$, $t = 1$. In Figure 9.10(a), R_3 has failed. S has executed $A(1)$ to send a to the three receivers, and this has resulted in a round 1 message from S to each receiver containing a. On receipt of the round 1 message, each receiver has used $A(0)$ to send the value received from S to the other receivers, and this has resulted in the six inter-receiver round 2 messages. Since R_3 has failed, we do not constrain the value contained in its round 2 messages. Using the naming scheme specified in $A(t)$, R_1 and R_2 assemble the vector of values shown, and using maj, R_1 and R_2 choose the same final value, a. In Figure 9.10(b), S has failed and sent different values to each receiver. In this case, the (normal) receivers exchange values and assemble the same vector, (x, y, z). As a result, all choose $\perp$ as their final value, satisfying G1. In Figure 9.10 we assumed that the failed node sent messages with unspecified values at the appropriate times. The result would not have changed if no message had been sent, since the received value would simply be $\perp$ in that case.

A node receives a number of values in round i, each one of which must be sent in the next round, using $A(t-i+1)$, to a different subset of $n-i$ nodes. To indicate which value must be sent to which subset, each message contains the sequence of identifiers of the nodes that have acted as relays for the message (*i.e.*, a node appends its identifier to the sequence when it relays the value). Values contained in messages that have been relayed through normal nodes will then be sent, in round $i+1$, to the appropriate subset of nodes. We make no assumptions about the content of messages arriving from failed nodes.

The proof of the correctness of $A(t)$ depends on the following lemma, which states a property of $A(t)$ when there is some number, k, of failed nodes, where $k \le t$.

Lemma: For any t and k, $A(t)$ satisfies G2 if $n > 2k + t$ and there are no more than k failed nodes.

Proof: The proof is by induction on t. Since the lemma refers only to G2, we need only be concerned with situations in which S is normal. Clearly, $A(0)$ satisfies G2, since S sends the same value to each of the $n-1$ receivers and the normal ones take this as the final value. Hence, we take as the inductive hypothesis that $A(t-1)$ satisfies G2 if the number of nodes exceeds $2k + (t-1)$ and there are no more than k failed nodes.

Suppose $A(t)$ is used in a network of n nodes, where $n > 2k + t$ and at most k nodes are faulty. S sends v to $n-1$ receivers. In step 2 each normal receiver uses $A(t-1)$ to send v to the other $n-2$ receivers. Hence, $A(t-1)$ is being used with $n-1$ nodes, at most k of which are faulty. Since $(n-1) > (2k + (t-1))$, the inductive hypothesis applies, and hence each normal receiver gets $v_j = v$ from

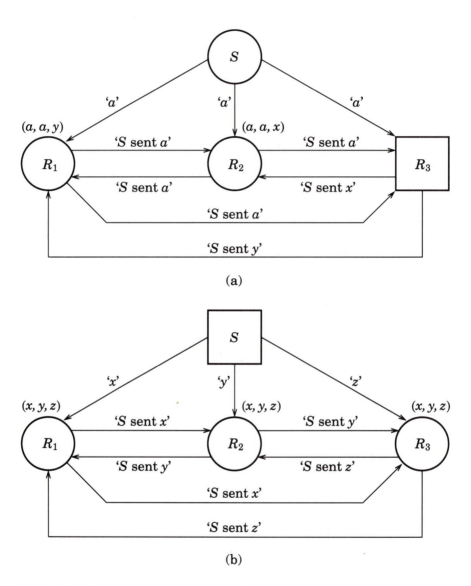

(a)

(b)

Figure 9.10: The result of executing $A(1)$ with $n = 4$ (a) when a receiver has failed and (b) when the sender has failed. Failed nodes are indicated by squares, normal nodes by circles.

each normal receiver, R_j. Each normal receiver receives $n - 1$ values. Since the number of failed nodes is k and $(n - 1) > 2k$, it follows that at each normal receiver *maj* returns v. Thus, $A(t)$ achieves G2. □

Theorem: $A(t)$ achieves G1 and G2 if there are more than $3t$ nodes, of which at most t have failed.

Proof: The proof is by induction on t. Clearly $A(0)$ satisfies G1 and G2, since S is normal in this case and sends the same value to each of the $n - 1$ receivers. Hence, we take as the inductive hypothesis that $A(t - 1)$ satisfies G1 and G2 if there are more than $3(t - 1)$ nodes, of which at most $t - 1$ are faulty.

If S is normal, we can use the lemma with $k = t$ to conclude that G2 is satisfied, and since G2 implies G1 in this case, the result holds. Thus, we need only prove that G1 holds when S is faulty.

When S is faulty there can be at most $t - 1$ faulty receivers. Since the total number of receivers is greater than $3t - 1$ and $(3t - 1) > 3(t - 1)$, the inductive hypothesis holds and we can conclude that $A(t - 1)$ can be used by the normal receivers to exchange the values they received from S. Hence, for any j, two normal receivers get the same value of v_j. Since normal receivers assemble the same vector of values, they all select the same final value. □

Note that when both S and R_i are normal, the vectors of values assembled by the normal receivers all satisfy the condition $v_i = v$. Normal receivers might have different values in their jth position, however, if R_j is faulty. (This follows from the fact that, since S is normal, as many as one third of the receivers might be faulty. Hence only the Lemma applies to communication among the receivers.) On the other hand, if S is faulty, the vectors assembled by normal receivers are identical.

The algorithm $A(t)$ involves $t + 1$ rounds, which can be shown to be a lower bound on the number of rounds necessary for reliable broadcast. Unfortunately, the number of messages in $A(t)$ grows exponentially with t. A wide variety of other algorithms have been developed that trade off these quantities or implement special features. An example of such an algorithm is described in the exercises.

9.6   Failures During Remote Procedure Calls

Even though actions at each individual site can be made atomic with respect to failures (crashes and decays) at that site, when a computation is distributed, new failure modes are possible. In this section we consider the following new failure modes:

1. *Message failure*: A transient failure involving the loss, duplication, or reordering of messages. Such a failure might or might not be masked from the user, depending on whether datagram or virtual circuit communication is being used.

2. *Partition failure*: A more permanent communication outage that prevents two operational sites from communicating (either directly, through a connecting link, or indirectly, through intermediate links and sites). More generally, the network is partitioned into two or more components, such that all sites in any one component can communicate with each other, but no site in one component can communicate with any site in another.

3. *Crash*: A crash can be *total*, when all sites fail, or *partial*, when some, but not all, sites fail.

To complicate matters further, it is often difficult for a normal node, u, to diagnose a failure situation. If an expected message has failed to arrive from a remote site, the problem might be due to any one of the above failures or it might simply be that the remote site or communication system is slow to respond. The appropriate action to take might be different in each case. For example, if the system is simply slow, u should continue to wait. If u believes that some failure has occurred and attempts to restart the remote computation, the restart might have different effects depending on the cause of the failure (or the delay, if no failure occurred). In some situations, the requested service might be performed twice.

As a first step in analyzing failures in distributed computations, we consider failures during a remote procedure call. (In Chapter 12 we deal with failures in general distributed transactions.) We assume that crashes and partitions can occur. In Chapter 8 we discussed why datagrams are a reasonable communication mechanism to support remote procedure call. Since most implementations of datagrams do not mask message failures, we must expect this type of failure as well.

An implementation of remote procedure call is shown in Figure 9.11. The call is handled by stubs at the caller and callee sites. The call message identifies the called procedure and contains the arguments. The reply message contains the results.

In Chapter 8 we pointed out that issues related to parameter passing and access to global variables stand in the way of achieving full transparency between local and remote procedure calls. Apart from such issues, however, in a failure-free environment the interfaces presented by local and remote procedure invocation are the same: parameters are passed to the procedure, the procedure is executed exactly once, and results are returned. We say that in a failure-free environment, both local and remote procedure call have *exactly once* semantics. Differences appear when we consider the effect of failures.

Since the implementation of a local procedure call involves no messages, the only failure we need consider in the local case is a crash. Since for local calls the calling computation and the procedure body execute at the same site, if that site should crash, its recovery protocol will recover both the calling computation and the body. Thus, for example, if the calling computation is failure atomic and commits, recovery ensures that the effect on program variables is that of exactly one execution of the procedure body, and if it aborts, the effect

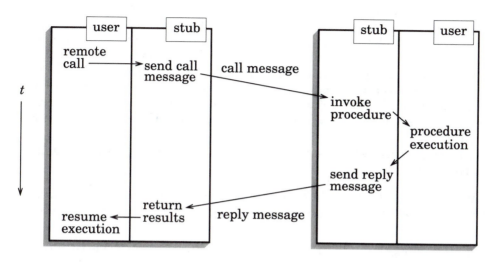

Figure 9.11: The actions at the caller and callee sites that result from a remote procedure call. Time progresses in the downward direction.

is that of zero executions.

By contrast, for remote procedure calls, the calling computation and the procedure body execute at different sites, each of which might separately crash or be prevented from communicating with other sites by message failures. Some applications require that the entire distributed computation, including the calling computation and the (remote) procedure body, be failure atomic; that is, the calling computation and the procedure body must either both commit (with the effect of having executed exactly once) or both abort (with no effect). We discuss how to satisfy this requirement in Chapter 12. Here we consider less stringent requirements. We assume the procedure body is failure atomic at its site (so partial execution is not an issue) but that the recovery protocol at the remote site is separate from the recovery protocol at the calling site (so, for example, the procedure body might commit at its site while the calling computation was still waiting for the return message from the invocation). We consider various recovery strategies at the calling site. As we shall see in the next two sections, new situations can arise that significantly complicate the semantics of remote calls. (For example, the calling computation might execute once when the procedure body has executed many times.) We refer to the effect of failures on the semantics of procedure invocation as *error semantics*.

We discuss the effect of failure on remote procedure calls in two steps. First we consider message failure; then we consider the effect of crash and partition failures.

9.6.1   Message Failure

Consider a remote invocation of procedure p. The calling stub can either return normally to the caller or return an exception. In either case the stub might first have attempted to compensate for errors that occurred. For example, if a call or reply message had been lost, the calling stub might have sent a duplicate call message. A variety of error semantics are possible in either the normal or the exceptional case. The error semantics of a normal return to a remote procedure call describe the postcondition of the call, while the error semantics of an exception return describe the precondition of the exception handler.

We define three types of error semantics for a normal return to a remote procedure call:

At least once semantics: The remote procedure has executed at least once, but may have executed many times; the results returned may be from any of the executions.

Last of many semantics: The remote procedure has executed at least once, but may have executed many times; the results returned are from the last execution.

Exactly once semantics: The remote procedure has executed exactly once; the results returned are from that execution.

The error semantics for an exception return might be as follows:

At most once semantics: The procedure has not been executed or has been executed once.

Maybe semantics: The procedure has been executed zero or more times.

Zero semantics: The procedure has never been executed.

At least once semantics provides minimal support for the caller. Figure 9.12 depicts a situation in which the values returned to the caller are not the result of the last execution of the procedure. The calling stub has timed out and, thinking that no response to the first call message is forthcoming, resends the call message. The reply message corresponding to the first call message subsequently arrives and the values it contains are returned to the caller. By the time the second reply message arrives, the caller might have already taken action based on the first (and, perhaps, terminated). If no reply message is received, an exception is returned to the caller with maybe semantics.

A more elaborate implementation is required to enforce last of many semantics. The calling stub assigns a sequence number to each call message, and that number is returned in the corresponding reply message. The calling stub records the number of the last call message sent and discards the reply message if its number is less than the stored value. The calling stub returns the values in the reply message to the caller when the numbers match. Once

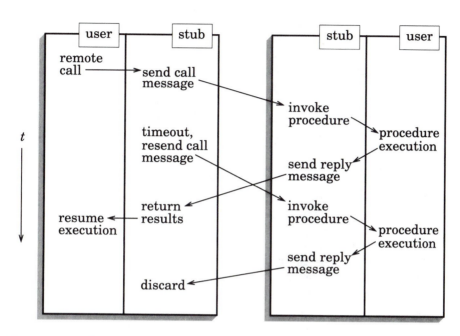

Figure 9.12: Last of many error semantics is violated, since the results returned to the caller do not reflect the final execution of the procedure.

again, if no reply message is received, an exception is returned to the caller
with maybe semantics.

This implementation of last of many semantics assumes that messages
are received at the callee's stub in the order sent. If messages can overtake
one another in transit, an early call message, $M1$, can arrive at the callee's
stub after the execution resulting from a later one, $M2$, has completed and
a reply message has been sent. The values returned in that reply message
will be delivered to the caller. If $M1$ subsequently causes the procedure to
be executed again, last of many semantics is not supported. Hence, if the
message system does not guarantee ordered delivery, the callee's stub must
itself detect out of order messages and discard them. This detection might be
done by recording the number of the last message received from the caller's
stub. Note that this information must be retained at the callee site even after
the execution of the procedure has completed, and the callee's stub must be able
to distinguish the call messages pertaining to one invocation of a particular
procedure by the user at the calling site from the call messages pertaining to
a subsequent invocation of the same procedure. Similarly, we assume that
only one execution of the procedure on behalf of a particular invocation is

in progress at a time. If this were not the case, the execution responding to the higher numbered call message, although initiated later, might finish earlier and once again cause a violation of last of many semantics. (Concurrent execution of the body introduces new problems, which are addressed in the next two chapters.)

Exactly once semantics can be implemented trivially by not allowing the calling stub to retry at all, but requiring it to immediately return an exception when it times out. If a response to the call message is received, a normal return is made and the caller can assume that p has been executed exactly once. If not, an exception is returned with at most once semantics (p might have been executed and the reply message been lost or arrived late). Unfortunately, this implementation does not provide much support for the caller. In a more supportive implementation, which allows the calling stub to resend the call message if it times out, the callee's stub saves a copy of the reply message sent when the procedure commits. If a subsequent call is received, the procedure is not re-executed; the reply message is simply resent. The callee site has to maintain information about the computed values after the invocation is completed, and it must distinguish between multiple call messages for the same invocation of p and call messages for a different invocation of p. If no reply message is received, an exception is returned to the caller with at most once semantics.

In the above three cases, when an exception is returned, the procedure might or might not have been executed. A more desirable condition would be to support zero semantics for exception returns. An implementation of zero semantics for exception returns together with exactly once semantics for normal returns is described in Chapter 12 in the context of failure atomicity of distributed computations.

9.6.2   Crashes, Partitions, and Orphans*

A new phenomenon arises when crashes or partitions occur in distributed systems: a procedure can be left in execution despite the fact that the caller no longer awaits its results. An example of the situation is shown in Figure 9.13. Procedure p can be executed at either site $B1$ or site $B2$. The caller invokes p at $B1$, which (unknown to the caller) makes a nested call to a procedure q at site C. Site $B1$ crashes, and when the caller becomes aware of the crash, it reinvokes p at $B2$. p once again invokes q at C, and this time execution of both q and p terminate normally, returning a result to site A. The first invocation of q is called an *orphan* because the process that invoked it no longer exists. The possibility that an orphan might be executing after the completion of a call has a major impact on error semantics. For example, since the orphan might still be executing after the result is returned to A, last of many semantics is not supported. Furthermore, it is difficult for C to recognize that the two invocations of q are related (and delay initiating the second until the first completes), since the call messages are sent by distinct processes (note that

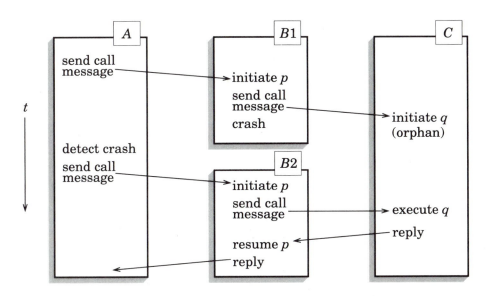

Figure 9.13: An orphan invocation resulting from a crash.

this is not a case of multiple call messages arising from the same invocation of q). Similar situations can arise if a partition separates the caller from the callee.

Orphans not only complicate error semantics, they waste resources as well. In addition, for certain applications we must consider the impact of an orphan on the consistency of the data on stable storage, and on the consistency of the orphan's view of that data (for example, the orphan might not terminate if it sees inconsistent data – data that does not satisfy its preconditions).

We now present two orphan elimination algorithms, which attempt to identify and terminate orphans. In the first, called *extermination*, site A keeps in stable storage a list of all nodes to which remote calls from A have been directed. If A crashes, orphans will (likely) exist at all nodes on the list. On recovery, A makes a remote call to an extermination procedure at each node, B, on its list, asking B to terminate the orphaned invocations. The extermination procedure at B makes a recursive call to those nodes on its list containing children of invocations that B initiated, so that the entire calling hierarchy can be eliminated. One problem with this approach is that termination has to wait for A's recovery, as well as the recovery of any other node that might have crashed in the calling hierarchy. Since the algorithm depends on message passing, it is also vulnerable to partitions.

In the *expiration* approach to orphan elimination, an expiration time interval is passed in the call message by the caller to the target node. If the invocation is still executing when the expiration time interval has elapsed, the target node terminates the computation. A calling stub attempting to implement last of many semantics waits for the expiration time interval to elapse before resending the call message. Two advantages of this approach are that no additional messages are required (hence, the algorithm works in spite of partitions) and that termination of orphans is not delayed by the crash of a node in the calling hierarchy. A disadvantage is that if the expiration time interval is too small, unnecessary aborts will occur, while if it is too large, orphan elimination is delayed. Furthermore, it assumes a degree of synchronization between local clocks.

The two approaches can be combined to retain the advantages of each. Large expiration time intervals are used in conjunction with extermination. Hence, if the extermination algorithm does not complete because of crashes or partitions, orphans will eventually be eliminated through expiration.

9.7 Clock Synchronization*

We have seen that synchronous algorithms rely on the assumption that at any instant of time the values of clocks at different sites do not differ by too much. Furthermore, we have discussed two specific asynchronous algorithms that assume clock synchronization: the duplicate detection algorithm for discarding old packets traveling through a network and the expiration approach to orphan elimination. In this section we describe two approaches to clock synchronization.

We assume that each processor is driven by a sequence of clock pulses and that these pulses are used to advance a register called a clock. Ideally, the value of the clock is incremented by the equivalent of one second during each second of real time. In actuality this will not be the case, and furthermore, the pulse rate may drift over time. To deal with this problem, we assume that the clock can be reset to compensate for the accumulated error.

We assume that the clocks at all normal sites initially contain approximately the same value. We further assume that the clock pulse rates are roughly the same at normal nodes and that the rate is such that a clock is advanced in a reasonable approximation to real time. Since these rates cannot be exactly the same, however, even if all sites are normal, the clock values will diverge over time if steps are not taken to resynchronize them. In clock synchronization algorithms, sites periodically exchange information about their clock values, and each site uses the information it receives from other sites to compute a new value to assign to its clock. All sites might not base their computations on exactly the same set of values – because of errors introduced by message delays and the fact that the resynchronization algorithm itself is not executed instantaneously at all sites – but, assuming the values are initially roughly equal and resynchronization is done often enough, the clocks must remain approximately synchronized.

The problem is compounded by failed nodes, which might behave unpredictably. In the worst case a failed node might behave maliciously, reporting totally different information about its clock value to different sites (a more benign form of such a situation arises if node i successfully reports its clock value to j but, because of a communication failure, k does not receive i's clock value and assumes a default value instead). As a result, the computations at different normal nodes might yield significantly different values. For resynchronization to work under these circumstances, we must limit the number of such faulty clocks. If n is the total number of nodes and t the number of failed nodes, we assume (as we did in our discussion of the agreement algorithm) that $n > 3t$.

Resynchronization algorithms should achieve two goals:

G1: At any time the values of normal clocks should be approximately equal.

G2: A normal clock should maintain a reasonable approximation to real time.

The second property is necessary to eliminate the trivial solution in which all clocks are kept fixed at the same value.

9.7.1   Interactive Convergence Algorithm*

The first algorithm we discuss is the Interactive Convergence Algorithm, in which each site acquires a clock value from every site and (essentially) averages these values to determine a new value for its clock. A site makes no attempt to ensure that the set of values it obtains is the same as the set obtained by another site. Instead, since a failed node might send totally different clock values to different sites (and, as a result, cause the averages computed at those sites to be significantly different) and, since (by assumption) the clock values of normal nodes will be approximately the same, a normal node simply discards values that differ from its own by too much.

More precisely, each normal node reads the value of every node's clock and sets its clock to the average of these values, except that if it reads a value that differs from its own by more than some specified constant δ, it replaces that value by its own clock value in the average value computation.

We have not explained how a node can read another node's clock. For simplicity, we initially assume that a node has direct access to all clocks and can read them without error. In addition, we initially assume that the resynchronization algorithm is carried out instantaneously and simultaneously at all sites.

If we assume that when resynchronization is initiated, normal clocks differ by no more than δ, we can demonstrate that when resynchronization completes, the difference between those clocks will have been reduced. Hence, if resynchronization is done often enough, the difference between normal clocks at any time can be bounded by δ. The algorithm relies on the assumption that clocks are synchronized at start-up time.

Assume that normal clocks differ by at most δ when resynchronization begins. Consider two normal nodes, i and j. Each gathers clock values from every other node. If k is a normal node, i and j get the same value for k's clock (since we have assumed that the algorithm is executed instantaneously and simultaneously). If k is faulty, i and j might get different values for k's clock. However, since by assumption i's clock and j's clock differ by at most δ and, since a site discards any reading that differs from its own by more than δ, the values used by i and j for k's clock cannot differ by more than 3δ. Hence, the averages computed by i and j cannot differ by more than $3\delta t/n$. Since $n > 3t$, the new values of the clocks at i and j will be closer after resynchronization than before.

We have made several unrealistic assumptions in describing the algorithm. First, we have assumed that all clocks are read at the same instant. In reality a node reads the clocks at other nodes during the course of executing the algorithm, and the time it takes to execute the algorithm, T, might not be negligible. As a result, even if there are no faulty clocks, the sets of values averaged by different sites will not be identical. Hence, the averages they compute will differ, and the above argument for convergence no longer holds. We can replace the assumption that all clocks are read at the same instant by the more realistic assumption that, since the rates of normal clocks are roughly the same and T is small, the difference between the values of two normal clocks over the course of a T second interval is approximately constant. Thus, if resynchronization is based on differences, the time at which a clock is read has no impact on the outcome of the algorithm.

Let $\Delta_{j,i}$, $i \neq j$, be the difference between the value of j's clock and the value of i's clock as computed by i, and let and $\Delta_{i,i} = 0$. For each j, i reads j's clock and immediately subtracts the value of its own clock to calculate $\Delta_{j,i}$. Then i adjusts its clock by adding the average of the n values $\overline{\Delta_{j,i}}$ where

$$\overline{\Delta_{j,i}} = \Delta_{j,i} \text{ if } |\Delta_{j,i}| \le \delta \text{ and } \overline{\Delta_{i,j}} = 0 \text{ otherwise} \tag{9.8}$$

A second unrealistic assumption is that i can read j's clock without any errors caused by message delays. In a distributed system, the value of j's clock is conveyed to i in a message, and hence when i calculates $\Delta_{j,i}$, it is using an old value of j's clock and the current value of its own clock. If we assume that ϵ is the maximum error in reading a remote clock (*i.e.*, ϵ is the maximum time between the instant j reads its clock and the instant i calculates $\Delta_{j,i}$), the true difference between the two clocks will exceed δ when the calculated difference exceeds $\delta + \epsilon$. Therefore we should replace δ with $\delta + \epsilon$ in (9.8).

The Interactive Convergence Algorithm maintains a bound, δ, on the difference between the values of normal clocks. Hence, the smaller the value of δ, the more successful the algorithm is. There are several factors that limit the extent to which we can reduce this value. If ρ is the maximum difference between the clock pulse rates of two normal clocks and if R is the time between successive resynchronizations, two normal clocks can diverge by as much as ρR between successive resynchronizations. Hence, ρ limits the extent to which δ can be reduced. Similarly, since the error in reading a clock is not exactly ϵ, but is simply bounded by ϵ, the correction in the calculation of $\overline{\Delta_{j,i}}$ might cause us to include the values of clocks that differ from i's clock by more than δ. As a result, we have weakened our ability to defend against the effects of faulty clocks and our ability to reduce δ.

9.7.2   Interactive Consistency Algorithm*

In the Interactive Convergence Algorithm, a site discards values that differ too greatly from its own (to reduce the difference between the average values computed at different sites as a result of the values transmitted by failed nodes). However, since values from failed nodes might not differ sufficiently to be discarded, sites still might not be averaging the same set of values, thus limiting the effectiveness of resynchronization.

An alternative approach is to use an agreement algorithm to ensure that all normal sites receive the same set of values. Simply taking the average of these values, however, would not ensure G2, since the value that all normal nodes use for a failed clock might be significantly different from the value of a normal clock, and hence the resulting average might not keep pace with real time. Rather than devising a scheme for discarding bad values before taking the average (as we did in the Interactive Convergence Algorithm), we can use the median of the values instead. If only a minority of the values are bad, the median will produce the value of a normal clock or the value of a faulty clock that lies between two normal clocks. In fact, the medians at all normal nodes will be the same up to the effect of errors introduced by delays.

If, as before, we start with the simplifying assumptions that resynchronization is done instantaneously and simultaneously and that clocks can be read without error, the Agreement Algorithm $A(t)$, where $n > 3t$, can be used to distribute the value of a particular clock to all other nodes. Each node, i, uses $A(t)$ to broadcast the value of its clock to all other nodes. We have described this step in terminology that conforms to our treatment of the Byzantine Generals Problem but it is equivalent to saying that each node reads i's clock and uses $A(t-1)$ to send the value it has read to all others. Using an agreement algorithm guarantees that all normal nodes agree on a value of each clock. Each node then resets its clock to the median of its set of values. Since the sets are the same at all nodes, all clocks will be set to exactly the same value.

If we eliminate the simplifying assumptions, we are immediately faced with a fundamental problem. $A(t)$ is a synchronous algorithm that unfolds in a series of rounds. Support of such an algorithm requires that clocks be synchronized to within a known maximum skew (recall the discussion of synchronous algorithms in Section 9.5.4). Hence, a certain degree of clock synchronization is needed to support the clock synchronization algorithm itself. To reason more easily about this circularity, we make the simplifying assumption that the time to execute the resynchronization algorithm is small compared to the time between resynchronizations, R. This assumption allows us to ignore the drift occurring during resynchronization and to use the maximum skew immediately prior to resynchronization (which is equal to the maximum skew immediately after resynchronization plus ρR, where ρ is the maximum difference between the rates of nonfaulty clocks) to dictate the interval of time allotted to each round of $A(t)$.

Suppose now we eliminate the assumption that a node can read another node's clock exactly. Then, even if all nodes are normal, the $n-1$ values of i's clock assembled by j will not be precisely the same, and if the function *maj* is based on majority, it will yield $\perp$. Hence all clocks will be resynchronized to $\perp$, thus violating G2. We can compensate for this imprecision in reading clocks by using the median function for *maj* in $A(t)$.

As with the Interactive Convergence Algorithm, we can deal with the fact that not all nodes read i's clock at the same instant by requiring that the nodes exchange clock differences instead of clock values. For example, suppose $n = 4$ and $t = 1$. In the first round, each node, i, sends the value of its clock to all other nodes, j. For each such value received, node j calculates $\Delta_{i,j}$ and uses $A(0)$ to send it to all other nodes in the second round. Hence, assuming node 2 is normal, it obtains three estimates of the difference between its clock and the clock at node 1: $\Delta_{1,2}$, $\Delta_{1,3} + \Delta_{3,2}$, and $\Delta_{1,4} + \Delta_{4,2}$. (For example, the second estimate is obtained by adding $\Delta_{1,3}$, which has been received in the second round from node 3, to $\Delta_{3,2}$, which node 2 has calculated from the value of node 3's clock received in the first round.) Node 2 calculates a value for node 1's clock by adding the median of these numbers to its own clock. All normal nodes get approximately the same value for each clock in the system (since clocks cannot be read exactly), and each node resets its clock to the median of these values.

9.8   Bibliographic Notes

Our discussion of the *happened-before* relation, logical clocks, and distributed mutual exclusion closely follows Lamport's presentation in [80]. A discussion of the distributed synchronization problem that takes failures into account is presented by Schneider, [116], who also describes the use of state machines in distributed synchronization [117]. A complete treatment of the architecture of communication systems can be found in texts by Tanenbaum [129] and Stallings [127]. An analysis of the theoretical limits that exist for achieving reliable communication is provided by Aho, Wyner, Yannakakis, and Ullman [8] and Halpern and Zuck [61]. Atomic broadcast protocols that preserve different ordering properties are described by Chang and Maxemchuk [31], Birman and Joseph [22], and Peterson, Buchholz, and Schlichting [111]. Gossip messages were introduced by Fischer and Michael [47]. Our discussion closely follows an optimized algorithm by Wuu and Bernstein [141]. The material on stable storage is based closely on the work of Lampson and Sturgis [87], [85], while background for the material on recoverable storage can be obtained from Gray [57] and from standard database texts such as Elmasri and Navathe [43] or Date [34]. The survey paper by Kohler [78] also covers this subject. The material on fail-stop processors is taken from the work of Schlichting and Schneider [114]. The basic work on malicious failures was done by Lamport, Shostak, and Pease [84] and Dolev [42]. Our treatment is based on the former. An excellent overview of research on agreement problems (up to 1983) has been compiled by Fischer [46]. The solution to the Byzantine Generals Problem given in the exercises is due to Bar-Noy and Dolev [15]. Material on the error semantics of remote procedure call can be found in Nelson's Ph.D. thesis [102], as well as in the publications on the Argus system [89], [90], [93]. A detailed model can also be found in the work of Spector [125]. Orphan elimination algorithms are described by Nelson [102] as well as by Liskov, et. al. [94] and McKendry and Herlihy [98]. The clock synchronization algorithms discussed here were developed by Lamport and Melliar-Smith [83]. A more recent synchronization algorithm having optimal properties is described by Srikanth and Toueg [126].

9.9 Exercises

1. For each of the events in the three processes in Figure 9.1, give the value of the logical clock of the process executing the event when that event occurs. Assume that the logical clock in each process ticks once between each event in that process.

2. The *birthtime* of a process is the value of the logical clock at its site when it is initiated. Two processes $\mathcal{P}_1$ and $\mathcal{P}_2$ satisfy the relation $\mathcal{P}_1$ *older-than* $\mathcal{P}_2$ if the birthtime of $\mathcal{P}_1$ is less than that of $\mathcal{P}_2$. Design a distributed mutual exclusion algorithm that satisfies requests in the *older-than* order: if the process making some request, r_1, is *older-than* the process making the request r_2, then r_1 will be granted the resource first.

The following four exercises refer to the stop-and-wait protocol described in Figure 9.2 with the exception that we assume sequence numbers have unbounded size and therefore modulo 2 arithmetic is not used. Let A_{-1} and M_{-1} denote the null element.

3. Show that the assertion

$$(\sigma = \mu_{sndr\_seq}) \wedge ((\forall i)(M_{i+1} \in \sigma) \Rightarrow (A_i \in \rho\,')) \wedge (s = M_{sndr\_seq})$$

is a loop invariant in *Sender*, and use the proof to show that I_s (9.3) is a program invariant. (Hint: Prove that it is implied by each assertion in your proof.)

4. To simplify the following proof, assume that in the code for $\mathcal{R}eceiver$, $r\_ack.seq$ is initialized to 0. Using (9.3), prove that the assertion

$$(\sigma' = \alpha_{rec\_seq-1}) \wedge ((\forall i)(A_i \in \sigma') \Rightarrow (M_i \in \rho)) \wedge$$
$$((rec\_seq \neq 0) \Rightarrow (r\_ack = A_{rec\_seq-1})) \wedge$$
$$((rec\_seq = 0) \Rightarrow (r.seq = 0)) \wedge (\rho = \mu_{rec\_seq-1})$$

is a loop invariant of $\mathcal{R}eceiver$ and that I_r (9.2) is a program invariant. (Hint: Prove that it is implied by each assertion in your proof. Your satisfaction proof should include the assertion

$$(rec\_seq - 1) \leq r\_ack.seq \leq rec\_seq$$

as a conjunct of the postcondition of the receive statement.)

5. Using I_s (9.3), I_r (9.2), and your proof in problem 9.4, prove that the assertion

$$(\delta = \overline{\rho}) \wedge (\rho = \mu_{rec\_seq-1})$$

is a loop invariant of $\mathcal{R}eceiver$, thus demonstrating that the application at the receiver's end gets the sequence of messages sent.

6. Using I_s (9.3), I_r (9.2), and your proof in problem 9.4, deduce that the assertion

$$\sigma' - \rho' = A^*_{rec\_seq-2}$$

is a precondition of the send statement in $\mathcal{R}eceiver$ that sends a particular acknowledgement for the first time and that

$$\sigma - \rho = M^*_{sndr\_seq}$$

is a precondition of the send in *Sender* that sends a particular message for the first time, thus demonstrating that a one bit sequence number field is sufficient.

7. Give an example of a routine, R, and two assertions, Q_1 and Q_2, such that R is idempotent with respect to Q_1 but not with respect to Q_2.

8. The following design has been proposed for an immediate-update system that combines the features of stable storage and recoverable storage. Instead of using primary and secondary storage (a disk and a tape), the system uses two primary storage media (two disks), $D1$ and $D2$. $D1$ is used to store the write-ahead log. As with stable storage, program variables are stored redundantly on both $D1$ and $D2$. The plan is to use background writes to update program variables on $D2$, thus avoiding the need to wait for two writes, as is required by stable storage systems. When the action commits, a forced null write is made to $D2$, forcing all the background writes to complete. The

advantage of this approach over recoverable storage is that if the first copy of the data should decay, the second copy is immediately available for use. Specify the design of the system in more detail, and contrast the errors that it corrects for and the disasters that it is vulnerable to with those of stable storage.

9. Find the total number of messages sent during the Agreement Algorithm, $A(t)$, when there are n sites.

10. Compare the number of I/O operations performed by committed transactions in immediate-update and deferred-update systems.

11. Suppose, in the model used to solve the Byzantine Generals Problem, no limit can be placed on the length of time it takes for a normal node to respond to a message. Give a scenario in which the Agreement Algorithm, $A(t)$, fails. Give an informal argument showing that no other algorithm will work under these circumstances.

12. Explain why, in the Agreement Algorithm, $A(t)$, if the source node is faulty, the vectors assembled by normal receivers are all identical, whereas if the source is normal this is not necessarily true.

13. Demonstrate that the following algorithm, due to Bar-Noy and Dolev [15], solves the consensus problem when $n \geq (2t+1)(t+1)$ and there are at most t failures. Assume that the initial value assigned to a process, p, is stored in a variable, x_p. The processes are divided into $t+1$ disjoint groups, each containing at least $2t+1$ processes. Let the groups be called $G_1, G_2, \ldots, G_{t+1}$. The algorithm is divided into t rounds. In round i, $1 \leq i \leq t$, only processes in G_i and G_{i+1} are active:

> Each process $p \in G_i$ sends the present value of x_p to each process in G_{i+1}.
>
> Each process $q \in G_{i+1}$ sets x_q to the *maj* function of the values it received from G_i. If it did not receive a value from some process, it uses 1 for the value for that process. In the case of a tie, it sets x_q to 1.

In round $t+1$:

> Each process $p \in G_{t+1}$ sends the value x_p to all processes (in all groups).
>
> Each process q sets x_q to the *maj* function of the values it received. If it did not receive a value from some process, it uses 1 for the value for that process. In the case of a tie, it sets x_q to 1.

At the end of round $t+1$, each process p decides the value it has stored in x_p.

14. In the following program A is an N dimensional vector of integers. Prove that the assertion

$$((\forall j)\ (1 \leq j \leq N) \Rightarrow (A[N] \geq A[j]))$$

is a postcondition of the program. Prove that the program can be used as its own recovery action. Assume that A is stored in stable storage.

```
begin
  i := 1;
  do i < N →
    begin
      if A[i + 1] < A[i] → A[i], A[i + 1] := A[i + 1], A[i];
      else skip; fi;
      i := i + 1;
    end;
  od;
end;
```

15. Give a scenario in which an orphan procedure body sees inconsistent data and does not terminate.

16. Show that, if step 2 of the Gossip Message Receive Algorithm is eliminated, row i of the time table at site i can be used as a logical clock.

10

Transactions on Untyped Databases

A *database* is a collection of data items. Many applications require that a database be maintained to describe the state of some part of the real world. Frequently the accuracy of the database is critical for life and property – for example, in an air traffic control system or a banking system.

As a part of the application, programs must be designed to read or update the database, often in real time. In the context of such database systems, these programs are called *transactions* (they correspond to the actions discussed in Chapter 9) and are executed when some external event occurs that requires the database to be accessed (for example, a bank deposit). Each transaction must be designed so that it maintains the correctness of the relationship between the database and the real world. Systems of this type are called *transaction processing systems*. The database itself is at the heart of such systems, since it persists beyond the lifetime of any particular transaction.

Frequently the application requires that the transactions execute concurrently. It is this concurrent mode of execution that is of particular interest to us. Although we assume that each transaction preserves the correctness of the database when executed in isolation, the concurrent execution of transactions is not guaranteed to do so. Hence, special techniques must be used to guarantee correctness under concurrent execution.

A transaction processing system can be viewed as a special case of a shared memory system in which the shared memory contains the database and the concurrent processes are transactions. In Chapter 4 we saw that the arbitrary interleaving of processes could result in interference and that one way to eliminate interference is to restrict interleaving through synchronization. The nature of the required synchronization is determined by a detailed analysis of the semantics of the individual processes.

A somewhat different approach to the problem of interference is taken in transaction processing systems, since transaction semantics are generally not known in advance. Interleaving is now controlled by a concurrency control algorithm, which bases its decisions on the semantics of the individual database operations invoked by the transactions, rather than the complete semantics of the transactions. In this and the next two chapters we study a variety of such concurrency control algorithms. In this chapter we assume that no failures occur during the operation of the transaction processing system. In Chapter 12 we consider the effect of failures.

10.1   Serial Execution and Atomicity

The execution of a transaction results in the execution of a sequence of database operations and internal computations, followed by a commit or abort operation. A *database operation* identifies an item in the database and an action to be performed on that item (for example, read or increment). The operation can return values to the transaction and store values in the database. We define the *effect* of an operation to be the changes it makes to the database and the values it returns. All computations performed by a transaction are done in a temporary workspace private to the transaction. In addition to modifying the state of the database, a transaction can cause actions that are externally visible (for example, return information to the user). We define the *effect* of a transaction to be the changes it makes to the database and its external actions.

We say that a transaction works correctly when executed in isolation if, whenever it is started in a database state that satisfies some specified assertion (its precondition), it terminates and the final database state satisfies some other specified assertion (its postcondition). Thus the specification of a transaction is similar to the specification of an operation on an abstract data object. We assume that each transaction has been designed so that it works correctly when executed in isolation. We are concerned with ensuring that it still works correctly when executed concurrently with other transactions.

We make the further assumption that the concurrency control – the portion of the system that is responsible for ensuring correct concurrent operation – does not know the assertions that support a proof of each transaction's specifications. We refer to this information as *transaction semantics*. The reason for this assumption is that the concurrency control is usually supplied as a part of the database system and we do not want to have to redesign it for each new transaction processing application (or each enhancement of an existing application).

Interference is a major issue. Even though the concurrency control does not know the semantics of the transaction, it must ensure that the assertions describing the state at each of the transaction's control points are not interfered with. We distinguish between *external interference*, in which the pre- or postconditions of the transaction are interfered with, and *internal interference*, in which assertions attached to control points within the transaction are interfered with.

We deal with internal and external interference differently. If we were to view concurrent transactions as the components of a cobegin statement, the resulting arbitrary interleaving of the statements in different transactions would, in general, result in internal interference. Since we assume the concurrency control does not know transaction semantics, it does not have the information necessary to permit interleavings that do not cause interference. Hence, the cobegin model does not place strong enough restrictions on the interleaving of transactions.

Assume next that instead of viewing the execution of transactions in the context of a cobegin statement, we view the transactions as the components of a coenter statement (recall that the components of a coenter execute sequentially in some nondeterministically selected order). Since the operational semantics of coenter does not allow interleaved execution, internal interference no longer occurs. We must still ensure that external interference does not occur. The pre- and postconditions of each transaction can be partitioned into assertions that refer only to variables local to the transaction (and hence cannot be interfered with) and assertions that refer to shared database variables (and can be interfered with). To ensure that no external interference can occur, we require that assertions in the pre- and postconditions of each transaction that refer to shared database variables be invariant to the execution of each transaction. Under these circumstances, both external and internal interference do not occur.

As an example, recall that in the banking system described in Chapter 4, the postcondition of the withdraw transaction (Figure 4.6) is the conjunction of the assertion

$$Q_i : (totwdrn[i] = W_i + amtwdri) \land ((amtwdri \neq 0) \Rightarrow (amtwdri = wdri))$$

which involves only local variables and hence cannot be interfered with, and the invariant

$$I : (bal = \sum_i totaldep[i] - \sum_i totwdrn[i]) \land (bal \geq 0)$$

where bal is the shared database variable and $totaldep[i]$ and $totalwdrn[i]$ are auxiliary variables. The conjunction of these assertions allows us to assert the application-related property that bal is updated properly.

If assertions in the pre- and postconditions of each transaction that refer to shared database variables are invariant to the execution of each transaction and the operational semantics of coenter is enforced, the pre- and postcondition of each transaction will be true when the transaction is entered and exited, respectively. Hence, each transaction will execute correctly. Note that the concurrency control need not know what the pre- and postconditions are.

It is interesting to consider the abstract invariant discussed in connection with abstract objects in Chapter 3 in the context of the current discussion. An abstract invariant defines the domain of an abstract object. For example, if we view *bal* as an abstract object, a reasonable abstract invariant is $bal \geq 0$. Such an invariant, however, does not assure us that the value of *bal* reflects all the operations that have been performed on it. By contrast, the banking invariant, I, also specifies that the state of the database reflects the history of operations that have been performed on it.

In the database literature, the terms *consistency constraint* and *integrity constraint* are used informally to refer to any invariants defined on the database. For the database example, one consistency constraint might be $bal \geq 0$; another might be I. When we say that a database is *inconsistent*, we mean that there is some consistency constraint that it does not satisfy. Intuitively we see that if a database is inconsistent, its database variables do not satisfy the specified relationships or do not reflect the history of database operations (and hence the database does not accurately model the appropriate real world situation).

The type of execution enforced by coenter semantics is called *serial* execution. While we have argued that serial execution has nice semantic properties, it does not allow concurrency and therefore would result in large response times when service had to be provided to a number of users (since it does not allow efficient use of multiple processors). Hence, our goal is to build a concurrency control that allows interleaving (and thus does not enforce the operational semantics of the coenter) but still supports the formal semantics of the coenter (4.12). Thus we allow interleaved execution, but that execution must be equivalent to a serial execution in the sense that all transactions have the same effect as if they had run in some serial order.

Although we have assumed that the concurrency control does not know the semantics of the transactions, we assume that it does know the semantics of the individual database operations and can use that knowledge to determine allowable interleavings. We assume that database operations are executed atomically with respect to one another. Using operation semantics, the concurrency control can detect situations in which the order of a pair of database operations (executed by different transactions) in some execution can be reversed without changing the values they return or the state of the database when the pair has completed. The two executions are said to be equivalent (this definition will be made more precise shortly). We say that a pair of operations *commute* if they return the same values and leave the database in the same final state when executed in either order. Operations that commute can always be reversed, but, as we shall see, in some situations we can use more general properties to determine a set of operation pairs that can be reversed without changing their combined effect. Based on the set of operation pairs that commute, we can specify interleaved executions that are equivalent to serial executions, and it is these executions that the concurrency control is designed to permit.

For example, if $p_{1,1}$ and $p_{1,2}$ are two operations in transaction T_1 and $p_{2,1}$ and $p_{2,2}$ are two operations in transaction T_2, one sequence of interleaved operations is

$$p_{1,1}\, p_{2,1}\, p_{1,2}\, p_{2,2}$$

If $p_{2,1}$ and $p_{1,2}$ commute, this interleaved sequence is equivalent to the serial execution

$$p_{1,1}\, p_{1,2}\, p_{2,1}\, p_{2,2}$$

and thus can be allowed by a concurrency control. (Note that two operations on disjoint data items always commute.) The more information about operation semantics the concurrency control uses, the larger the set of possible interleaved executions it can recognize as equivalent and hence the more concurrency it can allow. Keep in mind, however, that each interleaved execution must be equivalent to some serial execution.

Since a concurrency control guarantees that all interleaved executions are equivalent to serial executions, one transaction does not see an intermediate state produced by another. Hence, a transaction sees either all the information written to the database by another transaction or none. We refer to this property as *concurrency atomicity*. An intermediate state produced by a transaction might not satisfy the consistency constraints of the database. If another transaction sees such an inconsistent state, it is not guaranteed to work correctly – for example, it may go into an endless loop – thus violating our model of a transaction processing system. This situation is avoided by imposing the requirement of concurrency atomicity.

Much of the design theory for concurrency control has been developed using the simplest model for database operations: each data item is an (untyped) record with operations *read*(x), which returns the value of the record x, and *write*(x), which stores a new value into the record x. The value returned by *read*(x) is the value written by the last preceding *write*(x), which we refer to as the *predecessor write*, or the initial value of x, if there is no predecessor write. Note that two read operations on the same record commute, as do two arbitrary operations on different records. In this chapter we concentrate on this untyped model.

The untyped model can be generalized to include *typed* databases, in which the database is assumed to be made up of instances of abstract data types and the database operations are the abstract operations of those types. For example, a data item x might be an integer with abstract operations *increment* and *decrement* or a queue with abstract operations *enqueue* and *dequeue*. We assume that these abstract operations are executed atomically. Given operation semantics, we can again determine properties related to commutativity. We no longer have to limit ourselves to such simple considerations as with read and write: two operations on the same abstract object can commute even though both change its value (for example, two *increment* operations on an integer data item). In the next chapter we generalize our discussion to include typed databases.

10.2　Recoverability

When a transaction successfully terminates, any changes it made to the database are made permanent and must not be lost, even if the system should subsequently fail (this requirement is frequently referred to as *permanence*). Not all transactions successfully terminate, however. A transaction might terminate unsuccessfully either because it executes an abort operation or because the system fails before the transaction completes. Since such a transaction might have partially updated the database variables, it might leave the database in an inconsistent state – one which does not satisfy the consistency constraints. Hence we require that each transaction be failure atomic (see Section 9.5). Either it successfully terminates and commits, in which case its database changes are made permanent, or it unsuccessfully terminates, in which case it must have the same effect as if it had never been initiated. In this chapter we consider unsuccessful terminations caused by aborts; in Chapter 12 we discuss failures. A transaction that has been initiated but has not yet committed or aborted is said to be *active*.

When a transaction aborts, any changes it made to the database must be nullified. We say that the transaction must be *rolled back*. Since a transaction can abort at any time it is active, it should not cause any irrevocable external actions (such as printing a receipt for a deposit transaction) before it commits.

This definition of the semantics of abortion is not as simple as it might appear.[1] Concurrency atomicity has already restricted transaction execution so that one transaction does not see an intermediate state produced by another. Suppose, however, that we allow final results written to the database by transaction T_2 to be read by transaction T_1 before T_2 terminates. If we then allow the sequence of events "T_1 commits, T_2 aborts" to occur, abortion semantics will not be supported. Since T_1 has committed, the information it has written must be preserved. On the other hand, that information may be a function of the information that T_1 read from T_2, and hence T_2 has (indirectly) affected the database state even though it aborted. Since we generally cannot prevent a transaction from aborting, we must design the concurrency control in such a way that the above situation cannot happen. Specifically, we cannot allow T_1 to commit in the above scenario. A concurrency control is said to be *recoverable* if it does not allow a transaction, T_1, to commit until every other transaction, T_2, that wrote values it read has committed. (Thus T_2 can abort any time before it commits.) We require all our concurrency controls to be recoverable.

Even though a concurrency control is recoverable, it may have another undesirable property: cascaded aborts. A concurrency control exhibits *cascaded aborts* if the abort of one transaction causes the abort of one or more other

---

[1]As we shall see in later sections, transactions can be implemented in either the immediate-update model or the deferred-update model described in Section 9.5. The discussion of abortion in the remainder of this section refers primarily to immediate-update systems in which abortion implies rollback.

transactions. Suppose again that we allow final results written to the database by transaction T_2 to be read by transaction T_1 before T_2 terminates. If T_2 now aborts, we must also abort T_1, since it read a value T_2 had written. In a more general situation, the abort of one transaction might require the abort of an unbounded number of other transactions – an undesirable situation. Thus we require that our concurrency controls avoid cascaded aborts. A concurrency control will avoid cascaded aborts if a transaction is not allowed to read a value written by an active transaction. This condition is more stringent than that for recoverability, which allows T_1 to read a value written by an active transaction, T_2, but then does not allow T_1 to commit until after T_2 has committed.

We can ensure both recoverability and no cascaded aborts by requiring an even stronger condition called strictness. A concurrency control is said to be *strict* if it does not allow a transaction, T_1, to read *or write* a value written by an active transaction, T_2. Clearly, a strict concurrency control is recoverable and does not exhibit cascaded aborts. The reason we require strictness is for efficiency in implementing rollback in certain situations. Ordinarily when we roll back the effect of a write of some data item, x, we expect to restore the value of x to its value just before the write occurred. Suppose we allow active transactions T_1 and T_2 to each write a new value of x (in that order). If T_1 aborts, we do not have to restore the value of x at all. If T_2 now aborts as well, we have to restore the value of x to its value just before T_1's write (not T_2's write). Although we could design the system to perform correctly in all such situations, the design of strict systems is much simpler, since we can always roll back a write by restoring the value of x to its value just before the write occurred.

Note that the notion of recoverability is motivated by purely semantic considerations (it is required by the semantics of abortion), while the notions of avoiding cascaded aborts and strictness are motivated by practical considerations.

10.3 Serializability

A *schedule* is a sequence of elements, each of which specifies a database operation and the identity of the transaction that performed the operation (when typed operations are considered in the next chapter, we will sometimes include the results returned by the operation). A transaction, T, executing in isolation can be described by a schedule in which each element identifies T and the elements are sequenced in the order in which they are performed on the database. The interleaved execution of a set of transactions can be described by a schedule that is the merge of the schedules of the transactions in the set. All the schedules we discuss are of this form. The identity of a transaction is omitted when it is irrelevant to the discussion.

To keep the discussion simple, the schedules we consider do not contain the

$T_1 : read(x)$ $read(y)$ $write(y)$
$T_2 :$ $read(x)$ $write(x)$

(a)

$T_1 : read(x)$ $read(y)$ $write(y)$
$T_2 :$ $read(x)$ $write(x)$

(b)

Figure 10.1: (a) A concurrent schedule and (b) its serialized version.

operations of transactions that have aborted. We are justified in doing this, since concurrency atomicity guarantees that one transaction does not see the partial results written to the database by another transaction that ultimately aborts and failure atomicity guarantees that any modifications to the database caused by an aborted transaction are rolled back.

A schedule is a projection of the information describing the execution of the transactions, since the internal computations performed by the transactions are not shown. We assume that these internal computations are deterministic and therefore the effect of a transaction is completely determined by the values returned by each of its reads (and by the values passed to the transaction on initiation). We generally do not include commit operations in schedules, since they have no effect (*i.e.*, they do not change the database state or return information).

Figure 10.1(a) is a pictorial representation of a schedule in which the operations of each transaction occupy a different line and time increases from left to right. The value of a record at any point in a schedule is the value written by the last preceding write or its initial value if there is no preceding write. A schedule corresponding to the serial execution of a set of transactions is called a *serial schedule*. The schedule shown in Figure 10.1(a) is concurrent (nonserial) because some of the operations of T_1 occur before those of T_2 and others occur after. Consider now the serial schedule shown in Figure 10.1(b). Assume that the schedules of Figure 10.1(a) and Figure 10.1(b) are executed starting from the same initial state. Since T_2 does not read or write y, the final state of the database and the results output by the transactions will be the same in both schedules. The schedule of Figure 10.1(b) is said to be a *serialized* version of the schedule of Figure 10.1(a).

More precisely, a schedule is said to be *serializable* if there exists an *equivalent* serial schedule. We consider two notions of equivalence. Two schedules are said to be *view equivalent* if and only if

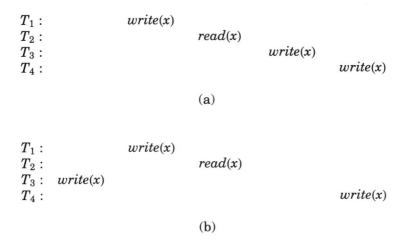

(a)

(b)

Figure 10.2: Two possible placements for T_3 in a view equivalent serial schedule.

1. They are merges of the schedules of the same set of transactions;

2. Corresponding read operations in the two schedules have the same predecessor write operations;

3. The final write operation to each data item in each schedule is the same.

Since each transaction reads values written by the same transaction in both schedules, it sees the same inputs in both cases (has the same *view* of the database) and hence computes the same results. Thus its effect is the same in both schedules. Furthermore, the database is left in the same state, since the final write operations in both are the same.

Consider the problem of determining whether a given schedule is view equivalent to a serial schedule. Figure 10.2(a) shows a projection of a concurrent schedule, S, which includes only the operations on a record, x. Note first that T_2 contains an operation $read(x)$ whose predecessor write is in T_1. Therefore, from the definition of view equivalence, T_2 must follow T_1 in any serial schedule that is view equivalent to S. Consider next the constraints implied by the other transactions. The write operations of T_1, T_3, and T_4 are said to be *blind* because each transaction does not read x before it writes. In addition, T_3's write is said to be *dead* because no other transaction reads the value T_3 wrote and it is not the final write operation in the schedule (hence the write does not affect other transactions or the final value of x).

As far as the effect of these four transactions on x is concerned, this schedule is view equivalent to a serial schedule in which the ordering of transactions is T_3, T_1, T_2, T_4. The operations on x are as shown in Figure 10.2(b). Note that T_2 has the same predecessor write, T_3's write is dead, and T_4 writes the same final value into the database. Furthermore, a serial schedule containing the subsequence T_1, T_2, T_3, T_4 contains the same sequence of operations on x as S [*i.e.*, as shown in Figure 10.2(a)], and so, as far as the effect of these four transactions on x is concerned, it too is view equivalent to S. Thus, if we consider only x, there may exist serial schedules view equivalent to S in which the write of T_3 occurs before that of T_1 and others in which it occurs after the read of T_2. Suppose the transactions of S interact in a similar way on another record, y. Again, there may be a binary choice in the placement of a write operation. In fact, if the transactions interact on n records in this way, there may be 2^n possible such choices, each of which may have to be individually checked to determine if it is view equivalent to S. By formalizing this reasoning, it can be shown that the problem of determining whether a schedule has a view equivalent serial schedule is NP-complete. Thus we cannot expect this computation to be part of a concurrency control algorithm.

Fortunately the problem faced by the concurrency control algorithm is not to determine whether a given schedule is serializable, but rather to respond in real time to requests from transactions and to take appropriate actions (for example, delay requests) so as to produce a final schedule that is serializable. This problem is computationally feasible. To describe the solution, we introduce the notion of a conflict.

For untyped databases, we say that an operation, p_1, *conflicts* with an operation, p_2, of a different transaction if they both access the same record, x, and if there exists a state of x such that the sequences $p_1 \, p_2$ and $p_2 \, p_1$ operating on that state either return different values or leave x in different final states. Clearly, if p_1 conflicts with p_2, then p_2 conflicts with p_1, and if two operations do not conflict, they commute. Conflicts can be described by the relation *does-not-commute-with*

$$p_1 \text{ conflicts with } p_2 \text{ if } (p_1, \, p_2) \in \textit{does-not-commute-with}$$

We define conflict in this way to conform to its usage in the next chapter, in which a more general notion than commutativity applies. Instead of the notation $(p_1, \, p_2) \in \textit{does-not-commute-with}$, we frequently use the equivalent notation $p_1 \, \textit{does-not-commute-with} \, p_2$. Also, if operations of T_1 and T_2 conflict, we simply say that T_1 and T_2 conflict.

Hence, for untyped databases, *does-not-commute-with* contains all pairs of operations on the same record in which at least one element of the pair is a write. The only pair of operations on a particular record that is not in the relation is two reads. The relation is shown in tabular form in Figure 10.3, where an X in the row corresponding to operation p_1 and the column corresponding to operation p_2 means that $(p_1, \, p_2) \in \textit{does-not-commute-with}$.

Two schedules are said to be *conflict equivalent* if and only if

1. They are merges of the schedules of the same set of transactions;

2. Conflicting operations are ordered in the same way in both schedules.

Operation of Transaction T_2

		read	write
Operation of	*read*		X
Transaction T_1	*write*	X	X

Figure 10.3: Conflicts between read and write operations on the same record for untyped databases are based on the relation *does-not-commute-with*, here denoted by X.

Operations that are ordered differently in two conflict equivalent schedules commute and hence have the same combined effect in both schedules.

Two schedules that are conflict equivalent are also view equivalent, but the converse is not necessarily true. To see that conflict equivalence implies view equivalence, we first note that both notions of equivalence have the same first condition. Second, the third condition for view equivalence follows from conflict equivalence, since two write operations conflict. Finally, consider a read operation, R, in two conflict equivalent schedules, S_1 and S_2, and assume that in S_1 R's predecessor write is W_1 while in S_2 it is W_2. W_1 and W_2 must be ordered identically in the two schedules, since they are conflict equivalent. Assume the ordering is W_1, W_2. Then R and W_2 must be ordered differently in S_1 and S_2. But this violates the second condition of conflict equivalence, so R must have the same predecessor write in both schedules.

That view equivalence does not imply conflict equivalence can be seen from the schedule shown in Figure 10.4, which is view equivalent to the serial schedule T_2, T_1, T_3. The two schedules are not conflict equivalent, however, since the write operations to x by T_1 and T_2 in the two schedules occur in opposite orders. Note that although these two writes conflict, they do not affect the final value of x and are not predecessor writes to any read; that is, they are blind, dead writes.

Conflict equivalence is thus a more restrictive concept than view equivalence and therefore implies less concurrency. In other words, a concurrency control based on conflict equivalence must disallow certain schedules, even though they are view equivalent to serial schedules. Still, for the practical reasons outlined above, concurrency controls are virtually always based on conflict equivalence, and henceforth when we use the word "equivalence" we mean conflict equivalence.

Because transactions that access only disjoint database items can be ordered arbitrarily, a serializable schedule can be equivalent to more than one serial schedule. Although any serial order will preserve consistency, we limit ourselves to concurrency controls that produce schedules that are serializable in the order in which the transactions have committed, called the *commit or-*

$$T_1: \qquad\qquad write(y)\ write(x)$$
$$T_2: read(y) \qquad\qquad\qquad\qquad write(x)$$
$$T_3: \qquad\qquad\qquad\qquad\qquad\qquad write(x)$$

Figure 10.4: A schedule that demonstrates that view equivalence does not imply conflict equivalence.

$$T_1: \qquad\qquad read(x)\ write(x) \qquad commit$$
$$T_2: read(x) \qquad\qquad\qquad\qquad\qquad read(y)\ commit$$

Figure 10.5: A schedule that is serializable, but is not serializable in commit order.

der. We select this particular order for two reasons. The first is efficiency. We have already stated that in order to implement recoverability efficiently, we require that the concurrency control be strict (*i.e.*, a transaction is not allowed to read or write a value that was written by an active transaction). Strictness does not imply serializability in commit order, as shown by the schedule in Figure 10.5. The schedule is strict and is serializable in the order T_2, T_1, but is not serializable in the commit order T_1, T_2, since T_2 read x before T_1 wrote it and hence T_2 must be before T_1 in the serial order. As we shall see in subsequent sections, serializability in commit order corresponds to a condition even stronger than strictness: in addition, a transaction is not allowed to write a value that was written *or read* by an active transaction (*i.e.*, a transaction is not allowed to perform any operation on a value on which a conflicting operation has been performed by an active transaction). As we shall also see, this stronger condition leads to quite simple implementations.

The second reason for selecting commit order is less technical. We can argue that the user has an intuitive expectation that the transactions have executed in commit order. For example, transactions frequently have irrevocable external actions visible to the user (a deposit transaction outputs a receipt), and the user expects the equivalent serial order to be consistent with the order implied by these external actions. Hence, if the user initiates one transaction after the external actions of another have been observed, the user expects the second to occur after the first in the equivalent serial order (a withdraw transaction should see the results of a previous deposit transaction for which a receipt has been issued). Since we cannot allow a transaction to have an irrevocable external action and then abort, transaction designs usually require all such actions to occur at commit time. Hence one way to ensure that the order implied by such external actions is the same as the serial order is to serialize in commit order.

10.4 Models for Concurrency Controls

To proceed further we must specify in more detail how the concurrency control interacts with the transactions and how the transactions interact with the database. Hence, in this section we deal with implementation issues. Like the failure atomic systems discussed in Section 9.5, transaction processing systems can be characterized as either immediate-update systems or deferred-update systems:

> In *immediate-update systems*, a write operation immediately updates the appropriate record in the database, and a read operation returns the value of the appropriate record in the database. Although it appears that a read might return a value written by an as yet uncommitted transaction, and hence the concurrency control would not be strict, we shall see that the concurrency control algorithm prevents this situation from occurring. Before an immediate-update system performs a write operation to a record, it copies the original value into its write-ahead log. If the transaction aborts, the write-ahead log is used to roll back any changes made by the transaction to the database.

> In *deferred-update systems*, a write operation does not update the appropriate record in the database immediately, but instead the information to be written is saved in the transaction's intentions list. A read operation returns the value of the appropriate record in the database unless the transaction has written that record, in which case the value from its intentions list is returned. Note that a value returned by a read is either a value the transaction itself has written or a value written by a committed transaction. If the transaction commits, its intentions list is used to update the database.

Concurrency controls require that transactions request permission to perform certain operations. The nature of these operations differs depending on the control. The concurrency control can grant, delay, or deny the request (denial implies that the transaction is aborted). Note that in a deferred-update system, a concurrency control might grant a request to write, but the data record is actually updated at a later time when the transaction commits. The write operation is recorded in the schedule when the record is updated, not when the request is granted. Concurrency controls can be characterized as either pessimistic or optimistic.

> In a *pessimistic* system, whenever a transaction attempts to perform some database operation, it must request permission from the concurrency control. However, the transaction can commit at any time without requesting permission.

> In an *optimistic* system, a transaction can perform any database operation it wishes without requesting permission from the concurrency control. However, the transaction must request permission to commit.

In both systems, a transaction can abort without requesting permission at any time before it commits.

We study three of the four combinations of these models: the immediate-update pessimistic system, the deferred-update optimistic system, and the deferred-update pessimistic system. (As will become clear, the immediate-update optimistic system is not a sensible alternative.)

We assume that the concurrency control bases its response to a request from a transaction, T, on the nature of the conflicts that granting that request would cause.

In a pessimistic system, a request asks the concurrency control to perform a database operation. Granting a request of a transaction, T, that conflicts with a previously granted request of an active transaction, T', would fix the ordering between T and T', since the two operations do not commute. Because the order in which the two transactions will commit is not yet known, granting T's request might destroy the ability of the concurrency control to create a serialization consistent with the commit order. We need not be concerned with conflicts with committed transactions, since they precede T in the commit order and, correspondingly, their operations precede the operation T has requested.

In an optimistic system, a request asks the concurrency control to commit a transaction. Committing a transaction, T, causes all operations done by T prior to the commit to become part of the schedule of committed transactions produced by the concurrency control. (If T had been aborted, these operations would simply be deleted.) Hence, the concurrency control needs to be concerned that T's operations can be consistently ordered with respect to the operations of previously committed transactions.

For each model, we consider which conflicts can possibly occur and organize the concurrency control so that it never grants a request that prevents a schedule from being serializable in commit order.

There is some confusion in the literature about the use of the word "conflict." As we have defined it, two database operations in a schedule conflict if they return different values or leave the database in a different state when their order is reversed. For untyped data, we have seen that this definition implies that two operations conflict if they access the same record and one is a write. The issue of reversal arises because we are interested in constructing an equivalent serial schedule. Since transaction execution can be interleaved in the original schedule, it might be necessary to reverse the order of the operations in order to construct a serial schedule. We want the operations to return the same values and leave the database in the same state after their order is reversed, and hence we want them to be nonconflicting. In the context of a particular concurrency control, however, certain operations might be guaranteed to occur in commit order and hence the question of reversal does not arise (for example, we will see that write operations in a deferred-update optimistic concurrency control always occur in commit order). Thus the concurrency control need only check for a subset of the conflicts. In the literature, discussions of a particular concurrency control frequently use the word "conflict" to refer only to the subset that must be checked by that control. Rather than introduce new terminology, in what follows we rely on the context of the discussion to differentiate these two meanings of the word "conflict" and are explicit when that is not sufficient.

10.5   Immediate-Update Pessimistic Systems

Our first goal in discussing each system model is to consider which conflicts can occur in the model. As an example, assume we have an immediate-update pessimistic system in which T_1 and T_2 are active transactions; that is, neither transaction has committed or aborted. Assume that T_2 has written some record, and T_1 makes a request to read that record.

We have already seen that, to ensure strictness, we must require that T_1 not read the value written by any active transaction such as T_2. Our reasoning was based on the possible scenario "T_1 commits, T_2 aborts," which does not support recoverability. We stated that to ensure strictness, we would require that the transactions be serializable in commit order. In the context of that requirement, a second bad scenario is "T_1 commits, T_2 commits," for we would then require serializability in the order $T_1 T_2$, but since T_1 read a value written by T_2 and the order of these operations cannot be reversed without changing the value returned by the read, T_1 must follow T_2 in any serialization. Hence, based on either scenario, such a request by T_1 must be considered a conflict.

Even if we did not insist that the transactions be serialized in commit order, we would want to declare T_1's request a conflict. A write by T_2 followed by a read by T_1 on a record, x, fixes the order between T_1 and T_2 in any serialization. If subsequently T_1 and T_2 were to request access to another record, y, the concurrency control would have to remember the order it had already fixed between the two transactions and ensure that accesses to y did not contradict that order. Such a concurrency control could be designed and might be efficient as long as the database resided at a single site and there was a single concurrency control for all items. Later, however, we discuss more general transaction processing systems in which there are a number of independent concurrency controls, each responsible for a different subset of the data items (perhaps the items are at different sites, or they are abstract data types for which each instance of a type has its own concurrency control). For these systems, we want each individual control to make its decisions without consulting other controls. To allow such independent controls, we require that each control make its decisions such that the sequence of database operations it permits to active transactions does not determine an ordering among them. Then, since each control makes decisions that do not fix an order among the transactions, any order is possible among the active transactions – including,

Active Transaction T_2
Has Previously Requested

		read	*write*
Transaction T_1	*read*		X
Requests	*write*	X	X

Figure 10.6: Conflicts between read and write operations on the same record for immediate-update pessimistic concurrency controls for untyped databases are based on the relation *does-not-commute-with*, here denoted by X.

for example, the order in which they commit.

Stated somewhat differently, if we design an immediate-update pessimistic concurrency control so that it maintains the invariant "requests granted to active transactions do not impose an ordering on them," then the schedule will be equivalent to a serial schedule in which the transactions are ordered in commit order.

Any pair of database operations on the same record, except for a pair of reads, conflict. Hence the conflict relation for an immediate-update pessimistic system, shown in Figure 10.6, is the *does-not-commute-with* relation of Figure 10.3.

An immediate-update pessimistic concurrency control can perform one of the following actions when it receives a request from a transaction, T_1, that conflicts with a request that it has previously granted to an active transaction, T_2.

It can not grant the request and cause T_1 to *wait* until there does not exist an active transaction that has been granted a conflicting request (T_1 waits at least until T_2 has committed or aborted; it might wait longer if other transactions are also waiting for T_2 to complete and are awakened before T_1).

It can abort T_1 or T_2 (and roll back any changes it has made using the write-ahead log) and then restart it (in which case the conflict no longer exists). If the requestor is aborted, it is said to *die*; if the transaction with which the requestor is in conflict is aborted, the requestor is said to have *killed* it.

Using one of the above actions, a concurrency control never grants a request that is in conflict with a previously granted request of an active transaction. From this property, we can prove the following result for immediate-update pessimistic concurrency controls:

Any schedule produced by an immediate-update pessimistic concurrency control is serializable, and one possible serial order is the commit order of the transactions.

To prove this result we first recall that schedules can contain operations of transactions that have not completed. When we say that such a schedule is serializable, we mean that it is equivalent to a schedule in which the operations of committed transactions are not interleaved and occur before those of uncommitted transactions. Henceforth, our notion of a serial schedule includes such schedules.

We can use an inductive argument to demonstrate the result. We perform the induction on the number, i, of committed transactions in a schedule. Consider the base case, $i = 1$. Since, prior to the time of the commit, all transactions are active, it follows that the concurrency control has not granted any request that conflicts with any other request. Hence, the operations of the committed transaction can be transposed with those of other transactions to produce a serial schedule. Because every pair of operations that is so transposed does not conflict and hence is in the *commutes-with* relation (the complement of the *does-not-commute-with* relation), each transposition does not affect the values returned by the operations and leaves the database state unchanged. Thus the final schedule is equivalent to the original schedule.

Assume now that all schedules (produced by an immediate-update pessimistic concurrency control) that contain exactly i committed transactions are serializable in commit order. Consider a schedule, S, containing $i+1$ committed transactions and let T be the last transaction to commit. Let $S = S_1 \circ S_2$, where S_1 is obtained by truncating S at the operation executed immediately prior to T's commit. Then S_1 contains i committed transactions and, from the induction hypothesis, is serializable in commit order. Let S_1^{ser} be the serial schedule equivalent to S_1. Thus S is equivalent to the schedule $S_1^{ser} \circ S_2$. This schedule has the property that all operations of T follow the ith commit. Furthermore, all operations of T must commute with all operations of any uncommitted transactions in S. Hence, the operations of T can be transposed in such a way that they follow those of all committed transactions and precede those of all uncommitted transactions. Once again, every pair that is so transposed is in the *commutes-with* relation and thus each transposition does not affect the values returned by the operations and leaves the database state unchanged. The schedule so constructed is a serial schedule equivalent to S.

Note that because of the way we have constructed the conflict relation (both read and write requests conflict with prior writes to the same data item), all immediate-update pessimistic controls are strict (and hence recoverable).

When a transaction makes a request to perform a database operation on a particular record, the concurrency control must be able to determine all the operations that have been performed on that record by currently active transactions so that if a conflict exists, it can be detected. For this purpose, we assume that the concurrency control associates with each record, x, a data structure called the *lock set*, $L(x)$, describing those operations. From the definition of the *does-not-commute-with* relation, it follows that if $L(x)$ is not empty,

$T_1 : read(x) \quad write(x) \qquad\qquad\qquad read(y)[wait]$
$T_2 : \qquad\qquad\qquad read(y) \quad write(y) \qquad\qquad\qquad read(x)[wait]$

Figure 10.7: A schedule that exhibits deadlock.

it can contain either multiple requests to read x or a single request to write x.

Similarly, we associate with each record, x, a data structure, the *wait set*, $W(x)$, which records the identity of all transactions that are waiting to perform an operation on that record. A request to access x can be regarded as a call to a routine in the concurrency control that manipulates $L(x)$ and $W(x)$. This routine must be executed as a critical section.

By appropriately choosing among the allowable actions that a concurrency control can take when a conflict is detected, we can design a number of different immediate-update pessimistic concurrency controls, some of which are described in the following subsections. All of our designs adhere to the following structure:

General Structure of an Immediate-Update Pessimistic Concurrency Control

1. If a request to access data item, x, does not conflict with an operation of a currently active transaction, grant that request and store a description of the requested operation in $L(x)$.

2. If a request causes a conflict, perform the actions prescribed by the particular algorithm.

3. When a transaction commits or aborts, for each data item, x, that the transaction has accessed, remove the description of the transaction's operations from $L(x)$. Examine each request in $W(x)$ in sequence, executing step (1) or (2) as appropriate.

10.5.1 Dynamic Immediate-Update Pessimistic Systems

A primitive control might use the approach that, whenever a conflict occurs, it just aborts and restarts the requesting transaction. Although this approach produces serializable schedules, it is needlessly harsh. A less drastic approach is to make the requesting transaction wait until the transaction with which it conflicts commits or aborts. This waiting has one potential complication: it can cause deadlock. Figure 10.7 shows such a deadlock situation. T_1 has written x and requested a read of y and been made to wait for T_2, while T_2 has written y and requested a read of x and been made to wait for T_1.

Combining the two approaches, the concurrency control can make the requesting transaction wait (recording the requestor's identity in the wait set) until the other transaction commits or aborts, unless that waiting would cause a deadlock, in which case it restarts the requesting transaction. The concurrency control can detect when making a transaction wait would cause a deadlock by maintaining a *wait-for* graph in which nodes represent transactions and an edge from the node labeled T_1 to the node labeled T_2 indicates that T_1 is waiting for T_2 to commit or abort so that T_1 can access some record. A cycle in the wait-for graph indicates a deadlock.

This protocol can exhibit another form of undesirable behavior called *cyclic restart*, in which, for example, a request of T_1 conflicts with an operation of active transaction T_2, causing T_1 to be aborted and restarted; later a conflict is detected between T_2 and the restarted version of T_1 causing T_2 to be aborted and restarted, and the cycle repeats indefinitely. Cyclic restarts can be difficult to detect since no process is ever waiting.

A better approach is to assign to each transaction, T, a *timestamp*, $TS(T)$, which is the value of the clock when it is initiated. A restarted version of a transaction retains the timestamp of its predecessor. If $TS(T_1) < TS(T_2)$, we say that T_1 is *older* than T_2 and T_2 is *younger* than T_1. Using timestamps, we can construct the following protocol:

A Dynamic Concurrency Control Protocol

When a conflict occurs, the requesting transaction is made to wait.

If the waiting causes a deadlock, the youngest transaction in the cycle of waiting transactions is aborted and restarted (and its identity is removed from the wait set in which it was waiting).

Cyclic restart cannot occur, since the oldest transaction in the cycle will not be restarted. This protocol is referred to as a dynamic protocol because the equivalent serial order is determined dynamically as requests are made (and transactions are made to wait or or restarted).

10.5.2   Kill-Wait and Wait-Die Systems

The dynamic protocol requires that the concurrency control maintain the wait-for graph to determine when waiting will cause a deadlock. We define two other protocols in which the decision to make a transaction wait or restart is made using only the timestamps of the conflicting transactions in such a way that deadlock freedom is guaranteed (but we still require that the transactions be serializable in commit order). If a conflict is detected, the following actions are taken.

Wait-Die System

If transaction T_1 makes a request that conflicts with an operation of active transaction T_2:

if $TS(T_1) < TS(T_2)$ **then** *Wait* **else** *Die*

Kill-Wait System

If transaction T_1 makes a request that conflicts with an operation of active transaction T_2:

if $TS(T_1) < TS(T_2)$ **then** *Kill* **else** *Wait*

In the Wait-Die System, it is advantageous, in step 3 of the General Structure, to examine transactions in $W(x)$ in increasing age order (youngest, with largest timestamp, first) in order to avoid unnecessary transaction restarts. Similarly, in the Kill-Wait System, transactions should be examined in decreasing age order (oldest, with smallest timestamp, first).

Both systems never grant a request that creates a conflict and thus produce schedules that are serializable in the commit order. Neither system can exhibit deadlock, since in the Wait-Die system an older transaction can wait for a younger one but not conversely, while in the Kill-Wait system a younger transaction can wait for an older one but not conversely. Similarly, neither system can exhibit cyclic restart, since in both systems only the younger transaction involved in the conflict can be restarted, and it retains its timestamp in its new incarnation.

Both systems avoid deadlock at the expense of possible unnecessary restarts. For example, in the Wait-Die system, whenever a younger transaction makes a request that is in conflict with an older transaction, the younger transaction is restarted, even when making that transaction wait would not cause a deadlock.

Note that this use of timestamps does not imply that the equivalent serial order of the final schedule will necessarily be consistent with the timestamp order. The equivalent serial order will be consistent with the commit order of the transactions and may or may not be consistent with the timestamp order (for example, two transactions might access the same record, but the younger one might commit before the older one makes its access, and hence it would precede the older one in the serial order). In the next section we discuss a static concurrency control in which the serialization order is consistent with the timestamp order.

10.5.3 Timestamp-Ordered Systems

In timestamp-ordered concurrency controls, a unique timestamp is issued to each transaction when it is initiated, and the concurrency control guarantees the existence of an equivalent serial schedule in which transactions are ordered by their timestamps. We consider only timestamp-ordered, immediate-update pessimistic concurrency controls. We have already demonstrated that such controls must also have an equivalent serial schedule in which transactions are sequenced in commit order. Any difference between these two serial schedules involves transactions that can be serialized in either order. Timestamp-ordered concurrency controls are sometimes called *static* concurrency controls, since the ordering is determined by the timestamps (issued at initiation time) instead of dynamically, as the transaction executes.

In addition to the lock and wait sets, the static system stores with each record, x, two timestamps: $wt(x)$, the largest timestamp of any transaction that has committed and written that record, and $rt(x)$, the largest timestamp of any transaction that has committed and read that record. When a transaction, T_1, makes a request to read (write) x, the concurrency control compares $TS(T_1)$ with $wt(x)$ $(rt(x))$. If $TS(T_1)$ is smaller, some (inactive) transaction T_2 that has executed a conflicting operation and must follow T_1 in the equivalent serial order has already committed. If T_1's operation is a write, T_2 should have read the value that T_1 is writing; if T_1's operation is a read, the read should return a value that existed prior to the write executed by T_2. Thus, T_1 is too old to access the record and must be aborted and restarted.

If T_1 survives this test – $TS(T_1)$ is larger than the appropriate timestamp in the record – the Kill-Wait protocol is used with respect to transactions in $L(x)$. When T_1 commits, $rt(x)$ and $wt(x)$, must be updated for each data item, x, that it has accessed. Elements in $W(x)$ are examined in decreasing age order. Since conflicting requests between active transactions are resolved in favor of the older of the two transactions (the younger transaction is killed) the resulting schedule is serializable in timestamp order.

One difference between the way timestamps are used in static and dynamic protocols is that when a transaction is restarted in a static system it receives a new timestamp, whereas in a dynamic system it maintains its old timestamp. (Note that the timestamp-ordered control does not necessarily serialize in the order in which transactions are initiated, since if a transaction is restarted, it gets a new timestamp and hence will be later in the serial order.)

10.5.4 Locking and Two Phase Locking

We have been assuming that the concurrency control is invisible to the individual transactions. Each transaction simply makes read or write requests. When a request is granted, the concurrency control automatically records the request in a lock set, which serves to lock the corresponding data item. Locks are removed automatically by the concurrency control at commit time.

Some transaction processing systems use a manual approach in which transactions explicitly make requests to lock and unlock data items. The lock and wait sets exist as before, and the concurrency control processes any lock or unlock requests and checks to make sure that a request is granted only if the

$T_1 : l(x)\ r(x)\ w(x)\ u(x)$ $l(y)\ r(y)\ u(y)$

$T_2 :$ $l(x)\ r(x)\ u(x)\ l(y)\ r(y)\ w(y)\ u(y)$

Figure 10.8: A schedule that is not serializable due to premature unlocking.

requesting transaction holds the appropriate lock. The important difference between these two approaches is that in the manual approach a transaction can (explicitly) unlock a data item before it commits.

Premature unlocking can result in unserializable schedules. For example, consider the schedule shown in Figure 10.8, where $l(x)$ is a request to lock x and $u(x)$ is a request to unlock it. T_1 accesses x, unlocks it, and then accesses y. Between the two accesses, T_2 makes conflicting accesses to both data items. As we noted earlier, this schedule is not serializable, since each transaction must follow the other in any serial order. This situation could not have happened if locks were handled automatically by the concurrency control, since locks are not released until commit time. To avoid this situation in a manual system, transactions must never lock a record after unlocking a record.

A transaction is said to maintain a *two phase locking* protocol if it obtains all its locks before performing any unlocks (it first goes through a locking phase, then an unlocking phase). As seen from the example, two phase locking is necessary in order to guarantee serializability. The argument for sufficiency involves showing that a schedule, S, produced by a two phase locking protocol is equivalent to the serial schedule, S^{ser}, in which transactions are ordered in the sequence in which their last lock requests are satisfied in S (but not necessarily in commit order). Consider two transactions, T_1 and T_2, in S, and assume that T_1's last lock request is satisfied before T_2's. If they do not access common records, they can be ordered arbitrarily. If they do, then because of the two phase assumption, all records accessed by both must have been accessed first by T_1. Hence all conflicting accesses dictate the same order in an equivalent serial schedule, and this is their order in S^{ser}. Thus we have

Two Phase Locking Theorem

A locking protocol produces serializable schedules if and only if it is a two phase locking protocol.

Two phase locking protocols are more general than the concurrency control protocols presented in the last section in that they permit serializable schedules in which data items can be unlocked before a transaction commits. This additional generality is not as useful as it might appear, since we have already noted that a system is nonrecoverable if, before committing, a transaction unlocks a record it has modified. However, a transaction can unlock a record it has only read without destroying recoverability.

10.6   Deferred-Update Optimistic Systems

An optimistic algorithm consists of a sequence of several steps. In the first step, a task is executed under some (optimistic) assumption that simplifies the performance of the task. For example, in a concurrency control the assumption is made that conflicts with concurrent transactions do not occur, and hence we need not be concerned with locking or waiting. Transactions read and write (to an intentions list) without requesting permission from the concurrency control. The second step validates the first step by checking to see if the assumption was actually true. If not, the task must be redone – redoing the task implies rollback in the concurrency control case. If the assumption is true, validation results in commitment. For those applications in which the assumption is true most of the time, rollback will be rare and the optimistic algorithm will result in efficient operation.

This approach stands in contrast to the pessimistic approach, in which execution of the task is done cautiously: no simplifying assumptions are made in the first step, each request for database access is checked in advance, and appropriate actions are taken immediately if conflicts are detected. Hence, no second step is required in the pessimistic approach.

Optimistic concurrency controls generally use a deferred-update approach, since database accesses are unchecked and writes may have to be rolled back. Writes are stored in an intentions list and do not update the database immediately. Hence a third step is needed for a transaction that modifies the database: if the transaction is successfully validated, the intentions list is written to the database. Since the database is not modified during the first step, this step is referred to as the *read phase*. The second step is referred to as the *validation phase*, and the third step as the *write phase*. Thus, a transaction's writes are performed (and appear in a schedule) during its write phase. For simplicity, we assume that if a transaction is successfully validated, it enters its write phase immediately and that only one transaction is in its validation or write phase at a time. Thus the validation and write phases are executed as a single critical section. The three phases of a transaction are shown in Figure 10.9(a).

The validation phase ensures that any schedule, S, produced by an optimistic concurrency control is equivalent to the serial schedule, S^{ser}, in which committed transactions are sequenced in commit order and their operations precede those of uncommitted transactions. That is, it ensures that all the operations of each transaction return the same values in S as they would in S^{ser} and that the final database state is the same.

Transaction T_1 will successfully validate, and hence commit, if operations it executed during its read phase (recall that no write operations are performed to the database during the read phase) do not conflict with operations of transactions that were active during its read phase but committed before T_1 entered validation. If transaction T_2 completed its write phase before T_1 started its read phase, as shown in Figure 10.9(b), the two transactions were not concurrently active. In this case, all of T_1's operations follow all of T_2's

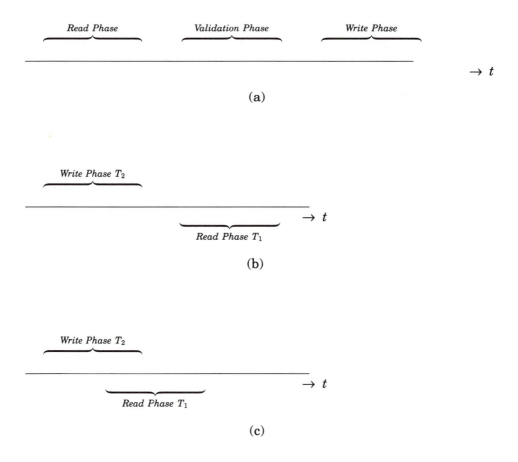

Figure 10.9: Transactions in an optimistic concurrency control: (a) the three phases of a transaction, (b) transactions that do not conflict, (c) transactions that may conflict.

operations in both S and S^{ser}, and no conflict has taken place. However, if T_2 completed before T_1 entered validation, but T_2 had not completed its write phase before T_1 started its read phase, as shown in Figure 10.9(c), a conflict occurs if T_1 read an item that T_2 wrote. T_1's read *might* have preceded T_2's write of that item, which is contrary to the commit order, T_2 T_1. Hence, T_1 cannot be allowed to successfully validate.

Figure 10.10 shows the conflicts that the validation phase must check for in an optimistic concurrency control. The validating transaction, T_1, tests for conflicts between its read operations and write operations of concurrent transactions that committed while T_1 was in its read phase.

Note that when T_1 validates, the only check that is made is that T_1's op-

**Transaction T_2 Committed
While T_1 Was Active**

		read	write
Transaction T_1	*read*		X
Requesting to Commit	*write*		

Figure 10.10: Conflicts between read and write operations on the same record for deferred-update optimistic concurrency controls for untyped databases.

erations during its read phase (*i.e.*, its read operations) do not conflict with operations of a concurrent transaction, T_2, that has previously committed. Validation need not check for conflicts involving T_1's write operations. Although a conflict occurs if T_1 writes a record that T_2 read or wrote, we are guaranteed by the structure of a deferred-update optimistic algorithm that T_1's write (during its write phase) followed T_2's read (during its read phase) or write (during its write phase) and hence, assuming T_1 commits, the operations occurred in commit order (*i.e.*, their order is the same in both S and S^{ser}). Thus, even though T_2's operation *does-not-commute-with* T_1's write, T_1 can be successfully validated, since these operations need not be interchanged in constructing S^{ser}. (The same point can be made in a different way: T_1's write is performed at a time when T_2 is no longer active, and hence the conflict is of no concern.)

We can demonstrate the equivalence of S and S^{ser} using an argument similar to that given in Section 10.5 for pessimistic concurrency controls. In this case, however, the induction is performed on the number of transactions that have completed (rather than the number that have committed), since in an optimistic system writes appear in the schedule after commitment.

We only sketch the argument. The base case is similar to the induction step and is omitted. The inductive assumption is that all schedules (produced by an optimistic concurrency control) that contain exactly i completed transactions are serializable in commit order. Consider a schedule, S, containing $i+1$ completed transactions and let T be the last transaction to complete. Let $S = S_1 \circ S_2$ where S_1 is obtained by truncating S at the last write of the ith transaction. Then, from the induction hypothesis, S_1 is serializable in commit order. If we let S_1^{ser} be the serial schedule equivalent to S_1, it follows that S is equivalent to the schedule S_3 given by $S_1^{ser} \circ S_2$. S_3 has the property that all operations of T follow the completion of the ith transaction and the only write operations beyond that point are those of T (since the write operations of incomplete transactions have not been transferred to the database). To demonstrate that S_3 is equivalent to a serial schedule, we transpose T's operations to the left over the read operations of incomplete transactions. Equivalence is not preserved by a transposition involving conflicting operations. However, the only case in which equivalence is not preserved occurs if a write of T is transposed with a read of an incomplete transaction, T'. But if such a transposition is necessary, T' will be aborted when it requests validation, since it will have read an item written by a concurrently active transaction, T, that committed at an earlier time. Hence S is equivalent to S^{ser}.

We have made the assumption that only one transaction is in its validation and write phase at a time (this is called the *serial validation assumption*). Hence the equivalent serial order of committed transactions is the order of entry into the validation phase (*i.e.,* the commit order) and no two transactions can simultaneously be executing their write phases. Although this serial validation assumption simplifies validation, it creates a bottleneck that restricts concurrency.

An alternative, *parallel validation assumption* avoids the bottleneck by allowing multiple transactions to execute their validation/write phases concurrently. Parallel validation complicates the validation process, since conflicts between concurrent write phase operations must now be checked for in the validation phase. When a transaction, T, enters validation, it distinguishes between a concurrent transaction, T_1, that has already committed and a concurrent transaction, T_2, that entered validation at a prior time and is still executing its validation or write phase. As with a serial validation algorithm, the concurrency control outputs schedules that are serializable in the order in which transactions enter validation. Thus T will follow both T_1 and T_2 in an equivalent serial order. The check that must be made with respect to T_1 is the same as would have been made under the serial validation assumption: that T's read operations do not conflict with T_1's write operations. With respect to T_2, T must (1) make this same check and (2) determine that its write operations do not conflict with T_2's write operations, since T and T_2 might execute their write phases concurrently. If conflicts are detected in either (1) or (2), T must be rolled back. Since T follows T_2 in the equivalent serial order and since T_2 has completed its read phase when T enters validation, it is not necessary to check for conflicts between T_2's read operations and T's write operations.

The optimistic approach has two advantages compared with the the pessimistic approach: (1) individual transactions do not have to request permission to perform read or write operations (although this savings must be balanced against the cost of the validation phase), and (2) the overall system has no waits and hence no deadlocks. There are two potential disadvantages. First, the cost of rollback may be substantial, since the transaction's entire computation must be redone. With pessimistic controls, conflicts are discovered earlier in the computation, so even if rollback is required, only part of the computation must be redone. The significance of this additional cost depends on the extent to which the optimistic assumption is true (*i.e.,* on the number of conflicts that actually occur). Second, since the read phase of a transaction, T_1, might occur concurrently with the write phase of a committed transaction, T_2, it is possible for T_1 to not see the effects of T_2 atomically (*i.e.,* it might see some records before T_2 wrote them and others after). Hence T_1 might see an inconsistent database state. In this case, a conflict exists between a read of T_1 and a write of T_2, which will be detected during the validation of T_1, and T_1 will be rolled back. However, since T_1 sees an inconsistent state, it may behave unpredictably (for example, it might enter an infinite loop) during its read phase. This problem can be dealt with by designing the read phase of each transaction so that it terminates even when it sees an inconsistent database or by using a more sophisticated optimistic system (for example, a multi-version system – see exercises), which is beyond the scope of our discussion. Note that optimistic controls are strict (and hence recoverable), since a transaction is allowed to read (or write) only records that have been written by committed transactions.

10.6.1   Implementations of Optimistic Systems

An implementation of a serial optimistic concurrency control assumes the existence of a counter, C, which is incremented each time a transaction commits. When a transaction, T, enters its read phase, it copies the current value of C into a local variable, $Start(T)$. While executing its read phase, T compiles a set, called its *read set*, $RS(T)$, which identifies all data items that T read, and a set, $WS(T)$, called its *write set*, which identifies all data items that T intends to modify (the names of the items in its intentions list). When T enters its validation phase, it copies the current value of C into the variable $Complete(T)$. This value becomes the transaction number, $tn(T)$, of T, if T commits. T is allowed to commit if its read operations have returned the same values as they would in the serial schedule in which T follows the transactions that have previously committed, ordered in accordance with their transaction numbers.

When T enters its validation phase, the concurrency control uses the values of $Start(T)$ and $Complete(T)$ to check whether a conflict of the type indicated in Figure 10.10 with a concurrently active transaction has taken place. The algorithm shown in Figure 10.11 is the validation and write phases of T and is executed as a single critical section. To implement this protocol, the concurrency control must retain $WS(T')$ for each committed transaction, T', until all transactions that started before T' completed its write phase have themselves committed or been restarted.

Another equivalent approach to designing an optimistic concurrency control stores with each record, x, the transaction number, $tn(x)$, of the last (committed) transaction to have written to x. The algorithm shown in Figure 10.12 is the validation and write phases of T and is executed as a single critical section. This new protocol finds conflicts exactly when the first one does. Thus it also produces an ordering consistent with the commit order.

Note that it would be possible to modify this second protocol so that when a transaction, T, accesses a data item, x, and it is found that $Start(T) \leq tn(x)$, T is immediately aborted. Such a protocol would not be optimistic, however, since T is now requesting database operations. An optimistic variation of the

$Complete(T) := C$;
For all committed transactions T' such that
     $Start(T) \leq tn(T') < Complete(T)$
   if $(RS(T) \cap WS(T')) \neq \phi \rightarrow$ restart T and exit;
   [] $(RS(T) \cap WS(T')) = \phi \rightarrow$ **skip**; **fi**;
commit;
$tn(T) := Complete(T)$;
For all data items x such that $x \in WS(T)$
     update x using T's intentions list;
$C := C + 1$;

Figure 10.11: An implementation of an optimistic concurrency control.

$Complete(T) := C$;
For all data items x such that $x \in RS(T)$
   if $Start(T) \leq tn(x) \rightarrow$ restart T and exit;
   [] $Start(T) > tn(x) \rightarrow$ **skip**; **fi**;
commit;
For all data items x such that $x \in WS(T)$
   begin
     update x using T's intentions list;
     $tn(x) := Complete(T)$;
   end;
   $C := C + 1$;

Figure 10.12: An alternative implementation of an optimistic concurrency control.

second algorithm can be obtained by simply recording the value of $tn(x)$ at the time T accesses x. If when T enters validation the value of $tn(x)$ stored with x is found to have changed, T is aborted (since another transaction has written x and committed since T accessed it).

10.7   Deferred-Update Pessimistic Systems

Deferred-update pessimistic concurrency controls have some of the properties of both of the previous models we have discussed. Writes are made to an intentions list and performed (and appear in the schedule) after the transaction commits. As in other pessimistic controls, however, a transaction must request permission to read and write (to its intentions list), but can commit

Active Transaction T_2
Has Previously Requested

		read	write
Transaction T_1	*read*		X
Requests	*write*	X	

Figure 10.13: Conflicts between read and write operations on the same record for deferred-update pessimistic concurrency controls for untyped databases.

without requesting permission.

Figure 10.13 shows the conflicts that a deferred-update pessimistic concurrency control must check. Assume that T_1 and T_2 are active transactions and that T_2 has executed a (deferred) write on record x. A subsequent request by T_1 to read x constitutes a conflict, since the value that would be returned is the value written by the last committed transaction, but this would not be the correct value if T_2 should later commit before T_1 (recall that commit requests cannot be delayed). Like the deferred-update optimistic algorithm, the deferred-update pessimistic algorithm does not have to deal with a conflict between two write requests to the same record by concurrently active transactions, since the new values will be transferred to the database at commit time in commit order.

At first glance, the considerations for the deferred-update pessimistic concurrency control appear identical to those for the deferred-update optimistic concurrency control, but there is an important difference. With the optimistic control, a test for conflict is always made between a validating transaction and a transaction that has already committed, and hence we know that, if validation is successful, the validating transaction will follow the committed transaction in the serial order. With the pessimistic control, a test for conflict is always between two transactions that are active at the time a database operation is requested, and at that time we do not know the order in which the transactions will commit. Thus, in the optimistic control, the conflict between a write of a validating transaction and a read of a committed transaction can be ignored, since we know that the write will follow the read in both S and S^{ser}. A pessimistic control, however, must take action in this case, since the writer might commit before the reader.

As with the optimistic algorithm, we can formalize the above discussion by defining a relation to identify those conflicts with which a deferred-update pessimistic concurrency control must be concerned. As shown in Figure 10.13, the relation contains elements of the form $(read(x), write(x))$ and $(write(x), read(x))$ where the first element corresponds to a requested operation and the second to an operation that has been granted to a concurrently active transaction.

Using this conflict relation, we can design a deferred-update pessimistic concurrency control using any of the protocols used for immediate-update pessimistic controls – for example, dynamic, Wait-Die, Kill-Wait, timestamp. Note that all deferred-update pessimistic controls are strict (and hence recoverable), since a transaction is allowed to read (or write) only records that have been written by committed transactions.

10.8   Predicate Locks

We have assumed that each database operation not only names the function to be performed (read or write) but also names the target record. In some database systems, however, operations do not name individual records, but instead designate a record(s) by specifying a relationship that must exist among the values stored in the record(s). Such operations frequently occur in relational databases, but can occur in other types of databases as well. For example, a database operation in a relational database for a banking system, *read(accounts, name = Mary)*, might return the set of all tuples (records) in relation *accounts* that satisfy the predicate

$$P \; : \; name = Mary \tag{10.1}$$

P is referred to as the *read predicate* of the operation. Since Mary might have more than one account at the bank, the read might return more than one tuple. In general, a predicate specifies a set of tuples, each of which satisfies the predicate.

Conflicts take a different form with operations of this type. For example, assume the relation *accounts* contains a tuple for each account, with attributes *accountnumber*, *name*, and *balance*, and there is a relation, *depositors*, containing a tuple for each depositor, with attributes *name* and *totbal*, in which the value of the *totbal* field is the sum of the balances of all that depositor's accounts. An audit transaction, T_1, for Mary might perform the operation *read(accounts, name = Mary)*, sum the balances in the tuples returned, perform the operation *read(depositors, name = Mary)*, and finally check that the value of *totbal* is equal to the sum. A new account transaction for Mary, T_2, might add a new tuple, *t*, to *accounts* using the operation

$$add(accounts, \; accountnumber = 10021, \; name = Mary, \; balance = 100)$$

and then update *totbal* by 100 in the appropriate tuple in *depositors*.

The operations on *accounts* performed by T_1 and T_2 conflict, since the addition of *t does-not-commute-with* the read operation of T_1. Thus, if the read is executed first, *t* will not be returned; otherwise, it will. If, for example, we wish to implement an immediate-update pessimistic control, our understanding of a lock set has to be modified. Invalid results will be obtained if T_2 is allowed to interleave its execution between the time T_1 reads *accounts* and the time it reads *depositors*. We cannot prevent this interleaving by associating a lock set with each tuple, since even if T_1 locks all tuples in *accounts* that it has read (*i.e.*, that satisfy P), T_2 can still subsequently add t. Hence, we need a mechanism that locks tuples that satisfy P but are not in *accounts*. Such tuples are referred to as *phantoms*. In the example, t is a phantom if T_1's read precedes T_2. (Phantoms do not occur only in relational databases but can occur in any database in which operations exist to add or delete data items.)

To deal with this situation, we introduce the notion of a predicate lock on a relation. In general, we regard a relation, R, as a subset of the Cartesian product set $D = D_1 \times D_2 \times \cdots \times D_n$, where D_i is the set of all possible values of the ith attribute of R (its domain). A *predicate lock*, P, is (defined by) a predicate associated with a database operation on R. The predicate specifies a subset of the tuples in D: a tuple (not necessarily in R) is in the subset if and only if P is true when the values in each of the tuple's fields are substituted for the corresponding attributes in P. When a predicate lock, P, has been obtained, all the tuples specified by P are locked.

The predicate lock associated with a read is the read predicate. The situation is illustrated in Figure 10.14. We have locked and then read all the tuples in R that satisfy P. The tuples returned by the read are the tuples in $R \cap P$. but the lock applies to all tuples in P.

The write operations of a relational database are add tuple and delete tuple (we assume that tuple modification is accomplished by a delete followed by an add). As with read, a predicate, P, is a parameter of delete. All tuples in P are locked, and the tuples in $R \cap P$ are deleted. In the case of add, the predicate lock is the tuple to be added. For example, the predicate lock associated with adding t to *accounts* is

$$P_t : (accountnumber = 10021) \wedge (name = Mary) \wedge (balance = 100) \qquad (10.2)$$

We now interpret the notion of a conflict somewhat more generally: instead of requiring that conflicting operations designate the same data item, we now require that the predicate locks associated with conflicting operations on the same relation have non-null intersections. For example, on the *does-not-commute-with* relation (Figure 10.6) the read operation *read(accounts, name = Mary)* conflicts with the write operation *delete(accounts, balance < 1)* (which deactivates all accounts with balance less than one dollar), since there exist tuples in D satisfying both predicates (*e.g.*, the tuple satisfying *accountnumber* = 10000, *name* = *Mary*, and *balance* = .5). Such tuples might be in *accounts* and hence we cannot be sure that the read commutes with the delete. On the other hand, the read operation does not conflict with the write operation *delete(accounts, name = John)*, since the predicate locks associated with the two operations have a null intersection.

With an immediate-update pessimistic concurrency control for the banking example, when T_1 reads *accounts*, it obtains a read lock on P (10.1). Later, when T_2 attempts to add t to *accounts*, it requests a write lock on predicate P_t (10.2). Since $P \cap P_t$ is not null, a conflict exists and the write lock cannot be

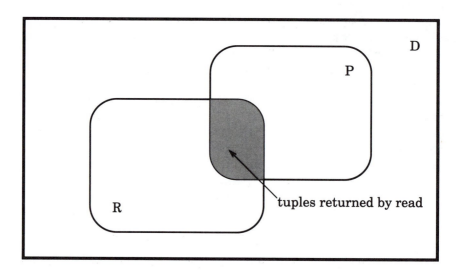

Figure 10.14: A read predicate, P, specifies a subset of D. Some of the tuples in the subset might be in R and others might not.

granted. t is a phantom (it does not exist in *accounts*), and the predicate lock P prevents it from being concurrently added.

For immediate-update pessimistic systems, we associate with each relation, R, a lock set, $L(R)$, which contains the locks associated with all requests that have been granted to currently active transactions. Each element of $L(R)$ is a predicate. When the lock associated with a request for a database operation conflicts with an element of $L(R)$, the concurrency control can take any action that would be appropriate for a single record lock (*i.e.,* wait, kill, or die). A similar interpretation holds for deferred-update optimistic and pessimistic systems.

One difficulty in using predicate locks is that if no constraints are placed on their form, the problem of determining when two locks conflict is recursively unsolvable. However, for most applications, the predicates of interest can be expressed in a simple form. We define a *simple predicate* as a boolean combination of *atomic predicates*, where an atomic predicate has the form

$$< attribute\ name > < relational\ operator > < constant >$$

or

$$< attribute\ name > < relational\ operator > < attribute\ name >$$

An example of a simple predicate for a relation, *faculty*, with attributes *salary*, *title*, and *name* is

$$P' : (salary \geq 25000) \wedge (title = AssociateProfessor) \qquad (10.3)$$

The problem of determining whether or not two simple predicates conflict is computable.

An example of a nonsimple predicate is one whose truth for a particular tuple in a relation depends on the value of another relation. Thus, in addition to *faculty*, the database might have the relation *location* with attributes *name* and *city*, and *P'* (10.3) might be augmented with a conjunct further restricting tuples in *faculty* to those corresponding to individuals living in New York (*i.e.*, for which there exists a tuple in *location* having the same value in its name field such that *city = NewYork*).

10.9   Bibliographic Notes

Much of the material on transaction management is based on the early report by Gray [57]. An excellent survey of the area of concurrency control for untyped databases can be found in the work of Bernstein, Hadzilacos, and Goodman [21] and Bernstein and Goodman [20]. A more theoretical treatment of the subject, with discussions of the complexity issue and view equivalence, can be found in Papadimitriou [107] [108] and Yannakakis [142]. Two phase locking and predicate locks were first discussed by Eswaren, Gray, Lorie, and Traiger [44]. For more information on specific algorithms, the reader is referred to Rosenkrantz, Stearns, and Lewis [113] (Kill-Wait and Wait-Die) and Kung and Robinson [79] (optimistic algorithms). In particular, the optimistic parallel validation algorithm is described in [79]. Other optimistic algorithms are described by Sinha, Nanadikar, and Mehndiratta [121] and Agrawal, Bernstein, Gupta, and Sengupta [5]. Forward and backward validation are discussed by Herlihy [64]. A number of simulation and analytic studies comparing the performance of various concurrency control algorithms have been reported. Examples are the work of Agrawal and DeWitt [7], Agrawal, Carey, and Livny [6], and Carey and Livny [28].

10.10   Exercises

1. Give an example of an interleaving of the deposit and withdraw transactions discussed in Chapter 4 that is allowable under the methods of that chapter, but would not be allowed by the concurrency controls described in this chapter.

2. Show that if transactions do not have blind writes, view serialization is the same as conflict serialization.

3. Show that if transactions do not have blind writes, there will never be a write-write conflict in an immediate-update pessimistic concurrency control.

4. Give an example of a schedule produced by a timestamp-ordered immediate-update pessimistic concurrency control in which the timestamp order is different from the commit order.

5. Assume that in addition to the operations *read*(x) and *write*(x), a database has the operation *copy*(x, y), which (atomically) copies the value stored in record x into record y. Design a conflict relation for a deferred-update pessimistic concurrency control for this database.

6. Assume an immediate-update pessimistic concurrency control that always restarts a transaction if its request causes a conflict with an operation of an active transaction. Show a schedule in which cyclic restart occurs.

7. Consider the following protocol for a timestamp-ordered, immediate-update pessimistic concurrency control, in which there are no lock or wait sets. Show that the protocol is not recoverable.

   Store with each record, x, the maximum timestamp of any (not necessarily committed) transaction that has written that record, *wt*(x), and the maximum timestamp of any (not necessarily committed) transaction that has read that record, *rt*(x).

   When a transaction makes a request to read or write a record, if the timestamp of the requesting transaction is smaller than the timestamp in the record, restart the requesting transaction; otherwise, grant the request.

8. Consider a pessimistic concurrency control that restarts a transaction if it makes a conflicting request. Exhibit a schedule in which a transaction is restarted by this protocol but would be allowed to commit by an optimistic concurrency control.

9. Exhibit a schedule in which an immediate-update pessimistic concurrency control makes a transaction wait but then later allows it to commit, while an optimistic concurrency control restarts the transaction.

10. Show that if transactions have no blind writes, the conflicts that arise in a deferred-update pessimistic concurrency control are the same as those in an immediate-update pessimistic concurrency control.

11. Give a pseudo-code algorithm for an optimistic concurrency control under the parallel validation assumption.

12. Propose a modification to the parallel validation optimistic concurrency control that does not roll back a validating transaction when a write/write conflict is detected.

13. Design an immediate-update optimistic concurrency control based on the following ideas:

    Each transaction is required to complete all its read operations before it performs its first write. Writes are made directly to the database, not to an intentions list. After writing, the transaction enters validation and is aborted if a conflict is detected. (You must state how rollback is accomplished.) The transaction copies the value of the counter, C, into a local variable, *StartRead*, on initiation and copies it again into a local variable, *StartWrite*, when it starts writing. When the transaction commits, C is incremented, and the incremented value is taken as the transaction number. The transaction numbers and the values in these variables are used to determine when a conflict has occurred.

14. Assume that transactions are partitioned into those that only read the database – read only transactions – and those that both read and write the database – read/write transactions. Instead of requiring that the concurrency control produce schedules that are serializable, we might require only that the concurrency control produce schedules in which

    (a) Read/write transactions are serializable.

    (b) Read only transactions see a view of the database that is the result of a serial schedule of the read/write transactions, but not necessarily the serial schedule of (a).

    Give an example of a (nonserializable) schedule containing two read/write transactions and one read only transaction satisfying (a) and (b) in which the read only transaction sees a database state that is not the result of any prefix of the equivalent serial schedule of the read/write transactions.

15. The particular optimistic algorithm we have described uses *backward* validation: a validating transaction checks for conflicts with previously committed transactions. An alternative approach is referred to as *forward* validation. In this approach, a validating transaction checks for conflicts with currently active transactions and is rolled back if such a conflict is detected. The conflict relation is the same as for the backward validation method. Show that the forward validation method works, but is subject to cyclic restart.

The following three exercises refer to a concurrency control model known as a *multi-version* concurrency control. In the multi-version model, several versions of a record might be stored in the database, reflecting successive stages in the history of the record. When a transaction makes a request to read a record, the control is allowed to satisfy that request with any version that was written by a committed transaction – not just the version produced by the last committed transaction that wrote that record. For example, in a conventional immediate-update pessimistic system, if active transaction T_1 has written a record and T_2 makes a request to read the record, a conflict exists and T_2 waits. In a multi-version system, T_2's request might be satisfied using the version of the record that existed before T_1's write. That version is sometimes referred to as the *before image*. The requirement for serializability still exists (although not the requirement of serializability in commit order), so if the control satisfies a read request with an earlier version, it must then satisfy other requests so that the schedule is serializable in some order. To ensure such serializability, the control might use different conflict relations for those transactions for which the order has been fixed (by the satisfaction of previous requests) than for those for which it has not. For the above example, T_2 must precede T_1 in any equivalent serial order.

The multi-version model has the potential of increased efficiency (the first exercise), but can lead to serializations that are not in commit order (the second exercise) and non-intuitive behavior (the third exercise). Note that for the first exercise we partition transactions into read only transactions and read/write transactions, while for the second and third exercise we do not.

16. Design a multi-version immediate-update pessimistic concurrency control with the following specifications. Transactions are partitioned into read only transactions and read/write transactions. For read/write transactions, the concurrency control follows the protocol given in the text for immediate-update pessimistic concurrency controls. A read only transaction, T_1, that requests to read a record that an active read/write transaction, T_2, has already written, is given the version of that record before T_2 wrote it, and the concurrency control guarantees that there exists an equivalent serial order in which T_1 precedes T_2. Such concurrency controls have the advantage that read only transactions are never made to wait and are never restarted.

17. Design a multi-version concurrency control that produces recoverable schedules that are serializable, but the commit order is not always one of the possible serial orders.

18. Design a multi-version immediate-update pessimistic concurrency control such that, when a transaction, T_1, requests to read a record that a concurrent transaction, T_2, has already written, T_1 is given the version of the record before T_2 wrote it, and the control guarantees that an equivalent serial order exists in which T_1 precedes T_2. Suppose this control is used in a banking application. Design a schedule that leads to the following non-intuitive behavior (even though the schedule is serializable): you deposit money in your account; your transaction commits; later you start a new transaction that reads the amount in your account and finds that the amount you deposited is not there. (Hint: At least three transactions are needed to obtain this behavior.)

Transactions on Distributed and Object Oriented Databases

In Chapter 10 we discussed how a transaction can be made to execute atomically in a concurrent environment. In this chapter we extend our discussion in two directions:

We examine how concurrency can be enhanced by using the semantic properties of the data items stored in the data base;

We study databases in which the data is distributed across a network.

As we shall see, these two topics have some interesting connections.

We have already noted that the concurrency control does not use information about transaction semantics, and hence it can allow only interleaved schedules that are equivalent to serial schedules. These interleaved schedules are determined by the commutativity of the individual database operations. The greater the commutativity among the operations, the larger the class of interleaved schedules that are equivalent to serial schedules. With typed or object oriented databases, the data is organized as a collection of instances of abstract types and the database operations are the abstract operations of the types. The semantics of the abstract operations can be used to detect commutativity that would otherwise not be apparent. For example, if a record in an untyped database contains an integer, an increment operation can be implemented as a read followed by a write and, if we use the approach described in the previous chapter, concurrent increment operations on the same integer will appear to conflict. If, instead, the data is organized so that integers are instances of an abstract type and increment is an abstract operation on the type, the control can take advantage of the fact that two increment operations commute and hence concurrent increment operations do not conflict. The control need not know the semantics of the transactions to obtain this increased concurrency.

The distribution of data in a network introduces new issues in the organization of a transaction processing system. Our view of a network is one in which each node is an autonomous and coequal computer system that controls access to a portion of the database. A transaction is now distributed: it is decomposed into subtransactions, each of which executes at a single site. Although each site can provide its own independent concurrency control for the subtransactions executing at that site, some coordination must be imposed on the sites as a whole. We must guarantee that a distributed transaction is atomic: either all subtransactions of the transaction commit or none do. We must be concerned about distributed deadlock. Finally, we must guarantee that the subtransactions of different distributed transactions serialize in the same order at all sites.

11.1   Typed Databases

In this section we assume that the overall structure of the concurrency control is the same for typed databases as for untyped databases. In particular, we assume a concurrency control (in a nondistributed system) in which requests from transactions are granted or delayed by a centralized control that deals with them sequentially. We also assume that database operations are done atomically. Hence we can use the reasoning of Chapter 10 to show that if the concurrency control makes its decisions so as not to fix an order among the active transactions, the final schedule will be serializable in commit order. In the next section, we consider object oriented and distributed systems in which the concurrency control is distributed: each object or site has its own local concurrency control. As we shall see, for such systems we must reason more carefully about the serializability of the final schedule.

Typed databases can have one property that distinguishes them from untyped databases. In untyped databases each database operation (read or write) is *total*: it can be carried out successfully regardless of the state of the target record. By contrast, in typed databases some operations might be *partial*: they can be executed only in a subset of database states. For example, money cannot be withdrawn from an empty bank account; hence the withdraw operation for a bank account abstract data type is a partial operation.

In the special case when all operations in a typed database are total, the conflict relation for the typed and untyped cases is the same: *does-not-commute-with*. For example, Figure 11.1 shows the conflict relation for database items of type integer. Note that increment and decrement commute (neither returns a value and the final database state is independent of the order of execution), and hence, for example, (*increment, decrement*) ∉ *does-*

	increment	decrement	read	write
increment			X	X
decrement			X	X
read	X	X		X
write	X	X	X	X

Figure 11.1: Conflicts between abstract operations on a data item of type integer are based on the relation *does-not-commute-with*, here denoted X.

not-commute-with whereas *(read, increment)* ∈ *does-not-commute-with*.

Figure 11.2 shows the conflicts that the various concurrency controls described in Chapter 10 must check for when they are used to control access to an integer type. As with untyped data, in an immediate-update pessimistic concurrency control [Figure 11.2(a)], requests for database operations can cause any of the conflicts of the *does-not-commute-with* relation.

Figure 11.2(b) shows the conflicts for an optimistic concurrency control. As with untyped databases, the conflicts for an optimistic control are a subset of those for an immediate-update pessimistic control (assuming all operations are total). For example, we need not be concerned with the conflict between *increment* and *read*, since the increment of the validating transaction (T_1) has not yet been installed in the database and therefore the committed transaction's (T_2's) read must have returned the correct value. Thus the reasoning for the increment and decrement operations is similar to that for write in the untyped system. The role of an intentions list is more complex with typed data. We defer a discussion of this issue to a later section. Similar reasoning can be used to obtain the conflicts for a deferred-update pessimistic control, as shown in Figure 11.2(c).

11.1.1 Partial Operations

As we saw in Chapter 3, a particular abstract operation might not be executable in all states of an instance. We defined the predicate $WP_a^j(t)$ to be the weakest precondition constraining the state of an instance, t, so that the termination of the jth abstract operation, p_j, is guaranteed. We now address the question of what action to take in a database consisting of instances of abstract types when a transaction invokes an operation on the instance and $WP_a^j(t)$ is false. One alternative is to take the approach used in Chapter 5 and make the transaction wait for a concurrent transaction to change the instance's state. This approach implies that the termination of one transaction depends upon the execution of another transaction – contradicting our assumption that each transaction, when executed in isolation on a consistent database, must terminate. Another alternative is to abort the operation and

		Active Transaction T_2 Has Previously Requested			
		increment	*decrement*	*read*	*write*
Transaction T_1	*increment*			X	X
Requests	*decrement*			X	X
	read	X	X		X
	write	X	X	X	X

(a). Immediate-update pessimistic concurrency control

		Transaction T_2 Committed While T_1 Was Active and Had Requested			
		increment	*decrement*	*read*	*write*
Transaction T_1	*increment*				
Requesting to	*decrement*				
Commit	*read*	X	X		X
	write				

(b). Deferred-update optimistic concurrency control

		Active Transaction T_2 Has Previously Requested			
		increment	*decrement*	*read*	*write*
Transaction T_1	*increment*			X	
Requests	*decrement*			X	
	read	X	X		X
	write			X	

(c). Deferred-update pessimistic concurrency control

Figure 11.2: Conflicts for database entities of type integer.

the requesting transaction. While this alternative is a possibility, abortion does not provide the user with any information about its cause. For example, a banking system might use the type *account* having operations *deposit* and *withdraw*. Rather than simply abort a transaction that attempts to overdraw an account, it might be more appropriate for the withdraw operation to return an error status to the transaction and for the transaction to print a message and terminate normally. Hence, a third alternative is to return status information with each operation. Negative status is returned if p_j is invoked in a state in which $WP_a^j(t)$ has the value false, and positive status is returned otherwise. We consider only this last alternative.

Up to this point it has been sufficient to consider an operation as simply an action – *e.g.*, read, decrement – without being concerned with data or status information. Now we must deal specifically with this information. We denote a particular instance of an operation by $t.p(\overline{x}):stat$, where *stat* is the status returned. Since we want our notation to capture both the data passed to the instance and the data returned, we assume for simplicity that there are no in out parameters. Furthermore, we do not differentiate between in and out parameters and we take $\overline{x}$ to represent the actual values passed to or from the particular occurrence of the operation in question. When it is obvious which instance of an abstract type is being operated on, we drop the dot notation. Thus an operation that dequeues 3 from a particular instance of an integer queue is denoted *Dequeue(3):ok*. An invocation of *Dequeue* when the queue is empty is denoted *Dequeue(x):no*, where, in this case, the value of *x* is of no concern.

It is convenient to represent the state of an instance as the sequence of all operations on the instance performed by committed transactions in commit order. In practice, one would use a more compact representation of the state to actually store in the database. For example, the sequence

$$Enqueue(5):ok, \quad Enqueue(7):ok, \quad Dequeue(5):ok, \quad Enqueue(9):ok$$

represents a queue with value < 7, 9 >. It is clearly preferable from the point of view of efficiency to store the value rather than the sequence.

A sequence of operations on an instance is referred to as a *history*. Operations of transactions that have been aborted or restarted are not included in a history, since we assume that their effect has been nullified. Not all histories are possible. For example, the semantics of the queue data type disallows the history *Enqueue(3):ok, Dequeue(2):ok*. A history that conforms to the semantics of the data type is referred to as a *legal history*. (Note that a history is the sequence of operations on a single object instance, while a schedule is the interleaved sequence of operations on all object instances in the database.)

This notation allows us to state the condition for serializability in a simple way. First consider a database consisting of a single instance of an abstract type. A schedule, S, is serializable in some order, O, if the serial schedule constructed from the operations of S in which transactions are ordered as in

O is a legal history. For example, the schedule

$(Enqueue(5){:}ok)_1$, $(Dequeue(5){:}ok)_2$, $(Enqueue(7){:}ok)_2$, $(Dequeue(7){:}ok)_1$

where we have used subscripts to distinguish between the operations of the two transactions T_1 and T_2, is not serializable in the order T_1 T_2, since the history

$(Enqueue(5){:}ok)_1$, $(Dequeue(7){:}ok)_1$, $(Dequeue(5){:}ok)_2$, $(Enqueue(7){:}ok)_2$

is not legal. This statement of the serializability condition can be easily extended to apply to a database with an arbitrary number of instances of (possibly distinct) types by simply requiring that each projection of S onto operations at a single instance be serializable in the same order.

The data and status associated with an operation can be used to extract an extra measure of concurrency. We illustrate this additional concurrency through the use of status information only, but the principle can be applied to the data returned as well. For example, withdraw and deposit operations do not commute: the status returned by a withdraw might change from negative to positive if it is interchanged with a subsequent deposit. However, if we differentiate withdraws returning positive status from those returning negative status (attempted overdrafts), we can take advantage of the fact that successful withdraws do commute with deposits (using a suitably generalized definition of commute). Since successful withdraws are much more common than attempted overdrafts, a significant amount of additional commutativity can be recognized, and this translates into a sparser conflict relation and less waiting or rollback. Concurrency controls that use information returned to determine conflicts are called *operation-based* concurrency controls. Concurrency controls that do not use return information and base their decisions only on information available at invocation time are called *invocation-based* controls.

In this chapter we consider operation-based controls, since they are capable of achieving more concurrency. We shall see in Section 12.7.2 that invocation-based controls have advantages in certain situations. Figure 11.2 is an example of an invocation-based conflict relation.

Figure 11.3 gives the abstract specification of an instance, *bal*, of the *account* data type. We consider a successful withdraw and an attempted overdraft to be distinct operations and assume that a local variable, *s*, is used to receive the status information. A concurrency control that considers conflicts between these operations is operation based, since a successful withdraw can be distinguished from an attempted overdraft only when the status has been returned.

A complication is introduced by this approach: operations defined in this way are partial, and hence the notion of commutativity must be extended. For example, while $bal.withdraw(x)$ is total (*i.e.*, it executes in all states,

(1) The invariant, I_a, is

$0 \leq bal$

(2) The initial value is

$bal_{init} = 0$

(3) The weakest preconditions for termination of each procedure are

$WP_a^{deposit(x):ok}(bal) \equiv true$
$WP_a^{read(x):ok}(bal) \equiv true$
$WP_a^{withdraw(x):ok}(bal) \equiv (bal \geq x)$
$WP_a^{withdraw(x):no}(bal) \equiv (bal < x)$

(We assume that the value of x is nonnegative.)

(4) Axiom schemas specifying the semantics of each procedure are

$\{P_{bal+x,\ ok}^{bal,\ s}\}\ bal.deposit(x):ok\ \{P\}$

$\{P_{bal,\ ok}^{x,\ s}\}\ bal.read(x):ok\ \{P\}$

$\{P_{bal-x,\ ok}^{bal,\ s}\}\ bal.withdraw(x):ok\ \{P\}$

$\{P_{no}^{s}\}\ bal.withdraw(x):no\ \{P\}$

(We assume that the value of x is nonnegative.)

Figure 11.3: An abstract specification for an instance, bal, of type $account$ involving the use of status information.

although it sometimes returns negative status), $bal.withdraw(x):ok$ is executable only in a state in which x is less than or equal to bal. (Note that, since we use only status information, we do not specify data values in denoting operations.) Thus, if the sequence $bal.withdraw(x):ok$, $bal.deposit(y):ok$ is defined in some state, the sequence $bal.deposit(y):ok$, $bal.withdraw(x):ok$ is also defined in that state. However, the reverse is not true: the sequence $bal.deposit(y):ok$, $bal.withdraw(x):ok$ might be defined in some state in which the sequence $bal.withdraw(x):ok$, $bal.deposit(y):ok$ is not defined (since the amount deposited might be needed to cover the withdrawal). Hence we must expand our notions of commutativity and of conflicts. As we shall see, the required generalization is different for immediate-update and deferred-update systems.

11.1.2 Immediate-Update Pessimistic Systems

In an immediate-update, pessimistic, operation-based concurrency control, whenever a transaction, T, invokes an operation on an instance, t, the status is computed and used to determine if a conflict exists with a prior operation of an active transaction. If no conflict exists, the operation is performed; otherwise a conflict is declared. Any of the protocols described in Chapter 10 can be used to deal with the conflict. If no conflict exists, the operation is added to lock set, $L(t)$, and the results (data and status) are returned to T, which resumes execution.

To describe conflicts, we define the *right-commutes-with* relation, which generalizes the notion of commutativity to deal with partial operations in an immediate-update pessimistic system. We say that an operation p_1 of T_1 *right-commutes-with* an operation p_2 of T_2 if, for every state in which the sequence $< p_2, p_1 >$ is defined, the sequence $< p_1, p_2 >$ is also defined and leaves the instance in the same final state. (Keep in mind that our notion of an operation includes data and status, and thus the operations are returning the same information in both cases.) Hence, when active transaction T_2 has executed p_2 and transaction T_1 makes a request to perform p_1, that request can be granted, since the operations could have been performed in the opposite order. As a result, the operations do not determine an ordering between the transactions. Note that *right-commutes-with* is not symmetric. A requested operation, p_1, conflicts with a prior operation, p_2, of an active transaction if (p_1, p_2) is an element of the complement of *right-commutes-with*, which we refer to as *does-not-right-commute-with*.

For example, if we assume that a queue has an unbounded length, the operation *Enqueue(x):ok* is defined in all states [*i.e.*, there is no operation *Enqueue(x):no*]. *Dequeue*, however, can return two distinct status values and thus yields two distinct partial operations, *Dequeue(x):no* and *Dequeue(x):ok*, depending on whether or not the queue is empty when the operation is invoked. Conflicts between operations on an arbitrary queue are indicated in Figure 11.4, where an X in the row corresponding to operation p_1 and the column corresponding to operation p_2 means that $(p_1, p_2) \in$ *does-not-right-commute-with*. For example, (*Enqueue(x):ok, Dequeue(x):ok*) $\notin$ *does-not-right-commute-with*, since T_2 successfully removed an element prior to the enqueue operation of T_1 and will remove the same element if the order of operations is reversed. On the other hand, (*Dequeue(x):no, Dequeue(x):ok*) $\in$ *does-not-right-commute-with*, since the transactions will get different responses if the operation order is reversed. Finally, (*Dequeue(x):ok, Dequeue(x):no*) $\notin$ *does-not-right-commute-with*, since the sequence *Dequeue(x):no, Dequeue(x):ok* is not defined in any state.

Active Transaction T_2
Has Previously Requested

		Enqueue(x):ok	Dequeue(x):ok	Dequeue(x):no
Trans-	Enqueue(x):ok	X		X
action T_1	Dequeue(x):ok	X	X	
Requests	Dequeue(x):no		X	

Figure 11.4: Conflicts between operations on a queue for an immediate-update pessimistic concurrency control are based on the relation *does-not-right-commute-with*, here denoted by X.

As with untyped databases, an immediate-update pessimistic system uses a write-ahead log to abort a transaction. However, the concept of the write-ahead log must be generalized for typed databases. We assume that for each operation defined on an object, there is also defined an *undo operation*, which reverses the effect of that operation. For example, the undo operation for *increment* is *decrement*. The undo operation for *dequeue* would be *replace* (which inserts an entry at the head of the queue). Before a transaction performs an operation on an object, it places an undo record containing the corresponding undo operation in its write-ahead log. To abort, it performs all the undo operations in the log in reverse order. (As before, when it commits, it discards the write-ahead log.) One seeming complication is that, since two concurrent operations that do not conflict can both update the same instance, an aborting transaction might want to undo an operation after some other transaction has performed a subsequent operation on the same instance. However, since the two operations do not conflict, they must right commute. Hence we can assume that the operation performed by the aborting transaction was performed last, and thus that the undo operation will work correctly.

11.1.3 Deferred-Update Optimistic Systems

In a deferred-update optimistic system, a transaction in its read phase sees the results of all committed transactions and stores information about its proposed updates in an intentions list. For an untyped database, an intentions list is a list of do records containing the new values to be installed in each of the records modified by a transaction (when it commits). As with write-ahead logs, this view must be generalized for typed databases. Each do record must now contain the operation to be performed (instead of the resulting value). Thus the intentions list contains do records corresponding to the entire sequence of operations that a transaction has executed on a particular instance.

To understand why the intentions list must contain the entire sequence of operations, recall that in a typed database each operation can both return a value and modify the state of the instance, and the new state it produces can be a function of the old state. A state can be stored as a value, a sequence of operations (which would produce that value), or some combination of the two. However, when a transaction invokes an operation, the value of the instance must be calculated in order to determine the results produced by the operation. Assume g is the (committed) history of the instance at the time a particular operation, p, is invoked by T (during its read phase) and h represents the sequence of operations that T has already performed on that instance. Then the state seen by p can be represented by the sequence $g \circ h$. For the purpose of executing p, we must reduce $g \circ h$ to a value. Consider the following two approaches. We can represent the committed state as a value in the database (rather than as the sequence g), maintain the sequence h as an element of T's intentions list, and apply h to the value in the database when p is executed. Alternatively, we can store the value represented by $g \circ h$ in the intentions list directly and update that value each time T executes an operation. However, since a concurrent transaction might commit while T is in its read phase, g might change between two successive operations of T, and the value in the intentions list would no longer be correct.[1] Hence, to guarantee that p sees the current state as produced by all committed transactions, the first approach (of representing the committed state as a value and separately maintaining the list h) is preferable to the second.

Since we focus our discussion on a single instance, we (loosely) refer to h as the intentions list (when, in fact, it is the entry in the intentions list for the instance). We assume that when T commits, its intentions list is used to atomically update the actual state of the object in the database. We represent this updating as the concatenation of h to g. (As before, T aborts by discarding its intentions list.)

Intentions lists for untyped databases with only read and write operations are a special case. Since read does not change the state of a record, it need not be stored in an intentions list. Write produces a new record state, but the new state produced by a write operation is not a function of the old state as it is with more general operations such as increment. Hence, the intentions list for a single record can be reduced to a single element: the value written by the last write performed by the associated transaction. When T performs a read of some record, if T has not previously written to the record, the database value is returned. If T has written to the record, the value stored in T's intentions list is returned. Although a concurrent transaction that commits during T's read phase might change the value of the record in the database, that value is not seen by any read of T that follows any of T's writes.

In a deferred-update optimistic concurrency control (using the serial valida-

---

[1]As an example, assume that the object is an integer whose committed state when T starts is 2. Suppose that the only operation in h is an increment operation, and that another transaction, T_1, commits while T is in its read phase. If T_1 also does an increment (this does not conflict with T's increment), then the committed state changes to 3. The value in T's intentions list is now wrong.

tion assumption), a transaction, T_1, must be validated against all transactions that committed while T_1 was executing its read phase. Suppose T_2 is such a transaction, and suppose that the two transactions access some instance t. T_2's intentions list, h, for t is used to (atomically) update t's state when T_2 commits. If the interleaved schedule is to be serializable in commit order, then (for each instance) we must show that the serial schedule of transactions in commit order is a legal history. (Since we are focusing on a single instance, the schedule of transactions and the history of the instance are the same.)

Assume T_1's intentions list is the sequence $p = <p_1, p_2, \ldots, p_n>$. Since T_2 committed during T_1's read phase, T_2's intentions list must have been concatenated with t's committed history between the execution of some pair of successive operations, p_i and p_{i+1}, that T_1 executed during its read phase. It could also have taken place before p_1 (in which case T_2 precedes T_1 as in the serial schedule) or after p_n (which is a special case of the following argument). Thus we have that, for $1 \le j \le i$, p_j saw the state $g \circ p^{j-1}$, while for $j > i$, p_j saw the state $g \circ h \circ p^{j-1}$, where p^j is the sequence $<p_1, p_2, \ldots, p_j>$ and p^0 is the null sequence. To guarantee that the interleaved schedule is equivalent to a serial schedule in which transactions are ordered in commit order, we must demonstrate that $g \circ h \circ <p_1, p_2, \ldots, p_n>$ is a legal history. Hence, we must demonstrate that the first i operation invocations would have generated the same results if T_2 had committed before T_1 entered its read phase.

Based on this reasoning, we can define the following relation that must hold between the operations of a validating transaction, T_1, and the operations in the intentions list of any transaction that committed during T_1's read phase. Since we assume we do not know what intentions lists can actually be produced, we state the condition for arbitrary sequences, h.

Does-Not-Depend-on Relation

A relation C is a *does-not-depend-on* relation if, for all legal histories g and all operation sequences h_1 and h_2 such that

$g \circ h_1$ and $g \circ h_2$ are legal, and
each operation in h_1 is in relation C to all operations in h_2 (*i.e.*, each operation in h_1 does not depend on any operation in h_2),

$g \circ h_2 \circ h_1$ is also legal.

(Intuitively we see that if no operation in h_1 depends on any operation in h_2, then h_2 can be inserted before h_1 without changing the results generated by h_1.)

In general, a number of transactions will commit while T_1 executes its read phase. Each successive commit causes an intentions list to be appended to the history, but the condition guarantees that this insertion does not change the results of T_1's operations up to that point.

If two operations are related by the complement of a *does-not-depend-on* relation, which is called a *depends-on* relation, we say they conflict. It can be

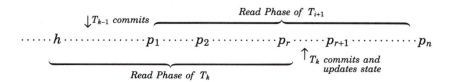

Figure 11.5: The sequence in which operations are invoked by transactions using an optimistic concurrency control.

shown that a *depends-on* relation is the most general conflict relation for an optimistic concurrency control. Unfortunately, however, since the definition of *depends-on* involves sequences of operations rather than pairs of operations, it can be quite difficult to deduce such a relation for an arbitrary abstract data type (or even to prove that a given relation is a *depends-on* relation). We now define a relation that is a special case of a *does-not-depend-on* relation (and hence its complement can be used as a conflict relation) but that is easier to use, since it is defined between pairs of operations. We say that an operation p_1 *forward-commutes-with* an operation p_2 if, for all states g such that $g \circ p_1$ and $g \circ p_2$ are both legal, the sequences $g \circ <p_1, p_2>$ and $g \circ <p_2, p_1>$ are also legal and represent the same state. Note that this relation is symmetric.

If each operation of a validating transaction, T, *forward-commutes-with* each operation of every transaction that committed during T's read phase, T can be allowed to commit. To see why the *forward-commutes-with* relation guarantees equivalence between the serial and interleaved schedules, we use an induction on the number of transactions in the interleaved schedule, S. Assume inductively that the serial schedule constructed from the operations of the first i transactions, $T_1 T_2 \ldots T_i$, to commit in S is legal. Consider T_{i+1} with intentions list $p_1 p_2 \ldots p_n$. Assume that in S, p_1 was executed (during T_{i+1}'s read phase) in the state g, which is the history produced by the serial execution of $T_1 \ldots T_{k-1}$. If no transaction commits during T_{i+1}'s read phase, $(k - 1) = i$ and all operations of T_{i+1} follow the operations of T_i in S. Thus, by the inductive hypothesis, the result is true for $i + 1$.

Suppose that T_k, $k \leq i$, is the first transaction to commit during T_{i+1}'s read phase and that the commit happens between the occurrence of p_r and p_{r+1}. Figure 11.5 shows the sequence in which operations are invoked during the execution of S. Note that, since the concurrency control is deferred update, the sequence does not represent the order in which operations are performed on the instance and so an operation does not necessarily see the effect of its predecessors in the sequence. For simplicity we assume that T_k's intentions list, h, is a single operation. (The argument extends trivially to an arbitrary intentions list.) The operation corresponding to h was invoked at the time corresponding to where the h appears in the figure but is performed at the time when T_k commits, denoted by $\uparrow$.

Transaction T_2 Committed
While T_1 Was Active

		$Enqueue(x){:}ok$	$Dequeue(x){:}ok$	$Dequeue(x){:}no$
Trans-	$Enqueue(x){:}ok$	X		X
action T_1	$Dequeue(x){:}ok$		X	
Requesting	$Dequeue(x){:}no$	X		
to Commit				

Figure 11.6: Conflicts between operations on a queue for a deferred-update concurrency control based on the relation *does-not-forward-commute-with*, here denoted by X.

In S, p_1 was executed in the state g, which is the history produced by the serial execution of $T_1 \ldots T_{k-1}$, whereas h may have seen an earlier state, g', which is a prefix of g. (For example, in Figure 11.5 h does not see the effect of T_{k-1}.) The inductive hypothesis, however, guarantees that $g \circ < h >$ is legal, since $k \le i$. Since both $g \circ < p_1 >$ and $g \circ < h >$ are legal, and since T_{i+1} successfully validates with respect to T_k, p_1 *forward-commutes-with* h and hence the histories $g \circ < h > \circ < p_1 >$ and $g \circ < p_1 > \circ < h >$ are legal and both represent the same state. Next we note that both $g \circ < p_1 > \circ < h >$ and $g \circ < p_1 > \circ < p_2 >$ are legal, and since validation ensures that h and p_2 also forward commute, the argument can be repeated once more to show that $g \circ < h > \circ < p_1 > \circ < p_2 >$ and $g \circ < p_1 > \circ < p_2 > \circ < h >$ are legal and both represent the same state. Thus, if the argument is repeated r times, we can show that $g \circ < h > \circ < p_1, p_2, \ldots, p_r >$ is legal and represents the same state as $g \circ < p_1, p_2, \ldots, p_r > \circ < h >$, and thus we can serialize T_k before T_{i+1}. (If h consists of more than one operation we can move each operation separately using the previous argument.) The same argument can be used to show that $T_{k+1} \ldots T_i$ can be serialized before T_{i+1}, demonstrating the desired result.

We have shown that the complement of the relation *forward-commutes-with*, which we call *does-not-forward-commute-with*, can be used to designate the conflicts for a deferred-update optimistic concurrency control. That relation for the queue abstract data type is shown in Figure 11.6.

Note that the conflict relations for optimistic controls given in Figure 10.10 for the read-write system and in Figure 11.2 for the integer data type are *depends-on* relations but not *does-not-forward-commute-with* relations. For example, two write operations do not forward commute but do not conflict in either of those systems. (Recall that we reasoned intuitively to show that these conflict relations were correct. However, we might find it difficult to apply such intuitive reasoning to a more complex data type and might be required to use the formal notions of *depends-on* or *does-not-forward-commute-with* relations.)

11.1.4   Deferred-Update Pessimistic Systems

The conditions governing the correct behavior of a deferred-update pessimistic system are closely related to those of its optimistic counterpart. As in the optimistic case, when a transaction commits, its intentions list, h, is concatenated to the state g, so the initial operations of a concurrently active transaction see a committed state g, while later operations see a committed state $g \circ h$. The difference arises from the fact that the concurrency control must decide whether a conflict exists without knowing the commit order of the active transactions. Thus, when transaction T_1 makes a request to perform some operation on a data item on which active transaction T_2 has already had a requested operation granted, the control does not know whether T_1 will commit before or after T_2. Hence it does not know whether T_1's operation should not *depend-on* T_2's or T_2's should not *depend-on* T_1's. It must therefore make the worst case assumption and not let either operation *depend-on* the other. Suppose T_1 has executed the sequence $p_1 p_2 \ldots p_i$ on an instance of an abstract type and this sequence is a prefix of its (final) intentions list, h_1, and similarly, T_2 has executed the sequence $q_1 q_2 \ldots q_j$ on the instance and this sequence is a prefix of its (final) intentions list, h_2. Then the sequences $g \circ h_2 \circ p^i$ and $g \circ h_1 \circ q^j$ must be legal for all possible values of i and j.

It can be shown that the most general conflict relation for a deferred-update pessimistic system is the symmetric closure of a *depends-on* relation. However, once again it is difficult to deduce such a relation for an arbitrary abstract data type, and we seek a special case of such a relation that is easier to find. Using the same reasoning as with the optimistic case, we can show that the *does-not-forward-commute-with* relation can be used as the conflict relation for a deferred-update pessimistic system. This relation is already symmetric. Thus the conflict relation shown in Figure 11.6 can also be used for a deferred-update pessimistic system.

Note that the conflict relations for deferred-update pessimistic controls, given in Figure 10.13 for the read-write system and in Figure 11.2 for the integer data type, are symmetric closures of *depends-on* relations and not *does-not-forward-commute-with* relations (two writes would conflict in the symmetric closure of the *does-not-forward-commute-with* relation).

11.1.5   Reasoning About Conflict Relations*

We have shown that the relations *right-commutes-with* and *forward-commutes-with* can be used to define conflicts in immediate-update and deferred-update systems, respectively. In all the examples we have discussed, the data type has been simple enough that we could reason about the commutativity of its operations intuitively. In a more general situation, we can use the methods of Chapter 3 to formally specify the operations and prove the desired properties.

Consider the formal specification of the *account* data type given in Figure 11.3. To show that a deposit operation *forward-commutes-with* another deposit, we first observe that deposit is a total operation and then derive triples for the composition of two deposit operations in both orders (for simplicity, we assume that P does not involve the variables that receive the status information). If the triples are the same, the two operations forward commute.

$$\{P^{bal}_{bal+x+x'}\} \; bal.deposit(x){:}ok \; ; \; bal.deposit(x'){:}ok \; \{P\}$$
$$\{P^{bal}_{bal+x'+x}\} \; bal.deposit(x'){:}ok \; ; \; bal.deposit(x){:}ok \; \{P\}$$

The two preconditions are the same because addition commutes.

To show that $deposit(x'){:}ok$ $right\text{-}commutes\text{-}with$ $withdraw(x){:}ok$, we first show that in any state, g, such that $g \; \circ \; < \; withdraw(x){:}ok, deposit(x'){:}ok \; >$ is legal, $g \; \circ \; < \; deposit(x'){:}ok, withdraw(x){:}ok \; >$ is also legal. Since the first sequence is legal, $WP_a^{withdraw(x):ok}(bal)$, which is $bal \geq x$, must be a postcondition of g. Then, since

$$(bal \geq x) \Rightarrow (bal + x' \geq x)$$

we can use this postcondition, the Rule of Consequence, and the Assignment Axiom to conclude that the deposit transaction in the second sequence can be described by the triple

$$\{bal + x' \geq x\} \; bal.deposit(x'){:}ok \; \{bal \geq x\}$$

Therefore, $WP_a^{withdraw(x):ok}(bal)$ must be a precondition of the withdraw operation, making the second sequence legal as well. To show that the two sequences yield the same state, we annotate the composition of the two operations in both orders:

$$\{P^{bal}_{bal+x'-x}\} \; bal.withdraw(x){:}ok \; ; \; \{P^{bal}_{bal+x'}\} \; bal.deposit(x'){:}ok \; \{P\}$$
$$\{P^{bal}_{bal-x+x'}\} \; bal.deposit(x'){:}ok \; ; \; \{P^{bal}_{bal-x}\} \; bal.withdraw(x){:}ok \; \{P\}$$

Both sequences are characterized by the same pre- and postconditions, since addition and subtraction commute.

11.2   Distributed and Object Oriented Databases

In a distributed database system, data is stored at a number of sites, perhaps widely separated geographically, in a network. Such systems are useful when the organizations they support are themselves distributed and each component maintains its own portion of the data. Communication costs can be minimized by placing data at the site at which it is most frequently accessed. System availability can be increased, since the failure of a single site need not prevent continued operation at other sites.

A transaction is generally not restricted to accessing only the data at the site at which it is initiated, but can access data at other sites as well. We assume that the distribution of data is invisible to the user. The user sees the system as a single integrated database. By making the distributed nature of the database invisible, we make it possible to move data around the network without disturbing the user interface. So that data can be accessed at several sites, a *distributed transaction* consists of a set of subtransactions called *cohorts*. A unique cohort executes at each site at which data is to be accessed. In addition, a *coordinator* is created at the initiator site to create and control the cohorts and communicate with the user. If the initiator site has data to be accessed, a cohort exists at that site as well. Note that, since each cohort of a transaction executes at a different site, cohorts access disjoint subsets of the database.

Cohorts can perform arbitrary computations, and hence the computation performed by the distributed transaction can itself be distributed. Furthermore, the subtransactions can execute concurrently and can pass intermediate results to one another. It should be noted that even if a distributed transaction runs in isolation (*i.e.,* there are no concurrent transactions), it may behave nondeterministically, since decisions made by a subtransaction can, for example, be based on the order in which messages from its cohort subtransactions arrive. This type of nondeterminism is a departure from our assumption of deterministic behavior for conventional (nondistributed) transactions.

The user views a distributed transaction as a single unit that is performed atomically. Thus, as in the case of a centralized system, the job of the concurrency control in a distributed transaction processing system is to respond to requests in such a way as to produce a globally serializable schedule.

For example, consider the nationwide distribution system of a hardware manufacturing company. The company maintains a network of warehouses at different sites throughout the country, and each site has its own local database that stores information about that site's inventory. A customer at some site might initiate a transaction requesting 100 dozen widgets. The transaction might read the record containing the number of widgets currently in the local warehouse and find that there are only 10 dozen. The transaction might (tentatively) reserve those and then spawn subtransactions at one or more of the other warehouses to reserve additional widgets until the full 100 dozen have been reserved. After 100 dozen have been located and reserved, the records in each of the sites at which widgets have been reserved would be decremented and appropriate shipping orders would be generated. If 100 dozen cannot be located, all reserved widgets should be released and the transaction should return failure status to the customer.

Since a distributed transaction must be atomic, it must either commit at all sites or abort at all sites. In the example, either all sites at which widgets have been reserved decrement their local databases or none do.

A complication that arises in distributed systems is that one or more of the sites (or communication links) may fail while the others remain operational. We discuss failures in database systems in the next chapter. In this chapter we assume no failures. We do assume, however, that a transaction can abort (and hence must be recoverable), and once a transaction commits (at all sites), the system must ensure that database changes at all sites are made permanent.

A simple approach to designing a distributed transaction processing system is to designate one of the sites as a central concurrency control site. All requests (at any site) are sent to the central site, which responds in the same way as would a centralized concurrency control. In fact such a system is just a centralized concurrency control in which the database is distributed. Unfortunately, this simple approach has a number of significant drawbacks: it requires a very large amount of communication among sites and is particularly vulnerable to failure of the central site.

A better approach, and the one we follow, is to assume that there is a local concurrency control at each site. Whenever a cohort makes a request to perform an operation at some site, the local concurrency control at that site makes its decision based only on local information available to it, without communicating with any other site. Each local concurrency control separately uses the techniques we have previously described to ensure that there exists at least one serializable schedule of cohorts at its site and that there are no local deadlocks or cyclic restarts. The overall design of the system must then ensure that transactions are serialized globally (*i.e.,* that there is a particular serial ordering on which all sites can agree) and there are no distributed deadlocks or cyclic restarts.

This model of a distributed system is quite similar to a commonly used model for object oriented transaction processing systems. For our purposes, an *object* is simply an instance of an abstract data type that incorporates its own concurrency control mechanism. A transaction is a computation involving operations on objects. The sequence of operations invoked by a transaction on a particular object is analogous to the sequence of operations executed by a subtransaction in a distributed system. As with distinct sites in a distributed database, we assume that the concurrency control at each individual object separately ensures that there exists a serial schedule of operations at its object. The overall design of an object oriented system must ensure that whenever each individual concurrency control guarantees that the schedule of operations performed locally is serializable, the schedule of operations across all objects is also serializable and there are no deadlocks or cyclic restarts. A system that guarantees this property will function correctly whether the objects are located at a single site or distributed in a network.

Virtually all of the discussion in the remainder of this section applies to both distributed transaction processing systems and object oriented transaction processing systems. We use the terminology of distributed systems, but the application to object oriented systems should be obvious (and in most cases just requires substituting the word "object" for the word "site").

If we assume that each local concurrency control separately serializes the cohorts at each site and ensures that there are no local deadlocks or cyclic restarts, the overall design of the system must ensure the following:

Atomic Termination. Either all cohorts of a distributed transaction must commit or all must abort.

No Global Deadlocks. There must be no global (distributed) deadlocks or cyclic restarts involving multiple sites.

Global Serialization. There must be a global serialization of all transactions. We would like the serialization to be such that one possible ordering is the commit order, but as we shall see, we have to slightly generalize the concept of commit order.

Our plan is that each of the local concurrency controls be one of the models discussed earlier: the immediate-update pessimistic, deferred-update optimistic, or deferred-update pessimistic. We assume initially that each site uses the same model, but as we shall see, this restriction can be relaxed. We discuss each of the above design issues separately.

11.2.1 Atomic Termination

A distributed transaction can commit only if all its cohorts commit. Even though a cohort is prepared to commit, it cannot commit by itself because some other cohort might still be executing and later might be aborted (for example, it may be deadlocked) or rolled back (if it fails to validate). In such cases the entire distributed transaction must be aborted. Thus when a cohort has completed, it must wait for all others to complete.

To ensure that the transaction commits atomically, the coordinator and its cohorts execute a protocol called an *atomic commit protocol*. We describe a particular atomic commit protocol called the *two phase commit protocol*. In Chapter 12 we discuss other atomic commit protocols that are appropriate for dealing with certain types of system failures.

The two phase commit protocol is initiated by the coordinator. In the first phase the coordinator sends a message to all cohorts telling them to prepare to commit. Each cohort replies with a *vote* indicating whether or not it is ready to commit. With a pessimistic control, a cohort is ready to commit if it has not been aborted. With an optimistic control, a cohort is ready to commit if it has been successfully validated. Once a cohort replies that it is ready to commit, that decision cannot be reversed (*i.e.*, the local concurrency control at the cohort site cannot abort the cohort). If the coordinator receives messages from all the cohorts saying that they are ready to commit, it decides to commit the transaction and sends each cohort a second message telling it to commit.

Two Phase Commit Protocol

Phase One

The coordinator sends a *prepare* message to all cohorts.

Each cohort waits until it receives the *prepare* message from the coordinator. It then votes *ready* or *aborting* and sends the corresponding message to the coordinator, depending on whether it is a pessimistic or an optimistic control:

Pessimistic control – If the cohort has been aborted, it decides abort and sends an *aborting* message. If not, it sends a *ready* message and enters a state in which it cannot be aborted by the local control.

Optimistic control – The cohort executes its validation phase. If validation fails, it decides abort and sends an *aborting* message; otherwise it sends a *ready* message and enters a state in which it cannot be aborted by the local control.

The coordinator waits to receive votes from all the cohorts and then enters the second phase of the protocol.

Phase Two

If the coordinator receives at least one *aborting* vote, it decides abort and sends an *abort* message to all cohorts. If all votes are *ready*, it decides commit and sends a *commit* message to each cohort. Then it terminates.

The actions taken by a cohort when it receives an *abort* or *commit* message depend on whether it is an immediate-update or deferred-update control:

Immediate-update control – If a cohort receives an *abort* message, it decides abort and rolls back any changes it made to the database. If it receives a *commit* message, it decides commit. In both cases, it then releases all locks, discards its write-ahead log, and terminates.

Deferred-update control – If a cohort receives an *abort* message, it decides abort, discards its intentions list and terminates. If it receives a commit message, it decides commit, executes its write phase, discards its intentions list, and terminates. If the control is pessimistic, locks must also be released.

The two phase commit protocol ensures that either all cohorts commit or all cohorts abort. Suppose now that two concurrent distributed transactions, T_1 and T_2, are executing their commit protocols simultaneously. If both commit and have several cohort sites in common, the phase 2 commit messages might arrive in different orders at the common sites. Hence, at one site it may appear that T_1 has committed before T_2, while the other site sees the commits as having happened in the reverse order. This eventuality has an impact on the problem of ensuring a global serialization as we shall see shortly.

11.2.2   Distributed Deadlock

Pessimistic concurrency controls that employ waiting are subject to deadlock and those that employ restarts are subject to cyclic restart. Assuming that each local concurrency control (perhaps using techniques described in the previous chapter) does not produce local deadlock or cyclic restart, we want to ensure that the overall system is not subject to distributed deadlock or cyclic restart. For example, a simple distributed deadlock between two distributed transactions, T_1 and T_2, both of which have cohorts at sites A and B, would result if the concurrency control at site A made T_1's cohort wait for T_2's cohort while the concurrency control at site B made T_2's cohort wait for T_1's cohort. Note that a distributed deadlock is somewhat different from a deadlock in a centralized system, since the subtransactions of a distributed transaction can run concurrently, whereas in the centralized case we assumed that a transaction was purely sequential. Hence, in the above example, T_2's cohort at site A not only holds some resource for which T_1's cohort is waiting, but can actually progress, since it is not delayed by the wait of its cohort at site B. Deadlock still occurs, however, since T_2 cannot release its locks until it commits globally, which will not happen if its cohort at site B is waiting.

In general, a distributed deadlock cannot be eliminated by restarting a single cohort, since the cohorts of a distributed transaction may have communicated with one another before the deadlock occurred and the state of some cohort may be dependent on the state of the cohort to be terminated. Thus, the entire distributed transaction must be restarted. Given this situation, cyclic restart on a global scale is possible.

Several techniques can be used to detect a distributed deadlock. In one technique the system maintains a distributed wait-for graph, which is updated whenever a cohort is made to wait at any site. Another technique is called probe chasing. A cohort of T_1 informs its coordinator that it is waiting for a cohort of T_2. The coordinator of T_1 sends a probe message to the coordinator of T_2. If the coordinator of T_2 has also been informed by one of its cohorts that it is waiting for a cohort of T_3, then the probe message is relayed by the coordinator of T_2 to the coordinator of T_3. A deadlock is detected if the probe returns to the coordinator that initiated the probe.

The timestamp technique can be used to avoid (as contrasted with detect) deadlock. We assume that each site has a local clock (this need not be a logical clock, nor need it be tightly synchronized with the clocks at the other sites). Whenever a transaction starts, the coordinator uses the current value of the local clock to construct a timestamp. To ensure that all timestamps are globally unique, the coordinator's (unique) site identifier is appended to the clock value to form the timestamp. If a transaction is restarted, it maintains its original timestamp. When a distributed transaction creates a cohort at a site, it sends along the value of its timestamp. Then if a conflict occurs at a site, the concurrency control at that site can use the timestamps of the two transactions to make a decision about waits or restarts. Suppose T_1 and T_2 have conflicts at sites A and B. Since the concurrency controls at each site have the same information available to them, they can make consistent decisions to avoid distributed deadlock or cyclic restart. For example, they can use a strategy based on the relative size of the timestamps.

The three centralized immediate-update pessimistic systems we have discussed that use timestamps to resolve conflicts are the Wait-Die, Kill-Wait, and Timestamp-Ordered systems. All of these can be used as the local concurrency control in a pessimistic distributed system with the assurance that no global deadlocks or cyclic restarts will occur. When a Kill-Wait control is used in a distributed system, it is referred to as a *Wound-Wait* system. The *Kill* primitive in the protocol is replaced by *Wound*, where *Wound* means that the transaction, T, with which the requesting transaction has a conflict is restarted, unless T has started the two phase commit protocol, in which case the requesting transaction waits. In the Wait-Die and Wound-Wait systems, the purpose of the timestamps is to allow consistent decisions (with respect to deadlocks and cyclic restarts) to be made by the local concurrency controls, not to determine the serial order of the transactions.

Distributed optimistic concurrency controls are subject to deadlock and cyclic restart that can occur as a result of executing the two phase commit protocol. When a cohort of T_1 at site A, T_{1A}, receives a *prepare* message, it may happen that a cohort of T_2 at that site, T_{2A}, has already entered validation. If a serial validation algorithm is used, T_{1A} must wait until T_2 either commits or aborts globally. Since it is possible for cohorts of the two transactions at site B to request validation in the opposite order, a deadlock can occur. Such a deadlock can be eliminated if a parallel validation algorithm is used. However, a new problem is then introduced. If the cohorts enter validation in opposite orders at the two sites, T_{1A} validates against T_{2A} at A, while T_{2B} validates against T_{1B} at B. If conflicts exist at the two sites, both transactions will be aborted, and a cyclic restart is possible. We return to this problem shortly.

11.2.3   Global Serialization

The concurrency control at each site independently schedules operations so that the cohorts at that site are serializable. The resulting interleaved schedule at any particular site will in general be equivalent to a set of different serial schedules. In each such schedule the cohorts at the site are totally ordered. Hence each such schedule defines a total order on the transactions as a whole, which we refer to as an *ordering*. Such an ordering is associated with a site and involves only those transactions having cohorts at that site. We refer to the set of orderings corresponding to the set of serial schedules equivalent to the particular interleaved schedule that has occurred at a site as the *possible orderings* at that site.

Although all sites individually guarantee the serializability of their schedules, we require a stronger condition: that the global schedule of operations at all sites be serializable. We must first be clear about what we mean by a global schedule. We imagine that there is some (conceptual) global clock that denotes real time, and we order operations in the global schedule according to the real time at which each operation is completed. Operations that occur simultaneously at different sites must involve distinct objects. Hence we can order them arbitrarily in the global schedule.

Any serial schedule, S^{ser}, that is equivalent to the global schedule places a total ordering on the distributed transactions, which in turn places a total order on the cohorts at each site. That total order must be one of the possible orderings at each site if S^{ser} is to be equivalent to the global schedule.

Two orderings (of possibly different sets of transactions) are *consistent* if they order the transactions present in both in the same way. For example, if site A has cohorts of the distributed transactions T_1, T_2, T_3, T_4, and T_6 and site B has cohorts of T_2, T_3, T_4, T_5, and T_7, the ordering $T_1 T_2 T_3 T_4 T_6$ at A is consistent with the ordering $T_2 T_5 T_3 T_4 T_7$ at B. Since a pair of consistent orderings order their common transactions in the same way, we can combine them into a set of possible total orderings of the transactions in both. Each ordering in the set is consistent with each ordering in the pair. In the previous example this set would contain $T_1 T_2 T_5 T_3 T_4 T_6 T_7$ and $T_1 T_2 T_5 T_3 T_4 T_7 T_6$. We say that A and B *agree* on each element of this set. By combining all pairs of consistent orderings, we obtain the set of all orderings on which A and B agree, and we can then combine these with the possible orderings at C, etc., until all sites have been included. If the resulting set of possible orderings of all transactions (on which all sites agree) is not empty, any of its elements, O, can be used to form a serial schedule equivalent to the global schedule of all of the (distributed) transactions (since the projection of O onto the cohorts at any particular site is one of the possible orderings at that site).

Our concern is that, since each site operates independently and might even employ a different concurrency control algorithm, there might be no ordering on which all sites agree. To ensure that local serializability at each site implies global serializability, we require all concurrency controls used in the system to share a common property, called a *local atomicity property*, defined as follows:

Local Atomicity Property

If the concurrency controls at each site all independently satisfy the same local atomicity property and the system uses an atomic commit protocol (such as the two phase commit protocol), the global schedule is serializable.

We can define different local atomicity properties depending on how we require the individual controls to serialize their local transactions. We define two such properties below.

Our plan is to design the overall system so that all the local controls agree on some ordering of the transactions. We must decide what ordering that will be. One obvious choice is the global commit order: the real time order of commit operations performed at coordinator sites. Unfortunately, if a two phase commit protocol is used, phase two *commit* messages for distinct transactions that have cohorts at common sites may arrive in different orders at those sites. For example, the coordinators for T_1 and T_2 might reside at sites C_1 and C_2

and cohorts for both transactions might execute at sites A and B. The *commit* message for T_1 from C_1 might arrive at A before the *commit* message for T_2 from C_2, while the order of *commit* message arrivals might be reversed at B. Thus the global commit order is not necessarily apparent at each site.

We introduce a new relation that can be used to define a partial order among transactions and show that it can be used as the basis of a local atomicity property. We say that *a transaction T_1 precedes a transaction T_2 at some site* if the cohort of T_2 at that site invokes some database operation after the site has received the *commit* message from T_1's coordinator. Note that the *precedes* relation is defined in terms of when an operation is invoked, not when the operation is actually performed. For example, a transaction using an optimistic concurrency control invokes an update operation during its read phase, but that operation is actually performed during its write phase (after it has committed).

If T_1 *precedes* T_2 at some site, T_1 must be before T_2 in the global commit order. However, the converse is not true. If T_1 and T_2 do not conflict, T_1 might be before T_2 in the global commit order, but not related by *precedes* to T_2 (all operations of both transactions might have been invoked before either commits). Because a transaction cannot invoke any additional operations after it commits, it can never be true that both T_1 *precedes* T_2 and T_2 *precedes* T_1 at one site; hence *precedes* is a partial order at each site. Note that, regardless of the concurrency control, transactions that have conflicting operations at some site are related by *precedes* at that site (since if T_1 conflicts with T_2, in a pessimistic system T_1 must wait for T_2 to commit, while in an optimistic system T_1 cannot successfully validate unless T_2 has completed prior to T_1's read phase). Furthermore, the order imposed by the conflict is the same as the *precedes* order at that site.

We now define an atomicity property based on the *precedes* relation and show that it is a local atomicity property. We say that a control at a site is *dynamic atomic* if it serializes in *all* orders consistent with the *precedes* relation at that site.[2]

To show that dynamic atomicity is a local atomicity property, we need only show that the union of the *precedes* relations at all sites is a partial order. Hence, there must be at least one total order, O, that is consistent with the union and therefore consistent with the *precedes* relation at each site. The global schedule is equivalent to the serial schedule based on O. To show that the union of the *precedes* relations at all sites is a partial order, we show that it cannot be the case that T_2 *precedes* T_1 at some site A, and T_1 *precedes* T_2 at some other site B. We assume the system uses a two phase commit protocol. If T_2 *precedes* T_1 at A, it follows from the ordering of events in the commit protocol that "T_2's commit event at its coordinator" *happened-before* "at least one operation invoked by T_{1A}" and that "all operations invoked by

---

[2]Since the *precedes* order agrees with the commit order for all transactions that have conflicted, we can use the same reasoning as in the previous chapter to argue that the user has an intuitive expectation that the transactions have executed in *precedes* order.

T_{1A}" *happened-before* "T_1's commit event at its coordinator." If it were also true that T_1 *precedes* T_2 at site B, we could draw the opposite conclusions as well. Since *happened-before* is a partial order, we have a contradiction, and we conclude that the union of the *precedes* relations at all sites – which we refer to simply as the *precedes* relation – is a partial order. Thus, dynamic atomicity is a local atomicity property.

As we shall see, all of the previously discussed controls that have conflict relations based on the commutativity of operations are dynamic atomic and hence can be used, without change, in distributed systems that employ an atomic commit protocol. In fact, it follows from the definition of local atomicity that different concurrency controls can be used at different sites as long as the control at each site is dynamic atomic.

We shall also see that deferred-update controls in which conflicts are based on a *depends-on* relation are not dynamic atomic. However, there is another local atomicity property that these controls satisfy. The property makes use of a globally unique timestamp assigned to each transaction at commit time and referred to as a *commit timestamp*. We say that a local control is *hybrid atomic* if the assigned timestamps are consistent with *precedes* and the local control serializes in timestamp order. Hybrid atomicity is clearly a local atomicity property, since all local controls produce serializations consistent with the same timestamp order.

We now show how to apply these ideas to design distributed controls based on the three (local) models we discussed earlier.

11.2.4   Immediate-Update Pessimistic Systems

We want to prove the following theorem:

Immediate-update pessimistic concurrency controls are dynamic atomic.

To see why the theorem is true, suppose T_{1A} and T_{2A} are subtransactions at site A of two distributed transactions, T_1 and T_2, and that A uses an immediate-update pessimistic algorithm to produce the (interleaved) schedule, S. Suppose further that T_{1A} and T_{2A} executed operations p_{1A} and p_{2A}, respectively; that p_{1A} follows p_{2A} in S; and that p_{1A} *does-not-right-commute-with* p_{2A}. Then T_{1A} must follow T_{2A} in any serial schedule equivalent to S. Either T_{1A} and T_{2A} are concurrently active or they are not. If they are concurrently active, an immediate-update pessimistic control delays p_{1A} until after the *commit message* for T_{2A} has arrived at A. Hence T_2 *precedes* T_1. If T_{2A} and T_{1A} are not concurrently active, T_{1A} is not initiated at A until after the commit message for T_{2A} has arrived, and hence T_2 *precedes* T_1 in this case as well. Thus, if conflicting operations constrain T_{1A} to follow T_{2A} in any serial schedule equivalent to S, T_{1A} is also constrained to follow T_{2A} in any serial schedule consistent with *precedes*. Thus, *precedes* imposes on the ordering of subtransactions in a serial schedule equivalent to S all the constraints that are imposed by conflicts between operations of the subtransactions at A. (*precedes* might impose additional constraints as well: it might be the case that T_2 *precedes* T_1 even though none of the operations of the cohorts conflict.) Thus, equivalent serial schedules consistent with *precedes* are a subset of those consistent with the conflicts occurring at any site.

Since the conflict relation for immediate-update pessimistic systems, *does-not-right-commute-with*, is based on operation commutativity (so that if two operations do not conflict, they commute and can be placed in either order in an equivalent serial schedule), S is equivalent to any serial schedule of subtransactions at site A that preserves the order of conflicting operations. It is therefore equivalent to any serial schedule of subtransactions at site A that is consistent with (the union of) the *precedes* relation.

We have shown that (1) the union of the *precedes* relations at each site is a partial order and hence there is at least one total order consistent with it and (2) all such total orders must be consistent with the ordering of subtransactions imposed by the conflict relation at each site. Hence, *any* such total order can be used as the basis of a serial schedule, S^{ser}, equivalent to the global schedule.

Since all immediate-update pessimistic concurrency controls are dynamic atomic, we can construct a distributed transaction processing system using a two phase commit protocol and an arbitrary immediate-update pessimistic control at each site and be assured that it will produce schedules that are globally serializable.

11.2.5   Deferred-Update Optimistic Systems

Consider first the special case in which conflicts are based on the *does-not-forward-commute-with* relation instead of the *depends-on* relation. Note that with an optimistic control, if validating cohort T_{1A} conflicts with cohort T_{2A} that completed before T_{1A} started its read phase, T_2 *precedes* T_1 at site A. If the two transactions were concurrently active, T_{1A} will fail validation and be restarted, and it is only the operations of the restarted version that are being related by *precedes*. Hence, as with the immediate-update pessimistic control, any serial schedule consistent with the *precedes* relation orders conflicting operations in the same way as they are ordered in S. Furthermore, *does-not-forward-commute-with* is based on commutativity, so that if two operations do not conflict, they can be placed in either order in an equivalent serial schedule. Hence a site serializes in all orders consistent with its *precedes* order. We can therefore use the same reasoning as for the immediate-update system to prove the following theorem:

All deferred-update optimistic systems that use a conflict relation based on *does-not-forward-commute-with* are dynamic atomic.

Thus, as long as we use *does-not-forward-commute-with* as the conflict relation, we can combine an optimistic control with any of the immediate-update pessimistic controls in a distributed system.

Suppose now that we want to use a *depends-on* relation as the conflict relation for an optimistic system. Since this relation is not commutative, the above reasoning breaks down, and we can show that systems based on the *depends-on* relation are not dynamic atomic (*i.e.*, a particular control does not serialize in all orders consistent with its local *precedes* order). For example, suppose two transactions invoke write operations on the same object during their read phases. Since writes do not conflict, the transactions can both commit. If the control were dynamic atomic and operations were invoked in such a way that neither transaction *precedes* the other, the transactions would have to be serializable in either order. However, since the two write operations do not commute, the transactions can be serialized only in their commit order. Hence the control is not dynamic atomic. (Note that the designs for the read-write controls in Chapter 10 and the integer data type given in this chapter use general, noncommutative, *depends-on* relations and hence are not dynamic atomic.)

Since the control cannot guarantee to serialize in *all* orders consistent with *precedes*, our approach is to single out a particular order, O, consistent with *precedes* and insist that the schedule at each site be equivalent to a serial schedule in which transactions are ordered in a way that is consistent with O. (This is not an unreasonable requirement: O will be consistent with the *depends-on* order, since if two transactions are ordered by a conflict at a site, *precedes* (and hence O) will order them in the same way at that site.) By requiring all sites to serialize with respect to O, we guarantee a common order for nonconflicting transactions. Continuing the above example, if transactions T_1 and T_2 write on a particular object at site A and also write on a (different) particular object at B, we can be sure that the writes of T_1 will be executed in the same order with respect to T_2 at both sites.

O is determined using logical clocks. We assume that when a cohort completes its read phase, it sends a *complete* message to its coordinator indicating that it is ready to enter the commit protocol. When all cohorts have indicated completion, the coordinator chooses the current value of its logical clock (with its site identifier appended) as the timestamp, $TS(T)$, of the transaction (and all its cohorts) and initiates the two phase commit protocol. (The site identifier must be appended to the logical clock to guarantee uniqueness, as described in Section 9.1. For simplicity, we ignore this detail in this chapter.) The coordinator sends $TS(T)$ to all cohorts in the *prepare* message. Suppose that T_2 *precedes* T_1 at site A and that the coordinators of T_1 and T_2 reside at sites C_1 and C_2, respectively. The sequence of messages is shown in Figure 11.7 and indicates that if e_i is the event "$TS(T_i)$ is chosen", then e_2 *happened-before* e_1. It follows that if T_2 *precedes* T_1 at some site, $TS(T_2) < TS(T_1)$. Therefore timestamp order is a total order that is consistent with *precedes*, and we choose it for O.

A variety of algorithms can be used to guarantee that each site serializes in timestamp order. In one such algorithm, each site remembers the timestamp, TS_{max}, of the last cohort that committed at that site. If a site receives

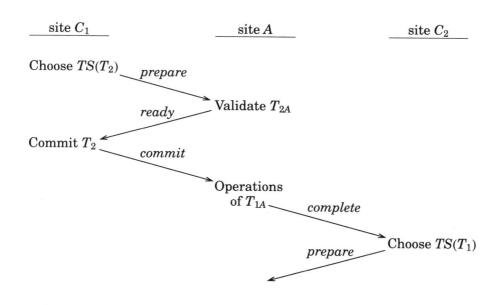

Figure 11.7: Timestamp order is consistent with *precedes*. Since T_2 *precedes* T_1, it follows that $TS(T_2) < TS(T_1)$

a *prepare* message with a timestamp smaller than TS_{max}, it aborts the cohort and responds with an *aborting* message. If the timestamp of the validating transaction is greater than TS_{max}, the control performs the usual validation procedure. Hence we are assured that transactions are validated – and therefore serializable – in timestamp order.

This algorithm suffers from the inefficiency that aborts occur because of the way timestamps happen to be chosen and not necessarily because of conflicting operations. In an alternative approach, a cohort, T_{1A}, is validated in the normal way with respect to a cohort, T_{2A}, that committed at an earlier time with a smaller timestamp. However, a *reverse validation* procedure is used if T_{2A} has committed and subsequently T_{1A} enters validation with a timestamp satisfying $TS(T_2) > TS(T_1)$. The reverse validation procedure checks whether any operation of T_{2A} *depends-on* any operation of T_{1A}, and if so, it aborts T_{1A}. If cohorts are to serialize in timestamp order and if p_{2A} *depends-on* p_{1A} (where p_{2A} and p_{1A} are operations of T_{2A} and T_{1A} respectively), then p_{1A} should have been a part of the state of the object seen by T_{2A}. Since this was not the case, an abort situation exists. Normally T_{2A} would be aborted, but this is not possible, since it committed at an earlier time; hence we abort T_{1A}.

We must also consider the case in which T_{1A} requests validation when T_{2A} is in its validation or write phase. We saw in Section 11.2.2 that this situation can lead to deadlock if a serial validation algorithm is used and T_1 and T_2 also have cohorts at site B. Suppose a parallel validation algorithm is used. If T_{1A} enters validation after T_{2A} and $TS(T_2) > TS(T_1)$, then T_{1A} will reverse validate against T_{2A}. Similarly, if T_1 and T_2 have cohorts at B that enter validation in the opposite order, then T_{2B} validates in the normal way against T_{1B}. As described in Section 11.2.2, this scenario can lead to cyclic restart if the cohorts at both sites conflict. We can use the timestamps to eliminate cyclic restart by requiring that (1) if a cohort of an older global transaction detects a conflict with a concurrently validating cohort of a younger global transaction at a site, the older cohort waits until the younger either commits or aborts (if the younger cohort commits, the older cohort aborts; if the younger aborts the older continues its validation phase); and (2) if the younger cohort detects the conflict, it aborts itself. This abort might be unnecessary, but the conditions under which the situation arises are narrow (both transactions must be global, they must be concurrently validating, and it must be the younger of the two that detects the conflict), and hence the probability of an abort of this type is small.

The reverse validation approach has a significant complication. Assume that T_{2A} has already committed at site A, and T_{1A} with a smaller timestamp requests validation and successfully passes the reverse validation procedure. Thus T_{1A} can be allowed to commit. However, since T_{1A}'s timestamp is smaller than T_{2A}'s, its updates must precede T_{2A}'s (even though T_{2A} has already committed). Note that, since the operations in the two transactions do not commute, no other order is possible. Conceptually, if we assume that the state of each object is maintained as a history (in timestamp order), an out-of-order commit request can be honored by inserting the intentions list of the requesting transaction in the history in timestamp order. In practice, however, we need an implementation that requires less storage.

We can obtain such an implementation using logical clocks. We maintain the committed state of an object as a value stored in the database plus a — preferable short — list of intentions lists (in timestamp order) to be applied to that value, where each intentions list contains the sequence of operations performed on the object by the corresponding transaction and includes the timestamp of the transaction. The plan is that when the site knows that, for some particular intentions list, h, no active transaction can possibly commit with a timestamp earlier than that of h, it incorporates h into the committed state of the object and then discards h. To implement that plan, the site maintains a lower bound on the possible commit timestamps of all transactions active at its site. The lower bound is computed separately for those active transactions that have not yet entered their commit protocol and those that have. Those transactions that have not yet entered their commit protocol will commit with a timestamp larger than that of the local site's logical clock, since the send of a *complete* message by a cohort at that site to the coordinator *happened-before* the assignment of a timestamp to the corresponding transaction by the coordinator. Thus for those transactions that have not yet entered their commit protocol, the lower bound on their commit timestamp is the current value of the logical clock at the site. For a transaction that has entered its commit protocol, the site remembers the logical clock value that it sent along with the *complete* message and uses that as the lower bound, since the commit timestamp for the transaction must be greater than that value.

11.2.6   Deferred-Update Pessimistic Systems

In the special case where conflicts are based on the *does-not-forward-commute-with* relation instead of the more general *depends-on* relation, we can use exactly the same reasoning as for deferred-update optimistic controls to prove the following theorem:

> All deferred-update pessimistic systems that use a conflict relation based on *does-not-forward-commute-with* are dynamic atomic.

Hence, in this case, a deferred-update pessimistic control can be used in conjunction with any other dynamic atomic control in a distributed system.

As in the optimistic case, deferred-update pessimistic systems in which the conflict relation is the symmetric closure of a *depends-on* relation are not dynamic atomic. As before, however, we can use logical clocks to construct an algorithm that is hybrid atomic. When the coordinator in the two phase protocol sends the *prepare* message, it sends along the value of its logical clock (with site identifier appended), which is used as the timestamp of all cohorts.

Each site is required to serialize cohorts in timestamp order. As with optimistic controls, the order in which *commit* messages arrive at a site might be different from the timestamp order. However, in contrast to the first type of optimistic control we considered, which aborts transactions that request to commit out of order, a pessimistic control must grant all commit requests, even if they are out of timestamp order, and must nevertheless perform the commits in timestamp order. This is the same situation that occurred in the second type of optimistic control, and we can use the same design. The state of each object is maintained as a history (in timestamp order), and an out-of-order commit operation is honored by inserting the intentions list of the executing transaction in the history in timestamp order. The fact that a *depends-on* relation has been used to determine conflicts ensures that the resulting schedule is legal. As before, in practice, we must use a compaction algorithm such as the one described in the previous section.

11.2.7   Summary

Although the description of the design theory for distributed and object oriented systems may seem complex, the final results of that theory (in the failure-free case) are surprisingly simple and practical. If the concurrency control at each site or object uses a conflict relation based on the commutativity of database operations, the concurrency control algorithm at each object or site can be chosen independently (and can be immediate or deferred update, pessimistic or optimistic). A protocol to ensure atomic commitment is used to synchronize the cohorts at commit time. Global deadlocks, which may arise as the result of waits imposed by pessimistic controls, can be resolved using timestamps, wait-for graphs, or timeout.

If we do not want to restrict local deferred-update systems to using conflict relations based on commutativity, but instead want to allow conflicts based on a *depends-on* relation, again each site can independently select any deferred-update control (pessimistic or optimistic). The only complication is that additional measures must be used to ensure a common serial order. We have seen that logical clocks are useful for that purpose. Perhaps surprisingly, such a distributed system can also include sites that use immediate-update controls or deferred-update controls with commutativity-based conflict relations. These sites will not use the timestamps sent during the commit protocol, since their controls are dynamic atomic. But, since they serialize in all orders consistent with their local *precedes* order, they will certainly serialize in timestamp order, which is consistent with *precedes* at each site.

One reason for this simplicity is our requirement that a concurrency control make no decisions that would fix an order among active transactions. Thus the control at each site can make its decisions arbitrarily, and the transaction order can be determined at commit time by the commit protocol.

11.3 Nested Transactions*

In the model of distributed transactions we have been discussing, a transaction is decomposed into a two-level tree structure consisting of a coordinator (at the root) and a set of cohorts (as leaves) that execute concurrently and can communicate with one another in arbitrary ways. Only cohorts access data; the coordinator provides overall control. We now present a more structured approach to decomposition called *nested transactions*. A nested transaction is more general than a distributed transaction in that it can consist of an arbitrary tree of subtransactions. The root of the tree is referred to as the *top-level* transaction, and the terms parent, child, ancestor, and siblings have their usual meanings. Subtransactions that have no children are called *leaf* subtransactions. All leaves need not be at the same level. A number of models for nested transactions have been proposed. The model presented here is particularly simple and easy to reason about.

1. A top-level transaction (and all its progeny) is atomic with respect to its environment and preserves database consistency. The hierarchical structure within a nested transaction is invisible outside of that transaction.

2. A parent and its children execute concurrently. A subtransaction (and all its descendents) appears to execute as a single atomic unit with respect to its parent and its siblings.

3. Subtransactions have their own local data space in which to perform private computations. Only leaf subtransactions can access or update the database. Non-leaf subtransactions create and manage lower level subtransactions, but do not access data directly.

4. The only communication among subtransactions occurs at the time of creation and termination.

5. Subtransactions can abort or commit independently. The commitment of a subtransaction is conditional: if a parent aborts, all of the subtransactions of that parent (even those that have committed) are aborted. When a top-level transaction commits, the entire transaction is said to have committed, and all the database changes made by its committed descendents are made permanent.

6. When a subtransaction aborts, it has the same effect as if it had not executed any database operations. A subtransaction can abort without causing its parent to abort.

The main differences among the various models for nested transactions have to do with whether or not a parent can execute concurrently with its children and whether it can access the database. The model presented here allows such concurrent execution, but restricts database access to leaf nodes. It is a generalization of the distributed transaction model in that non-leaf nodes act as a hierarchy of coordinators and leaf nodes act as cohorts. Whereas in the distributed transaction model cohorts reside at distinct sites and hence access disjoint regions of the database, in this model each leaf can access the entire database (the nested transaction might, of course, be distributed across a network, in which case a particular leaf might have only a portion of the database available to it).

In the distributed transaction model, either all cohorts must commit or all must abort. In contrast, item 5 states that the children of a particular parent can commit or abort separately. However, in both models, if a parent (*i.e.,* the coordinator in the distributed transaction model) aborts, all children abort.

Item 1 states that a top-level transaction must preserve database consistency. As in the distributed transaction model, individual subtransactions need not. Data made inconsistent at the time one subtransaction commits may be restored to consistency by a subsequent subtransaction in the same nested transaction, thus allowing the top-level transaction to preserve consistency. For example, a transaction for transferring funds from one account to another might consist of two subtransactions, one that debits the source account and the other that credits the target account. The constraint that the sum of the balances of the two accounts be invariant to the execution of the top-level transaction is violated by each of the subtransactions.

In addition to providing concurrency and modularity within a transaction, the nested transaction model provides isolation between the various subtransactions, so that individual subtransactions can be aborted without restarting the entire transaction. By contrast, the distributed transaction model requires that the entire transaction abort if any of its subtransactions abort. Item 4 is important here, since if subtransactions were allowed to communicate intermediate results during their lifetimes, they could not be separately rolled back.

The effect of an abortion as stated in item 6 has implications that do not arise in conventional transaction systems. As in a conventional system, abortion involves the rollback of all database operations performed by the subtransaction. However, with nested transactions, the parent is notified of the abort (this notification corresponds to the status information discussed earlier in connection with typed databases). The information that its child has aborted might influence the parent's subsequent actions. For example, the parent may infer something about the state of the system (a site has died) or the state of the database (the value of some variable is negative). Hence, in the general case, it may not be possible to say that an aborted subtransaction has the same effect as if it had never been created. To make this stronger assertion, we must restrict the parent in such a way that its actions are not conditioned on the status of its descendents.

We discuss in Chapter 12 how to implement atomicity as described in items 5 and 6 in the context of both abortion and failure.

With conventional transactions, we assume that the only transaction semantics utilized by the concurrency control is that any serial schedule of transactions is correct. Hence an execution is correct if it is equivalent to a serial schedule. We take a similar approach with nested transactions in that we require that all schedules produced by the concurrency control be equivalent to serial schedules. However, a serial schedule in the context of nested transactions is more complicated because of the concurrency that can occur within a single transaction.

In constructing the parent, the designer thinks of each child as performing an atomic activity (item 2). Hence, from the parent's point of view, a child is an operation. If the child is created in such a way that it can run concurrently with the parent, the designer has (implicitly) asserted that the parent will produce the correct result if the child (as a whole) is interleaved between any pair of successive atomic constructs of the parent that are executed concurrently with the child. If several children have been created by the parent in such a way that they execute concurrently, the designer has asserted that the parent will produce the correct result if the children execute atomically with respect to one another in any (nondeterministically selected) order. Hence, the serial execution, in any order, of concurrent siblings can safely be assumed to be correct. Note that not all children run concurrently. The parent might create one after the termination of another. Such an ordering is enforced by the structure of the parent, however, and is therefore not a concern of the concurrency control.

We define a *serial behavior* for a nested transaction as a schedule in which concurrent siblings execute atomically with respect to one another and each child executes atomically with respect to its parent. Hence a number of serial behaviors are possible for a transaction, and all are assumed to be correct. A schedule of a set of nested transactions is serializable if it is equivalent to some serial schedule in which the subschedule of operations of each individual transaction is some serial behavior of that transaction.

It is the responsibility of the concurrency control to ensure that only serializable schedules are produced during execution. Several of the concurrency controls we have described can be adapted to nested transactions. For example, consider an immediate-update pessimistic control for an untyped database. Leaf nodes acquire locks when they access the database. Locks are acquired and passed within the hierarchy of subtransactions in accordance with the following rules:

An Immediate-Update Pessimistic Control for Nested Transactions

1. When a subtransaction makes a request to read a record, a read lock is granted only if all subtransactions holding a write lock on that record are its ancestors (and hence, since they are not leaf nodes, cannot write the record).

2. When a subtransaction makes a request to write a record, a write lock is granted only if all subtransactions holding a read lock or a write lock on that record are its ancestors (and hence, since they are not leaf nodes, cannot read or write the record).

3. All locks obtained by a subtransaction are held until it aborts or commits. When a subtransaction aborts, its locks are discarded. When a subtransaction commits, its locks are inherited by its parent.

4. Conflicts can be resolved by any of the methods discussed earlier. Note, however, that if timestamps are used to resolve conflicts (*e.g.*, using a Kill-Wait protocol), each subtransaction must have a different timestamp.

It follows from these rules that if ST_1 and ST_2 are active siblings, no lock held within the subtree rooted at ST_1 can conflict with a lock held within the subtree rooted at ST_2. Hence, concurrently active siblings are not ordered by the database operations that have been performed within their subtrees. By the arguments presented in Chapter 10, it follows that the siblings will be serializable and thus execute atomically with respect to one another. The fact that a child is atomic with respect to its parent follows, since they access disjoint data items (the parent does not access the database at all). Hence, the desired semantics of the nested transaction model is enforced by the concurrency control. Lock checking can be performed using a lock set as described in Chapter 10.

This design can be easily modified to deal with pessimistic controls on typed databases using the *right-commutes-with* relation to define conflicts for immediate-update systems or the *forward-commutes-with* relation for deferred-update systems. In this case items 1 and 2 of the immediate-update pessimistic control are modified to a single rule, which states that a subtransaction can execute an operation on an object, and hence acquire the corresponding lock, only if all subtransactions holding conflicting locks on that object are its ancestors. Since all of these controls are dynamic atomic, independent local controls can be used at different sites or different objects.

11.3.1   Utility of Nested Transactions*

Nested transactions are particularly useful when a transaction requires a considerable amount of processing on a complex set of objects. For example, in a database describing a large software project, a top-level transaction that changes one line of the Requirements Document might create a large number of concurrent subtransactions to explore the implication of that change throughout the specification, design, and implementation modules in the project database. By contrast, a traditional financial transaction might just update a single field of a single record when a bank deposit occurs.

By using a nested structure, a transaction designer can build a transaction in a modular manner – an important design advantage. Transaction throughput can be increased because of the concurrency among subtransactions. Wasted computations caused by aborts can be reduced, since a parent can continue to execute despite the abortion of one of its children. For example, if the failure of a site causes a subtransaction to abort, the overall transaction need not abort. The parent might be able to create another child at an alternative site to do the task the first child was supposed to do.

Nested transactions can also be used as a way of implementing the coenter statement. The operational semantics of the coenter requires the serial execution in arbitrary order of its component statements. If the coenter is implemented as a nested transaction, so that the process entering the coenter is the parent and each component statement is a child subtransaction, the concurrency control in the nested transaction system will allow interleavings among the component statements, while at the same time guaranteeing that the overall execution is equivalent to a serial execution. By contrast, a straightforward implementation of the coenter might not allow any interleavings at all.

11.4   Transactions in Argus*

Argus is an integrated language and system that supports "*distributed programs*: programs in which modules reside and execute at communicating but geographically distinct locations" [91]. The language supports such features as nested transactions and locking, while the system implements the features of the language and is concerned with issues such as resiliency of data to node

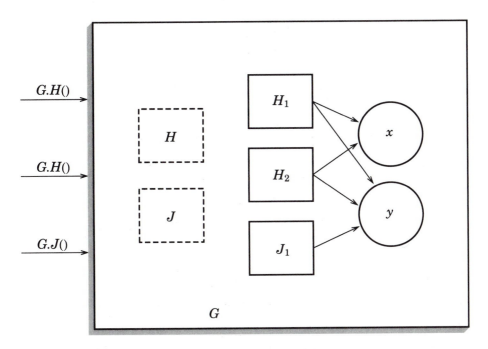

Figure 11.8: A guardian, G, with two handlers, H and J, and two data items, x and y. H has been invoked twice, and J has been invoked once.

failures. We concentrate on the synchronization aspects of the language.

An Argus program is a collection of *guardians*. A guardian is a module that exists at a single node and encapsulates data and the programs that access that data. These programs are called *handlers*. Handlers implement (abstract) operations that can be performed on the encapsulated data. Only the guardian's handlers (and asynchronously executing background tasks supported within the guardian) have direct access to the guardian's data (since data cannot be exported from the guardian and the arguments of calls made by a handler are passed by value). A handler in one guardian can be invoked from another using a remote procedure call, which causes a new process to be created in the guardian to execute the handler. Since calls occur asynchronously, several handlers can be executing concurrently within a guardian. In Figure 11.8 guardian G encapsulates two handlers, H and J, and two data items, x and y. Two invocations of H are executing concurrently with an invocation of J.

The unit of atomic computation in Argus is referred to as an *action*. Top-level actions (corresponding to transactions) can be created in-line with the statement

enter topaction *body* **end**

while nested (sub)actions (corresponding to subtransactions) can be created in-line using:

enter action *body* **end**

The coenter statement is used to create concurrent subactions. For example, a top-level action for transferring money from one account to another might involve two subactions as follows:

> **coenter**
>   **action** *withdraw(acc1, amt)*
>   **action** *deposit(acc2, amt)*
> **end**

A handler call creates two actions: a (parent) call action at the caller and a (child) handler action at the callee. The handler action executes the handler body; the call action manages communication for the caller.

Since it is expected that subactions will usually commit, normal termination of the body of a subaction is taken, by default, to be commit. An abort must be explicitly specified. Thus, a subaction can terminate normally by executing return and can abort by executing abort return.

In contrast to the model for nested transactions in the previous section, Argus requires a parent action to wait until all its children (which may have been created in-line or concurrently) terminate before it resumes. Furthermore, data access is not limited to leaf subactions: any action, parent or leaf, can access the data encapsulated within its guardian. Since a parent waits until its children terminate, such accesses by a parent cannot be concurrent with the execution of any of its children.

11.4.1 Locking and Synchronization*

Synchronization is achieved through locking. Since locking is expensive, not all data items can be locked. Only data items declared as *atomic objects* have associated locks; hence, the serializability of concurrent subactions can be guaranteed if all shared objects are atomic. Argus provides built-in types, such as atomic arrays, which have the same operations as ordinary arrays but provide synchronization as well. For built-in atomic types, operations are classified as readers or writers. The appropriate lock is implicitly requested by the subaction when it invokes an operation (*i.e.,* the lock requests are handled automatically in the language), and the subaction waits until the lock has been granted. Locks are granted and passed within the hierarchy of the nested transaction in accordance with the locking rules for an immediate-update pes-

simistic control for nested transactions described in Section 11.3. These rules
guarantee that sibling actions execute atomically with respect to one another.
The atomicity of a child with respect to its parent follows trivially, since a
parent waits while its children are active.

The language provides no mechanism for avoiding or detecting deadlock
other than the use of timeout.

The locking mechanism for built-in types is primitive in that it only distinguishes between readers and writers. Furthermore, once a write lock has been
obtained by a descendent of a top-level action, T_1, it will inhibit any concurrent action that is a descendent of a distinct top-level action from accessing the
object until T_1 commits (although abortion might cause the lock to be released
earlier). Since the transaction as a whole might be a lengthy computation involving many objects, a particular locked object might be inaccessible to other
actions for a long time.

As we have seen, considerable additional concurrency can be obtained if the
semantics of operations are taken into account. To obtain this concurrency,
the designer of an abstract atomic type must recognize when operations on
an instance of the type commute. Recall that operations are implemented
by handlers and are executed as subactions. If operation p_1 is invoked at a
particular guardian while operation p_2 is in progress and the two operations
commute, p_1 should be able to access the data structures representing the
instance as soon as p_2 completes (e.g., assuming p_1 and p_2 are descendents of
two distinct top-level actions, p_1 can perform its access before p_2's top-level
action commits). Since the language does not provide a mechanism (other
than action termination) for releasing the write lock held on an instance of a
built-in type, it is difficult to construct highly concurrent atomic objects from
built-in types.

To deal with this issue, Argus allows the specification of user-defined atomic
types, which can use a more sophisticated locking mechanism based on the
semantics of the operations for the type. A user-defined atomic type can be
defined to consist of some combination of built-in atomic and non-atomic types
together with a set of user-defined operations encapsulated within a guardian.
As a part of the implementation of a user-defined atomic type, the designer
has the responsibility for

Determining which pairs of operations cause a database conflict;

Checking for conflicts (e.g., managing the lock and wait sets) and implementing lock inheritance;

Assuring that the atomic commit and abort events work correctly (for
example, if an action aborts, any changes it made to an instance of the
type must be rolled back).

The language supplies several constructs that can be used for this purpose,
but ensuring the correctness of such implementations is the responsibility of
the designer.

11.4.2   Abortion and Failures*

When a subaction aborts, any changes it made to atomic variables must be rolled back. For variables of user-defined atomic types, the designer of the type is responsible for implementing some rollback mechanism. For variables of built-in atomic types, the system implements rollback using a mechanism based on *versions*. The value of a variable is stored in its *base* version. Instead of updating the base version, a subaction creates a new, *current* version of the variable. If the subaction aborts, the current version is discarded; if the corresponding top-level action commits, the current version replaces the base version.

To accommodate the fact that a write lock might be concurrently held by a subaction and its ancestors, a stack of current versions is maintained (recall that the semantics of the language requires that all ancestors be blocked). When a parent initiates a subaction, the parent's current version is on top of the stack. The subaction keeps its current version on the stack (right above its parent's version). If the subaction aborts (returning control to the parent), the subaction's version is popped off the stack and the parent's version is left on top of the stack for the parent to use. If the subaction commits (returning control to the parent), the subaction's version is left on top of the stack and becomes the parent's current version.

Since handler calls are treated as actions, the nested transaction structure provides exactly once semantics for normal return and zero semantics for exception return. If the action commits, the parent knows that the handler has executed exactly once. If communication with the target node cannot be properly established or maintained or if the target node crashes at any point, the handler aborts and the parent is assured that the handler call has not affected the state of the called guardian. For example, if the handler action commits but the reply message is not received, the call action will abort. Since, in the nested transaction structure, the final commitment of an action is conditioned on the commitment of all ancestors, the handler action will ultimately be aborted.

The language provides two mechanisms by which guardians can be made resilient to node failures:

A subset of its variables can be declared to be *stable*, causing their base versions to be stored on stable storage while the stack is kept in volatile memory.

A *recovery procedure* can be declared within each guardian. When a guardian is restarted after a node failure, its recovery procedure is automatically called and has access to the (base versions of) stable variables; it can use these stable variables to re-initialize the remaining nonstable variables (presumably the stable variables have been selected to make this reinitialization possible). When the recovery process completes, the guardian becomes available for handler calls.

To keep the base versions up to date, a two phase commit protocol is used. Current versions of all objects (in all guardians) modified by subactions of a top-level action are written to stable storage before completion of the first phase and are transferred to the base version when the top-level action commits. Adaptations of a two phase commit protocol to deal with various types of failures are discussed in Chapter 12.

11.5   Bibliographic Notes

Much of our development of typed data and distributed systems is based on Weihl's Ph.D. thesis [131] and on related work by Weihl and Herlihy [132], [134], [133], [64], and [65]. Rosenkrantz, Stearns, and Lewis [113] discuss using the Kill-Wait and Wait-Die systems for distributed systems. An optimistic concurrency control algorithm for distributed systems is described by Agrawal, Bernstein, Gupta, and Sengupta in [5]. Gray [57] discusses the two phase commit protocol. Its use in the Argus language is described by Liskov in [90]. Nested transactions are studied extensively in Moss's Ph.D. thesis [101]. Our treatment is based on work by Fekete, Lynch, Merritt, and Weihl [45]. Liskov led the development of Argus. She has written an overview of the system [91]. A more detailed treatment appears in papers by Liskov [93] and Liskov and Scheifler [90]. The mechanisms for constructing user-defined atomic types are described by Weihl and Liskov [135]. More information on algorithms for distributed deadlock detection can be found in [77].

11.6   Exercises

1. A database is to be designed using a *double buffer* data type. A double buffer consists of two buffers, each of which can store one element and is initialized to some default value. The database operations are *put(e)*, which stores an element into the first buffer (and overwrites what is there), *copy*, which copies an element from the first buffer to the second buffer, and *get(x)*, which copies the contents of the second buffer into *x*. All operations are total. Find the *does-not-commute-with* relation for this type, and design the conflict relations for immediate-update pessimistic, deferred-update pessimistic, and optimistic controls.

2. A database system is to be designed using a *set* data type. The database operations are to be *insert(element)*, *delete(element):ok*, *delete(element):no*, and *is−member(element)*. *delete* returns the status *no* if the given element is not in the set and deletes the element from the set otherwise. *is−member* is a boolean function that returns *true* if its element is in the set and *false* otherwise. Find *does-not-right-commute-with* and *does-not-forward-commute-with* relations for this type. Design the conflict relations for immediate-update pessimistic, deferred-update pessimistic, and optimistic controls.

3. Show how the relations in the previous exercise would change if the conflict relation were allowed to use the value of the argument of the operation (for example, a conflict between an *insert* and a *delete* could depend on whether the same element was being inserted and deleted).

4. A database system is to be designed using a *stack* data type. The database operations are to be *push(element)*, *pop(element):ok*, *pop(element):no*, and *is–empty(element)*. *pop* returns the status *no* if the stack is empty. *is–empty* is a boolean function that returns *true* if the stack is empty and *false* otherwise. Find *does-not-right-commute-with* and *does-not-forward-commute-with* relations for this type. Design the conflict relations for immediate-update pessimistic, deferred-update pessimistic, and optimistic controls.

5. Design an abstract specification (analogous to that shown in Figure 11.3) for the queue data type of Figure 11.4. Prove that each pair of nonconflicting operations in that figure satisfies the *right-commutes-with* relation.

6. Describe what happens during the validation of transaction T_1 in the following scenario. Assume a deferred-update optimistic system is controlling access to an instance of a queue data type

> Initially the queue is empty. T_1 is initiated, performs an enqueue operation to put x in the queue, then performs a dequeue operation that retrieves x from the queue. Later T_2 is initiated, performs an enqueue to put y in the queue, then commits. Still later, T_1 requests to commit.

7. Give a history that shows that each of the pairs indicated by X in the following diagram is in the *depends-on* relation for a queue data type. Argue intuitively that the blanks are not in the relation. Show that the relation is not a *does-not-forward-commutes-with* relation.

**Transaction T_2 Committed
While T_1 Was Active**

		enqueue	dequeue:ok	dequeue:no
Trans-	*enqueue*			
action T_1	*dequeue:ok*	X	X	
Requesting	*dequeue:no*	X		
to Commit				

8. A database system is to be designed using a *write once variable* data type. The database operations are to include a write, which can only be performed once and writes a value into the variable, and a read, which can only be performed if the variable has previously been written and returns the value of the variable. Since these operations are partial, the concurrency control assumes there are four operations: *write(x):ok*, *write(x):no*, *read(y):ok*,

and *read(y):no*. Find *does-not-right-commute-with* and *does-not-forward-commute-with* relations for this type.

9. State how the *precedes* order and the commit order are related to the equivalent serial order produced by a centralized system and a dynamic atomic distributed system.

10. Prove or disprove the following statement: Any conflict-based concurrency control is dynamic atomic if (1) Whenever any operation in one transaction, T_1, conflicts with a prior operation in another transaction, T_2, the control produces a schedule such that T_2 *precedes* T_1; and (2) the conflict relation is commutative, so if two operations do not conflict, they can be put in either order in an equivalent schedule.

11. Show that a Wound-Wait system will still work correctly if Wound is defined as follows: If a Wound message reaches a site at which a transaction has neither aborted nor entered its commit protocol, that transaction is restarted only if it is waiting; otherwise it is allowed to proceed until it either enters its commit protocol or becomes involved in a conflict that would normally cause it to wait, in which case it is restarted.

12. In a nested transaction, a child might abort after sending its parent some information it had read from the database. If the parent subsequently uses that information, the semantics of abortion – as described in item 6 of the description of nested transactions – will not be supported. Suppose we change the semantics of abortion so that, instead of being treated as if it performed no database operations, an aborted subtransaction is treated as if it were a read only subtransaction that performed the reads that the aborted subtransaction made before it aborted. Show how the immediate-update pessimistic concurrency control can be extended to deal with this new requirement.

13. Design immediate-update and deferred-update concurrency controls for general typed databases that support nested transactions.

14. Design a time stamped concurrency control that extends the algorithm described in Section 10.5.3 to support nested transactions.

15. We want to implement an abstract data type for an integer, i, with abstract operations *increment* and *decrement*. The concrete implementation of i is a 32-bit computer word, w, with concrete operations *read* and *write*. We want to design a lock-based, immediate-update pessimistic concurrency control for the system. We assume there are two levels of concurrency controls: w has a concurrency control with *read* and *write* locks, and i has a concurrency control with *increment* and *decrement* locks. The *increment* and *decrement* operations commute and hence do not conflict with each other. However, individual *increment* and *decrement* operations must be

atomic with respect to each other. The plan is to use the *read* and *write* locks to ensure that the higher level *increment* and *decrement* operations are atomic with respect to each other.

The system is to work in this general fashion. When a transaction wants to perform an increment on some integer i, it calls the *increment* operation, which is a program containing *read* and *write* operations on the word w that implements the integer. The *increment* operation first obtains an *increment* lock from i's concurrency control. Then, when the program for the *increment* operation needs to perform a *read* or *write* operation, it obtains the appropriate *read* or *write* lock from w's concurrency control. A (perhaps unexpected) feature of this system is that, when the program for the *increment* operation is complete, it can release the *read* and *write* locks it had obtained on w, even though the transaction containing that *increment* operation is still active (but the transaction must keep the *increment* lock until it commits or aborts).

Give a complete description of the design of this *multi-level* concurrency control, and show that it works correctly.

16. We want to add the operation *square* to the abstract data type for an integer discussed in the previous problem. *square* conflicts with both *increment* and *decrement*. Give a design for a multi-level concurrency control that includes this new operation.

12

Failures and Replication in Distributed Databases

In Chapter 9 we discussed techniques for making the basic components of a computer system resilient to certain types of failures. Then we showed how to use these techniques to make computations executed at a single site failure atomic. We dealt with arbitrary computations, which we referred to as actions, and procedures, which might be invoked either locally or remotely. In this chapter we extend that discussion to transactions. The extension introduces two new factors. First, since transactions can execute concurrently, we must consider the effect of concurrent execution on strategies for dealing with failure. Second, since transactions can execute in a distributed environment, we must develop new strategies to make distributed transactions failure atomic.

In distributed systems, failures might not be total. To the extent possible, we want the surviving portions of the system to remain operational and continue to process transactions. Furthermore, when the failed portions are repaired and restarted, it must be possible to integrate them into the system in such a way that the database remains consistent and the effects of committed transactions are not lost. Hence, we require that, even when failures have occurred, each transaction see a database state that contains the effects of all transactions that committed before it.

The replication of data at different sites in a network is a technique for dealing with failures. Although data stored at a failed site might be inaccessible, a copy of the data can be accessed at another site. Data replication is also useful as a means for enhancing the responsiveness of a distributed database.

If a copy of a data item is stored locally, the need for network communication can be avoided. The need to keep replicas consistent and up-to-date, however, introduces some new problems, which we study in this chapter.

12.1   Recovery in Centralized Systems

In Chapter 9 we discussed crashes (benign processor failures) and decays (loss of the contents of a random access mass storage device), together with algorithms for making an arbitrary computation (an action or procedure) resilient to such events. In Chapters 10 and 11 we discussed concurrent transaction processing systems in a failure-free environment. In Chapter 9 we did not discuss the impact of failures on the concurrent execution of transactions or on distributed transactions. In this chapter we extend the discussion of failures to include concurrency and distribution.

We require that transactions satisfy the following two conditions related to failure:

1. Each transaction is *failure atomic*: if a crash interrupts its execution, either all its changes are made to the database or none are.

2. After recovery from a decay, the database reflects the updates of all the transactions that had committed before the failure, serialized in commit order.

The methods described in Chapter 9 for achieving failure atomicity for non-concurrent actions at a single site use the same immediate-update and deferred-update techniques described in connection with the concurrency controls of Chapters 10 and 11 (based on undo and intentions lists). It should be clear from the discussion in those chapters that these methods also provide failure atomicity for concurrent transactions executing at a single site. Crash recovery at a site supporting the concurrent transactions involves aborting (and hence rolling back) all the transactions that were active when the crash occurred. The recoverability property of the concurrency controls guarantees that each transaction can be individually rolled back (since recoverability guarantees that no values an uncommitted transaction has written to the database have been read by a transaction that has committed).

We can apply these same methods to distributed transactions that were active but not in their commit protocol when the crash occurred. (An *abort* message is sent to each site at which a cohort of an aborted transaction is executing, and these methods are applied at that site.) Those transactions that were in their commit protocol when the crash occurred require different recovery procedures, which we discuss in the next sections.

The second requirement can be achieved using either stable storage or recoverable storage. Stable storage is appropriate for *non-stop* applications (such as the stock market), where the database must always be available even when errors occur. Recoverable storage is used for less time-critical applications, where its reduced storage costs are important.

In extending the concepts of stable storage to a concurrent environment, it is important to ensure that both careful pages of a stable page are updated consistently. If two *StablePut* operations to the same stable page were executed concurrently, the two *CarefulPut* operations in each *StablePut* could conceivably be interleaved. This interleaving does not happen in the deferred-update systems we have described, since updates of only one transaction at a time are transferred to the database (at commit time). Similarly, interleaving does not occur in an immediate-update system, since we assume that all operations are executed atomically. For example, if a request by transaction T_1 to perform operation o_1 has been granted and T_2 makes a request to perform nonconflicting operation o_2, although T_2's request can be granted, we assume that the object will perform the operations atomically with respect to one another. Thus, stable storage will be updated correctly.

Recoverable storage is different from stable storage in that update entries are written to the journal in background, and hence the updates from different concurrent transactions might be arbitrarily interleaved in the journal. However, since commit records are appended using forced operations, they appear in the journal in commit order. Thus, to recover after a decay has occurred, it is sufficient to assemble the update records for each transaction and to apply them as a unit to the primary device in the order in which the commit records appear in the journal. Thus, the updates are applied in commit order, which is the same order in which the transactions were serialized.

12.2 Failures in Distributed Systems

When a transaction is distributed, failure atomicity requires that all subtransactions agree on whether to commit or abort – even when failures occur. We are particularly concerned that when crashes or communication failures occur, different cohorts do not make inconsistent decisions (in which some abort and some commit). We assume that decays are dealt with using stable or recoverable storage (and may require aborting active transactions). Furthermore, we assume that not all sites crash.

In Chapter 9 we considered two types of communication failures: message failure, in which messages are lost but might be received if re-sent, and partitions, in which sites are prevented from communicating with one another. In this chapter, we discuss protocols for recovering from failures. A site that fails to receive a message draws some conclusion about what caused the failure (*e.g.*, the sender has crashed). To reduce the number of possible causes and hence to create a situation in which the site can take the most informed action, we assume that (transient) message failures are masked by lower levels in the communication hierarchy. Hence, the only communication failures seen by the transaction processing system are partitions.

We assume that messages that arrive at a site are held in volatile memory and hence are lost when a crash occurs, and that any messages that arrive while a site is not operational are simply lost. Furthermore, we assume that the time to restart a site is long compared to the message delivery time, so any messages a site sent before crashing will not still be arriving at their destinations at the time the site is restarted.

We assume that messages sent from one site to another are delivered in the order sent. We further make the worst case assumption that there is no atomic broadcast facility. When a site, S, wants to communicate the same message to several sites, it must unicast the message to each of those sites separately. Thus, S might fail after only a subset of the messages has been sent, or a partition might prevent some of the messages from being received. We assume that the sender is not notified when a message is not delivered.

Both crashes and partitions become apparent when a site times out while waiting to receive a message from another site. In general, the site cannot ascertain whether the failure to receive the message is due to a crash or a partition. This assumption is key to the reasoning underlying the protocols we describe later, since a site might respond differently if it could distinguish between these two types of failures. We assume that while waiting for a message or after the timeout period has elapsed, a site can attempt to communicate with other operational sites.

Timeout might also occur because the sender or the communication network is slow – a situation that cannot be ruled out in an asynchronous system. A timeout due to a slow sender or communication network is referred to as a *false timeout*. Unfortunately, the possibility of false timeouts puts a severe restriction on the ability of any commit protocol to reach agreement. Therefore we generally assume that the timeout period is set sufficiently long so that, when a timeout occurs, some crash or partition actually exists (*i.e.,* false timeouts do not occur).[1]

12.3   Atomic Commit Protocols

The strategy for dealing with failures in distributed systems is through the use of atomic commit protocols. The two phase commit protocol introduced in the last chapter is an example of such a protocol. In this chapter, we extend the two phase commit protocol to deal with failures and then present the three phase commit protocol, which has advantages in certain situations.

The atomic commit protocols we consider all have the property that a coordinator asks each cohort to vote whether it wants to commit or abort. Note that there may exist a cohort at the coordinator site, but the coordinator itself

---

[1]For some types of reasoning, false timeouts can be viewed as partition failures if we assume the system is designed so that when a timed-out message finally arrives, the receiver knows enough to ignore it. As shown in footnote 3 in Section 12.4, however, our reasoning sometimes requires us to distinguish false timeouts from partitions.

is not a cohort and does not vote (it does, however, decide to commit or abort on the basis of cohort votes). With a nested transaction, not all subactions participate in the vote. The top-level transaction corresponds to the coordinator, and participating subactions are the cohorts. A subaction participates if it and all its ancestors except the top-level transaction have (conditionally) committed. The protocol does not involve any subaction having an aborted ancestor (such a subaction is assumed to have aborted when its ancestor aborted).

After sending its vote, and after perhaps several other rounds of communication with the coordinator, a site eventually decides that it will commit or abort. During the time period after a cohort site has sent its vote to commit, but before it has enough information to know what the decision will be, it is said to be *uncertain*; that period is called its *uncertain period*. As we shall see, it will be necessary to modify this definition somewhat when we discuss the three phase commit protocol.

We assume that failures can occur before the protocol was initiated or while it is being performed. We want an atomic commit protocol to have the following properties:

Properties of an Atomic Commit Protocol

1. All sites that reach a decision reach the same decision. (A stronger property – that all sites that are operational reach the same decision – is desirable but, as we shall see, not always achievable, since a site might be operational but unable to reach any decision at all.)

2. If there are no failures and all sites vote to commit, the decision of all sites will be to commit.

3. If any site votes to abort, no site can decide to commit (even if failures occur).

4. Once a site has made a decision to commit or abort, it cannot reverse that decision (even if failures occur).

When we say that a commit protocol is *robust* for a particular type of failure, we mean

For all executions in which failures of the given type have occurred, if all failures are repaired (and no new failures occur), all sites will eventually reach a (consistent) decision.

A site must depart from the normal execution of a protocol when a failure occurs. Special protocols are required to recover from failures. A *timeout protocol* is executed if a site times out while waiting for a message. A *restart protocol* is executed by a site recovering from a crash. In either case, as a part of the protocol, we allow the site to communicate with other sites. In addition, we assume that each site maintains a journal in stable (or recoverable) storage of the significant events that have occurred during the commit protocol. This journal enables a site executing the restart protocol to determine how far it had progressed before crashing.

If the restart protocol does not involve communication with other sites, we say that it exhibits *independent recovery*. Independent recovery is desirable, since it permits a site to reach a decision without depending on communication with other sites (which might not be possible because of partitions or crashes).

Unfortunately, no atomic commit protocol can exhibit independent recovery when at least two sites fail. To see this, suppose to the contrary that such a protocol exists. Then, at every point in the protocol, each site must be in one of two states: S_c, in which it will (independently) decide commit if it should fail in that state and then later recover, or S_a, in which it will decide abort. When the protocol begins (before any site has received a message initiating the protocol), all sites are in S_a, since no site can assume on restart that all cohorts voted yes. On the other hand, if a decision to commit has been made at some site, all sites must be in S_c. Since messages are sent individually to each site, only one site can change state at a time. Thus there must be a time when the first site, s_1, changes its state from S_a to S_c, while all the other sites remain in S_a. If, at this instant, s_1 and one other site should fail, upon recovery these sites would make inconsistent decisions – thus contradicting the assumption that the protocol exhibits independent recovery. Protocols do exist that exhibit independent recovery when exactly one site fails but, since these protocols are not robust for more than one site failure, they are of little practical value.

If an operational site cannot complete the commit protocol until some failure is repaired, we say that the protocol exhibits *blocking*. Hence, a site executing a protocol that exhibits blocking might have to wait for the repair of a failure as a part of its timeout protocol. Blocking is undesirable, since when a site blocks, the decision to commit or abort is delayed (and, hence, records might remain locked) for an arbitrarily long period of time.

As we shall see in the next section, the two phase commit protocol exhibits blocking under certain circumstances. We can use an argument similar to that used in connection with independent recovery to show that any atomic commit protocol that is robust for partition failures exhibits blocking.[2] However, as we shall see when we discuss the three phase commit protocol in Section 12.6, non-blocking protocols do exist when the only failures are site crashes (still assuming no false timeouts).

When false timeouts can occur, an even stronger negative result about blocking can be deduced. From properties 2 and 3 it follows that, to reach a commit decision, the vote of every operational site must be considered. In an asynchronous environment a site, A, might be arbitrarily slow, and hence any site that times out while waiting to receive a message from A cannot

---

[2]If we assume that undelivered messages are returned to the sender, it can be shown that there exist nonblocking protocols that are robust for partitions that divide the network into exactly two partitions, but no such protocols exist for general partitions. All of these results are proved in Skeen and Stonebraker [124].

conclude that a failure has occurred (*i.e.,* false timeout is possible). Hence, if A is operational but slow to communicate its vote, other sites must delay making a decision, since property 2 forbids them from deciding abort. Since a slow response from A cannot be distinguished from failure, the remaining sites must wait even if a failure prevents A's vote from being communicated. Since waiting for a failed site is blocking, property 2 implies that in an asynchronous environment there does not exist a non-blocking atomic commit protocol when even a single failure can occur (whether that failure is due to a crash or a partition). This is exactly the situation discussed in Section 9.5.4, where we stated the result that agreement is not possible in the totally asynchronous case if even a single benign failure occurs.

12.4   Two Phase Commit Protocol

We described the two phase commit protocol in Section 11.2.1 under the assumption of no failures. We now repeat that description in a slightly different format that emphasizes waiting periods.

Two Phase Commit Protocol with No Failures

1. The coordinator sends a *prepare* message to all cohorts.

2. Each cohort waits until it receives the *prepare* message from the coordinator. It then votes *ready* or *aborting* and sends the corresponding message to the coordinator. If the vote is *aborting*, it decides abort.

3. The coordinator waits until it receives votes from all the cohorts. If at least one vote is *aborting*, it decides abort and sends an *abort* message to each cohort. If all votes are *ready*, it decides commit and sends a *commit* message to each cohort.

4. Each cohort that voted *ready* waits to receive a message from the coordinator. If that message is *commit*, it decides commit. If that message is *abort*, it decides abort.

The uncertain period for each cohort starts when it sends a *ready* message in step 2 and ends when it receives a *commit* or *abort* message in step 4.

To extend this protocol to deal with failures, we must supply a timeout protocol for each waiting period (steps 2, 3, and 4) and a restart protocol in case a site should fail. If a cohort times out while waiting at step 2, it can be certain that no decision to commit has yet been taken at any site (since it has not yet voted). Hence, it can decide to abort and thus prevent any site from reaching a commit decision (since such a decision requires *ready* votes from all sites). A similar situation exists if the coordinator times out while waiting at step 3, and hence the coordinator can decide to abort and send an *abort* message to all cohorts. If a cohort times out at step 4, the situation is more serious, since it is in its uncertain period. Since we have assumed that false timeouts do not occur, either the coordinator has crashed or a partition separates the cohort from the coordinator. In both cases the cohort cannot communicate with the coordinator. Unfortunately, the coordinator may have decided before the failure occurred but, because of the failure, be unable to communicate that decision to any cohort. Since the cohort's decision must be the same as that of the coordinator, the cohort must block until it can determine if the coordinator has made a decision and, if so, what that decision was. The cohort can try to communicate with other cohorts in an attempt to find a cohort that is not in its uncertain period. If it finds such a cohort, it can use the state of that cohort to make its decision. Otherwise it must block. Thus we have

Timeout Protocol for Two Phase Commit Protocol

Timeout at step 2: The cohort decides abort.

Timeout at step 3: The coordinator decides abort and sends an *abort* message to every cohort from which it received a *ready* vote.[3]

Timeout at step 4: The cohort attempts to communicate with the other cohorts. If it finds a cohort that has not voted yet, both cohorts decide to abort. If it finds a cohort that has decided abort or commit, it makes the same decision. If all other cohorts it finds are also in their uncertain period, it blocks until communication can be established with some site that has decided.

We must also supply restart protocols for the coordinator and cohorts.

Restart Protocol for Two Phase Commit Protocol

If the restarted site had decided abort or commit before crashing, it completes the appropriate processing.

If the restarted site is a cohort that has not yet voted or is the coordinator and it has not yet decided, it decides abort.

If the restarted site is a cohort that crashed in its uncertain period, it attempts to communicate with a site that has decided and uses that decision. If it can find no such site, it blocks.

Note that the protocol does not exhibit independent recovery.

The two phase commit protocol satisfies the four requirements for an atomic commit protocol and is robust under both crashes and partitions. Unfortunately, the protocol exhibits blocking, even though we have assumed no false timeouts. Blocking occurs only when the coordinator crashes or a cohort is unable to communicate with the coordinator.

---

[3]Our reasoning depends on the assumption that false timeouts do not occur, since if the coordinator times out at step 3, it can assume that a failure has actually occurred. If, instead, no failures had occurred and all sites had voted to commit, but a false timeout at step 3 prevented one site's vote from reaching the coordinator on time, the protocol would decide abort – in violation of property 2 of an atomic commit protocol.

12.5   Extended Two Phase Commit Protocol

The two phase commit protocol can block when the coordinator crashes or when a partition occurs. In this section we present an extension of the two phase commit protocol that does not block under any single site crash (including that of the coordinator). It can block, however, when the coordinator and at least one cohort crash or when a partition occurs. Once again, we assume no false timeouts.

In the two phase commit protocol, when a cohort times out during its uncertain period (and, hence, cannot communicate with the coordinator), the coordinator might have made a decision and then crashed before it could communicate that decision to any cohorts. Under these circumstances the cohort must block. The basic idea of the extended two phase commit protocol is to avoid this situation by establishing the following property, which we call *NB1* (for non-blocking):

NB1: Whenever at least one operational site is in its uncertain period, the coordinator (whether it is operational or not) cannot have decided to commit.

Thus, if the coordinator should crash while all cohorts are operational and in their uncertain period, they can all safely decide to abort in their timeout protocols (and thus avoid blocking), since the coordinator cannot have decided commit and therefore can decide abort when it is restarted.

To achieve this property, we add one more message to the two phase commit protocol. In step 3 of the extended protocol, when the coordinator sends *commit* messages to all cohorts, it has not itself decided commit. Each cohort, after committing, sends a *done* message to the coordinator. After receiving a *done* message from at least one cohort, the coordinator decides commit.

Extended Two Phase Commit Protocol with No Failures

1. The coordinator sends a *prepare* message to all cohorts.

2. Each cohort waits until it receives the *prepare* message from the coordinator. It then votes *ready* or *aborting* and sends the corresponding message to the coordinator. If the vote is *aborting*, it decides abort.

3. The coordinator waits until it receives votes from all the cohorts. If at least one vote is *aborting*, it decides abort and sends an *abort* message to each cohort. If all votes are *ready*, it sends a *commit* message to each cohort.

4. Each cohort that voted *ready* waits to receive a message from the coordinator. If that message is *commit*, it decides commit and sends a *done* message to the coordinator. If that message is *abort*, it decides abort.

5. The coordinator waits until it receives a *done* message from at least one cohort. Then it decides commit.

The uncertain period for each cohort starts when it sends a *ready* message in step 2 and ends when it receives a *commit* or *abort* message in step 4. We now define an uncertain period for the coordinator, which starts when it sends the first *commit* message and ends when it receives the first *done* message (since, as in a cohort's uncertain period, within that period the coordinator is prepared to decide commit but the final disposition of the transaction is in doubt).

To extend this protocol to deal with failures, we must supply a timeout protocol for each waiting period (steps 2, 3, 4, and 5) and a restart protocol in case a site should crash during the execution of the protocol.

The timeout procedures for step 2 and 3 are the same as before. If a timeout occurs while a cohort is at step 4, the cohort is in its uncertain period and can conclude that the coordinator has crashed or is unable to communicate because of a partition. Therefore the cohort communicates with the other cohorts. If we assume a single site crash (in which case it must be the coordinator that has crashed) or an isolated coordinator (a coordinator isolated from all cohorts because of a partition), all cohorts must be operational and able to communicate with each other. If any cohort has decided, they all make that same decision. If all cohorts have timed out and none have decided, they all decide abort (since the coordinator could not have decided commit because of property *NB1* and a cohort decision to abort is consistent with the restart and timeout protocols for the coordinator, given below, that might cause the coordinator to abort). Hence, under the assumption of a single crash or an isolated coordinator, the protocol is nonblocking.

If, in addition to being unable to communicate with the coordinator, a cohort, $C1$, that has timed out at step 4 is unable to communicate with at least one cohort, $C2$ (either because $C2$ has crashed or because the two cohorts are separated by a partition), and all cohorts with which $C1$ can communicate are undecided, then $C1$ must block until either (1) it can communicate with a site that has made a decision (in which case it decides in the same way) or (2) it can communicate with all cohorts and finds them all to be undecided (in which case all cohorts can decide to abort). Blocking is necessary, since the coordinator might have decided abort or it might have sent a *commit* message to a cohort that committed and then crashed or became isolated. In either case a decision might have been made, and $C1$ must know what that decision is.

If the coordinator times out at step 5, but has received at least one *done* message, the protocol can proceed and the coordinator decides commit (since it knows that a cohort has committed). If it has received no *done* messages (all cohorts have crashed or are isolated by a partition), it is in its uncertain period and must block, since it is possible that either some cohorts decided commit and then crashed (or were isolated) or all crashed (or were isolated) before receiving the coordinator's *commit* message and will therefore abort when restarted (or in their timeout period if they were isolated). When a failed cohort is restarted, it has the responsibility of finding out what decision was made. Thus, we have the following protocols.

Timeout Protocol for Extended Two Phase Commit Protocol

Timeout at step 2: The cohort decides abort.

Timeout at step 3: The coordinator decides abort and sends an *abort* message to every cohort from which it received a *ready* vote.

Timeout at step 4: The cohort communicates with other cohorts. If any have decided, the cohort decides in the same way. If communication can be established with all cohorts and none have decided, all decide abort. If communication cannot be established with one or more cohorts (because of a crash or partition) and all other cohorts are undecided, the cohort blocks.

Timeout at step 5: If at least one cohort returns a *done* message, the coordinator continues with the protocol. If no *done* messages have been received, the coordinator blocks.

Restart Protocol for Extended Two Phase Commit

Case 1: If the restarted site had decided abort or commit before crashing, it completes the appropriate processing.

Case 2: If the restarted site is a cohort that has not yet voted, it decides abort.

Case 3: If the restarted site is a cohort that crashed in its uncertain period:

a. It attempts to communicate with a site that has decided and uses that decision.

b. If it can communicate with all cohorts and none have decided, it aborts.

c. Otherwise it blocks.

Case 4: If the restarted site is the coordinator and it was in its uncertain period when it crashed, it attempts to communicate with all cohorts to which it has sent *commit* messages:

a. If it succeeds in communicating with a cohort that has committed or aborted, the coordinator makes the same decision.

b. If it can communicate with at least one cohort and no cohort with which it communicates has decided, it reenters the Extended Two Phase Commit Protocol at step 3 by sending a (new) *commit* message to all cohorts. Then it continues in the protocol as before. [Since the coordinator had received *ready* messages from all cohorts before crashing, it knows that no failed or isolated cohort can have decided abort (Case 2). Since it has communicated with at least one undecided cohort, it knows that the cohorts collectively could not have decided abort if they timed out at step 4 or restarted (Case 3b). It cannot just decide commit, since that might violate *NB1*.]

    c. If it cannot communicate with any cohort, it blocks. [The cohorts might have decided abort if none received the *commit* message (Case 3b) or commit if at least one had (step 4).]

Note that this protocol does not exhibit independent recovery.

    The description we have just given needs to be expanded to deal with a situation caused by the form of our definitions. For simplicity we have assumed that if data is to be accessed at the site at which a transaction is initiated, a *local* cohort is created at that site in addition to the coordinator. Thus the coordinator and local cohort coexist at the same site, and the situation in which the coordinator site crashes and all the cohorts are operational can never occur. To deal with this case, we enhance the protocol as follows:

    In step 3, instead of sending *commit* messages to all cohorts, the coordinator sends *commit* messages to all cohorts except the local cohort.

    In step 5, when the coordinator commits, it also commits the local cohort.

(Note that property *NB1* is still satisfied.) Since the coordinator cannot crash without the local cohort's crashing as well and, since the two cannot be separated by a partition, we assume that the local cohort cannot time out. For cohorts other than the local cohort, we enhance the Timeout Protocol as follows:

    Timeout at step 4: The cohort attempts to communicate with other (nonlocal) cohorts. If it can communicate with all of these cohorts and none have decided, they all decide abort.

We enhance the Restart Protocol as follows:

    In Case 3b, if a nonlocal restarted cohort can communicate with all other nonlocal cohorts and none have decided, they all abort.

    The extended two phase commit protocol satisfies the four requirements for an atomic commit protocol and is robust under crashes and partitions. Blocking can occur only when the coordinator and at least one cohort fail, when all the cohorts fail, or when a partition occurs.

12.6   Three Phase Commit Protocol*

The three phase commit protocol is an extension of the two phase commit protocol that does not block when sites fail but is not robust for partitions (two sites might make inconsistent decisions when a partition occurs). Initially we assume no partitions; later we discuss the effect of partitions. As we shall see, the protocol can be extended to be robust for partitions, but then it loses its nonblocking property. We also assume no false timeouts.

    In the two phase commit protocol, when a cohort times out during its uncertain period (because the coordinator has crashed), the coordinator might have already decided commit or abort, so the cohort is blocked until the coordinator is restarted. In the extended two phase commit protocol, the coordinator cannot have decided commit when a cohort, $C1$, is in its uncertain period, so $C1$ need not block so long as it can communicate with all cohorts. If, in addition to the coordinator, a cohort, $C2$, has crashed, $C1$ must block. To design a protocol that exhibits no blocking under arbitrary site failures, we establish the following property, which we call *NB2*:

NB2: Whenever at least one operational site is in its uncertain period, no other site, either operational or failed, can have decided commit.

Hence, if all operational sites discover that they are in their uncertain period, they can all decide abort, since they know that no failed site can have decided commit. (Remember, we have assumed no partitions, so all operational sites can communicate with one another.) To establish *NB2*, we add another phase to the protocol.

Three Phase Commit Protocol with No Failures

1. The coordinator sends a *prepare* message to all cohorts.

2. Each cohort waits until it receives the *prepare* message from the coordinator. It then votes *ready* or *aborting* and sends the corresponding message to the coordinator. If the vote is *aborting*, it decides abort.

3. The coordinator waits until it receives votes from all the cohorts. If at least one vote is *aborting*, it decides abort and sends an *abort* message to each cohort. If all votes are *ready*, it sends a *precommit* message to each cohort.

4. Each cohort that voted *ready* waits to receive a message from the coordinator. If that message is *precommit*, it sends an *acknowledge* message to the coordinator. If that message is *abort*, it decides abort.

5. If the coordinator sent *precommit* messages in step 3, it waits until it receives an *acknowledge* message from each cohort. Then it decides commit and sends a *commit* message to each cohort.

6. Each cohort that sent an *acknowledge* message waits until it receives a *commit* message. Then it decides commit.

The uncertain period of a cohort starts when it sends a *ready* message at step 2 and ends when it receives the *precommit* or *abort* message at step 4. Thus, while a cohort is waiting at step 4, it is uncertain.[4] The uncertain period of the

---

[4]The definition of the uncertain period must be modified for the three phase commit protocol. We still say that a cohort is in its uncertain period during the time period after it has sent its vote to commit, but before it has enough information to know what the decision will be. However, now we say it need only know what the decision will be under the assumption that it does not fail between the time it leaves the uncertain period and the time the decision is actually made. As

coordinator starts when it sends the first *precommit* message and ends when it receives the first *acknowledge* message. While a cohort is waiting at step 6 for the *commit* message, we say it is *committable*.

This protocol has the interesting property that the contents of the messages in steps 5 and 6 are known to the recipients before the messages are received. Their significance is that they transfer an assertion to their recipients: the sender is in a particular state. Hence, the recipient can make certain inferences about the state of the overall system.

The receipt by the coordinator of an *acknowledge* message sent by some cohort tells the coordinator that that cohort is no longer in its uncertain period. Thus, after the coordinator has received *acknowledge* messages from all cohorts, it knows that no cohort is in its uncertain period, and thus it can commit and send the *commit* message. Since the coordinator does not send *commit* messages until it receives *acknowledge* messages from all cohorts and a cohort does not decide commit until it receives a *commit* message, it follows that when a site is in its uncertain period, no other site has decided commit. Thus, *NB2* is achieved.

To extend this protocol to deal with crashes, we must supply timeout and restart protocols. Since the three phase commit protocol has the property that sites never block, an operational site (one that has not crashed or one that has crashed and been restarted) always proceeds to a decision. Therefore, the restart protocol is simple: the restarted site contacts a site that has not crashed or a restarted site that has decided and uses its decision. Since we have assumed that not all sites fail, such a site can always be found. Hence, in the remaining discussion, we can disregard restarted sites.

The timeout protocols for steps 2 and 3 are the same as for the two phase commit protocol: since no site can have decided commit, the site that times out can decide abort. When a timeout occurs at step 5, a cohort, *C*, has crashed after sending a *ready* message, but before sending an *acknowledge* message. The coordinator knows that *C* is not operational and that it and all other cohorts are prepared to commit. The coordinator decides commit, and sends a *commit* message to each cohort. Note that *C* might have crashed during its uncertain period (before receiving the *precommit* message) but, since it is not operational, *NB2* is not violated.

Timeouts at steps 4 and 6 are due to failures of the coordinator. When a site times out at step 4, the coordinator might have failed after sending *precommit* messages to some but not all cohorts. Those cohorts that do not receive precommit messages will time out at step 4 while in their uncertain periods, whereas those that receive precommit messages will time out at step 6 and are committable. When a site times out at step 6, the situation is more complex. As above, the coordinator might have failed after sending *precommit* messages

---

we shall see below, a cohort may have passed its uncertain period and know that the decision will be commit if it does not fail – but if it does fail before the decision is made, the final decision will be to abort. (Specifically, it fails while waiting at step 6, the coordinator also fails, and all other cohorts are operational and time out at step 4.)

to some but not all cohorts, in which case some cohorts may also be timed out in step 4. Alternatively the coordinator might have failed after sending *commit* messages to some but not all cohorts, in which case some cohorts have committed. Thus when a site times out at either step 4 or step 6, it cannot independently make a commit decision because it cannot be certain that it will not violate *NB2* (since other sites might be in their uncertain periods). Furthermore, it cannot independently decide abort either. This is easily seen in the case of a site timed out at step 6, since such a site knows that some other site might have already committed. In the case of a site timed out at step 4, it might seem that an independent decision to abort is possible, since no cohort can have committed. Let us refer to such a decision as *D*. To see that *D* cannot be allowed in a nonblocking protocol, consider the plight of a site *A* timed out at step 6. It knows that some other site might have committed (if the coordinator failed before sending all commit messages) and also that some other site might have aborted (using *D*). Hence, *A* cannot make an independent decision and must contact other cohorts. If *A* discovers that any cohort *B* has failed, *A* must block, since *B* might have failed after deciding commit or abort. Thus if *D* were allowed, the protocol would block, contrary to our requirement that the three phase commit protocol be nonblocking. Therefore, in order to proceed to a decision without blocking, sites that time out at either steps 4 or 6 execute a *termination protocol* (described next). The timeout protocol is as follows:

Timeout Protocol for Three Phase Commit Protocol

Timeout at step 2: The cohort decides abort.

Timeout at step 3: The coordinator decides abort and sends an *abort* message to every cohort from which it received a *ready* vote.

Timeout at step 4: The cohort executes the termination protocol.

Timeout at step 5: The coordinator decides commit and sends a *commit* message to every cohort from which it received an *acknowledge* message.

Timeout at step 6: The cohort executes the termination protocol.

The termination protocol is executed only when the coordinator has failed. The basic idea is that the operational cohorts elect one of themselves to be the new coordinator. (We discuss how such an election can take place in Section 12.6.1.) The new coordinator polls the operational cohorts to find out where they were in the commit protocol. The only tricky situation arises when the poll determines that all operational cohorts are in their uncertain period. In this case it follows from *NB2* that no site could have decided commit, but some (non-operational) sites could have decided abort. The following scenario leads to this situation: the original coordinator receives an *abort* vote from cohort *A* and therefore it and *A* decide abort, then *A* fails, and then the coordinator fails before it sends *abort* messages to any of the operational cohorts. Hence, if the poll finds that all the operational cohorts are uncertain, the new coordinator must decide abort and send *abort* messages to all operational cohorts. Thus we have the following protocol:

Termination Protocol for Three Phase Commit

1. The operational sites elect a new coordinator.

2. The new coordinator polls the operational sites to find out where they are in the commit protocol.

3. The new coordinator takes the following actions:

> If any cohort has not voted or has aborted, the new coordinator decides abort and sends an *abort* message to all cohorts.
>
> If any cohort has committed, the new coordinator decides commit and sends a *commit* message to all cohorts.
>
> If all operational cohorts are uncertain, the new coordinator decides abort and sends an *abort* message to all cohorts.
>
> If some cohort is committable (and, hence, all cohorts had sent *ready* messages) but none have committed, the new coordinator sends *precommit* messages to all uncertain cohorts, waits for them to send *acknowledge* messages, and then decides commit and sends *commit* messages to all cohorts.

The new coordinator will never make a decision that is inconsistent with any decision that might have been made by the original coordinator. (As we have seen, *NB2* is needed to reason about the coordinator's decision when all cohorts are uncertain.) The new coordinator might itself fail during the protocol, in which case the surviving cohorts restart the termination protocol. Note that no blocking occurs (assuming not all sites fail).

The robustness of the three phase commit protocol to site failures is based on the assumption of no partitions. Suppose a partition occurs that divides the operational sites into two disjoint components such that all sites in one component are uncertain and all those in the other are committable. The sites in each component separately perform the termination protocol. The sites in one component will decide abort and those in the other will decide commit – an inconsistent decision that violates property 1 of an atomic commit protocol. Thus, the three phase commit protocol is not robust for partition failures.

We can design a version of the three phase commit protocol that is robust for partitions, but the new version exhibits blocking. The basic idea is that a coordinator, the original or a new one, blocks until it can communicate with at least a majority of the sites or with a cohort that has decided.

12.6.1 Electing a Coordinator*

Given a set of communicating sites, the goal of a coordinator – or leader – election algorithm is for the sites to select one of their number as a coordinator. In some respects an election algorithm is similar to a mutual exclusion algorithm: all processes compete to enter their critical sections, and the process that enters becomes the coordinator. A difference is that fairness is not an issue in an election algorithm, since it is not important that each site eventually get to be coordinator. Note also that with mutual exclusion we generally assume that a process does not crash in its critical section, whereas an election algorithm is used to recover from just such an eventuality: the coordinator (the process in its critical section) has crashed and a new coordinator must be elected.

A considerable amount of research has been devoted to the leader election problem. In the most general model it is assumed that sites are vertices in an (arbitrary) graph and can communicate only with their neighbors. In this setting, leader election is closely related to algorithms for finding a spanning tree of the graph: the new leader is the root of the resulting tree. Our model is a special case of electing a leader in which the sites are vertices of a complete graph (*i.e.*, we have assumed that any nonfailed cohort can talk to any other nonfailed cohort).

Algorithms for electing a leader in a complete network generally assume that each site has a unique identifier and does not know the identifiers of other sites. There are two basic paradigms around which many of these algorithms are built. In the simpler paradigm, if a site, A, finds that it cannot communicate with the coordinator, it attempts to have itself elected the new coordinator. We refer to such a node as a *base* node. A base node broadcasts an *elect* message, containing its identifier, to all other sites. On receiving such a message, a base node, B, compares its site identifier with the received identifier. If B's identifier is smaller, it responds to A with an *accept* message. Otherwise, it responds with a *reject* message. Nodes that are not base nodes unconditionally respond with an *accept* message. When a site receives *accept* messages from all other sites, it becomes the new coordinator. Since we have assumed no false timeouts, if a base node does not receive a response to its message from some site, it can conclude that that site has crashed and ignore it.

Since *elect* messages are sent out in parallel and the longest sequence of messages is two, the time complexity is order 1. On the other hand, since in the worst case it is possible that all sites are base nodes, the algorithm has the property that the message complexity is order n^2, where n is the total number of sites.

A more message-efficient approach involves communicating with sites sequentially. In this case, election is based not on a comparison of site identifiers, but on the number of sites a base node has already captured. Each site, S, maintains the pair (*level$_S$*, *maxid$_S$*), where *maxid$_S$* is initialized to the site's identifier if the site is a base node and 0 otherwise and *level$_S$* is initialized to 0 at all sites. At a site that is not a base node, the pair contains the value of the lexicographically largest pair it has seen in any message it has received. All base nodes are initially active (the distinction between active and inactive base nodes is made in Case 1, below). Active base nodes attempt to capture other nodes, and the node elected leader is the active base node that has captured all other nodes. At any time a node can be captured by at most one node – its *owner* – and an active base node can take a captured node from its owner (and become the new owner) using the algorithm described below. At an active base node, S, $maxid_S$ is the node's identifier and $level_S$ is the number of sites the node has captured.

An active base node, A, sends the pair $(level_A, maxid_A)$ in the *capture* message it sends to site B.

Case 1: B has not already been captured:

> If the pair is lexicographically larger than B's pair (the site identifier is used to break ties), A captures B and B responds with an *accept* message. B records the identity of its owner, A, and copies A's pair into its own. A increments its level number on receiving the *accept* message, indicating that it has captured another node. If B is a base node, it becomes *inactive*. If B's pair is larger than the pair in A's *capture* message, B is not captured. B sends a *reject* message to A, and A becomes inactive (but it is not captured).

Case 2: B has already been captured:

> If B's pair is larger than the pair in A's *capture* message, B sends a *reject* message and A becomes inactive. If not, A contests for B with B's owner, C. B copies A's pair into its own and sends a message to C with A's pair. If A's pair is larger than C's, C is *killed* (it is not, however, captured) and becomes inactive. It returns a message to B indicating that it has been killed. B is then captured by A. B updates the identity of its owner and sends an *accept* message to A. If A's pair is smaller than C's, C sends a *reject* message to B, which relays it to A, and A becomes inactive.

A base node can become inactive in three ways: it is captured, killed, or it receives a *reject* message in response to a *capture* message that it has sent. An inactive base node stops sending capture messages, and its pair will be subsequently updated if it sees a larger pair in a message it receives. A base node becomes inactive when it becomes aware that another base node exists with a larger pair. An inactive base node will not be elected leader. It follows that for all sites, S, as far as S can tell, its pair $(level_S, maxid_S)$ is the largest such pair in the system.

The base node that captures all other nodes becomes the coordinator. (It knows when it has captured all nodes because it has received *accept* messages from all its $n - 1$ neighbors or has timed out if a neighbor has crashed.) Note that at all times the algorithm maintains the invariant that the sets of nodes captured by active base nodes are disjoint from one another. The reduction in message traffic is a result of the fact that, although the base node that becomes coordinator sends a number of messages proportional to n, by killing other base nodes it prevents them from also sending that many messages. Thus, the message complexity is less than n^2.

To determine the message complexity, we note that at most four messages are exchanged each time a base node captures another node. Suppose A becomes coordinator. Then, at most $4n$ messages are exchanged as a result of A's captures. In any run, $n/2$ is the largest level of any base node that gets killed (since the sets of captured nodes are disjoint and the killer must have a level at least as large as $n/2$). Similarly, $n/3$ bounds the level of the second largest base node to be killed. To see this, assume the contrary. Suppose B and later C are the last two nodes killed, and at the time they are killed, both have captured at least $n/3$ nodes. Then at the time B is killed, its killer must have captured at least $n/3$ nodes. In order for C's level to be greater than $n/3$ at the time it is killed, it must capture at least one node, D, previously captured by B, since its level cannot have been $n/3$ at the time B was killed. But this is not possible, since in order for C to capture D, C's pair must be greater than that of B at the time B was killed. Thus two nodes, each having a level greater than or equal to $n/3$, cannot be killed in the same run.

In general, the ith largest base node killed in a run cannot have a level greater than $n/(i+1)$. Since a base node having level k has caused at most $4k$ messages to be exchanged, an upper bound on the total number of messages exchanged in a run is $4\sum_{i=1}^{n} n/i$. Since, for large n, $\sum_{i=1}^{n} 1/i$ is approximately $\ln n$, it follows that the message complexity of the algorithm is $4n \ln n$. The time complexity is order n, since a sequence of at most $4n$ messages must be exchanged in order for a node to become coordinator, and these messages are sent without waiting for other messages. Furthermore, a node with a larger level is never killed by a node with a smaller level.

12.7   Replicated Databases

A common technique for dealing with failures is to replicate portions of a database at different sites in a network. Then if a site crashes or becomes separated from the network because of a partition, the portion of the database being maintained by that site can still be accessed by contacting a different site that holds a replica. We say that the *availability* of the data has been increased. Replication can also improve the efficiency of access to data, since a site can access the nearest replica.

Replication, of course, has its costs. First, more storage is required. Second, a replicated system must ensure that copies of a data item are properly updated. One way to achieve proper updating is to guarantee *mutual consistency*: all replicas are identical. If we view replicas as simply additional items in the database, mutual consistency can be expressed as a consistency constraint: if $x1$ and $x2$ are copies of a data item, then $x1 = x2$. As we have seen, consistency constraints can express much more complex relationships than just mutual consistency, and we speak of the consistency constraints as expressing the semantics of the database. In the context of replication, these general relationships are often referred to using the term *internal consistency*. In this view, then, mutual consistency is an example of internal consistency, and if we make the assumption that the concurrency control does not know database semantics (*i.e.,* it does not know which data items constitute a set of replicas), each transaction has the responsibility of maintaining mutual consistency. Hence, a transaction wanting to update an item must spawn subtransactions to update its replicas.

In an alternative view, mutual consistency is considered to be a special case of internal consistency that is recognized by the database system. The database system knows which data items are replicas and maintains mutual consistency. In this view, a transaction is unaware of replication. When it updates a data item, the system automatically updates the replicas. The portion of the system that assumes the responsibility for replication is called the *replica control*. We take this view of a replicated system, although – as we shall see – the replica controls we examine do not necessarily maintain mutual consistency.

The simplest replica control system is referred to as a *read one / write all* system. When a transaction updates a data item, the replica control updates all copies. On the other hand, when a transaction wants to read an item, the replica control can return the value of any one – presumably the nearest – of the copies. Read one/write all systems yield an improvement in efficiency over a nonreplicated system (where reads might have to access distant data items) if reads occur more frequently than updates.

Although this approach can increase efficiency, it does not increase availability for all operations. Since an update must access all replicas, if any site has crashed, the update cannot be completed. We now describe a different approach, in which operations need not access all replicas. Hence, a data item might still be available, even though some replica is inaccessible. To achieve this goal, we no longer insist on maintaining mutual consistency. Since replicas are no longer identical, the state of a data item must be constructed from its replicas. The replica control is responsible for doing this construction.

12.7.1   Replica Control for Untyped Databases

In this section we describe replication in the context of an untyped database that uses a lock-based deferred-update pessimistic concurrency control (the extension to immediate-update controls is easy). In the next section we show how the approach can be extended to typed databases.

The new approach is called the *quorum consensus* protocol. The basic idea is that when a transaction makes a request to read (write) a replicated record, the concurrency control first locks some subset, called the *read quorum* (*write quorum*), of the replicas before granting the request. If the size of a read quorum is p and the size of a write quorum is q, we require that $p + q > n$, where n is the total number of replicas. Thus, we ensure that there is a nonnull intersection between any read quorum and any write quorum for a particular record. As a result, whenever a read/write conflict occurs, it will be detected. (Recall that in Section 10.7 we pointed out that deferred-update systems do not have write/write conflicts.) We can easily generalize this idea by assigning a nonnegative weight to each replica of a record and then taking p and q to be the sum of the weights of replicas in the read and write quorums respectively, and n to be the sum of the weights of all replicas. Note that the read one/write all system can be viewed as a quorum consensus protocol in which each replica has unit weight and the number of replicas in a read quorum is 1 and in a write quorum is n.

Quorum consensus enables us to trade off the availability of the operations on a record. A read can be executed as long as p replicas are accessible. The availabilities of read and write are related, however. The more available read is, the less available write is.

When a write request is granted (and the transaction commits), only the records in the write quorum are updated. Hence, mutual consistency is not maintained and replicas at different sites may have different values. We assume that transactions have timestamps as described in Section 11.2.5 and that each record has the timestamp of the (committed) transaction that last wrote it. Since each read quorum intersects each write quorum, each read quorum intersects the write quorum of the most recent write. Therefore, at least one record in each read quorum has the latest timestamp and, hence, the current value. This value is returned by the replica control to a read request.

Assume that a record, R, is stored as a set of replicas in the system, and each replica contains a value and a timestamp. We assume a deferred-update pessimistic concurrency control that uses two phase commit, and we assume that each site maintains a logical clock (as described in Section 9.1). We view the interface between a transaction and the replicated database as consisting of both a concurrency control and a replica control, as shown in Figure 12.1. The replica control requests locks from the concurrency control in order to gather a quorum and manipulates the values of replicas.

Quorum Consensus Replica Control Protocol Assuming No Failures

1. When a transaction executing at site A makes a request to read or write a particular record, the replica control at A sends messages to the concurrency controls at sites (for example, B) at which replicas exist, requesting a read or write lock on that replica. If the concurrency control at B can grant the request, it places the lock in the lock set of the record and replies. If the request was a read, the reply contains the value of the replica and its timestamp.

2. When replies have been received from a quorum of sites, if the request was a read, the replica control supplies to the transaction the value with the largest timestamp. If the request was a write, the replica control places the write operation on its intentions list for that record.

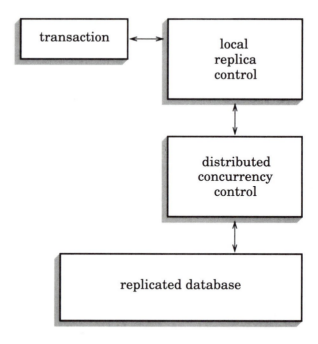

Figure 12.1: The relationship between replica control and concurrency control in a replicated database.

3. A transaction commits using the two phase commit protocol, where the cohorts are all of the sites at which it holds locks. The coordinator obtains a timestamp for the transaction by appending its site ID to the current value of its logical clock. With the *prepare* message, the coordinator sends the new value of the record, as well as the timestamp. If the transaction commits, each cohort updates the replica and its timestamp. Each cohort removes the transaction's locks from the lock set.

As with data abstraction, there exists a mapping between the set of replicas corresponding to a record – the concrete representation – and the record they represent – the abstract entity. The mapping function can be applied when the replicas satisfy a concrete invariant. In this case the concrete invariant specifies that all replicas with the same timestamp have the same value and that the number of replicas with the largest timestamp be greater than or equal to the size of the write quorum. If a set of replicas satisfies the concrete invariant, the mapping function specifies that the value of the corresponding (abstract) record is the value stored in the replica(s) with the largest timestamp in the set.

We observe that any serial execution of a set of transactions preserves the concrete invariant, and as a result of the quorum intersection requirement, the value returned by a read operation is the value of the record. Now assume that a set of transactions is executed concurrently. If we view the replica control as being a part of the transaction (*i.e.*, the first view described in Section 12.7), the reasoning in Chapters 10 and 11 shows that the concurrency control produces only schedules that are equivalent to serial schedules (the concurrency control is unaware of replication and manages locks on items without knowing – or caring – whether they are replicas of the same record or are distinct records). Furthermore, as shown in Section 11.2.6, each allowable schedule is equivalent to a serial schedule in which transactions are in a sequence consistent with both the *precedes* order and the order specified by the timestamps of each transaction. Thus we can conclude the following:

> Any schedule produced by a quorum consensus replica control protocol maintains the concrete invariant and can be serialized in an order consistent with both the *precedes* order and the timestamp order.[5]

As long as the control can assemble the necessary quorums for all operations, the protocol can proceed even when failures have occurred. Algorithms for dealing with deadlocks or blocking (which might occur during the commit phase) are not part of the replica control and are unaffected by replication.

When a site fails and is subsequently restarted, some of its replicas might have very old timestamps. The site need take no special recovery action, however, since the values contained in these replicas will not be used by any transaction until after they have been overwritten by some later transaction, at which time they will be current.

The protocol, although correct, has the rather untidy property that, after all the active transactions have committed and the system has quiesced, not all the replicas corresponding to some record have the same value. One way to eliminate this untidiness is to enhance the protocol so that after each transaction has committed, replicas not contained in the write quorum are updated in background. Hence, approximate mutual consistency is maintained. Gossip messages can be used for this purpose. Each event record contains the value and timestamp of a record that has been updated by a committed transaction. If a gossip message arrives when a replica is locked and the update contained in the message has a larger timestamp than the replica, the lock can be ignored and the replica can be updated, since the value of the locked replica cannot be the value of the record and, hence, will not be returned by the replica control to the transaction holding the lock.

When we use this method to obtain approximate mutual consistency, we can take a more optimistic approach to the quorum consensus algorithm. When performing a read operation, the transaction (optimistically) takes the value

---

[5]In the literature this condition is frequently referred to as *one-copy serializability* because the effect of the execution is the same as would have been obtained if there had been only one copy of each record.

of the nearest replica to be the current value and gathers a quorum (asynchronously) in the background. If it later discovers that it cannot gather a quorum or that the nearest replica was not current, it aborts and then restarts. This approach avoids the delay involved in quorum assembly and can speed execution if the probability is high that a replica is current. A high probability can be ensured if gossip messages are exchanged frequently enough.

12.7.2   Replica Control for Typed Databases

In this section, we extend the ideas of the previous section to replicated typed databases. Quorums are associated with each abstract operation and the sizes of the quorums are selected so that whenever a conflict exists, quorums intersect. When quorums are chosen in this way, a suitably generalized concrete invariant is maintained. Consider, as an example, the data type integer with operations increment and read. Read and increment conflict, but two increments or two reads do not. Thus, if a read operation accesses a quorum of p replicas and an increment operation accesses a quorum of q replicas, such that $p+q > n$, all reads will have enough information to determine the correct value of the integer and all conflicts will be detected. Note that $2p$ or $2q$ might be less than n, so quorums for two reads or two increments might not intersect.

Again we base our protocol on a deferred-update pessimistic concurrency control. As with the similar control described in Section 11.1.4, the state of a replica can be represented by a history of abstract operations invoked by committed transactions. Each entry in a history consists of an operation (*e.g.*, *Dequeue*(3):*ok*) and a timestamp (consisting of the value of the logical clock assigned to the invoking transaction when it committed, followed by the site ID of the coordinator).

One complication that might arise is that after a set of transactions has committed, no single replica contains a complete history of all the operations on the corresponding object instance. For example, suppose that a particular instance of an integer data type is replicated at four sites, and that $p = 3$ and $q = 2$. After two transactions have performed increment operations and committed, one possible configuration of the histories at the replicas is shown in Figure 12.2. The first invocation of increment assembled a quorum consisting of sites 1 and 2; the second used sites 3 and 4. The increment quorums happened not to intersect (which is allowable, since increments do not conflict), and hence no site has a complete history of the operations. However, there is enough information at any three sites (a read quorum) to determine the value of the integer.

We say that histories at two replicas of a single instance are *coherent* if, whenever they both contain entries for a particular operation, the entries are identical (including timestamps). Two histories can be merged only if they are coherent. The *merge* of two coherent histories is the history consisting of all the entries of both (in timestamp order) with duplicates deleted. By the *global history* of an instance we mean the merge of the local histories of all

site 1	site 2	site 3	site 4
1: increment	*1: increment*		
		2: increment	*2: increment*

Figure 12.2: One possible set of histories at four replicas of an integer after two increment operations have been performed by committed transactions with timestamps 1 and 2.

replicas of that instance. The concrete invariant that must be satisfied by a set of replicas corresponding to an instance requires that all local histories be coherent and that the number of histories in which a particular operation is recorded be greater than or equal to the quorum size of that operation. For a set of replicas satisfying the concrete invariant, the value of the data object is the global history.

When a transaction makes a request to invoke an abstract operation on some instance of an object, two conditions must be ensured. First, we must assemble that portion of the committed state of the instance that is relevant to the invocation (so that the invocation will yield the correct result). Second, we must ensure that conflicts do not exist with operations of concurrently executing transactions. Both of these conditions involve the use of a conflict relation. In Section 11.1.1 we discussed both invocation-based and operation-based conflict relations. Invocation-based conflict relations specify conflicts based only on information available at invocation time – the name of the operation (*e.g.*, *Dequeue*) – while operation-based conflict relations specify conflicts based on status returned as well [*e.g.*, *Dequeue(x):ok*]. An invocation-based approach is more natural for replicated data, since the status returned by an invocation cannot be known until a quorum has been assembled and histories merged. Hence, if we tried to use an operation-based approach, the information needed to determine the size of a quorum and the nature of a lock would not be available at the time the quorum was assembled or at the time the lock had to be inserted in the lock set. Thus, our plan is to associate quorums with invocations and place *invocation* locks (*e.g.*, a *Dequeue* lock), as contrasted with associating quorums with operations and placing *operation* locks (*e.g.*, a *Dequeue(x):ok* lock).

The problem of not knowing the status returned by an invocation when obtaining a lock does not arise in nonreplicated systems. For such systems we assume that we can atomically compute the status that would be returned by an invocation of an abstract operation (on a single instance at a single site) and then determine if that operation (*i.e.*, invocation plus status) conflicts with operations that were executed previously by concurrently active transactions (on that instance at that site). If a conflict exists, we discard the results computed by the operation and make the invocation wait.

Assuming we use an invocation-based conflict relation, the portion of the committed state of an instance that must be seen by the invocation, $o1$, is the subsequence of the global history consisting of those invocations, $o2$, such that $o1$ *depends-on* $o2$. Following our discussion in Section 11.1.3, if $o2$ is not in the *depends-on* relation to $o1$, it does not affect the results computed by $o1$ and, hence, need not be part of the state on which $o1$ bases its computation. Recall also that we showed that the *does-not-forward-commute-with* relation is a *depends-on* relation and therefore can be used as a conflict relation.

If $o1$ conflicts with $o2$, $o1$'s quorum must intersect $o2$'s quorum. Thus, $o1$ will see the state change produced by all conflicting invocations of committed transactions and will therefore compute the correct result. Note that for the integer object, *read does-not-forward-commute-with increment* and therefore their quorums must intersect, whereas *increment forward-commutes-with increment* and therefore their quorums need not intersect (a similar quorum assignment is appropriate for read and write operations on a record).

The replica control system is concerned with assembling the state and storing the final result of an operation. If p_o is the size of a quorum for operation o, then to ensure that the state seen by $o1$ includes each invocation, $o2$, of committed transactions that conflict with it, we require that $p_{o1} + p_{o2} > n$, where n is the total number of replicas.

Secondly, the concurrency control must guarantee that invocations of concurrent transactions on an instance do not conflict. When the concurrency control at a site receives a request to include a replica in a quorum for an invocation, the control must check to see whether that invocation conflicts with a lock currently held by an active transaction (which had previously included the replica in a quorum for an invocation it had requested). The conflict check can be organized in two ways. The first approach is to maintain invocation locks and perform the conflict check between two invocations. A lock request made on behalf of an invocation $o1$ is not granted if $o1$ *does-not-forward-commute-with* $o2$, where $o2$ is an invocation on the instance requested by a concurrently active transaction and therefore is an element of the lock set of the replica. For example, Figure 12.3 gives the conflict relation between the invocations *Deposit* and *Withdraw* on an instance of an account type. An invocation of *Deposit* conflicts with a prior invocation of *Withdraw*, since the results of a withdraw can depend upon whether or not a deposit is executed first.

The second approach requires that after invocation locks have been set, histories merged, and the result of an invocation computed, the status is sent to the quorum sites, which can then refine their invocation locks into operation locks to obtain more concurrency. [For example, a *Withdraw* lock can be refined into either a *Withdraw(x):ok* lock or a *Withdraw(x):no* lock.] The conflict check is then between invocations and either invocations (if a previously invoked operation has not yet returned its status to quorum sites) or operations (if it has). Extra messages are required to return the status information. The conflict relation shown in Figure 12.3 applies to the first approach, while the (more relaxed) relation shown in Figure 12.4 applies to the second. Note that, with status information known, an invocation of *Deposit* need not conflict with

Active Transaction T_2
Has Previously Requested

		Deposit	Withdraw
Transaction	Deposit		X
T_1 **Requests**	Withdraw	X	X

Figure 12.3: A conflict relation based only on invocations for an account data type.

Active Transaction T_2
Has Previously Requested

		Deposit(x):ok	Withdraw(x):ok	Withdraw(x):no
Transaction	Deposit			X
T_1 **Requests**	Withdraw	X	X	

Figure 12.4: A conflict relation between invocations and operations for an account data type.

a completed execution of *Withdraw* that returned *ok*.

A transaction invokes an abstract operation by calling the appropriate procedure in the object interface. The object interface calls the replica control to determine the relevant state of the instance of the object. The replica control determines the state by requesting the concurrency control to place an invocation lock at a quorum of replicas and then merging their histories to obtain a state to return to the object interface. If the operation modifies the state, an entry for the operation is appended to the entry for the instance in the transaction's intentions list (and, if operation locks are maintained, the result of the invocation is returned to quorum sites). When the transaction commits, its intentions list is sent to all replicas at quorum sites. Each such site incorporates operations executed by the transaction on the instance into the history at that replica. The organization is shown in Figure 12.5.

We summarize the protocol as follows:

Quorum Consensus Protocol for Typed Replicated Databases
Assuming No Failures

1. When a transaction executing at site A makes a request to invoke some abstract operation on an object instance, the replica control at A sends messages to the concurrency controls at sites (for example, B) at which replicas exist requesting an invocation lock for that operation on that replica. If the

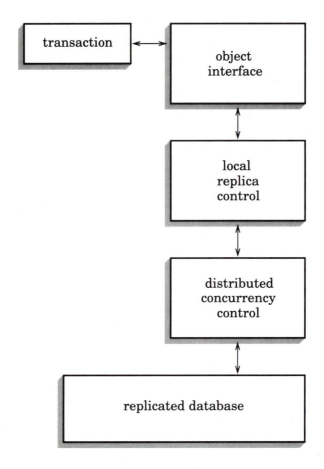

Figure 12.5: The relationship between replica control and concurrency control in a typed, replicated database.

concurrency control at B can grant the request, it places the lock in the lock set and replies. The reply contains the (committed) history of the replica at B. If it cannot grant the request, it places the request in the wait set.

2. When replies have been received from a quorum of sites, the replica control merges the histories, computes the relevant state of the instance, and supplies the object interface with that state.

3. The abstract operation is executed using the supplied state. If the operation modifies the state, the replica control appends the operation to the intentions list of the transaction. If operation locks are maintained, operation status is returned to each quorum site, which updates the appropriate

element in its lock set for the replica.

4. A transaction commits using the two phase commit protocol, where the cohorts are all of the sites at which it has obtained locks. The coordinator obtains a timestamp for the transaction by appending its site ID to the current value of its logical clock. With the *prepare* message, the coordinator sends its merged history and intentions list for the instance, as well as the timestamp. Each cohort merges the received history with the local history maintained at the replica. If the transaction commits, each cohort merges the intentions list for the object with the local history of the replica. Each cohort then removes the lock from the lock set.

To demonstrate the correctness of this protocol, we first observe that when a set of transactions is executed sequentially, each transaction maintains the concrete invariant. The only issue is whether each operation reads the appropriate state of the object instance, but, as we have discussed, this follows from the definition of the conflict relation and the quorum intersection property. Thus, the merged history used by the replica control to compute the state is adequate to perform the operation. Given that a sequential execution is correct, we can use the reasoning in the previous section to conclude the following:

Any schedule produced by a quorum consensus replica control protocol maintains the concrete invariant and can be serialized in an order consistent with both the *precedes* order and the timestamp order.

The comments in the previous section relating to failures and to approximate mutual consistency for untyped replicated databases apply in this case as well.

Example

Consider the *does-not-forward-commute-with* relation for a queue shown in Figure 12.6 (based on Figure 11.6). Note that the relation is between invocations and completed operations (whose status is known). Thus we have assumed that after each Dequeue operation is completed, its *Dequeue* lock is refined into either a *Dequeue(x):ok* or a *Dequeue(x):no* lock.

To use the queue in a quorum consensus protocol based on a deferred-update pessimistic concurrency control, we have to select quorums for each invocation with the required intersection property. The intersection property is expressed graphically in the figure: wherever an X appears in the conflict relation, the sum of the quorums in that row and column must exceed the number of replicas. For example, if the number of replicas is 5, quorums containing 3 replicas for both *Enqueue* and *Dequeue* are sufficient and allow the queue to be accessed even when two sites are inaccessible. Note, for example that, since two *Enqueue* operations conflict, we cannot make the *Enqueue* quorum less than 3.

Active Transaction T_2
Has Previously Requested

		Enqueue(x):ok	*Dequeue(x):ok*	*Dequeue(x):no*
Trans-	*Enqueue*	X		X
action T_1	*Dequeue*	X	X	
Requests				

Figure 12.6: The conflict relation for a queue in a deferred-update pessimistic concurrency control.

12.8   Bibliographic Notes

Two phase commit protocols were first discussed by Gray [57] and Lampson and Sturgis [87]. Three phase commit protocols were first analyzed by Skeen [123]. The theorem that all commit protocols that allow false timeouts exhibit blocking follows from a more general theorem by Fischer, Lynch, and Paterson [95], which states that there does not exist a solution to the consensus problem in an asynchronous network with only one faulty process (since in such a network it is not possible to distinguish a faulty from a slow process). The consensus problem is a generalization of the commit problem: in the commit problem, the processes agree to commit if and only if all cohorts vote yes, whereas in the consensus problem, arbitrary initial states (votes) can result in a particular final state (commit or abort) at all sites. A formal model for atomic commit protocols, together with several proofs, is contained in the paper by Skeen and Stonebraker [124]. The broadcast election algorithm described here is due to Garcia-Molina [52]. The sequential election algorithm was developed by Afek and Gafni [3], [2]. Improvements on these results are described by Singh [120]. The result on which many election algorithms for general networks are based is the algorithm for finding a minimum weight spanning tree developed by Gallagher, Humblet, and Spira [50]. The text by Raynal [112] surveys a number of such algorithms. The quorum consensus approach to replication was first described by Gifford [56]. The extension to typed data was described by Herlihy [62], who later presented an approach that integrated locking and quorum intersection considerations [63]. The algorithm described here is based on this work. An optimistic algorithm for exploiting approximate mutual consistency was developed by Agrawal and Bernstein [4].

12.9   Exercises

1. Discuss how the results of this chapter can be used to achieve exactly once semantics for normal returns and zero semantics for exception returns for remote procedure calls.

2. We pointed out in Section 12.1 that when recoverable storage is used in a transaction processing system, update records from different concurrent transactions might be arbitrarily interleaved in the journal. Show that for a pessimistic immediate-update system, recovery will work correctly if update records are copied from the journal into the primary storage in exactly the order in which they appear in the journal.

3. Suppose in an immediate-update system using recoverable storage the write-ahead log of a transaction decays and the system crashes before the transaction can commit or abort. What can be done to restore the primary device?

4. Prove that, under the assumption of no false timeouts, all atomic commit protocols that are robust for partition failures exhibit blocking.

5. Give an argument showing that the restart protocol of the two phase commit protocol (or the extended two phase protocol or the three phase protocol) works correctly when two or more sites are concurrently executing their restart protocols.

6. Give an induction proof that, in the termination protocol of the three phase commit protocol, no new coordinator makes a decision that is inconsistent with an earlier decision of another coordinator.

7. Show that if false timeouts can occur, the three phase commit protocol does not maintain the *NB2* property. [Hint: Consider a scenario in which the coordinator times out at step 5 and sends a *commit* message to all the cohorts from which it received acknowledgement messages when, in fact, all the sites and communication links are operational (but slow) and one of the cohorts has not yet received the *precommit* message.]

8. Design a restart protocol for the three phase commit protocol when all sites fail. [Hint: The protocol blocks until the cohort that was the last to fail recovers (since that cohort might have decided commit or abort immediately before it failed and a recovering cohort must know what that decision was). In order to determine which cohort was the last to fail, each cohort keeps a list (in stable storage) of all cohorts it knows to be alive (non-failed). Assume that all cohorts have failed and subsequently some subset of them has restarted. Show how this subset can use their lists to determine if the last cohort to fail is in the subset.]

9. Assume an atomic broadcast capability exists. Design a three phase commit protocol that exhibits independent recovery with no blocking for single site failures (assuming no false timeouts).

10. In a distributed atomic commit protocol, no coordinator exists. Each cohort executes a protocol that involves communicating with the other cohorts and, based on the results of that communication, decides to commit or abort. The following distributed version of an atomic commit protocol without failures has been proposed [122]:

    (a) Each cohort sends a *prepare* message to all other cohorts.

    (b) Each cohort waits until it receives the *prepare* message from every other cohort. It then votes *ready* or *aborting* and sends the corresponding message to all of the other cohorts. If the vote is *aborting*, it decides abort.

    (c) Each cohort waits until it receives votes from all the cohorts. If at least one vote is *aborting*, it decides abort. If all votes are *ready*, it sends a *precommit* message to each cohort.

    (d) Each cohort that voted *ready* waits to receive messages from all the other cohorts. If it receives *precommit* messages from all cohorts, it decides commit.

    Design timeout and restart protocols that do not block for site failures (as long as at least one site does not fail). Derive a bound on the total number of messages sent in the worst case.

11. You are given the task of implementing an atomic commit protocol for a system in which failure atomicity is critical to system operation. Although failures are relatively rare, both crashes and partitions occur. Discuss the design issues involved, compare the systems we discussed, and recommend one of them.

12. Design a quorum consensus protocol based on a deferred-update pessimistic concurrency control for records with read and write operations. Assume that, instead of a timestamp field, each record has a version number field, which is updated whenever the record is written.

13. Design a quorum consensus protocol based on an immediate-update pessimistic concurrency control for records with read and write operations.

14. In the quorum consensus protocol for typed replicated databases, when a cohort grants a lock request on an object, it sends its committed history for the object to the coordinator (step 1). The coordinator merges the committed histories from all cohorts (step 2) and returns the merged history to each cohort with the *prepare* message (step 4). Explain why, in step 4, the cohort must merge the history it receives with its own history, instead of simply using the received history.

15. Consider a quorum consensus protocol in which a record is stored as five replicas. A read quorum and a write quorum each contain three replicas. Give an example of a scenario that satisfies the following conditions:

    Three different transactions write to the record. Then two of the replica sites fail, leaving only three copies of the record – *all of which contain different values*.

    Show that the protocol continues to execute correctly.

Bibliography

[1] *Reference Manual for the Ada Programming Language*, Jan. 1983. ANSI/MIL-STD 1815A.

[2] Y. Afek and E. Gafni. Time and message bounds for election in synchronous and asynchronous complete networks. In *Proc. 4th ACM Symposium on Principles of Distributed Computing*, pages 186–195, 1985.

[3] Y. Afek and E. Gafni. Simple and efficient distributed algorithms for election in complete networks. In *Proc. of the 22nd Annual Allerton Conference on Communication, Control, and Computing*, pages 689–698, 1987.

[4] D. Agrawal and A. Bernstein. A nonblocking quorum consensus protocol for replicated data. *IEEE Transactions on Parallel and Distributed Computing*, 2(2):171–179, April 1991.

[5] D. Agrawal, A. Bernstein, P. Gupta, and S. Sengupta. Distributed optimistic concurrency control with reduced rollback. *Distributed Computing*, 2(1):44–59, Apr. 1987.

[6] R. Agrawal, M. Carey, and M. Livny. Concurrency control performance monitoring: Alternatives and implications. *ACM Transactions on Database Systems*, 12(4):609–654, Dec. 1987.

[7] R. Agrawal and D. DeWitt. Integrated concurrency control and recovery mechanisms: Design and performance evaluation. *ACM Transactions on Database Systems*, 10(4):529–564, Dec. 1985.

[8] A. Aho, A. Wyner, M. Yannakakis, and J. Ullman. Bounds on the size and transmission rate of communication protocols. *Comp. and Maths. with Appls.*, 8(3):205–214, 1982.

[9] M. Alford, L. Lamport, and G. Mullery. *Basic Concepts*, volume 190 of *Lecture Notes in Computer Science*, chapter 2, pages 7–44. Springer Verlag, 1982.

[10] B. Alpern and F. Schneider. Defining liveness. *Information Processing Letters*, pages 181–185, Oct. 1985.

[11] G. Andrews. Synchronizing Resources. *ACM Transactions on Programming Languages and Systems*, pages 405–430, Oct. 1981.

[12] K. Apt and N. Francez. Modeling the distributed termination convention of CSP. *ACM Transactions on Programming Languages and Systems*, pages 370–379, July 1984.

[13] K. Apt, N. Francez, and S. Katz. Appraising fairness in languages for distributed programming. In *Sypmosium on Principles of Programming Languages*. Springer Verlag, 1987.

[14] E. Ashcroft. Proving assertions about parallel programs. *Journal of Computer Systems Science*, pages 110–135, Jan. 1975.

[15] A Bar-Noy and D. Dolev. Families of consensus protocols. In *Proc. of Third Aegean Workshop on Computing*, pages 380–390, 1988.

[16] J. Barnes. *Programming in Ada*. Addison-Wesley, second edition, 1984.

[17] A. Bernstein. Output guards and nondeterminism in Communicating Sequential Processes. *ACM Transactions on Programming Languages and Systems*, pages 234–238, Apr. 1980.

[18] A. Bernstein. Predicate transfer and timeout in message passing systems. *Information Processing Letters*, 24:43–52, Jan. 1987.

[19] A. Bernstein and P. Siegel. A computer architecture for level structured operating systems. *IEEE Transactions on Computers*, pages 785–793, Aug. 1975.

[20] P. Bernstein and N. Goodman. Concurrency control in distributed database systems. *ACM Computing Surveys*, 13(2):185–222, June 1981.

[21] P. Bernstein, V. Hadzilacos, and N. Goodman. *Concurrency Control and Recovery in Database Systems*. Addison-Wesley, 1987.

[22] K. Birman and T. Joseph. Reliable communication in the presence of failures. *ACM Transactions on Computer Systems*, 5(1):47–76, Feb. 1987.

[23] A. Birrell and B. Nelson. Implementing remote procedure calls. *ACM Transactions on Computer Systems*, Feb. 1984.

[24] P. Brinch Hansen. The programming language Concurrent Pascal. *IEEE Transactions on Software Engineering*, pages 199–207, June 1975.

[25] P. Brinch Hansen. *The Architecture of Concurrent Programs*. Prentice-Hall, 1977.

[26] G. Buckley and A. Silberschatz. An effective implementation for the generalized input-output construct of CSP. *ACM Transactions on Programming Languages and Systems*, pages 223–235, Apr. 1983.

[27] Alan Burns. *Programming in Occam 2*. Addison-Wesley Publishing Co., 1988.

[28] M. Carey and M. Livny. Conflict detection tradeoffs for replicated data. *ACM Transactions on Database Systems*, 16(4), Dec. 1991.

[29] N. Carriero and D. Gelernter. How to write parallel programs: A guide to the perplexed. *Computing Surveys*, 21(3):323–358, Mar. 1989.

[30] N. Carriero and D. Gelernter. Linda in context. *Communications of the ACM*, 32(4):444–459, Apr. 1989.

[31] J. Chang and N. Maxemchuk. Reliable broadcast protocols. *ACM Transactions on Computer Systems*, 2(3):251–273, August 1984.

[32] E. Clarke. Proving correctness of coroutines without history variables. *Acta Informatica*, 13:169–188, 1980.

[33] P. Courtois, F. Heymans, and D. Parnas. Concurrent control with readers and writers. *Communications of the ACM*, pages 667–668, Oct. 1971.

[34] C. Date. *An Introduction to Database Systems*, volume II. Addison-Wesley, 1983.

[35] E. W. Dijkstra. Cooperating sequential processes. Technical Report EWD-123, Technological University, Eindhoven, 1965.

[36] E. W. Dijkstra. Solution of a problem in concurrent programming control. *Communications of the ACM*, page 569, Sept. 1965.

[37] E. W. Dijkstra. The structure of the THE multiprogramming system. *Communications of the ACM*, pages 341–346, May 1968.

[38] E. W. Dijkstra. Hierarchical ordering of sequential processes. *Acta Informatica*, 1(2):115–138, 1971.

[39] E. W. Dijkstra. Guarded commands, non-determinacy and formal derivation of programs. *Communications of the ACM*, pages 453–457, Aug. 1975.

[40] E. W. Dijkstra. *A Discipline of Programming*. Prentice-Hall, Inc., 1976.

[41] E. W. Dijkstra. Termination detection for diffusing computations. *Information Processing Letters*, pages 1–4, Aug. 1980.

[42] D. Dolev. The Byzantine Generals strike again. *Journal of Algorithms*, 3(1):14–30, Jan. 1982.

[43] R. Elmasri and S. Navathe. *Fundamentals of Database Systems*. Benjamin/Cummings, 1989.

[44] K. Eswaren, J. Gray, R. Lorie, and I. Traiger. The notions of consistency and predicate locks in a database system. *Communications of the ACM*, 19(11):624–633, Nov. 1976.

[45] A. Fekete, N. Lynch, M. Merritt, and W. Weihl. Commutativity-based locking for nested transactions. Technical Report MIT/LCS/TM-370.b, Laboratory for Computer Science, Massachusetts Institute of Technology, Cambridge, Mass., July 1989.

[46] M. Fischer. The consensus problem in unreliable distributed systems (a brief survey). Technical Report YALEU/DCS/RR-273, Yale University, New Haven, Conn., June 1983.

[47] M. Fischer and A. Michael. Sacrificing serializability to attain high availability of data in an unreliable network. In *Proc. of the ACM SIGACT-SIGMOD Symposium on Principles of Database Systems*, pages 70–75, 1982.

[48] N. Francez. Distributed termination. *ACM Transactions on Programming Languages and Systems*, pages 42–55, Jan. 1980.

[49] N. Francez. *Fairness*. Springer Verlag, 1986.

[50] R. Gallagher, P. Humblet, and P. Spira. A distributed algorithm for minimum weight spanning trees. *ACM Transactions on Programming Languages and Systems*, 5(1):66–77, Jan. 1983.

[51] J. Gallier. *Logic for Computer Science*. Harper and Row, 1986.

[52] H. Garcia-Molina. Elections in a distributed computing system. *IEEE Transactions on Computers*, C-31(1):48–59, Jan 1982.

[53] N. Gehani. *Ada: Concurrent Programming*. Prentice-Hall, 1984.

[54] D. Gelernter. Generative communication in linda. *ACM Transactions on Programming Languages and Systems*, 7(1):80–112, Jan. 1985.

[55] R. Gerth and W. de Roever. A proof system for concurrent Ada programs. In *Science of Computer Programming 4*, pages 159–204. Elsevier, 1984.

[56] D. Gifford. Weighted voting for replicated data. In *Proceedings of the 7th Symposium on Operating Systems Principles*, pages 150–162. ACM, Dec. 1979.

[57] J. Gray. *Notes on Database Operating Systems*, volume 60 of *Lecture Notes in Computer Science*, pages 393–481. Springer-Verlag, 1978.

[58] D. Gries. *The Science of Programming*. Springer-Verlag, 1981.

[59] D. Gries and G. Levin. Assignment and procedure call proof rules. *ACM Transactions on Programming Languages and Systems*, pages 564–579, Oct. 1980.

[60] A. Haberman, L. Flon, and L. Cooprider. Modularization and hierarchy in a family of operating systems. *Communications of the ACM*, pages 266–272, May 1976.

[61] J. Halpern and L. Zuck. A little knowledge goes a long way: Simple knowledge-based derivations and correctness proofs for a family of protocols. In *Proc. 6th ACM Symposium on Principles of Distributed Computing*, pages 269–280, Aug. 1987.

[62] M. Herlihy. A quorum-consensus replication method for abstract data types. *ACM Transactions on Computer Systems*, 4(1):32–53, Feb. 1986.

[63] M. Herlihy. Concurrency versus availability: Atomicity mechanisms for replicated data. *ACM Transactions on Computer Systems*, 5(3):249–274, Aug. 1987.

[64] M. Herlihy. Apologizing versus asking permission: Optimistic concurrency control for abstract data types. *ACM Transactions on Database Systems*, 15(1):96–124, Mar. 1990.

[65] M. Herlihy and W. Weihl. Hybrid concurrency control for abstract data types. In *Proc. 7th ACM SIGACT-SIGMOD-SIGART Symposium on Principles of Database Systems*, pages 201–210, Mar. 1988.

[66] C. A. R. Hoare. An axiomatic basis for computer programming. *Communications of the ACM*, pages 576–580, Oct. 1969.

[67] C. A. R. Hoare. Procedures and parameters: An axiomatic approach. In *Symposium on Semantics of Programming Languages*. Springer Verlag, 1971.

[68] C. A. R. Hoare. Proof of correctness of data representations. *Acta Informatica*, 1:271–281, 1972.

[69] C. A. R. Hoare. Monitors: An operating system structuring concept. *Communications of the ACM*, pages 549–557, Oct. 1974.

[70] C. A. R. Hoare. Communicating Sequential Processes. *Communications of the ACM*, pages 666–677, Aug. 1978.

[71] C. A. R. Hoare, editor. *INMOS Limited OCCAM 2 Reference Manual*. Prentice Hall International Series in Computer Science. Prentice Hall, 1988.

[72] J. Howard. Proving monitors. *Communications of the ACM*, pages 273–278, May 1976.

[73] K. Hwang and F. Briggs. *Computer Architecture and Parallel Processing*. McGraw Hill, 1984.

[74] J. Keedy. On structuring operating systems with monitors. *Operating Systems Review*, Jan. 1979.

[75] J. Kessels. An alternative to event queues for synchronization in monitors. *Communications of the ACM*, pages 500–503, July 1977.

[76] R. Kieburtz and A. Silberschatz. Comments on Communicating Sequential Processes. *ACM Transactions on Programming Languages and Systems*, pages 218–225, Oct. 1979.

[77] E. Knapp. Deadlock detection in distributed databases. *ACM Computing Surveys*, 19(4):303–328, Dec. 1987.

[78] W. Kohler. A survey of techniques for synchronization and recovery in decentralized computer systems. *ACM Computing Surveys*, 13(2):149–184, June 1981.

[79] H. Kung and J. Robinson. On optimistic methods for concurrency control. *ACM Transactions on Database Systems*, 6(2):213–226, June 1981.

[80] L. Lamport. Time, clocks and the ordering of events in a distributed system. *Communications of the ACM*, 21(7):558–565, July 1978.

[81] L. Lamport. A new approach to proving the correctness of multiprocess programs. *ACM Transactions on Programming Languages and Systems*, 1(1):84–97, July 1979.

[82] L. Lamport. Control predicates are better than dummy variables for reasoning. *ACM Transactions on Programming Languages and Systems*, pages 267–281, Apr. 1988.

[83] L. Lamport and P. Melliar-Smith. Synchronizing clocks in the presence of faults. *Journal of the ACM*, 32(1):52–78, Jan. 1985.

[84] L. Lamport, R. Shostak, and M. Pease. The Byzantine Generals Problem. *ACM Transactions on Programming Languages and Systems*, 4(3):382–401, July 1982.

[85] B. Lampson. *Atomic Transactions*, volume 105 of *Lecture Notes in Computer Science*, chapter 11, pages 246–265. Springer-Verlag, 1981.

[86] B. Lampson and D. Redell. Experience with processes and monitors in Mesa. *Communications of the ACM*, pages 105–117, Feb. 1980.

[87] B. Lampson and H. Sturgis. Crash recovery in a distributed data storage system. Technical report, Xerox Palo Alto Research Center, Palo Alto, CA, Apr. 1979.

[88] G. Levin and D. Gries. A proof technique for Communicating Sequential Processes. *Acta Informatica*, 15:281–302, 1981.

[89] B. Liskov. On linguistic support for distributed programs. In *Proc., IEEE Symposium on Reliability in Distributed Software and Database Systems*, pages 53–60, July 1981.

[90] B. Liskov. Overview of the Argus language and system. Technical Report Programming Methodology Group Memo 40, Laboratory for Computer Science, Massachusetts Institute of Technology, Cambridge, Mass., Feb. 1984.

[91] B. Liskov. Distributed programming in Argus. *Communications of the ACM*, 31(3):300–313, Mar. 1988.

[92] B. Liskov, M. Herlihy, and L. Gilbert. Limitations of synchronous communication with static process structure in languages for distributed computing (revised). Technical Report Programming Methodology Group Memo 41-1, Massachusetts Institute of Technology, Cambridge, Mass, Sept. 1985.

[93] B. Liskov and R. Scheifler. Guardians and actions: Linguistic support for robust distributed programs. *ACM Transactions on Programming Languages and Systems*, pages 381–404, July 1983.

[94] B. Liskov, R. Scheifler, E. Walker, and W. Weihl. Orphan detection. In *Proc. 17th IEEE Symposium on Fault Tolerant Computing*, July 1987.

[95] N. Lynch M. Fischer and M. Paterson. Impossibility of distributed consensus with one faulty process. In *Proc. 2nd ACM Symposium on Principles of Database Systems*, pages 1–7, 1983.

[96] Z. Manna and A. Pneuli. Adequate proof principles for invariance and liveness properties of concurrent programs. *Science of Computer Programming*, 4:257–289, 1984.

[97] R. McCurley. A valid rule for auxiliary variable transformations. Technical Report GIT-ICS-89/11, School of Information and Computer Science, Georgia Institute of Technology, 1989.

[98] M. McKendry and M. Herlihy. Time driven orphan elimination. In *Proc. 5th Symposium on Reliablility in Distributed Software and Database Systems*, pages 42–48. IEEE, Jan. 1986.

[99] E. Mendelson. *Introduction to Mathematical Logic*. Wadsworth & Brooks/Cole Advanced Books and Software, third edition, 1987.

[100] J. Misra and K. Chandy. Termination detection of diffusing computations in Communicating Sequential Processes. *ACM Transactions on Programming Languages and Systems*, pages 37–42, Jan. 1982.

[101] J. Moss. *Nested Transactions: An Approach to Reliable Distributed Computing*. PhD thesis, Department of Electrical Engineering and Computer Science, Massachusetts Institute of Technology, Cambridge, Mass, Apr. 1981.

[102] B. Nelson. Remote procedure call. Technical Report CMU-CS-81-119, Department of Computer Science, Carnegie Mellon University, May 1981.

[103] G. Nelson, editor. *Systems Programming With Modula-3*. Series in Innovative Technology. Prentice Hall, 1991.

[104] S. Owicki. Specifications and proofs for abstract data types in concurrent programs. Technical report, Digital Systems Laboratory, Departments of Electrical Engineering and Computer Science, Apr. 1977.

[105] S. Owicki and D. Gries. An axiomatic proof technique for parallel programs I. *Acta Informatica*, 6:319–340, 1976.

[106] S. Owicki and L. Lamport. Proving liveness properties of concurrent programs. *ACM Transactions on Programming Languages and Systems*, pages 455–495, July 1982.

[107] C. Papadimitriou. Serializability of concurrent database updates. *Journal of the ACM*, 26(4):631–653, Oct. 1979.

[108] C. Papadimitriou. *The Theory of Concurrency Control*. Computer Science Press, 1986.

[109] G. Peterson. Myths about the mutual exclusion problem. *Information Processing Letters*, pages 115–116, June 1981.

[110] J. Peterson and A. Silberschatz. *Operating Systems Concepts*. Addison Wesley, second edition, 1985.

[111] L. Peterson, N. Buchholz, and R. Schlichting. Preserving and using context information in interprocess communication. *ACM Transactions on Computer Systems*, 7(3):217–246, Aug. 1989.

[112] M. Raynal. *Distributed Algorithms and Protocols*. John Wiley and Sons, 1988.

[113] D. Rosenkrantz, R. Stearns, and P. Lewis II. System level concurrency control for distributed database systems. *ACM Transactions on Database Systems*, 3(2):178–198, June 1978.

[114] R. Schlichting and F. Schneider. Fail-stop processors: An approach to designing fault-tolerant computing systems. *ACM Transactions on Computer Systems*, 1(3):222–238, Aug. 1983.

[115] R. Schlichting and F. Schneider. Using message passing for distributed programming: Proof rules and disciplines. *ACM Transactions on Programming Languages and Systems*, pages 402–431, July 1984.

[116] F. Schneider. Synchronization in distributed programs. *ACM Transactions on Programming Languages and Systems*, 4(2):125–148, Apr. 1982.

[117] F. Schneider. The state machine approach: A tutorial. Technical report, Department of Computer Science, Cornell University, Dec. 1986.

[118] F. Schneider and G. Andrews. Concepts for concurrent programming. In *Current Trends in Concurrency*, volume 224 of *Lecture Notes in Computer Science*, pages 669–716. Springer Verlag, 1985.

[119] K. Shumate. *Understanding Concurrency in Ada*. McGraw-Hill, 1988.

[120] G. Singh. Efficient distributed algorithms for leader election in complete networks. In *Proc. of 11th IEEE Int'l Conference on Distributed Computing Systems*, 1991.

[121] M. Sinha, P. Nanadikar, and S. Mehndiratta. Timestamp based certification schemes for transactions in distributed database systems. In *Proceedings of ACM SIGMOD Conference on Management of Data*, May 1985.

[122] D. Skeen. A decentralized termination protocol. In *Proceedings of Symposium on Reliability in Distributed Software and Database Systems*, July 1981.

[123] D. Skeen. Nonblocking commit protocols. In *Proceedings of ACM SIGMOD Conference on Management of Data*, June 1982.

[124] D. Skeen and M. Stonebraker. A formal model of crash recovery in a distributed system. *IEEE Transactions on Software Engineering*, SE-9(3):219–228, May 1983.

[125] A. Spector. Performing remote operations efficiently on a local computer network. *Communications of the ACM*, 25(4):246–260, Apr. 1982.

[126] R. Srikanth and S. Toueg. Optimal clock synchronization. *Journal of the ACM*, 34(3):626–645, July 1987.

[127] W. Stallings. *Data and Computer Communications*. MacMillan, 1988.

[128] A. Tanenbaum. *Operating Systems: Design and Implementation*. Prentice-Hall, 1987.

[129] A. Tanenbaum. *Computer Networks*. Prentice Hall, second edition, 1988.

[130] D. Walden. A system for interprocess communication in a resource sharing computer network. *Communications of the ACM*, 15:221–230, Apr. 1972.

[131] W. Weihl. *Specification and Implementation of Atomic Data Types*. PhD thesis, Dept. of Computer Science, Massachusetts Instiute. of Technology, Cambridge, Mass, 1984.

[132] W. Weihl. Distributed version management for read-only actions. *IEEE Transactions on Software Engineering*, SE-13(1):55–64, Jan. 1987.

[133] W. Weihl. Commutativity-based concurrency control for abstract data types. *IEEE Transactions on Computers*, 37(12):1488–1505, Dec. 1988.

[134] W. Weihl. Local atomicity properties: Modular concurrency control for abstract data types. *ACM Transactions on Programming Languages and Systems*, 11(2):249–283, Apr. 1989.

[135] W. Weihl and B. Liskov. Implementation of resilient, atomic data types. *ACM Transactions on Programming Languages and Systems*, 7(2):244–269, Apr. 1985.

[136] N. Wirth. Modula: a language for modular multiprogramming. *Software - Practice and Experience*, 7:3–36, 1977.

[137] N. Wirth. Toward a discipline of real-time programming. *Communications of the ACM*, pages 577–583, Aug. 1977.

[138] N. Wirth. *Programming in Modula-2*. Springer-Verlag, second edition, 1983.

[139] W. Wulf, R. London, and M. Shaw. An introduction to the construction and verification of Alphard programs. *IEEE Transactions on Software Engineering*, pages 253–264, Dec. 1976.

[140] W. Wulf, M. Shaw, P. Hilfinger, and L. Flon. *Fundamental Structures of Computer Science*. Addison Wesley, 1981.

[141] G. Wuu and A. Bernstein. Efficient solutions to the replicated log and dictionary problems. In *Proc. of the 3rd ACM Symposium on Principles of Distributed Computing*, pages 233–242, 1984.

[142] M. Yannakakis. Serializability by locking. *Journal of the ACM*, 31(2):227–244, 1984.

Index

DATE DUE